Best Wishes

Arnold Palmer

DUNHILL
World of Professional Golf 1983

DUNHILL
World of Professional Golf 1983

MARK H. McCORMACK

SPRINGWOOD BOOKS · LONDON

First published 1983
by Springwood Books Ltd,
Chewter Lane, Windlesham, Surrey

Typeset by Inforum Ltd, Portsmouth
and printed by The Camelot Press, Southampton

ISBN 0 86254 119 0

ACKNOWLEDGEMENTS

Thanks are due to the following
for permission to use the photographs
in this book:
  Peter Dazeley
  Will Hertzberg
  Jim Moriarty
  United Press International
  Fred Vance
  Valery Picture Agency
  Wide World Photos

Contents

1. The Year in Retrospect

Pebble Beach, that gorgeous strip of California coastline that Robert Louis Stevenson described as 'the most felicitous meeting of land and sea in creation', needs nothing to enhance its esteem in the world of golf as one of the game's hallowed shrines, a spot to which anybody who plays or merely follows and loves golf dreams of visiting. It's a mecca for the devotees. Even though not the traditional private club with expansive clubhouse facilities which the U.S. Golf Association and the PGA of America usually seek for their major events, Pebble Beach has been the venue for three U.S. Amateur Championships, a PGA Championship and now two U.S. Open Championships. The sagas of these six major tournaments have embellished the reputation Pebble Beach has attained through its tremendous exposure as the anchor course of the Bing Crosby National Pro-Am for 37 years. Virtually every great of the game, professional and amateur, has done battle with Pebble Beach and, even when the weather is benign, which is not often, most would agree with Jack Burke's assessment back in the 1950s that 'it's like fighting Rocky Marciano . . . every time you step onto the course, you're a cinch to take a beating'. The roll of winners at Pebble Beach includes many of those greats, headed by Jack Nicklaus with his Open, Amateur and three Crosby titles, and they and so many others have contributed memorable moments to the lore of the game from appearances there.

Yet, I suspect that when golf's historians of the future look back on the 1900s, one player and one shot — one soft, little 18-foot chip shot — will stand out above everything else that has ever happened at that golf jewel on the Monterey Peninsula and that probably ever will. Such was the impact of a touchy wedge lob that went into the cup for a deuce at the devilish 17th hole and righted Tom Watson just when he needed it to overtake Nicklaus in the ferocious pressure of the final holes of the U.S. Open Championship. Very simply, it won the Open for Watson and almost certainly will prove to have been the most important stroke ever by one of the game's most brilliant players. 'It was the best shot I've ever hit,' Watson concurs. 'It had more meaning than any single shot I've hit in my career.'

It gave Tom the most important title in golf for the first time, just when it looked as though it might escape him again. What long-range negative effects such a failure might have had on Watson's career and reputation, of course, can only be imagined. Obviously, though, the long-sought triumph in the Open had a positive influence as he went on to win the British Open a month later, achieving a same-season double of the world's two most prestigious championships that had only been accomplished by Bob Jones (twice), Gene Sarazen, Ben Hogan and Lee Trevino before him. Coupled with victories in the Los Angeles Open and Heritage Classic, the twin Open titles clearly established Watson once again as the game's No. 1 player in 1982. Unlike the preceding year, when Bill Rogers was acclaimed Player of the Year in some important quarters, Tom Kite in others and when Watson and still others had records to further fuel the arguments, Watson's superiority in 1982 was little disputed. His earnings did taper off a bit as he finished fifth on the U.S. and World Money Lists, but the men ahead of him were more active on the tour. Besides, Tom's total was still a healthy $417,048. Only four players in the world won more often than he did and their victories didn't really match up in calibre of tournament, course and field to Watson's on the two fine Open courses, at Riviera for the Los Angeles win and at Harbour Town for the Heritage.

In terms of the future, it now appears that the upper strata of the career-victories records are within his reach. At 33, with at least a solid decade of full-schedule action ahead of him if he so chooses, Tom already has 28 official U.S. titles to go with his four British Open Championships and two other non-Tour wins.

To dredge up 1982 challenges to Watson's pre-eminent position, which he has occupied since 1977, one would turn to the performances of Tom's American compatriots, Raymond Floyd and Craig Stadler, who enjoyed the finest seasons of their varied careers. Many similarities existed beyond the fact that they finished one-two and dominated the World Money List, Floyd collecting $738,699, a new single-season record, and Stadler banking $664,372. Floyd won a major (the PGA Championship) and the richest event of the year (the Sun City Challenge in southern Africa) while Stadler landed the other major (the Masters) and America's premier money tournament (the World Series of Golf). Both also won twice on the PGA Tour, Floyd in the Memorial and at Memphis, Stadler at Tucson and in the Kemper in Washington, D.C. They also had an interesting give-and-take involving two of those tournaments. Stadler beat Floyd in a sudden-death playoff in the World Series, the $100,000 prize insuring his No. 1 finish on the U.S. money list. Then, Floyd turned the tables at the end of the year, again meeting and that time defeating Stadler in a sudden-death playoff in the Sun City Challenge, that $300,000 bonanza producing the World Money List record. Coincidentally, both playoffs went four holes.

The two men are at different stages of their careers, although the age of 40 doesn't seem to be bothering Floyd one bit. He has never played better over such extended periods as he did in the 1981 and 1982 seasons. His triumph in the PGA Championship was every bit as solid as his two previous victories in the 1969 PGA and the 1976 Masters. He got the bit in his mouth the first hot day at Tulsa's Southern Hills with a sparkling 63 and showed once again what a great front-runner he is, shattering and tying a flock of course and tournament records and coming up just a stroke short of the PGA's 72-hole record. Still, one wonders how long a player can keep grinding it out so successfully, recalling that Raymond has been on the PGA Tour full-time since 1963.

In contrast, Stadler is just 29 and that Masters Championship could well be just the first of a string of major titles for this very promising golfer of prodigious talent. Two incidents during 1982 convinced me of this. I talked to Arnold Palmer after he had played with Stadler in the second round of the Masters and he unequivocally forecast Craig's ultimate victory. Several months later, I played with Stadler for the first time myself and saw firsthand why the other pros are high on him. His putting touch that day in the Bruce Rappaport Pro-Am at Gleneagles, Scotland, bordered on the incredible and I was equally impressed with his straightness and length. Although much has been made of his temper, which flashes on and off so quickly, I find Craig's personality infectious. He has a sort of devil-may-care attitude toward his golf and seems totally undisturbed by the unflattering Walrus tag he has acquired. In fact, when I consider his ample middle, I think of how much 'stomach' he showed at Augusta when he gathered himself together after blowing his big lead to beat Dan Pohl with a solid playoff par. In recent years, we have seen quite a few one-season flashes who dropped back a few paces and remained consistent players at their lesser level. It will surprise me if this happens to Stadler.

A case for No. 1 could conceivably be made, too, for Calvin Peete, who in a single season established himself as the most successful black golfer in history, eclipsing the achievements of such of his racial predecessors as Lee Elder and Charley Sifford and doing it at the age of 39. Peete, who didn't even take a serious whack at a golf ball until he was 23 years old and required three tries before qualifying for the PGA Tour, won more tournaments than any other player in the world in 1982. He was the fourth highest money winner in America with $318,470 and No. 3 in the world with $455,140, and led the World Stroke Averages list at 70.28. Although not a classic swinger, Calvin is probably the most accurate shotmaker in golf today, as his leadership in 1981 and 1982 in two key statistical categories testifies. A money-winner in six figures since scoring his first Tour victory at Milwaukee in 1979, Peete was the leader both years in driving accuracy and greens hit in regulation. From late May on in 1982, Calvin added a putting stroke to the mix and went on a tear. He won again in Milwaukee and in the Anheuser-Busch Classic in Virginia in July, the B.C. Open in September, the Pensacola Open in October, then went to Japan as a member of the first Goldwin Cup team (the successor event to the U.S.-Japan ABC Cup Matches that our International Management Group people helped to pioneer there in the 1970s), shared the individual title and contributed importantly to the U.S. team victory, then capped the trip with a sixth win in the Dunlop Phoenix, Japan's richest tournament.

Tom Kite continues to do everything except attach titles in quantity to his record. The U.S. Tour's Mr. Consistency, who is more than halfway toward his second million in a 10-year career that has produced just five world titles and no majors, nearly duplicated his 1981 performance in 1982. Although yielding the money leadership in the U.S. to Stadler, he generated a $341,081 season from 24 in-the-money finishes in 25 starts, a second straight Vardon Trophy-winning season with a 70.21 stroke average. Yet, just as in 1981, he won only one tournament, again during the early-season Florida swing. In 1982, it was in the Bay Hill Classic from a chip-in birdie that bested Nicklaus and Denis Watson in a playoff.

Actually, you could attach the term, consistency, to the 1982 PGA Tour in general. As in the previous year, only five players won for the first time on the tour and three of them — Bobby Clampett, Bob Shearer and Payne Stewart — already had pro titles from other world circuits. Which leaves Hal Sutton, obviously the Rookie of the Year who capped his $252,903 international season with victory in the remodeled Disney World Classic, and Tim Norris. Sutton's excellent season was no surprise. Apparently, all the amateur standout of 1980 needed to get his professional game into high gear was to resolve his marital problems and whet his playing appetite again. The victory came after several near-misses, mostly late in the year in the U.S. and Japan, and Hal smashed Jerry Pate's rookie-year Tour record by more than $80,000. The Norris win, on the other hand, was as surprising as anything that happened in golf in 1982, not just the victory but the scores he shot. The 24-year-old, who missed the first three months of the season with a hand injury and finished only three of the next 14 tournaments he entered, then won the 15th, the Hartford Open, with rounds of 63, 64, 66 and 66 for 259, the lowest score on the PGA Tour since Mike Souchak set the record of 257 in the 1955 Texas Open. Norris won just $11,000 over and above his Hartford check for the season.

We can feel more comfortable with our predictions of greatness for Clampett after his 1982 season. Even though his earnings were little different from his first full year of 1981, the 22-year-old Clampett broke the victory ice on the U.S. Tour in 1982 at the late-season Southern Open and, perhaps more significantly, made solid runs at the U.S. and British Open Championships, leading the latter after the second and third rounds. Could it be that we have a Clampett/Watson analogy? Consider the 1974 U.S. Open at Winged Foot, where Watson, in just his third season and also then still winless on the Tour, was the third-round leader and had an even worse finish than Clampett's closing 77 at Troon. We all know what has followed that Winged Foot disaster for Watson.

Five other pros were multiple winners on the PGA Tour in 1982, only one of whom, Lanny Wadkins, falls into the category of veteran. Wadkins, one of four former Wake Forest players who had $250,000-plus seasons in 1982, had another big upsurge in an erratic, 12-year career that has brought him PGA, Tournament Players and World Series championships. After two lean seasons, the 33-year-old Virginian fashioned his best season ever, winning three events — the Tournament of Champions and the Phoenix and Buick Opens — for the first time and having his best ever year financially with $445,140 on the World Money List. Bob Gilder, generally considered a journeyman pro with just two victories during his first six seasons, erupted with three impressive victories in America and a share of the individual title with Calvin Peete in the Goldwin Cup Matches in Japan. His scoring in those four events was sensational — 13 of 14 rounds in the 60s and winning scores of 271 in the Bank of Boston Classic in Massachusetts, 266 in the Byron Nelson Classic and a record 261 in the Westchester Classic, in which he started 64-63-65 and double-eagled the 18th the third day.

Jay Haas made his season with wins two autumn Sundays apart in the Hall of Fame Tournament and the Texas Open, while Wayne Levi won early (Hawaii) and late (LaJet). Both players, like Gilder, now have five victories on their U.S. records. Payne Stewart, a qualifier in early 1981 whose career was nurtured on the Asia Circuit, had his first victory. Stewart, 25, who won the Indian and Indonesian Opens just before earning his U.S. privileges, scored three triumphs in 1982, winning the Quad Cities Open and the unofficial Magnolia Classic the same week as the Master, then the Resch's Classic in Australia in the autumn. Scott Hoch started his year ignominiously as an armed robbery victim in a Tucson motel but ended it brightly with two victories during a three-week November stay in Japan. In between, Hoch landed his second

U.S. title at New Orleans, where he was the beneficiary as persistent storms forced shortening of the USF&G tournament to 54 holes.

Gary Hallberg, of whom big things have been expected off his great collegiate career at Wake Forest, had to go out of the country to find success in 1982. Hallberg, 24, did not even finish half of the U.S. tournaments he entered and won just $36,192, barely making the list of 125 money-winners earning exempt status for 1982. However, he captured the Chunichi Crowns, Japan's richest spring tournament, and a small event in France called the Preservatrice Fonciere Open. Peter Jacobsen and Vance Heafner were two other non-winners in the U.S. who nonetheless impress me with their potential. Like Hallberg, Jacobsen won abroad, besting Seve Ballesteros in a stirring duel to win the late-season Johnnie Walker Trophy tournament in Spain for the second year in a row, but the personable Peter, a 28-year-old man who exudes charm and wit, also had an excellent season in America. A run of high finishes from mid-season on led him to a $145,832 season in the U.S. and a $183,850 one overall. In his second full season, Heafner climbed over the $100,000 mark and should maintain momentum in that direction.

Perhaps one or two of them would dispute it, but the 1982 season carried a downbeat for quite a few regulars on the American circuit. Jerry Pate, for instance, will surely take umbrage. But, I can't help watching Pate in action, that fluid swing so much like that of Gene Littler, and wondering when he is really going to burst forth. Jerry won his eighth U.S. title — the important Tournament Players Championship — and had another big year at the pay window with $380,759 in world earnings, but he is too good a player not to harness his sometimes happy-go-lucky attitude and expand his accomplishments in the major arenas. It has been too long since the U.S. Open at Atlanta in 1976. Bruce Lietzke had much the same kind of year as Pate, although I am not as high on his future prospects, particularly when hearing that he was expressing thoughts of departing the Tour even while winning the Canadian Open. He had won three times in 1981 and challenged for the No. 1 spot on the money list down to the final weeks, but, with just the victory at Glen Abbey, his earnings tailed off measurably in 1982 to $233,264.

Matters were much more disappointing for two other stars of 1981, the winners of the two Open Championships. Bill Rogers, the pleasant Texan whose victory in the 1981 British Open was the jewel among his seven wins during the year, struggled practically all year with his game, never won and seriously challenged only in the U.S. Open at Pebble Beach, where he slipped back to third place well into the final round. Rogers plunged to 36th on the World Money List with $172,839. David Graham, who was so impressive in winning the U.S. Open at Merion, salvaged something from his season in October in Paris, when he won the restructured and expanded Lancome Trophy tournament, which is now an official part of the European Tour as a tournament of that circuit's champions plus a few invitees. Graham's earnings dropped to $132,920. What happened to Rogers and Graham is often something that goes with the territory. Winners of major championships frequently find their performances declining temporarily afterward when they fulfill heavy exhibition and foreign appearance obligations and opportunities.

For the present at least, Curtis Strange seems to be settling into the pattern of

Tom Kite — consistent money-winner, infrequent title-winner. Strange, the other figure in the Wake Forest quadrangle, went through a second straight season without a victory but won $533,503 during those two years. One hopes that the flak he took when he was singled out in public print for an incident of rude on-course behavior will have a salutary rather than a negative effect on the mental approach Curtis brings to his physical talents.

Two veteran players of proven ability seem to have established living patterns that carve out sizeable segments of time with their families at the expense of constant pursuit of titles and major riches. Nearly a decade ago considered by many to be golf's next superstar, Johnny Miller seems content with his occasional returns in spurts to the brilliance of the early 1970s. The world's leading money-winner in 1981, primarily because of his $500,000 victory in the first Sun City Challenge at years's end, the 35-year-old Miller carried the impetus into the early weeks of the 1982 PGA Tour, winning at San Diego, finishing third in the Crosby and losing a playoff to Watson in the Los Angeles Open in successive weeks. However, Johnny played only 14 times in the remaining months of the season and well in just three of them, finishing the year, nonetheless, with $262,853. Hale Irwin, 37, was a little busier, winning in Florida's Inverrary Classic in March with a remarkable long-range trouble shot on the final hole and in a small, late season Brazil Open, but the income of the two-time U.S. Open champion was down heavily from 1981 and his overall record was mediocre.

The decline and fall of Ben Crenshaw and Hubert Green extended through 1982, Crenshaw's the more devastating and puzzling. The soft-spoken Texan came to the Tour a decade ago with all the credentials and an enthusiasm for the game in all of its phases, even its history. A sure-fire star, everybody agreed. But, Crenshaw kept coming up a shot or two short in so many major tournaments, often betrayed by his long game. By 1982, it had deteriorated so badly that, even though it hadn't also eroded his silken putting stroke, he played only the two fall Texas tournaments in San Antonio and Abilene after the PGA Championship in early August and did not do well in either of them. Other than the 1981 Mexican Open, Crenshaw has not won since the fall of 1980 at Napa, California. Green really had only one good shot at a title in 1982 — at Hartford where, as defending champion, he finished second but six shots behind winner Norris. Hubert dropped to 54th on the U.S. money list with just $77,448, a far cry from the 1973–1979 period when he was never worse than 13th in the rankings. I am not overly surprised at this sad development for Hubert, since I have long felt that his nervous playing mannerisms and unorthodox methods would eventually catch up to him, as they have to others with such characteristics in their games.

What of the superstars whose exploits have been documented through the 16 previous editions of this annual? Jack Nicklaus just keeps rolling along, perhaps having a poor tournament a few more times than he used to but still very obviously capable of winning a 20th major championship (counting his two U.S. Amateurs) as he came so close to doing at Pebble Beach before Watson's coup de grace. Just as was transpiring before Nicklaus won the Open and PGA in 1980, the 'over the hill' remarks were astir again when Jack ended the 1981 season without a victory among his 18 starts at home and abroad, even though he won more than $300,000. Nicklaus put it all to rest again in 1982 when he took the Colonial National Invitation tournament, one of the few older events on the Tour that he had not won before, and made several other serious bids besides the one in the Open, notably his playoff loss to Tom Kite at Bay Hill. His earnings again exceeded $300,000. Jack hardly sounded like somebody on the verge of retirement when he remarked at a late-season press conference that 'physically, there is no reason why I can't play for quite a while. The thing is whether I want to give up the things I have to give up to retire. Right now I can't wait to get started (in the new season)'.

Things did not go as well for Gary Player and Lee Trevino in 1982. One of golf's more remarkable streaks ended when Player won just once in 1982 — the early-season South African PGA Championship. Until then, Gary had won at least twice a season for 27 years in a row. Now 47 years old, the sprightly winner of 123 tournaments around the world, including nine majors, played just 11 times in America in 1982 and won only $22,059. His earnings elsewhere, though, boosted his total to $100,894. Recurring back problems plagued Trevino through much of a winless 1982, his first season without a victory since he won the U.S. Open in 1968 in his first full year on the PGA Tour. Lee's overall earnings dipped to $160,241. Surgery seemed to relieve his problems and enabled him to tune up in the two October tournaments in Texas for a strong showing in the Sun City Challenge in which he fell just a stroke short of joining the Floyd-Stadler playoff. He made it doubtful that he would be a fully active player in 1983, though, when he accepted a role as chief color commentator on 12 NBC golf telecasts and took himself out of those dozen events as a player.

Arnold Palmer had a $100,000 season, but achieved most of it on the fast-growing Senior Tour, which in 1983 was to include 18 events and carry more than $3 million in prize money. Even though he won twice in his 10 starts (he now has 84 pro titles) and was his usual self as a gallery magnet everywhere he went, Palmer was overshadowed by Miller Barber, whose four wins included the USGA Senior Open, and Don January, whose three numbered the PGA Seniors and a runaway with Sam Snead in the better-ball Legends of Golf.

The American Tour underwent its most drastic change in its modern history for 1983, yet it was barely perceptible to any except those directly involved with the Tour, its players and the tournaments. To simplify, the Tour established a sequence of exemptions good for the year for all of its tournaments and eliminated all Monday qualifying that had the lives of so many marginal players on constant edge and created countless problems for Tour officials and tournament sponsors. Yet, Tour administrators were still left with one serious headache — a large number of reasonably-able pros who didn't earn exemptions, both young men on the way up and many Tour veterans on their way down, all still wanting action and a chance to earn a livelihood in gold. One answer was the planned establishment of a 10-tournament secondary tour called the Tournament Players Series, for which many of them would be eligible. However, it was going together slowly at year's end, at that point including two events that have existed on the regular Tour for years — the Magnolia Classic opposite the Masters and the Tallahassee Open opposite the Tournament of Champions — and just three new events in Baltimore, Albuquerque, New Mexico, and Chattanooga, Tennessee with $200,000 purses. Commissioner Deane Beman floated a trial balloon on the concept of a 'split tour' for a second time in 1982, its main virtues being the new cities and additional players it would put into the big league. The proposal again drew strong opposition from existing sponsors, who didn't care for any idea that might deprive them of a chance to have all of the star players in their particular tournaments. With many of those top pros also in opposition, Beman deflated the balloon and Tour headquarters went back to the drawing board. Still, presuming the 10 events of the Tournament Players Series were booked and counting the Seniors schedule, the Tour had 72 events under its jurisdiction in 1983. I am not sure that the split tour is the best method for expansion, although I recognize that something must be done along those lines in the interest of progress. I have long pushed for some sort of an international tour with a separate administration. Perhaps this is the route that should be taken.

Golf remained healthy and interesting in other parts of the world as well in 1982. Greg Norman, the powerful and extremely promising Australian who has designs on success in America and full international recognition, topped the European Tour's Order of Merit, that circuit's alternative to the U.S. Tour's money list, but, if you go subjective rather than statistical, you really have to give Severiano Ballesteros at least a draw with him in Europe. The Order of Merit does not include the Suntory World Match Play Championship because of its highly-limited field and Ballesteros captured that important title for a second year in a row to go with his official victories in the Madrid and French Opens. That equalled in numbers Norman's wins in the Dunlop Masters, State Express Classic and Benson & Hedges International, all in Britain. From an overall standpoint, the edge goes to the Spaniard, who exudes the brilliance and magic of a superstar talent and would surely challenge America's best if he were ever to get his commercial activities and geographic dilemmas sorted out. Seve was 13th or better in six of his nine American starts in 1982, finishing second to Stadler in the Kemper Open and in a third-place tie in the Masters. A second and a third in two of Japan's lucrative late autumn tournaments led Ballesteros to a $352,312 year on the World Money List, ninth in position and first among non-Americans. Norman also played an international schedule, but was overshadowed at home in his few appearances and did well in just one of his American starts, tying for fifth in the PGA Championship. He finished the year 23rd on the World Money List at $226,059.

Nobody else really stood out in Europe, as the three men generally considered at or near the level of Ballesteros and Norman managed only a victory apiece, although Nick Faldo missed the initial Continental segment while playing with some success in the early months in America. His victory came in the Haig Whisky Tournament Players Championship after Sandy Lyle had successfully defended in the Lawrence Batley the week after the British Open and Bernhard Langer did likewise in the German Open.

Europe had new faces, too. Gordon Brand Jr. won twice — in the Bob Hope British Classic and the Coral Classic — and, although it came thousands of miles away, British and Irish golf fans hailed the late November victory of 18-year-old Ronan Rafferty, the rookie pro from Ireland, in the Venezuelan Open. The Caracas tournament was one of the events formerly played in the

South American Tour, which splintered in 1982 because of the unrest and economic problems of that continent. We learned otherwise only of the aforementioned win by Hale Irwin in the Brazil Open and of John Cook in the Sao Paulo Open, also in Brazil.

Calvin Peete went to Venezuela to play after returning from Japan, planning to get in another tournament before joining Bob Gilder at Acapulco to represent the U.S. in the World Cup Matches there. Peete never reached Mexico as he suffered a serious reaction to a bee sting at Caracas and returned to the States after that tournament. That set World Cup officials scrambling again. They had done a lot of contact work before settling on Gilder and Peete originally and went back at it to come up with Bobby Clampett as Bob's partner.

Actually, that was a relatively minor problem among the many Executive Director John Ross and his staff faced in economically-strapped Mexico. (Would you believe T-shirts lettered 'Wordl Cup'?) All of the grand plans of Cup officials to get more of the world's leading players back into the international competition went down the drain when the Sun City Challenge, with its field of 10 of the world's biggest stars, was lodged into the same early December dates. For one reason or another, Langer, Lyle and Faldo passed up the event and, with their seasons still going, the top players from Japan and Australia also skipped it. Taiwan sent no team because of its running dispute over the name and flag of its team and Mexico declared ahead of time that it would not admit South Africans. So, the infusion of considerable prize and guarantee money had no helpful effect on the field whatever and the World Cup is once again in jeopardy. Which is not to detract overly from the victory of the Spanish team of Manuel Pinero and Jose-Maria Canizares and the individual triumph of Pinero, who had won the European Open earlier in the season.

Over the last quarter century, many young pros in South Africa had appeared to challenge Gary Player's exalted position — and failed. Dale Hayes, Bobby Cole, the Hennings come to mind. With Gary's career now winding down, a takeover seems more likely, although none of the leading prospects appears to have the tools to reach Player's peak level. The results of South Africa's relatively-brief 1982 season indicate that Mark McNulty may be the best of the lot. McNulty, who miraculously survived without serious injury a high-speed collision with a bus, won four of the seven events on the Sunshine Circuit shortly thereafter. He and Denis Watson, who nearly won at Bay Hill, were to return to America for another full-time shot at the PGA Tour, along with Nick Price, who qualified in the fall a few months after his ill-fated run at the British Open Championship at Troon. Between them, Watson and Price took the two Sunshine titles that McNulty and Player didn't. South Africa also reminds us of the passing of time. Gary Player's son, Wayne, was to launch his pro career on the 1983 Sunshine Circuit.

While Greg Norman was making his mark primarily in Europe in 1982, two other Australians were performing well elsewhere. As already noted, Bob Shearer was one of five men who won their first titles in America in 1982, but that underplays it. The 34-year-old pro, who had won the 1981 Australasia Order of Merit with two late-season victories in New Zealand, returned to

America the next March and within two months had won the Tallahassee Open and more than $100,000. By the time he went back to Australia for the important events in the later-year months, he had insured his position as the leading foreign money-winner in America. But, the best was yet to come — a solid victory in the Australian Open, an earlier win in the New South Wales Open and the No. 1 spot again on the Order of Merit.

In the latter role, he edged Graham Marsh, who had perhaps his best-ever Australian year, yet marred it when he chose to play in the rich Dunlop Phoenix tournament in Japan instead of the Australian Open, in effect forfeiting his shot at the Order of Merit title. Marsh, long one of the game's real globe-trotters, played more in his homeland in 1982 than he had in years and he won four times — the South Australian and Queensland Opens, the Australian Masters and the Australian PGA Championship. He was severely criticized by some fellow pros and others for his intention to bypass the Open, particularly since he heads the players organization in Australia. The criticism was deserved. For years Graham has been making speeches urging support for Australian golf when commercial interests might dictate otherwise. In failing to seek and find a proper way to skip the big Japanese event (which he surely could have done) and play in his country's national championship, Marsh was being unpardonably hypocritical. Even though missing out on the Australasia Circuit title, Marsh still had a most worthwhile season. His four Australian wins and a fifth victory in Japan in the Mitsubishi Galant tournament boosted him toward $191,363 in income for 1982. Terry Gale, who lost the 1981 Order of Merit when Shearer won those New Zealand tournaments, landed both of them in 1982 to cap his finest season. He had earlier taken the Western Australian Open and the Yomiuri in Japan on his way to a $131,442 year.

Until 1982, Tsuneyuki Nakajima's international reputation had been mostly negative, the result of the 13 he scored in the 1978 Masters at the 13th hole and the nine he took at St. Andrews' famed Road Hole in the British Open a few months later. His accomplishments in 1982 should tend to blot out those two indiscretions. The 28-year-old golfer, who had been on the verge of a big season for years, broke loose with five victories that helped him supplant Isao Aoki as Japan's No. 1 player in 1982. Nakajima earned his place as the No. 14 money-winner in the world — $287,202 — with an astonishing record on consistency. He played in 31 tournaments on the Japanese Tour and was 10th or better 25 times, fifth or better 20 times and out of the money only twice.

Nakajima is just one of several of the younger Japanese pros mounting bids to overtake Aoki, who has served as a great ambassador for his country in the international field for many years. Although he trailed only Nakajima on the Japanese Tour money list and won $255,711 world-wide, Isao managed only one victory, appropriately in the Japan Match Play Championship, which he has won four of the last five years. In America, he placed third in the World Series. Another remarkable showing of 1982 also occurred in Japan, where 45-year-old Teruo Sugihara demonstrated why he has won more tournaments than any other Japanese pro by adding five and running his total to 45. Masahiro Kuramoto, another of those serious contenders for the No. 1 spot in Japan, failed to duplicate his sensational rookie year of 1981, but still won twice, one the Japan PGA Championship, and displayed his ability for the world to see when he played solidly in the British Open and finished fourth.

Taiwan's most promising player — Lu Hsi Chuen — struggled through his first winless season in his four-year pro career, but two of his older countrymen had considerable success. Both Hsu Sheng San and Hsieh Min Nan had three-tournament winning streaks in the Orient. Hsu achieved his in the heart of the Asia Circuit season on his way to the seasonal championship, while Hsieh ran off his triple in the stronger competition of the Tokai Classic, Golf Digest and Bridgestone tournaments on the Japanese Circuit. The former World Cup winner, now 42, also edged Hsu to win the Philippine Open early in the season and wound up 21st on the World Money List with $231,293, more than any other Taiwanese player ever accumulated in a single season.

It was all very fitting when JoAnne Carner routed her elite opposition with a five-stroke victory in the Chevrolet World Championship of Women's Golf, the tournament we of International Management Group founded in 1980 to bring together the 12 best female players for a 72-hole shootout late in each season. In the first place, it did exactly what it was supposed to do — crown the year's best player. Carner clearly was that person, winning four other titles on her way to the first $300,000-plus season in the history of the Ladies Professional Golf Association and the No. 1 position on the money list in a runaway with her official $310,399 and $356,900 from all sources. Even more significantly, the win, her 35th, put the 43-year-old veteran into the LPGA Hall of Fame, just the 10th player in history to achieve that status. The $50,000 JoAnne received from that victory at Shaker Heights Country Club in suburban Cleveland was the check that carried her past Beth Daniel's previous record of $231,000. Daniel, who also won five times during 1982 and was third on the LPGA World Money List with $242,263, had captured the Chevrolet World Championship the first two years. When you consider that Big Momma, as Carner is affectionately known, has won all of those tournaments and more than a million dollars in just 12 years since turning pro in 1970 at age 31, and doing that after monopolizing before then with five Amateur Championships, one surely agrees with *Golf World*'s editorial suggestion that JoAnne 'is the next logical female candidate for the World Golf Hall of Fame'.

The comeback of Sandra Haynie accelerated in 1982. The 39-year-old Texan, who won her first title in six years and almost $100,000 when she returned to competitive golf in 1981, played in 1982 like she did back in the 1960s and early 1970s. Sandra picked off two individual titles, including the major Peter Jackson classic, teamed with Kathy McMullen to win the Ping Team Championship and finished second in five other tournaments en route to a $264,074 season, the first time in 22 seasons that she had even been in six figures on a money list.

The 1983 season, when the LPGA approaches $7 million in prize money and goes on all three major American TV networks for the first time, should give a strong inkling about the future of Nancy Lopez, whether her second marriage, this time to Houston baseball player Ray Knight, will settle her back into the form that brought her domineering success until her private life soured and slowed her down for parts of the 1981 and 1982 seasons. She did win twice in 1982, though, in fact taking the second victory in November, the Mazda in Japan, while on a sort of honeymoon trip. Patty Sheehan, 1981's Rookie of the

Year, continued to improve in 1982, winning three times and, like Daniel, Haynie and Sally Little, topping the $200,000 mark in winnings. Jan Stephenson, another LPGA star who was preoccupied in 1982 straightening out her marital life, still played well enough to capture two tournaments, including the PGA Championship, and Kathy Whitworth passed Mickey Wright with her 82nd and 83rd victories in the Women's International at Hilton Head and the Lady Michelob at Atlanta. The surprise of the year came in the most prestigious of all the events, when unheralded Janet Alex, who had not won during her first four seasons, took the U.S. Women's Open at Del Paso in Sacramento, California.

The LPGA also may have the brightest newcomer in American pro golf in 1983 with the arrival of Juli Inkster, a 22-year-old Californian out of San Jose State, who turned pro in the fall of 1982 after winning her third consecutive Women's Amateur championship at the Broadmoor in Colorado Springs, the first time anybody had tripled that tournament in almost 50 years.

Until they come to America to play, little is known about the fast-developing women pro golfers of Japan for lack of news of that circuit. Still, enough information has filtered out for us to know that the most frequent winner in the entire world of golf in 1982 played the Japanese LPGA circuit. Tu Ai Yu, a 28-year-old Taiwanese pro, won nine tournaments in Japan in 1982, challenging the No. 1 status now being accorded to Ayako Okamoto, although the two did not go head to head through most of the season because Okamoto played in America — and with considerable success. She won the Arizona Copper Classic in Tucson, Arizona, early in the year and wound up with $87,768 in overall earnings. Okamoto, 31, now has 24 victories on her record, but still has a long way to go to catch Japan's best known woman golfer, Chako Higuchi, who has 59 titles.

Our final look at the 1982 pro golf season here is through the medium of the individualistic Mark H. McCormack Rating System, a procedure we devised and have applied to the world of men's pro golf since 1968. Everybody has his own idea about how golfers should be ranked. This one is predicated on the three most recent seasons, rather than a single one, as a measure of staying power . . . an avoidance of direct use of money winnings and of stroke averages at all because of their inconsistencies as gauges . . . and a point system that stresses bonuses for victories, strengths of fields and statures of tournaments. The structure of the point system accompanies the following standings, which show:

THE TOP 25 GOLFERS IN THE WORLD

Position	Player, Country	1980	1981	1982	TOTAL
1	Tom Watson, U.S.	134	89	143	366
2	Raymond Floyd, U.S.	21	118	150.5	289.5
3	Severiano Ballesteros, Spain	62.5	83.5	124	270
4	Tom Kite, U.S.	21	90	146.5	257.5
5	Craig Stadler, U.S.	35.5	46.5	165.5	247.5
6	Jerry Pate, U.S.	49.5	93	102.5	245
7	Jack Nicklaus, U.S.	56.5	68.5	112.5	237.5

8	Bill Rogers, U.S.	25	152.5	31.5	209
9	Isao Aoki, Japan	67.5	93	45	205.5
10	Curtis Strange, U.S.	46.5	50.5	101	198
11	Bruce Lietzke, U.S.	16.5	117.5	57	191
12	Greg Norman, Australia	43.5	77.5	67	188
13	David Graham, Australia	27	95	63	185
14	Graham Marsh, Australia	22	50	85	157
15	Bernhard Langer, West Germany	27.5	86	36.5	150
16	Calvin Peete, U.S.	2.5	13.5	131	147
17	Lanny Wadkins, U.S.	6	10	130	146
18	Lee Trevino, U.S.	94	36.5	13	143.5
19	Larry Nelson, U.S.	35.5	48	54.5	138
T20	Masahiro Kuramoto, Japan	—	65	69.5	134.5
	Bob Gilder, U.S.	21.5	15.5	97.5	134.5
	Tsuneyuki Nakajima, Japan	10.5	22	102	134.5
T23	Sandy Lyle, Great Britain	36.5	35	60.5	132
	Hale Irwin, U.S.	16	90	26	132
25	Johnny Miller, U.S.	9.5	63	56.5	129

POINT CATEGORIES

Class 1: The U.S. and British Opens, the Masters, the PGA Championship.
Class 2: U.S. Tour events in which at least 13 of the 15 leading money-winners of that particular year competed.
Class 3: U.S. Tour events in which from 10 to 12 of the leading money-winners competed.
Class 4: All other U.S. Tour events.

(Certain events carrying particular status or with especially strong fields are placed in higher categories or assigned special point scales. Otherwise, all other non-U.S. Tour events go into Class 4.)

POINT ASSIGNMENTS

1982 — *Class 1*: Top 10 finishers — 30 points for winner, 24 for second, down to 16 for 10th. *Class 2*: Top 8 finishers — 25 points for winner, 19 for second, down to 13 for eighth. *Class 3*: Top 6 finishers — 20 points for winner, 14 for second, down to 10 for sixth. *Class 4*: 12 points for winner, 6 for second, 5 for third.

1981 — *Class 1*: Top 10 finishers — 25, 29 to 11 points. *Class 2*: Top 8 finishers — 20, 14 to 8 points. *Class 3*: Top 6 finishers — 15, 9 to 5 points. *Class 4*: Top 3 finishers — 10, 4, 3 points.

1980 — *Class 1*: Top 10 finishers — 20, 14 to 6 points. *Class 2*: Top 8 finishers — 12, 9 to 3 points. *Class 3*: Top 6 finishers — 11, 5 points to 1 point. *Class 4*: Top 3 finishers — 8 points, 2 points, 1 point.

Several men other than Jack Nicklaus and Tom Watson have headed the U.S. and World Money Lists during the last 15 years, but the dominance of those two great players has been clearly reflected in these ratings. One or the other has been No. 1 in this evaluation exercise since we devised it in 1968, Nicklaus for the first 10 years and Watson since then, Tom finishing on top for the fifth time at the close of the 1982 season. His margin this time, though, was his slimmest since he first took over from Nicklaus by 18 points in 1978 and his point total was the lowest since he became the leading man. He had a new challenger in 1982, too. Raymond Floyd, who wasn't even among the top 25 in 1980, then jumped in at the ninth position in 1981, finished second, 76.5 points behind Watson.

These rankings also verify Seve Ballesteros' stature as the leading non-American golfer. The Spaniard, who has climbed steadily since his first appearance among the top 25 in the 10th position in 1977, placed third in 1982, just 19.5 points behind Floyd but comfortably ahead of two other Americans who made big strides in 1982. Tom Kite jumped from 14th to fourth place and Craig Stadler, who made the list for the first time at 23rd position in 1981, finished fifth. Winning only the Tournament Players Championship in 1982, Jerry Pate slipped from fourth to sixth place, while Nicklaus, now one of just two players who have been in the ratings every year, recovered from 12th in 1981 to seventh position. Lee Trevino, the other man with the unbroken record in the rankings, plunged from fifth to 18th place after his poor 1982 season and Gary Player dropped out of the top 25 for the first time. Their relatively-unsuccessful years skidded Bill Rogers from second to eighth and Isao Aoki from third to ninth.

In all, nine non-Americans placed among the elite 25 — Australians Greg Norman (12th), David Graham (13th) and Graham Marsh (14th), Japanese Masahiro and Tsuneyuki Nakajima (tied for 20th), German Bernhard Langer (15th) and Sandy Lyle of Great Britain (23rd) in addition to Ballesteros and Aoki. Four entered the select 25 circle for the first time — Calvin Peete and Bob Gilder as well as Kuramoto and Nakajima — while Lanny Wadkins returned after a one-year absence, coming in at 17th right behind Peete. Gilder was in a three-way tie at 20th place. Besides Player, Ben Crenshaw, Mike Reid, Lon Hinkle, Andy Bean and Lu Hsi Chuen fell out of the standings.

Finally, before dispatching the reader into the nitty gritty of the 1982 year of golf around the world in the chapters that follow, we call attention to a decision that, in its way, has taken the game full cycle at the Masters. Heeding the appeals of many of the leading players, officials at Augusta National decided that, for the first time in 1983, they would permit the players to bring their own caddies, if they so desired, rather than be required to use a man out of the Augusta National caddie pool, which has had more and more unqualified men of late. The irony is that the Masters, which has always had black caddies exclusively but for so many years was the target of criticism because it had never invited a black player to the tournament until Lee Elder ame in 1975, will have its first white caddies in 1983.

2. The Masters

Who can forget the agony of Ed Sneed in 1979? Confronted with the challenge of making only one par in the last three holes to win a green jacket, he was unable to do it, bogeying them all and then losing on the second hole of sudden death to Fuzzy Zoeller in a three-way playoff that included Tom Watson. Zoeller and Watson had been paired and stood watching at the scorer's tent as Sneed missed the five-foot putt that would have given him the Masters. Standing on the green itself, also watching, was Craig Robert Stadler, Sneed's playing partner, who had shared the 36-hole lead with Sneed before self-destructing, a habit of his during his formative years of the Tour. He was probably glowering as he watched Sneed putt and perhaps his thoughts were miles away, since he had already holed out, but the one thing that surely never occurred to him was that three years later he, Craig Stadler, would be in precisely the same position as Sneed and that he . . . well, we'll get to that in due time. So much happened before Stadler reached the 72nd green.

For instance, the pairing of Tom Kite and Jerry Pate went off at 7.30 in the morning. That's a U.S. Open hour, not Augusta, Bob Jones' gathering of friends in sunlight among flowering dogwood and azaleas. For instance, John Schroeder, Bill Rogers and Calvin Peete teed off at 11.30. A threesome? And off the 10th tee? For instance, Mark Hayes was putting for a birdie on 18 from only eight feet away. He missed and his putt for a par was from 35 feet. His putt for a bogey was from 40 feet and he finally sunk a five footer for a six. Nor was this an isolated catastrophe. The greens at the 1982 Masters were, as Tom Weiskopf put it, like chipping to a table top. Jack Nicklaus compared them to the hood of a car. Add to this some difficult pin placements — 'unfair,' the players called them — and an opening-day typhoon that created a river down the middle of the course and you had 77–77 (Bill Rogers) making the cut and, when it was over, only six players under par.

During the early days of the Masters, the greens at Augusta National were as fast as any short of a U.S. Open. There were no measuring devices; this is merely the perceptions of players who were there, then and now. Certainly the score required to win became lower. With one exception, 280 always won in the '40s, and 283 was the average winning score in the '50s. But over the past 15 years, 283 would have won only twice and one of those years, 1972 when Nicklaus won with 286, the greens were infected with a leafy strain called poa annua, making putting a bit like Russian roulette. The last eight years the average winning score had been 276.6. Double digit red numbers proliferated the leaderboards around the course.

To combat lowering scores, Masters officials kept tinkering with the course. Various tees were moved about to either lengthen a hole or make a dogleg more pronounced, pines and bunkers were inserted to put more pressure on the tee shot. Finally, between the 1980 and '81 tournaments, Augusta National's Bermuda grass greens were torn up and replaced with bent. There was some panic just before last year's event when several greens had virtually no grass. Frantic work made them passable but it wasn't until this year that the course, according to management, became 'close to where Bob Jones would like it to be played.' Tom Kite put it another way. 'The course is still on Washington Road,' he said, 'but it's not the same. All the good stuff I've built up for five years has gone for naught. Now there will be situations where I'll have to make up a shot I don't know.' In practice Johnny Miller stroked a putt up the hill on the 18th green, turned to say something to a playing partner and was astonished to find that the ball was now behind him. Said Ray Floyd: 'If they put the pins Thursday where they did today (Tuesday) you'll have some peculiar things happening out there.'

And finally, Nicklaus: 'The course is more like I would like to see it played,' he said, sounding like a Bob Jones echo. 'The green speed is the only change necessary if there are sensible pin placements. If they put the pins where they have in recent years, I would not call that sensible, nor would the scores be sensible. Now you're going to have to think a lot more about what you should do with your tee shots and second shots. Before it didn't make much difference if you were putting 20 feet uphill or 20 feet downhill.'

On the eve of the tournament, Hord Hardin, chairman of the Masters committee, announced one change in the rules concerning qualification for invitation. A 14th category was added which includes all players on the top 30 of the previous year's money list not otherwise qualified. Bobby Clampett and Tom Purtzer would have been at Augusta had the rule been in effect this year, having finished 19th and 27th in 1981. The players were naturally pleased although Tom Watson thought the number might have been the top 20, not 30. There are two ways of looking at the change, although in itself it is not really significant. The addition of Clampett and Purtzer would indeed improve the quality of the field, no doubt about that, but it also makes the field a bit more like the Tournament Players Championship or even the Tucson Open. Earning your way to Augusta has always been a goal for all players and the easier it becomes, the less of an achievement it is. As I say, this change does not matter a lot, but should Masters officials someday yield again and allow, say, the top 60, it would be sad.

On Tuesday a freak snowstorm hit the northeast, trapping many would-be Masters voyagers and preventing them from arriving until late Wednesday. And that seemed to set the tone for the week . . . weather. Wednesday afternoon at Augusta, assuming the weather is benign, is always a pleasant time. You can watch most of the golfers play the par 3 course — Watson won this year in a three-way playoff with Peter Jacobsen and Jerry Pate — and then wander back to the clubhouse veranda and speculate who will win the tournament. *The Augusta Chronicle* annually polls its writers and a group of local club pros and not surprisingly, Watson was the player most often mentioned. After all, his last five years at Augusta included first (twice), second (twice) and 12th, a record that compared favorably to the best of Nicklaus, Arnold Palmer and Ben Hogan. Furthermore, he had just won the Heritage Classic, indication that his game was set.

Other players mentioned prominently were Tom Kite, based on his consistency at Augusta — top 10 in six of seven years; Jerry Pate, winner of the TPC;

Ray Floyd, Seve Ballesteros and, of course, Nicklaus. None of the eight writers or 10 club pros picked Craig Stadler, although one club pro, Dave Franklin of Goshen Plantation Country Club, had him as a third pick and two writers picked him as a dark horse. Stadler came to Augusta as the third leading money winner behind Pate and Kite and a reputation as a hothead who could toss away a lead as quickly as he could toss away a golf club.

I digress with a brief but significant memory. I was at Baltusrol for the 1980 U.S. Open. During the second round I was strolling up the 18th fairway with a friend, left side, when a player hacked the ball out of the deep rough toward the green and then hurled his club rather violently toward his caddie. It was Stadler, angry as usual, not the sort of behavior one likes to see at any tournament, much less the U.S. Open. But the reason I so well remember the moment is that much to my surprise, some hours later, I learned that Stadler had shot a 67 and that he had made par on the final hole. A par for a 67 in the U.S. Open. I remember thinking I'd hate to see him after he'd shot a 77.

Which is a score Craig Stadler shot a lot of during the early years of his pro career. He played his college golf at the University of Southern California and in 1973 won the U.S. Amateur. He turned pro two years later, tried the PGA's fall qualifying school, failed, but got his card on his second try in the spring of 1976. He earned only $2,702 that first year and while the figure rose every year, reaching $73,392 in 1979 for the 55th on the money list, he seemed headed for a career of mediocrity, a burly, red-faced young man with a walrus mustache who was saddled with an uncontrollable temper.

But in 1980 his talent for the game broke out, although his temper was— and still is— a dominating characteristic. Stadler contends his anger is no problem. 'When I make a mistake or throw away some shots, I'll get mad and maybe bang my club into the ground, but when I get ready to hit the next shot, I've forgotten it,' Stadler said recently. Maybe it was his marriage or the birth of his son that motivated him. He won the Bob Hope Desert Classic in 1980 shortly before his son Kevin was born and the Greater Greensboro Open not long after. The next year he won the Kemper and both years he finished eighth on the money list with more than $200,000.

He began 1982 in style, winning at Tucson, and he let several other opportunities slip away, most notably the Crosby. He held a five-stroke lead on Jim Simons with nine holes remaining, but when the two of them reached the 17th tee, the lead was gone. Then, as a national television audience looked on, Stadler hooked his tee shot onto the rocks of Carmel Bay and as he did so, he turned violently away, saying something that surely wasn't printable. Simons won the tournament. But Stadler's game continued on a high level. At Augusta he said: 'My confidence is as high as it has ever been. I won that first tournament and playing well every week has boosted that confidence even more. There's really no difference in my game, but my golf course management is getting better. I'm getting the most out of my game.' He also had a comment about the greens. 'Sure they're fast,' he said. 'That's the way I like them.'

Thursday morning dawned, but only barely. It was dark and, worse, it was cold. Temperatures at nearby Daniel Field airport were in the high 40s. There was a definite threat of rain and it felt as if it might even snow, so icy was the breeze. And yet a sizable crowd with sizable umbrellas at the ready turned out to watch Byron Nelson, in a shockingly purple sweater, and Gene Sarazen, all in powder blue, hit the traditional first shots. Sarazen was using the orange ball, making it quite a colorful beginning. Nelson had a 40 for the front nine, which is all he played, Sarazan a 45, and as it turned out there were a number of players who would have traded Byron for this first-nine score. Someone asked Nelson about the condition of the greens. 'Fastest I've ever seen the greens here,' he said, and Nelson goes back to the first years of the tournament.

At 9.30 the pairing of Dave Eichelberger and John Schroeder launched the tournament proper. Observing them and the next several groups play the first hole, it was obvious that the course was going to play a lot longer than normal. The players looked like condemned prisoners as two by two they trooped up to the first green. The pin was set at the back and almost without exception the approach shots were falling short, a sign perhaps that the air was heavy or that they feared balls hit too far into the green might roll right over.

The rain began to fall at a few minutes after 10 and up went the umbrellas, always a colorful scene but one not recommended for golf watching. Together with the darkness and the cold — and virtually every player said it was the cold that made the day a nightmare — the scene was unreal. This was Augusta, it was April and there were the world's best golfers out there, but it was as if nothing was really happening. No cheers, no applause, perhaps because it takes two hands to clap and everyone was holding on to an umbrella. Or else was wearing mittens, or socks in place of mittens. Players began producing an odd assortment of hand-warmers, huge gloves that would be removed for a shot and quickly put back on. There had been two memorable rainstorms during the 1970s — Saturday of '73, when heavy rains all day prevented the third round from really getting started and in 1979, when late in Friday's second round, a torrential downpour ended play for the day. But it had been sultry that day. As Hale Irwin said later this Thursday after struggling in with an 80: 'I'm sure I've played in heavier rain. I'm sure I've played through stronger winds and I'm sure I've played when it was colder. But I don't think I've played when all three conditions combined to make things as miserable as it was out there today.'

At 11.36, with the rain now falling heavily, Fuzzy Zoeller teed off on a round which a good four hours later would make him 'the first-round leader.' His day had a certain symmetry to it; six birdies, six pars, six bogeys. Zoeller seemed headed for a sub-par round when he went two under after a birdie at the par-five 15th, but he bogeyed both 16 and 18. On 16, after a short tee shot, he chipped to two feet, but his short putt missed and wound up six feet away. Ever the comic, Zoeller said later: 'It looked good going by the hole. You can always tell a pro — he never leaves it short. I hit it firm because if I had babied it I would have lost the ball to the right.' Zoeller's last competitive round had been an 84 at Greensboro. Asked about it, he said: 'To begin with, I don't think that was me that shot that 84. It must have been somebody else. Actually I was trying to get my handicap squared away. Now maybe I'll get some strokes in the pro-ams.'

Through noon the rain kept coming. It slackened a bit around one, then began again. Morris Hatalsky limped home with a 73, thanks to superb putting. Old Gay Brewer had the same score on a round that resembled Zoeller's, five birdies, six bogeys. 'I made more putts today than I ever have for 18 holes,' said

Brewer, proving that not everybody was bedeviled by the greens.

Nicklaus went off at exactly one o'clock, parred the first two holes, then chipped in for a birdie at three. A bogey at seven put him back to even par for the front nine. Four pairings behind him, Watson started off with a birdie and held on to that through nine holes. One group back, paired with Curtis Strange, Stadler also fashioned a 35 for nine, due largely to some long par putts. On the eighth hole, for instance, Craig drove into the fairway bunker on the right side, came out, tried to hook a fairway wood onto the green and caught a tree branch, hit his approach shot 30 feet from the pin and dropped the putt for an easy par. Buoyed by that, he knocked his approach on nine close to the pin and sank the putt.

When he reached the 10th tee, he found a collection of his fellow pros waiting. It was now shortly after four in the afternoon and the golf course was now largely under water. It was getting darker and colder every minute and even if the rain had magically stopped it would have been impossible for every player to complete his round before evening. And now a strange thing happened. As the rain increased one more notch to an absolute torrent, the players simply stopped playing. There was no official siren; it was just that so much water was falling that golf was impossible. Nicklaus stood huddled under an umbrella on the 11th fairway, conferring with an official about where he could get a drop, since his tee shot and much of the surrounding area was now a lake. Waiting behind him on the tee was Arnold Palmer and the French amateur, Philippe Ploujoux.

And then suddenly everyone was trooping back the long hill toward the clubhouse, caddies sloshing along behind their players. It was like walking up the middle of a stream and after a while there was no point in trying to keep dry because it was too late. The day was over with 36 players still to complete their rounds, the last of whom were Jack Renner and Ron Streck, at the seventh when play was suspended.

Soon after came the announcement that play would be resumed at 7.30 the next morning and that the entire field would begin round two at 11.30, going off in threesomes from the first and 10th tees. Naturally the groupings could not be made until all first rounds had been completed. So Zoeller had the low score for 18 with his 72, while Hatalsky, Brewer, Greg Norman and Peter Oosterhuis were one stroke behind at 73. Oosterhuis was two-under after a birdie at 12, but bogeys at 13, 14, 16 and 18 (together with a birdie at 15) cost him an amazingly good round.

Unofficial first-round leaders with their front-nine, one-under 35s were Stadler, Watson, David Graham and Seve Ballesteros. At even par were Nicklaus, his amateur playing partner Jodie Mudd, the perfect name for the day, and Bernhard Langer, who had finished second to Bill Rogers in the 1981 British Open. The prospect of finishing their first rounds at 7.30 did not thrill the players. 'You think it was cold this afternoon" asked Tom Kite, who had a 37. 'Wait until tomorrow. You'll be able to drive the 10th green because all that casual water will be ice. We won't have to worry about any of the water hazards.'

One man would not be returning Friday. Herman Keiser, age 67, had decided to use his lifetime pass as a former champion (1946) and participate in the tournament one last time. 'To revive old memories,' is how he put it. That was certainly his prerogative, but one would have thought Masters officials would have paired him with, say, Doug Ford, another past champion and have sent them off in the final pairing. Instead they matched him with Mark Hayes, going off at 10.33, prime time. 'I was hoping it was his son,' said Hayes. It took Keiser five shots to reach the first green, he hit five balls in the water during the round and three-putted 'seven or eight times.' The sad total: 93. At the end his hands were numb. 'I couldn't play tomorrow if they offered me first prize,' he said. However the pairing did not seem to bother Hayes. His 74 was a good score on this bad day.

Keiser won high score honors, but not by much. Frank Conner broke 90 by one stroke while Jim Thorpe beat him by one for an 88. You reach 88 by carding, among other things, a triple bogey, four doubles and nothing like a birdie. 'It's a darn shame to work this hard to get here and then shoot a number like that,' said Thorpe. 'It was one of those days when an old fashioned football game would have been better.' And most of the field would have agreed. Of the 39 players who finished, 77.5 was the average score. All in all, a dismal day.

Friday brought on and off sun and bone-chilling temperatures. The scene around the practice putting green looked more like a Monday qualifying round for rabbits, except that the players on the green were Nicklaus, Miller, Balles-teros, Pate, Kite and so on. But there were no crowds, just small clusters of people dressed for a November football game. At 7.15 the golfers began the trek out to where they had marked their balls the evening before, another curious sight. Just as there had been no obvious order to stop play the day before, there was no apparent signal to begin. 'I thought they'd shoot off a gun,' Kite said on the 10th tee. 'Clifford Roberts had the last gun,' answered Jerry Pate as all within earshot winced.

Wandering down the 10th hole into Amen Corner, the wet ground made a squishing sound when you took a step, rather like walking on soggy cornflakes. I wasn't around for the first Masters, or any of those pre-World War II tournaments, but this is what it must have been like. Winnie Palmer and Barbara Nicklaus, both bundled appropriately, chatted as Jack prepared for his first shot of the day, probably the most difficult one on the course — the second at 11. With the pond guarding the left front of the green, it is not exactly like hitting your tee shot at one. Arnold was back at the tee, waiting for Nicklaus to hit. On a normal day, the two wives would be in the area, but so would 5,000 or so other people and the chances of the two women meeting would be small. This looked more like a club tournament.

Nicklaus, after dropping his ball over his shoulder, hit a Hogan-type shot just off the right fringe and got down in two for a par. He then hit a six-iron 10 feet from the pin at 12. As he did so, Palmer hit his approach Palmer-type 20 feet from the flag at 11 and it was a treat to watch the two old warhorses roll in birdie putts at approximately the same moment. And watch is the word. At 12 I was able to stand immediately against the ropes when Palmer drove, something you can only do if you are one of those fans who arrive at dawn and take one position for the full day.

By 8.15, the sun had come out through patches of blue sky and an hour later the skies were clear, the temperature going up from, say, Boston in November to Augusta in April. Nicklaus failed to make birdies at 13 and 15, and two par-fives, but he put his tee shot at 16 two feet from the pin, dropped the putt and went to two under par. At 18 his six-iron approach gave him an eight-footer which he made. Three under, 69 for the two-day opening round, the only score in the 60s as it turned out and three strokes better than the next best, Zoeller's 72. Golf tournaments are rarely won before Sunday, but there have been exceptions and one that comes to mind involved the same man on the same course exactly 10 years earlier. On that year of the bumpy greens, Nicklaus went out in 37 Thursday morning, then shot 31 on the back nine. His 68 put him in a lead he never relinquished and he finished the tournament as the only player in red figures.

Lest you think the course on Friday morning was playing easier than it had the day before, ask Watson, Stadler, Kite and Hale Irwin if they agree. Watson, you'll remember, was one under after nine. Friday morning he bogeyed 10 and 11, but settled down to reach the 16th tee at even. The 16th is the par three whose fairway is mostly water and if you don't use enough club . . . plop. In went Watson and by the time he had holed out, he had a triple-bogey six. Rattled, he added two closing bogeys to finish with 42 for the back nine and 77 for the round. He had lost seven strokes to Nicklaus over the final three holes. 'I've used up my allotment of mistakes for the entire tournament,' he said.

Stadler, also with 35 for the front nine, got nailed with two double-bogeys sandwiched around a bogey. At 12 he was in the water. At 13, trying for the green in two, he found the ditch. Then he nearly topped his drive at 14, was short in two, pitched poorly and three-putted. A birdie at 16 got him home in 40 and 75 for the round.

'I went in and had breakfast,' said Stadler, 'then tried to go out and make up some shots. It really wasn't a letdown that did me in. In the morning, a couple of shots I felt I hit good didn't turn out good. I did not hit that many bad ones.'

Kite added a 39 to his 37 for a 76, but that was better than Irwin, who had a 41 for an 80 and Miller, who was 42 for an 81. But the biggest disaster among those who have known glory was Andy North, winner of the 1978 U.S. Open. His back nine, most of it shot Thursday afternoon, included only one par, a three at the 12th. His line score, for the record: 653–756–465—47. That's three double bogeys, five bogeys and one par.

But there were success stories, too. Jack Renner rolled in a 40-foot birdie putt at 18 Friday morning and found himself tied for second with Zoeller at even par. Renner, in the true style of a Rod Funseth a few years back, immediately established himself as a definite non-favorite, saying the course was too long for him. Informed he was playing in a threesome with Nicklaus later that morning, he said: 'Now I've got the Bear where I want him. I'll bet he's shaking in his boots.'

Curtis Strange was paired with Stadler and had posted a 39 when play was suspended. Friday morning he three-putted the 10th, then hit into the water at 12. He managed to salvage a bogey, but even so he was five over after 12 holes. Unshaken, he birdied the next three to get in with a 35 and a respectable 74.

One stroke lower were two Australians, Greg Norman and David Graham and a Spaniard, the long-hitting Ballesteros. Seve had played the last five holes in even par to keep his one-over standing. 'I think they changed the greens here because I won,' he said. When that riposte drew only a few chuckles, he added a cautionary 'that's a joke' to make certain he didn't wind up with the wrong kind of headlines. 'You cannot try to make putts,' he said. 'You must putt defensively and that's not my system.'

Friday's 'afternoon round' was a splendid illustration how quickly fortunes can be made and lost on a golf course. Last year Watson and Nicklaus had had a monumental swing on the back nine of Saturday's round when Jack went from five ahead to four behind to only one behind within a few holes. The Friday 'morning round' had seen Nicklaus gain nine shots on Watson to lead 69 to 77. By Friday evening all of that margin had disappeared as the two switched scores to tie at 146, two over par. Watson, off on No. 1 in the first group with Jay Haas and Bruce Lietzke, played an errorless 18, although his start was a little shaky. 'The first thing I wanted to do was break my bogey string,' he said later, but when he left his approach at the first hole 50 feet from the pin, he was tested. But Watson, the best putter in the game, rolled it up to five feet and dropped the putt for the par, then made another five-footer for the first of three birdies at two. The others came at six, an eight-foot putt doing the job and 13, on in two and two putts.

'I had some bad breaks but I got away with it,' Watson said later. 'A bogey-less round—I'll take that again for two days and win it. I knew that if we got any wind, even par would be the score to bear.'

And there certainly was wind. By the time Nicklaus teed off at 1.06 with Renner and Zoeller, the flags were flapping. The first thing Jack did wrong was not birdie No. 2 on a round when a large percentage of the field was. There is a misconception that Nicklaus plays Augusta National as a par 68 because he can reach the four par 5s in two. That may have been true a decade ago, but now he is not as long off the tee and three of those holes, the second, eighth and 15th, are longer. The second hole in particular has given Jack fits in recent years and his two-year record there stands at seven pars and one bogey, a poor showing for a hole that plays at 4.68, second easiest (after 13) on the course. Privately he admits he is psyched by the woods on the left, so that he uses a three-wood off the tee for accuracy. Thus his drives are failing to catch the downhill bend of the 555-yard hole, longest on the course, and he has not been reaching the green in two. Hence the lack of birdies. Things really began to go wrong for Nicklaus when he three-putted both par-threes, the fourth and sixth, then knocked his approach into one of the many bunkers that guard the seventh green and failed to get down in two. A birdie at eight got him back to two over for the round and he turned in 38. That was bad, but there was worse to come.

Up ahead, the pack had closed in. No, not Zoeller and Renner, who had been tied for second. They were to shoot 76 and 75 respectively on their ways to respectable but harmless showings. The same was true with most of those opening-round 73s. Brewer shot 80 and eventually finished third from last, ahead of two other Masters champions, Bob Goalby and Arnold Palmer. Hatalsky, Oosterhuis, Norman and Graham were also dropping from immediate view. No, the leaders were coming from those further behind, with the exception of Ballesteros.

Seve moved into the tournament lead when Nicklaus bogeyed the seventh. He had made a birdie at two by coming out of the left-hand bunker in front of

THE MASTERS / 29

the green and sinking a four-footer. He three-putted the fourth to lose that stroke, but got it right back with an eight-foot birdie putt at five. That was the beginning of a remarkable one-putt string. He saved pars at the sixth and seventh, then made another birdie at eight when he chipped to six feet. At nine his approach shot spun back off the green as so many do, but he holed a 15-footer, turning in 34 to make him one-under for the tournament.

The sixth straight one-putt green, an eight-footer at 10, saved still another par. He missed a birdie try at 12 from eight feet, parred 13 and then — disaster. His nine-iron approach to the two-tiered 14th green spun back off the green. His chip reached the top of the hill but then trickled back to where he was standing. Now he got the ball over the ridge but was still 12 feet away. He sank the putt for a tough bogey. At 15 he played his second shot safely short of the pond that guards the green, then pitched over but short and watched helplessly as that one spun back into the drink. A drop, a pitch and two putts gave him a double-bogey seven. Three pars and he was in with a second straight 73 for 146. 'When I laid up at 15 I was in between a pitching wedge and a sand wedge,' he said later ruefully. 'I tried an easy pitching wedge but hit it fat.'

Playing directly ahead of Ballesteros was Ray Floyd, ever dangerous. He had finished his Friday morning first round at 74, two over, and when he started bogey, bogey in round two, it was easy to put him out of your mind. Never put Ray Floyd out of your mind. That bogey at two was his last until the final hole, where he three-putted, but in between he birdied all three par 5s, none of which he reached in two. That gave him an even par 72 and 146 for two rounds.

Let's pick up Nicklaus. Turning in 38, he birdied the 10th, no easy task, with a 15-footer, so that veteran Bear watchers were primed for another scourge of the back nine, one such as they had seen only that morning. Instead he immediately double-bogeyed 11, which is not unique, but he did so without going in the water. He drove, hit his iron right off the green as he had done that morning, but then left his chip 30 feet short of the cup. From there he three-putted for a six. He followed that with a bogey at 12, failed to birdie either par-five and limped home with his 77 and 146. 'Finishing the first 18 with 69 gave me some freedom,' he said, 'but I kind of used it up. I knew it would be a difficult afternoon for playing golf. No, I'm not surprised to be close. In fact, I thought I might still be leading it.'

Instead, there were three men ahead of him and three others tied at 146. Kite was at 145 after a second round he described as being like a ride on the bull at Gilley's Bar and Grill in Houston. The good news was that he had eight birdies. The bad was three bogeys and a double-bogey. 'At one point today I definitely thought I was out of the tournament,' Kite said. He was five over through 27 holes and was facing a back nine he had already had a 39 on that morning. Then he began dropping putts and he birdied five of six holes from 12 through 16, parring the 14th. Only a bogey at 18, where he stubbed a chip shot from inches off the green, cost him a share of the lead. 'This morning I was hitting the ball poorly,' Kite said, 'so I hit a couple of buckets of balls. Halfway through the second bucket my father saw something and I started to hit it solid.'

Curtis Strange and Craig Stadler played together in the first round, were five and four over par respectively during the early morning and by evening were both back to even par, tied for the lead. Strange, you will remember, rallied to a

74 for the first round and kept on burning. He birdied the second, then rolled in a long putt from off the green at three. 'It was like stealing a shot,' he said. 'You don't expect something like that. You just smile and go on to the next tee.'

By the 16th tee he was two under and leading the tournament, having birdied the back nine par-fives, but he three-putted 16 and also bogeyed 18 when his approach wandered into the righthand bunker. 'It's amazing how quick it can turn around,' he said. 'You go from being the worst player in the world to leading the Masters.'

Stadler, like Kite, owed his position to a spasm of birdies. After his 75 and a bogey at three during the afternoon, he was just one of a score of players trying not to slip too far beyond par when he made birdie putts of 15 and 10 feet at six and seven, parred eight and then hit a pitching wedge two feet from the hole at nine and a five-iron a foot away at 10. Eight straight pars got him in with a 69 and 144. 'I was just playing my own game,' Stadler said. 'I knew the course would catch up with the other guys. I didn't worry about what he (Nicklaus) did.'

At this point let us have a moment of silence for Mark Hayes, who had an eight-foot birdie to gain a share of the lead with Strange and Stadler. Putting right to left, the ball broke in front of the cup and trickled downhill, stopping 35 feet away. His next effort stopped five feet short, hesitated, then rolled back close to the same spot. Putt No. 3 went by and he finally sank his fourth putt for a double-bogey and three strokes behind the leaders.

Among those leaderboard names who missed the cut were Irwin, Miller, Mahaffey and Crosby. Crosby? Nathaniel, Bing's boy, was in Augusta because of his exciting victory nearly a year before in the U.S. Amateur. And his name was on the leaderboard at the start of play Thursday, a Masters tradition. Alas, it came down quickly (and mercifully) as he posted an 85 with no threes and a 78. At Augusta he was as much in demand as the top players, constantly surrounded by media and autograph seekers. 'I started signing my name "Nathaniel",' Crosby said. 'Then I shortened it to "Nate" and finally just the initials "N.C." Otherwise I never would have gotten to the first tee.'

Saturday, cool and clear at first but later hot, was one of those wild days golf tournaments sometimes produce when it seems as if everyone in the field has a share of the lead at one time or another. It was a day when red made its appearance on the leaderboard, when roars echoed about the course as birdies rolled home. And then, at day's end, just when it seemed as if 10 players would be within three strokes of the lead, Craig Stadler said goodbye to the field.

The harbinger that this would be a day for scoring — there were 21 rounds under par — came when Bob Gilder set off fireworks on the front nine. Gilder, a 31-year-old pro of modest accomplishments, had opened with a 79, then made the cut by shooting 71. Teeing off around noon Saturday, he began bogey, birdie, bogey, which does not seem like much fireworks, but he then ripped off four straight birdies, thanks to irons that set up a series of putts 12 feet or less. He had good chances on the next two holes, just missing from 15 feet or so, but the outgoing 33 left him only three over for the tournament.

When he bogeyed 11, his round seemed to be slipping away, but then came another rash of birdies, again thanks to approaches that gave him makeable putts. He birdied everything between 13 and 17 except the 16th, four out of five, and when he parred the last hole, he was in with a 66 and even par for the tournament. As Gilder sat in the press hut describing his round to the media, he was — depending on the exact moment — tied for the lead, one shot out or two shots out. That's how quickly things were happening.

'I've had a good round with irons before,' Gilder said, 'but I don't think I've ever had one where I hit the ball so close consistently.' Naturally he was pleased, but he added this cautionary note as he surveyed the leaderboard. 'There's a lot of gold to be played out there. Some other guys could have good rounds.'

Even as he spoke, Dan Pohl was winding up his own very good round, a record-breaker in fact. No one has ever done what Pohl did at Augusta on Saturday, April 10, 1982. Pohl, who had just turned 27 a few days earlier, is noted as perhaps the longest hitter on the tour. No wins. Top 60 guy the past two years. He had shot a pair of 75s and was working on a 73 when he stepped to the 13th tee, just one of the people trying to make the top 24 finishers and get himself an invitation next year.

His drive at the par-five was perfect and when he hit a five-wood 10 feet below the cup, his playing partner, Keith Fergus, also on in two, said they both had a chance for crystal, referring to the goblets the Masters rewards all those who make eagles. 'Well,' said Pohl, who did not know about it, 'we'll have to coax this baby in.' Which he did. On 14, after a huge drive, he hit a pitching wedge just past the pin. The ball hit and then spun back into the cup for a second straight eagle, something not Nicklaus, Palmer, Hogan nor anyone else has ever done in a Masters. Having been seven over after 48 holes, he was now three over after 50. And the binge was not over. At 15 he tapped in a two-footer for a birdie, then dropped a 15-footer at 16. Two pars gave him a 67 and 217, one over and one back of Gilder. 'I'm real excited,' Pohl said understandably as many in the press section wondered if he pronounced his name 'Pole,' which he does, or 'Pool.' He remarked, 'I hit shots the way I feel I should. If I'm feeling that way tomorrow, I won't be playing for second.' How right he was.

Jerry Pate and Tom Weiskopf, both at three over par for the tournament, went off together at 1.06, five groups from the end. Weiskopf was making his celebrated reappearance as a player at Augusta, having been present the year before as an announcer for CBS. Until Saturday he (and Pate) was just one of 11 players lurking three and four shots off the pace, but after five holes his name was on the leaderboard, thanks to birdies at one, four and five. He left his tee shot at six some 50 feet from the hole, three-putting for a bogey, but that was his only mistake of the day. Birdies on the back-nine par-fives got him home in 68 and 215, one under. 'It was difficult being here last year and not competing,' Tom said. 'But I'm back again now, I have the experience to win and I'm playing well.'

Pate was playing even better. In mid-round, he was actually leading the tournament, thanks to a 33 on the front side and two more birdies at 12 and 13. Most of these were due to sensational putting, a 30-footer and two 20-footers, for instance. His only bogey of the day came at 14, a problem hole for so many players. He felt he hit an approach 'Trevino would have been proud of,' a little low cut shot, but the ball came up a tad short and spun back to the front of the green, from where he three-putted. But he got the stroke back by sinking a putt of 10 feet at 17 for a birdie and avoided trouble at 18 after driving in the right woods. A five-iron faded just in front of the green, a pitch and putt got him home in 67 and two under for the tournament. At the moment he holed out, he was tied for the lead with Stadler and Ballesteros.

The Spaniard demolished Augusta's par-fives on the way to a 68, racking up three birdies and an eagle, reaching the green in two on all but the eighth, where he chipped to eight feet. At 15 he nailed a four-iron within four feet of the pin for an eagle. Five-under on the par-fives. He also had birdies at the fourth and seventh, but they were sandwiched around bogeys at five and six, where each time approach shots fell short. He also three-putted the 11th from the right fringe. Asked to assess his position, Seve quipped: 'Better than last year,' when 78–76 rounds sent him home Friday night.

Stadler and Strange, tied for the lead at the start of the day, both parred the first. Then one of them birdied two while the other double-bogeyed it, a three-shot swing. One went on to shoot 67, the other 73, but golf is a funny game. It was Stadler who had the disaster at two and still brought home the subpar round. You will remember that on Friday morning he had two double-bogeys and a bogey in one three-hole stretch and still fought back to lead by nightfall. Now, with a drive in the left woods and no great success at recovery, he was two over for the tournament, which meant about a half dozen players were now ahead of him and a half dozen more either tied or one stroke back. A perfect time to pack it in, just as he had in 1979, when he had tied for the 36-hole lead and then shot a 79.

But Stadler did not lay down. During the next 16 holes he made seven birdies and no bogeys and, amazingly, none of those birdies were on the par-fives. On five and nine he hit approach shots $1\frac{1}{2}$ feet from the pin. At 10 he got lucky. His drive was in the trees on the left, his approach in a bunker, his explosion . . . in the cup. A 10-footer at 12 put him two under and he stayed there until he reached 16. At that moment the leaderboard had 10 names bunched within two strokes of each other, presenting the prospect of a real dogfight on Sunday. But then Craig Stadler went and spoiled it.

At 16 he sank a 15-footer for a birdie. 'That was a tough one,' Stadler said later. 'It broke about $1\frac{1}{2}$ feet.' At 17 an undistinguished approach left him 40 feet away, three-putt territory. Stadler sent the ball on its way. Plop. 'I had no right to make that one,' he said. 'It just stayed on line and went in.' On 18, he was 35 feet from the flagstick. 'Well,' he said to himself, 'I might as well make this one. I just had to get it started and not run it way by. Those last three holes put a cushion on the lead.'

By making six birdies in the last 10 holes Saturday, Stadler had surged from the crowd to lead by three. Then came Pate and Ballesteros and a stroke behind them, Weiskopf and Floyd, who had posted a quiet 69. A stroke further back were Gilder and Watson, who felt reasonably happy with his 70 but had to admit that Stadler's 67 was impressive. 'Craig's played well all year,' he said. 'While he's never been in position to win a Masters before, he's learned how to handle pressure.'

And Nicklaus? 'When I walked off the course I thought I'd be three off the lead,' Nicklaus said after finishing birdie, birdie for a 71. 'I felt pretty good about it. Now I look up and see he went birdie, birdie, birdie, so I'm six back. Craig's a good player. His day is just arriving.' That's as close to a concession speech as you're likely to hear Nicklaus give. His major problem Saturday was putting as he failed six times to drop putts of six feet or less. As it turned out, six strokes back was not too far to catch Stadler. But it took someone other than Nicklaus to prove that.

Sunday's weather was a repeat of Saturday, cool in the morning but warming toward noon. Early scores indicated the course would not be a repeat, however, as subpar rounds were few. Bill Rogers had a 70 after three straight 77s, as did Wayne Levi and Morris Hatalsky, but when the day ended, there would be only three rounds below that. One, a 69, was by Larry Nelson, and it served to move him from 16th to seventh. A second 69 came from Kite, who had apparently fallen from contention with a 73 Saturday. Kite put together a great front-nine 32 to move from two over to two under, three strokes behind the leader — although the leader was making some birdies of his own — but a 37 coming home left him with only a good round when he needed a superb one. The third round in the 60s? We'll get to that.

The first players to tee off Sunday with a solid chance to catch Stadler were Nicklaus and Strange. Nicklaus parred the first, then in his continuing struggle with the second hole, drove far left, his ball hitting a limb. It fell to earth a mere 150 yards from the tee, from where it was a wood to the bottom of the hill, an approach into the bunker, out onto the green, putt, putt and goodbye, Jack. He finished with a 75, tied for 15th. Strange birdied two holes on the front nine, but he also bogeyed three. His 72 got him a tie for seventh.

Behind them were Watson and Pohl. 'I just felt like it wasn't going to be my day,' said Watson and his bogey at the first hole confirmed it. 'I've started rounds with bogeys and shot 65s,' he also said, but not when he failed to make a birdie on the front. His 71 was not enough and he wound up tied for fifth.

Of the challengers, only Dan Pohl looked like a player intent on winning the Masters. He birdied one, he birdied two and he birdied nine, and all the rest were pars, so that he turned in 33 and was two under for the tournament. The others — Floyd, Gilder, Ballesteros, Weiskopf and Pate — all started shakily. Floyd parred the first two holes, missing the birdie on two when many in the field were making one, and gradually drifted out of sight, shooting a 74 to wind up tied with Nelson and Strange for seventh. Gilder, who had played himself into contention with that marvelous 66, bogeyed the first hole on his way to 75 and 14th place.

Ballesteros, playing with Weiskopf, and Pate, paired with Stadler, both bogeyed the first hole, too, so that Stadler, when he parred the hole, had a quick four-stroke margin. The pin on one was cut left near an embankment. 'I knew it was dangerous to go for the flagstick,' said Pate later. 'But I felt so good I had to try it. The wind got it and blew it too far left.'

Ballesteros and Weiskopf both birdied two, but right behind them Stadler did, too, reaching the green in two and two-putting. When Pate failed to get his birdie, driving into the fairway bunker, he had lost two strokes in two holes and was five back. And so it went. Bogeys were made, but not by Stadler. Pate got another at the fourth, as did Weiskopf. Stadler parred the hole, as he had the third, where he came out of the fairway bunker onto the green. He remained six under with a par at the dangerous fifth hole, while well up ahead, Kite was two under, as was Ballesteros. Weiskopf and Pohl were at one under, Pate even.

Already comfortably ahead, Stadler now made a move to leave the field altogether. At the par-three sixth, he hit a six-iron 20 feet from the cup and hole high, important on that multilevel green. In went the putt and he was now seven under. At the seventh, his sand wedge approach gave him a 15-footer and he made that, too. And no response from his challengers. Only pars from Pate, Weiskopf and Ballesteros. Up ahead, Pohl, with his birdie at nine, joined Kite, on 12, and Ballesteros, on eight, at two under, tied for second. For the fourth straight day Stadler failed to birdie the par-five eighth and for the first time he failed to birdie nine, but he did get pars to turn in 33, eight under. His closest challenger was Kite, who had birdied 13 to go three under.

There then came a wait on the 10th tee while down the fairway, everyone was looking for Weiskopf's golf ball. He had driven left into the trees in a section of the course where spectators are not permitted, so there was no one close at hand to spot the ball. Two players, two caddies and at least two officials searched the area while folks in the gallery yelled across the fairway to say where they thought the ball had gone. Poor Tom. The ball was never found, he had to drive again and when he made a bogey, it came out a seven because of the two-stroke penalty.

Stadler, when he had a chance to play, parred 10. Pate made his first birdie of the day to go one under. Two holes ahead, Pohl rolled home a 12-footer at the 12th to go three under, which put him alone in second place because Kite had bogeyed 15. This was the crusher for him, for one expects to birdie the par-five hole, and if he had, and if he had parred in . . . well, that's a lot of ifs. Kite's drive at 15 left him 'right at the go point,' but he decided not to try to carry the pond with his second. He laid up, hit his third shot just over the green, saw his chip just miss going into the cup and then blew the short putt. As he did so, he bent from the waist in despair, like a man doing his morning stretching exercises. A final bogey at 18 brought him in at one under, tied for fifth with Watson.

On 13, Pohl came as close to a double-eagle as the two a's in Sarazen. He had a 10-footer for an eagle and missed that, but his tap-in birdie made him four under, reducing Stadler's lead to four strokes. Stadler almost played the 11th too cautiously. His approach certainly was in no danger of going into the pond on the left, but it left him some 70 feet from the pin and his first putt wound up six feet away. But in it went and he had now gone 28 holes without a bogey — ever since that double-bogey at two on Saturday — during which time he had made 10 birdies. Taking it back even further, after making a double-bogey at 14 in the first round (Friday morning), Stadler played 51 straight holes with only a second-round bogey at the third hole and that double-bogey in the third round on two. And during that stretch he made 14 birdies — 11 under.

It was only appropriate to mention these statistics at this point because when Stadler teed off at 12, seven holes between him and the green jacket, things changed dramatically. He missed the green with his tee shot, chipped to five feet, but this time missed the putt. He was now seven under. When Stadler had been strolling down 11, he said later, he had let his thoughts wander. 'It seemed like everyone else was playing for second,' he said. After the bogey at 12 he told himself to 'get back to business.'

There didn't seem to be any real danger, however. Pohl had hit his approach shot at 14 over the green and it had given him a bogey. Back to three under and a four-stroke lead for Stadler. Ballesteros had three-putted 10 for one bogey and another bogey at 12 had put him back to even. Pate was still one under and Weiskopf, poor man, was in the process of taking a second triple-bogey. To his credit, he had rallied from his first disaster with a birdie at 11, but then he bogeyed 12. At 13 he went into the woods, stayed in the woods, hit across the fairway into the gallery, chipped into the ditch, took a drop, hit on and took two putts. That's an eight. He finished with a 75, not a bad score with two triples on the card. 'Par those two holes and I tie for the lead,' Tom said later. As it was, he tied for 10th.

Stadler was unable to birdie the 13th and indeed was slightly lucky to get his par. Trying for the green in two, he fell short, but he was able to hit his ball out of the hazard guarding the green and two putt for the five. Up ahead, Pohl, who needed at least a birdie at 15, hit his second shot into the pond, but after taking a drop, he chipped the ball close enough to make the putt and save par. Still three under. A few moments later he nearly made a hole-in-one at 16 and the tap-in birdie got him back to four under.

Back to Stadler at 14. On in two, his first putt from some 30 feet left him a short but tricky putt, one that broke sharply to his left. He missed and now the margin was down to two strokes and the panic was on. There isn't a golfer in the world who wouldn't love a two-stroke lead with four holes to play, but when that lead was five or six strokes just an hour before, the margin doesn't seem nearly as secure. To make matters worse, the man playing alongside Stadler, Pate, finally began to exert some pressure. While Stadler was again unable to birdie the par-five 15th, Pate did, so that now he was two under, three back.

The last three holes which had treated Stadler so kindly the day before now lay between him and the championship. Three pars would certainly do it, even should Pohl make one more birdie and Pate two. More likely, he could afford a bogey. At 16 Pate tightened the screws with a tee shot some 15 feet from the cup. Stadler's own tee shot was a trifle strong and found the bunker to the back right of the green. His sand shot out looked marvelous at first, but it trickled by the cup, kept moving, caught the downhill slope of the green and finally stopped 40 feet from the cup. His putt missed. Pate's putt did not. Stadler made his second — and one was beginning to believe that nothing would go in at this point — and he was down to five under. Pate was three.

Even as Stadler was bogeying 16, Dan Pohl had a 20-foot birdie putt at 18 that would have tied him for the lead. But the instant he stroked the ball it was clear it would never reach the cup. 'I thought I was playing for second place,' he said later. 'I thought I was three strokes behind.' Evidently Pohl, playing in his first Masters, had failed to check the leaderboard as any veteran would do, for even had Stadler's bogey at 16 not been posted, his bogey at 14 had, so that Pohl could have seen he was closer than he thought. In any case, he holed his second putt at 18 to finish at four under. It was then that he learned he had a real chance to win. An official told him he had three options; to stay where he was and watch the final groups play 18, to go to the locker room and wait there, or go over to the nearby practice putting green. Pohl did that.

Ballesteros, who had also been dormant for most of the day, had birdied 15 to get back to one under and now he birdied 17 to get to two under. It seemed a case of too little, too late, and indeed it was, even with a third birdie at 18 to go three under, but it served to emphasize the Stadler nightmare wherein suddenly everyone else on the course was making birdies while he could do nothing right. For instance, his good drive on 17 rolled into a divot, meaning there was no way to know exactly how the ball would react to the next shot. Justly, it came out normally, Stadler reaching the green and two-putting for a par. Pate also made a par to remain two back.

Now one more par would do it. That's all that Ed Sneed needed in 1979. That's all Arnold Palmer needed in 1961 (and instead got a double bogey, Gary Player winning.) Stadler's drive was solid and his approach with a five-iron left him 30 feet below the pin, normally close to the front bunker on Sundays but this year set to the back right of the two-tiered green. His first putt was woefully short, leaving him six feet away. Now Pate, who needed a two-stroke swing on the hole, had a real chance. But his 20-footer for a birdie stopped two feet short, never given a chance. He tapped in to tie Ballesteros for third.

The very moment that Stadler hit his second putt there was no doubt it would not go in. The stroke was tentative, a stab and the ball sort of wandered its way left of the cup. Stadler sagged, his big shoulders slumped. He looked physically ill. He had been tested and had been found wanting.

As the ball failed to drop, crowds of people began racing toward the 10th green where the Stadler-Pohl playoff would begin. After signing his scorecard and getting a pep talk from his wife, Sue, Stadler walked over to the 10th tee surrounded by guards, looking much like a man walking to his own execution. One had to feel sympathy for him at that moment. He had carried the burden of the lead for two long days. Pohl, like Fuzzy Zoeller three years before, had simply backed into the lead. Now he, again like Zoeller, had a chance to win in his first Augusta appearance.

A coin toss came up tails and Stadler drove first. Both players were long, Pohl the longer. Stadler's six-iron put him 40 feet away. Now one great iron such as he hit at 13 or 16 would give Pohl the Masters. But, perhaps feeling the pressure of the moment, his approach drifted to the right fringe of the green, far from the pin which was to the left. Pohl elected to chip the ball and the ball died six feet short. Over to Stadler. There was never any real thought that he could make his putt, but he did get it close enough to tap in. Back to Pohl. He took his time lining it up, his first putt in nearly an hour.

To the side, Stadler watched. 'I thought, "Is he going to make it or isn't he?" He hit a good putt, but then I thought, "Oh my God, he missed it!" Then I didn't know what to do. It took me 10 seconds to realize what had happened.'

What had happened is that Craig Stadler had won a Masters he very much deserved to win. Not long after, in the gathering darkness around the practice putting green, Tom Watson slipped a giant green jacket on the new champion. It was the biggest jacket available in the closet where they are kept. 'Exactly what size is that jacket?' Stadler was asked later.

'I don't know,' he replied, 'and I'm not about to take it off and find out.'

3.   The U.S. Open

While competitive golf as we know it today began in 1860 with the British Open, it has its roots in earlier forms. Before we had the formal stroke play tournaments involving a large number of players, we had money matches involving, for the most part, just two players, and occasionally four men in better-ball matches. Challenge matches probably go back to the origins of the game, sometime in the 14th or 15th century, but we don't know anything about them until the middle of the 19th century, when the feather-ball era was giving way to the gutta-percha ball period.

One of the earliest matches we know of was between Willie Dunn, of Musselburgh, Scotland, and Allan Robertson, of St. Andrews. During June of 1843, Robertson and Dunn played a 20-round match — 20 rounds, not 20 holes — over St. Andrews, two rounds a day for 10 days, the winner decided by the number of rounds won. Robertson won, two rounds up with one to play.

Robertson was the first of the great professional players. He was born in 1815 and died in 1858. At his death it was said that he never lost a match. That probably isn't true; Horace Hutchinson, in his book *Golf*, in the Badminton Library series, claimed that Robertson lost twice to Old Tom Morris, but for rather insubstantial amounts of money.

It is unfortunate, in a way, that Morris and Robertson played so few matches against one another, for they were probably the best golfers of their day. More often than not they were on the same side, which is understandable since Morris began his career in golf as an apprentice to Robertson as a maker of clubs and feather balls. In their most famous partnership, Robertson and Morris played the twins Willie and Jamie Dunn in a three-round match for £400. The first round was played at Musselburgh, the Dunns' home course, the second at St. Andrews, the home course of Robertson and Morris, and the last at North Berwick, neutral ground. The Dunns won the first round and Robertson and Morris won the second. With eight holes to play in the third round, the Dunns were four up, but Robertson and Morris won six of the last eight and the match.

While Robertson and Morris were the leading partners, the principal rivals seem to have been Robertson and Willie Dunn, said to have been the longest driver of the day. They played four singles matches that we know of, and Robertson won them all.

As far as we can tell today, this was the first of the great rivalries. By the end of the 1970s and into the early 1980s, we had another, this one between Jack Nicklaus and Tom Watson. Since the middle 1960s, Nicklaus had been the best player in the game. In the middle to late 1970s, Watson came along and, many believed, replaced him. Watson had one flaw in his record, however. He had not won the U.S. Open Championship. When he did win the Open at Pebble Beach in June of 1982, he at once rounded out his own record, established a further claim as the best in the game, and continued his rivalry with Nicklaus.

Jack finished second by two strokes. Watson won by holing a pitch shot from the rough alongside the 17th green during the last round. It was an unlikely shot to hole, and it will be remembered for a long time.

Over the last five years, Watson and Nicklaus have given us some of our most exciting moments. The last round at Pebble Beach was not the least of them. Although Watson went into the last round tied for the lead with Bill Rogers, the most stirring challenge came from Nicklaus. It fell two strokes short only because of Watson's melodramatic finish — two birdies on the last two holes where par or worse seemed likely. Watson won with scores of 72–72–68–70—282; Nicklaus shot 74–70–71–69—284. Bill Rogers, Bob Clampett, and Dan Pohl tied for third, at 286. The rivalry between Nicklaus and Watson is the latest in a long series that is the very core of the traditions of golf — rivalries that include those between Nicklaus and Trevino, Palmer and Nicklaus, Hogan and Snead, Hogan and Nelson, Jones and Hagen, Hagen and Sarazen, and, in the late 19th and early 20th centuries, among Harry Vardon, J.H. Taylor and James Braid.

Vardon, Taylor and Braid were known as the Triumvirate, and theirs may have been the most intense and overpowering rivalry the game has known. In their day, the British Open was the only tournament in the world worth winning. For a period of 21 years, they dominated the British Open so thoroughly that only five other men were able to win. From 1894, when Taylor won his first, until 1914, when Vardon won his last, the three of them won 16 British Open championships. Vardon, who ranks with Nicklaus, Hogan, and Jones as the best who ever played the game, won six, his first in 1896 and his last in 1914, a period covering 18 years. Taylor, who arrived as a great player before the other two, won five, from 1894 through 1913, and Braid also won five, his first in 1901, his last in 1910. Three times within that period they were the leading three finishers — in 1900, 1901, and 1906, and three other times when one of them won, another was second.

They breathed their last gasp as the Triumvirate in 1914, at Prestwick, where the British Open began in 1860. Vardon shot 73 to lead the first round, and Braid and Taylor were a stroke behind at 74. Never a solid putter, Braid shot himself out of contention with 82 in the second round, but Taylor and Vardon were still in the thick of it. Vardon won because Taylor hit his ball into a bunker that Braid had designed when he was called in as an advisor before the Open. Over the years, Braid and Taylor had become fast friends, often travelling to tournaments together, but when that bunker cost Taylor the championship, he declared that Braid should be buried in it with a niblick through his heart.

While the British Open was the natural setting for this rivalry, it extended beyond one tournament. They met in exhibition matches and in other competitions, one of the most notable a foursomes match with Vardon and Taylor, representing England, against Braid and Sandy Herd, for Scotland (Herd had won the British Open in 1902). The match was played in 1905, 36 holes at each of four courses. The match began at St. Andrews. The Scots finished two up, but when the second 36-holes was played the following week at Troon, the Englishmen won 14 of the 36 holes, lost none, and had a 12-hole lead. The match was effectively over. The Scots won five holes back at Royal Lytham and St. Annes, but when the final round was played at Deal, in southeastern

England, Taylor and Vardon won, 13 and 12.

When World War I began, in August, 1914, the British Open was suspended for the duration (indeed, it wasn't played again until 1920) and the great rivalry ended. We were not to see its like again, although Bob Jones and Walter Hagen gave us some exciting moments in the Roaring 20s. Jones, of course, was an amateur and Hagen, the best of professionals. Their rivalry was more in the public mind than on the golf course. During the 20s, Hagen won five PGA championships and Jones won the U.S. Amateur five times. In addition, Jones won the U.S. Open four times and the British Open three, and Hagen won the British Open four times and the Western Open five. (Don't sluff off that Western Open; we must never forget that during the 1920s and 1930s, the Western Open was every bit as important as the Masters is today.)

Even though Hagen won the U.S. Open twice and the British Open four times, he did not win any of them when Jones was in the field. Hagen won his two U.S. Opens in 1914 and 1919, before Jones was ready, and his four British Opens when Jones stayed home. Jones played in only four British Opens and won three of them.

Since Jones was an amateur and Hagen a professional, they did not meet for a national championship in match play, but they did play against each other once. In 1926, a challenge match was arranged between them primarily to promote the sale of real estate in Florida. The match was over 72 holes and Hagen won, 12 and 11.

Byron Nelson and Ben Hogan came along in the 1930s and early 1940s. Boyhood friends who grew up together as caddies at the Glen Garden Country Club, in Fort Worth, Texas, they became the two best players on the Tour. Their rivalry reached its peak in 1945 when they battled throughout the year with neither gaining a clear edge. By 1946, Nelson had worn his nerves raw and he was ready to retire to his ranch in Texas. The PGA was to be his last hurrah before his retirement, and when he and Hogan were placed in opposite halves of the draw, it was possible that they would meet in the final. The opportunity was ruined when Porky Oliver defeated Nelson in the quarter-finals. Hogan defeated Oliver in the final, winning his first major championship.

Twice before Hogan had come close. Halfway through the 1942 Masters, Nelson led Hogan by eight strokes, but while Neison played the last 36 in 72–73—145, Hogan shot 67–70—137, picking up those eight strokes and forcing a playoff. Playoffs then were over 18 holes. Three strokes ahead after five holes, Hogan played the sixth through the 13th in even par but lost six strokes. Around Amen Corner, the 11th, 12th, and 13th, Hogan shot birdie, par, birdie, and lost a stroke. Nelson birdied all three. Nelson won the playoff by one stroke.

It is said the intense rivalry between Nelson and Hogan had strained their personal relationship, so that when Nelson retired, they were no longer friends. It was different between Hogan and Snead, the rivalry that naturally followed when Nelson retired. Hogan and Snead never were friends.

Nelson, Snead, and Hogan were all the same age, each born in 1912, Nelson in February, Snead in May, and Hogan in August, and they had all begun playing the Tour in the late 1930s. Both Nelson and Snead developed earlier than Hogan. Nelson won the Masters in 1937 and the Open in 1939. Snead won the 1942 PGA Championship, and in 1946 went to St. Andrews and won the British Open. Hogan, however, won the 1948 U.S. Open, which Snead had never been able to win. Two months after Hogan had nearly been killed in his collision with a bus in Texas in February of 1949, Snead won his third major championship, the 1949 Masters. After months of speculation that Hogan might never play competitive golf again, he made his comeback in the Los Angeles Open, the first event on the 1950 Tour. He shot 73 in the first round, and then three consecutive 69s. Snead caught him with 66 in the last round, forcing an 18-hole playoff. Snead won, 72–76.

Jimmy Demaret won the 1950 Masters, but over the next four years, Hogan and Snead alternated at Augusta, Snead winning in 1952 and 1954, and Hogan in 1951 and 1953. Hogan was only two strokes off the lead after 54 holes in 1950, but, evidently weary, he shot 76 in the last round (he and Nelson tied, incidentally). Snead went into the last round in 1951 leading Hogan by a stroke, but Hogan shot 68, Snead 80, and Hogan won. Snead came back to win the next year when Hogan shot 79 in the last round against Snead's 72. Hogan won in 1953, and then they tied after 72 holes in 1954 after Hogan went for the flag at the 11th and hooked the ball into the water, taking a double-bogey six. Another playoff. Trailing by only a stroke at the 16th, Hogan three-putted and Snead won again.

That effectively ended their rivalry — at least for such high stakes. Then Arnold Palmer came to the front and a few years later he was joined by Nicklaus. Their rivalry reached a peak early. When Palmer won the 1960 U.S. Open, Nicklaus, still an amateur, was second. Two years later Nicklaus won the Open, defeating Palmer in a playoff. Palmer had won his third Masters that year, and he was succeeded in 1963 by Nicklaus. Palmer won his fourth Masters in 1964; Nicklaus then won the next two. Their rivalry, although it was relatively brief, created an intense amount of interest in the game. More and more cities bid for tournaments, and prize money climbed steadily. Galleries changed, too. Where fans in the past showed their approval of a shot by polite, enthusiastic applause, they now cheered and screamed as if they were at a football game. They even called encouragement to the players before they played a shot. The world moves on.

Then Lee Trevino came along. In one three-week period in 1971, Trevino won, in order, the U.S. Open, defeating Nicklaus in a playoff at the Merion Golf Club in Philadelphia, the Canadian Open, and the British Open. Nicklaus came back the next year to win the U.S. Open, and although the final margin was by three strokes over Bruce Crampton, the final round began with Nicklaus at 216, Trevino, Crampton and Kermit Zarley at 217, and Palmer and John Miller at 218. Being this close to the lead wasn't expected of Trevino. He had spent the previous week in a hospital, recovering from bronchial pneumonia, and had not arrived at Pebble Beach, the site of the Open, until late on the Tuesday before the Open began. He was still weak, and he simply couldn't keep up. He shot 78 and finished five strokes behind Nicklaus. A month later at Muirfield, Trevino won his second consecutive British Open, but Nicklaus had a chance to tie with two holes to play. He needed a birdie on the 17th, a par 5, but he hooked his tee shot into rough, made par and missed catching Trevino by a stroke.

Two years later, in the PGA at the Tanglewood Golf Club near Winston-Salem, North Carolina, Nicklaus and Trevino hooked up in what was their last head-to-head battle. After shooting 73 in the first round, Trevino trailed Nicklaus by four strokes. He picked up three of them in the second round and then went a stroke ahead with 68 in the third round. With two holes to play, Trevino led Nicklaus by two strokes, but when he three-putted the 17th, Nicklaus thought he had a chance to catch up on the 18th. Trevino, though, two-putted from 18 feet and saved his lead. The following year, in mid-summer of 1975, during the Western Open, Trevino, Jerry Heard, and Bobby Nichols were struck by lightning, and while Trevino came back to win the next year, he was not the player he had been, and the rivalry cooled down.

At about this time, Tom Watson began to project himself into the picture. He and Nicklaus had their first important encounter in the 1977 Masters. Nicklaus went into the last round trailing Watson by three strokes, shot 66 — six under par — and gained only one stroke. Watson shot 67. Playing behind Nicklaus, Watson was able to see how Jack was playing. When Jack holed a birdie putt at the 13th, Watson became angry. As Nicklaus walked off the green, he raised his arm to the crowd, but at the same time he seemed to look back toward Watson. Tom thought that Jack had challenged him. Watson was fuming, but instead of collapsing, as he might have done a few years earlier, he lashed an iron right at the flagstick. The ball hit on the green, but the shot was too strong and the ball rolled off the back of the green. Watson chipped back and holed a short putt for his par. Nicklaus explained later that he was simply waving to the crowd to acknowledge their applause, and that he would never do what Watson thought he had done. Watson apologized, and their rivalry never did take on the sourness of the Hogan–Nelson relationship.

Later that year, Watson and Nicklaus played in the British Open. Those who saw it will never forget it. The British Open was played at Turnberry in 1977, restored after use as an air base during World War II, but Britain was in a period of drought, and the golf course was not nearly as demanding as it might have been. The rough was light and thin, the greens were true and nicely paced, and the breeze was light and never from the most demanding quarter. Nevertheless, only Watson, Nicklaus, and Hubert Green were under par, and Watson and Nicklaus both shattered the standing record. Watson shot 268, eight strokes lower than the record Arnold Palmer set at Troon in 1962, and Nicklaus had 269.

Watson and Nicklaus played stroke for stroke through the first three rounds, with 68, 70, and 65. Twice during the 65, Nicklaus, perhaps the most reliable putter among the great players, missed from three feet. As the drama of the last round unfolded, Watson fell three strokes behind by the fourth hole, and while he was able to catch up at the eighth, he was two down again after the 12th. Watson won a stroke back with another birdie at the 13th, but when he pulled his four-iron tee shot to the left of the 15th green, Nicklaus looked as if he would take command.

Watson then played the critical shot of the week. Using his putter from a few yards off the green, he rapped the ball smartly through the light rough and watched as it rolled fully 60 feet dead at the hole. It hit the flagstick and dropped into the cup. Even again.

Watson went ahead by a stroke on the 17th, a 515-yard par 5, rifling a three-iron onto the green, a shot that Nicklaus could not match. Watson made his birdie four, but Nicklaus missed his putt after a delicate chip from light rough and dropped behind for the first time.

The tension grew as they moved to the 18th hole, the 72nd of the championship. Watson, with the honor, played a safe enough tee shot, but Nicklaus came off the ball and hit into prickly gorse alongside the fairway. As a measure of the man, he managed to play an eight-iron onto the right edge of the green. Watson, meanwhile, from a good lie in the fairway, stroked a seven-iron to three feet.

Now, with the championship in the balance, Nicklaus stroked his 32-footer right into the hole for the birdie. Watson would have to hole his putt to win. He did.

Now that I look back on it, I am amazed that these two men could have played so superbly through such tension. I certainly have never seen anything like it, nor do I expect to ever again. Think of it; Watson shot Turnberry in 68, 70, 65, and 65, and Nicklaus shot 68, 70, 65, and 66. It was the golf duel of the age.

Their confrontation at Pebble Beach in 1982 was nothing like that — and yet there was a striking similarity at the end. It was different in that neither Nicklaus nor Watson tore the golf course apart as they did at Turnberry, and until he zoomed out of the pack on the first nine of the last round, Nicklaus was never higher than seventh at the end of any round. At the end, though, there was Watson once again holing an improbable shot after missing the green of a par-three hole, and winning on the strength of an unexpected birdie.

To recreate the scene. At the end of 54 holes, Watson and Bill Rogers were tied for the lead at 212, and Nicklaus was tied for seventh place, three strokes behind. When he lost a stroke to par on the first hole, Nicklaus seemed to be on his way out of contention. It is never wise to count Jack out of a big championship when he is within striking distance of the lead. He pulled himself together, and in a remarkable stretch of pressure golf, he birdied the next five holes. He finished the day with 69 and 284, four under par. Watson began the round four under par, and when he bogeyed the 16th hole, hitting his tee shot into a fairway bunker, he was still four under par and tied with Nicklaus.

Then came the shot. The 17th at Pebble Beach is a par three that played at 175 yards for the first and third rounds, and 209 yards for the second and fourth. Watson played a two-iron from the tee, but came over the top slightly and hooked the ball. When it came down, the ball hit into rather short rough just off the edge of the green and settled between two bunkers. At first I thought Watson had lost his opportunity to win the Open this day, that he would certainly have trouble making his par, and even if he could, that he would be back the next day for a playoff. But when the ball was found lying fairly cleanly on top of the grass, not buried deep, a par there was likely.

Watson surprised us all. His caddie told him to hit it close, but Watson said that he would hole the shot. He did just that. Using his sand iron, he lobbed the ball softly onto the edge of the green. It rolled straight for the hole, hit the flagstick and dropped into the cup for the birdie two. The Open was his. Another birdie on the 18th did nothing but extend his margin to two strokes over Nicklaus.

This was not the most stirring moment in Open history, but it will rank among them, and it was fitting, in a way, that it happened at Pebble Beach, for Watson had played the course so many times while he was an undergraduate student at Stanford University, in Palo Alto, California, about an hour and three-quarter's drive north. When Watson was in college, he would make an occasional trip to Pebble Beach, leaving Palo Alto before dawn so that he could tee off by seven in the morning, when he would have the course to himself. The usual program for Stanford students would be to play 36 holes, and then play the first through the fifth, cut over to the 14th hole, whose fairway crosses behind the fifth green, play the approach to the green with, perhaps, an eight-iron, and then play in from the 15th. They would then have played 45 holes for one green fee.

That program is one of the world's bargains, for Pebble Beach is one of the world's marvels. It is usually ranked along with Merion Golf Club, in Philadelphia, Pennsylvania, and Pine Valley Golf Club, in Clementon, New Jersey, about 40 miles east of Philadelphia, as the three best golf courses in the United States. The best golf courses in the world are generally believed to be Muirfield, in Scotland; the composite course at Royal Melbourne, in Australia; Royal County Down, in Newcastle, Northern Ireland; and I rather believe that Carnoustie belongs in this company, although its condition is not all it should be. As I walk Pebble Beach, however, especially those glorious holes along the cliffs at the water's edge, I'm inclined to believe that this is arguably the best of them all.

Pebble Beach ranges along the craggy bluffs of the Pacific Ocean near the village of Carmel, about 110 miles south of San Francisco. It was designed in 1919 by Jack Neville, a real estate salesman who had won the California State Amateur a couple of times. It was built on land owned by Del Monte Properties, an organization formed by Samuel F.B. Morse, nephew of the inventor of the telegraph. In the years before California became a state, political power centered around Monterey, just a few miles north of Pebble Beach, but when gold was discovered in the foothills of the Sierra Nevada Mountains, at Sutter's Mill, power shifted northward, to Sacramento. This was the beginning of the California Gold Rush and a chaotic dash westward. Inevitably, most of this new wealth drifted to San Francisco, and before long, a transcontinental railroad became more than a convenience: it was a necessity. The line was completed in 1869, and by 1880, 30 years after California became a state, a spur line had been built to a fashionable resort near Monterey modeled after Newport, Rhode Island. The Hotel Del Monte, a very large building of Victorian architecture, was the jewel of the Monterey Peninsula. It attracted not only the well-to-do of San Francisco, but of the Eastern United States as well. Among the amusements for the guests, the hotel had a rather modest golf course, but its most appealing attraction was its riding trails and carriage paths through the forests of pine, cypress and eucalyptus, winding along the wild, rocky shore of the Pacific.

Morse was a man of vision. An Easterner, he had gone to Yale, and in 1906 he was captain of the football team. He came West in 1914 to work with the Pacific Improvement Company, a subsidiary of the Southern Pacific Railroad, which owned the resort. Given the assignment of disposing of the railroad's real estate holdings, Morse decided to buy seven thousand acres of it, including seven miles along the ocean, for $1.3 million. He also had the vision to see that golf would become important to resort operations, and while the course at the Hotel Del Monte was pleasant enough, Morse wanted something better. Now he had a real stroke of genius. Instead of selling the prime acreage that ran along the bluffs above Carmel Bay for homesites, he decided to build his new course there. To what extent Morse knew golf is not certain, but he did know that Jack Neville, one of his real estate salesmen, was a very good amateur player, and that, evidently, was enough to know. Morse gave him the assignment. Neville had learned the game by playing with Macdonald Smith, his brother George, and Jim Barnes, all of whom worked together at the Claremont Country Club, near Oakland, where Neville's father was a member. Neville had played some golf at Monterey, and after a ride over 17-Mile Drive, where he saw the beauty of the place, he determined that this was where he wanted to spend his life. In 1915 he became a real estate salesman for Pacific Improvement. Morse found him there.

For three weeks Neville walked the property, working out the routing of the holes. They began simply enough. A log cabin, the original Del Monte Lodge, had been built as a refreshment stand for those riding the 17-Mile Drive. With Morse in tow, Neville walked along a path that led from the cabin and drove stakes into the ground for the tees and greens of the first two holes. Those ran parallel to the shoreline, but they are a couple of hundred yards inland from the bay. Having reached that point, Neville had to decide whether he should continue inland or turn toward the coast. He turned toward the sea, with a shortish par-four hole that doglegs slightly left, and created the first loop of the figure eight routing. In a way, Pebble Beach resembles North Berwick, an ancient course on the Lothian coast of Scotland, near Edinburgh. It, too, is built on headlands, above the Firth of Forth, and it has a simple figure eight design. Like many courses in the British Isles, Pebble Beach moves out from the clubhouse and doesn't return until the last hole.

The fourth, the first of the seaside holes, moves along the edge of the cliffs, and although it is only 327 yards from tee to green, it is no pushover. The cliffs range along the right, a nest of bunkers is set in the drive zone to the left of the fairway, and the small green is set in a cluster of bunkers, with a sheer drop to the beach and to the right. We then come to the fifth, an uphill par three of 170 yards through a narrow chute between very tall trees. The hole seems out of place, and, indeed, it wasn't supposed to be there. When Morse took over the property, he bought up a subdivision of 80-foot lots, but the owner of a tract along the bay refused to sell. Neville and Morse had intended to build a downhill par three along the shoreline, beginning behind the fourth green. It is a shame they couldn't carry out their plan. Late one afternoon I slipped inside the ropes that keep spectators away from the fairway and the green of the fourth and stole a peek. From what I could see and imagine, it would have been lovely.

Now begins a series of classic holes, starting with the sixth, a moderate length par five of 515 yards that rises to a high escarpment above Stillwater Cove, a yacht basin. The course then plunges down to the edge of Carmel Bay with the seventh, a 120-yard par three that is frightening. The tee is set high above the green level, but the green itself is the smallest on the course. It probes into the bay, a peninsula bordered on its three sides by frothy surf that pounds the rocky shoreline. In troubled weather the green is framed by lacey spray. Bunkers guard the front.

In calm weather, the shot to the green is a nine-iron or a wedge, but when the wind blows in from the Pacific, it could call for a very long iron. Beginning here, you are playing golf of the most demanding order. Every shot flirts with the cliffs along the edge of the bay. The eighth is intimidating. It is a 425-yard par four that begins at the base of the slope that leads downward to the seventh green. The tee shot is blind, it must reach the crest of a plateau, and it must be played with great control, not only for direction, but for distance as well. A shot that goes too far could drop off the edge of a savage chasm that plunges 80 feet straight down to a cove where the waves churn against the cliffs. While the fairway swings left and serpentines around the cove, the green is off to the right. The second shot must carry the gorge and settle on a smallish green protected by bunkers. Let the second shot leak to the right, and the ball could fall to the beach; hit the shot timidly and it could ricochet off the rocky bluff and into the sea; make sure of the carry and go beyond the green, and you are in pretty bad shape there, too, for now you must play your third shot back toward the cliff's edge. The eighth hole, in short, is a magnificent test of nerves and skill. It just might be the best par-four hole in all of golf. If not that, then it is one-third of the most demanding series of three holes in the game.

Both the ninth and 10th follow the edge of the cliffs over land that pitches and rolls and tilts slightly toward the sea. At 450 yards, the ninth is the longer of the two and its fairway the wider. Two steep-faced bunkers are set to the left of the fairway, beginning about 235 yards from the tee and running for perhaps 20 yards. The fairway at this point is a little more than 30 yards wide. With the fairway tilting toward the bluffs, this is a very testing tee shot, indeed. The natural tendency is to stay away from the right and the plunge downward to the beach, but the bunkers on the left are difficult because of their high frontal walls.

At 436 yards, the 10th is shorter, but it has many of the same problems as the ninth. Its fairway, however, is narrower than the ninth's around the area of the fairway bunker, which is much larger and elongated. The green of the 10th is more closely guarded. A pear-shaped bunker cuts off a portion of the front and wraps around to the side. Then a deep semi-circular begins a yard or two behind the frontal bunker and encloses half the green, curling around the back and onward toward the right front. From the right, a depression covered with thick, deep kikuyu grass intrudes across the front. The shot, therefore, must carry to the putting surface.

You are now at the outer reaches of the course. From there it moves inland, weaving among the cypress, eucalyptus, live oaks, and Monterey pines before returning to the sea again at the 17th, a par three with an hourglass-shaped green set at an angle to the line of flight, bordered on three sides by bunkers and with the rocky coastline just beyond and to the left, where so many fine rounds have been shattered by a mis-played shot.

We come then to the 18th, a glorious finishing hole along the coastline. It measures 548 yards, and it has nearly everything golf-course architecture has up its sleeve. The waters of the bay range along the left, large bunkers are set on the right in the drive zone, with out-of-bounds farther right. Trees stand in the fairway where a good drive should land, and more trees protect the right front of the green. Bunkers nearly envelop the green. Like the 14th, this is a true three-shot hole. Should a player come to the 18th needing to make up a shot and try to reach the green in two, he would have to avoid all those hazards and obstacles on both his first and second shots, and the second would have to hold a green set above fairway level. During the Crosby Pro-Am some years ago, Gene Littler, needing a birdie on the 18th, went for the green with a wood and hooked his ball into Carmel Bay. In a qualifying round for the California Amateur, a player needed 13 to reach play. He hit two in the water on the left, then two more out of bounds to the right and made 16. In the 1968 Pacific Coast Amateur, a stroke play event, another player needed seven to win. He hooked his tee shot into the water, made 10, and finished third. In the early rounds in the 1982 Open, Fred Couples and Frank Conner each made nine, and five others made eight, including Gary Player and his son Wayne.

While the design and layout of Pebble Beach was Neville's alone, he was given assistance by two other good amateur golfers. Douglas Grant, a contemporary of Neville's, helped him with the original bunkering, and H. Chandler Egan, a Chicagoan who had won the Amateur in 1904 and 1905, remodeled and re-bunkered every green, toughening the course for the 1929 Amateur, the first national championship played at Pebble Beach. (As a matter of golf trivia, in each of the two years he was Amateur champion, Egan defeated one of our most gifted golf course architects in the first round. In 1904 it was A.W. Tillinghast, who gave us Baltusrol and Winged Foot, among many others, and in 1905 he defeated Charles B. Macdonald, the creator of the National Golf Links of America, one of our early modern courses.)

Pebble Beach, however, is a public course, and over the years 21 bunkers were eliminated so that play could be speeded along. When the 1972 Open was scheduled for Pebble Beach, the USGA summoned Neville, who was then 81, to help recreate his original design. Three new tees were built, one of them to extend the length of the 10th hole, and six bunkers were added or enlarged. Still, Neville felt the course was softer than his original design.

Other matters changed during the 1970s. Morse died in 1969, and shortly afterward Del Monte Properties changed its attitude toward the golf course. Instead of a place for guests of the Del Monte Lodge to play golf, as it had been under Morse, it became a profit center. Del Monte Properties became The Pebble Beach Corporation, and later it was bought by Twentieth Century Fox. Other changes came along in quick order. The golf cart was perceived to be essential to the financial well-being of the corporation, and soon black ribbons of asphalt threaded across the landscape. More and more players were crammed onto the course; play began at dawn and went on until dusk, and some groups didn't finish rounds that were taking six hours to complete. Cost of green fees outraced the rate of inflation. By the time the 1982 Open began, a round of golf at Pebble Beach cost $50 for persons staying at the Lodge, $70 for others. The price included a motorized cart, thank heavens.

With such heavy play, the condition of the course suffered, and it took a supreme effort by the grounds crew and some concessions from the administrators to have Pebble Beach in shape for the Open. Even though Pebble Beach is laced with cart paths, the carts ordinarily are allowed to roam at will. For three weeks before the Open, however, they were restricted to the paths. That helped with the fairways. Then, three weeks before the Open, only guests at the Lodge were allowed to play, and then only if they had made golf reservations when they made room reservations. Those who hadn't booked a starting time when they booked their rooms weren't allowed to play. This cut down on play from 60 to 70 percent.

Throughout early spring, the greens had been slow and bumpy. As the Open neared, the grounds crew rolled them and topdressed them with sand. By the time the Open began, they still weren't at their best, but the ball was rolling fast and true, and the fairways had been cut down to half an inch, ideal height for crisp, clean shots.

Meanwhile, two changes in the bunkering had been made since 1972. A pot bunker was added to the cluster in the drive zone of the fourth hole, and the bunker to the right of the drive zone at the 16th was extended toward the green, a sheer wall three feet high was built at the front, and the ground within the bunker was pitched toward the green. A ball that goes in now rolls toward the base of the vertical wall, and if it rolls close enough to the front, the player is left with no shot to the green; he must play out sideways to the fairway. This was to become significant.

We are still too close to it now to make an objective and sound judgement, but the 1982 Open may have been among the more significant championships in the game's extensive history. We won't know until we see if Tom Watson wins it again. Walter Hagen is often given credit for saying that any golfer can win the Open once, but only a great player can win it more than once. Until 1982, Watson had not yet won the Open, although he had won the Masters twice and the British Open three times (he won his fourth British Open a month after the U.S. Open). For many years it has been dogma that a player cannot be considered among the great ones without winning the U.S. Open. I don't believe it myself because, for one thing, Sam Snead must be included on anyone's list of the great players, and yet Sam did not win the Open. For another, Watson had already established himself as the leading player in the game despite continued failures in the U.S. Open.

By the time the field had gathered for the 1982 U.S. Open, Watson had won 30 tournaments since joining the PGA Tour in the fall of 1971. He had won the Masters twice, in 1977 and 1981, and the British Open three times, in 1975, 1977, and 1980. He had also been named player of the year four times, had been the Tour's leading money winner four consecutive years, from 1977 through 1980, and had won the Vardon Trophy for having the lowest scoring average in 1978, 1979, and 1980. In 1980 he had won $530,808, the most ever in one season. But his failure to win the U.S. Open nagged at him. Winning it ended a series of frustrations. He had been in position to win several times. He had his first chance in 1974, when he took the third round lead at Winged Foot, in Mamaroneck, near New York City. Even though he was playing first class golf, he seemed to lack confidence. When he finished the third round, he asked a friend if he thought he could win.

'Do *you* think you can?' the friend asked.

Watson said yes, but the next day he three-putted twice on the first nine, shooting 38, and when he bogeyed both the 11th and 12th holes, he fell three strokes behind Hale Irwin, the eventual winner. Trying to catch up, Watson played some so-called 'loose' shots, came back in 41, shot 79 for the round, and finished five strokes behind Irwin. He was in position again the following year, at Medinah, near Chicago. Leading the field after 36 holes, Watson once again saw his game fall apart. At the beginning of the third round, he three-putted the first hole from 20 feet and then missed a one-foot putt on the second. He hit only nine greens, shot 78, claimed gallery members called 'Remember Winged Foot' to him, and dropped from contention. In 1980 he went into the last round trailing Nicklaus and Isao Aoki, the co-leaders, by two strokes, but he put himself in a hole immediately by pushing his drive into trees along the right side of the first fairway at Baltusrol and losing a stroke to par. While he got that stroke back with a birdie on the second, he three-putted twice on the first nine and missed several short putts on the second. When he finally made his second birdie, he was on the 16th hole and no longer a factor.

Again in 1981, at Merion, he was in the hunt, only four strokes off the lead after 36 holes. He was a stroke under par after 14 holes of the third round, but on the 15th, a shortish par four that doglegs right, he hooked his tee shot out of bounds, made seven, and finished the round nine strokes off the lead.

Those earlier failures, in 1974 and 1975, were easily excused; Watson was still a young man. They could be excused for another reason as well. Two weeks after he collapsed at Winged Foot, Watson won the Western Open, his first victory as a professional, and then a month after he failed in the 1975 U.S. Open, he won his first British Open, defeating Jack Newton in a playoff at Carnoustie. He showed then that he had the courage and the strength of will to shake off the effects of earlier failures and win.

The failures of 1980 and 1981 were not so easily excused, because by then Watson had established himself as something special. After 1981, though, some people thought that Watson, like Snead, might never win the Open and might spend the rest of his career in hopeless and frustrating pursuit of it, the championship he wanted above all others. That speculation has now been interred.

Most of those in the 1982 Open had played Pebble Beach many times in the Crosby Pro-Am, and they knew that the trick to scoring well is to make your birdies early and then hold on. Of the seven players who were under par 72 in the first round, five scored better on the first nine than the second. Bill Rogers shot 34 on the first nine, 36 on the second. Bobby Clampett, Calvin Peete, and Terry Diehl had 34–37. Among the others, Isao Aoki shot 33–39; Butch Baird had 35–37; David Graham 34–39; Jack Nicklaus and Jack Renner 35–39; Bob Shearer 34–41; Gil Morgan 35–40; Ben Crenshaw 35–41; Chip Beck 36–40; Mark Hayes 36–42; Severiano Ballesteros 38–43; and Frank Conner 36–47. Wayne Player, Gary's son, had all kinds of trouble with that second nine. He shot 37–44—81, in the first round and 36–43—79 in the second.

Naturally some others went the other way. Bill Brodell, for example, shot 49 on the first nine but solved the mysteries of the second nine well enough to come back in 39.

Danny Edwards had the best first nine of the day. Playing in the 10th group of three players off the tee on Thursday morning, he began his round with a birdie three on the first hole, an eagle three on the second, a par four on the third, birdie three on the fourth, par three on the fifth, and a birdie four on the sixth. Five under after six holes. Three more pars and he was through the first nine holes in 31. He followed a par four on the 10th with another birdie three on the 11th, then two more pars on the 12th and 13th. With five holes to play he was six under par — par in for 66. His game turned around on the 14th hole, a par five of 565 yards that doglegs right and turns away from the ocean. Like the 18th, this is a true three-shot hole, and Edwards missed the green with his third. After pitching on and putting to within a foot of the cup, Edwards missed the putt and made seven, two over par. His misery was just beginning. After three-putting the 16th, he needed three strokes to reach the green of the 17th, the par three, and made five. Within five holes he had lost five strokes. He was back in 40 and finished only one stroke under par.

When the day ended, Edwards was tied with Clampett, Peete, Diehl, and Jim King, a former Tour player who was then teaching at a club in Miami. They were a stroke behind Rogers, the reigning British Open champion, and Bruce Devlin, who was 44 at the time and spending more time talking about golf as a television commentator than playing it.

Rogers had a very eventful first nine consisting of four birdies, two bogeys and only three pars. He began by making his par on the first and picked up two strokes with birdies on the second and third. Two pars followed, but then he birdied the sixth, lost strokes on both the seventh and eighth, and then rifled a one-iron eight feet from the stick on the ninth and holed the putt for another birdie. He played nine consecutive pars coming back, even though he hit only five of the nine greens. The key hole probably was the 10th, where he drove into the rough, missed the green with his second and could only come within 50 feet of the cup with his third. He holed it to save par.

Rogers had been something of a disappointment through the early part of the year. After finishing in a tie for second in the 1981 U.S. Open and then winning the British, he fully expected, as he said, to come on like gangbusters in 1982. It didn't work out.

'I haven't played that well this year,' Rogers said. 'One week I'd drive well but not putt worth a darn. The next week I'd putt well but wouldn't be able to drive. I haven't put it together and I've pressed a little. A 70, though, makes me feel good.'

Devlin, too, was feeling good. 'If anyone had told me I'd be co-leader of the U.S. Open after the first round, I'd have told them they were mad,' Devlin said. 'I've only played in five other tournaments this year, and I played miserably in all of them. I haven't enjoyed it, but I wanted to qualify for the Open.'

When he was playing the Tour full time, I always felt that Bruce Devlin had a vast potential. I also felt that except for a year or two he didn't live up to that potential. In 1970, he won the Cleveland Open, the Bob Hope Desert Classic, and Australian PGA. He teamed with David Graham, another Australian, to win the World Cup, and won the Alcan, a short-lived tournament that was played at Portmarnock, near Dublin, Ireland, that year. It looked as if he had arrived. Then, in 1971, he became ill in mid-year with two cases of walking pneumonia, and a chronic sinus condition began to bother him once more. He didn't win a tournament that year. In 1972 he showed signs of revival, finishing eighth in a Florida tournament, fifth in the Masters, and then won the Houston Open and the USI Classic and lost a sudden death playoff to Graham in the Cleveland Open. Devlin was in his middle 30s by then, and he had become interested in golf course architecture. To the surprise of a great many people, he quit the Tour and played only a limited schedule. Looking back on it now, he questions whether it was the right thing to do.

'I just wasn't enjoying playing that much, but, no, quitting wasn't the smartest move I've ever made. I've suffered the consequences.'

He had played in 16 tournaments in 1981, which was about normal for him, and he had played in eight 1982 tournaments before the Open, missing the cut in four. Driving had been one of his problems, but he solved it on the evening before the Open began. On the practice tee, Devlin was approached by Julio Campagni, a salesman for one of the equipment companies. Campagni had seen Devlin spraying his shots, and he offered him one of the new metal drivers to try. Devlin had six drivers with him, and since none was working well, he figured he might just as well give the metal club a try. He hit the first ball and it flew straight. He tried another, and it, too, went straight. Every ball he hit went straight. Warming up the next morning, he hit a few more balls with the metal club, and just like the night before, they flew straight. So he put the club into his bag.

After a routine par four on the first hole, Devlin very nearly scored a double-eagle two on the second, at 506 yards the easiest par on the course. He split the fairway with his tee shot and then went for the green with a three-wood second. The ball lipped the cup and stopped only three feet from the hole. He rolled in the putt for the eagle. While he was off to a fine start, his round looked as if it might slip away from him when he bogeyed the sixth and double bogeyed the short seventh. But Devlin kept his composure and birdied the 11th, 15th and 16th to finish two under par.

'I hit a lot of fine irons,' Devlin said, 'and I hit some indifferent shots, too. I had a lot of chances for birdies. If you have a lot of chances, you'll make some of them.'

While Devlin's position as a co-leader was the biggest surprise of the day, we had some others at the other end of the scale. Craig Stadler had come into the Open as one of the favorites because of his victory in the Masters in April, but he shot a disappointing 76. Jerry Pate limped in with 79, Raymond Floyd, who was enjoying a very good year, shot 78, Hale Irwin had 76, Hubert Green 78, Jim Simons, who had won the Crosby early in the year, shot 81, and Gary Player shot 78, a round that included an eight on the 18th.

Watson had not torn Pebble Beach apart, and even though he shot 72, it was such an erratic round that I had some doubts he would be a contender. He had only eight pars, and with four holes to play he was three over par, on his way to 75, or perhaps worse. He began by losing strokes on both the first and third holes, won them back with birdies on the fourth and fifth. One of the great putters in the game, he three-putted the 14th from 25 feet.

Just when all seemed lost, Watson turned his game around. He played a sand wedge to 10 feet on the 395-yard 15th and holed it, drove into the fairway bunker at the 16th but had enough room to clear the front wall with a nine-iron and hit the ball within a foot and a half for a second birdie, and then played a medium iron to within 15 feet on the dangerous 17th, a par three that was playing 175 yards that day. He holed that one for a third consecutive birdie. A par five at the 18th, where he missed a chance for a fourth consecutive birdie from five feet, and he finished with even par 72.

In retrospect, those last four holes were probably the most important of the championship. Obviously they saved Watson; had he finished that first round with 75, he could have been so discouraged that he might not have been able to make up those strokes over the next 54 holes.

Under the windy and overcast conditions of the first day, 16 men played Pebble Beach in par 72 or better — seven were under par, nine were even par. Although it was still overcast and brisk the second day (it would remain that way throughout the week), the wind had become more quiet and the scoring improved noticeably. Sixteen players broke par 72 in the second round and eight more shot 72. Furthermore, while no one was under 70 the first day, six broke 70 the second day. Larry Rinker, a young professional from Florida, had 67, the lowest score of the day (indeed, it was the lowest of the four days, matched by Peter Oosterhuis and Lanny Wadkins in the third round, and by Gary Koch in the fourth).

Rinker comes from a golf-oriented family that is based in Stuart, Florida, about 40 miles north of Palm Beach. His father is a low-handicap amateur, his sister Laurie was United States Girls' Junior champion in 1980, and his sister-in-law, Kelli Rinker, plays on the LPGA Tour. Rinker's 67 followed an opening 74 and thrust him into the thick of it. When the day ended, he was in the unaccustomed position of being in second place, two strokes off the lead, and while that might have seemed strange, it was no more strange than the overall picture. The lead was held by Devlin, who followed his opening 70 with 69, giving him a halfway total of 139. Rinker was along in second place, with 141, followed by Scott Simpson, with 142, and, at 143, Lyn Lott, Calvin Peete, Andy North, and Bill Rogers. Of those seven, only Rogers, and perhaps Peete, could be classified as less than a surprise.

Watson, with a second 72, and Nicklaus, with 70, were tied, at 144, with Tom Kite, Bobby Clampett, and George Burns. Burns had one of the more unusual rounds in Open history. After a par four on the first hole, be birdied the next six with some superb iron play. He holed no putts from longer than 10 feet, and, indeed, on the par five sixth hole, he two-putted from eight feet for his birdie after being on the green in two with a three-wood second. His pitching wedge on the fourth stopped 18 inches from the cup, and his six-iron to the par three sixth was only a foot from the hole. No one could document a player ever before making six successive birdies in the Open. Burns was out in 30, but, like Edwards in the first round, he lost it all on the second nine, shooting 42 and finishing with 72. 'I felt like two different men,' Burns said.

Devlin was the first man to break 70. Off the first tee at 10 minutes before eight in the morning, Devlin quickly dipped three under par with birdies on the second, third, and fourth. After making his pars on the fifth and sixth, Devlin played a nine-iron to three feet on the seventh for a fourth birdie. Another par on the eighth, and he needed one more four to make the nine-hole turn in 32. On the ninth, though, Devlin pulled his tee shot into the bunker. Because of the high front wall, it looked as if he might have to sacrifice a shot and simply play out sideways to the fairway. Instead, Devlin hit a superb four-wood that cleared the lip of the bunker and soared toward the green. It wasn't enough club; the ball fell short and buried in the face of a greenside bunker. Devlin tried to dig it out with a pitching wedge, but the shot failed. He did work it loose, however, and, switching to a sand iron, he very nearly holed it to save his par. The ball stopped about six inches past the cup, and Devlin holed it for a bogey. It was one of those holes that could have cost him many more strokes than it did, and if there is such a thing as a saving bogey, this was it.

Three under par now, Devlin bogeyed three of the next four holes. But as quickly as he lost strokes, he picked them up again. He made a birdie from 15 feet on the 15th, and played a two-iron onto the 17th green just 10 feet from the hole for another birdie. Two under par now, Devlin split the fairway with his tee shot on the 18th, played his second shot short of the green, and pitched on with his wedge. As soon as he hit the pitch he knew it was a good shot, but he didn't realize how good it really was. The ball came down on the green, hopped twice, and then disappeared into the hole. Unfortunately for Devlin, it didn't stay in; the ball hopped right out again and rolled about 40 inches away. No eagle, but another birdie and 69.

Pleased as he was with the ending, Devlin was just as happy about the beginning of his round. 'I was off to a marvelous start,' he said, 'but then I couldn't stop the bleeding.' Asked if any one hole could be considered the key to his round, Devlin replied that the 14th was the turning point, even though he made only a par five. 'I put together three good shots in a row. I needed them because I had just bogeyed four of the last five holes. Making par was a turning point.'

While Devlin almost let his game get away from him on the second nine, Watson appeared to be falling apart in the early going. He played the first nine in 38, two over par, the result of some very loose iron play. Three times he was in bunkers, and on the ninth hole he took two strokes to get out of the sand. He had to hole a 20-footer to save his bogey. Once again he saved himself with late birdies on the incoming nine, holing from three feet on the 14th and from 20 feet on the 17th. He finished with another 72, and at 144, he was five strokes behind Devlin.

Far from being discouraged, however, Watson took a positive outlook. 'This is the best position I've been in since I led at Medinah in 1975,' he said. 'I had a bad start, yes. I just got out of the box poorly. The man who wins here will have to have a lot of patience. I just didn't play 90 percent today; maybe about 65 or 70 percent. My iron play was not that good. Nobody's going to play 100 percent this week.'

Nicklaus was much more consistent. His 70 was made up of three birdies and a single bogey. He dropped a stroke on the 13th, a 393-yard par four that runs parallel to the sea and where the tee shot must be placed on the left side of the fairway to open the green for the approach. Nicklaus drove into the right rough and had to carry across a bunker with his sand iron in order to reach the green. From the rough he was able to put very little spin on the ball, and so it rolled off the back edge. From there, Nicklaus played a little chip that stopped three and a half feet from the hole. He missed the putt.

Nicklaus made no putts of any length throughout the round; indeed, he had made nothing of consequence through two rounds. He made his first birdie on the third, where his seven-iron stopped 18 inches from the hole. Another seven-iron to four feet resulted in a birdie on the 10th. He made his final birdie on the 14th with a pitching wedge to 12 feet.

There was another development of interest in this round. Amateurs normally are obscure in the Open, since they so seldom have any bearing on the outcome, and they usually are so little known that spectators have no interest in them. Each year the Amateur champion of the previous year is paired with the Open champion of the previous year, as a reward, for one thing, and, not incidentally, so that the USGA can call some attention to him (the conduct of an amateur championship was one of the principal reasons for the creation of the USGA). In 1982, though, there was no need to go any unusual lengths to call attention to the Amateur champion. In September of 1981, the Amateur championship had been won by Nathaniel Crosby, the youngest son of Bing Crosby. Nathaniel was 10 years old in 1972 when the Open was played at Pebble Beach. His father had him by his side as he walked the course in the Jack Nicklaus gallery during the first round. Since Bing's death, Nathaniel had taken over as host to the Crosby Pro-Am, which winds up at Pebble Beach each year. He is, in short, a very popular figure, and, if anything, his presence attracted attention to David Graham and Bill Rogers, the other members of the group, rather than their attracting attention to him. Their gallery was not only large, but it included a good many of the best looking girls on the grounds.

When he won the Amateur in 1981 it was considered pretty much of a fluke, even though he consistently came back after being down to some players who were considered very much better than he. It was generally conceded that in any listing of the best amateur in the country, Nathaniel might not even be mentioned. Even when he shot 77 in the first round of the Open it was a bit of a surprise; hardly anyone expected him to break 80.

Nathaniel Crosby, however, is made of some pretty solid stuff. He's gritty and determined, and he showed it by coming back in 37. I doubt, however, that even those who know him best were ready for what he did the next day. Five over par going into the second round, Nathaniel birdied two holes on the first nine, going out in 34, and after 13 holes he was only three over par for the distance and right in there among the best players in the game.

At the 14th hole, Nathaniel's tee shot failed to carry a fairway bunker on the right side, just where the hole turns for its uphill run to the green. The ball caught in the grass at the top of the bunker; not in the sand, but still against the rise of the bank. Taking an iron, Nathaniel tried to play toward the green; a decent shot would have put him in position to reach the green with his third and set up a routine par five. Somehow, though, the ball slammed against the face of the rise and rolled back down into the sand. One stroke gone. His third shot was very well played, back into the fairway, leaving him only a pitch to the green, which sits about 10 feet above the level of the fairway and is protected on the left by a deep bunker. His fourth shot was hit thin, and instead of reaching the green, the ball fell short. He was lying four and still wasn't on the green. He evidently misjudged the fifth shot and hit the ball over the back of the green into rough of only moderate length. Going with his wedge once more, he barely moved the ball. He was on in seven and two-putted for nine. In one hole he had gone from three over par to seven over, and now it was not so much a question of being among the leaders as whether he would survive the 36-hole cut. He couldn't afford to drop another stroke.

Throughout the Amateur, Nathaniel had made the shots he had to make, and he showed once again in this very difficult situation that his upbringing as a member of a very prominent family had developed in him remarkable poise for one so young. He played the last four holes about as well as they could be played, holing a birdie putt from a little over 20 feet on the 15th, and having legitimate opportunities for birdies on the other three. His approach to the 16th left him about 25 feet from the hole, he missed a birdie on the 17th from 15 feet, and his putt on the 18th stopped only inches short of the hole. He finished with 73, one over par with a nine. His 36-hole total of 150 kept him in the field for the final 36 holes.

Scores of 151 made the cut, and, as usual, some very prominent players didn't make it. The last two rounds would be played without Bruce Lietzke; Hubert Green, the 1977 champion; Mark Hayes; Jerry Pate, who won in 1976; Lee Trevino, not enjoying a good year; Gary Player, as well as his son Wayne; Seve Ballesteros, who shot 160 for two rounds; and Arnold Palmer.

Overnight rain softened the greens for the third round, the wind died, and even though it was still overcast, it was an ideal day for scoring. The 66 players left in the field took advantage of it. Twenty-one of them broke par; 14 were under 70, and 10 others were even par for the day. When the round ended, Watson and Rogers were tied for the lead at 212, four under par, but 13 others were within five strokes of them. Bruce Devlin, David Graham, George Burns and Scott Simpson were tied at 214, and Jack Nicklaus and Calvin Peete were another stroke behind, at 215.

Six players either led or had a share of the lead throughout the day. Andy North, who had won the Open at Cherry Hills in Denver, in 1978, began the day at 143, a stroke under par, but when he rolled in a birdie putt on the seventh he went four under and took over the lead. Just as quickly he disappeared from view. He dropped strokes on the eighth, ninth, 11th, 12th, and 13th, went eight over par on the last 11 holes, shot 42 on the second nine and 77 for the day. From one under he went to four over.

Scott Simpson, who was two strokes under par after 36 holes, held a share of the lead early in the third round when he went to three under par, but he lost strokes on the 10th and 11th and finished the day with 72, right back where he started — two under par, with 214.

Bobby Clampett, a hometown boy, also went to three under par and a share of the lead on the first nine, but he lost three strokes after the 10th hole, and he, too, finished with 72.

Larry Rinker was another. After playing a superb round of 67 on Friday that put him in second place, three under par, Rinker began the third round with a birdie four at the second to go four under par. He lost a stroke at the fifth and two more at the ninth, shot 75 and finished with 216. He was soon lost to sight.

Poor Bruce Devlin. After making 11 birdies through the first two rounds, he made none at all in the third. He did have three bogeys, though, and shot 75, the kind of score expected of him when the championship began. The driver that had been so reliable through the first two days deserted him on the third. Despite his misfortunes, he ended the day only two strokes off the lead.

No one had been able to win the Open in successive years since 1950 and 1951, when Ben Hogan won first at Merion, defeating Lloyd Mangrum and George Fazio in an 18-hole playoff, and then came back the next year to win at Oakland Hills Country Club, near Detroit, perhaps the most severe course the Open has ever been played on. David Graham had won at Merion in 1981, and while his first two rounds at Pebble Beach could not be called inspiring — a 73 in the first round with two balls out of bounds on the 14th, and 72 in the second — he was still on the edge of contention. In the third round he thrust himself squarely among the contenders with a solid 69.

He began the day slowly, dropping a stroke at the third where he hooked his tee shot severely and was lucky to be able to play his second shot in the direction of the green. His ball had settled among the trees and in a depression near the 16th green. He was able to pitch out across the fairway to the right rough, and then needed three more strokes to finish. It looked as if he would drop another stroke at the fifth, the par three, where he missed the green, but he chipped back and holed a slippery eight-footer for his par. Off and running now, he birdied the next two holes and made the turn for home in 35, one under par. A bogey at the 10th, where he hooked his drive into a fairway bunker, cost him one stroke, but he birdied the 14th, 16th, and 18th to finish with 34 and 69.

Graham had a difficult year after winning the 1981 Open, so difficult that listening to him made you wonder if winning was worth it — particularly if you expect to make money from being the U.S. Open champion. Professional golf, however, is played for the money, and Graham found that anyone who wants it must work for it. He spent 20 weeks on the road, traveling to Europe, the Far East, South America and Australia playing in tournaments and exhibitions. 'I wanted to go to parts of the world where people might never have seen the U.S. Open champion,' he explained. While he took in close to $1 million ('I went after as much as I could'), his game suffered. He put pressure on himself constantly, trying to play as well as he did when he shot 67 in the last round at Merion. He believes he set too high a standard for himself and, particularly in Australia, he was in a no-win situation. 'If I won, well, they all said I was supposed to win. If I didn't, I was still supposed to win. Someone once asked me what I'd do if I won a tournament that gave me a 10-year exemption on the Tour. I said I'd take six months off. I won two (the 1981 Open and the 1979 PGA), but I didn't take time off. I'd like to take six months off now, because I feel like I've been working 15 years without a vacation.'

Rogers, meanwhile, continued to play much better than he had early in the year, making five birdies and two bogeys. He was hot at the beginning of the round, reaching the second green in two, then holing a 15-footer at the fourth and a 12-footer at the sixth. Out in 33, Rogers began the home nine by dropping a stroke at the 10th, where he drove into the right rough. After making his pars on the next three holes, he birdied the 14th from three feet and the 15th by holing a 30-footer. A routine par on the 16th and Rogers was four under par for the day, five under for the tournament. Now, on the 17th, he was a little quick with his hands and hooked his tee shot onto the right collar of the green. A poor chip left him eight feet from the hole, and he missed the putt.

With a chance to go five under again by holing a five-footer on the 18th, Rogers missed the putt.

Still, it was a satisfactory round, good enough to give him a share of the lead.

In the meantime, Nicklaus was playing some rather steady but dull stuff. While he continued to hit greens and place his ball within reasonable distances of the holes, he wasn't dropping his putts. After a birdie at the second, Nicklaus ran off seven consecutive pars before dropping a 20-footer for a birdie at the 10th. Two under for the round, he lost another stroke on the 12th, a very difficult par three of 204 yards, where he missed from two and a half feet after his three-iron was short and in a bunker. He had the ball inside 20 feet on each of the last four holes, but he didn't make a birdie. He shot 71 for the round, 215 for the 54 holes and went into the last round three strokes out of the lead, apparently heading nowhere.

On the other hand, Watson was finally in top form and beginning to move. It is a common belief that the third round sets up the tournament for you, that the thing to do is play cautiously through the early rounds, avoiding risks and playing with patience, taking birdies when they come to you but not taking chances when they can be avoided. Watson had played that way so far, and then in the third round his irons became more assured and the putts began to fall. He began very slowly by missing the first green and taking a bogey and then missing the second green and settling for a par five. Four birdies on the next six holes turned everything around. He birdied the third from 12 feet and came out of the fairway bunker to the right of the fourth to 15 feet for a second birdie. After pars on the fifth and sixth, Watson birdied the seventh from 16 feet and the eighth from 18 feet, playing a four-wood from the tee and a five-iron across the chasm to the green. He missed the ninth green and lost a stroke there, failing to hole from four feet, but he was out in 34, his best first nine of the week.

Coming back he had three birdies, but the 14th hole caused him problems again. He had bogeyed this hole in the first round and came back the next day with a birdie. Here he drove into the right rough, dug the ball out with a seven iron and, using his seven-iron again, he seemed to hit his third shot a little fat and left it short of the green. From there he pitched on and two-putted from 15 feet.

He closed out his round with a birdie on the 18th, playing a three-wood from the tee, a four-iron, and then a pitching wedge to 10 feet. He had played the round with seven birdies and three bogeys, out in 34, back in 34 for his 68.

'Obviously I like my position,' he grinned. 'I had a good feeling about my golf swing, and I can't wait to get out there tomorrow. The Open championship is very important to me. I would love to win it on this course.'

Nicklaus was in the fourth-from-last group off the tee on Sunday, paired with Peete. He hit a very good drive down the fairway and in excellent position for his approach, which he would play with a pitching club. For the second straight day he was a little short; the ball hit the lower right corner of the green and spun back off into some shaggy grass at the top of a slope. As he walked toward his ball through sustained applause, Nicklaus smiled and waved to the gallery. Looking at him you would think he was out for a friendly Sunday round rather than playing for the national championship.

Great player though he is, Nicklaus sometimes seems helpless when he misses a green. Here, facing a simple little shot, he played a miserable chip that never once seemed to move in the direction of the hole and left him at least 12 feet from the cup. He missed the putt, taking five. When he failed to birdie the second, it seemed obvious that this was not to be Jack's Open.

On the other hand, it is never wise to underestimate this remarkable man. His resolve is so strong, his will so powerful, he can't be dismissed if there are still holes to be played. Just as quickly as he threw two strokes away (a par on the second is the same as a lost stroke, for it is a relatively easy birdie), he put together a string of five consecutive birdies, from the third hole through the seventh, and before anyone was quite prepared for it, Nicklaus was four under par for the day, five under for the distance. At that moment he was tied for the lead with Bill Rogers, who had completed the fifth hole. Watson, who was paired with Rogers as the last twosome off the tee, was at four under with Devlin. Devlin was playing a hole behind Nicklaus, paired with Scott Simpson. When Bruce birdied the sixth hole he went five under par, and he was tied with Rogers, who had just completed the fifth (George Burns and David Graham were between the two groups).

Devlin, however, lost one stroke on the seventh and two more on the ninth and was never in it again. He shot 74 and finished with 288, six strokes behind Watson.

Nicklaus had been playing superb shots to make those birdies. He had holed only one sizeable putt, from 24 feet on the fourth. On the third he played a sand wedge to 15 feet, and on the fifth, the uphill par three, his six-iron stopped just two feet from the hole. Since he had to make up ground quickly, he decided to take a chance on the sixth and go for the green with a one-iron from a very close lie. The shot came off nicely, and he two-putted from 35 feet for his fourth consecutive birdie.

Really rolling now, Nicklaus chose a sand iron for his tee shot on the seventh and played a lovely high pitch that dropped 11 feet from the hole. He rolled it in for a fifth birdie.

With each successive birdie, spectators began joining the Nicklaus gallery, and when he went to the eighth tee, it was difficult to get a good look at him through the crowd. Here he played a good enough drive (you only want to reach the top of the hill so that you can have a clear view of the green), but his approach drifted a little right and stopped a step or so off the edge of the green. It had hopped into some of the higher rough though, and Jack had some difficulty finding it. When he did, he played another mediocre shot and bogeyed. Par on the ninth and Nicklaus was out in 33 and four under for the tournament. Another par at the 10th, and then Nicklaus, most uncharacteristically, dropped another stroke. I say it was uncharacteristic because Nicklaus for many years had been the most dangerous fourth-round player in the game, to say nothing of being the most reliable putter. He lost a stroke on the 11th because he three-putted from 20 feet; his first putt glided three feet past the hole, and he missed coming back.

Watson, meanwhile, was making no headway either. He had gone ahead of Rogers briefly with a birdie at the second, dropping him to five under par, but he lost it just as quickly at the third, where he was bunkered. Rogers birdied the fourth with a nifty pitch about eight feet from the hole, but he gave back the stroke at the ninth. Watson had lost a golden chance for a birdie at the seventh where he missed a birdie chance from two feet. Both men were out in 36 and still at four under par.

No one wins a major golf competition without a touch of luck, and when Watson looks back on what he accomplished at Pebble Beach, he will have to pause a while over the 10th hole. This could very well have been the pivotal hole of the championship.

Every man has his weakness; with Nicklaus it is the short game, with Watson it is the driver. It was the driver that put him out of business in the 1981 Open, that cost him so dearly in the 1980 Open, and that caused him to miss the cut in the 1979 Open. Even in 1982 he had strayed a bit in the early going (he hit only five fairways in the first round), but after nine holes of the final round, he had not missed a fairway. A man of no more than average size (5 foot 9, 160 pounds), he is, nevertheless, very powerful. His forearms are massive, reminding one of Ben Hogan. With this arm strength, Watson is able to generate terrific clubhead speed, and he drives the ball a very long way. On the 10th, he crushed his tee shot and sent it 30 to 40 yards past Rogers, leaving him only a seven-iron to the green.

Close as he was to the green, though, Watson had to play his shot from a downhill lie, and when he came into it, something happened. The ball was both short of the green and to the right. When it was in mid-flight, it looked as if it might drift over the edge of the cliffs and fall to the beach, 40 or 50 feet below. Instead it settled on a shelf well below the level of the green, nestled among the kikuyu grass, a very coarse strain that is the devil to play from. A very quick player, Watson took hardly any time, and with a sand wedge he pitched the ball onto the collar of the green, still short of the hole. From 20 or 25 feet, Watson used his putter and holed it to save his par four.

Without that saving putt, there is no telling how Watson's confidence would have been affected; what came later might not have happened as it did.

While Watson was working out his problems satisfactorily, Rogers was having trouble. Well behind Watson after their tee shots on the 10th, Rogers pulled his second into a bunker to the left of the green, but he could not salvage his par, lost a stroke there, and another at the 12th. He had made three bogeys in four holes and was effectively out of it. He had chances, certainly, for he missed several holeable putts, one on the 13th from no more than 12 feet, and another on the 16th, from perhaps closer, but Rogers never seemed to be on the correct side of the hole to make a putt. His seemed always to be the slippery, downhill route to the hole, and, as a consequence, he had to stroke the ball cautiously. The cautious don't make many putts when they're needed.

By now, of those who began the last round with a shot at the championship, all but Graham had fallen back. Burns began his day by putting his approach to the first in almost the same position as Nicklaus had earlier, and where Nicklaus made a bogey five. From a shorter distance, Burns three-putted for six. He was out in 37, playing very unsteady golf, and then got worse. He shot 43 on the second nine, 80 for the round. Simpson bogeyed eight and nine and was out of it.

Graham, though, was holding on. Two under par when the day began, he played the first nine in 35, with three birdies and two bogeys. He stood on the 10th tee three under for the distance. Pars on the next three and he was still three under, just a stroke behind Watson, who was playing the 11th hole. That was as close as Graham would come. He dropped two strokes on the 13th, and from that moment, the 1982 Open was between Watson and Nicklaus.

When Watson finished saving his par on the 10th, Nicklaus was making his par on the 12th. Watson was four under par, Nicklaus three under. Once again on the 11th tee, Watson hit a very powerful drive. The hole measures 382 yards, and at least two-thirds of the distance is uphill. The ground flattens out toward the end, and the green is set behind mounded bunkers that shut off the right front. The best entrance is from the left. This is where Watson played his drive, and when he walked up to his ball, he had only a sand wedge left. He played a very nice shot 22 feet from the hole and made the putt for a birdie.

Five under par now, two ahead of Nicklaus. Not for long; as quickly as Watson made his birdie on the 11th, he dropped the stroke on the 12th, a difficult par-three hole of 204 yards to a flattish green with a broad bunker across the front, another to the side, and two more behind the putting surface. Because of its length, the tee shot calls for a long iron, and because the green has so very little back-to-front cant, the shot should come in high and drop relatively straight down if it is to remain on the green. Watson's shot drifted to the right and dropped into the bunker. Over the previous few years the PGA Tour had developed a series of statistical yard sticks designed to measure a player's abilities in a number of categories, such as driving distance, driving accuracy, and greens hit in regulation. One of the categories was 'sand saves,' the ability to get down in two from a bunker. Watson ranked first in 1981. He would have won no prize for this recovery, however. He left it well short of the hole and bogeyed. Back to four under, only one stroke ahead of Nicklaus.

Another long drive on the 13th set up a routine two-putt par, but at about the time Watson and Rogers were walking onto the green, a roar from up ahead told us that Jack had birdied the 15th to go four under par and into a tie for the lead. On to the 14th for Watson.

Tom hit another good drive, well past the left-to-right turn of the dogleg, and then played an iron for his second shot, leaving it well short of the green. If he could gauge his pitch just right, he should have a decent chance for a birdie. First the ball must clear the bunker. While Watson could see the top portion of the flagstick from where he stood, he was so far below the level of the green that he could not see the cup. Between the cup and the front edge, the green has some nasty little pitches and rolls. From where I was standing, it looked as if Watson's pitch hit on the downslope of one of those rolls, failed to take up, and rolled directly to the back of the green, stopping on the collar. Watson was 35 to 40 feet from the cup, facing a very testy putt. As I said before, no man wins a major tournament without some luck, and it was running in Watson's favor today. After taking account of the line and walking about a little with his typically quick stride, Watson settled himself over the ball and stroked it right into the cup. Five under once again and clear of the tie.

Another routine par at 15 and Watson was three holes from home and the Open Championship. Just three more pars. Still playing superb tee shots, Watson hadn't missed a fairway through the first 15 holes. All good things come to an end, though, and here Watson hit his only off-line drive. The ball bounced into the remodeled fairway bunker on the right, but instead of staying at the back of it, as it had on Thursday, allowing him room to play to the green and make a birdie, it rolled to the front, very close to the high frontal wall. From where his ball lay, Watson had no choice but to play out sideways to the fairway and pitch on with his third shot. When he played from the sand, he was left with a slight downhill lie, and once again his pitch rolled to the back of the green. He was 50 feet from the hole, and on that heaving green he would do very well to get down in two. Once again he settled himself over the ball and stroked a very good putt. The ball had just the right pace, breaking from left to right just before it reached the cup. He was left with a putt of no more than 18 inches. When he holed the putt, he and Nicklaus were tied, and with two very demanding holes coming up, it seemed certain that the 1982 Open would be settled by a playoff the next day. That is, of course, if Watson would be able to score pars on the last two holes.

As Watson tapped in his putt, the gallery raced for the 17th tee. I was able to work my way to the ropes in a position just behind the tee markers, in line with the green, and from where I stood I would be able to see directly down the line of flight of the ball. Rogers was up first and, using a wood, he played a nice soft draw that rolled to the back of the two-sectioned green within birdie range. Watson next. He drew a two-iron from his bag, and after the normal preliminaries, he settled himself, drew the club back with his usual quick rhythm and lashed into the ball with terrific force. The ball shot off toward the green on a line just a trifle to the right of the flag, but as it began to descend it started a turn to the left. I remember thinking that with that little draw, Watson's ball would be right against the flagstick. Even as I was thinking this, the ball kept moving to the left, and it became obvious that he had hit it with a slightly closed clubface (Lord knows I've hit enough like that to recognize the affliction). The ball hit the collar, and here luck was with Watson again. If you take a good look at the left side of the 17th green at Pebble Beach, you see that except for two or three yards, it is bordered by sand from well to the front all the way around to the back. Watson's ball settled in the grass, between the two bunkers that envelop the green so well.

Nicklaus had finished his round a few minutes earlier, but he had remained behind the 18th green waiting to see what Watson would do. He was watching on a television monitor in the scorer's tent, and when Watson missed the green, he was certain that he would either win outright or that he and Watson would be in a playoff the next day.

Watson's ball was perhaps 15 or 18 feet from the hole, and when he walked up to it, he could see it was sitting up and that he could work the leading edge of his sand iron under it. As he was looking over the shot, his caddie said to him, 'Get it close'.

'I'm not going to get it close,' Watson replied, 'I'm going to make it.'

After a last look Watson swung his sand wedge softly. The ball popped up, hit the green and began running toward the cup. As he saw the line the ball was following, Watson bent his knees, sensing it might go in, and called, 'That's in the hole.' When it hit the flagstick, Watson flung his arms skyward and began to dance around the green.

The crowd roared, and nearly everyone leaped to their feet, sensing they had just seen one of the more memorable moments in sport. It was among the more electrifyiing moments I've ever lived through, and it will be something I'll always remember. It lifted the 1982 Open above others of the last several years, and as the legend of that shot grows, this Open might rank among the greatest ever.

Before we go on, you should know that the ball didn't go into the hole simply by chance, and that when Watson told his caddie that he was going to hole it, he wasn't pumping himself full of false courage.

'I've practiced that shot for hours, days, months, years,' Watson claimed some time later. 'It's a shot you have to know if you're going to do well in the Open, where there is high grass around the greens.'

With that shot, Watson had broken clear of the tie, and now he had one more hole to play. He would take no chances with the 18th; a three-wood from the tee, seven-iron well short of the green, and then a nine-iron on, about 20 or 22 feet past the pin. He lagged the putt, trying to roll it close, but his luck was too good; the ball ducked into the hole for another birdie and a two-stroke victory over Nicklaus.

As Watson walked off the green, Nicklaus was still there, waiting for him. They shook hands, Nicklaus smiled and said, 'You little son-of-a-blank, you're something else. I'm proud of you.' With his arm across Tom's shoulders, Nicklaus walked him to the scorer's tent.

While nothing will ever erase the memory of that marvelous confrontation at Turnberry, the final round of the 1982 U.S. Open must rank among the great encounters ever. It left us hungry for more. It is not likely, however, that we will see very much more. Nicklaus was 42 in 1982 and Watson was 32. Nicklaus is a remarkable man, but, like any other great rivalry, this too will end eventually.

4. The British Open

It was all a matter of coincidence, of course, but the week of the 1982 British Open was a week of high history, tense drama, and strange events. It began, that week of July 11, with the return of the mighty cruise liner *Canberra*, steaming into Southampton with some 2,500 British troops returning from the brief and unpleasant Falkland Islands war with Argentina. She was greeted by tens of thousands of cheering people jammed along two miles of the waterfront.

The Italian soccer team provided some of the week's excitement, beating West Germany 3–1, to become the surprise winner of the World Cup in Spain. And when it came to strange events, nothing could out-do the story that surfaced on Tuesday — that a man had broken into Buckingham Palace undetected, and actually had spent about a half-hour chatting with the Queen in her bedroom.

It all seemed to set the tone for the week, and indeed the 111th Open Championship at Royal Troon, on Scotland's Ayrshire coast, followed suit in drama, tension, and strangeness. It ended with Tom Watson winning his fourth Open while standing beside the 18th green on Sunday believing that indeed, if he hadn't already lost, he had nothing better to hope for than a playoff.

'I had my second-place speech all prepared,' Watson was to joke later.

Other Opens may have topped this one for sheer drama and excitement — Watson's victory over Jack Nicklaus in the head-to-head duel at Turnberry in 1977, and Lee Trevino's victory over Nicklaus at Muirfield in 1972, just to name two. But the 1982 Open must go down as perhaps unmatched for sheer surprise.

First there was Bobby Clampett, the young, mop-haired Californian, a disciple of the mechanical approach to golf. He crushed proud old Royal Troon with a 67 in the first round, crushed it again with a 66 in the second, and there he stood — this young man who had yet to win on the American Tour — five shots clear. Then he stumbled to a 78, but still clung to a one-shot lead on South Africa's Nick Price, himself a surprise contender. The bookies had offered him at 200-to-1 odds before the Open. And while Clampett was on his way out with a closing 77, Price moved into the lead, only to surrender it down the stretch where he dropped four shots over the final six holes. The coveted trophy thus fell into the hands of Tom Watson, who had already finished and who was waiting nervously beside the final hole for, at best, the playoff that was never to come.

For all of the surprise of his victory, Watson was a gallant and graceful champion. He was delighted with the title, but he was ever the realist in his press interview. 'It's a marvelous feeling,' Watson said, 'but I didn't so much win this one as have it handed to me on a plate by Nicky Price. I feel great empathy for both Nick Price and Bobby Clampett. I've been in the position of

Clampett. I've been in the position of Price. I imagine there will be some crying tonight. I know I cried. You hate to have it happen to you, but you learn from it. It made me a tougher player.'

In retrospect, it seemed that Watson wasn't even in the chase until Price's game began to fail on the final holes. This was an illusion, of course, for Watson, Price and others had played very well. The illusion was the result of Clampett's dazzling 67–66 start, whose smoke obscured all else. Actually, nobody was in the chase at that point. While Clampett was shooting that 11-under-par 133 for the first 36 holes, just a shot off Henry Cotton's Open record of 132 set in 1934 at Royal St. George's, Watson was scoring 69–71—140, a strong 4-under.

Watson would go on to win at 4-under 284, a shot ahead of Price and Peter Oosterhuis, and write yet another chapter in what is fast becoming a legendary career. Watson has thus joined four-time winners of the Open — Willie Park, Old Tom Morris, Young Tom Morris, Bobby Locke, and Walter Hagen. He also became only the fifth player in history to win the difficult 'double' — the U.S. and British Opens in the same year — joining Bobby Jones, who did it in 1926 and 1930; Gene Sarazen, 1932; Ben Hogan, 1953, and Lee Trevino, 1971.

Watson has taken all his four Open titles on Scottish soil. He had won at Carnoustie in 1975, at Turnberry in 1977, and at Muirfield in 1980. The 1983 Open will be played at Royal Birkdale, in England, and Watson probably will be the favorite, but all eyes will be on him when the Open returns to Scotland in 1984, to St. Andrews.

Ironically, the way the oddsmakers and the scriptwriters had it calculated, there were really just two men in the picture to begin with. With all due respect to one of the strongest fields ever assembled for an Open, this was to be nothing more than another Watson–Nicklaus shootout. Undying in the minds of all was their battle in the 1977 Masters Tournament, which Watson won, and then his victory in the 1977 Open in that breathtaking struggle at Turnberry. The format was to be repeated as recently as the 1982 U.S. Open championship at Pebble Beach. This time it was Jack Nicklaus waiting beside the 18th green for the playoff that never came, for Watson refused to fold. Instead, he made one of the great shots in the history of the game, a delicate little chip from greenside rough that popped up, bounced, and rolled into the cup for a birdie-two at the 17th. That gave Watson a one-shot lead, and he birdied the seaside 18th for good measure to win his first U.S. Open by two.

So dramatic justice fairly cried for another rematch. The sentiment was widely noted, and it even appeared in the form of a bold headline across the cover of a pre-Open press guide: 'Young Tom's Goin' Bear Huntin' Again'. The cover carried two pictures — Tom Watson on the left, and Jack Nicklaus, the Golden Bear, on the right.

Nicklaus arrived at Troon in high appetite, like an old Western gunfighter. 'I've been shot up too many times lately. Maybe it's my turn to come out blasting,' he said. Having thus pleased the press, he pulled things back into his personal perspective. 'It's not just a fight between the two of us,' Nicklaus said. 'There are far too many good players around for us to think this title is just between Tom and me. Anyway, a lot of people have been playing much better than I have this year. I'm here because I think I can win. I don't think in terms of beating other people. For me, the fun still remains in preparing myself as best I can so that on that final afternoon I'm in the middle of it all. That's why I worked so hard for the month before this championship. I want to be somewhere in there when it happens. Being involved is the great charge. At the moment, I am playing very well and I am happy with my game. But I couldn't tell you just how well anybody else is playing because I really don't pay that much attention.'

Nicklaus did seem to be well on his game. He had won the Colonial National Invitation in May on the American Tour, breaking a victory drought that stretched back to 1980 when he won both the U.S. Open and the American PGA Championship, his last previous major victories. He had enough high finishes in his abbreviated playing schedule to sit well up in the U.S. tour money rankings and statistical ratings. And returning to the British Open had him in a good humor. 'This is my favorite tournament in golf,' Nicklaus said. 'I love to play here. It is different, it is fun. It's by the sea, by the sand dunes — conditions we never play at home. We've come back to the home of golf.'

For all of Nicklaus's high spirits and sharp game, the rematch that was made in heaven was not to be.

The days leading up to the Open itself are, in their own way, every bit as thrilling for the fans as the actual play. It is then that the breath comes a little tighter, and the writers and broadcasters begin to hone their final speculations, trying to peer into the future.

The tension of those approaching days grips the players, too, probably more so, and it grips none more than the first-timers because it is a time of dreams come true. The young Swedish amateur, Magnus Persson, put it well on the eve of his first Open: 'I cannot believe I will now be playing alongside Nicklaus, Watson, and Trevino.' He was one of three Swedish amateurs who came to the Open seeking experience, which suggests that the Swedes, despite their short playing season, are enjoying a sharper appetite for golf. Joakim Sabel shot 71–80 and missed in the qualifier. Per Andersson made it through on 72–70—142, to join Persson (70–68—138). Both failed to make the 36-hole cut in the Open. Persson shot 83–73—156, and Andersson 81–79—160.

Possibly the best-known amateur in the field was Nathaniel Crosby, 20, son of the late Bing Crosby, famed American entertainer and great friend of golf. Crosby, the 1981 U.S. Amateur champion, was knocked out in the first round of the 1982 British Amateur at Royal Cinque Ports in June. Crosby arrived too late for a practice round because he was playing in the U.S. intercollegiate championships. 'I did not want to let my university down,' Crosby said, explaining his tight schedule. 'I did not have a clue how to handle the (links) course at Deal.' He was the low amateur at the U.S. Open at Pebble Beach, but his experience at Royal Troon was less satisfying. He began by losing his very first tee shot in his first practice round. It might have been a sign of difficulties to come. He went on to shoot 82–84—166, and he finished last among those who missed the 36-hole cut.

Only one amateur was to make it the entire 72 holes — Britain's Malcolm Lewis. He carded 74–74–77–75—300, 12 over par but six shots above last place.

The bookies had installed Watson as the pre-Open favorite, generally at 4-to-1 odds. Among other observers, however, it was not so open-and-shut a case. Their speculations, part of the wonderful fabric of the Open, were the heady stuff of those last days before tee time. Who would — or could — conquer Troon? The press pretty well followed form and picked Watson. But others thought otherwise. Wrote one magazine correspondent '. . . Watson has not been at his best, and a player not at his best won't win at Troon.' The writer rummaged around and came up with some strong candidates — Nicklaus, Jerry Pate, and Tom Kite, but Spain's Severiano Ballesteros, the 1979 Open champion at Lytham, was his final pick. Ballesteros was also the pick of another, who prudently added as his 'saver' Raymond Floyd. This was Peter Haslam, writing in Britain's *Golf World*, and he was the only one even to raise the name of the young man from California. 'Watch out for newcomers Bobby Clampett and Jack Renner,' Haslam wrote.

The name of Nick Price was never raised. Price stood 86th on the European Order of Merit with £1,200 in winnings coming into the Open. He had won the 1980 Swiss Open, the 1981 South African Masters, and the 1982 Vaal Reefs Open in South Africa. The hefty 6-foot, 25-year-old was born in Rhodesia (Zimbabwe), and now was living in South Africa. He was playing in his sixth Open, exempt after being joint 23rd in 1981, his best previous finish. Price was discouraged with his play coming into the Open.

And so the stage was set. It would be man against Royal Troon, which offered both a treat and a solution on its famed crest. That crest shows five golf clubs entwined by a snake. And the solution was there for all who could read Latin in the club motto: Tam Arte Quam Marte. The loose translation: As much by skill as by strength.

For Clampett, skill meant a game built largely on the precepts of a book titled *The Golfing Machine*. Clampett long has credited the book's intellectual and mechanistic approach to the game for much of his success. In this Open he would say, 'I'm not so much an artist in golf, but more like a mechanic.' Clampett's powerful game, whatever its foundation, had carried him into a dream.

'Ever since I was 12,' Clampett was to say, 'I've watched the British Open on TV back home and wondered what it would be like to play on a Scottish links course. Now I know — and I love it'.

And defending champion Bill Rogers was to say: 'I don't know what course those fellows were playing on. I don't think it could have been here.'

Welcome to Royal Troon and the first round of the 111th Open Championship.

The four days preceding the first round were warm and sunny, and if any golfer suspected that he had been deceived by tales of capricious Scottish seaside weather, he had only to step outside his hotel that Thursday morning. It was as though the weather, too, had been waiting for the start of things. The wind was up, the temperature down into the mid-50s, and the rain had arrived. The wind was behind the golfers going out, and it cut into their faces coming home.

The reason for Clampett's delight for his first real trip across a Scottish links course was easy to understand. Teeing off shortly before noon, he posted his five-under-par 67 while others were confounded by the combination of mean course and mean weather. Watson and Price shot 69s. Lanky Anglo-Scot Ken Brown, who fought his way in through the qualifiers, was tied for third on 70. To find the first cluster of acclaimed players, one had to go back to the 73s for such as England's Nick Faldo, Australia's David Graham, and American Tom Kite; and to 74 for American Raymond Floyd and Scotland's Sandy Lyle.

The reason for Rogers' consternation was that he shot a 73 and felt that was a good showing under the circumstances, and then he found six shots and six men between him and the lead.

Clampett's 67 was all the more remarkable when viewed in comparison with the field and the conditions. Against a par of 36–36, Clampett went out with the wind at his back in 32, and fought his way home against it in 35. One of his playing partners, young Scottish professional Keith Lobban, went 34–47; Raymond Floyd had 34–40, and fellow American Bruce Leitzke 33–44. Such lopsided halves were the rule. Clampett was the exception.

'It was one of the best five rounds I've ever shot,' Clampett said, never suspecting that he was to add an astonishing sixth the very next day. 'My game plan,' he said, borrowing a phrase from American football to describe his strategy, 'was to get the ball into position for my second shot.' The raw score showed how well his plan worked, but it becomes even more clear on closer examination. Getting into position for his second shot — often by using irons off the tee — set up a round of wonderfully precise approach play that was backed up by a voracious putter.

Clampett needed only 26 putts in that first round, and 11 of them came on one-putt greens. He saved par twice from 15 feet, twice from four to five feet; and made seven birdies, one from 15 feet, the others from an astonishing seven feet or less.

The field for the 111th Open bristled with big names and was liberally sprinkled with former champions, so Clampett took everybody by surprise by breaking from the pack with that 67. This curly-haired blond from Carmel Valley Ranch on California's Monterey Peninsula was certainly no stranger to golf fans, however. He was just three months past his 22nd birthday at the Open, and he was in his second year on the U.S. Tour. He had had some strong finishes, but he had not won there. His only professional victory came as the individual titleist in the '81 U.S. versus Japan ABC Cup.

Clampett was regarded as a young man of immense potential, and most observers conceded it was only a matter of time until he would win, and win big. But few could be so rash as to think that anyone of his young age and brief experience would score his first victory in a major event. (Although Nicklaus and Jerry Pate were 22 when they won their first, the U.S. Open.) This sentiment was expressed in various ways. In Troon, for example, Clampett would be in a pre-Open group at 25-to-1 odds at Truesdale's betting shop, and at 33-to-1 at William Hills'. One newspaper carried selected starting times for the first round under the heading, 'When the Stars Tee Off,' and Clampett's name did not appear among them.

Clampett's reaction to playing Troon, aside from his joy at his 67, was much like those of other American first-timers who make their peace with the nuances of links play. 'This is a nice diversion from the courses we play in the

States,' Clampett said. 'I would compare Troon to Pebble Beach back home.' That might have been the key to his round. Clampett grew up playing in the wind on the Monterey Peninsula, jutting into the Pacific Ocean from California's coast. So he had known stiff winds and chill temperatures. He tied for third in the U.S. Open there in June, behind Watson and Nicklaus, barely a month earlier in his last competitive golf before the British Open.

Nick Price, less-heralded than Clampett, was probably more of a surprise coming in on 69 to join Watson in second place. He started with a birdie-three at No. 1, playing a two-iron off the tee, a wedge into the green, and sinking a 25-foot putt. A six-footer got him a birdie-four at No. 4. After losing a shot at No. 5, he turned in 34 with a birdie-three at No. 9 on a five-foot putt. Price exchanged bogey for birdie at the 10th and 11th, then struck a liberating blow at the par-four 15th, where his three-wood approach left him 60 feet from the hole and his putter put him into it. He had played the last six holes — they would be fateful later — in one under, when the wind and cold were at their harshest. Playing into that wind, which hurt so many, was much to Price's taste. 'I was not very good with the middle irons, so it was good for me, as I could hit the three-wood or the one-iron,' he said. If the wind had blown any harder, then 38 or 39 would have been a good incoming score.

'And that's where the tournament will be won,' Price said. 'The guy who finishes best over the last six holes . . .' It was a woeful prophecy that he himself would unwittingly fulfill just three days later.

Watson was delighted with his 69. 'A terrific score today,' he said, 'especially after starting off with three or four poor drives.' He started with a bogey five after changing his plans. He had intended to hit a two-iron off No. 1 tee, then went to the driver instead, and found the left rough. His sand wedge approach went over the green, and he pitched back to 20 feet and two-putted. The driver betrayed him again at No. 2, taking him into deep rough. He was 30 yards short in two, but he made an excellent pitch from a poor situation and saved par with a 12-foot putt.

Watson had a curious time heading into the turn. At No. 7, he hit his tee shot into the bunker at the famed No. 8 hole, the little 'Postage Stamp' par three. He played a nine-iron out and saved par with two putts from 20 feet. Then he took the same nine-iron at the 8th tee, hit it to about 10 feet, and got the fourth birdie of his outward 33.

Like Clampett, Watson was brilliant with the putter. He needed only 28 putts in the round, and eight of them were one-putters — six of them for birdies, two for pars.

The first round was the end of one highly regarded player, Jerry Pate. He shot an 81, then withdrew because of an injury to his left shoulder. 'I can't play this game with one arm,' he said. The first round was the beginning of the end for others, saddling them with scores too heavy from which to recover. Among them were Bernard Gallacher, Eamonn Darcy, Isao Aoki, and Gary Player, in a group at 75; Brian Marchbank, Hubert Green, and Terry Gale at 76; Nicklaus, a three-time champion, at 77, and Tom Weiskopf, who won in 1973, the last time the Open was held at Troon. He shot 79.

Nicklaus was not only disappointed, he was puzzled. He thought his game was in order. 'But I caught a flu bug last week and I haven't got my timing back yet,' he said. 'Every time I hit a good shot, I followed it up with a bad one. I just don't seem to have any interest, and that's not like me in a British Open.'

The 111th Open had its bittersweet moments. Two great former champions, Arnold Palmer and Lee Trevino, feared they may have been playing in their last British Opens.

Palmer has been generally credited with reviving the Open and returning it to its pedestal among world events when he elected to enter in 1960, in pursuit of what had been the uncatchable Grand Slam of golf — victories in the same year in the U.S. and British Opens, and the U.S. Masters and PGA Championship. No one has ever won all four in the same year, but Palmer was hot on the trail in 1960. He had taken both the Masters, in April, and the U.S. Open, in June — electrifying the world with his fierce final-round charge to a 65 in the Open. So the electricity followed him to the British Open at St. Andrews, where he was to miss by a single shot, falling to Kel Nagle's 278. Palmer would win the Masters twice more, in 1962 and 1964, but not the U.S. Open, and thus he would never again be in position to chase the Slam. Still, he returned to the British Open, and won it two years running, in 1961 at Royal Birkdale and in 1962 at Troon. Palmer was then the dominant name in golf, and his continuing quest for the Open attracted the attention that drew golfers from all over the world. The Open was again in golf's firmament.

Troon was the site of four previous Opens. In 1923, Arthur Havers won on 295; in 1950, Bobby Locke on 279; in 1962, Palmer set what was then the Open record, 276, and in 1973 Weiskopf matched it. (Watson and Nicklaus would both break it in their 1977 shootout at Turnberry, Watson winning, 268–269.) Troon was designated 'Royal Troon' in 1978, in honor of its centenary, and when the Open returned in 1982 the members were quick to salute Arnold Palmer's role both at their club and in the history of the British Open. They named him an honorary life member.

In a tightly emotional moment at ceremonies the Wednesday night before the first round, a packed audience at the clubhouse burst into applause at an odd moment. Palmer was giving his acceptance speech and his thanks, and at one point he fell silent, unable to continue. He wiped tears from his eyes and fought to bring his emotions under control. It was a poignant, awkward silence. Then the members voiced their rousing tribute.

Sir Robert Fairbairn, captain of Royal Troon, presented Palmer with a set of club buttons and ties and a history of the club's 104 years. He told the audience that British golf owed Palmer an enormous debt for restoring the Open to its lofty position.

Palmer, who played in all but six British Opens since 1960, accepted his honors in that slight Western Pennsylvania twang. 'I am very flattered and extremely proud and honored,' Palmer said. 'As a child, coming to the British Open was one of my greatest dreams — playing Troon and St. Andrews. This is something I know my father would have dearly loved . . .'

Palmer stopped, and broke down at the memory of his beloved father, the late Deacon Palmer.

'There is nothing I would rather do,' Palmer said, now back under control, 'than win the Open here again.'

'As a member, too,' came a voice.

Palmer's role in the British Open has been well catalogued over the years, and added to that lore came a tribute from the top, from Keith Mackenzie, Secretary of the Royal and Ancient Golf Club of St. Andrews, which conducts the Open. Two years earlier, the R & A had conferred an honorary membership on Palmer. 'Palmer's is one of the greatest roles ever played as far as the Open is concerned,' Mackenzie told the audience. 'He came over at a time when the prize money was very small and when, as the best player in the world, he could have been earning much more in the States. But because he came the whole stature of the Open changed. Arnold was the Pied Piper. He made everything happen.'

Palmer's devotion to the Open is such that not only was his entry the first received for 1982, Mackenzie said, but that he asked for the very same hotel room he had occupied in 1962. A repeat victory was not to be, but Palmer gave his fans a flash of the good old days and a reason to cheer with his opening one-under 71. It was only four off the pace and it left Palmer tied for seventh with such as Spain's Severiano Ballesteros, the 1979 champion; America's Johnny Miller, the 1976 champion, and 1982 Masters champion Craig Stadler.

Palmer was to rise steadily from there on rounds of 73, 78, and 74 for a 296 total, eight over par. That gave him a joint 27th, just one shot from the top 25 players and ties, who are exempt from qualifying the following year. A historic tale may hang from that one shot. 'I won't be back if I have to qualify,' Palmer told a group of writers in the Troon locker room, repeating his vow of several years.

Another door may already be opening for Palmer and for others. Mackenzie had already announced his intention 'to attract the best international field possible, by continuous detailed investigation into our exemption policy.' That statement suggests that additional exemptions may be made in certain cases. The R & A fears that with about 1,000 entrants seeking a place in a field of 150, some very good golfers might choose not to go through the expense of traveling to Britain to risk the qualifiers. It is thus conceiveable that Palmer could receive an exemption in the future.

There is already some support for such a notion, where Palmer is concerned. Writing in the '82 Open Souvenir Brochure, Michael Williams of *The Daily Telegraph* insisted that when Palmer won in 1962 '. . . he had already embarked on a pattern of visits that was to take our Open from a secondary role and restore it to its rightful place as a major championship as all the the other great golfers of the world chose to follow Arnie's example. For that, the championship should remain eternally grateful and offer an ever-open door to Arnie for as long as he wishes to play.'

Trevino may also have played in his last British Open, but for a far different reason. In fact, his appearance at Troon, while unrewarded by his scores, was nothing short of heroic. Complications arising from his spinal disk surgery of 1976 jeopardized his future as a golfer. He barely made it to Troon.

Trevino's usual problems since that back surgery have been stiffness and soreness. Exercise and proper warmup would see him onto the course. Indeed, despite his advancing years — he was 42 at Troon — he won numerous times since leaving the hospital, including the difficult and exclusive American Tournament Players Championship in 1980. This time, however, his problem was different. Trevino had gone to an oceanside course in Florida to prepare for the Open. There, he would find the stiff and capricious breezes he could expect at Troon, the better to hone his already considerable wind game. Suddenly, there was a new and intense pain in his back. Trevino feared he had suffered a new spinal problem, and he was relieved when doctors diagnosed it as not spinal, but muscular. Still, the pain was real enough. Certain back muscles around the old incision were going into spasm. 'It got so bad, I couldn't bend over to put on my shoes,' Trevino said. The spasms hit on the Sunday preceding the Open. By Monday at 10.30 a.m., Trevino was in hospital in Dallas, Texas. On Tuesday night, he arrived at Prestwick.

Forever the high-spirited wisecracker, Trevino described his hospital treatment for reporters, a treatment that consisted of acupuncture and medication to relieve the spasms. 'They had so many needles in me,' he said, 'that I looked like a porcupine. And the pills they've got me on! Whoo-ee — they've even got me talking slow.

'But,' he added, soberly, 'this is only temporary. Doctors said this treatment will last about 18 days, and then I'd have to do it again. Obviously, I can't go on like that.' And then he issued his personal prognosis, one that chilled golf fans everywhere. 'When I get back to the States, I will have a new kind of laser surgery,' Trevino said, 'and if it doesn't work you won't be seeing me on the golf course anymore. Maybe in the television tower, but not on the course.'

Trevino said doctors had diagnosed his problem this way: internal scar tissue from the original surgery was pressing on nerve endings, irritating them and triggering the disabling spasms. The laser surgery, they hoped, would burn off the nerve endings and thus solve the problem. Trevino underwent the surgery about two weeks after the British Open. It would take months, maybe longer, to see whether it was completely effective. There was some encouraging news quickly, however. Shortly after the laser treatment, Trevino appeared in a two-day charity event in Erie, Pennsylvania, late in August. He shot 66–67—133, seven under par, and finished second. He went from there to the B.C. Open, an American Tour stop, where he missed the cut. He reported no troubles with his back at either place.

Trevino was a memorable Open champion, the last to win twice, back-to-back. He beat Taiwan's Lu Liang Huan (Mr. Lu) at Royal Birkdale in 1971, then beat Jack Nicklaus at Muirfield in 1972, both times recording a 278. At Troon, there was no trace of fear or self-pity evident either in Trevino's game or his remarks. But the old Trevino game was not there. A quadruple bogey eight at the 10th sent him to an opening 78. He fought back for rounds of 72, 71, and 75, and his 296 total tied him with Arnold Palmer and put him one shot out of the top-25 category.

Bobby Clampett, generally serious in appearance, showed not only a flash of his huge potential in that first round, but also his sense of humor. He played dressed in plus-twos, the knee-length trousers popular years ago. They were, of course, the talk of Troon and of the press corps. In the press center during his post-round interview, he was asked to display them, and he stood up and announced, 'These are my knickers,' using the American word for them. The packed tent broke into laughter. 'We'll let him off the hook,' said Press Secretary George Simms, with a chuckle. 'Knickers are ladies' underwear.'

Clampett laughed at himself, then put his head into his hands in mock embarrassment.

So ended a day of harsh weather, high spirits, and a leaderboard that looked so unfamiliar to the British Open fans:

Bobby Clampett	67	Danny Edwards	71
Nick Price	69	Masahiro Kuramoto	71
Tom Watson	69	Arnold Palmer	71
Ken Brown	70	Seve Ballesteros	71
Bernhard Langer	70	Craig Stadler	71
Des Smyth	70	Jose-Maria Canizares	71
		Johnny Miller	71

It was more than just an unfamiliar leaderboard that captured the fancy of press and official alike. Early in Open week, the British press took one look at the contingent from across the Atlantic and promptly titled it the 'American Invasion'. George Simms said it was perhaps the largest and strongest American entry ever. The partial American boycott of 1981 — in response to alleged profiteering by commercial interests the preceding year — had ended with a rousing turnout.

This was the result of two factors: a record purse of £250,000 and the considerable efforts of R & A Secretary Keith Mackenzie and others in a campaign for moderation among the business concerns. Golfers, reporters and others involved in the Open reported that prices and food and lodging were not out of line.

Fully 39 American golfers were entered in the qualifying tests that week, and nine of them made it into the Open. There, they joined fellow Americans who were exempt from qualifying, bringing the U.S. contingent in the Open itself to 33. Of the nine Americans who made it through the qualifiers, five survived the 36-hole cut, and one went on to threaten. He was Tom Purtzer, a U.S. Tour regular. He scored 76–66–75–69 for a two-under 286 and a share of fourth place, two shots behind Watson.

Sportswriters were also part of the American invasion. Some 30 of them — probably the largest U.S. press group ever, Simms said — covered the Open. Several of the group had made the Open part of an extended European swing. They had covered the World Cup soccer matches in Spain and the tennis championships at Wimbledon, then headed for Troon. The Open thus was also a reunion for close friends in the U.S. and British press corps.

'It certainly does impress me,' Watson had said after Clampett's first-round 67, 'but it doesn't surprise me. Bobby is a very deliberate and serious golfer, and despite his lack of experience he really is capable of shooting the lights out of any golf course, any time.'

Coming from Watson, that was high tribute. And what was left of the lights, well, Clampett shot them out in the second round with a 66. It was described as a single-round record for Troon, although Nicklaus had shot a 65 in the final round of the 1973 Open. This led to some brisk discussion in the press center. This was not the same Troon course that Nicklaus played, officials explained. Numerous changes had been made for the 1982 Open. The most significant among them were these: the ninth green was moved to the right and raised four and a half feet to allow the back portion of the green to be seen from a perfect drive; a 'v' was cut in the big hill facing the 10th tee, thus eliminating another totally blind shot; new fairway bunkers were added to tighten the driving at the first, sixth, ninth, and 15th; entrances to the green were narrowed at the first, second and third; and a new tee was installed at the seventh, 11 yards back and to the right.

Whether Clampett's 66 is truly the record was stuff left for the purists to chew on, but not really for long. Incredibly, it was equalled by two others, also in the second round. But there is no doubt where it left Clampett — 11 strokes under par at 133, and five ahead of his nearest pursuer, the persistent Nick Price, who shot his second 69 for 138.

There were those who believed that the 111th Open was now over, and that the final two rounds would be a mere formality. It belonged to Clampett. This notion drew some interesting reactions, most notably those of Sandy Lyle and Ken Brown. Said Lyle: 'Anyone is catchable on a golf course — especially Troon, because this is a mean golf course.' And said Brown, with a snort: 'I'll throw in the towel if he is five shots ahead of me with three holes to play on Sunday, and not before.'

Still, it must have been a depressing feeling to the world's stars on Friday to be finishing up their breakfasts while looking at the obstacle awaiting them — Clampett's 66. The day dawned as a new and far more agreeable one, and Clampett was up and about at 5.30 that morning for breakfast. He was kept waiting for 15 minutes for balls to be brought to the practice ground at 6.15. When his tee time arrived, at 7.40, he was primed. If he had followed the oddsmakers at all, he would have learned that he had plunged from 33-to-1 in the pre-Open listing to a 5-to-4 favorite with Ladbrokes, and that Watson had gone to 5-to-2. Even the bookies weren't ready to believe Nick Price. Though he had tied for second in the first round, he improved to only 33-to-1.

Jumping at the opportunity of an early start and fair, sunny weather, Clampett warmed up with pars on the first two holes, then birdied the third and fourth, and then the sixth and seventh, and turned in 32. Coming in, he birdied 10 and 11, then bumped along to a bogey-birdie-birdie finish.

Clampett had stuck to his game plan, playing for position, and again his precise approach shots were rewarded by a hot putter. Where he had taken only 27 putts in the first round, now he needed just 26. Of them, 10 were one-putts, none longer than eight feet. His card showed eight birdies and two bogeys. Then, with his 133 safe in hand, he departed, leaving the field to shoot at him, and he went back to his room for a glass of milk, two ham-and-cheese sandwiches, and for some sleep. He had spent the better part of two hours with the press, possibly the longest press conference in Open history, veteran writers said.

Holding a big lead was nothing new to Clampett. In his only professional victory up to the Open, in the U.S. versus Japan ABC Cup, he shot 65–66 for a six-stroke lead and won by seven. In his college days as an amateur, he would win by as many as 13 shots. But the British Open is not a collegiate event, and no one knew that better than Clampett himself.

Price opened the second round with a bogey after bunkering his nine iron approach. He steadied himself with two following pars, then birdied the fourth on two putts from 30 feet, and birdied the fifth with his second 60-footer of the Open. He turned in 35, took a bogey five at No. 10, and then came to the hole he said got him going — the fearful 11th. There, he drilled a two-iron approach shot to about one foot and dropped the putt for an eagle three.

Friday was marked by the arrival of some new hounds to pursue Clampett. Sandy Lyle thrilled the Scots with a stunning 33–33—66 to match Clampett's fresh record. The key was an eagle three at the 11th, where he struck a four-iron to 12 feet and holed the putt. The 66 lifted Lyle from near-obscurity into a tie for fifth with Watson at 140.

And Lyle's 66 was barely cool when American Tom Purtzer poured his own 66 in on top of it. And what a beauty it was — a flawless jewel. Purtzer had run through 18 holes at Royal Troon with no score higher than par. Of the 60 golfers who completed all four rounds, his was the only round free of bogeys or worse. Purtzer would very nearly duplicate the feat, not the score, in the final round when his card of 69 was married by only one bogey, a five at No. 15. Purtzer had come from seeming nowhere — actually from an opening 76 — to join the hunt.

Ireland's Des Smyth (69) and West Germany's Bernhard Langer (69) moved in at 139, a joint third behind Price. A three-putt from 40 feet for a bogey at the 13th cost Smyth a share of second with Price. England's Peter Oosterhuis, who now lives and plays his golf in the States, came crowding in with a 67 for a share of the seventh with Ken Brown. Oosterhuis chipped in from 40 feet for a birdie three at the 15th, and only a missed five-footer at the 10th robbed him of a 66 and a bogey-free round.

Watson, meanwhile, posted a worthy one-under 71 and found himself drifting astern. His own game had slipped by two shots, and he fell five shots farther back and trailed Clampett by seven, 133 to 140. 'I played reasonably well, but I did not make the putts I made yesterday,' Watson said. 'I actually hit the ball closer to the hole.' He had birdied three of the four par fives in the first round, but this time he played them level par, in two birdies and two bogeys. At the sixth, his ball lay in an old divot hole and his approach skipped over the green. At the 11th, he pull-hooked his second into an unplayable lie in gorse and had to take a penalty drop. He closed the round in grim fashion, considering that Clampett lay comfortably snoozing back in his room. Watson was short with his approach to the 18th, then took two putts to get down after his chip, and he walked off with his third bogey (against four birdies) of the day.

'The third round is invariably the key,' Watson said later. 'And if Bobby starts making mistakes, I have got to play well and give myself a chance of catching him. When a player has such a commanding lead it makes you feel that you must play more aggressive golf. But I have no plans to change my game.'

The 36-hole cut was made at a 152 total. Among those who missed were Brian Marchbank (76–77), Ed Sneed (76–77), Maurice Bembridge (79–76), and Bruce Lietzke (77–78).

The challengers were moving in, but for unexpected reasons. Langer, for example, admitted to suffering from the putting 'yips,' yet it was his putter that carved out his 69. Apparently the long ones didn't trouble him as much as the short ones, for he holed from 30, 25, 25 (twice), and 10 feet. Des Smyth suddenly found strength in his short game, which had been his weakness through '82, and he could only offer, 'The trouble is that I have not got any confidence in my driver now, so I don't know what is going on.'

Clampett remained true to his game plan, and it showed. At the 10th, for example, he put his three-iron approach to three feet and holed for one of his eight birdies; and at the 11th, he deliberately played short with his second, then chipped dead for another. If there were signals of the doom to come, they were in the form of a bunkered drive at the 15th, where he said he felt cramped by the gallery, and a tee shot that flew the green at the par-three 17th. Both cost him bogeys.

So Clampett was to leave the course at 11 under par and holding a five-shot lead. History shows that such leads are far from completely safe in the Open. In 1963, Bob Charles won at Lytham after trailing Phil Rodgers by five, and Gary Player did the same after trailing Billy Casper at Carnoustie in '68. Over the past 20 years, only one man had a five-shot lead at the halfway point, however, and that was Gary Player, at Lytham in 1974. He went on to win by four.

If Troon was to present a new face as British Open champion, it was not being gracious to the old. For one, Bill Rogers, the 1981 champion, was suffering a troubled 1982 and never got his meticulous game off the ground. He shot 73–70–76–75—294 and tied for 22nd. His was the story of a man taxed not only by a disobedient driver but also by the pressures of fame that followed his triumph at Royal St. George's and his huge success of the 1981 season. The problem with the driver, Rogers said, was that early in 1982 he began feeling uncomfortable playing a draw off the tee, the right-to-left curve that he counted on for maximum distance. It was a shot that he had made fine use of the previous two years. It had helped him to an outstanding 1981, in which he was named the PGA Player of the Year in the States. In addition to his British Open title, he won (on the U.S. Tour) the Sea Pines Heritage Classic, the World Series of Golf, and the Texas Open. His high finishes included a tie for second in the U.S. Open. He won $325,411 in the U.S. alone, which was good for fifth place on the U.S. money list. But 1982 dawned with some confusion for him. Beyond the puzzling trouble with the driver, there was the worldwide acclaim. While flattering to his ego and enriching to his bank account, it proved also to be wearing and distracting. 'It has been a proud 12 months for me,' Rogers said. 'All the things that have happened with my British Open win have been fantastic. But all of a sudden people are watching what I'm doing and what has gone wrong, and reminding me every week what a great year 1981 was. I am tired of hearing of 1981.'

Another former champion, Tom Weiskopf, returned to Troon where he won the Open in 1973, the last time it was held there. His pride in that accomplishment is evidenced by his auto license plate. It says TROON. Weiskopf was relatively inactive on the U.S. Tour before coming to Troon, and he spoke of spells of a certain disinterest in the game. Besides the U.S. Open, he said he played in only two events since the Masters in April. He won the Western Open on the long and difficult Butler National course. Weiskopf always had been one of the most fiercely individualistic players in the game, and he revealed yet another aspect of that characteristic in a pre-Open press conference. He recalled that after opening with an 80, he withdrew from the Memorial, the tournament Jack Nicklaus founded near Columbus, Ohio. Asked what Nick-laus might think about his departure, Weiskopf replied, 'I don't care what Jack thinks.' He added that golf had not been and never would be the most impor-tant part of his life— that if, for example, he wanted to go fishing at the time of the British or U.S. Open, or the Ryder Cup match, then he would go.

When Weiskopf won the Open at Troon in '73, he shot 68–67–71–70—276, tying what was then the Open record set there by Palmer in 1962. Perhaps it was the rust of inactivity, but this time Weiskopf's game would not budge. He didn't make it beyond the 54-hole cut, carding 79–73–75—227. He was done in, principally, at the 468-yard par-four 13th, which he played in 5–6–6.

Bobby Clampett left the course after the second round a determined man. 'Golf is a challenge against yourself,' he said. 'I am not going to change my strategy, but I will continue to see how low I can score.'

Another voice trailed his ominously. Said Watson: 'Clampett will be feeling the pressure by tomorrow, if he is not feeling it already.' And one other statement hung in the air as the second round closed at Troon. If it was puzzling, it also had the ring of prophecy for both the speaker and the man he was speaking of. Said Nick Price: 'I wouldn't want to be where Bobby is. I wouldn't want to be leading now. I don't think I could handle it.'

The 1982 Open had its share of strange happenings, and among them were the tremendous swings of fortune that bore on two golfers. Rex Caldwell, one of the American qualifying brigade, had opened with an 84, yet came back in the second round with a 68, a swing of 16 shots that kept him afloat through the halfway cut right on 152. He would then bow out with a third-round 75.

Then there was the case of David Graham, the Australian who lives and plays in America, and who counts among his victories the 1979 U.S. PGA Championship and the 1981 U.S. Open. He moved into the hunt of this British Open with 73–70. Then he added 76–77. Few suffered so sharp and so severe a reversal. Bobby Clampett, hero of the first two rounds, was one.

Saturday began dully and with some light rain, and then it was almost as if Sandy Lyle's prayer had been answered. 'I hope the wind changes,' Lyle had said, 'and gives us a different golf course to play.' By the time Clampett and his challengers moved into action in the afternoon, the wind was coming in from the south-west. One observer of this phenomenon and the dangers it held was Chingy Maidment, a caddie for 50 years and something of an Open institution himself. He was custodian of the caddie tent for this Open, and at the shift in the wind, he stuck his head through the flap and proclaimed, 'This'll sort out 'oo can play golf.' Now the players would have to duel against the wind through the first six holes and hope to repair any damage coming home.

This problem endured through the morning and then the winds did an about-face for the rest of the round. For two glorious rounds Clampett was cruising along in full command of himself and Troon, the next he was careering around the course almost out of control. The decline began with only a slight shake that Saturday. He bogeyed the first hole. It was the first and only time he opened a round with a bogey. He got that back and more with birdies at the fourth and fifth (4–2), the latter on a 40-foot putt, signalling that for the first time, his surgical iron play had deserted him. Still, at this moment he was 12 under par for the Open and he held a seven-shot lead on Des Smyth, who had taken two birdies on the first four holes. He was eight ahead of Price, who opened bogey-bogey, and on Watson, who was level par for the round through the first four following a birdie, a bogey, and two pars.

Knowing fans sat back to let the Open run its course. They were set to salute the fourth youngest champion in Open history.

Then came the sixth hole, 'Turnberry'. It is a par five of 577 yards, the longest championship hole in Britain. It has a slight dogleg to the right, and the need for an accurate tee shot was sharpened by the addition of a new bunker beyond the existing one on the left. The hole was to play at something less than intimidating for the Open, at an average of 4.93 shots. Clampett himself had already played it 5–4. This time, it ambushed him.

Clampett hooked his drive into a bunker on the left. He tried to get out with a sand wedge but succeeded only in pitching the ball forward into another bunker. He barely escaped from that one, and he lay three, still 270 yards from the green. He hooked his fourth into deep rough, and his fifth landed in a greenside bunker — under the lip. He came out to 20 feet, and then two-putted. Clampett had made a triple-bogey eight. It was his only score over single bogey — and one of only two triples among the top 25 finishers — for the entire four rounds. Oosterhuis had the other triple, a seven at No. 10 in the third round.

The eight seemed to have a deeply sobering effect on Clampett. He played the next 12 holes in four over, with four bogeys and the rest pars. He shot 38–40—78. As Watson had warned, the third round would tell the tale. Clampett was not to make another birdie until well into the final round.

'To say the least, it was a challenging day,' Clampett said with a sigh. 'I did not play as well as I had in the first two rounds but I didn't think I played that badly. The game works out funny sometimes. Some days you have it going smoothly and hit a shot not quite perfect and get a good bounce. A couple of those didn't happen today. I hit a perfect tee shot at No. 1 right down the middle and it kicked left into one of the pot bunkers.' What he meant was that he was deliberately trying to lay up, and the trailing wind had carried him too far. 'It was the first time,' Clampett said evenly, 'that I ever hit a three-iron 260 yards.'

The 78 left him at 211, five under, but the lead that was five shots at the start of the round and that had swelled to seven, had melted to just one. Nick Price shot 74 and stood at 212, and tight behind came Des Smyth, 74—213, Sandy Lyle, 73—213, and with his freckles and ready smile, Tom Watson, 74—214.

The contenders' scores showed what had become of Troon after the wind shifted. Of those who went 72 holes, there were 17 rounds in the 60's through the first two days. In the third, there were just four subpar rounds, and they were all 71's — by Masahiro Kuramoto, Nick Faldo, Lee Trevino, and Keith Waters.

Price, who was paired with Clampett in the third round, was as surprised as anyone at his unravelling. 'When he took the eight at No. 6, I thought he was losing a bit of grip on his game,' Price said. 'I thought he could have played a lot better. When I saw the leaderboard and saw that no one was charging at Clampett, then I was waiting for Watson to do so.' Price didn't gain ground so much as have Clampett slide back to him. Still, Price's 74 in the stiff wind — 'It was stronger than the first two days,' he said — was a creditable card. After those two opening bogeys, he parred through the turn, birdied No. 10 from six feet, bogeyed No. 13 with two putts, and parred in.

Meanwhile, a sub-drama was unfolding in the person of Japan's Masahiro Kuramoto. If there is such a thing as being too small to play championship golf, Kuramoto must be it. Yet there he was in the thick of things. Kuramoto, 27, who turned professional just a year earlier, stands five feet, four inches tall, and weighs just 147 pounds. It would seem there isn't enough strength in that small a body to tackle a course like Royal Troon, but if any other proof were needed beyond his 71–73–71 through three rounds, his play at the scary 11th should be enough. The par five of 481 yards demands an all-carry drive over 230 yards of no-man's land growth. He routinely hits 260-yard drives. He played the 11th in two pars and two birdies.

'I am quite surprised to be where I am,' Kuramoto said, of his tie for sixth with Oosterhuis after three rounds, 'but I am not surprised at the way I am playing.'

As Price had said, with Clampett backsliding, eyes were on Tom Watson to make a charge. But like Price, the best Watson could do in the gusting winds was a 74, and he picked up ground even though he was shooting his highest round. 'This is the type of course that plays tricks with your mind,' Watson said. 'You want to get off to a good start early on, and if you don't then you say "My God! I've still got the back nine to play".'

Watson, who enjoys playing in stiff breezes, figures that the wind had come around 120 or 130 degrees early in the round, but he would not claim it as a deterrent to his game. 'The wind did not blow you over,' he said, 'and when you have a six-iron and a three-iron to the par fives, you ought to have at least one four, and I didn't produce.'

If Watson didn't mount a charge, it wasn't for lack of trying. He electrified the galleries at the first by lashing a drive that reached the green 362 yards away and stopped just 10 feet from the pin. He narrowly missed his eagle two, but got his birdie three. He gave the shot back on a three-putter at No. 3, then bogeyed the fifth after catching a front bunker and turned in one-over 37. He bumped along from the 10th, bogey-birdie-bogey-bogey-birdie, and if there was a British Open championship somewhere in his game, he had yet to find it.

'I'm a lot closer than I thought I would be, starting out today,' Watson said, 'but if I'm going to win it, I'll have to shoot in the 60's tomorrow — maybe 68.'

Said Clampett, who would be the Open champion if he could hang on for just one more round: 'I felt that the course was controlling me, not me it. I have to go out and control the course tomorrow.'

And said Price, the earlier doubts gone: 'I think I can win. I can believe in myself and I believe I have the ability to win.'

So for the final push, they lined up this way:

Bobby Clampett	67–66–78—211
Nick Price	69–60–74—212
Sandy Lyle	74–66–73—213
Des Smyth	70–69–74—213
Tom Watson	69–71–74—214
Masahiro Kuramoto	71–73–71—215

Peter Oosterhuis	74–67–74—215
Nick Faldo	73–73–71—217
Denis Watson	75–69–73—217
Fuzzy Zoeller	73–71–73—217
Tom Purtzer	76–66–75—217
Bernhard Langer	70–69–78—217

Sunday, July 18, arrived as a sunny, mild day, with temperatures in the mid-60's, with the wind about 10 knots, light and variable from the northwest. It was as though the weather had stepped back and said, 'Gentlemen, the stage is all yours. Go to it.'

The final round opened quickly as a duel between Clampett, at five under, and Price, at four under. It was a short duel. Compared to Clampett's skyrocketing first two rounds and the gripping struggle in the third, this one was over in an instant. Well back lurked Watson at two under. Clampett parred the first hole and Price birdied, and they were tied at five under. Clampett bogeyed the second and Price birdied, and suddenly the Open had a new leader for the first time in four days, or 56 holes. But even that was not to last. They matched pars at No. 3, and they were tied again at No. 4 in another two-shot swing on Clampett's birdie four to Price's bogey six. Clampett played the fifth through the ninth in bogey, par, bogey, bogey, bogey. The final breakdown had come.

He turned in 40 and sank out of sight. It will go down as one of the tragic moments in Open history. The young man who had led through three rounds, who only some 18 holes earlier was leading at 12 under par, now was back in the pack and never to escape. He had shot the first two rounds in 67–66, 11 under par. He shot the final two in 78–77, 11 over. He finished at par 288, tied for 10th with Jack Nicklaus. It was a finish Tom Watson would find uncomfortably familiar.

Price, meanwhile, was busy trying to solidify his hold on the lead. After pars at the fifth and sixth, he went birdie-bogey-bogey in the difficult effort and turned at four under, leading Watson and Smyth by one. Smyth had one bogey and one par on the front for a par 36. Sandy Lyle took himself out with a 39 on the front, though he was to have one last burst coming in that would give the leaders pause while it was happening. At that point, a chain reaction could have carried him to the title.

And the charge so long expected of Tom Watson still did not materialize. He birdied the fourth in an otherwise steady front nine and turned in 35, as did Kuramoto, who stood at two under and trailed Price by two.

Now the game was on. Coming down the final nine holes it was still anybody's championship. They lined up like this:

Nick Price	–4	Masahiro Kuramoto	–2
Des Smyth	–3	Peter Oosterhuis	–2
Tom Watson	–3	Bobby Clampett	–1
		Sandy Lyle	Level

What happened next would leave Price smiling bravely but obviously dejected. He would come into the press center and say, 'Sorry I couldn't buy you guys champagne.' The Open suffered its second collapse of the day during those final nine holes. Where Clampett's had been the result of a kind of erosion that began in the third round, Price's by comparison was brutally abrupt. Price ripped off three straight birdies coming out of the turn, and now the Open was surely in his hands. At No. 10, he birdied from three feet to go to five under. Smyth and Watson, playing ahead of him, had parred, and he led them by two shots. At No. 11, Price made a birdie four, two-putting from 20 feet, to drop to five under. Watson's long-awaited charge came — and went — right here. He made an eagle three, hitting a driver, then a three-iron 203 yards to three feet from the hole. Watson was now five under. Price led him by one and Smyth, who had birdied, by two. At No. 12, Price made a birdie three on a three-footer to drop to seven under. He led Watson, who parred, by two; and Smyth, who bogeyed, by four. Kuramoto, who played the same stretch in par-birdie-par, also was at three under and trailing by four. Lyle moved into the picture with some fireworks — an eagle three at the 11th and a birdie three at the 12th — to drop to two under. It triggered some wild cheering from his countrymen, but his charge was blunted by a bogey at the 14th, and he was to finish with 74—287, one under and joint eighth. Trouble arose for Price at the 13th, and though damaging by one shot, it seemed of no real consequence at the time. A poor drive cost him a bogey five and dropped him to six under. Watson, who parred the hole, remained at five under and trailed by one shot. Kuramoto and Smyth held steady with pars for three under. The 14th went by uneventfully. Price got his par three and Watson, his. Smyth and Kuramoto took themselves out of the running with bogey fours, while Oosterhuis nosed in with a birdie to join them at two under. It was now Price and Watson. Everybody took a deep breath.

Despite the mighty reputations of the par five 11th, the Railroad Hole, and the nasty little Postage Stamp eighth, it was the 15th that was the pivotal hole in the 111th Open. The 'Crosbie' is a par four of 457 yards, a slight dogleg right. A new bunker had been placed beyond the existing bunker on the left side of the fairway, putting an additional demand for accuracy on the golfer seeking maximum length off the tee. Of all the 18 holes at Troon, the 15th played the hardest in the 1982 Open — an average of 4.61 against its par of four. It was here that Nick Price crashed. Price drove into the rough, which luckily had been trampled by spectators. But that was his last bit of luck. He hit his second shot into a bunker. He came out, 20 yards onto the fairway. He hit his fourth 20 feet short of the pin. Then he two-putted. Price had taken a double-bogey six, his only double of the entire Open. The crash left him at four under, and in a tie with Watson, who had left the hole about a half-hour earlier with a bogey five.

Price parred the 16th, clinging to the tie. Then came the fatal 17th, a 223-yard par three. 'I hit a two-iron and tried to give it a bit extra,' Price said. The tee shot came up short. 'Then I hit a bad chip, about eight feet long,' he said. Two putts later he had a bogey four. He had dropped four shots in five holes, three of them in one three-hole stretch. Up ahead stood the new leader of the 111th British Open, Tom Watson, who did not become the leader until the 71st hole had been completed by someone else.

Watson had long since finished and had retired to the secretary's office to watch Price play the last several holes on television. When Price reached the

18th tee, Watson and his wife, Linda, came out to the greenside to see whether Price could get the birdie that would tie them. Price's approach shot to the 18th came to rest about 25 feet from the hole. Before a jammed, breathless gallery packed into the stands and nearly ringing the green, he studied the putt. Then he putted. When the putt missed, Linda and Tom Watson fell joyfully into each other's arms in quiet celebration of Tom's fourth British Open championship.

'I didn't expect to be the champion today,' Watson said later. 'When I missed a makeable birdie putt at the 18th, I figured, great, that's the way to finish second.' He did admit to one reservation about winning the way he did. 'It's a great feeling to win a tournament,' he said, 'but an even greater one to *win* it — like birdieing the last two holes, as I did at the U.S. Open.'

The astute will note that Watson had used the word 'empathy', not 'sympathy', in describing his feelings for both Clampett and Price. Watson knows the difference between them, both because he is a psychology graduate of Stanford University and because, as the saying goes, he has 'been there.' Watson only too well remembers his own early wounds. He led the 1974 U.S. Open at Winged Foot, but shot a closing 79 to lose. And in the 1975 U.S. Open at Medinah, he had an experience eerily similar to Clampett's in this British Open. Where Clampett started 67–66, Watson started 68–67. That gave him a record-tying 36-hole total of 135, and a three-shot lead. Then, just as Clampett, Watson closed with 78–77.

Recalling these, Watson offered an observation that, while not directed at Clampett and his dedication to *The Golfing Machine*, might serve as a signal. 'I just couldn't get the job done,' Watson said. 'I had a manufactured swing. It worked for two rounds, then it didn't work when the heat was on.'

The sobering punishment of failure, the will to succeed, hard work, and maturity — Watson put all these together to rise from his own ashes, and now he had in his overflowing trophy case the crown jewels of seven of the world's major titles. They consist of two Masters, one U.S. Open, and astonishingly, four British Opens in the span of eight years.

The 1982 Open attracted a total of 133,299, just 1,202 short of the record set at Royal Lytham in 1979, despite the difficulties presented by a rail strike. When the last of the fans went home, the final leader board read:

Tom Watson	69–71–74–70—284	–4
Peter Oosterhuis	74–67–74–70—285	–3
Nick Price	69–69–74–73—285	–3
Tom Purtzer	76–66–75–69—286	–2
Nick Faldo	73–73–71–69—286	–2
Masahiro Kuramoto	71–73–71–71—286	–2
Des Smyth	70–69–74–73—286	–2
Fuzzy Zoeller	73–71–73–70—287	–1
Sandy Lyle	74–66–73–74—287	–1
Jack Nicklaus	77–70–72–69—288	Even
Bobby Clampett	67–66–78–77—288	Even

Watson would leave Troon and return to the States for '10 days of rest and recuperation,' he said, and then begin preparing for an assault on the one major championship not yet in his bag, the U.S. PGA. He had a parting word, first. Remembering that he won the first event of his professional career, the Western Open, right after painfully losing the 1974 U.S. Open, he offered Bobby Clampett and Nick Price one last piece of advice as a sure cure for the crushing disappointments they had just suffered.

Said Watson, 'Win next week.'

5. The PGA Championship

The heat. That's what everybody thinks of first when they think about golf in Tulsa, Oklahoma, in August. Halfway through his stroll to his second PGA Championship at Southern Hills Country Club, Raymond Floyd admitted, 'The heat has gotten to me; I've about had it.' Bob Gilder, who was to dog Floyd — unsuccessfully — through most of the tournament, said, 'Four or five years ago, I'd have wilted, but I've gotten used to the heat. In 1977, I couldn't believe it. I couldn't walk out the door.'

The daily 100-degree heat had an effect on the outcome of the 1982 PGA Championship, but not the one that many thought it might. Instead of players being carried off the course because of heat prostration, it was Southern Hills that needed emergency treatment. In three previous national championships, the course had never been so badly manhandled. For instance, Floyd tied the tournament's 18-hole record, broke the 36-hole and 54-hole marks and came within a bunker shot of breaking the 72-hole record. Fred Couples shattered the nine-hole record and par was broken daily by an unprecedented number of players in the greatest assault Southern Hills has ever suffered.

Floyd, who won the 1969 PGA at Dayton, Ohio, in a virtual wire-to-wire performance, burst from the starting blocks with a seven-under-par 63 and never looked back as he won by three strokes over fast-finishing Lanny Wadkins with 63–69–68–72—272, one stroke off Bobby Nichols' record set at Columbus in 1964. That's eight under par for the tournament, making a mockery of the winning scores for the three previous national championships the pros played at Southern Hills. In the 1958 U.S. Open, Tommy Bolt's winning score was three over par. Dave Stockton won the 1970 PGA with a one-under score and Hubert Green took the 1977 Open with a two-under total.

Southern Hills had changed little from those earlier tournaments. The tee at the No. 11 hole had been extended back a few yards, but the par-three hole was still one of the easier on the course. The tee at No. 12 had been moved, but that alteration merely cut down the severity of the dogleg. What made the course a pasty for the pros was the weather. Because of the danger of losing the greens in the constant heat, they were syringed three times in the morning and hourly in the afternoon the first two days. This kept them soft, susceptible to almost any kind of shot. The syringing consisted of a man spraying the greens with a shower nozzle attached to a hose and the treatment not only cooled the greens, it also smoothed them.

The heat had another effect. 'It's good for fat men,' said the 6-1, 200-pound Floyd. 'In cold weather it takes me some time to get loose, but in hot weather I can be loose after hitting a couple balls. You also don't get fat hands in hot weather. You know, in cold weather your hands get fat and you don't have any feel.'

Nobody seemed to take this into consideration prior to the start of the tournament. After all, Bolt, Stockton, and Green are not fat men and they won at Southern Hills in almost the same conditions. The principal questions seemed to be: Could Tom Watson win three majors in one year? Could Jack Nicklaus win his 20th major? Could Larry Nelson become the first since Denny Shute in 1936–37 to win it two years in a row? Could Calvin Peete become the first black to win a major? Could Arnold Palmer win the only major that has escaped him? All valid questions that had a resounding 'no' tacked onto them when Floyd shot his opening 63.

Nelson had won a year earlier at Atlanta in similar weather and figured he could repeat. 'I'm playing better than I have in two years. My iron game is as good as it's ever been,' he said, 'although I'm struggling with my driver. My chances of repeating are good, if not better, than last year. I feel I'm a different player than I was a year ago. Last year I was maybe a 20-to-1 shot. This year I should be 15-to-1. Southern Hills is one of the few courses I have played on which you have to do everything well. It's a true test of golf, one of the truest in a major championship. It's not brutally long, it's a matter of where you hit the ball. The greens are severe, but it depends on where you are.

'The guys will be hoping to play somewhere around par for the week. There's one par-five most can reach and one par-five that nobody can reach on the back side. Last year, deciding between a two-iron and a four-wood was the only management necessary. This year, when you step on a tee you know every time you're going to use a driver. Game management is going to help. If I were a betting man, I'd bet on myself— I'm the only one who can control the outcome. I don't bet on horses, I don't bet an anything I can't control.'

Palmer, Billy Casper and Gene Littler received special invitations to the tournament. Like Palmer, Casper and Littler have finished second in the PGA Championship, but they've never won it.

'At best, my chances (of winning) are slim,' admitted Palmer. 'On the other hand, if I get off to a good start it could build confidence in my game. I think I could still win it. I'm back to hitting the ball farther again. I went to a lighter driver with a power shaft. It's further away, but I'm still not giving up. I've won the British PGA, the Australian PGA and the Canadian PGA, but I haven't won the U.S. PGA. I put a lot of pressure on winning the PGA, yes, but I haven't done it. This is my profession, the business I've been in all my life. It makes it very important to me. The fact I haven't done it, I can't do anything about it. But guys like Casper, who has won the Masters and a couple of Opens, haven't won it either. Not competing on a full-time basis makes it difficult to get my game up where it should be. I'm not saying if I compete regularly I would win, but my chances would be much better. For me to win here, I'd have to stay within one or two shots of the lead, then make a move on the last nine. I don't know if I could do it. It might get to me. On the other hand, I'd like to try.'

Nelson's hopes of repeating and Palmer's dreams went down the drain as both missed the cut, Nelson with 74–75 and Palmer with 74–76. Watson and Nicklaus fared better, but neither ever menaced Floyd. Peete had won twice — in the Milwaukee Open and Anheuser-Busch Classic — in the five weeks prior to the PGA and the 39-year-old former jewelry salesman loomed as a bonafide threat. At one time, Peete was a curiosity piece, a black man with diamonds in his front teeth. No more. 'I am being respected for the caliber of player I am now,' he said. 'I took the diamonds out of my teeth in 1980. I wanted people to recognize me for my play and not that.' He received a great deal of recognition at Southern Hills.

Southern Hills. It was dreamed up by a group of Tulsa businessmen who feared Tulsa Country Club would shortly become public land during the Depression in 1934. They asked oil baron Waite Phillips, who owned a great deal of land on the south side of town, to donate 300 acres and advance the capital to construct a new country club. Phillips said he thought the idea was 'ridiculous', but he agreed. Perry Maxwell, a noted course architect who lived in Ardmore, Oklahoma, laid out the course and it opened in May, 1936, a 6,964-yard, par 35–35—70 course with only two non-par-three holes without a dogleg. 'You've got to come out ready to play,' said Southern Hills pro Jim Lucius. 'The man who plays these first three holes better than the rest of the field for four days is likely to be crowned the champion.'

There were some fears the bent-grass greens would die because they were cut down to one-eighth of an inch during the heat, much lower than usual, but superintendent Bob Randquist said there was no danger of that. 'Some players said they saw dry wilt, but that's not the case,' said Randquist. 'If we went for a full day without water, we might lose some grass because typically the greens are not this low. We are not anywhere near losing a green. I realize that's the way (wet, soft greens) it has to be at this time of the year, but if we had some wind we would lose the softening effect. The PGA asked us not to go above 10 feet on the Stimpmeter. You can't use some pin locations if you go much past that.'

So everybody was painting Southern Hills as a monster that could be even worse than it was. And quickly it was exposed as a veritable house pet. Give golf pros a course with soft greens and no wind, never mind the length or the temperature, and they're going to rip it apart. And that's what happened at Southern Hills. Because of the doglegs and the menacing Bermuda rough, the driver was only a sometimes weapon. One-irons and three-woods got almost as much distance as the fairways got harder every day. The only problem was to avoid hitting through the fairways into the unforgiving rough.

Among the withdrawals before the start of play was Lee Trevino, the 1974 champion. Trevino has had back problems since being struck by lightning during the 1975 Western Open and underwent surgery to relieve a nerve problem in his back the weekend before the PGA. If he had only a sore back, Trevino would have loved the weather. The thermometer bubbled at 100, causing players to head for shade every chance they could. Despite the suffocating heat, of the 17 under-par rounds and the three even-par scores turned in the first day, only five came in the morning, before the sun really became searing.

Floyd and Bob Gilder were morning starters and they set a standard for the day, Floyd with a 63 and Gilder with a 66 that tied him with Australian Greg Norman, an afternoon starter, for second place. Gilder had an up-and-down tournament, constantly charging, retreating and charging again. But in the first round he was a model of consistency, five birdies — a 10-footer at No. 7 and a 20-footer at No. 6 his only putts longer than a yard — and a bogey. He finished with birdies at the 569-yard No. 16 and the 434-yard No. 18 and obviously figured his 33–33—66 would hold up as low round of the day.

'I'm used to being in the lead, it doesn't bother me,' said Gilder. 'I try not to think of this as a major. Everybody says the majors are tougher to win, but I think they're easier because not as many guys can win. I used the driver quite a bit; it's as good as any club in my bag. At 16, I was laying up with a five-iron. I had 283 yards to the pin . . . and I came up 10 yards short of the green. I never saw the course playing shorter than it is now.'

Gilder had hardly settled into the leader's chair when Floyd knocked him out of it with what he called 'the best round of golf I've played anywhere. And to have it happen in a major and on a golf course like this — it's something I'll always remember.'

Floyd's round began innocently, pars at the 447-yard No. 1, 459-yard No. 2 and 406-yard No. 3, the opening holes that held so much terror. But when he parred the 175-yard No. 6, Floyd began a tear unparalleled in PGA tournament history. From the sixth through the 14th holes, Floyd shot nothing but threes, a nine-hole, 27-stroke stretch that included five birdies. When the streak was broken with a par four at No. 15, he added two more birdies at the 16th and 18th holes for a five-under 30 on the back nine that tied the tournament's nine-hole record and a 63 that tied Bruce Crampton's record set at Firestone in 1975 and lowered Southern Hills' competitive record by two strokes. The old course record of 65 was set by Trevino and Floyd in the 1977 Open.

Here's how Floyd got his birdies: A pitching wedge to the green at the 383-yard No. 7 and a 16-foot putt, an eight-iron to the green at the 373-yard No. 9 and a 10-foot putt, pitching wedge and a three-foot putt at the 375-yard No. 10, five-iron and 15-foot putt at the 444-yard No. 12, five-iron to within two feet at the 465-yard No. 13, chip to two feet at the 569-yard No. 16 and a six-iron and 10-foot putt at the 434-yard No. 18.

'I didn't have a weakness,' said Floyd. 'I hit one bad shot — I blocked a drive at the third hole — but it was not that bad. It caught the trees and but for that it would have landed in the fairway. It was not a surprise to me to play well and I don't see any reason to lose it. Until I made the putt at seven, got it up and down at eight and made the birdie at nine, I might have shot 70 or so. Positive things can make you play well; you have to guard against the negative things. There are definitely keys in every round. I always thought you get a lift when you think you're going to bogey and you save it — that's better than making a birdie.

'It's the best round I ever played — no doubt. It was not perfect, but I can add up threes very fast. I'm known as a front runner. My psychology is that you've got to be playing well to get there, so what got me there, keep going. I like it. I like the pressure, the awareness; you're less apt to make mental errors. A lot are just teeing off and that puts pressure on them. They make a bogey and they're 9–10 behind. It gives me a psychological edge. If I were asked to bet last night that someone would shoot 66, I'd have bet somebody would have. The best players are here.'

Norman used his driver 'five or six times,' a surprising number considering how far he can hit a golf ball. One time was at the 447-yard opening hole. Norman hit his drive so far he had only 120 yards to the flag . . . and hit a pitching wedge to within four feet for a birdie. He birdied No. 6 and 7 with six-footers and offset a bogey at No. 10 with birdies at No. 16 (three feet) and

17 (10 feet). 'This is the same as my home town (near Brisbane, Australia) — 100 degrees and 80 percent humidity — so I'm used to it,' said Norman.

The most startling round of the day was turned in by Fred Couples, a 23-year-old second-year pro from Palm Springs, California who is one of the longest drivers on the Tour. Couples was paired with Rex Caldwell and Jim Booros and after 11 holes he was three over par and just trying to stay out of the way of Caldwell and Booros. Then he birdied No. 13 with a 10-foot putt and it was like hitting a gusher. He birdied the next five holes — No. 14 from 10 feet, No. 15 from two feet, No. 16 from 10 feet, No. 17 from eight feet and No. 18 from five feet. That gave him a six-under-par 29 — the first man to break 30 for nine holes in the tournament's history — and a 67 that moved him into a tie for fourth place with Caldwell and Nick Faldo.

'I was kind of sluggish for 10 or 11 holes. I felt good on the range and tried to attack the course,' said Couples. 'A lot had to do with playing with Rex and Jim Booros. Rex was making birdies and he said there wasn't any reason why I couldn't do it, too. It wasn't any fun early. I was in the rough a lot.'

'There were 12 birdies in our group on the back nine. It was unbelievable,' said Caldwell. 'You can't alter your game because of what someone else (Floyd) is doing. If you do, you can pack your bag, you're choking already.' Caldwell played erratically on the front nine, then birdies at holes No. 14, 15 and 16 got him under par. The threesome of Couples, Caldwell and Booros had a best ball of 58; despite Floyd's 63, his threesome, which included Hale Irwin and Gary Player, had only 61.

Jim Simons, Vance Heafner, John Jackson, Mark Pfeil and David Graham were at 68 and six others were at 69, including Peete. Watson had a 72 and said, 'I didn't keep the ball in play. I turned a 68 into a 72.' Nicklaus had a 74 and groaned, 'Basically, I got what I deserved. If you don't drive it in the fairway, you're history. But it's too early to say I'm history.' Nicklaus was one under par, then bogeyed No. 6, 8, 10 and 12 and double-bogeyed 13.

The heat, clicking cameras and golf carts constantly traveling the cart paths got to Floyd in the second round, but none of the players did. Oh, Simons got to within a stroke of him, but that was before Floyd teed off, and Gilder tied him, but only briefly. At the end of another steamy day Floyd had another record and still had a two-stroke lead over Gilder as he shot a 69 for 132. That broke the tournament's 36-hole record shared by Jerry Barber (1959), Bruce Crampton (1975) and Gil Morgan (1976) by two strokes. It should be noted that none of the last three went on to win.

As is the custom, the early starters of the first round played in the afternoon the second day and vice-versa. How much difference that made can be ascertained by the fact that of the 13 still under par for the tournament after 36 holes, only Floyd, Gilder and Heafner teed off after noon the second day.

Simons was the first to make a run at Floyd, which was surprising. Simons figures he does well in the majors because he is accurate off the tee and usually stays out of the high rough in a tournament such as the U.S. Open. But for some reason he has never done well in the PGA. Added to that is that since the Masters in April he hadn't played well. There were reasons. Simons is legally blind — he can't read the big E at the top of the eye chart without glasses — and he wears contact lenses, a soft one over a hard one in his left eye and a hard one in the right. He has a problem getting his eyes to shed tears and because of this he almost withdrew after the third round of the Bing Crosby Pro-Am early in the year after the soft lens dried and doubled up, causing excruciating pain in his eye. But he was in contention, so wearing wrap-around sunglasses between shots and putting drops in his eyes at almost every hole, he played the last round and won, overtaking Craig Stadler with a final-nine 32 at Pebble Beach to win his third Tour tournament.

Southern Hills was brighter than Pebble Beach, much brighter, so Simons wore those same sunglasses, looking much like a blind man without his dog. And after two holes of the second round he looked as if he needed somebody to show him the way. He hit a tree from out of the rough at the first hole and bogeyed and missed the green at the second hole for another bogey, leaving him at even par for the tournament. 'Yes, I was thinking of high numbers,' Simons replied to a question, 'because I haven't been playing well, but the 68 gave me more incentive. I got a bad break when I hit the tree at the first hole and I started thinking maybe things could be as bad today as they were good yesterday. The way I've been playing lately, my thoughts were to make the cut, not win the golf tournament.'

At the end of the day, his thoughts were of winning it. 'At this point I do think I can win,' he said. It was a nine-hole stretch, from the third hole through the 11th, that changed his mind. He whacked a six-iron over a tree to within 18 feet of the hole at the third hole and made the putt, touching off a birdie binge. At the fifth hole he sank a 15-footer for a birdie and at the seventh he tapped in a five-footer to go three under for the tournament. He missed the green with a four-wood at the 215-yard No. 8, but holed a 60-foot blast on the fly for another birdie. An eight-footer at No. 9 and five-footer at No. 11 got him to within a stroke of Floyd, who hadn't even gone to the practice range. Simons tried to get a little extra out of this drive at the long 16th and knocked it under the trees for a bogey that gave him a 67 and a tie for third place at 135 with Norman. 'For some reason, it was more of a struggle, maybe it was the heat,' said Simons. 'Maybe because I had the 68 yesterday I expected more of myself. If I had gone out and shot a 67 or 66 yesterday I wouldn't have expected a 67 today. When I was standing in the 18th fairway while they syringed the green, my legs almost gave out on me. The middle holes carried me. I feel I should do well in the Open and the PGA because of the high rough, but I've never done well in the PGA. But I never played well in the Crosby until this year. My iron play has been very good. When I had a chance to put the iron in for a birdie, I did it. I'm not as aggressive off the tee, but I've made my share of putts. If I made all my birdie chances, I'd be 15 under par.'

Norman got his bogeys and birdies in clusters, sandwiching bogeys at No. 15 and 17, both as a result of hitting bunkers, around a two-putt birdie at 16 for a 69. His other birdies all came on lengthy putts — 25 feet at the third hole, 15 feet at the sixth and 30 feet from off the edge at the ninth. 'I had a great chance to move on Ray, but I didn't make enough putts,' said the blond Australian. 'I feel pretty good. I'm not driving it that good, but I'm hitting my irons well, and the closer I hit them the more confident I get. There is pressure since I haven't won a major, but I can't put pressure on myself.'

Nick Faldo got to five under par for the tournament with a 30-foot birdie putt at the 13th hole 'that rolled in like a train,' but poor drives cost him bogeys at the 15th and 18th and left him with an even-par 70 that tied him with Jay Haas at 137. Haas had an unobtrusive 66, for when he finished all eyes were on Floyd and Gilder, who were waging a battle on the course.

Floyd got to eight under with an eight-foot birdie putt at the second hole, then took his first bogey of the tournament at the next hole after missing the fairway with a three-wood off the tee. Gilder got to within a stroke of him with a 35-foot birdie putt at the first hole and a 12-footer at the third and Floyd had to scramble to save par at the fourth hole to maintain his edge. Gilder offset a bogey at the fifth hole with a birdie at the ninth and Floyd also birdied the ninth, leaving them two strokes apart. Gilder made the difference one stroke by sinking a 12-foot birdie putt at the 11th hole, then bogeyed No. 12 and 13. Floyd bogeyed No. 13 — 'It was one of the few times a shot was not pictured in my mind,' he said — and when Gilder birdied No. 16 and 17 with short putts, they were deadlocked at seven under. It lasted only temporarily, until Floyd birdied No. 16 from 15 feet and Gilder bogeyed No. 18 after coming up with a buried lie in a bunker on his five-iron approach.

'I didn't drive it as well, but I had more control of my irons,' said Gilder. 'I was in the rough more than yesterday and didn't have as many chances to go for the green. I was missing the fairway on the tougher holes. But I was putting where I was looking, and I was looking pretty good. I went for the pin at 18. I felt if I made another birdie I'd put some heat on him. No. 12 and 13 were the crucial holes, but so are the others. The idea is to make some birdies and par the tough holes. The heat was stagnant at times. The sun was out and you'd be standing on the tee with no wind and it got hot. I must have gotten used to it. Four or five years ago, I'd have wilted.'

The heat got to Floyd, too. 'I played well from tee to green and I putted well, I hit a lot of putts that should have gone in. That was the difference in not shooting 65 today,' he said. 'The heat has gotten to me, I've about had it now. Including the practice tee, I was out there five and one-half hours in the sun with no breeze and the sun is higher in the afternoon and I couldn't get to the trees. I felt it, a couple of times I pulled the ball; I had to take a couple deep breaths.' The save at the fourth hole was pivotal, he admitted. 'Had I made a bogey there it could have been shocking. I hadn't made any bogeys and now I make two in a row. I hit my three-wood into the rough at the third hole and yesterday I didn't do that. And the putts I thought I made didn't go in; yesterday they did. I was on the green and about to putt at 16 when I saw on the leaderboard we were tied. But it doesn't matter. It's early, we have two rounds to go. Two shots aren't anything, one hole, a birdie against a bogey, a double-bogey against a par. Tomorrow everything will be happening together. There will not be the question of morning and afternoon.'

Morgan made the greatest jump in position in the second round, going from 99th place to 26th with a 66. Woody Blackburn made a hole-in-one with an eight-iron at the 169-yard No. 11 and he needed it. Blackburn had a 71 which gave him 145, the cutoff score. Watson, with 71, was at 141, nine strokes back, and Nicklaus, with a 70, was at 144 and seemingly out of it. There were a number of big names that were definitely out after missing the cut: Palmer, with a 76–150; Nelson, with 75–149; Stockton, Green, Tom Weiskopf, Gary

Player, Fuzzy Zoeller and Bobby Clampett. Here's the way the leaders stood at the halfway point:

Raymond Floyd	63–69—132
Bob Gilder	66–68—134
Jim Simons	68–67—135
Greg Norman	66–69—135
Nick Faldo	67–70—137
Jay Haas	71–66—137
Lon Hinkle	70–68—138
Fred Couples	67–71—138

Floyd had won the 1969 PGA title at the NCR course in Dayton, Ohio, by one stroke over Player after going into the final round with a five-shot advantage. It was in the 1976 Masters that he got the reputation of being a great front-runner. That year he kept expanding on his lead until he won by eight strokes and tied Nicklaus' tournament record of 271. Floyd is indeed a fine front-runner, which nearly everybody will admit is the most difficult position to play from. Most would rather be a stroke or two behind going into the final nine holes, then charge. Floyd left no room for that in the third round, the day on which he actually won the tournament. He finished the front nine birdie-birdie to double his lead over Gilder and Norman and at the end of the round he was five strokes ahead as a result of a 68 that gave him a 54-hole total of 200, another tournament record. That was two strokes lower than the 202 Floyd led with in 1969 and Nelson had in 1981, and his five-stroke lead tied the 54-hole record set by Floyd in 1969 and Watson in 1978.

Norman shot a 70 and Haas a 68 for a share of second place at 205 and Gilder dropped back to 206 with a 72, but after a slow start the day belonged to Floyd. He bogeyed No. 3 again after bunkering a seven-iron, then finished the front nine with a flourish, a 40-footer at No. 8 and a three-footer at No. 9. Birdies at No. 12 and 16 got him 11 under for the tournament and opened the gap to five strokes. Even a bogey at 18, on which he nearly sank a blast from a bunker, didn't hurt his lead. 'I played very well again,' he said in an understatement. 'I hit the ball solid and I had the ball close to the hole a lot. To shoot 68 on this golf course without making any putts — outside of No. 8 I made nothing — is very rewarding. On the other hand, I should be sitting here with a 10 or 11-stroke lead instead of five. I just feel I haven't made as many putts as I should have. This round could have been a 63 easily. I don't think I've ever lost a big lead, something over three or four.'

Norman played a rather ordinary round, two bogeys and two birdies, and would have had second place to himself had he not bogeyed No. 18. Haas followed his 66 with a solid 68, his only mistake a bogey at the second hole. 'I guess I'm going to have to shoot a 65 to have a realistic chance,' said Haas. 'And I've got to get them early. He (Floyd) has done this before. He's the kind of guy who, when he gets it going, keeps it going. The rest of us sit back, but he goes for the pin all the time.' Haas packed all his excitement into the final six holes, birdieing No. 13, 14 and 17 on putts of eight, 18 and 20 feet, respectively.

Meanwhile, Gilder followed his pattern, starting his round bogey, bogey, double-bogey, then birdieing No. 5, 7 and 9 on the way to a 72 that dropped him six strokes behind. In this round Peete first gained some attention. When he birdied No. 11 and 12 he was six back of Floyd and even though his 68–207 left him in arrears with 18 holes to go, he was in the chase — for a second place, as it turned out — the rest of the way. Peete said he hurt a knee at the 16th hole, but the injury proved minimal.

The best round of the day, which was not nearly as hot as the first two days (maybe only 95), was turned in by 53-year-old Gene Littler, a three-under 67 that moved him into the top 20 at 212. Wadkins had a 69 and was at 208 and was just a face in the crowd. Watson, at 212, had to wait another year for a crack at the only major he hasn't won, Simons had slipped out of contention with a 73 for a 208 that tied him with Wadkins and Seve Ballesteros and Nicklaus had disappeared with a 72–216.

Minutes after the threesome of Floyd, Haas and Norman had completed their round, lightning flashed, thunder sounded and the skies opened, sending the crowd of 25,870 rushing for their cars. The storm was to dump half an inch of rain on the course and maybe that sewed up Floyd's victory. On a dry, fast track, it's conceivable the leader could shoot a 75 or 76 and somebody behind him could have a hot round, but on a wet course it was unlikely that somebody such as Floyd would throw away a five-stroke lead.

Floyd played his poorest round of the tournament the final day, which maybe only proved he is human. By the 10th hole he had four bogeys, which is as many as he had in the previous 54 holes. Everybody behind him came out firing, but only a few connected and some of them were just aiming for a high finish. Peter Oosterhuis made the second hole-in-one of the tournament, with a two-iron at the 215-yard No. 8, and Jim Thorpe turned in one of the four eagles made at Southern Hills, a two at the 373-yard No. 9, but neither of them were in contention. The greatest threat Floyd got came from Couples, who drew to within two strokes when he eagled the No. 16 hole but immediately removed the threat by bogeying No. 17 enroute to a fine 66 and a tie for third place.

Floyd's competition was with Bobby Nichols' 1964 tournament record of 271 and he might have broken it had he not blanked out on a three-iron shot to the 18th green. And he would have tied it if a bogey putt from eight feet had not lipped out. As it was, he double-bogeyed the final hole for a 72 and a total of 272, one more than the record. 'I had a normal three-iron shot, but I never got to the ball. I don't remember standing over it,' Floyd said. 'Standing there in the 18th fairway, looking up at all those people and realizing I had the tournament won, I got caught up in the awe of the moment. It caught me quick, I should have backed off.'

The three-iron shot, the one he didn't remember, landed in the high rough near a greenside bunker and the rough was the thickest near the greens. Floyd tried to pop it on the green and flubbed it into the bunker. Now the shot at the record had all but disappeared. His recovery left him eight feet away with a chance to tie Nichols, but the putt refused to drop, just as so many had in the preceding 71 holes. But he had a 72 and a three-shot decision over Wadkins, a check for $65,000 and his third major triumph in three decades. And he said it wasn't easy.

'I think I took all the pressure away from the field. Everybody knows I can play out front. I had a five-stroke lead after three rounds and they could freewheel it,' said Floyd. 'They figured Ray Floyd's not going to lose. I really believe I was the only one with pressure on him. It was not easy, by any means. The thing was, it would be detrimental to my career to be reading everywhere tomorrow that Ray Floyd had blown a five-shot lead. That's a lot of pressure. People figure he's got a five-shot lead and can't lose it and that's a lot of pressure, too. There was a hell of a lot of pressure.'

If there was pressure, only Floyd was aware of it, but maybe that's the only way to explain his start in the final round. It was a little cooler after the overnight rain, in the low 90's, but the course was the way it had been for the first three rounds. The only thing that had changed was the attitude of the players. And Wadkins' attitude was that Floyd could be caught, even from eight strokes behind.

'When Raymond went to three over (for the round), I had just gotten to four under (for the tournament) and I thought I had a chance,' said Wadkins. 'Then I missed a 12 or 15-footer for a birdie at 14 and one from six or eight feet at 15. I thought if I could get to six under, then Ray had some tough holes left. I'm a realist, but when I won in 1977, Littler made five straight bogeys to help me. I know it can happen.'

Floyd missed the green at the third and fifth holes and bogeyed, reducing his lead to three strokes over Norman, who played the first five holes in even par. Wadkins birdied the second hole from 10 feet and the fourth from a foot, but in between he bogeyed the third after driving into the rough. He had picked up three strokes, but he still trailed by five.

Nobody else was doing anything to menace Floyd. Peete played the first eight holes in even par. Gilder triple-bogeyed the short sixth and though he staged another of his comebacks, that was fatal to his chances. Haas got off to a poor start, a ruinous 37 on the front. Floyd certainly gave them the opportunities to close the gap early. He hit the trees at the third hole and bogeyed, buried an approach in the bunker for a bogey at the fifth hole and hit what he called 'another bonehead shot' at the ninth hole and bogeyed. But he birdied the eighth hole and that proved important.

'I got off to a shaky start. No. 8 was the turning point,' he said. 'I was struggling and I hit a one-iron seven feet from the hole and I birdied as he (Norman) bogeyed. I used my driver at the ninth and got in trouble. I was fortunate to make bogey. And I blocked a four-iron shot at the 10th. At that point, I knew if I continued to go the way I was playing, I was not going to win the golf tournament. I had a talk with myself — if I told you what I said on the 12th tee they'd put me in one of those places. I've had hundreds of talks with myself and sometimes they don't work. This one did. I got very aggressive and I feel very proud I was able to gather up my round.'

Couples, playing four groups in front of Floyd, had birdied the sixth and 11th holes, but at that point he wasn't taken seriously. However, he dropped an 18-footer at No. 14 and sank a 20-foot chip shot for an eagle at No. 16 and, even though Floyd birdied No. 12, there was danger up ahead. 'Floyd had just birdied No. 12 to go eight under, then I chipped in and I thought 17 was a birdieable hole,' said Couples. 'I thought the way things were going, if I birdie there, I'd be in good shape.' But Couples pushed his drive into the deep rough on the other side of the creek that borders the right side of the fairway and could only punch it out toward the green. The bogey ended his bid, even though he got it up and down at 18 for a 66.

Meanwhile, Wadkins was playing and hoping. He birdied the 12th hole from 15 feet and made a three-footer for a birdie at 17, the finishing touches to a 67 and 275, seven strokes below the score he had tied Littler with at Pebble Beach in 1977. 'I hit a lot of good shots. The main thing is that the ones that were not very good at least were on the greens. You have to do that out here, even if you have a long putt. You have to keep it out of the rough,' said Wadkins. 'But when he smells it (victory), he's tough to catch. I thought I'd have to shoot at least a 64.'

The birdie at the 12th righted Floyd and he started lighting the candles on the cake with birdies at the 15th (eight feet) and 16th (15 feet) holes, putting him 10 under for the tournament and well within range of the 72-hole record. But strange things happen when a man walks down the final fairway knowing he has victory in his pocket. When Nichols set the record, he was being pursued by Nicklaus and Palmer. Floyd had only himself.

'I felt stronger today than in any round this week. I had the feeling I would shoot another low round,' Floyd said. 'I didn't think well. It was not my ball striking, I made mental errors. I used the wrong club a few times and when you do that you think, "What's wrong with me?" That's pressure. Records don't mean anything. Monetarily, they're worth two cents. I knew Couples was five under after 16 and I'm at 11 seven under, then I birdied 12. But I had the hard holes to play yet. Winning from wire to wire is difficult, but it's a position I like to be in. It's no surprise when I play well. When I play well, I expect to go out and play well again. When I'm shooting 68, 67, when I'm playing that way, I feel confident and feel in control.'

'I feel in the last two or three years I've been in a streak. I was 26 when I won my first PGA and I honestly can't say how I felt. But I remember the feeling when I won the Masters. I always wanted to win that, geographically so, because I'm from the South. This victory means a helluva lot to me because I haven't won a major since 1976 and it means I've won a major in three decades — not many have done that. When you set goals and achieve them, it's very, very rewarding. But I want to keep winning.'

After his triple-bogey, Gilder ran off five birdies, three bogeys and four pars over the final 12 holes for a 72 and a 278 that left him all alone in eighth place. Simons, making his best showing in a major as a pro, hit his drive in almost the same spot as Couples at the 17th hole and bogeyed for a 69 that tied him with Haas and Norman for fifth place at 277. 'That bogey cost me a lot of money,' lamented Simons, and indeed it did — $9,000, the difference between what he would have got for tying for third place ($25,000) and the $16,000 he got for tying for fifth.

Peete, turning in the best finish by a black man in a major, birdied the 16th hole and chipped to within a foot to save par at 18 and felt good about tying Couples for third place. 'I feel super about my finish. It's not like winning, but it's close. I'm proud of the way I played,' he said. Couples felt good, too. 'Ray Floyd says nobody remembers who came in second. When I get as good as

Watson and Floyd, I'll think that way, too, but I'll take that now,' said the young Couples.

Looking back over the tournament, it appears Floyd won by playing the middle six holes at Southern Hills better than any of the other contenders. He was eight under for the tournament over those holes and three under for the final six, although that is tempered somewhat by his meaningless double-bogey at 18 the final day. Haas played the last six holes in six under, but was two over on the middle six. Everybody figured the winner would have to play the first six holes well, but Floyd got only one birdie in four days and was three over for the tournament. Peete had six birdies and was five under, yet he was four strokes behind at the finish.

Floyd had 18 birdies in 72 holes, but Gilder (20) and Couples (17 birdies, one eagle) did better and Simons as well. In the final analysis, Floyd won because he did the best job of avoiding bogeys. In the majors, that's what it's all about.

6. The World Match Play Championship

The year of 1982 was not the vintage season that Severiano Ballesteros wanted. He had a promising start and won twice early in the European season, but autumn arrived and Seve had not added to his victory total. He was clearly disappointed, especially by his play in the major events. There was one remaining way that Ballesteros could reaffirm his position among the great golfers of the world. He could win the Suntory World Match Play Championship, the last of the year's major international tournaments. The prospects of his doing so were not good, even though Seve was returning as defending champion to the Wentworth Club in Virginia Water, Surrey, England. Only twice before had a golfer won in successive years, Gary Player in 1965–1966 and Hale Irwin in 1974–1975. There had been six different winners in the six years since Irwin's second title. In addition, Ballesteros was suffering the after-effects of influenza and his game was off. He had missed the 36-hole cut at his most recent tournament, the Sanyo Open. Said Ballesteros, 'I cannot play any worse than that'.

The result, of course, was that Ballesteros did win the World Match Play. He won with a performance that was something less than vintage, yet that did not detract from the significance of the accomplishment. 'I said before the year that I would win something big, and I kept my word,' Seve said, in the glow of his 37th-hole triumph over Sandy Lyle in the final, which was concluded with a near-miraculous 30-foot putt across a watery green. 'I must say I expected more this year,' Ballesteros continued. 'This makes it better.'

Ballesteros was three under par in miserable weather conditions while beating Lyle. In the semifinal, Seve was let off the hook by Lanny Wadkins (who subsequently earned third place, 3 and 1 over Tom Kite). He took the good fortune philosophically. He said at the presentation ceremony, 'Sometimes you play good enough to win and you lose. Sometimes you play badly enough to lose and you win. That's my case'.

The final was the first between two European golfers and was evidence of the improving standard of play on the European Tour. The American entrants perhaps did not play as well as they were capable, but Lyle's performance made it abundantly clear that Ballesteros no longer stands alone, as he once did, among world-class golfers. There are six to perhaps a dozen more in their category, including Nick Faldo, who was eliminated by Lyle in the first round with one of the most dramatic reversals in the championship's history.

With the notable exception of Tom Watson, the 1982 World Match Play contestants were the best to be gathered from the world of professional golf. The winner of the Open championships on both sides of the Atlantic, Watson did not play for several reasons, including his wife's pregnancy, another autumn commitment in Japan and our refusal to offer appearance money. Representing the United States were Masters champion Craig Stadler, PGA champion Raymond Floyd, Kite, Wadkins, Curtis Strange and young Bobby Clampett, who thrilled the British audiences three months earlier with his play in the first two rounds of their Open at Royal Troon. The American players occupied the first (Stadler), second (Kite) and fifth (Wadkins) positions on the U.S. PGA Tour money list. It would have been great to complete the top five with Watson, who held the fourth position, but we were extremely pleased with those players on hand.

As the defending champion, Ballesteros received the No. 1 seed and a bye into the second-round play. Other byes were presented to Floyd, Stadler and Greg Norman, the leader of the European Tour's Order of Merit and winner of the 1980 World Match Play. Other European representatives were Lyle, second on the Order of Merit, and Faldo, winner of the Haig Whisky Tournament Players' Championship. The Japanese entrant was Masahiro Kuramoto, who had placed joint fourth in the British Open. From South Africa there was Player, a five-time winner of the World Match Play and the current holder of the South African Open and PGA titles. Player was making his 18th appearance in 19 years of the World Match Play while this event was the first for five contestants: Stadler, Kite, Strange, Clampett and Kuramoto.

The pairings were determined as usual in a public drawing. The first match would be between the two youngsters who excelled in the British Open, Clampett and Kuramoto, with the winner to play Ballesteros. Two extremely tough competitors, Wadkins and Player, were set in match No. 2, having Norman awaiting the winner in the second round. The British rivals, Faldo and Lyle, were paired and the winner was scheduled to meet Floyd. The final quarter was all-American, Kite versus Strange, with the victor to play Stadler. The critics were much divided over the choice of an eventual World Match Play champion. Names most frequently mentioned were Norman and three Americans — Stadler, Floyd and Kite. Wadkins also received some consideration, about the same as Faldo and Lyle, while Ballesteros was regarded with skepticism.

Naturally, the duel between Lyle and Faldo was the dominant theme of the newspapers. The match provided the flavor of a prize fight and in some quarters was described in grander terms such as 'the heaviest British sporting collision since Seb Coe and Steve Ovett met at the Moscow Olympics'. Malcolm Folley of *The Mail on Sunday* brought Faldo and Lyle together for an interview the week before the championship. Lyle said, 'I'm sure the media will make the match sound like the clash between Coe and Ovett. But you can't classify whoever loses next week as a second-class golfer'. And Faldo said, 'Golf fluctuates too much to nominate either Sandy or myself as Britain's best golfer purely on the outcome of one match'.

Pride, more than anything else, was at stake. These were the young hopes of British golf, with one or the other expected to take the place once occupied by Tony Jacklin. Lyle believed he would be at an advantage because his drives were longer, 'with a good rip off the tee'. To that Faldo replied, 'Maybe he is about to learn there is more to golf than who hits the ball farthest'.

Impossible, one might think, for any match to live up to such an advance billing. Somehow, the match of Lyle versus Faldo did. It was one of the classics in the 19-year history of this championship, harkening memories of Player versus Tony Lema in 1965, when Gary came back from seven down with 17 holes to play. On this bitter, but fair Thursday, three of the four matches were determined by afternoon reversals, but the encounter between the young Britons was the only one destined to live long in memory. Six down after the first 18, Lyle recovered to win 2 and 1. The other results were Wadkins, 2 and 1 over Player after Lanny was three down at lunch; Kite, also 2 and 1 over Strange after being one down following 18 holes; and Clampett, 5 and 4 over Kuramoto.

Cautious might be the word to describe the play of Faldo and Lyle early in their match. Nick was level with par and two up after nine holes, then changed gears and played the last seven holes in five under par, coming home in 33, four under par, to establish his six-up advantage. Faldo's surge followed a bogey at the 11th where Nick missed the green and allowed Lyle to win the hole and close the margin to one. In his eagerness to draw level quickly, Sandy drove into an impossible position on the par-five 12th hole. Nick reached the green with a drive and three-wood, having two putts from 35 feet for the birdie. Faldo holed a five-footer at No. 13, and the margin went to four-up on Sandy's three-putt bogey at the next. Lyle had no chance for a birdie at the 16th, while Faldo sank a 10-footer.

Both required wedges for their third shots on the par-five 17th and both missed their putts for birdies. The closing par-five was especially notable. At the 18th, Lyle hit by far the longer drive and hit a five-iron from light rough that landed 18 inches short of the flag and rolled four feet past. Faldo played a two-iron to the right side of the green and holed a 30-foot putt for an eagle. Lyle then missed his four-footer.

During the interval between rounds, Lyle changed putters, from a heavy blade to a softer center-shafted model to accommodate the fast greens. 'My putting was what was really doing the damage', Sandy later explained. 'If I had been putting (well), maybe I would have been only three down. The greens were too fast for the blade. The ball was coming out too fast.' He reflected on the 13th hole when, having a 35-foot birdie attempt, he putted 15 feet past the hole. 'After that I got too tentative,' he said, 'and that's the worst thing you can do, really, to become too tentative. I had to change.'

At that point Lyle had a modest objective, 'trying to make a game of it and not to give him holes and lose 9 and 8'. Sandy started off with a nice putt, a four-footer for par that felt comfortable and gave him the confidence to play aggressively. An eight-foot birdie at No. 2 further brightened his outlook. The third hole was virtually a gift from Faldo following a poor wedge shot, then Sandy holed another good putt for birdie at the fourth and suddenly Faldo's six-up margin had been halved. At the fifth hole Lyle missed the green and saved his par from six feet after Faldo had blown his birdie opportunity from seven feet. 'That was what started the rot with Nick,' Lyle thought. The replacement putter again did its job with a 24-foot birdie on No. 6 and, by now, Faldo was visibly shaken. Nick tried a risky shot with his two-iron into the ninth green, pulled the ball into the trees and gave back another hole with a bogey to Lyle's birdie on a five-iron shot to eight feet. One up with nine to play.

Still, Lyle had not begun thinking about beating Faldo. He simply was trying to 'give it a rip' and was collecting nice dividends. His 18-footer at No. 10 slid past the hole but he squared the match at No. 11, holing from five feet as Faldo two-putted from 30 feet. A critical test came at the 12th, a hole that Lyle had played carelessly in the morning, and many times before that. 'Usually I thrash it into the trees and lose to a birdie,' Sandy said. 'Once I got past that hole with a good drive, I thought I could win.' The change of heart probably went unnoticed by the massive gallery because Faldo was equal to the moment. Both drove well and reached the green with their second shots in the 30 to 40-foot range, then holed out in twos for birdie-fours.

On the next hole Lyle went ahead, scoring his birdie from five feet. Faldo hit into the righthand bunker on the short 14th and they halved the hole in pars when Lyle, wisely cautious, left his 25-footer short of the cup. Sandy's margin went to two-up at No. 15, where Faldo hit into a bunker and bogeyed. In another bunker at the next, Nick stayed alive by holing the shot. Would this be the dramatic turning point for Faldo, who still had not forgotten his loss in 1980 to Norman after holding a four-hole lead with 11 to play? Unfortunately for Nick, the answer was negative.

Having the honor on the 571-yard 17th, Faldo allowed Lyle to breathe deeply by driving into the trees, from which he was fortunately able to get a free drop, having line-of-sight relief over a Suntory sign. Lyle knew Faldo could not reach the green in two. Sandy took a one-iron off the tee, then a four-iron short of the green, even though he might have reached the putting surface with a hooked three-wood. 'I was playing safe and keeping it in play,' Lyle said. 'I would prefer a 90-yard wedge to a 10-yard wedge.' But Lyle's pitch was heavy, some 27 feet short of the hole. Faldo missed his birdie try from 45 feet. Lyle had one thought, 'to try to get as close as possible and then on to 18 to win with a four.' Sandy did better than that. He holed the improbable shot to end the match with his eighth birdie. The ball bounced twice and went in the hole. Had Lyle scored another birdie at 18, as anticipated, he would have scored 63!

'It's been a while since I've played as well at Wentworth,' Lyle said. 'But I had to — I was six down. I had to give it a rip. The first three or four holes kept my morale going, but I never expected to win. It is very enjoyable, to come back from the dead virtually.' Lyle knew that his rival's sentiments were then the opposite. Said Sandy, 'He's going to feel sore for a few weeks. I could see Nick getting dejected. I didn't expect to win all those holes and I'm sure he didn't expect to lose them. It's unbelievable what can happen in match play. It often happens at Wentworth, and it happened today.'

While the duel overshadowed the first day's other encounters, there were nevertheless three more good matches. In match No. 1 was the pairing of Kuramoto and Clampett. Kuramoto won an astounding six tournaments in his first year and two more in 1982, and Clampett had just secured his first American Tour title in the Southern Open. They had, according to Clampett, 'played quite a bit of golf together,' first meeting in the 1970 Sunnehanna Amateur, where Kuramoto gained notice by shooting 65. Later, Kuramoto played collegiate golf in the United States at East Tennessee State University and, Clampett said, 'always impressed me. It's no surprise that he has won eight tournaments on the Japanese tour'.

Kuramoto is a very quick player, as the British journalists noted, but Clampett did not think that was a factor in his 5-and-4 thrashing. 'Basically, that's his style of play,' Bobby said. 'I don't think Massey has ever been nervous. I was (nervous) this morning and starting a little this afternoon. But this is a big tournament, it's the first time either of us had been here, and we both wanted to win.' Their duel was curiously formless. Of the first 14 holes, only two were halved. 'It was a topsy-turvy match,' Clampett said, 'I played a little better in the afternoon, especially on the first seven or eight.' Two up after a birdie on the 18th, Clampett in the afternoon won two of the first four holes and three of the first seven, moving to a five-up advantage. He simply out-played the Japanese and had the occasional master stoke, such as his 25-foot putt for eagle to better Kuramoto's birdie on the fourth hole. From there on, Clampett held his margin. 'I felt Massey wasn't in position on enough holes to beat me,' Bobby said. 'I had position on almost every hole and I think that's the secret in match play — to out-position your opponent. If you can be in better position, your odds are better to win.'

In match No. 2 Player recalled some of the magic from his past and was on the verge of another miracle at Wentworth, a course that always will be associated with his name. Dressed all in black, except for a white cap, Gary went round in 67 in the morning to break for lunch three up on Wadkins. If there was a turning point, that was the 17th, where Player was looking to be five ahead and missed a six-foot putt while Lanny sank one from twice the distance, winning the hole with a birdie. 'Even though I was three down, I felt very good because I played so well. I was two under and didn't putt well. I missed two six-footers,' said Wadkins, who had won the Phoenix Open, Tournament of Champions and Buick Open on the 1982 American Tour.

During the afternoon round, Wadkins raised his game to the heights that Player once was able to do while Gary, approaching his 48th birthday, bowed out with a performance more typical of a year in which he seldom played sharply. Wadkins took only six holes to climb from three-down to all-square in the match. Lanny won two holes with pars, one with a birdie and most remarkably, had another birdie to halve the fourth. At No. 4, Wadkins hit a great-looking three-iron shot that went through the green, hit a water sprinkler on his return chip and then holed from 18 feet. 'Maybe,' Lanny said, 'that putt was just justice.' Wadkins lost the seventh to Player's birdie, halved the ninth with par on a sensational wedge shot and leveled the match again at No. 10, the par-three, when Gary's tee shot lodged in a tree. Player spotted his ball through binoculars and conceded the hole.

Wadkins took the lead at No. 12, hitting a four-wood to the edge of the green and two-putting for his birdie, while Player was short of the green in two and missed a four-foot putt. The clinching shot came when Wadkins holed from a bunker at the 15th, and Player again conceded, just when it appeared that the hole would be halved in bogeys. 'Gary had a bad lie,' Lanny recalled, 'and I was thinking that I didn't want to be stupid and leave it in the bunker. It was a great bunker shot.' Two ahead, Wadkins continued to the 2-and-1 victory by halving the next two holes in pars.

Very little notice was taken of the No. 4 match of the first day. Neither Kite nor Strange held much magnetism for the British spectators, considering the occurences in the matches ahead. Known for his victory in the 1980 European Open as well as for his No. 1 position on the 1981 American Tour, Kite was three down to Strange after just nine holes of the morning round and it seemed that Curtis was as much a master of match play as he was in his youth while winning twice in the prestigious North and South Amateur in Pinehurst, North Carolina.

Kite was far off his notably consistent game in the early going. He lost two holes with bogeys and one with a double-bogey on the first nine. Strange also lost a hole with a bogey, and made the only birdie of the pairing at No. 6. Kite played the second nine without a five on his card, three under par including birdies at the two closing par-gives. Going out in level par was sufficient for Kite to square the match in the afternoon, and Tom secured the 2-and-1 decision by winning No. 12 with a birdie and No. 15 with a par. All other holes were halved in pars.

For openers, it was a great day and there was much more ahead with the introduction of the seeded players: Ballesteros against Clampett, Norman against Wadkins, Floyd against Lyle and Stadler against Kite. All were first-time World Match Play meetings. Ever the student, Clampett was 'looking forward to finding out why he's such a good player.' Wadkins meanwhile was undaunted in facing the No. 1 man from the European Tour. 'Hitting the ball the way I am, it really depends on putting,' said Lanny, one of the great streak players. 'If I can make some putts, I'll be okay.' The British followers were most concerned not about Norman, but about whether Lyle would be too emotionally drained to be ready for the test. 'It will be an equally tough match tomorrow,' Sandy said, 'and I don't even know how Floyd is playing.'

A record crowd of 12,500 spectators came out for the second round and they surely were not disappointed in witnessing the progression of Lyle along with victories by Ballesteros, Wadkins and Kite. The defending champion was the only one of the seeded players to win, taking the measure of Clampett 2 and 1. Floyd was beaten by Lyle 3 and 1; Norman was crushed 6 and 5 by Wadkins and Stadler lost to Kite 4 and 3.

Ballesteros was one down to Clampett after the morning round, three over par to two over. 'I played like a professional in the afternoon. I played like a 24 handicapper in the morning,' Ballesteros said. The Spaniard was six under par for the afternoon round. There was nothing particularly notable about their first 18. It will suffice to say that Clampett gained his lunchtime advantage with birdies on the last two holes. Ballesteros had a par at 17 and a birdie at 18. Seve was out in 32, three under par in the afternoon, and then was one ahead. They halved seven of the eight remaining holes, both scoring birdies on the two par-fives, and Ballesteros also birdied No. 15 for his winning margin.

The notorious third green provided an unforgettable experience for Clampett. The green is double-tiered with an extremely steep slope. The hole was cut close to the slope on the upper level. Bobby left his approach short of the green. He should have run the ball up the slope but instead tried to pitch it to the hole with his distinctive pitch shot in which he opens the blade of his club and skids it under the ball. He underplayed the shot fractionally and the ball rolled all the way back and off the green again. He tried again, with the same result. On the third try, Clampett made the upper tier with a conventional pitch, but that was purely for personal satisfaction because Ballesteros, who was near the cup in three, had won the hole and squared the match.

Ballesteros went ahead at No. 4 with an eagle-three, hitting a five-iron to within 12 feet of the hole. 'That brought my confidence back,' Seve later said. 'That was the key.' They halved the remaining outward holes, both with birdies at No. 8, and continued with halves until No. 15, where Ballesteros made his victory-clinching birdie from 20 feet.

With Norman not playing well, all Wadkins needed were pars through the morning to build his four-up advantage. Norman was two over par, including birdies on the last two holes, and Wadkins was two under. Greg drove the ball well enough, but his iron play was below his standard. He improved after lunch but so did Wadkins, who hit two of the best shots of the championship. Lanny won the first three holes of the afternoon to be seven ahead, and had a masterful stroke at No. 3, a two-iron of 198 yards, uphill and into the wind, that finished six inches from the flag. 'To put it over the hump on top was what I was trying to do,' Lanny said. 'To get to six inches was a bonus.' (Coming from Clampett against Ballesteros, such a shot might have altered the course of the championship.) The other brilliant blow by Wadkins was his four-wood on No. 12, which was on the flag every inch of the way and finished four feet from the hole. 'That was game, set and match,' Wadkins said. 'I thought it was going in the hole.' Lanny closed out the match, 6 and 5, with a par at the next hole.

In the eight holes between those two shots, Wadkins was never in trouble, but knew he couldn't relax either. Norman won the eighth and ninth holes with birdies, and that was enough of a reminder for Lanny. 'I had played match play enough in my amateur career to know a lot of things can happen,' Wadkins said. 'I knew Greg was such a good player, capable of birdies on four or five holes in a row, that if I made a couple of mistakes, he could blow right past me.'

After Norman, Wadkins had no apprehension about facing Ballesteros, to whom he lost 3 and 1 in the 1979 World Match Play. 'At least I've played Seve,' Lanny said. 'I've played a lot of golf with Seve over the years (including the final round when Ballesteros took his first American victory in the Greater Greensboro Open). With Greg, I didn't know what to expect. We've been friends for a while and our wives have been friends, but we have never played.'

In contrast to those two great shots by Wadkins, a couple of Lyle's errant shots were the focal points of his 3 and 1 victory over Floyd, who felt he had been against two opponents, Sandy and the crowd. On two occasions Raymond felt that the natural partisanship had tipped over to outright interference to Lyle's advantage. At the 10th hole of the afternoon, Lyle's ball hit into the crowd and rebounded favorably. Then at No. 17, Floyd insisted that Lyle's drive was headed out of bounds until the ball was kept in play by a spectator. 'That crowd was hostile,' Raymond said. 'It was something I've never experienced in this country before. How can you be happy when your opponent's ball is going out of bounds and it ends back on the fairway?'

On the par-three 10th Floyd hit 27 feet from the hole after Lyle, apparently having missed the green, was on the fringe 35 feet away. Raymond snapped, 'Why didn't they put it in the hole?' Sandy retorted, 'Because I didn't pay them enough money.' Lyle won the hole with a par, going four up, when Floyd three-putted.

Floyd came back to win the 12th and 13th holes, only to then hit a disastrous shot at No. 14. Raymond hit a wedge to four feet on his third shot at No. 12, scoring a birdie, while Lyle got a par after leaving his wedge shot 25 feet from the hole. Floyd birdied the next from five feet after a five-iron approach and Lyle got a one-putt par. Raymond's tee shot at the short 14th was far off the mark. 'It was very fat,' Lyle said. 'He mistimed it. That was about the only bad shot he hit all day, and it was at a vital stage.' Sandy won the hole with a par, but another in his series of wayward second shots enabled Floyd to take No. 15 with a par. Lyle thus remained two ahead. Both got pars on the 16th and Floyd was left to win the 17th and 18th holes in order to stay in the match.

Seeing the flight of Lyle's approach shot, Raymond believed he at least had won No. 17. Sandy hooked the shot toward the gardens out of bounds. The ball disappeared into the crowd for a few seconds before rolling back on the fairway. Lyle then hit a wedge to within eight inches of the hole and Floyd conceded the birdie and the match before departing with a noticeably brief handshake. 'I don't think my ball would have gone out of bounds,' Lyle maintained later. 'And I think there were other things that upset Ray. He was annoyed about the cameras clicking and he was really annoyed with himself when he lost the 14th.'

Clearly, however, Lyle was inspired by the crowds. 'They have been fantastic,' Sandy said, 'and I have needed a bit of an uplift to keep me going a few times.' Lyle took their encouragement and won three successive holes starting from No. 15, two with birdies, and was two ahead at lunch. He maintained an advantage through the afternoon as the gallery became increasingly larger and sometimes boisterous. 'I suppose they were a bit one-sided,' Lyle said. 'But Ray must have expected that when he played me on my home ground. Of course, they were partisan.'

The victory set the stage for a rematch in the semifinal against Kite, who beat Lyle 3 and 2 in a memorable Ryder Cup duel. Kite had 10 birdies in that match and Lyle, eight. 'It will be a bit of a grudge match, although Tom is a nice guy,' Sandy said. 'I just want to get even with him for the golf he played last year. I don't feel sore about it. I played well, got beat and good luck to the chap who beat me. There are holes here he can't reach. I must be the favorite. Yet he's straight. If I'm hitting well, I can be straight also.'

When Kite entered the press center following his 4 and 3 decision over Stadler, the first mention was of the forthcoming match. 'Sandy told me early in the week he wanted a rematch,' Kite related, ' and I know he will come out tomorrow with blood in his eyes. Sandy has a lot going for him. The match with Nick Faldo was a boost and now, beating Raymond, he's riding high. I have proved I can beat Sandy, but he's such a good player, such a strong player, and this golf course is so long. The match a year ago will certainly have no bearing. His game has changed, my game has changed and we will be playing for ourselves rather than our countries.'

Kite, the winner of one 1982 tournament in America, the Bay Hill Classic, said his match against Stadler 'proved to be much easier than I thought it was going to be. It was a good match, an interesting match, but Craig didn't play well at all and I gave him opportunities. We both played so poorly early in the afternoon, it was a joke. At the third Craig did something I have never seen him do. He topped an iron. At the next hole Craig ran a putt by five feet and missed. From that point on, I played well.'

One ahead after the morning round and still one ahead through six holes of the afternoon, Kite then settled down and finished his match in clinical style. He won the seventh, eighth and ninth holes, two with pars, then lost No. 10 to Stadler's 28-foot birdie. Kite's birdies at the 12th and 13th holes provided a five-up margin and from then on, it was a matter of time. Stadler managed a birdie to win No. 14, but Kite closed him out with a par to halve the 15th hole. Tom was glad to get off lightly. 'When you have a close match,' he said, 'it takes something out of you physically and mentally. Last night I got into the tub and I was afraid I would go to sleep. I would slide right under and miss my tee time. But match play, I love it.'

Another dark, winter-like day was in the offing for the semifinals, but it was still a memorable occasion for the European Tour players and spectators. Ballesteros overtook Wadkins for a 3 and 1 victory while Lyle demolished Kite 8 and 7. Seve admittedly 'played just good enough to win' but Lyle was so far ahead that he didn't realize he had won until an official announced the result.

Wadkins was two-up on Ballesteros after the morning round. Lanny sank putts of 16 and 25 feet on the 15th and 16th holes, respectively, for the birdies that produced his advantage. Ballesteros had squared the match three times previously after taking an early lead with his seven-iron shot to three feet at the short second hole. Lanny immediately drew level at the third when the Spaniard missed the green and bogeyed. Seve three-putted the next par-three hole, the fifth, and went one-down. Their match was squared again with Ballesteros' wedge to five feet to birdie No. 6. Another bogey dropped Seve to a one-hole deficit at the eighth. There, he missed the green and missed a par-saving three-footer while Wadkins had an easy two-putt par from eight feet. At No. 9, Lanny three-putted from 40 feet to bring the match back to level. A three-putt bogey from 23 feet cost Ballesteros the 11th hole. Both birdied No. 12, then Wadkins lost the 13th by missing the green and then his three-foot putt. After his wins on the 15th and 16th holes, Lanny had an opportunity to further increase his lead at No. 17 but failed on an eight-foot birdie attempt. Ballesteros, with the pressure off, was left to birdie from three feet and win the hole. The situation was reversed at the 18th hole. Seve missed from six feet and Wadkins holed from three feet to restore his margin to two ahead.

The key to the afternoon round, and the match, was that Ballesteros failed to hit a green from the 10th through 15th holes yet did not lose any of those holes to Wadkins, who missed three modest putts, one from seven feet and two from four feet. It reminded one of what Lanny said earlier in the week, that he was striking the ball well enough and his success would depend only on his putting. Eventually, Wadkins' drives did him in, but it was the putter that caused his desperation.

Ballesteros won three holes in a row on the first nine of the afternoon, then dropped the next hole. He won No. 9 and was one up with nine holes remaining. Seve birdied the par-five No. 4 from six feet, won the short fifth when Wadkins missed the green, and birdied the sixth from eight feet. Wadkins won No. 7 with a routine par as Ballesteros three-putted for a bogey from 35 feet. Lanny took three strokes to reach the ninth green and Ballesteros again won with a par.

Ballesteros did not reach another green in regulation figures until the 16th hole, yet remained one ahead. On the six holes in question, three were halved in pars and three were halved in bogeys. Ballesteros went out of bounds off the tee at No. 12. He got the half by sinking an eight-foot putt for bogey. Wadkins then missed his four-footer. 'That was a crazy hole,' Seve said later. 'I should have tried to hit up the right side, and chip and putt for a birdie. I was too ambitious. I tried to go over the trees (left). I was lucky to halve the hole.'

Wadkins missed putts from four feet at No. 14 and seven feet at No. 15, then Lanny took his driver at the 16th tee and hit into a bunker. He came out to the left of the green, under some branches in the brush. He chopped the ball out backhanded with his putter and just barely cleared the undergrowth. Lanny's chip did not make the slope and came rolling back to his feet. He picked up the ball and conceded the hole. At No. 17, now two behind, Wadkins tried to rip a drive down the left side in an attempt to reach the green in two. The tee shot sailed through the trees and over the fence, where it was later found and identified by a spectator in a garden. Hitting a provisional ball, Wadkins reached the green in five strokes and conceded the hole and the match to Ballesteros' three.

'I think we both were a little tired,' Ballesteros said, in defense of their lackluster play. 'It was very difficult all day, cold and windy. We had problems with cross winds, right to left. The course played very long also, because it had rained for so many days.'

Ballesteros was simply pleased to be in the championship match. 'I must say I didn't play great, but it was enough to be in the final,' Seve said. 'I can't be worse than second and it's been a long time since I've seen second. Before, I've played better and didn't reach the final. That's the game.' Ballesteros noted, 'Sandy is going very well. One problem is that he hasn't practiced the last few holes.'

True, Lyle played six fewer holes than Ballesteros in his rout of Kite. Sandy was in almost total command, winning the first three holes and going on to the 8-and-7 verdict. Kite's play was almost a parody of his golf in beating Lyle in the Ryder Cup matches. Sandy did not have a score above par on his card until the first hole of the afternoon. He won those first three holes of the morning because Kite bogeyed all. Tom failed on par-saving putts from six feet at the first and second holes and took three strokes to reach the third green. Both birdied the par-five No. 4 and continued with halves in pars until No. 9, where Kite missed a saving putt from six feet again, dropping to four down. Kite hit into the trees off the 10th tee and lost that hole with another bogey. Sandy won the 13th with an 18-foot birdie, moving six ahead, and they played out the remainder of the round with pars, failing to birdie either of the par-five closing holes.

Lyle got a minor scare in the afternoon when he bogeyed the first hole and lost No. 2 to Kite's birdie. But Tom then made an extraordinary error, or series of errors, reminiscent of Clampett against Ballesteros on the second day. He lost No. 3 when he seemed more likely to win the hole. He made the most of a poor drive by hitting a lengthy approach shot, just short of the green. Lyle played a good third shot onto the upper tier of the green after driving into a bunker, and Kite, by all appearances, was in command of the situation. Who could then believe that Tom took four attempts to get his ball on the top level? Three times, his chip-and-run failed to reach the crest of the steep slope and came rolling back to his feet. He finally chipped over the green, and a possible four became an eight. If Lyle had lost that hole, who knows what might have happened. 'It was a relief going to the fourth tee,' Sandy admitted.

What did happen was that Lyle won the seventh hole with a par, the eighth with a 12-foot birdie and closed out the match with an eight-foot birdie at No. 11. By then, Sandy had lost track of the score, so sure was he of a victory. He started walking towards the 12th tee, not knowing it was over. 'Honestly, I didn't realize I had won it,' he said, 'until the Marshal gave the score and we shook hands.' Lyle credited Kite's poor start to misfortune. 'He hit some good shots and didn't come up with pars. He hit some really good-looking putts that didn't go in,' Sandy said. 'I made a few silly mistakes of my own, but I played quite well, all in all. I drove well and got my one-iron working well.'

Thus Lyle was set for his second World Match Play final, having lost to Greg Norman in 1980. 'At least I've had the experience of playing in a final at the Suntory,' he said. 'It's not so much of an occasion for me. The last time, it was an occasion and Norman made the shots when he needed them.'

The final developed into one of the great 'occasions' in the World Match Play Championship. Although scoring was greatly affected by the weather and 11 holes were won with pars, that did not diminish the magnitude of the match, which did not end until the first extra hole when Ballesteros sank a 30-foot birdie putt across the soggy first green. That was the only birdie of the week on that hole and followed a resurgence by Lyle which featured five birdies on the closing seven holes.

The match was an absorbing encounter, including fluctuations in the morning round caused as much by error as virtue. Lyle took the first advantage, winning No. 2 with a par after Ballesteros hit into a bunker on that par-three hole. Seve got back to all-square at the third hole, also with a par, because Lyle took three strokes in reaching the green. Ballesteros drove out of bounds and lost No. 4 with a bogey while Lyle birdied there. The Spaniard struck back with a four-iron to eight feet and won the fifth hole with a birdie, but promptly hit into a bunker on his approach to the sixth. Lyle hit a wedge to seven feet, holed the putt and went one ahead for the third time. That margin lasted only two holes. Sandy bogeyed No. 8 and Seve birdied, making the putt from six feet. They finished the first nine with Lyle having 34, one under par, and Ballesteros, level par.

Lyle took the lead for a fourth time at No. 10, scoring a birdie with a five-iron from six feet. They had pars at the 11th and 12th holes. Ballesteros missed a six-footer on his birdie try at the par-five No. 12, while Lyle took three strokes to reach the green and failed on his 15-footer. Sandy allowed Ballesteros to draw level again at No. 13, three-putting for bogey from 23 feet. Neither had good birdie chances on the next two holes, then Ballesteros won three in a row to have a three-up advantage at lunch. At No. 16, Seve holed an 18-foot birdie. Sandy hit his one-iron approach out of bounds on the 17th, enabling Ballesteros to win that hole with a par. Seve reached the 18th green with a driver and three-iron, then two-putted from 35 feet for the birdie. Lyle hit into the sand on his approach and made a par. Ballesteros shot 70, two under par, and Lyle shot par 72.

The afternoon play began with three holes won with pars, two by Lyle. Ballesteros took three strokes to reach the first green and missed a three-foot putt. Lyle three-putted No. 2 from 55 feet for a bogey then, after a five-minute rain delay, Seve missed the green at the third hole for another bogey. Ballesteros made his third bogey of the round with a poor tee shot, missing the green at the par-three No. 5 and his margin was one. The scoring was not distinguished because of the high winds and rain on the already-waterlogged course, but the match was as tight as anyone could wish. They halved the sixth and seventh holes. Lyle missed a 10-foot birdie chance at No. 6 and Ballesteros missed a five-footer at the seventh, where both scored bogeys. Seve won the eighth and ninth holes to regain his three-up margin from the morning round. Both finished the nine in 37, two over par. Lyle three-putted the eighth from 33 feet and Ballesteros holed a 30-footer for birdie on the ninth.

They scored pars on No. 10, then Ballesteros blew an opportunity at the 11th to go four ahead and lost the hole, reducing his lead to two. Seve left his 15-footer for a birdie out to the left and missed a three-footer for par coming back. He forgot that misery at No. 12, holing a massive 45-footer for an eagle. 'The ball was going at a fair pace,' Lyle said later. 'It would have been seven or eight feet past if it hadn't gone in.' Although three down, Sandy made a birdie on the hole, beginning his run of five birdies in seven holes that would erase Ballesteros' margin. Lyle made a 10-footer at the 13th and Ballesteros' eight-footer was out on the high side. Sandy holed from 24 feet on No. 14, while Seve took two putts from 60 feet, having an awkward first putt across the ridge from the lower level. 'I had my adrenalin going then,' said Lyle, who had cut the deficit to one. 'Along before the 13th I wasn't feeling good about the match. But there was hope. I had done it from six down (against Nick Faldo) and I knew I could do it from three down.'

Another rain squall erupted as they were playing the 15th hole. Lyle's birdie string ended, and Sandy had to even struggle for a par. He had a 45-footer that 'never got going' and was 10 feet short of the cup. Ballesteros tried a 12-footer for birdie and missed to the right by inches and Lyle was left to make his pressure-packed putt to save par and halve the hole. Sandy squared the match with his birdie on No. 16. Ballesteros was in the right rough off the tee, 20 yards behind Lyle, and hit onto the green, 14 feet short of the flag. Sandy hooked his approach onto the green and was 18 feet away. He holed that putt, raising his arms to the tumultuous applause. The crowd quiet again, Ballesteros left his 14-footer out to the right by two inches. There was no break in his line, as Seve expected.

Ahead were the two par-fives. Lyle hit a good one-iron off the 17th tee and Ballesteros drove into the left fairway. Both hit second shots to the right, away from the flag. Seve chipped first, 15 feet beyond the cup. Then Lyle did the same, over to the fringe, 18 feet from the hole. 'Seve opened the hole to me,' Sandy later remarked, 'then I opened the hole to him.' Lyle's putt was out to the left and Ballesteros' putt, out to the right. They took pars and continued to No. 18.

Both drove well on the closing hole, with Lyle 20 yards ahead of Ballesteros on the left side. Ballesteros took a three-wood and hit to the right front of the green. The pin was back left. Lyle's one-iron approach was pin high on the same side as Ballesteros. Neither were within 25 yards of the hole, although Lyle was marginally closer. Seve struck a very good putt, however, and left it 30 inches short. Sandy's attempt was also short, by about three feet. They putted out and went on to the extra hole, as the rain began to pour again.

If the first hole were to be won by either, the overwhelming odds were that it would be with a par. As noted earlier, there had been no birdies on the 471-yard hole all week. Lyle's tee shot was right and Ballesteros' shot, left, about 25 yards behind. As they walked towards their second shots, a heavy storm struck for a few minutes, almost flooding the low-lying areas. Ballesteros' wood to the green skipped across the water before settling 30 feet from the flag. Lyle hit a low cutter with his one-iron, off the bank on the left and in good position behind the flag, just beyond pin-high.

The players waited for the crew with squeegees to sweep the water away. The rain had almost stopped by the time Ballesteros addressed his putt, a right-to-left breaker that Seve was merely trying to get close. 'There was so much water on the green,' he said, 'I didn't know what the speed would be.' To Seve's surprise — and everyone else's, especially Lyle's — the ball rolled directly into the cup and Ballesteros raised his putter joyfully. Lyle had to try to duplicate the near-impossible and could not. Two years before, Sandy had lost to Norman on the 36th hole. He had now been beaten by Ballesteros on the 37th, losing but coming closer to that elusive first victory by a British player in the World Match Play.

'Nobody likes losing, but at least I gave my all,' said Lyle, whose esteem had risen greatly over the four days. 'I don't feel bitterly disappointed. He made a birdie and I ran out of holes.' Demonstrating the best in sportsmanship, Lyle refused to say that Ballesteros had been lucky. 'It went in the middle of the hole. It couldn't be that lucky,' Sandy said. 'No, I really didn't expect him to make it, but weird things can happen in this game, as has been shown this week.'

Ballesteros returned the compliment. 'You can't play better golf than that,' Seve said. 'He made five birdies in seven holes, a tremendous comeback.'

7. The U.S. Tour

When the 1982 PGA Tour ended, Calvin Peete must have wished he was as young as Hal Sutton and Hal Sutton had to be envious of Calvin Peete's ability to hit a golf ball almost any place he wanted. Craig Stadler, Raymond Floyd and Tom Watson were the dominant figures on the Tour, but Sutton and Peete were the ones they were talking about after the season had run its course. Peete, with victories in the Milwaukee, B.C. and Pensacola Opens and the Anheuser-Busch Classic, tied Stadler for first place in tournaments won with four. But Stadler's were more lucrative — the Masters, the World Series of Golf ($100,000) and the Tucson and Kemper Opens — and it paid off with the Arnold Palmer Trophy, which goes to the year's leading money winner. Stadler and Floyd, who won the PGA Championship in one of only three tournaments in which the winner led from wire to wire, fought a good battle for the money prize, a battle that was climaxed with Stadler's sudden-death victory over Floyd in the World Series.

With Player of the Year now determined by a set process (so many points for placings in each tournament and extra points for the majors), there was no doubt about the winner. It was Watson for the fifth time in six years off his triumphs in the British Open and U.S. Open. But if Peete had played better early in the year, perhaps he would have stolen Player of the Year from Watson with his second-half rush.

For that matter, Sutton might have done it for the same reason. The 1980 U.S. Amateur champion from Shreveport, Louisiana, struggled through the first six months of the season and hit the depths when he missed the cut in the British Open at Troon. Depressed by his showing and a marriage that ended in early divorce, he returned to Centenary College for consultation with Floyd Horgen, his old college coach. Horgen has a drill that brings out the flaws in a swing and when Sutton returned to the Tour he was a revived young man, his confidence restored. After tying for second place behind Peete in the next-to-last tournament of the year, Pensacola, Sutton won the last, the Disney World Classic, in a playoff with Bill Britton. The $72,000 check gave the 24-year-old pro $237,434, demolishing Jerry Pate's record for winnings by a rookie of $153,102 set in 1976. In 31 tournaments, Sutton placed in the money 25 times, had a first, three seconds, one third, one fourth, one seventh and one ninth. He averaged 71.06.

Sutton was only one of the record-setters. The others: Bob Gilder, who set a mark for the opening 54 holes of a tournament with 192 in the Westchester Classic; Curtis Strange, whose $263,378 was the most money won by a player without a victory (old record: $230,500 by Bill Rogers in 1979); number of $200,000-plus winners in a season (15) and number of $300,000 winners (seven).

There was a record $15,089,596 paid out in official money – up $914,183 from the year before — and nearly one-sixth of it was divided up among Stadler ($446,462), Floyd ($386,809), Tom Kite ($341,081), Peete ($318,470), Watson ($316,483), Gilder ($308,648) and Lanny Wadkins ($306,827). It may be significant that of those seven, only one, Stadler (29), was under age 30 at the end of the season and one was over 39, Floyd (40). Peete was 39, and he has to be an inspiration to anybody who has attempted something and met with failure more than once. Peete started playing golf when he was 23, which is rather late, and failed twice before earning his Tour card. In his first six years on the Tour, he had won only once, the 1979 Milwaukee Open. Now he's the most accurate man on the Tour. He repeated as the leader in driving accuracy, hitting fairways .813 percent of the time, and succeeded himself as the Greens In Regulation champ by hitting them almost three-fourths (.724) of the time.

Like Peete, there were others who found the secret to success and held onto it. Stadler had won only three previous tournaments in his career before he came up with his four-win season. Gilder had won only twice, then did better than that in 1982 with victories in the Byron Nelson, Westchester and Bank of Boston events. Jay Haas, like Peete and Sutton, came on strong at the end of the year to win the Hall of Fame and Texas tournaments, giving him five victories in his career. Wayne Levi became the first man to win a PGA tournament while playing a colored ball when he took the Hawaiian Open and late in the year came back to add the LaJet Classic, a fine performance by a man who had started the year as a 'rabbit' after scoring three victories in 1979 and 1980.

Watson, Floyd and Wadkins each won three times on the U.S. Tour. Watson's trio gave him 28 for his career, moving him into 12th place on the all-time standings past Walter Hagen and Henry Picard, who each have 27. Watson was 33 at the end of the season and still had maybe 10 years of his career in front of him. But it's doubtful whether he will ever equal the achievements of Jack Nicklaus, something Watson admits. In his 21st year on the Tour and playing a limited schedule, Nicklaus won the Colonial Invitation and $232,645, good for 12th place. He also placed second in three tournaments, giving him 69 victories and 51 seconds during his pro career. When the 1982 season ended, he was a little less than $8,000 shy of $4 million in U.S. Tour earnings. Nobody else in any sport has done as well over such a long period of time.

Nicklaus would turn 43 shortly after the 1983 season began, posing the question of how much longer he can play so well. If anybody is looking for a successor, they might look at some of those who stepped into the limelight in 1982. Sutton, of course. Only 24, his future may be unlimited. Bobby Clampett, of whom much was expected when he joined the Tour late in 1980, scored his first victory as a pro in the Southern Open. Gilder, Haas, Pate, Wadkins, Strange and Bruce Lietzke still have many good years in front of them and Kite's career may be just shifting into high gear. Kite won one tournament, the Bay Hill Classic, and had three seconds in 1982 and in the last two years has earned more than $700,000 while winning only twice and placing second numerous times. And again he won the scoring title, averaging 70.21 to Peete's 70.33.

The year was not without the unusual. Jim Simons, legally blind and contemplating withdrawing after the third round because of an excruciating pain in his left eye, came on to shoot a 32 on Pebble Beach's back nine in the final round to overtake Stadler and win the Bing Crosby Pro-Am; Tim Norris, a little-known second-year pro, shot the best 72 holes of the year, a 25-under-par 259, and won the Hartford Open from wire to wire; Australian Bob Shearer, on the verge of leaving the Tour, won at Tallahassee and placed second in two of the next three tournaments; Payne Stewart, twice a winner in Asia, won in the U.S., taking the Quad Cities Open; Lietzke, only 31, talked about retirement while winning the Canadian Open and Ben Crenshaw, his golf game in such a shambles that he left the Tour early, a disillusioned man, took the putting championship with an average of 28.65 a round, yet placed 83rd among the money winners with $54,277.

As the season ended, the winds of change were in the air. In 1983, the Tour was to consist of all exempt players; no more Monday qualifiers. A second tour was in the works and a split tour was more than just a gleam in Commissioner Deane Beman's eyes. With only one qualifier a year, it figured that those with frivolous thoughts of joining the Tour would be unwilling to wait a year between qualifiers, the Tour adding only 50 new players each year. Such a system probably would have discouraged a Calvin Peete, but it should produce a stronger, more organized Tour.

Joe Garagiola Tucson Open — $300,000
Winner: Craig Stadler

To say Craig Stadler came out of the box with a rush would be an understatement of his showing in the first tournament of the 1982 season. He didn't just come out rushing, he was in full gallop. The No. 8 money winner of 1981 began with 65, 64, 66 and with a seven-stroke lead to play with, slacked off to a 71 and 266, a 14-under-par score that gave him a three-stroke triumph in the Joe Garagiola Tucson Open.

Stadler, whose only win in 1981 came in the Kemper Open, had played little in the fall segment of the tour. But nobody would have believed it off his first three rounds. The only ones who gave him trouble in the final round were Vance Heafner and Bob Gilder, but Gilder's threat turned out to be a computer error. And Heafner's charge, a 64 in the final round, was only good enough to get him a tie with John Mahaffey for second place.

If Stadler's steady play reduced the drama for the final rounds, there were enough sidelights earlier to keep everybody interested. To wit, the appearance of defending champion Johnny Miller, a robbery and colored golf balls.

Victims of the robbery were Scott Hoch and his wife, Sally. The night before the first round of the tournament, a man posing as a police officer knocked at their motel door. When they answered, he barged in, threatened to kill them if they looked at him and said the FBI was after him. He held them for an hour, then tied their wrists and left with $200 and jewelry. Sally soon got free and untied her husband. Shaken by the experience, Hoch shot a 73 in the first round, but he came back with 69, 66, 66 and tied for 15th place at 274.

Fluorescent orange and lime green balls, which had made an impression among amateurs a year earlier, finally found their way into the golf bags of the touring pros, giving an Easter egg feeling when some groups got their shots on the green. The only thing different about the balls is their color — otherwise, they are the same size, same compression.

Miller had to travel halfway around the world to make the tournament. On Sunday, he won $500,000 in the Sun City Challenge in Bophuthatswana, but his playoff with Severiano Ballesteros caused him to miss his flight home. He finally arrived in Salt Lake City on Tuesday and the next morning he departed for Tucson, arriving in time to make his tee time for the pro-am.

Miller has won the Tucson Open. He might have won it again if not for jet lag and Stadler. Miller shot a creditable 277 and said, 'The tour probably won't start for me until Phoenix.'

Meanwhile, Stadler's lead went from one stroke to four strokes, to seven strokes and the only battle in the final round was for second. At one time or other, 14 players had a shot at it — for a while the scoreboard showed Gilder only a stroke behind, although he was actually six back — with Heafner and Mahaffey, who had a 65, tying at 269.

Bob Hope Desert Classic — $304, 500
Winner: Ed Fiori

It was almost as if the 1981 season had continued for Tom Kite in the Bob Hope Desert Classic. Just as he was so often in 1981, Kite was a contender but not a winner. A combination of his own mistake at the final hole of regulation and a shocking birdie putt by Ed Fiori at the second hole of a sudden-death playoff saw to that.

Fiori, whose wife, Debbie, was back home in Sugarland, Texas, awaiting the birth of their first child, was one shot ahead with a 268 after 72 holes, but the Hope is a 90-hole tournament played over four fine courses. When they teed off at the 90th hole it was Kite who was out front. Fiori was a stroke behind; Rex Caldwell, two back.

Kite's drive at the par-five 18th hole at Indian Wells was down the right side of the fairway and not very far — 'I was trying to hit it too hard and hit it on the neck,' he said — and it left him with no chance to reach the green in two. Kite played short of the lake protecting the green with his second shot, then hit his third well past the hole, out of birdie range. Fiori carried the water with his second shot, 20 feet from the hole. After Kite failed on his attempt to win the tournament, Fiori two-putted for a birdie that tied them at 335, a record-tying 25 under par.

Meanwhile, Caldwell stayed in the chase until a little past the beginning of the final nine, looking for a break. With two holes to go, it looked as if he was out of it when he heeled his drive into the crowd, the ball stopping in a clearing near TV trailers. He was 250 yards from the green and had a patch of trees between him and the fairway. But Caldwell hit a marvelous four-wood shot that knifed through the trees, hit the fairway and ran . . . onto the green, where it hit the hole and stopped less than a foot beyond it. The stunning shot moved Caldwell to within a stroke of Fiori, but he knew he probably needed an eagle at the final hole to have any chance of catching Kite. He parred and settled for third place at 337.

The playoff began at the par-three No. 15, which both birdied from four feet. At the 354-yard No. 16, Kite hit a perfect second shot, the ball landing on the green, then sucking back to within about four and a half feet of the hole. Fiori, who puts his right hand so far under when he grips a club that it's amazing he doesn't hook all the time, hit his approach onto the green, too, but 30 feet short of the cup.

'I thought I'd two-putt and he'd make his and it would be all over. I really didn't think I'd make mine,' said Fiori. But make it he did and when Kite missed his short one, the rotund Fiori had $54,000 for his third victory on the Tour.

Fiori and Kite were part of the crowd in the early rounds. Caldwell and Tateo (Jet) Ozaki, brother of Japan's more famous Jumbo Ozaki, jumped out in front in the first round with 64s at Indian Wells, the easiest of the four courses (the others are Bermuda Dunes, La Quinta and Eldorado and they all were in top condition for the tournament). Kite's 66 the second day put him at 134, two strokes out of the lead, and Fiori was a stroke behind him after a 65. Ozaki was in the lead with a 68–132 and Caldwell was second with 64–69—133.

Kite, aided by a 142-yard nine-iron shot that found the hole for an eagle two at the 18th hole (his ninth) at La Quinta, moved a stroke in front with a 66 for 200 and Fiori remained a step behind him with a 66 at Bermuda Dunes for 201 after 54 holes. Jet went into the start of a tailspin with 70, but Caldwell stayed close at 203 with a 70.

In the fourth round, Kite and Fiori switched places, Fiori taking over the lead at 268 with a 67 at Eldorado and Kite moving a shot back with a 69 at Indian Wells. Somebody pointed out to Fiori that if the Hope had been a regular tournament, one of 72 holes, he would be the winner, and he sighed, 'Yeah, I know.' For him, the real tournament was just beginning.

Phoenix Open — $300,000
Winner: Lanny Wadkins

No matter what his politics, put a golf club in Lanny Wadkins' hands and he's anything but a conservative. When Wadkins hits a ball to the green, he doesn't want to just get it close — he wants to put it in the hole. If he has an under-par round going, he wants to get it under 60.

Sometimes such tactics backfire and sometimes they pan out, and when they click the result is something on the order of Wadkins' performance in the Phoenix Open. He shot an eight-under-par 63 in the third round, aided by a hole-in-one, and then fought off a challenge by Jerry Pate in the final round for a six-stroke victory, the first for the 32-year-old pro since the Tournament Players Championship in 1979.

Wadkins' rounds went like this: 65 and two strokes out of the lead; 70 in the second round and still two strokes behind; 63 the third day and a four-shot lead, and 65 that was the icing. He had a 72-hole total of 263, which is 21 under par, and it was a most satisfying win. In 1972, Wadkins had lost to Homero Blancas in his first visit to Phoenix and placed second there the next two years.

Wadkins had to take a supporting role to Larry Nelson and the weather for the first two rounds. Nelson, the reigning PGA champion, carved out a 10-birdie 63 in the first round, but had to wait a day to learn how good that was as a cold rainstorm curtailed play, forcing the late starters to complete their round the next day. As it turned out, it was very good as only Tom Purtzer, with a 66, came close when the scores were counted on Friday. The second round was played on Saturday and Nelson let many chances elude him on the incoming nine, but his 70 was good enough to maintain his two-stroke margin at 133.

Wadkins had been bothered by a thumb injury for two years and to compensate for it he had shortened his swing. That enabled him to get a handle on his game and with it came renewed confidence. That was apparent at the 18th hole in the third round. Wadkins was seven under for the round when he hit a long drive far left. With a lake to the right of the green, the prudent golfer would have laid up, playing for a par at the par-five hole. Not Wadkins. He went for it, came up short, then got down in two for a 63 and a 198 total that put him four shots up on Morris Hatalsky, who had a 68.

By the 18th hole, Wadkins was riding a cloud of euphoria, pumped up by an ace at the 231-yard No. 13, a two-iron shot that took one bounce and dove into the cup. 'I felt good about my round, but compared with Lanny, I felt like I shot 100,' said Hatalsky.

Pate shot a 64 and lost a stroke to Wadkins, leaving him six in arrears, but he and Hatalsky had plans to catch Wadkins in the final. The only problem, it turned out, was that Wadkins heard what Hatalsky said on a TV interview. Hatalsky said he thought it would be difficult for Wadkins to come back with another fine round in the final, 'and I really got so pumped up I didn't go to sleep for an hour,' said Wadkins. 'I was determined I was going to shoot a helluva round.'

Pate applied the pressure with an eagle at the first hole and birdies at the third and fourth in the final round and that moved him to within three strokes of Wadkins. But Wadkins birdied No. 9 and 10, 'and I felt after I birdied those two holes, I had a comfortable lead,' said Wadkins.

It wasn't so comfortable. Pate birdied No. 10, 11 and 12, but he bogeyed No. 13 and that proved fatal. 'I lost my momentum. I birdied 14, so if I had birdied 13, I would have had a shot at it,' groaned Pate. 'I know it would have taken a 60, but the way I was playing I could have shot that.'

The way Wadkins was playing, even 60 wouldn't have been good enough for Pate. Wadkins and Pate both shot 65 and at the end all it got Pate was a good payday ($32,400) for second place.

Wickes-Andy Williams San Diego Open — $300,000
Winner: Johnny Miller

Of Johnny Miller's first 20 victories on the tour, 13 had come in tournaments (excluding Hawaii) on the West Coast. Only one tournament had eluded his grasp — the San Diego Open. No more.

Miller added the San Diego crown with a vintage Johnny Miller performance and for the second time in a month he defeated Jack Nicklaus by a stroke. In the Sun City Challenge in Bophuthatswana at the end of December, Miller and Severiano Ballesteros finished a stroke in front of Nicklaus, then Miller won the sudden-death playoff on the ninth hole and picked up $500,000. In the San Diego Open, Miller also edged Nicklaus by a stroke, but not before Nicklaus threw a scare into him with a closing 64.

'What were you trying to do? Pucker me a little?' asked Miller of Nicklaus after his 65–67–68–70—270. Until Nicklaus made his charge, it looked as if Miller's challenge would come from the three Toms who chased him after three rounds — Kite, Weiskopf and Watson. But, like the Miller of old, Johnny went into the final round oozing confidence. 'I'm probably the best front-runner in the world,' he said matter-of-factly.

Miller built up that confidence early. He blasted out a seven-under-par 65 on Torrey Pines' North course in the first round, tying him with Fuzzy Zoeller for the lead. The North course is the easier of the two courses used for the tournament, but the first round was played amid cold rain and wind.

Nicklaus was back in the pack with a 69, but he didn't go without notice. It was the first time he played in the tournament in 10 years after a tiff with the city over the redesigning of the courses. Nicklaus had huddled with the city planners when they decided to renovate the two municipal courses, but when it came time to seek bids, the city, Nicklaus noted, didn't invite him. Billy Casper got the job, and, said Nicklaus, 'I don't see much change. This still could be a sensational golf course.'

After Miller moved into a three-stroke lead with a 67 and a 36-hole total of 132, he also had something to say about the course: 'This is a U.S. Open course. It's as tough as Pebble Beach. This could be one of the premier courses in the world if they had a good tree-planting program.'

A 68 the third day gave Miller 200 and a three-stroke lead on Kite, who had a 66, and four on Weiskopf, who chipped in at the final hole for a 68. But Kite and Weiskopf moved aside as Nicklaus came barreling through in the final round. Nicklaus trailed by seven strokes at the start of the round, but 'I thought if I shot a 64 or 65 I'd have a chance of winning the tournament,' Nicklaus said.

Nicklaus eagled the ninth hole, capping a 32 on the front side, but he gained only two strokes on Miller. Birdies at No. 10 and 11 preceded a bogey, and the bogey was to prove fatal. Nicklaus reached the green at the par-five No. 18 with a three-wood second shot and dropped an eight-foot putt for his second eagle of the day. That gave him a 72-hole total of 271 and gave Miller, playing several groups behind him, a score to shoot at and somebody other than Kite to be concerned about.

Kite got to within a shot of Miller with a 15-foot birdie putt at 15, but Miller matched it minutes later with an eight-footer of his own. Trailing by two, Kite attempted to reach the 18th green with his second shot and came up short, his ball bouncing into the lake.

All Miller needed to win was a par and after a good drive, he had to make a decision. He had 212 yards to the front of the green. Go for it? Miller laid up, hit a wedge to within 20 feet and two-putted for par.

Bing Crosby National Pro-Am — $300,000
Winner: Jim Simons

Jim Simons set two records in the Bing Crosby Pro-Am: For the tournament, with a 72-hole, 14-under-par 274, and best score by a man playing much of the time with one eye.

Without his contact lenses or glasses, Simons is legally blind (see Chapter 5, The PGA Championship). In the third round, at difficult Spyglass Hill, Simons had to remove the contacts in his left eye. In addition to the eye trouble, Simons had tendonitis in his left shoulder. But he's had trouble with his shoulder throughout his career, a souvenir from some horseplay during his senior year at Wake Forest, and he's learned how to play with, or despite, it.

In the final round, Simons wore dark glasses between shots, but he could see enough to understand that maybe Craig Stadler was going to run away with the tournament. An eight-under-par 64 at Cypress Point in the third round had given Stadler a two-stroke lead on Simons with 18 holes to go and that edge quickly became five strokes after eight holes of the final round.

Meanwhile, Simons was plugging away, waiting for a break, or getting ready to accept second place. The breaks came and soon it was Stadler who was trying to catch up. At the par-four No. 9 hole, Stadler hit a ball into a bunker and took a double bogey. He still led by one when they approached the green at the par-five No. 14 and when they walked off he trailed by a stroke. Stadler's wedge hit the green and went over and he played a poor chip back. Simons' shot to the green might have had the same fate, but the ball struck the flagstick on the first bounce and stopped two feet away. Simons birdied, Stadler bogeyed.

Simons came up short with his approach at the 15th green and ultimately bogeyed when his three-foot par putt slipped past the hole. Now they were tied and that's the way they stood when they came to the par-three No. 17, a hole backed by the Pacific Ocean. Stadler used a four-iron and hooked it left of the green into the rocks on the beach. After taking a drop, Stadler holed a 10-footer for a bogey, but his hopes had vanished. Simons used a three-iron off the tee and hit his ball six feet from the hole. Simons agonizes on the greens, but putts fairly well and this one he dropped, giving him a two-stroke lead for the final hole.

Using his metal-wood, a stainless steel club with more loft than a driver and a clubface that gives the ball less spin, Simons split the fairway at No. 18 and got a meticulous par for a brilliant 66. Stadler used a driver on his second shot in an attempt to reach the green, but he came off it and hit his ball to the right of the green. He also parred.

Until Simons and Stadler got into their head-to-head battle, much of the tournament talk was about odd-colored golf balls the pros were using. Fluorescent orange balls and bright lime green balls were in such profusion during the Crosby that at times it looked as if the Easter bunny had visited a green. Jerry Pate made a hole-in-one with an orange ball and a one-iron at the 233-yard No. 16 at Cypress Point, the famous hole that has the ocean for a fairway, but Pate failed to survive the 54-hole cut. (The first three rounds of the Crosby are played on three different courses with the pros paired with amateurs. Only the top 60 pros and the leading 25 teams play the final round at Pebble Beach.)

Bruce Leitzke, using a lime green ball, tied Forrest Fezler for the first-round lead at 66 and George Burns, with 67–69—136, took over the second day, a stroke in front of Simons and Hall Sutton. Then came Stadler with an eagle and six birdies for his eight-under 64 at Cypress. The Tucson Open winner looked as if he was headed for his second victory of the year, but even in perfect weather — the Crosby was played in its best weather ever — Pebble Beach has bite, and Stadler got bit.

Hawaiian Open — $325,000
Winner: Wayne Levi

The Hawaiian Open is one of golf's television delights. Fans sitting in front of the TV sets in the northern and eastern parts of the mainland put another log on the fire and sigh for the beginning of their golf season as they watch the touring pros play with swaying palms, gentle surf and saronged women serving as backdrops. And, to be sure, the telecasts are good public relations to attract the tourist trade to the Pacific islands.

It's just as well the first two rounds of the 1982 Hawaiian Open at Waialae Country Club were not telecast. Bad PR. Instead of trade winds and sunshine, the course was hit by a Kona wind, which in the Eastern United States would be translated into a Nor'easter, and the Kona brought rain. Enough rain the night before the first round that the start of play was delayed 90 minutes while the water on course worked its way through the lava and earth. And even though everybody teed off that day, 72 didn't complete their round as rain intervened.

But when the mainlanders turned on their sets on Saturday and Sunday for the final two rounds the only problem they saw was the wind . . . and a leader playing an orange golf ball. Not just using an orange ball, but winning with it. His name was Wayne Levi and he made history when he used what its manufacturer calls an 'optic orange' ball for an 11-under-par 72–68–67–70—277, the first touring pro to win with anything but a white ball.

That Levi's total was 13 strokes higher than turned in by Hale Irwin in his victory a year earlier was due to changes in some bunkers and tees and more rough, plus the weather. The leader with a five-under-par 67 the first day was Bobby Clampett, who played when the weather was at its worst. Andy North, with two eagles en route to a second straight 69, and Greg Powers, with a 66, tied for the second-round lead at 138, a stroke in front of Clampett, Tom Watson and Scott Simpson.

North came up with another eagle in the third round as Levi carved out five birdies for a 67 that tied them for the lead at 207. But the field was bunched up behind them and, with the playful wind a member of the cast, everybody had a chance. An eagle at the ninth hole gave Levi a one-stroke lead with nine holes to go, but the battle was just heating up. North caught him with birdies at 10 and 11 and Ben Crenshaw pulled within a shot with an eagle at 13. Levi dropped back with a bogey at 12 and Simpson took his place with a birdie at 13.

Then they started dropping off. Crenshaw three-putted 14 and bogeyed 15. Simpson hit over the green at 15 and bogeyed. North three-putted 15 and Levi made a six-footer for birdie, putting Levi on top for keeps at 12 under par. A bogey at 16 cut his margin over North, Clampett and Simpson to a stroke, but North bogeyed 16 and 17, Clampett hit his tee shot out of bounds at the 200-yard 17th and the best Simpson could do was keep in step with Levi to take second place at 278.

'I'm very proud of myself for the way I hung in there,' said Levi afterward, and well he might have been. After failing to land among the top 60 money winners the year before, he was a Monday morning 'rabbit' — but the win ended that travail and the victory with a colored golf ball earned him a niche in golf lore.

Glen Campbell Los Angeles Open — $300,000
Winner: Tom Watson

For 70 holes, the Los Angeles Open title was in the hands of Johnny Miller . . . and he let it slip away. Again in the playoff, it was his . . . but Tom Watson took it away.

With two holes to go at Riviera Country Club, as a national television audience watched what it thought was the anticlimactic finish to a battle involving Miller, Watson and Tom Weiskopf, Miller led by two strokes and seemed on his way to his second victory of the season. He bogeyed the 71st hole, but he still led by one after Watson missed a birdie. The final hole was a repeat of the preceding one. Miller missed the green and bogeyed and Watson parred to tie. Watson shot a four-under par 67 to Miller's 69 and they deadlocked at 271. Weiskopf had faded from the chase some holes back, placing third with a 73 for 275.

So it was back to the 15th tee for the playoff, one that matched the golden boy of the middle 1970s and the dominating figure of the late 1970s in a sudden-death duel that extended TV to almost 3½ hours. And came within seconds of having its ending clipped off by the network.

The first two holes of the playoff were vintage Watson: In a bunker and out for pars and halves. At No. 17, Watson's approach came up 45 feet short of the hole; Miller's was 12 feet to the left. If there were to be a winner decided before the telecast ended, it looked as if it would be Miller. But Watson holed his putt. There was no way Miller could match him. His putt was hit weakly and slipped off to the right of the cup. The $54,000 he earned for his first victory in eight months moved Watson into second place on the all-time PGA Tour money list, past Lee Trevino and behind only Jack Nicklaus, with $2,622,384.

Until his final putt, Watson's play was somewhat overshadowed by others. Terry Mauney, who had won a little more than $61,000 since 1972, opened with a tournament-record 63, eight under par, and was rewarded with a silver putter and $1,000 by the tournament sponsors. Mauney didn't break par again, finishing far behind.

Weiskopf broke on top the second day with 67–67—134 for a two-shot lead over six players, among them Watson and Miller. That round might have given an indication of what was to come for Miller. Tied with Weiskopf with one hole to go, he double-bogeyed the 18th.

Weiskopf had his problems in the third round. At the par-three 16th, he hit his five-iron tee shot onto a cart path. He got a free drop, but the ball wound up in a hole. 'I bumped that out and was restricted by a tree,' he said. 'I whiffed the next — the gallery said I didn't, but I did.' Then, with his back to the green, he hit the ball between his legs. The result was a triply-bogey but Weiskopf got two of the strokes back by birdieing the final two holes for a 68 that tied him with Miller for the lead at 202.

Watson had troubles, too. Bogey at No. 11, double-bogey at No. 13, bogeys at 14 and 15. But he birdied No. 17 and matched Weiskopf's 68, leaving him two behind. And through 16 holes of the final round he still trailed by that margin, waiting for a crack in Miller's armor. When it came, he made the most of it.

Doral-Eastern Open — $300,000
Winner: Andy Bean

The Tour went from the West Coast to the East Coast and for Andy Bean it was resurrection time. Almost exactly a year before, Bean had broken a bone in his left thumb when his club hit a tree root in the Los Angeles Open. He won the Bay Hill Classic a week later, but his left hand was in a cast for three months and he didn't play for eight months.

His victory in the Doral-Eastern Open stirred up the rules-conscious telephone callers among those who watched the final round on television. So much so that there was some doubt Bean had won when he posted his final round 69 for 279 and maybe Scott Hoch, Mick Nicolette and Jerry Pate would have to go out in a sudden-death playoff for the title.

The confusion stemmed from an incident at the 14th hole. Bean hit his drive into the rough at Doral Country Club's Blue Monster course and the ball settled among some tree roots. Naturally shy of situations such as that, Bean first ascertained whether he could hit the ball without hitting a root, then tried to figure out what kind of shot he could make from under the trees. He took a practice swing and knocked some leaves and twigs off a tree with his backswing.

The phone calls immediately started coming into the Doral clubhouse, the callers saying he had improved his line of play. Not so, said Warren Orlick, former PGA president, a rules official who was standing nearby. Bean, who had penalized himself when his ball moved during the Crosby Pro-Am in 1981, costing him a playoff, asked Orlick if he had done something wrong when he heard a murmur from the crowd, but Orlick said no.

'The (TV) camera showed something that wasn't wrong,' noted Bean. 'I was standing about two feet from where I would stand to hit the ball.' Jack Tuthill, the TPA Tour tournament director, said he talked to Orlick and Bean and 'what happened did not improve his line of play.'

So Bean punched the ball out to the fairway and still bogeyed the hole. When Hoch, Nicolette and Pate heard about the incident, none protested. The bogey cut Bean's lead to one stroke over Pate and when Bean followed with another bogey at 15, they were deadlocked. But Pate bogeyed No. 16 and Bean parred in for the win.

'I felt I had the tournament all day, until the 16th,' said Pate. But others, principally Craig Stadler, felt that way earlier. Stadler opened with 66–69 for a two-stroke lead on Bean and fought back from a poor start in the third round to remain in front. Another stumbling start dropped Stadler back in the final round before birdies at holes No. 6, 7 and 8 got him to within a stroke before he plummeted on the back nine.

Nicolette, like Hoch a non-exempt player, chipped in from 60 feet at the first hole and hit a one-iron to within eight feet and dropped the putt at the second hole for birdies that gave him the lead in the final round, then made 16 straight pars. Hoch stayed a shot behind Nicolette until he nearly holed a seven-iron shot at the 17th and said, 'I never had any serious feelings about winning.' Pate did and, if only Bean had stood two feet closer to his ball in the rough at 14, he would have got an extra shot at doing it.

Bay Hill Classic — $300,000
Winner: Tom Kite

When he was at his peak, the gag was that Arnold Palmer listed God as a personal friend. That was why all those putts dropped. If Arnie wanted the sun to shine, he'd say, 'God, let there be sun,' and the sun came out. If he wanted it calm, or if he wanted it to rain, all he had to do was ask.

The funny thing was, sometimes this seemed true. People can cite instances when an overcast day turned sunny when he stepped to the first tee and when the rain stopped as he began a round or started after he completed one.

But if Palmer had an 'in' with God in his playing days, he lost it when he became a tournament sponsor. His Bay Hill Classic seems to always get treated like an unwelcome guest. In 1980, winner Dave Eichelberger had to wear a ski hat and pantyhose to stay warm. In 1982, the weather for the tournament might have been even worse, though not as cold.

Bay Hill was 'immaculate,' said Jack Nicklaus, and the field was strong— 19 of the top 21 money winners, plus foreign stars such as Gary Player, Bernhard Langer, Seve Ballesteros and Isao Aoki. And the weather was strong, too — rain, tornado warnings, cold, and more rain. The tournament carried over an extra day because of its constant starts and stops and the climax was about as shocking as the weather, Tom Kite chipping in on the first hole of a sudden-death playoff with Nicklaus and Denis Watson.

Bad weather caused a 55-minute delay in play the first day. Fog held up the start of play for 68 minutes in the second round and rain and lightning called a halt for the day with half the field still on the course. The remaining players completed their second round on Saturday, then the survivors prepared for a 36-hole windup on Sunday. But once again the weather interfered, a delay of almost four hours pushing the final 18 holes over to Monday.

Through all this, Nicklaus and Ray Floyd, at 42 and 39, respectively, two of the elder statesmen in the field, played surprisingly well. Nicklaus shot 69–67–67—203 — 10 under par — and Floyd had 68–70–66—204. Nicklaus led by one with one round to go and said, 'I've been in contention to win all year, but this is my best shot to win because I'm leading going into the last day.'

Denis Watson was in third place, three strokes behind. Kite, with 69–70–70, trailed by six and looked only as if he was in line for another good pay day. Nicklaus was playing well and it looked as if only Floyd had a genuine shot at overtaking him.

However, Nicklaus preceded birdies at No. 15 and 16 with four bogeys and a double-bogey and limped in with 75—278 the last day. Watson blew a few birdie putts on the last five holes on the way to a 72—278. Kite, finding himself unexpectedly in the chase, birdied No. 15 and 17 for a 69 — one of seven under-70 rounds the last day — and made it a trio at 278. Floyd just missed making it a foursome in the playoff when he hit his tee shot into the water at 17 and took a 76 for 279.

The playoff ended with the suddenness of a lightning flash. At the 426-yard No. 15, Nicklaus hit his approach 24 feet from the cup, Watson put his 15 feet away and Kite caught the fringe, 20 feet from the hole.

Nicklaus' putt touched the cup, but refused to drop. 'I couldn't believe he missed; it was perfect,' said Kite. He found it almost as difficult to believe he won seconds later when he holed his chip shot and picked up the $54,000 winner's check after Watson failed in his attempt at a birdie.

'You're not supposed to win by chipping in. I did to Jack and Denis what others have done to me a few times,' said the weekly challenger but only one-time winner in 1981.

'I just had to play good golf to win the tournament and I didn't,' groaned Nicklaus. 'I've had four frustrating weeks. I've done something right in these last few tournaments but not enough right to win.'

Honda-Inverrary Classic — $400,000
Winner: Hale Irwin

Hale Irwin hadn't planned on playing in the Inverrary Classic. But, well, the first two rounds of the Bay Hill Classic took three days and it didn't make a whole lot of sense to go home to St. Louis to work on his game, then hurry back for the Tournament Players Championship.

Irwin also didn't plan on hitting his drive into the woods at the 72nd hole of the Inverrary. In fact, that's where he didn't want to hit it. 'The most unforgiving place to be off the 18th tee is to the right in the woods,' Irwin said. So Irwin hit his drive into the woods on the right.

Hale was in two places he hadn't planned on being — in the Inverrary tournament and off in the woods at the 18th hole — and he made the most of them. He pulled off a sensational shot from out of the trees for a birdie and won with 65–71–67–66—269, a 19-under-par score that tied the course record. Tom Kite and George Burns, both with a chance to catch him, failed and deadlocked for second at 270, Burns' low as a pro.

It was strange that Irwin had planned not to play at Inverrary, for he had played the Lauderhill, Florida, course well in the past. He set the 18-hole record with a 62 in 1979 and finished third, he was second in 1974 and third in 1978.

As good as his opening round was in 1982, it only tied him with Kite for second place. Bob Proben, a second-year touring pro, opened with a 64. But the first round was delayed by rain and was completed on Friday. As a result, the second round was played Saturday, and maybe the long time between rounds affected Proben. At any rate, he shot an 81 and missed the cut. 'No matter what I did, it was wrong,' he lamented.

Kite, whose only win in 1981 came at Inverrary, grabbed the lead by one stroke over Burns after 36 holes and Irwin trailed by four. But the last day was 36 holes because of the earlier rain delay and maybe that's where Irwin's stamina from his days as a football player at the University of Colorado paid off. Burns, also a football player in college (Maryland), went three ahead with a 67 in the morning round the last day. But Irwin had just started warming up on the final nine in the morning. He birdied 10, 11, 12, 14, 15 and 16 as he came in with a six-under 30.

Eight pars, followed by birdies at nine, 10, 11 and 12, on putts of 25, eight, 20 and 30 feet, put him in the leading pack and, when Burns bogeyed 14 after Irwin birdied it, Irwin, Burns and Kite were deadlocked for the lead at 18 under par. 'I should have hit my driver off the tee at 14. But I got conservative and hit a one-iron. That bogey, and when I didn't birdie the (par-five) 15th, were the turning points,' said Burns.

Irwin was playing ahead of Burns and Kite and was hitting his drives straight as an arrow . . . until the final hole, a dogleg right. Irwin's tee shot went into the woods, some 145 yards from the pin. 'I had a shot to the green, if you used your imagination a little,' he said.

Irwin used his imagination and a choked-down five-iron to get the job done. He punched the ball low to keep it under a tree and drew it a little. It came skimming out, hit short of the green and ran up to within three feet of the hole. The resultant birdie gave him a one-shot lead and Burns and Kite couldn't match it.

'I can't recall a shot that good under those conditions,' Irwin said. 'I knew I had to make birdie at 18 because I didn't want to go back out for a playoff.'

Tournament Players Championship — $500,000
Winner: Jerry Pate

Long after they forget the complaints that were uttered about the greens, long after they recall the introduction of 'stadium golf,' long after they think of the way the tournament was won, golf fans will remember the first Tournament Players Championship at the Tournament Players Club in Ponte Vedra, Florida, as the one in which the commissioner of pro golf, the course architect and the tournament winner all went for a swim after it was over.

Jerry Pate vowed if he won he was going to throw designer Pete Dye into the water, alligators or no alligators. And after his two-stroke victory, secured by birdies on the last two holes, he made good on his promise, first pushing Commissioner Deane Beman (who wasn't totally unprepared for the swim) into the water at the 18th green, then throwing in Dye, then following with a belly whopper himself, the way he did after winning the Memphis Open the year before.

It was all great fun for the 30,000 or so spectators seated in the amphitheater near the 18th green and for the television watchers around the world. 'There were no doubt a few professionals watching who were hoping that the water was 10 feet deep and neither could swim,' wrote Ron Coffman in *Golf World*. 'Especially Dye.'

After playing the TPC at wind-swept Sawgrass, the players thought any course would be an improvement and eagerly looked forward to moving to the 6,857-yard Tournament Players Club course, born by the will of Beman and sculpted by Dye. After one round, they weren't so sure. The course has water and wasteland at every hole. It has small greens, pot bunkers and mounds and some of the greens are shaped in such a way that only the most precise shot is rewarded. And it has three of the most wicked finishing holes in golf.

No. 16 is a 497-yard par-five that is reachable in two, but a long bunker and water abut the right and rear of the green. No. 17 is only 132 yards, but it has an island green and woe to anybody who misses it. Only a small bunker guards the front of the green; the rest is supported by railroad ties, a Dye trademark. No. 18 is 440 yards bordered by water on the left from tee to green.

It was chilling to think what the scores would be like with windy weather. As it turned out, the weather was about as good as it gets in northeast Florida in March, yet Pate's eight-under-par 280 was looked upon as a near miracle. Pate hit the greens 54 times during the 72 holes and made 18 birdies. He also holed out from bunkers for two more birdies.

Ed Fiori gave an indication of what sort of tournament it would be in the first round. He was eight under par when he came to the short 17th, hit a ball in the water, took six and was not heard from the rest of the week. There were a number of high scores posted at various holes, not just the final three, during the week. Roger Maltbie tried to hit a shot backwards between his legs at the par-three No. 8 in the third round and the ball hit his leg. The four strokes over par he took was the number he finished behind Pate. Victor Regalado went 7–7 at No. 17 the last two days.

Lyn Lott and the ever-present George Burns led the first round with 67s. Fog caused a delay of the start of the second round for more than two hours, forcing some of the late starters to complete their round Saturday morning. One of those who had to come back early was Jack Nicklaus, who played the last seven holes in five over par and missed the cut along with Lee Trevino, Arnold Palmer, Gary Player and Johnny Miller. Lott, with a 71, still had a piece of the lead, but now he was tied at 138 with Scott Simpson, Tim Simpson, Vance Heafner, Hale Irwin and Jay Haas. Tim Simpson and Haas both had 66s.

Ray Floyd, the tournament's defending champion, had 148 and thought he had missed the cut. So he went home to Miami. When he received a call Saturday morning that he was still in the tournament, he chartered a plane to Jacksonville, got to the course by helicopter, made it to the first tee two minutes before he was to tee off ... and passed half the field with a 71. But the tournament was still up ahead of him and the leaders were undergoing a change.

Little-known Brad Bryant had played more practice rounds on the course than perhaps anybody in the field and showed he had gained a lot of knowledge of how to play it as his 71 tied him with Bruce Lietzke for the 54-hole lead at

210, three ahead of Pate and Irwin. 'Whoever wins will have to show a lot of heart and have a lot of guts,' said Lietzke.

With two birdies early in the fourth round, Leitzke got to eight under par, but bunkers at No. 8 and 9 slowed him. Meanwhile, Pate, Lietzke's brother-in-law, picked up a stroke with a 35 on the front nine and got to within one with a 10-foot birdie putt at No. 12. At No. 14, Pate holed a 20-footer for birdie and moments later Bryant also birdied there, putting Pate, Bryant and Lietzke in a tie for the lead. Bryant bogeyed No. 15, setting up a tense battle over the final three holes.

Pate went for the green with his second shot at the par-five 16th, but pulled it behind a stand of trees and figured not making birdie was fatal. But as he stood on the tee at 17, he saw Lietzke put his second shot in the water on the 16th. Given new life, Pate, who had birdied No. 17 twice in earlier rounds, cut an eight-iron into the green and smoothly tapped a downhill 15-footer that found the cup for birdie and a two-stroke lead.

It wasn't over, but it looked as if Pate could win with a bogey at No. 18. Instead, he went for the bundle, hitting a perfect drive, then smacking a five-iron to within two feet of the cup for a cinch birdie two and a 67. Scott Simpson birdied the last three holes, the 18th from 20 feet, to tie Bryant for second place at 282. Then Beman, Dye and Pate went for a swim.

Sea Pines Heritage Classic — $300,000
Winner: Tom Watson

It was the way it sometimes was when the Sea Pines Heritage Classic was played on Thanksgiving weekend. The weather for the 1982 Heritage at Hilton Head, S.C., was more like a harbinger of winter than an early hello to spring.

Except for the first day of the tournament, the weather, in a word, was miserable. Wind and falling temperatures froze the blood in the veins and by the end of the week the players were dressed as if they were playing in the Eskimo Open rather than in a tournament which usually is accompanied by blooming azaleas. It was not surprising that one of the tour's best bad-weather players, Tom Watson, emerged the winner, but even he had problems enroute to his second victory of the year.

When he came to the 14th hole in the final round, Watson was nursing a three-stroke lead. He had seen Craig Stadler and Doug Tewell stumble with five-irons, so he used a four-iron for a 142-yard shot into the wind. Plunk — into the water. But a fine nine-iron got him off with a bogey. There were two ways of looking at what Watson did at that hole: Either the bogey cost him first place without a playoff or the escape from a possible double-bogey kept him from losing by a stroke.

As it was, Watson and former tennis pro Frank Conner tied at 280, four under par, and Watson won in the gloaming with three straight pars in the sudden-death playoff. It was the third straight playoff win for Watson, starting with the Atlanta Classic in 1981 and continuing through the 1982 Los Angeles Open.

Watson shot 69–68 and Conner 71–66 in the first two rounds, then moved up as the others succumbed to the unseasonable weather. Veteran Buddy Allin and third-year tourist Mike Donald took advantage of the only good-weather day to shoot seven-under-par 64s in the first round. Donald stuck around to eventually tie for 11th place, but Allin, who bought a new set of irons the night before the first round, plunged with the thermometer.

Despite a strong wind and falling temperatures, a dozen players broke 70 in the second round and five were deadlocked for the lead at 137 — Watson, Conner, Fred Couples, Mike McCullough and Tommy Valentine. As Couples stepped aside with bogeys at the 15th, 16th and 17th holes, Conner took over the lead after 54 holes with a one-under 70. But the biggest excitement was stirred up by Jodie Mudd, a collegian at Georgia Southern, who, teeing off at 7.22 a.m., when the day was at its coldest, blazed out a 66, one of the four under-70 rounds turned in that day. Mudd ultimately tied for 11th.

The weather was still the primary topic in the final round. Howard Twitty and Greg Powers were the first grouping and to stay warm, they fairly flew around the course, playing in 1.46. Ben Crenshaw hit four balls into the water at the 14th hole and took an 11 . . . then drowned another ball at the 15th on the way to a triple-bogey eight. He staggered in with an 87, his high as a pro.

Meanwhile, Watson had built up a three-stroke lead with an eagle at the second hole, a birdie at the seventh and a bogey at the 11th and a bogey by Conner at the seventh. But a bogey at 15 and three putts at 16 cut his lead to one stroke and Conner erased it by sinking a 40-footer for birdie at 17. Conner sent the tournament into overtime by saving par with a fine pitch at the final green, but a poor pitch at the same hole in the playoff permitted Watson to two-putt for the victory.

Greater Greensboro Open — $300,000
Winner: Danny Edwards

Those who played at Hilton Head thought they brought the bad weather with them as Mother Nature once again kicked up her heels in the middle of the Greensboro Open. This time it was wind, gusting up to 45 mph and blowing so hard it was impossible to keep the numbers on the scoreboards during the third round. Wind knocking shots about so that the only way to play was to aim for the fat part of the greens.

Only two rounds under par were turned in at Forest Oaks Country Club in the third round and only three the final day. Ironically, the three who were at the top of the heat when it was over were three young men who looked as if a strong wind could blow them away — Danny Edwards, with a three-under 285; Bobby Clampett, 286, and Jack Renner, 287.

Edwards opened with a 66 before the wind kicked up and rode that round to his second individual victory, both at Greensboro (he won there in 1977, too). The 66 tied him for the first-round lead with Keith Fergus, but it was Denis Watson, a South African with hay fever that was irritated by the pine pollen, who charged in front after 36 holes with a 65 for 137, one in front of Edwards.

Then the wind started blowing . . . and, oh, did it blow! Only Jim Booros and Mark Calcavecchia, with 71s, broke par in the third round. Edwards shot an even-par 72, which was good enough to give him a three-stroke lead over Watson, Clampett and Lanny Wadkins.

With the wind continuing to howl, anything under par was guaranteed to move a player past bunches of players in the final round. Ben Crenshaw got in with a 69 for 289 more than two hours before the last groups neared the clubhouse and for a time it looked as if he might be the winner. But Renner birdied the 18th hole for a 70 and then it was his turn to wait.

Edwards and Clampett were paired together and Edwards was four under and two ahead of Clampett as they came to the final three holes. Clampett dropped a 15-footer for birdie at the 16th, cutting the difference to a stroke . . . then he gave the stroke back with a poor tee shot at the 17th.

Edwards drove into a fairway bunker at the 426-yard 18th and Clampett was straight down the middle. Edwards' shot out of the sand caught the top of the bunker, leaving him still 90 yards from the green. Clampett had life. Bobby tried to cut a seven-iron into a pin cut deep in the green, but hit the ball over the green. When Edwards put his third 30 feet from the hole, Clampett was faced with the necessity of holing his chip shot to force a tie and he couldn't do it.

'The Masters had been on my mind all week. It's been in my mind since December,' said Clampett, noting that the winner gets an invitation to the Masters. The invitation went to Edwards, but he didn't appear very elated. 'It's a nice tournament. I look forward to playing in it,' he said simply.

Magnolia Classic — $75,000
Winner: Payne Stewart

It was only an 18-foot putt for par early in the final round of the Magnolia Classic, but it was the springboard for Payne Stewart's first victory on the PGA Tour. 'The long putt on No. 5 was the big key, no doubt about it,' said Stewart after he turned a three-stroke deficit into a three-stroke victory at Hattiesburg, Missouri, Country Club. We learn from our mistakes. A year earlier, Stewart, 25, led the Southern Open after two rounds and was in position to win until he bogeyed the last three holes. 'I feel like I learned something from that experience. I consider myself a good enough player to win tournaments and make a living on this tour,' said Stewart after turning in a 10-under-par 270 for a three-shot margin on Bruce Douglass and Jay Cudd.

In addition to how to handle pressure, Stewart learned you treat a course with respect, even a course as short as the 6,594-yard Hattiesburg Country Club, as he relearned again. Most of the players in the tournament, staged at the same time as the Masters, were Monday 'rabbits' — how appropriate for a tournament that ended on Easter — but there were a few name players, such as Dave Hill and his brother Mike, Bob Charles and Jerry Heard. The tournament has produced a number of stars, including just four years before, Craig Stadler, who was winning the Masters as Stewart won at Hattiesburg.

Stewart's 65 in the first round left him a stroke behind another second-year pro, Don Levin, and his 67 in the second round knotted them for the lead. But the third day Stewart found his troubles among the trees and came out with a 71 that left him three behind Douglass, who tied the course record with a seven-under-par 63 that day and came within a fraction of an inch of bettering it and collecting $2,000 from a company offering the money for that feat. 'If you putt well, you can do anything,' said Douglass, happy with the lead, and undismayed that his 15-foot birdie putt at the final green missed dropping by half an inch.

Stewart used his three-wood and one-iron instead of his driver in the final round and had the benefit of being paired with Douglass. They matched each other stroke for stroke through the first five holes, but Stewart's last stroke at No. 5 was the 18-footer for par and Douglass failed on a birdie putt from 14 feet. Then Stewart went birdie, birdie, birdie on the next three holes while Douglass went par, bogey, bogey and Stewart had the lead. He took a firm grip on it when Douglass bogeyed No. 10 and 11. 'I knew the only way I could lose was to beat myself, and I was making sure I wasn't going to do that,' said Stewart after turning in a 67.

Mony Tournament of Champions — $350,000
Winner: Lanny Wadkins

It's not often a man wins a tournament as prestigious as the Tournament of Champions and plays a secondary role, but it happened to Lanny Wadkins, thanks to the wonders of television. Wadkins won by three strokes over Ron Streck with an eight-under-par 67–72–68–73—280 at LaCosta Country Club 30 miles north of San Diego, California, but when he finished it appeared his margin was only one stroke over Streck, whose three-putt bogey at the 18th hole seemed to have handed Wadkins his ninth Tour victory.

However, the TV viewers could see Streck talking to PGA Tour Deputy Commissioner Clyde Mangum in the score tent as Wadkins played the 18th hole and some of them must have realized they had played a part in upholding the integrity of golf. For indeed they had.

Streck was in a group immediately ahead of Wadkins in the final round and after each bogeyed No. 15, Streck was eight under par for the tournament and led Wadkins by a stroke. Both parred No. 16, or so it seemed. Streck had knocked his drive under a tree and while a TV cameraman zeroed in on his every move Streck moved branches and took various stances, seeking a way to hit the ball. Under the Rules of Golf, a player is permitted to move branches of a tree while taking his normal stance to play a shot, but they don't say a person has to see the ball. When he took his stance, Streck had a branch in his mouth and he moved it aside before hitting a fine shot down the fairway.

That's when the phone calls started coming in to the tournament headquarters. Two-stroke penalty, the callers said, and much to the dismay of Streck, they were correct. But had the tournament not been on TV, maybe nobody would have known he had broken a rule. Mangum didn't know what happened, but when the phone calls started, he asked for a videotape replay.

'According to the tape, when Ron went in, he moved a branch out of his mouth when he straightened up, then he hacked away, moved in and did the same thing again. I'm sure Ron was not trying to get away with anything. But we cannot ignore the evidence,' said Mangum.

'It would have been more fair if I was told about what happened on the 17th tee. I'm not saying I didn't deserve the penalty; I was so intent on hitting the ball I didn't realize I had done anything. A branch got in my mouth when I got in between the branches and I must have pushed it out of the way without thinking. Was I supposed to eat the course?' said Streck. It was impossible to inform him of the penalty at the 17th tee because the calls didn't start to come in until he had started down the fairway. At the 17th green, Wadkins sank a birdie putt from about 40 feet and it looked as if he were in a tie for the lead. When Streck three-putted the final green, it looked as if all Wadkins had to do to win was par the hole. He parred it, sinking a putt of maybe an inch under the three-footer Streck had missed moments earlier.

Then came the announcement that Streck had been penalized two strokes and instead of finishing in second place by himself, Streck had to share the position with Andy Bean, Craig Stadler and David Graham. The two strokes were costly for Streck, who had been plagued by poor health much of the winter and had gone to LaCosta with only $5,720 in winnings for the year. He picked up $26,162, but the extra two strokes cost him more than $14,000.

Wadkins' opening 67 gave him the lead and he played well — he made only three bogeys in the first 45 holes — as one after the other players took their shots at the lead. Tom Watson began 69–68, then fell back; Peter Oosterhuis went 72–66, then collapsed, and Tom Kite threw in a 65 in the third round, but it came between two over-par rounds. In the end, it was between Wadkins and Streck . . . and the TV audience. Stadler, fresh off a victory in the Masters, had to cope with the demands on his time attendant with such a triumph and took three rounds to find himself. Then he shot a tournament record-tying 64 to snatch a share of second place.

Wadkins' career has been up and down. No. 5 on the money list in 1973 in his second year on the Tour, he fell to 54th the next year after having his gall bladder removed. He won the PGA Championship and World Series of Golf in 1977 and the following year dropped to 61st after incurring a rib injury. No. 10 on the money list in 1979, he plunged to 58th in 1980 because of a thumb injury. 'I can't look back. I've had a rewarding career. I've had problems, but I've been able to come back and win tournaments,' he said. And everybody admitted he won the T of C fair and square, but it was a runner-up who got much of the attention.

Tallahassee Open — $100,000
Winner: Bob Shearer

On the 42-hour journey from Australia to Florida for the Tallahassee Open, Bob Shearer had made up his mind: it would be either his last or next-to-last tournament on the U.S. Tour as a regular. As it turned out, it wasn't either. A 50-foot putt for an eagle three at the 71st hole caused a change in plans as Shearer won the Tallahassee Open by one stroke over Hal Sutton and Denis Watson with a 16-under-par 272 on rounds of 69, 69, 68 and 66 over the 7,024-yard Killearn Golf and Country Club course. It was the 33-year-old Australian's first victory on the U.S. Tour and he said it would mean a lot to his prestige in his home country because 'people there tend to judge you on how you do in this country.'

In Australia, they know he can play. He had won 14 tournaments during his career and had accumulated more than $75,000 on the Australian Tour before departing for America. The fact a man can make a living on the Australian Tour now and that he has a son ready to enter school had made Shearer decide his days on the U.S. Tour were numbered. But the Tallahasse victory assured him an exemption through 1983.

Killearn was a soft touch under perfect weather conditions. It took 141, three under par, to make the cut and Larry Rinker shattered the course record with a 10-under 62 the first day. But Rinker didn't break 70 in the other three rounds and wound up 10 strokes behind. Bob Byman shot 67, 69, 66 for a 54-hole total of 202, which put him four strokes ahead of Shearer. But the race was just heating up. Byman held the lead until the turn in the final round, but then the people immediately behind him began birdieing and he didn't. Watson birdied No. 11 and 12 and Sutton birdied 10, 11 and 13, putting all three at 14 under, and Bobby Wadkins made it a quartet. But Wadkins then went in reverse, Watson birdied No. 13 and when Sutton three-putted 13 the former U.S. Amateur champion was two strokes behind.

Meanwhile, Shearer, who went out in 35, began his move. He birdied the par-three No. 11 from 10 feet and dropped a four-footer at 11 for another bird. Disaster stared him in the face at the par-five No. 13 when he buried his third shot in a greenside bunker. But he blasted out and saved par with an eight-foot putt and in retrospect that par was about as important as the eagle that was to come later.

Shearer bogeyed No. 14, but bounced back for birdies at the next two holes. Now it was a two-man race, Shearer trailing Watson by a stroke. The long-hitting Watson popped up his drive at the 506-yard No. 17 and the door swung open for Shearer. Watson was unable to reach the green in two and ultimately missed an eight-foot birdie putt. Shearer was in the rough off the tee, 228 yards from the green. A fine five-wood got him to the green, 50 feet from the cup. 'I looked up and the putt was halfway there and on track,' said Shearer about the putt that dropped and put him one stroke in the lead. Watson, playing up ahead of Shearer, made a routine par at the final green. Instead of playing safe, Shearer went for the pin and his five-iron shot bounced over the green, leaving him with an uphill 40-foot chip shot. A chip and four-foot putt, and it was all over. 'I told myself two things could happen on the putt and the second one wasn't so bad because I'd still be in a playoff if I missed,' said Shearer.

USF&G Classic — $300,000
Winner: Scott Hoch

It used to be called the New Orleans Open and now it had a new sponsor and it was the USF&G Classic. But it could have been called the WIESR Classic, as in Won't It Ever Stop Raining? Poor weather, usually in the guise of rain, had been following the PGA Tour in 1982 and at New Orleans it was more of the same . . . in buckets. Only the pro-am was played in good weather. Thursday's scheduled first round was rained out. The second round on Saturday was halted with 30 players still on the course and that night it seemed as if the Gulf of

Mexico had moved in as six inches of rain fell on the course, wiping out any possibility of playing on Sunday. So the tournament was reduced to 54 holes, much to the chagrin of defending champion Tom Watson and the delight of Scott Hoch.

Hoch won by two strokes over Watson with 67–69–70—206 and Watson and Bob Shearer tied for second place at 208. 'I just wish we had one more round to go,' said Watson after his third-round 67. It was the second victory on the tour for Hoch, a former Wake Forest star. However, his first win had come in the Quad Cities Open two years earlier and in 1981 a poor year had cost him his tour card, putting him among the Monday 'rabbits.' He had tied for first place in the USF&G qualifier with a 65 and when he walked off the 18th green the following Monday with a $54,000 check in his hand, he was assured a place on the tour through 1983.

Coming on the heels of the Tournament of Champions and prior to the opening of the tour's swing through Texas, the tournament at Lakewood Country Club usually lacks a number of the big-name stars. But this year it had Watson and Jack Nicklaus, making one of his rare appearances in New Orleans, and that figured to be enough to hype the gate. But as if the rain wasn't enough, Nicklaus splashed to a 71–76 in the first two rounds and did not play the final 18 holes.

After Thursday's rainout, Shearer, fresh off a victory in the Tallahassee Open, fired a 66 in the first round and led Hoch and Jim Colbert by a stroke. When the second round was completed Monday morning, Hoch was in the lead and Shearer trailed by a stroke. Hoch was in the lead to stay, but Shearer made it interesting on the last four holes. Trailing by two strokes, the Aussie drove into the water at the 15th hole, but salvaged a par with a fine pitch. Then he birdied the 16th by hitting an iron to within tap-in distance, cutting Hoch's lead to one stroke. Now Shearer was on the scent of a second straight victory. Hoping to catch Hoch, Shearer tried to hole a long birdie putt at the short 17th, but the ball ran by the cup and he missed it coming back, a three-putt bogey that took the pressure off Hoch.

Byron Nelson Classic — $350,000
Winner: Bob Gilder

They said adieu to Preston Trail Country Club in the Byron Nelson Classic at the Dallas, Texas, course and Bob Gilder left a lasting impression, one that will long be pointed to when the members reminisce about the 15 years the club played host to the touring pros. Gilder found the range in the first round and locked in on it as he scored a 67–65–67–67—266, a 14-under-par score that lowered by three strokes the tournament record set by Buddy Allin in 1974 and tied by Tom Watson in 1975. Gilder won by five strokes over Curtis Strange, turning in a nice bit of front running after building up a three-stroke lead going into the final round.

The tournament, which has had more than its share of bad weather over the years after replacing the old Dallas Open, was scheduled to move to Cottonwood Valley Country Club in 1983. During its time at Preston Trail, it came up with an acre of highlights, including three straight victories by Watson, a protege of Nelson. This time Watson had to settle for a third-place tie with Dan Halldorson and David Graham at 273 as Gilder mechanically added to his lead each day.

Strange and George Archer shot 65s in the first round, putting them two ahead of Gilder, but after that the 31-year-old Gilder took control. A storm began to build and the wind kicked up in the second round and Bob held his breath, hoping the round wouldn't be washed out. But they got the round in and Gilder's 65 moved him one stroke ahead of Archer, who said of his recent showings, 'I'm tired of my friends asking me why I had that 79 to spoil a good tournament.' Archer didn't have a round that bad, but he failed to break 70 in the final two rounds and tied for sixth place. Graham turned in one of the more startling rounds of the year the second day — a 69 that began with four birdies on the first six holes, followed by five straight bogeys and an eagle.

His 67 in the third round put Gilder three up on Strange, who rebounded from a 72 for another 65, after 54 holes. 'It's awful nice to have a three- or four-shot lead. The other guys have to make the birdies to try to catch you,' said Gilder, a quiet man who prefers to stay out of the limelight. 'I was the guy who was supposed to make some birdies and put some pressure on him, but I just couldn't get the putts to go in,' said Strange after his final-round 69 left him at 271, five strokes behind Gilder and two ahead of the trio in third place.

Gilder's 199 was a Preston Trail record for 54 holes and, with nobody pressing him, he was able to shoot for the 72-hole record the final day. He continued to play flawlessly (he hit 54 greens during the tournament) and dusted off the field and the old tournament record with birdies at No. 15 and 17. 'I was a little nervous at the start, but when the putts didn't drop for Curtis, that made it easier and easier as the round went on,' said Gilder. 'I took two weeks off before coming here and I didn't play during the whole time. I only hit practice balls twice, but I felt good coming here.' If he had felt any better, he might have broken Mike Souchak's PGA Tour record of 257 set at another Texas course.

Houston Open —$350,000
Winner: Ed Sneed

To paraphrase a line from an old song, Bob Shearer was too hot not to cool down going into the Houston Open. He had won the Tallahassee Open, had tied for second at New Orleans and tied for sixth in the Byron Nelson Classic. And after 54 holes of the Houston Open the Australian looked as if he were headed for his second victory on the U.S. Tour. Shearer was five strokes ahead and steaming after three rounds. Then the fire went out in his boiler, letting Ed Sneed step in and win on the first hole of a sudden-death playoff, Sneed's first win in five years. Shearer had a total of 20 birdies in the first 54 holes, then got none in the final 18 as he soared to a 75.

That opened the door for Sneed, who got in the tournament through a sponsor's exemption. Sneed, who had placed 92nd on the money list in 1981, represents Michelob on the tour and the beer-maker sponsored the Houston

Open. The tournament is played at The Woodlands, a lush course north of Houston that is usually easy pickings. A 2½-hour rain and lightning delay during the first round softened the course and Sneed put his putter to work for a seven-under-par 64. That put him one stroke ahead of Scott Hoch, who had nine birdies in a 65. 'I can't remember the last time I led a tournament,' said Sneed, completely forgetting he was in front after three rounds of the 1981 Los Angeles Open. A 70 in the second round expanded his lead to two strokes over Shearer and Peter Oosterhuis, but he didn't lead again until the final hole of the tournament.

Shearer came up with a 64 of his own in the third round and after rounds of 69, 67 and 64, he was five in front of Sneed, who had a third round 71. It looked as if the only question in the final round was who would finish second. However, Shearer's fires had gone out and with a little luck and a little help from Shearer, Sneed gradually took over.

Shearer's slide began when Sneed birdied the second hole, then knocked in a 25-footer at the sixth hole that cut the margin between them to three strokes. Sneed bogeyed No. 7 but didn't lose ground as Shearer three-putted. At No. 11, the cross-handed-putting Shearer three-putted again, reducing his lead to two strokes. 'I could feel what was happening, but there wasn't a thing I could do about it,' said Shearer. At No. 12, Shearer three-putted again and now Sneed was breathing down his neck. At No. 13, Sneed hit his tee shot into a fairway bunker and went from there to rough and then to a greenside bunker. His fourth swing buried the ball even deeper in the sand and it looked as if his charge had vanished. But on his explosion, the ball popped onto the green and went into the hole for a bogey. 'That had to be the key, a bogey,' said Sneed. 'I could have so easily made seven. There was absolutely no skill involved in that shot. I just hit it as hard as I could and the ball went in.'

However, Shearer's lead was back up to two strokes and only five holes remained. But Sneed had life and he made the most of it, catching Shearer by birdieing the 15th hole from six feet and No. 16 from five feet. Both escaped from bunkers to par No. 17, then once again it looked as if Shearer was headed for victory. At No. 18, Shearer hit a 285-yard drive straight down the middle and Sneed drove into the rough. Sneed's second shot stayed in the rough near the green and Shearer approached to 18 feet. But Sneed got it up and down and they tied at 275, nine under par, when Shearer two-putted. Back they went to the par-three No. 15 to start the playoff, much to the delight of Sneed, who had birdied the hole in the last two rounds. Sneed hit a seven-iron to within four feet of the hole and, after Shearer two-putted from 25 feet with a fine comebacker, Sneed ended it.

Colonial National Invitation — $350,000
Winner: Jack Nicklaus

Jack Nicklaus had played in the Colonial National Invitation Tournament nine straight years and had come up empty. 'It's always been a difficult course for me,' he said. So he didn't play it for seven years. Nicklaus came back in 1982. The course hadn't changed. Colonial Country Club in Fort Worth, Texas, is almost 7,200 yards long with a par of 70 and the gallery makes it the best

THE U.S. TOUR / 131

girl-watchers' tournament on the Tour. But Nicklaus had changed. At 42, he was no longer the dominant player on the Tour and he hadn't won since the 1980 PGA championship at Oak Hill in Rochester, New York. But Nicklaus ended his drought, shooting a vintage Nicklaus round of 67 in the final round to beat out another long-time non-winner, Andy North, by three strokes with 66–70–70–67—273.

Vance Heafner led the first round with a 65, putting him one stroke ahead of Nicklaus and Lennie Clements, a 'rabbit' who was the last man to get in the tournament, receiving an invitation when Mike Morley withdrew. Arnold Palmer brought back memories of the old days and his showdowns with Nicklaus when he opened with a 66.

But Heafner and Palmer quickly dropped out of contention. A hot, swirling wind took its toll in the second round, but neither the wind nor being paired with Nicklaus bothered Clements, who took a one-stroke lead over Nicklaus and Tom Kite with a 69 for 135. Clements recovered from a mid-round slip for birdies at the 16th and 17th holes as 'everybody on the leaderboard was having trouble,' he said.

North, who hadn't won since the 1978 U.S. Open, took command in the third round. Nicklaus kept hitting the greens, but North kept making the putts. North shot a 67 to Nicklaus' 35-putt 70 and with one round to go North was two up on Nicklaus, Jerry Pate and Danny Edwards. North ran out of birdie putts in the final round and Nicklaus collected a few due him. Nicklaus birdied the first two holes and the round quickly developed into a two-man duel between Nicklaus and North. The duel ended when Nicklaus birdied the 16th hole while North bogeyed the 15th and Nicklaus breezed in from there. North hung on for a 72 and second place, beating out Pate by a stroke.

Georgia-Pacific Atlanta Classic — $300,000
Winner: Keith Fergus

There are 18 holes on the Atlanta Country Club course, but those who were in contention for the Georgia-Pacific Atlanta Classic (née Atlanta Open) champ-ionship the last day looked at it a different way. For them, there were 17 holes and one nightmare. The nightmare was the 448-yard No. 15 and, as fate would have it, that was the hole Keith Fergus, Ray Floyd, Larry Nelson and Wayne Levi had to contend with when play resumed after a two-hour rain delay in the final round. No. 15 is a dogleg right, with a hill of rocks, trees and out of bounds on the right and a creek skirting the fairway on the left before crossing in front of the green. 'It's not the place you want to have to begin after a delay,' said Floyd.

Of the four struggling for the title, Fergus might have been the most apprehensive while at the same time the most excited. Fergus was just happy to be in position to win. After a fine season in 1981, he was having trouble— 'I've been struggling all year,' he said— and had won only $29,000 prior to Atlanta. 'My confidence level wasn't that high coming in here, but I got off to a pretty good start on Thursday and even with a 72 on Friday I didn't feel too bad,' he said.

His opening round of 66 deadlocked him for the lead with Nelson and a 72 dropped him to five strokes behind when Nelson followed with a 67. At that point, it began to look like Nelson's tournament. Nelson's home is just off the 18th fairway of the course and while everybody had to sit out the rain delay where they could, Nelson was able to sit it out in the comfort of his den. It began to look even more like the PGA champion's tournament when he shot a 68 in the third round, giving him a three-stroke lead over Fergus and Peter Jacobsen and four over Floyd. And to top it all, Nelson is a great front-runner, a man who had never lost a tournament when he led it going into the final round.

However, nobody bats 1.000 in golf and Sunday wasn't Nelson's day. He missed birdie putts under five feet at the third and fifth holes and, when they made the turn for home, Fergus and Levi trailed him by only a stroke and Floyd was charging. 'If Larry had made those early putts, it would have put a lot of pressure on us,' said Fergus. So now we come to the fateful 15th. Nelson and Fergus were tied for the lead and Floyd and Levi trailed by a stroke when the skies opened. When play resumed two hours later, they had to work the kinks out of their backs and hit a drive that would keep their ball in play on a hellacious hole. None of them did. Floyd hit his approach into the creek and limped off the green with a double-bogey, dropping him three strokes behind. Levi, his playing companion, hit his tee shot into the hill and out of bounds, then knocked a ball into the hazard. The resultant eight crushed his hopes.

While all that was going on, Nelson and Fergus had to wait on the tee, wondering what their fate would be. They did little better. Nelson drove into the hazard, then three-putted for a seven. Fergus escaped with the least damage, bogeying after hitting his tee shot onto the hill, then chipping out to the fairway. That put Fergus one stroke ahead and with everybody bleeding, it looked as if he could coast in. But Floyd wasn't finished. He birdied 16 from 12 feet, holed a 25-foot chip shot for a birdie at 17, then came within an eyelash of sinking another birdie putt at 18. Now he was deadlocked with Fergus for the lead and had to sweat out Fergus' final hole. Fergus had a 15-footer to win, but it hit the lip and stayed out and the astounded Fergus said, 'I hit the putt you dream about hitting if you've got one to win a championship. I knew it was in. I had the tournament won.'

He didn't, of course, but when he got another chance he didn't muff it. Floyd's 68 and Fergus' 69 tied them at 273, one stroke ahead of Levi and two ahead of the disappointed Nelson. On the first hole of the sudden-death playoff, both hit the green, but Floyd's 40-footer was short and Fergus was perfect on a 20-footer. 'It was the same putt I had at 18,' said Fergus, who tripled his winnings for the year with the $54,000 first prize.

Memorial Tournament — $380,445
Winner: Raymond Floyd

The home of the Memorial Tournament in Dublin, Ohio, Muirfield Village Golf Club, demands well-placed drives, accurate iron shots, a feather-like putting touch and has scared many who have played it.

One of those it frightened was Raymond Floyd. 'I love the golf course, I love the conditions, I love the atmosphere, I love the tournament. I've just never been able to do well. I've never felt like I knew how to play the course,' said Floyd, whose best finish in previous Memorials was a tie for eighth. Which made it all the more gratifying for Floyd when he won by two strokes with a seven-under-par 281 total that was just a stroke off the tournament record.

Roger Maltbie knew how to play the course. He won the first Memorial in 1976. Although his career went into a slide after that year, Maltbie showed he hadn't forgotten how to play Muirfield Village in the first 36 holes. However, Maltbie slipped in the final two rounds and tied for second place with Wayne Levi, Peter Jacobsen and Gil Morgan.

The weather no doubt played a part in Maltbie's fall. Rain forced a suspension of play three times in the third round — for Maltbie, once on the practice tee, twice on the course. The constant stop-and-go in the eight and one-half hour day, plus an eagle two at the 18th hole by Morgan, cost Maltbie all of the six-stroke lead he held after 36 holes. 'Warming up three times for one round of golf is not easy to do. It was a struggle all the way,' admitted Maltbie. Until that fateful round, the 31-year-old Maltbie had a firm grip on his second Memorial championship.

The threesome of Arnold Palmer, Sam Snead and Gary Player was the feature attraction through the first 36 holes — Snead was serenaded by Tom Watson and Ben Crenshaw at the first tee in honor of his 70th birthday — but it was Maltbie who got the attention on the course.

The first rain delay of the week came during the first round on Thursday and softened the course, taking some of the sting out of the greens. As a result, there were an uncommon number of under-par rounds shot the first day, the lowest a four-under 68 by Maltbie. Floyd had an eagle and four birdies, but at the end of the day he was back in the pack at 74 and in danger of missing the cut. Floyd, who had lost in a playoff to Keith Fergus at Atlanta the week before, survived the cut with a 69, but after 36 holes he was even further back, trailing Maltbie by nine.

Maltbie tied the course and tournament record with a six-under 66 the second day for a 134 total that was three strokes below the tournament record set by Jim Simons in 1978. Maltbie bogeyed the first hole, then played seven-under-par golf the rest of the way with six birdies and an eagle three at the par-five 15th, where he hit a 3-wood to within a yard of the hole. That gave him a six-stroke advantage on the field, but at Muirfield nothing is safe.

Maltbie was on the sixth fairway when rain caused a two-hour delay in the third round, but by the time he walked off the 11th green with a double bogey he was deadlocked for the lead with Floyd, Morgan and Bob Gilder. But Roger birdied the 15th from 25 feet and when Morgan bogeyed No. 14 and Gilder three-putted the 18th it looked as if Maltbie would still have a lead, albeit tenuous, at the end of the day. However, Morgan's 167-yard four-iron approach at 18 went into the cup for an eagle and a 67 that deadlocked him with Maltbie, who had a 75, for the lead at 209, which equaled the tournament record for 54 holes. Floyd, with a 67, was a stroke behind and the field was bunched up behind him.

The final round quickly turned into a dogfight. Floyd made it a three-way tie for the lead with a birdie at the first hole, then Morgan went ahead with a birdie at the second. But Morgan double bogeyed No. 4 and bogeyed No. 5 and with nine holes left Maltbie and Floyd were tied for the lead and Morgan and Jacobsen were a stroke back. At the 10th, Morgan birdied, Floyd bogeyed and Maltbie double bogeyed. It looked as if it were Morgan's tournament to win.

Floyd made a marvelous par at the 11th hole, hitting a three-wood shot to the green after topping a shot in a fairway bunker. That was a pivotal hole, for it kept Floyd in the chase. Maltbie birdied No. 11, then Morgan gave up a stroke at 12, although it could have been more as he dropped a 30-foot putt for bogey after hitting his ball in water. It was again anybody's tournament.

Floyd made a 20-footer for birdie at the 13th hole, putting him in the lead by himself for the first time. And anybody knows when Floyd takes the lead, especially late in a tournament, he's difficult to dislodge. A sand shot to within a foot of the hole at the long 15th gave him another birdie and he increased his lead to two when he saved par with a perfect pitch at the par-three 16th as Morgan bogeyed. The rest was routine.

Kemper Open — $400,000
Winner: Craig Stadler

As Craig Stadler stood on the 18th tee in the final round of the Kemper Open at Congressional Country Club in Bethesda, Maryland, he thought there was something wrong with his driver. The clubhead felt loose. Sure enough, it came off in his hands. Stadler laughed, asked for his three-wood, then hit a drive about as far as a normal person would with a driver . . . and wound up birdieing the downhill, 465-yard par-four hole.

Stadler might have been distressed over the loss of his favorite driver, but at that point he had little to worry about. He had a six-stroke lead and the birdie just gave him a seven-stroke victory over Seve Ballesteros, who edged past Jack Nicklaus and Gil Morgan on the final nine holes.

The Kemper must come at the right time of the year for Stadler. In 1979, the last year the Kemper was staged in Charlotte, North Carolina, Stadler was tied for the lead after 54 holes. In 1980, he was deadlocked for first place with two holes to go and eventually finished three strokes behind John Mahaffey and in 1981 he won the Kemper by six strokes. This time his margin was a stroke greater over a course whose par had been increased from 70 to 72 as a result of the sixth and 10th holes being made par-fives. Stadler had 72–67–67–69—275, giving him 10 rounds out of his last 11 in the 60s in the tournament.

'The only trouble I have at Congressional is on the 11th hole (a 395-yard dogleg left), where I have to hook the ball,' said Stadler, who normally fades the ball off the tee.

Jack Nicklaus is a fader, too, and he underscored the fact Congressional is good for those who fade the ball when he shot a course record 30–35—65 in the second round to take a two-stroke lead over Stadler at the halfway point. But Nicklaus fell to three behind with a 72 in the third round and said, 'I guess I'm now in a position I play best from — I hope.' He wasn't; a 74 in the final round left him tied for third.

It was Nicklaus' first appearance in the Kemper since 1974 and for two rounds he played as if he were about to win his second tournament of the year.

Morgan and Gavin Levenson, a little South African, grabbed the first-round lead with 68s, but Nicklaus jumped into the lead with his 65 the second day, birdieing Nos. 3, 4, 5, 7, 8 and 9 en route to a six-under 30 on the front and beginning the back nine with a birdie at No. 10. That gave him 137, but Stadler was on his tail at 139.

On a rainy Saturday, Stadler pounded out another 67, one of only five under-par rounds shot during the miserable day, and his 54-hole total of 206 gave him a three-stroke lead on Nicklaus and four on Morgan. Rain had fallen the night before the third round and play was delayed for two hours and 10 minutes before the leaders teed off on Saturday. It was the seventh consecutive week and the 14th time in 23 weeks that a tournament had been delayed because of rain.

Stadler, Nicklaus and Morgan fought it out over the last 18 holes and Stadler refused to fold. When Nicklaus birdied the second hole, Stadler answered him with a 40-foot chip-in birdie — his second of the tournament — at the third. Stadler birdied Nos. 6, 7 and 8 and Nicklaus bogeyed No. 9 and birdied No. 10. At this point, Nicklaus' fire seemed to die. Stadler birdied No. 15 after Nicklaus three-putted 13 and from there it was no longer a contest. When Stadler birdied No. 13, he was in front by seven strokes. He could have played the 18th hole with a seven iron and won.

Danny Thomas Memphis Classic — $400,000
Winner: Raymond Floyd

At age 39 and in his 20th year on the Tour, Raymond Floyd was just approaching a peak. He had lost in a playoff for the Atlanta Classic, won the Memorial and after sitting out the Kemper Open, he came back to capture the Danny Thomas Memphis Classic, giving him two firsts and a playoff loss in four weeks.

The Memphis Classic, played at the 7,249-yard Colonial Country Club, came the week before the U.S. Open and, for many, was a tuneup. After Floyd's 67–68–67–69—271 and six-stroke triumph, the odds on him in the Open went down and his money winnings went up. Floyd won $72,000, making him only the sixth to pass the $2 million mark in Tour winnings. (The others are Jack Nicklaus, Lee Trevino, Tom Watson, Hale Irwin and Tom Weiskopf).

Despite all the money he won, Floyd was incensed about being fined $200 by the PGA Tour for slow play in the third round. Floyd, Mark Lye and Jim Nelford had received notices they had been levied the fines in envelopes posted on their lockers before the fourth round. Floyd doesn't look at mail before a round and didn't know about it until Nelford mentioned it to him on the practice range. Nelford, who had had a 63 in the second round, shot a 72 and Lye a 71 in the third round while Floyd turned in a 67. Floyd was rightly incensed after he read his notice and hurried to the PGA Tour headquarters to plead his case.

'It's ridiculous, and inconceivable that I would be guilty of slow play,' said Floyd. 'If they fine me $200, then they've got to fine them $2,000 each. I'm taking 67 and waiting for them because they're having all kinds of trouble. I guess they feel it's just equitable to fine all three of us . . . I'm going to beat this if it's the last thing I do. This will go to the Supreme Court before I pay it . . . This is an insult to my intelligence . . . Slow play is one of our most serious problems, maybe the most serious. Slow play is the worst I've ever seen and I'm talking about this year . . . When I came out here (in 1963) we averaged 3½ hours for a round of golf; it took us 5 hours and 15 minutes to play Friday and Saturday. It's ridiculous.'

Floyd and Lye tied for the first-round lead with 67s, but after Floyd took a three-stroke lead with 135 after 36 holes, it became merely a battle for second place. Floyd expanded his advantage to five strokes after 54 holes and said 'The most frustrating thing that could have happened to me would have been to blow a five-shot lead and lose. I wouldn't have slept for a week.' Others were saying things like 'They ought to give him the money on the first tee, take his name off the leaderboard and let the rest of us have some fun.'

Floyd played solid golf for 11 holes in the first round and even though he three-putted No. 12 and drove through the fairway at No. 13 for bogeys, he still led by four. His only moment of fright came when he almost hit his tee shot into the water at the short 15th and Mike Holland, a rookie touring pro, chipped in for birdie. But Floyd dropped a 15-footer for par and said, 'If I had missed that putt, it may have been different.'

Jolted, Floyd birdied the final three holes on putts of six, five and 12 feet to leave Holland six strokes behind and in second place at the end. Curtis Strange fired a 69 that got him third place at 278 and said, 'I played as good as I can and finished third. That tells you how good Holland played . . . and it certainly tells you about Floyd.'

Westchester Classic — $400,000
Winner: Bob Gilder

In the Westchester Classic in Rye, New York, spectators and players alike learned that one shot in an earlier round can virtually finish off a tournament even before a stroke is taken in the final round.

Bob Gilder hit The Shot and it was a beauty, a 258-yard wallop with a three-wood at the 18th hole in the third round that went into the cup for a rare double-eagle two and turned what had been a reasonable chase into a one-man stroll. The shot gave Gilder a share of the PGA record for 54 holes and took the heart out of his closest pursuers, dropping Tom Kite six strokes behind and Peter Jacobsen eight. Kite shot 66–64–68 in the first three rounds, yet found himself losing ground daily to the sizzling hot Gilder, who began 64–63–65.

Gilder eventually won by five strokes with a final round 69 for a total of 261 that missed by four strokes the Tour record for 72 holes set by Mike Souchak in the 1955 Texas Open. Gilder flirted with Souchak's records all week, missing his 36-hole mark of 126 by one stroke and tying his 54-hole mark of 192. Gilder had bogeyed only three holes in the first three rounds, but after his double-eagle it was difficult to maintain his intensity while riding a six-shot cushion.

'Bob's been on an emotional high for so long. He played sloppy coming in, but it was probably due to wanting to get it over with. We all knew he had it locked up,' said Jacobsen, who fought Kite for second place, a battle that ended in a dead heat.

Gilder led from wire to wire, hopping off to a one-stroke lead with a six-under-par 64 over the 6,329-yard Westchester Country Club course in the first round and taking a three-shot advantage on Kite and Jacobsen after 36 holes even though Jacobsen tied the course record with a 62 that included only two long putts, a 25-footer at the 14th hole and a 20-footer at No. 15. As the trio came to the 18th tee in the third round, Kite trailed by four strokes and Jacobsen by five. When Gilder connected with his three-wood, Kite said, 'It's in the hole,' but golfers often say that about a well-struck shot. This time, however, he was correct.

'I knew I had hit it fairly hard, but I thought I had hit it a little thin. I didn't think it would make it (to the green),' said Gilder. 'They (the fans) yell a lot even when you're just close to the cup. I didn't know it was in until a few seconds later. It was my first double-eagle ever. It really put a cap on my day.'

And, as it proved, to his second victory of the year. He birdied holes Nos. 5, 6 and 7 in the final round, putting him 21 under par for the tournament. Had Gilder parred in from there, he would have tied Souchak's 72-hole low. He gave it a good try, parring until the 15th hole. But he bogeyed that 470-yard par-four, the same hole he had bogeyed in the first round. At the 18th, the double-eagle hole the day before, Gilder again went for the green with a 3-wood, but this time the ball went into a bunker and he bogeyed.

'It was tough to play today,' said Gilder. 'I felt comfortable after the three straight birdies and felt if I birdied No. 9, I might have a shot at the record. I felt strong for the first 15 holes, but I got a little tired after that.'

Western Open — $350,000
Winner: Tom Weiskopf

It had not been a good year for Tom Weiskopf, with only a little more than $67,000 in winnings halfway through the 1982 Tour. At age 39, Weiskopf was the subject of talk that maybe his career was on the decline. All that ended when Weiskopf won the Western Open with two of his greatest shots ever under pressure that produced a birdie at the final hole and a one-stroke victory over Larry Nelson. It was only his second PGA Tour triumph in $3\frac{1}{2}$ years. The victory, and the way he scored it, had Weiskopf literally leaping for joy afterward.

'I'm excited, as excited as I can remember. This is the best I've played from tee to green and I also putted well,' Weiskopf said. 'I've never hit a more important shot on the last hole than that. I can't hit it better than that. Those were the two best swings in succession I've ever made.'

Considering the circumstances, they might have been the two best anybody has made. The scene: Nelson led by one stroke as they stepped to the 18th tee, a 450-yard par-four that yields birdies reluctantly. Salt Creek is on the left and a tree stands in the middle of the fairway. Weiskopf doesn't normally use a driver off the tee, but this time, needing a birdie, he did. He rapped it 280 yards down the middle, 30 yards past Nelson, who hit his into the rough.

'I had 200 yards to the pin, so I used a five-iron because I had a flyer lie in the rough,' said Nelson. 'But when I got over my ball, somebody in the crowd yelled and I had to step away and I lost my concentration.' The result was a poorly hit shot that came up short on the fringe of the green, 45 feet from the hole.

'I knew I had to play the hole aggressively. I was thinking birdie at the tee, hoping I'd have a 15 to 20-foot putt,' said Weiskopf. With 170 yards to the pin, he chose a six-iron and hit it perfectly, through the woods and over the creek and seven feet from the cup. When Nelson three-putted, leaving Weiskopf seven feet from victory instead of a playoff, Tom stroked the putt unerringly.

His $63,000 check pushed his PGA Tour career earnings to $2,137,056, placing him fourth on the all-time list. He gave much credit to Jack Nicklaus and Ken Venturi, two men who weren't even in the tournament. Nicklaus, he said, showed him patience in the U.S. Open at Pebble Beach two weeks earlier and he had come across a note on the basics that Venturi had written in 1970 and it proved to be a source of inspiration.

Weiskopf needed all the inspiration he could get. With the British Open on the horizon, some of golf's big names had bypassed the Western, at one time a tournament considered major. Butler National has always been one of the toughest courses on the tour, but rain had softened the greens and the winds remained calm. It appeared there would be some records broken and Weiskopf provided the final one, his 12-under-par 67–67–70–70—276 breaking by one stroke the record Ed Fiori had set a year earlier.

But it was no waltz. Bob Gilder, who had recorded a sensational victory at Westchester the previous week, was still flying as he opened with an eight-under 64 that included 10 birdies, an eagle, two bogeys and a double bogey. 'I sure didn't expect this, even after last week. I can't explain it. It's just happening, that's all,' said Gilder. Yet Bob had only a two-stroke lead.

Gilder came back with a 71 that left him with a one-stroke lead on Weiskopf, but a 74 in the third round, which included a missed shot when he tried to hit his ball out of bushes, ruined him, although he did finish third, two strokes behind Weiskopf. The leaders after 54 holes were Weiskopf and Nelson at 206 and they remained in a virtual deadlock until Nelson pulled a stroke in front with birdies at the 14th and 15th holes, setting the stage for the final-hole dramatics.

When it was over, the tall man from Ohio explained what had been happening with him throughout the year. 'I started out the year playing very well, then I had some problems, private and personal, and I stayed off the tour two months. There was some speculation about these problem, but they weren't serious. I believe in spending time with my family. Golf isn't my entire life. My priorities and life-style are different than they were early in my career,' he said. 'You have no idea what this means to me. I needed it badly. It proved to me not only that I can win, but that I can win after leaving the tour as I did this year to be with my family.'

Greater Milwaukee Open — $250,000
Winner: Calvin Peete

Once, he was an oddity on tour — a black man with diamonds embedded in his front teet. A man who began playing golf when he was 23, who took three tries

before he got his Tour card in 1975. His breakthrough came in the 1979
Greater Milwaukee Open, when he scored his first victory.

His name is Calvin Peete and he's no more a curiosity, but a man who can
play golf very well. In 1981, Peete was first in driving accuracy and first in
hitting greens in regulation and a man can make a good living excelling in those.
Now here he was back again at the site of his first win, the diamonds gone from
his teeth and leading the Tour in fairways hit and No. 2 behind Jack Nicklaus in
greens hit. Peete showed what accuracy can produce as he scored steady rounds
of 70, 66, 69, 69 for a 14-under-par 274 and a two-stroke victory over Victor
Regalado at the 7,000-yard Tuckaway Country Club course.

Tuckaway has wide fairways and huge greens and seems more tailored for
the long hitters, rather than the short-but-accurate type such as Peete. And
with many of the better players out of the country competing in the British
Open, it seemed an appropriate time for some little known player to step into
the limelight. That man was Richard Zokol, a former winner of the Canadian
Amateur. Zokol wears a headset with a radio attachment while he plays golf
and but for a poor finish might have been the first man to win a Tour event to
the accompaniment of *Pomp and Circumstance*.

Zokol opened with a seven-under 65 that included eight birdies and shared
the first-round lead with Terry Diehl, Jay Cudd, Scott Simpson and David
Edwards. Peete was virtually unnoticed with a 70. Zokol, of course, drew most
of the attention, mainly because nobody plays golf while listening to a radio and
perhaps because some figured he was just a flash who would quickly disappear.
But Zokol stuck around, shooting a 69 and tying Diehl for the second round
lead at 134 as Peete moved to within two strokes with a 66.

Zokol tuned in for a 70 and Wayne Levi scored his third consecutive 68 in the
third round, tying them for the lead after 54 holes at 204. But neither Zokol nor
Levi were able to hold on, Zokol taking a fourth-round 75 and Levi a 76,
although Zokol hung on until he played the final three holes in four over par.
Levi took himself out of it with three successive bogeys in the middle of the
round.

The final day became a struggle among a nervous Peete, Diehl and Regaldo
and Peete admitted 'It was the tightest I have ever been. I felt even more
pressure than in my third qualifying school. It was those last five holes. I knew I
couldn't make one mistake.'

Peete was ahead by a stroke when he bogeyed No. 16, dropping him into a
deadlock for the lead with Diehl. Nervous or not, Peete hit a marvelous
four-iron to within six feet of the hole at No. 17 and when he dropped the birdie
putt as Diehl three-putted, the tournament was his.

Quad Cities Open — $200,000
Winner: Payne Stewart

Payne Stewart sticks out in a tournament because he wears plus-fours —
knickers, some Americans call them — but when he wins, it's while people are
looking the other way.

After a brilliant amateur career that included the Missouri State Amateur championship and a share of the Southwestern Conference title while a student at Southern Methodist University in 1979, Stewart turned pro, packed his clubs and headed for the Asian tour, winning the Indian Open and Indonesian Open in 1981. He joined the PGA Tour in 1981 and won a modest $13,400, not enough to earn him exempt status.

His second year on Tour began much better. He won the Magnolia Classic played opposite the Masters and even though the money and the title were regarded as unofficial, the money spends. Stewart's second victory on the Tour came in the Quad Cities at Coal Valley, Illinois, and even though this one also is played at the same time as a major — the British Open — it's an official event even if it is pretty much bereft of top players. If the tournament lacked the big names, it didn't lack excitement — there was a new name atop the scoreboard at the end of every day. Tim Graham led the first round with a 65, Jeff Mitchell was one of three (the others were Barry Jaeckel and Butch Baird) who shot course-record 63s in the second round for a 36-hole total of 132 that gave him the lead and a 71 tied him with Calvin Peete, still flying high after a win at Milwaukee the previous week, and new bridegroom Pat McGowan for the 54-hole lead at 203.

Meanwhile, Stewart was shadowing the leaders with 66, 71, 68 and trying to ignore the pain in his back. Stewart hurt his back in a diving accident as a five-year-old and it has troubled him ever since. But the pain was forgotten as Stewart had his day in the final round, matching the course record with a 63 for a 72-hole 268 that gave him a final margin of two strokes over McGowan and Brad Bryant, who finished with 67 and 66, respectively.

Maybe his victory was pretty much overshadowed by Tom Watson's win in the British Open, but Stewart earned $36,000, nearly doubling his season winnings, and had assured himself an exempt status through the 1983 season. Maybe the latter was the most gratifying. Even though he had won the Magnolia, he had to qualify for the Quad Cities and got in with a 68.

Anheuser-Busch Classic — $350,000
Winner: Calvin Peete

There's this about golf: A man will spend endless hours on the practice tee and putting green trying to get his game together and when it happens — if it happens — he'll ride a crest for maybe two or three tournaments until the process begins again.

That's the way it was for Calvin Peete in the Anheuser-Busch Classic at the renovated Kingsmill Golf Club course in Williamsburg, Virginia. Peete had won the Milwaukee Open two weeks earlier and had followed with a fine showing for three rounds in the Quad Cities Open the next week. That seemed to mark the end of his peak, but it wasn't, as he demonstrated with a two-stroke victory, his third on the Tour and only his second outside Milwaukee.

There had been many complaints about the Kingsmill course upon the Anheuser-Busch move from California to Virginia a year earlier and obviously they fell on receptive ears. Kingsmill was extensively changed under the guidance of architect Ed Ault. The green at the par-five No. 3 hole had been moved to bring water into play near it, the No. 4 hole was improved from tee to green, the No. 5 green was rebuilt and the hated No. 8 green was vastly improved. All very well and good, but there was little time to praise the changes before the weather stepped in and reduced the tournament to a 54-hole event with no change in the payoff, much to the delight of Peete.

'I want to thank Anheuser-Busch for making this a 54-hole tournament. I don't think I could have made another 18,' said Peete after he won by two strokes over Bruce Leitzke and three over Hal Sutton and Rik Massengale with a 10-under-par 66–68–69—203. Peete had two reasons for feeling thankful: an ailing back had been giving him trouble and the third round had made a mess of his nerves.

Leitzke jumped off to the first-round lead with a 65, then gave way to Peete in the second round on a stormy day that ended with 93 of the 156 players still on the course when play was stopped and the tournament was reduced to 54 holes. After the second round was completed on Saturday, Peete was two in front of Bill Rogers and Massengale with 134 and hadn't made a bogey. 'That's incredible on this course. He's due,' noted Rogers.

Peete's string of bogey-less holes finally ended at the third hole in the final round after he nearly hit his third shot into the water. Sutton and Payne Stewart, another man riding a high after a win in the Quad Cities, quickly took the opportunity to tie him for the lead. However, Stewart met disaster with double bogeys at the seventh and eighth holes and Sutton retreated with a double bogey at No. 8. Peete shoved them even further behind with birdies at the sixth and eighth holes.

Soon Peete had other challengers. Leitzke, who had slipped with a 74 in the second round, went out in a two-under 34 and birdied No. 10 and 13. When Peete bogeyed No. 10, Leitzke was within a stroke of him. Massengale tied Leitzke with a birdie at No. 11 and Sutton made it a trio in second place with birdies at Nos. 12 and 13. Soon it became a three-man tie for first as Lietzke birdied the 177-yard No. 17 with an eight-foot putt and Sutton two-putted the 506-yard No. 15 for birdie.

Now the pressure was on the 39-year-old Peete and he was equal to it. A six-iron to within 12 feet of the hole at No. 14 gave him sole possession of the lead and he cinched it with a birdie at No. 16, sinking an eight-footer following a marvelous five-iron shot.

'I knew when I looked at the leaderboard at 18 that I didn't have much of a chance. Those last three holes don't require any strength and Calvin just had to play to his strengths,' said Lietzke, who finished with a blazing 66. Peete's strengths are hitting fairways and greens, and that's another thing about golf: A man who consistently hits fairways and greens has to win from time to time.

Canadian Open — $425,000
Winner: Bruce Lietzke

Bruce Lietzke must be one of the most pessimistic and at the same time one of the most happily married men on the PGA Tour. On almost every shot during his march to the Canadian Open championship, Lietzke insisted he couldn't win because 'I lack the killer instinct.' And when it was over, when he had set a course record and won by two strokes over Hal Sutton, the 31-year-old Lietzke talked as if he were ready for retirement.

'I find that occasionally I don't enjoy playing under the pressure I played under today,' said Lietzke after he had toured the Glen Abbey course in Oakville, Ontario, with a seven-under-par 68–68–68–73—277, three shots below the old course record. 'If I don't enjoy it, I don't want to stay out there.'

Of course, most everybody analyzed that as retirement talk, but during the PGA Championship a week later Lietzke took the time to point out he wasn't talking retirement, that he was only contemplating cutting back the number of tournaments he would play. Lietzke had talked similarly in 1973, the year before he turned pro. He had been playing golf since he was five and when he graduated from the University of Houston he was tired from all the golf he had played in high school and college. His 'retirement' lasted six months.

This time, Lietzke had another reason: 15 months earlier he had married the sister of the girl who was married to Jerry Pate and he was enjoying wedded life so much he wanted more time to spend with his wife. 'My enthusiasm for the game has dwindled in that I've found something more interesting than golf — a wife,' he said.

If the bloom of being married had not yet worn off, neither had Lietzke's ability to win a tournament, despite his daily admonition he couldn't hang on to the Canadian Open lead. For a while in the final round, as he stumbled to a two-over 73, there were those who agreed with him. But for three rounds he played superbly, straying from the inconsistent style that had marked his play during much of 1982.

Glen Abbey's greens were so bad in 1981 that many of the top players refused to come back, including Masters winner Craig Stadler and U.S. and British Open winner Tom Watson. One bad year can make a reputation for a course. But Glen Abbey's greens were much improved and the scoring reflected their condition. Greg Norman, Bruce Douglass and alternate Brad Bryant tied for the first round lead with 67s, but Lietzke tied Sutton for the lead after 36 holes as they both shot two 68s for 136.

Lietzke outshot Sutton by four strokes with his third 68 on Saturday, giving him a two-stroke lead on Tommy Valentine. 'On the last day I was hoping to go from nine under par to 13 and break away, but I guess I lack the mental toughness,' said Lietzke.

Despite the improved greens, the 7,060-yard Glen Abbey course is still a difficult track. Lietzke never lost his lead in the final round as he shot a 73 to Valentine's 74. Sutton closed with a 71 and Charles Coody with one of his better rounds of the summer, a 67, but all that got them was, respectively, second place and a tie for third.

Sammy Davis Jr.-Greater Hartford Open — $300,000
Winner: Tim Norris

Tim Norris' triumph in the Greater Hartford Open was one of those success stories that make the heart beat a little faster. They come up maybe once or twice a season on the PGA Tour and when they occur everybody is delighted, even the losers.

Norris was a 24-year-old second-year tourist from El Paso, Texas, whose career seemed to be going in reverse when he arrived at the immaculately groomed Wethersfield, Connecticut, Country Club. He had won $32,424 in 1981, but he had missed the first 14 tournaments of 1982 and here it was mid-August and he had earned only $3,550. The bills kept piling up. Many players pass up Hartford, played the week after the PGA Championship, so Norris was able to pick up a spot by tying for 20th in the qualifier with a 70. Nobody knew it at the time, but Norris was off and running.

He shot out of the gate with an eight-under-par 63 and never stopped as he added 64, 66 and 66 for a 25-under 259 that broke the tournament record by six strokes and gave him a decisive six-stroke edge on Ray Floyd, the newly-crowned PGA champion. En route, Norris also set tournament records for 36 and 54 holes and with four holes remaining he was in step with Mike Souchak's all-time tour record of 257. He led all the way, a remarkable performance by a young man who never had led even one round of a Tour event previously.

'He got a few breaks when he needed them, but believe me, folks, that's the way you win golf tournaments. Let me assure you he played a mighty solid round today and made the putts when he had to,' said Floyd. 'His victory was no fluke.'

Norris, who grew up in Fresno, California, said he 'majored in golf' at Fresno State and was a college All-American. And he brought out that ability at Hartford. He said 'I was off last week and I got my attitude in shape. I told myself I'd better get myself in gear or I wouldn't be around next year.'

His eight-birdie 63 in the first round gave him a one-stroke lead and he went from there. The next day, he had five birdies and an eagle in a 64 for a 127 total that broke the tournament record for 36 holes by one stroke and left him three strokes ahead of Floyd, who had gone 65–65. Norris and Floyd were paired for the final two rounds, but Floyd's presence didn't bother Norris. 'He doesn't scare me. Bring 'em all on,' said Norris. Poverty and bill collectors can harden a pro golfer to the point he is not awed nor shaken by being paired with one of the greatest players in the game.

Norris showed his talk wasn't mere bravado as he shot a 66 to Floyd's 67 in the third round and widened his lead to four strokes while setting a tournament record of 193 for 54 holes. The biggest gainer was Dana Quigley, who blasted out a tournament-record 61 — eight birdies and an eagle — but Quigley began the day far behind after starting 70–69.

Defending champion Hubert Green had crept to within five strokes of Norris with three straight 66s and it looked as if the pressure from veterans such as Floyd and Green might make Norris crack in the final round. There were a few times he might have, but he got just enough breaks to keep his composure.

Norris came within two inches of an eagle with an eight-iron shot to the first hole in the final round. At hole No. 2, Floyd was 10 feet away from an eagle when Norris pulled out an astounding birdie. His tee shot went into the trees, his second hit a chair and his third went into a bunker. His fourth went into the hole for a birdie that Floyd called 'definitely the tournament; it deflated my balloon.' Norris produced some similar dramatics at the eighth hole — his second shot sailed over the green and hit a marshal squarely on the forehead and caromed back onto the green, 30 feet from the hole for an easy par.

Floyd eliminated himself with a double bogey at the fifth hole and Norris widened his lead to seven strokes with birdie putts of 35, 25, 10 and 25 feet at holes Nos. 10, 11, 12 and 13. Now he was 27 under par and all he had to do was par in to tie Souchak's record. But bogeys at the 15th and 18th holes cost him that. No matter. He had won $54,000, had assured himself a place on the all-exempt tour in 1983 and 'now we can pay off all our credit-card bills for the first four or five months of the year,' he said.

Buick Open — $350,000
Winner: Lanny Wadkins

In 1981, Lanny Wadkins limped away from the Buick Open in disgust, leaving after a third round 78, his game in disarray. And that was the beginning of his 1982 season, the 33-year-old Virginian's best in 12 years on the Tour. He departed from the Buick because he had aggravated tendonitis in his thumb and headed for some putting sessions with Phil Rodgers. 'The injury made me change my grip, and that improved it, and working with Rogers improved my putting,' Wadkins said after he returned and conquered.

Wadkins scored his third victory of the year at the 7,001-yard Warwick Hills course in Grand Blanc, Michigan, winning by one stroke over Tom Kite and boosting his earnings for the year to $290,138, a personal high. It was the fourth time Kite had finished in second place, continuing a 'streak' he had started a year earlier. 'I'm disappointed, but far from frustrated,' said Kite. 'It means I've played very well.'

Indeed, Kite played well — 71–67–69–67—274. But Wadkins played a little better — 66–71–71–65—273. Wadkins likes the longer, tougher courses. He had placed sixth in the U.S. Open at Pebble Beach, was second in the PGA at Southern Hills and had won the Tournament of Champions at LaCosta. He had taken a week off after the PGA and arrived at Warwick Hills in good spirits. His 72-hole total broke by one stroke the course record set by Julius Boros 19 years earlier, but Wadkins had to come from behind to win.

John Cook, who had been struggling so much that he went to a cross-handed putting style, opened with a 65 that put him one stroke ahead of Wadkins and Curtis Strange, but Cook didn't break 70 again as he tied for eighth place, six strokes behind Wadkins. Strange, awaiting the birth of his first child, took the lead with a 69—135 at the halfway point, and now Wadkins trailed by two.

Payne Stewart caught Strange at 204 after 54 holes with a 67 as Strange came back with another 69. At this point, Wadkins trailed by four and Kite was three back. The tournament was just beginning.

Wadkins birdied three of the first seven holes and Kite started out birdie, birdie in the final round, putting them both 11 under par for the tournament. Strange also got off to a good start, birdieing the first and third holes to go 14 under. However, Strange played the next 14 holes in three over before finishing with a birdie at the last hole as Wadkins and Kite slipped past him. Wadkins birdied four in a row starting at the 10th hole, including an amazing 70-footer at the par-three No. 11 that Wadkins said 'gave me momentum.' Wadkins gave one stroke back by three-putting No. 15, but regained it by birdieing No. 16 with a 10-footer.

Now it was down to Wadkins and Kite with Wadkins playing in a group up ahead. As Wadkins played 18, Kite was at 17 and they both got into trouble. Wadkins pushed his drive and hit his second into a bunker. At the par-three 17th, Kite also pushed his tee shot and made a fine recovery from a difficult spot, putting the ball seven feet from the hole. Wadkins' explosion shot left him 18 feet away from a par and it looked as if he, not Kite, was destined to place second. But Wadkins dropped his curling putt and Kite missed his and it was Wadkins who drove off in the new white convertible auto, a complete turn around from the way he had left the area a year earlier.

World Series of Golf — $400,000
Winner: Craig Stadler

Mainly because of television, there probably never will be a genuine climax to the PGA Tour. The season ends with the Walt Disney World Classic in Orlando, Florida, which would be a fitting climax to settle such matters as the money-winning championship and Player of the Year honors. But late October is football time in the United States and television is unavailable for a climactic golf tournament.

So we have the World Series of Golf being played on the final weekend of August, with eight tournaments remaining on the schedule. Despite the $100,000 first prize, only twice since the new format was adopted in 1976 has the year's money champion won the Series — Jack Nicklaus in 1976 and Tom Watson in 1980.

But no matter, the gathering at Firestone Country Club in Akron, Ohio, will have to do and the 1982 edition produced a battle that would have done justice to any season-ending tournament. The Masters champion, Craig Stadler, and the PGA champion, Raymond Floyd, the top two money winners, battled it out for not only the tournament title but perhaps also the money and Player of the Year crowns. And they got right down to the wire and beyond, Stadler winning on the fourth extra hole after they were the only ones under par after 72 holes.

For the record, Stadler shot 70–68–75–65—278 and Floyd 69–71–68–70—278. Stadler won $100,000, giving him $428,101 for the year, and Floyd collected $55,000, pushing his earnings to $386,809. Floyd took a three-stroke lead into the final round and Stadler came from five back to catch him, then won on the 76th hole with a par.

That is only the final statistics and they tell only part of the story. The World Series of Golf is a very select event, open only to those with special credentials — multiple winners, 'major' winners, etcetera. So while the others took a break, 26 players — 25 pros and 1981 U.S. Amateur champion Nathaniel Crosby — gathered at Firestone to battle for the richest first prize on the Tour. Since the Series departed from its four-man format, Firestone had had its reputation as one of the most difficult courses on the Tour tarnished. In 1982, the pride came back. An absence of rain and the presence of some wind made the course hard and the greens fast and treacherous. As a result, only 17 under-par rounds were turned in during the week and the two-under-par winning score was the highest since the field was expanded.

Floyd, Australia's Bob Shearer and Japan's Masahiro Kuramoto tied for the first-round lead with 69s as some of the would-be challengers stumbled and fell. Defending champion Bill Rogers and TPC champion Jerry Pate shot 76s and neither recovered. Watson opened with a 75 and followed with a 74 that ended his hopes. Nicklaus made several charges, birdieing three of the first four holes on Thursday and Saturday, but every time he fell into a pit of double bogeys. Nicklaus had five double bogeys, 'and when have I ever made five double bogeys in one tournament? I haven't made five double bogeys all season,' he groaned.

Stadler's 68 in the second round gave him a share of the lead with Shearer, and Stadler said, 'Considering the way I played, it was a fantastic round. I didn't play worth a damn.' Stadler hit only four fairways, yet the round could have been better. He sank a 93-yard wedge shot at No. 11 for an eagle two, then gave those strokes back at the long No. 16 after hitting his ball into the water.

Floyd trailed by two strokes going into the third round, but when the day was over he was three in front and heads were starting to nod as if the tournament were all but over. Hey, Raymond Floyd doesn't lose when he's three ahead with one round to go, does he? Well, maybe nobody told Craig Stadler that. At any rate, Floyd, with a 68, and Watson and Tom Weiskopf, with 69s, were the only ones who broke par on a day on which tricky pin positions combined with a gusting wind to make Firestone about as difficult as it can be. Floyd picked up seven shots on Stadler, who had a 75, and five on Shearer, who turned in a 73.

Floyd played well in the final round, an even-par 70 that forced everybody else to come up with a sub-par round if they were to challenge. But Stadler played brilliantly, a five-under 65 that was just enough to force a playoff as Floyd unexpectedly slipped in the stretch. Stadler went after Floyd immediately, birdieing holes No. 1, 2 and 3 on putts of six, 15 and 20 feet. A 20-footer at No. 6 gave Stadler a four-under 31 on the front nine and erased the difference between him and Floyd, who went out in 36.

Now it was a tournament again, Stadler and Floyd one under for the tournament and Isao Aoki at even par. Aoki chipped in for birdie at No. 11, but bogeyed No. 12 and that's when his tank went dry. Floyd pulled in front with a 25-footer at the 10th hole, but Stadler deadlocked it again with a six-footer at No. 13, and that was his last birdie. Floyd came out of a bunker for par at No. 13 and took a one-stroke lead with a six-foot birdie putt at 14, but he missed the green at the 221-yard No. 15 and it was a dead heat between him and Stadler on the last three holes, both missing birdie putts at No. 18.

Stadler scrambled just to stay even with Floyd on the first three holes of the playoff. After they parred No. 14, Stadler chipped close for a matching par at No. 15 and another fine chip at No. 16 kept him alive as Floyd missed a 15-foot birdie putt by an eyelash. Stadler's ability with the chipping wedge ultimately won it for him. Both missed the green at No. 17, the fourth playoff hole, and Floyd had the better lie, almost in the same place where he had been during the final round of regulation play. Stadler, as usual, chipped close for a tap-in, but

Floyd's chip came out hot, leaving him with a 15-footer for a half, which he barely missed.

'I just kept up my scrambling ways,' said Stadler. 'Raymond had the better hand in the playoff. He just made the first mistake.'

B.C. Open — $275,000
Winner: Calvin Peete

Calvin Peete, who had been standing on the edge of greatness, took a step onto it in the B.C. Open at the EnJoie Golf Club in Endicott, New York. Peete scored his third victory of the year by a resounding seven-stroke margin over Jerry Pate and the number of golfers who have won three tour events in one season is not lengthy. Perhaps his triumph in the Milwaukee Open could be shrugged off because it came with many of the top players off to the British Open, but his win in the Anheuser-Busch certainly was over a representative field and victory No. 3 was a masterful one over a field that included World Series and Masters winner Craig Stadler and TPC champion Pate.

Peete did what he does best. That is, hit fairways and greens. And at the 6,966-yard EnJoie course a man is rewarded. Pate and Fuzzy Zoeller found that out as they scattered too many tee shots and watched Peete pull away from them in the final round en route to a 19-under-par 69–63–64–69—265 that set a tournament record as Pate straggled in seven strokes behind and Zoeller took third place eight strokes back. Peete earned $49,500, pushing his earnings for the year to $281,361, No. 6 on the money list. And all this from a man who came out of poverty and took up golf rather late in life.

Peete's victory left no doubt, but it was not as easy as it looks on paper. He didn't lead until after the third round and he didn't really take command until Pate and Zoeller began making double bogeys in the final round.

Mike Smith, a 32-year-old tour sophomore, grabbed a two-stroke lead over Pate and Tom Kite with a 65 in the first round, then went into reverse. Peete was four strokes back, but he quickly moved up with a 63 in the second round. That was better than everybody except Zoeller, who had nine birdies and lowered the course record by a stroke with a 62, giving him a two-shot edge on Peete at 130. Peete almost matched Zoeller's record-setter, a bogey at the 17th hole denying him a share.

Peete came right back with almost an identical round, a 64 that gave him the 54-hole lead by a stroke over Zoeller. Big blow for Peete was an eagle two at the 441-yard No. 13, where he holed a 3-iron shot.

The final round began as a battle among Peete, Zoeller and Pate, and Peete's problem at the first hole was a tipoff of what was to come. Peete went over the green and double bogeyed, putting Zoeller in the lead. But from there Peete played solidly as Pate and Zoeller had their adventures, taking the lead and adding to it. Zoeller hit the water and double bogeyed at No. 2, then double bogeyed Nos. 9 and 10. Pate bogeyed No. 9 and double bogeyed No. 12. Meanwhile, Peete got a big shove with a birdie at the ninth hole and from there it was free sailing.

The PGA Tour statistics are not always accurate guages, considering they take in only the first two rounds of a tournament, but in this case they gave a good indication of why Peete won. He tied Peter Jacobsen for first in greens hit in regulation, led in percentage of sub-par holes, tied Zoeller and Kite for first in putts per round and was fourth in fairways hit. It all added up to the fact that steadiness is perhaps the most important friend a touring golfer can have. It's not how far you hit it, but where you hit it that determines how often you hit it. Just ask Calvin Peete.

Bank of Boston Classic — $300,000
Winner: Bob Gilder

Bob Gilder used to say he didn't yearn for the glory and the attention winning brings. He just wanted to cash in weekly checks, maybe win a tournament here and there and earn the respect of his peers. And during his first six years on tour he got his wish. He won the second tournament he played in, the 1976 Phoenix Open, and three times earned more than $100,000 in a season. But fans had a difficult time distinguishing him from Tom Purtzer, a teammate at Arizona State University, or many of the fine young players cruising around the edges of the Tour.

But in 1982 Gilder's career took off and his feelings went in a different direction. He won the Byron Nelson Classic and the Westchester and played well in the U.S. Open and PGA. Now everybody knew who he was and he found with success comes even more money . . . from exhibitions, endorsements, etcetera. And you've got to grab them when you can.

Gilder scored his third victory of the year — one more than he scored in his first six years on Tour — in the Boston Bank Classic at Pleasant Valley Country Club in Sutton, Massachusetts, and the $54,000 prize increased his winnings for the year to $296,598, which is about half as much as he earned his first six years. And the way he won, either leading or hanging around the lead for all four rounds, indicated Gilder has come of age as a touring pro.

Gilder was the only one of the top 10 money winners to sign up for the Boston Bank and showed he got where he was by his ability to handle pressure. He shot a 13-under-par 67–67–70–67—271 and won by two strokes over crowd favorite Fuzzy Zoeller, but he was in the midst of a jam all the way.

George Archer, who took only 11 putts on the back nine, and Ed Sneed tied for the first-round lead with 66s and Gilder was almost inconspicuous at 67 as 42 players broke par. Archer had an early tee time the second day and made it look as if the later starters would be far behind when they stepped to the No. 1 tee as he birdied the third through seventh holes and added a birdie at No. 12 that put him at 11 under, which is the score Jack Renner won the tournament with in 1981. But Archer hit his tee shot out of bounds and took a double bogey at the 15th hole and followed that with a bogey at 16 for a 68 and 134 that tied him for the lead with Gilder. Afterward, Gilder was angry because he had missed short putts at the 16th and 18th holes.

Mike McCullough, 37 and in the 10th year of a lacklustre career, shot a seven-under 64 in the second round following an opening 72 and a 66 in the third round gave him the lead as Gilder fell two strokes behind. McCullough was contemplating leaving the Tour 'unless I win a tournament. I've been looking for employment outside of golf. At age 37, where in hell am I going to go in golf?' McCullough didn't get his victory as he slipped to a 72 in the final round and tied for third place with Gil Morgan.

Meanwhile, others had moved into contention — Brad Bryant, who had led the Monday qualifiers with a 64, came up with another 64; Peter Jacobsen had put together 67–66 in the middle rounds and Zoeller kept breaking 70. The contenders quickly got sorted out from the pretenders in the final round. Jacobsen started off bogey, double bogey and McCullough bogeyed the third hole. Archer, who had trailed by a stroke, and Bryant never got started and slowly faded.

Zoeller eagled the fourth hole and birdied the fifth and sixth and Gilder played the front nine in a three-under 33. When Zoeller bogeyed No. 10, Gilder led by two and said 'I figured someone's going to step up and catch me. I said, "Just be ready." I was just sitting there thinking they've got to come to me, they're going to have to make birdies down the stretch. It was on their shoulders.'

Nobody did and when it was over Gilder said, 'Being as low-keyed as I am and not being flamboyant hurts my salability, but winning doesn't hurt. It makes it easier to be loose.'

Hall of Fame — $250,000
Winner: Jay Haas

Almost from the time they returned to Pinehurst, North Carolina, after a two-decade absence, the touring pros must have figured that some day they would leave. The World Open marked the return of the Tour in 1973 and the Hall of Fame tournament in 1982 marked the end of the pros' annual visit to the small North Carolina golf resort town. Jay Haas, almost a native son, will go down in history as the last to win it.

Several things led to the demise of the tournament. For the first three years after the World became the Hall of Fame, the tournament had a national sponsor, but when Colgate pulled out, the tournament struggled. Miles away from a major city and lacking members to drum up ticket sales, Pinehurst found it difficult to attract the necessary crowds. The club had changed hands and in the process the course had undergone changes, including a shift from Bermuda greens to bent grass and back. The course was not as good as it once was, but it still had a charm and anybody who ever picked up a golf club wanted to play it.

However, the Hall of Fame's dates were in mid-September, a bad time for golf in the football-happy U.S. It also didn't help that rumors had spread that the greens on Pinehurst's No. 2 course were still not good. 'We were told they weren't even greens, but mud,' noted Ed Sneed. Because of the condition of the greens, the pins had to be placed in some peculiar places in order to have grass around them. Yet 28 players broke par in the first round, led by John Adams with a four-under-par 67. With most of the big names missing, Jerry Pate withdrawing because of injury after the first round and PGA champion Raymond Floyd missing the cut (74–74), people named John Adams got their chances to step into the limelight and Adams made the most of his.

Adams was in the fifth year of a lackluster career, 132nd on the money list. His principal goal was a spot among the 125 who would qualify for the all-exempt Tour in 1983. He made that goal, tying Haas after 72 holes with an eight-under 276 before losing on the second hole of a sudden-death playoff. And for four days he didn't act like a young man who had never before been in contention for a tournament championship. Naturally, everybody expected Adams to fade quickly after his hot start, but Adams wouldn't accommodate them. He shot a 69 in the second round and shared the lead with Jack Renner, who had a sizzling 64, and Lance Ten Broeck, whos trung together two 68s. Haas had two 70s and was hardly noticed at 140, four strokes back. 'I just wanted a decent tournament,' said Haas.

Adams looked as if he was about to take the plunge everybody expected when he bogeyed two of the first three holes in the third round, but he recovered for an even-par 71 that left him in a deadlock at 207 with Renner. Curtis Strange had pulled to within one stroke of the lead with a 69 and Haas' third straight 70 left him three behind. Now all the characters who were to play a part in the Hall of Fame's final act were gathered for what was to be an exciting finish.

Allen Miller, like Adams a man fighting for a place on the 1983 Tour, thrust himself into the battle by birdieing three of the first four holes in the final round, but Miller soon cooled off, although his fourth-place finish did guarantee him a place among the top 125. Renner quickly removed himself from the chase en route to a 74. So now it was Strange and Haas, former teammates at Wake Forest University in nearby Winston-Salem, and Adams, the Man from Nowhere (actually, Altus, Oklahoma), in a race to the wire. Strange and Adams matched each other shot for shot, both turning in 69s. When Haas made brilliant saves of par at the 12th and 13th holes, he found himself one stroke ahead of the field and nervous. 'I stayed nervous the rest of the way,' he said.

When he arrived at the par-three No. 17, Haas was in a tie for first place with Strange and Adams and he quickly broke it by hitting a five-iron to within six feet of the hole and sinking the putt for birdie. 'Boy, I got nervous. I've won three on Tour and one unofficial, but I've never been through this,' he said as he sat down and awaited his fate. At the 18th hole, Strange put his approach 15 feet from the hole and Adams knocked his 20 feet away, putting them both within range of forcing a playoff. Adams fought down the butterflies and holed his birdie putt, the ball just making the hole. Strange left his putt short, a victim of the slow greens.

Playoff time, and Haas might have been more nervous than Adams. 'But when I got on the tee with Adams I was thinking, "I've won before, he hasn't and experience counts",' said Haas. Maybe it does, for after they parred the first extra hole, Haas won at the second when Adams mis-hit an iron, chipped 10 feet past the hole, then barely missed the cup.

Haas, the nephew of veteran touring pro Bob Goalby, was born in St. Louis, Missouri, but he settled down in Charlotte, North Carolina, after graduating from college and that's only about 100 miles from Pinehurst. Perhaps it was fitting that the last Hall of Fame tournament was won by a neighborhood player.

Southern Open — $250,000
Winner: Bobby Clampett

It wouldn't be correct to say a star was born when Bobby Clampett won the Southern Open. The only question was what took him so long to win a tournament. From the time he won the California State Amateur and was low amateur in the U.S. Open in 1978, great things had been predicted for the curly-haired blond from Monterey, California. He showed the great expectations were not unfounded when he played his way onto the Tour by winning $10,190 late in 1980 and placed eighth among the 1981 money winners with $184,710.

Clampett was eighth in scoring with an average of 70.77 and placed second four times and third twice in 1981 . . . but he didn't win a tournament. Until the Southern Open, 1982 was pretty much of a repeat — a second in the Greensboro Open and bitter disappointment in the British Open after leading by five strokes at the halfway mark. Finally, success, and Clampett attributed his two-stroke triumph over Hale Irwin in the Southern Open to his misfortune in the British Open. 'My confidence was hurt a lot by the British experience,' Clampett admitted, 'but it's the type of experience you can turn around in your favor.'

When his time to win finally came, Clampett knew how to handle it, shooting a six-under-par 64 at Green Island Country Club in Columbus, Georgia, in the face of an outstanding 61 by Irwin in the final round. 'When you shoot a 61, you don't figure that is going to lose the golf tournament,' groaned Irwin. Clampett turned in rounds of 65, 69, 68 and 64 for 266 and said, 'It was a nice feeling to finally come out on top. It's been a weight on my shoulders.'

Clampett led at the beginning, sharing the first-round lead with Lance Ten Broeck, and at the end, but in between his first victory as a pro was in question. John Fought, with 67–66, led after the second round. Fought had left the Tour after missing the cut in six of his first eight tournaments in 1982 and took a job as an accountant in his home town of Portland, Oregon. When he thought he was ready, he returned and said, 'Now I enjoy it; everything is gravy now.' But Fought didn't break par the last two rounds. George Burns, with a 66, went in front by one stroke with a 201 after 54 holes, one ahead of Clampett. Burns shot a creditable 68 in the final round, but Clampett came out in the plus-twos, argyle socks and shirt he wore in the final round of the British Open, just to show he wasn't superstitious. Now, if he hadn't shot a 64 and if he hadn't won, well, who knows?

Texas Open — $250,000
Winner: Jay Haas

When last the Tour had seen Jay Haas, it was at the Hall of Fame tournament two weeks prior to the Texas Open when he beat John Adams in a playoff after they had finished one stroke in front of Curtis Strange. Maybe their stars run in the same orbit, for at Oak Hills Country Club in San Antonio, Texas, Haas and Strange again were at the top of their games . . . and again Haas came out the winner.

Speaking of replays, the Texas Open had another: in 1981, Bill Rogers and Ben Crenshaw, old friends, met in a playoff won by Rogers; now here were old friends — Haas and Strange both went to Wake Forest University — again battling it out for the tournament championship. Haas won by three strokes with 63–67–67–65—262 and didn't have a single bogey. 'I was just riding the wave of a couple weeks ago,' said Haas after his opening round following a one-week layoff. That gave him a two-stroke lead and the wave continued.

Craig Stadler, shooting for the money-winning championship, opened with a 65 and although he ultimately wound up in a tie for 18th, the $2,519 he won seemed to sew up the money title as his main challenger, Raymond Floyd, missed the cut for the second week in a row. With three tournaments to go, Stadler had $443,820 and Floyd $386,809.

Meanwhile, Haas had his lead cut to a stroke by Strange, D.A. Weibring and Keith Fergus after 36 holes and Strange made it a two-man deadlock with a 66 in the third round. With Leonard Thompson in third place, just two strokes back, it was an all-Wake Forest battle in the final round. 'It's kind of like last year, when Rogers and Crenshaw, good friends, were in a playoff,' noted Strange.

The head-to-head showdown never developed. Haas kept making birdies and pars en route to a 65, Strange shot a 68 and Thompson slipped to a 71 and a tie for fifth place. With two straight victories and more than $194,000 in winnings, what had looked like an ordinary season for Haas suddenly had become his best. Strange had more money — $263,000 — but was facing his second consecutive winless season . . . and probably hoping Jay Haas would take the week off the next time Strange played.

Lajet Classic — $350,000
Winner: Wayne Levi

He was among the top 15 money winners and had won a tournament many months earlier, but Wayne Levi had an identity problem before he captured the LaJet Classic. Aside from the players on Tour, few people knew who he was. Although he was the first to win a tournament while using a colored ball — the Hawaiian Open in February — even that notation was taken from him. Most people thought the first was Jerry Pate, who was pictued in most of the advertisements for the orange-colored golf balls.

By the time the LaJet tournament at the Fairway Oaks Country Club in Abilene, Texas, was over, the people in Texas knew him and he gave indication the rest of the world will get acquainted in 1983 as he won wire to wire. The $63,000 prize put him in ninth place among the money winners with $268,631, by coincidence just a little more than $5,000 behind Pate.

The LaJet is a tournament that evolved from one of those rich pro-ams that provide a sure payday to those fortunate enough to get invited to them. It was started by three oil barons who like golf and the $350,000 purse was unusual for a tournament so late in the year. The players are treated royally and with only two tournaments to follow it the LaJet had added importance — the money-winning championship and the Vardon Trophy for scoring average were still up for grabs.

Raymond Floyd virtually handed over the money title to Craig Stadler. Floyd shot 72–74, then left for his home in Florida, believing he had missed the cut. Earlier in the season, in the TPC, Floyd had gone home after figuring he had missed the cut, but after learning he had made it he was able to return in time for the third round (getting from one part of Florida to another is not as difficult as traveling from Florida to Abilene, Texas). So Stadler gained $2,642 on Floyd, giving him a lead of almost $60,000. Tom Kite outscored Tom Watson, 293–295, dropping Watson out of a virtual tie with Kite for the scoring lead.

Levi, 29, had won more than $100,000 in 1979 and 1980, but had missed the coveted top 60 in 1981. A year earlier, he had failed to break par in any round of the LaJet. This time, he broke it every round. On an unusually calm day, Levi fired an eight-under-par 64, birdieing 10 of the last 13 holes, to take the first-day lead by one stroke over Mike Morley, who used two eagles to fashion a 65. A dry, hot Texas wind swept Fairway Oaks the second day and obviously Floyd didn't calculate what it would do to the scores as he beat an ill-advised retreat home. Only five players turned in scores under 70 as Levi doubled his lead with a 71, two ahead of Bruce Devlin, who opened 67–70 in a valiant bid to land an exempt berth in 1983. The wind slowed to a cool breeze from the north in the third round and once again Levi doubled his lead. This time the man closest to him was Bobby Cole, like Devlin a man shooting for exemption. Cole, whose wife, touring pro Laura Baugh, had given birth to their first child a few months earlier, had a 69 for 207, four behind Levi.

Levi said he was nervous before the final round, but it didn't show in his play. Maybe because he made two birdies in the first six holes and by then had a seven-stroke lead on the field. Birdies at 11, 13 and 14 removed all the suspense as Levi turned in a 68 for 271 and won by six strokes over Thomas Gray, a second-year pro who earned his biggest paycheck — $37,800 — by finishing 66–67.

Pensacola Open — $200,000
Winner: Calvin Peete

People such as Pete Brown, Charley Sifford and Lee Elder laid the groundwork, but it was Calvin Peete who really proved a black man can win on the PGA Tour with regularity. Elder won four tournaments and nearly $1 million in 15 years on the Tour. When Peete captured the Pensacola Open in a runaway, it marked his fourth victory of the year and raised his earnings for the year to more than $317,000.

Peete joined Craig Stadler as the only four-time winners in 1982 by a seven-stroke margin over another man on a roll, Hal Sutton, at Perdido Bay Country Club. It was Peete's second seven-stroke win of the year. The other came in the B.C. Open, the third of his four victories, following the Greater Milwaukee Open and the Anheuser-Busch Classic. From the beginning of July until the end of October, nobody played better than the 39-year-old Peete — not Player of the Year Tom Watson, nor the money champ, Stadler.

Peete showed the ability to sink his teeth into a tournament, then when he was in position to win, to do just that, his uncanny accuracy pushing his pursuers out of the way. That's what he did in the Pensacola Open, a tournament with a modest purse but some big-name players — Watson, Jerry Pate and Bob Gilder — and also many not so well known. Two of the latter, Brad Bryant and Steven Liebler, shot eight-under-par 64s the first day, giving them a one-stroke lead on Peete and a few others. Liebler came back with a 66 for a 36-hole 130 and Peete hung on his tail with a 66 of his own. Meanwhile, Sutton had opened 66–67 and when he shot a 68 on Saturday he jumped into a two-stroke lead on Peete, Jim Colbert and Mike Sullivan as Liebler came apart with a 74. Peete shot 72.

Sutton's lead didn't last long the final day. Peete birdied the first and third holes and when Sutton bogeyed the fourth Peete was ahead and shifted into overdrive. With a clear field in front of him, Peete shot a seven-under 65, the best round of the day, for a 72-hole 268. Sutton had to settle for a tie for second place with Dan Halldorson at 275 as he struggled to a 74 while Halldorson came in with a 67. The $17,600 he collected gave Sutton the record for most money ever won by a first-year Tour player, $165,434, topping Pate's record of $153,102 in 1976.

Walt Disney World Classic — $400,000
Winner: Hall Sutton

From the way he had been playing, it was only a matter of time until Hal Sutton would win his initial Tour tournament. It finally came in the final tournament of the season, the Walt Disney World Classic at Orlando, Florida, but Sutton had to share the moment with some of those who won what amounted to little more than change. Sutton, the 1980 U.S. Amateur champion, capped a magnificent first year on tour by defeating little-known Bill Britton on the fourth hole of a sudden-death playoff, but he couldn't have been much happier than Britton, Antonio Cerda or Larry Mize, who were involved in a different money match. Sutton's $72,000 check gave him $237,434, the most money won by a first-year pro on the PGA Tour.

Jack Nicklaus had won the Disney tournament in 1971, 1972 and 1973 when it was an individual event. From 1974 through 1981, it was a team tournament and the money was 'unofficial'. In 1982, the Disney went back to an individual format on the order of the Crosby — the pros played with amateur partners for the first three days on Disney World's three courses (Magnolia, Palm and Buena Vista) and those who survived the 54-hole cut played the final round at Magnolia. For those seeking a place among the top 125 money winners and an exempt spot on the 1983 Tour, it could have been distracting playing with amateurs the first three days, but it didn't seem to bother Britton, who was 116th on the money tree going into the final tournament of the year.

Britton broke 70 in every round, finishing with an outstanding 64 the final day, and might have won had Sutton not holed a clutch 15-foot birdie putt at the 72nd hole for a 67 that tied him with Britton at 269. After they both parred the first extra hole, Britton missed a seven-foot birdie putt at the second that would have won it and eventually bowed to Sutton's 12-foot birdie putt at the fourth extra hole after leaving his first shot in the wet sand of a bunker near the green. But Britton won $43,200, moving him to $57,328 and 57th place on the money list.

Two of the hottest players on the Tour, Calvin Peete and Jay Haas, shot 66s and shared the first-round lead with Terry Diehl. Peete had another challenge: If he hit 52 greens, he would break away from a tie with Peter Jacobsen (not entered in the Disney) and win the 'Greens In Regulation' title for the second straight year. He was almost a shoo-in to take the 'Fairways Hit' crown again. An 18-under score for the 72 holes would give him the lowest average for the year, but he couldn't win the Vardon Trophy because one of the conditions is that a man must have at least a high school education to qualify for PGA membership and Peete, who had passed his high school equivalency test earlier in the year, had not passed it early enough to qualify for the Vardon. But no matter. Peete slipped after his opening round and, although he hit 57 greens and took the GIR and fairways hit championships, he wasn't a factor in the tournament.

Haas, who had played only 27 holes the week prior to the tournament, continued to wield a hot putter as he shot a 66 the second day for a one-stroke lead on Howard Twitty and two on Sutton, Dan Pohl and J.C. Snead. And when he came back with a 65 the third day he had a five-stroke cushion on Sutton and Nelson going into the final round. It looked as if his third victory of the year was assured.

But Haas' putter went cold in the final round and Sutton and Britton got hot. Sutton had blown a two-stroke lead in the Pensacola Open the week before by playing conservatively the final day and said, 'I was determined not to let that happen again. I told myself I would be as aggressive all day as I knew how to be.' Playing aggressively, Sutton birdied three of the first four holes. Even so, Haas was still two strokes to the good as they made the turn for home.

Then, disaster for Haas. He bogeyed Nos. 10, 11 and 12 and suddenly found himself deadlocked for the lead with Sutton and Nelson, with Britton, Twitty and Don Pooley a mere shot behind. Britton played the back nine in a six-under 30, birdieing Nos. 15 and 18 and finishing 19 under par. Haas and Sutton both got 18 under by birdieing No. 14, but Haas missed a 2½-foot birdie putt at 16 and had no more birdies left in his bag. Sutton had one left, a 15-footer at the final green that sent the tournament into extra holes.

After Sutton's victory in the playoff, the only matter left was figuring out who did and who didn't make the all-exempt Tour for 1983. John Fought, finishing fast, took the 125th and last spot with a $1,108 payday that gave him $28,596 and made a sad man of South African Gary Levenson. Although Fought already was assured a place on the Tour because he had won two tournaments in 1979, by finishing 125th he knocked Levenson, who missed the cut, down to 126th, just $185 behind him. Cerda won $6,400, moving him from 131st to 117th, and Mize picked up $9,200, going from 152nd to 124th. 'I feel like I won the tournament,' Cerda said.

World Cup — $64,500
Winners: Spain (Team), Manuel Pinero (Individual)

When Manuel Pinero and Jose-Maria Canizares hoisted the huge championship trophy after winning the 29th World Cup, the little Pinero had to struggle to hold up his end, but there was no way he was going to call for help. His golfing skills had earned him the individual trophy and helped him and Canizares win the team title for Spain, and national pride brought renewed strength to tired muscles at the crowning ceremony. 'I'd play in the World Cup even if there weren't prizes like this,' said Pinero, holding aloft the two $10,000 checks he collected. 'When my country asks me to play on her team, the honor is enough.'

Pinero won $10,000 as the individual champion, winning by one stroke over Canizares and Bob Gilder with a three-under-par 281 over the Pierre Marques Golf Club course in Acapulco, Mexico. The other check was his share of the team prize after he and Canizares had held on in a tense final round for a 563–566 decision over the United States entry of Gilder and Bobby Clampett. But for a while in the final round it appeared that the Spanish twosome might have its pockets picked by the Americans. Calvin Peete was Gilder's original partner in this 50-nation tournament founded to spread international goodwill, but Peete had to withdraw because of a reaction to a bee sting he suffered the week before in Venezuela. It took many phone calls to find a replacement for Peete before Clampett was reached. Clampett arrived only the day before the tournament was to begin and the U.S. had to pull out of the pro-am, cutting into Clampett's practice time.

There are always small crises at the World Cup because some nations turn it into a political event. South Africa was refused visas for its representatives and Taiwan withdrew because its team could not play as the Republic of China. But after these small matters were settled, the golfers got down to business and in the Pierre Marques course they faced a formidable test. It's only 6,870 yards, but it underwent an extensive renovation by Robert Trent Jones that gave it four new greens and 36 additional bunkers. The ever-present heat and ocean breezes added to the difficulty. It is not a course a man can step on and immediately play well. The scores reflected as much — only 17 under-par rounds were turned in, three by Baldovino Dassu of Italy, who placed fourth at 283 with a final-round 74.

Canizares established a course record with a four-under 67 in the first round and Pinero broke it the next day with a 65. Canizares, who had a 75 the second day, shot another 67 in the third round and the Spaniards were then the only team under par at minus-nine. They had an 11-stroke lead on Gilder and Clampett. Bobby played steadily, if unspectacularly, in the first three rounds and Gilder had followed a second-round 74 with a 69. 'I can't believe we're over par, but this is not an easy course. They (the Spaniards) are playing very well,' said Gilder.

Paired with the Americans, the Spaniards widened their lead early in the final round. Canizares birdied the second hole and Pinero birdied Nos. 5 and 6. When Canizares followed with a birdie at No. 7, the Spaniards were ahead by 14 strokes. With six holes to go, the Spanish team still held what looked like a comfortable 11-shot lead. Then the tournament began. Gilder and Clampett both birdied the long 13th and they picked up three more strokes at No. 14 when Clampett birdied and both Spaniards bogeyed. When Pinero bogeyed No. 15, his team's lead was reduced to five. But Pinero and Canizares both saved pars with excellent bunker shots at No. 16, virtually assuring their team championship.

The individual outcome went right down to the final green. As they stepped to the tee at the 438-yard No. 18 hole, Pinero and Canizares were tied for the lead and Gilder was two strokes behind. Canizares hit a poor drive and Pinero knocked his second shot into a bunker, building the tension. Gilder lost a chance at a playoff when he missed a birdie putt from 10 feet, finishing with a 68, and Pinero won with a 73 by sinking a three-foot bogey putt after Canizares three-putted for a double bogey. Pinero had bogeyed four of the final seven holes, a performance he said was caused more by fatigue than pressure. Pinero, 30, won the European Open championship and said he had played in 'too many tournaments'. It was Spain's third World Cup victory in six years and the second time Pinero was a member of the winning team. He teamed with Severiano Ballesteros to win at Palm Springs, California, in 1976.

8. The U.S. Seniors Tour

The Senior Tour in America, PGA operated and otherwise, continues to grow in size and value. In 1982, it included 14 scheduled and recognized events that attracted full complements of leading world senior players, up two from the preceding year. In 1983, the number for the fourth season jumps to 18, carrying purses of more than $3 million. The strength, though, remains in the hands of six of the younger seniors, none of them over 55 years of age and all of them leading players in the late 1950s and 1960s when professional tournament golf came into its own. The six — Miller Barber, Don January, Arnold Palmer, Bill Casper, Bob Goalby and Gene Littler — were the leading senior money-winners in 1982 and among them won 12 of the 13 individual events, although Dan Sikes shared the title in the rain-shortened, 36-hole Hilton Head Seniors with Barber. Bill Collins intruded with his victory in the new Syracuse Classic and the astonishing Sam Snead paired with January in an overwhelming performance in the Legends of Golf early in the season at Austin, Texas.

Texans Barber and January actually commanded the stage most of the year. The 51-year-old Barber, the only one of the 'Big Six' without one of the game's major championships but with 11 U.S. Tour titles on his record, followed up his four-victory first season in senior golf with a repeat in numbers in 1982, leading the money-winners for the first time with $171,390. Miller had only one poor showing all year, producing this record as he played in all except one of the tournaments:

Vintage	1st	$40,000
Tampa	Tie 4th	5,150
Legends	6th	10,500
Marlboro	Tie 9th	3,250
Peter Jackson	6th	6,500
USGA Open	1st	28,648
Denver	Tie 3rd	7,000
Syracuse	Tie 33rd	1,342
Jeremy Ranch	Tie 2nd	12,500
World Seniors	2nd	14,000
Suntree	1st	22,500
Hilton Head	Co-1st	15,000
PGA Seniors	Tie 7th	5,000

January was not as active, competing in just 10 tournaments on the senior circuit but winning three of them — Tampa and the Legends (with Snead) early in the year and the PGA Seniors for a second time in December — and was never worse than seventh in any of those 10 starts. With second-ranking earnings of $158,508, January made almost $16,000 a start, an average few players in all of golf bettered in 1982. Palmer and Casper each landed two titles, Bill presumably well-satisfied with that considering the severe problems he had endured with his game but Arnold certainly not, since he let two others get away from him during the year. Palmer, as always a tremendous crowd magnet in all 10 of his appearances and the key to the success of senior golf, won easily in the Marlboro Classic and did another come-from-behind number in Denver, but experienced demoralizing finishes that let victory escape in the Vintage and PGA Seniors. Casper, finally exhibiting the kind of form, albeit revamped, that brought him more than 50 pro titles during his great career, scored back-to-back victories in the Jeremy Ranch Shootout and the Merrill Lynch-Golf Digest Commemorative, the latter in the year's only playoff over Bob Toski, but seriously threatened in only one other event.

Financially, Goalby had a better year than either of those double winners, placing third on the list with $119,474. He was never worse than seventh after a weak showing in the season-opening Vintage and nosed out Littler to score his lone 1982 victory in the Peter Jackson Champions. Gene's triumph came in the World Seniors Invitational at Charlotte, where he has won two of his four seniors titles, although not in 1981 when he was the leading senior money-winner. Three others scored victories in non-tour events of some consequence — Art Wall winning Doug Sanders' Pro-Amateur extravaganza in Houston, Bob Erickson the U.S. National Seniors in Carmel Valley, California, and Joe Jimenez the National 'Super Seniors' Pro-Amateur in Scottsdale, Arizona.

The dominance of the few is further evidenced by a compilation of the money won during the three years that a formal Senior Tour has existed. Five of the domineering six of 1982 head that table, all with a quarter-million dollars and headed by January with $352,106. Barber has banked $288,776 in just two seasons. He is followed by Goalby at $264,371, Littler at $263,307 and Palmer at $249,548. Casper, the youngest of the group who only became a senior in mid-1981, has collected $129,710.

This cast at the top is unlikely to change much in 1983. Gay Brewer was the only new senior of consequence in 1982 and had a reasonably good debut with $51,511 in nine starts. But, senior golf is still a few years away from the arrival of the next of the game's great players.

Vintage Invitational —$400,000
Winner: Miller Barber

Miller Barber picked up where he left off in 1981 when he played in his first Vintage Invitational, the rich event that launched the new seniors season in March at the plush new Vintage Club and course near Indian Wells in the Southern California desert resort area. The chunky Barber, who didn't turn 50 early enough last year to play in the Vintage, had won his last three seniors starts of 1981. He then made it four in a row at the Vintage, but he needed a little help from his friends.

It came in particular and with no willingness from Arnold Palmer on what is considered to be the Vintage's toughest hole — the 401-yard, uphill par-four

16th, on which the approach to a shallow green deep in canyon must carry a water hazard, yet avoid heavy grass behind and the rocks of Eisenhower Mountain on the left. Palmer had taken command of the tournament on the rainy Sunday, rare for the Palm Springs area, and seemed to have the tournament in hand when he put his tee shot in excellent position on the tight 16th.

Then, Arnie was visited by the dramatic, as he has been so often during his storied career, both positively and negatively. He hit his seven-iron approach 'fat' and the ball dropped into the water. A bad pitch and three putts later he had a seven. Pars on the final two holes weren't enough to stave off Barber, even though he and the other two contenders behind Arnie bogeyed that hole.

Barber got in with a 73 for 282, one stroke better than the 70s of Palmer and Art Wall and the 73 of Dan Sikes for 283s. It gave him the $40,000 first prize, the biggest individual prize in senior golf.

Palmer, who has enjoyed great success over the years in the desert west, was in the midst of things from the start of the $400,000 tournament. A three-birdie string helped him to a 69, good for a one-stroke lead over Sikes, two over Bill Casper and three over the ailing defending champion, Gene Littler, who had picked up a virus on a trip to the Far East.

The field just beat a thunderstorm Friday as Sikes caught up to Palmer, shooting a 71 while Arnie, missing a four-footer at the last hole, was taking a par 72 for his 141. Right behind were Littler (70) at 142, Barber (60) at 143 and Wall (70) and Bob Rosburg (60) at 144, the latter spoiling a blazing round with double-bogeys thanks to shots into the water at the 16th and 17th holes. (Rosburg was six over on the 16th for the tournament.)

The scoring perked up some under fair skies Saturday, Barber enjoying the weather the most as he ripped off a near-perfect, six-birdie 66 to jump into first place at 209. Sikes had 69 for 210, while Palmer, managing only a par 72, slipped to 213, joined there by Wall with his 69. The final round revolved around those four players, Don January and Casper unable to do anything from 215.

For 15 holes Arnie dominated play on the damp Sunday after he picked up two strokes on Barber by chipping in for a birdie on the first hole while Miller was bogeying. Arnie had closed to a single stroke at the turn and, with birdies at the 10th, 12th and 15th, had moved a shot into the lead before the disaster at the 16th.

As has been typical of the man amid adversity over the years, Palmer swallowed his disappointment and got in the last word at the presentation ceremony. Chiding Barber, he said: 'I noticed you thanked the great course, the great conditions, the great officials and the great gallery, but you didn't thank me.'

Michelob Seniors Classic — $125,000
Winner: Don January

It was much easier this time around. In fact, Don January was a very surprised man a year earlier even to win the Michelob Seniors at Tampa, Florida. 'When the day began, I figured my chances were slim and none,' said January, who had been six strokes behind with nine holes to play before leader Arnold Palmer ran into a rash of back-nine bogeys and Don beat Doug Ford in a playoff.

This year, the victory had no such theatrics as Don became the first player successfully to defend one of the senior tour titles. January started the day three strokes up on the field and finished the tournament with the same margin, recording five birdies on the first 12 holes and coasting home to a 69 and a 10-under-par winning score of 278. It was the rawboned, 52-year-old Texan's sixth victory in seniors competition.

It was also a rewarding week for another former PGA champion, Dow Finsterwald. Although he had to settle for second place, Finsterwald made his best senior tour showing to date at Tampa's Carrollwood Village Golf and Tennis Club, never exceeding par en route to his 281.

Miller Barber teed off in the Michelob carrying a four-tournament winning streak in senior golf (three in 1981 and the season-opening Vintage in 1982) and got a good start toward No. 5. He shot 68 and shared the first-round lead with J.C. Goosie, a well-known local pro and former tour player who organized the first successful mini-tour (Space Coast) in Florida years ago. Paul Harney had a 69, Finsterwald was among four players at 70, January well back at 73 and Palmer off to an even worse start with 74. He never totally recovered from that.

Goosie hung tough Friday with a 71, remaining in a first-place deadlock, but then with Art Wall, who shot 72–67 for his 139. Barber fell back with 74, but January began his move with a three-under 69 on the 6,529-yard course. An experienced wind player from way back, as are most Texans, January coped better than anybody else Saturday when 30 mph gusts breezed through Carrollwood. He fired a 67 and rocketed into his three-stroke lead at 209.

It was a magnificent round — 16 greens hit in regulation, five birdies, no bogeys. Don protested that he is not a good wind player despite what happened: 'When the wind blows like this back in Dallas, I like to stay indoors.' Nonetheless, he then had three strokes on Harney (69–72–71) and four on Barber (68–74–71), Wall (72–67–74), Bill Collins (70–70–73), Finsterwald (70–72–71) and Bill Casper (73–69–71).

January did face challenges on the front nine Sunday. Collins eagled the first hole and he and Harney were just two behind at the turn after Don three-putted the ninth green. However, after a shaky par at No. 10, Don ran off birdies at the next two holes — sinking a 12-footer at the par-five 11th and a four-footer off a six-iron tee shot at the par-three 12th.

'After that, I didn't shoot at the pins,' January recalled afterward. 'I figured I'd make pars and they'd have to make birdies.' That strategy produced the closing 69 and $20,000 victory. Finsterwald sank an 18-foot birdie putt on the final green for his 68—281 that edged Harney by a stroke. Paul finished with a 70, as did Barber and Collins, who tied for fourth position.

Legends of Golf — $464,000
Winners: Sam Snead and Don January

How can a tournament in which the victors win by 12 strokes over just 54 holes possibly have any drama or excitement left in it the last day? In most cases, it doesn't — a situation that has sponsors and, even more so, television producers singing the blues. Such would certainly have been the case in April at the Legends of Golf, a tournament that was created and exists primarily for television.

But there was a saving grace. The team that opened an eight-stroke lead after 36 holes of the rain-shortened tournament Saturday and rode it on to the final massive margin consisted of the winningest of the seniors — Don January — and the amazing Sam Snead, who was just a month away from his 70th birthday and has to be the only man ever in any sport to have scored victories in six different decades.

Nor was it a matter of the older man riding his younger (52) partner's coattails. Snead made 14 of the team's 27 birdies in reaching the record low score of 183 and, in the words of January, 'I can't see any athlete in any sport doing what Sam has done. I've never seen a player fly shots right at the flag hole after hole. Sam was on a roll.' Then, the Texan added in generous exaggeration, 'I just tried to stay out of his way.'

Starting with the PGA Seniors at the end of 1979, January had won six times before the Legends since senior golf became a serious endeavor, while Snead with Gardner Dickinson as his partner then, took the first Legends in 1978 and Golf Digest's Commemorative Seniors in 1980.

There is no telling how far under par Snead and January might have gotten if the tournament had gone the scheduled four rounds. After Snead had birdied the 15th and 16th holes Sunday, January said: 'Man, how many do you want to win by?' Sam's typical snappy response: 'You never know. Them folks up ahead might be cheating.'

Anyway, a stalled storm system over that part of the country plagued all of the pre-tournament activities at Austin's Onion Creek Club, the scene of the tournament since its inception, and left the 6,584-yard course unplayable for Thursday's first round. So it was cancelled and the 54-hole format established since double rounds were not feasible.

When action finally began Friday, January logged five birdies and Snead three as they shot 62, just a shot better than the first round of the defenders Gene Littler and Bob Rosburg, and three under Julius Boros and Miller Barber. By Saturday night, the contest for first place was over. Don and Sam generated a 60 for 122 and left the field behind, sputtering in disbelief. Boros and Barber shared the distant runnerup slot — 130 — with the unlikely team of Bob Toski and Chin Sei Ha, a naturalized Japanese better known by his native Chinese name of Chen Ching Po.

Any thoughts anybody might have had that January/Snead were catchable evaporated early on Sunday. Snead birdied the first hole, January the second and they were off and running toward their final-round 61 and 183 total. The race for second place did generate some interest for TV. It came down to the final hole, where Roberto DeVicenzo and Bob Goalby bogeyed, Littler and Rosburg parred and Toski rolled in a birdie putt. The result: a three-way tie for second at 195.

A bad starting round of 68 put the old pals team of Arnold Palmer and Dow Finsterwald too far behind and their closing 64 missed that tie by a stroke Barber and Boros, still not at full strength after a quintuple bypass operation last year, skidded to a closing 68 and 198. The winners needed little from their individual $50,000 checks to get home. January lives just up the road in Dallas and Snead, the Jack Benny of sports, if you believe all the stories, skipped the final press conference to accept a lift back to Florida on Palmer's Citation II jet.

Marlboro Classic — $150,000
Winner: Arnold Palmer

Arnold Palmer returned to one of his happier hunting grounds — New England — for the first time in almost six years and made that visit rewarding by capturing his 83rd professional victory and third in the senior realm. It came in June in the Marlboro Classic, a regular stop on the PGA Senior Tour in Massachusetts, just west of Boston, as Palmer fought off the challenges of Bob Rosburg, Bill Casper and one errant tee shot to score a four-shot win at Marlboro Country Club, its course a 6,174-yard layout with rolling fairways and good greens.

In victory, Palmer could reflect on his other New England achievements — his first U.S. triumph as a pro in 1956 and a second win in 1960 in the Insurance City Open at Hartford and later on a win in the first Kemper Open in 1968 just down the road from Marlboro at Worcester's Pleasant Valley.

Arnie never trailed in the Marlboro Classic, shaking loose from leadership deadlocks each of the first two days to run in front the rest of the way. The first tie was with the remarkable Sam Snead as both shot opening three-under-par 68s. Only three others — Bill Johnston and Charlie Owens at 69 and Doug Ford at 70 — broke par. However, it was not to be Snead's week. The 70-year-old marvel, who had lost his caddie at the first tee Thursday when he fell and broke a leg, fumbled his scorekeeping Friday, signed for an incorrect number at No. 15 after shooting 74 and, realizing it moments later, disqualified himself.

Meanwhile, Art Wall was replacing Sam as co-leader with Palmer by tying the course record with 66 while Arnie was lipping out a flock of putts en route to 70 for his 138. That put them three in front of Owens (69–72) and Casper (73–68) and four ahead of Bob Goalby, the defending champion; Peter Thomson and Johnston.

A third straight sub-par round lifted Palmer into permanent possession of the lead Saturday. With his two-under 69 and 207, Arnie moved three strokes ahead of Wall, who shot 72, and Bob Rosburg, who broke Art's day-old course record with a 65 for his 210. Still in the picture were Casper at 211, Thomson at 212 and Dan Sikes, a consistent challenger since the first 1982 event, at 213. Palmer was not happy with his putting, but Rosburg had no complaints about his, as he fashioned the 65 with his own recovery touch and stroke on the greens.

Palmer was as steady as the moderate rain that fell all day, but was unspectacular in the early going Sunday, running off seven pars before making birdie at the par-five eighth, parring the next two holes and recording his second and final birdie of the round at the 11th. With consecutive birdies at the seventh, eighth and ninth, Rosburg remained close and Casper challenged early on the back nine, but the issue was settled by Arnie's lone flirtation with trouble at the 15th hole.

His tee shot wound up behind trees and his recovery left him 60 yards short of the pin with playing partner Rosburg on the green eyeing a birdie putt. It was the only green Palmer missed all day. However, he lofted a sand-wedge shot six inches from the cup for a tap-in par and Rosburg left his eight-foot birdie putt just short. Arnie's final three pars for 69 gave him his 276 and four-shot victory over Casper, who also finished with 69, and Rosburg, who had a closing 70. Thomson (69) and Sikes (68) tied for fourth at 281.

So, Palmer had another New England win for his record and $25,000 for his bank account after what he said 'was really a dogfight all the way until the last few holes.'

Peter Jackson Champions — $200,000 (Canadian)
Winner: Bob Goalby

Bob Goalby and the Peter Jackson Champions produced yet another example of the danger of assuming victories in golf and, for that matter, in any sport while it is still humanly possible to lose. The Peter Jackson was the fifth stop on the 1982 senior tour, taking many of the veteran players on a nostalgic return in late June to Winnipeg, Manitoba, and St. Charles Country Club, where they had played in the Canadian Open 30 years earlier.

Goalby, still five years away from the start of his professional career at that time, was not among them, of course, but was quite pleased with Peter Jackson's choice of venue by week's end. The 53-year-old Illinois native and former Masters champion became just the fifth multiple winner of individual events in the three years that senior golf has had a tour of sorts, but turned a rout into a scare at the very end. (Miller Barber, Don January, Arnold Palmer and Gene Littler were the others who had more than single titles on their individual senior records at that time.)

Scattering record-making scores all over the place, Goalby moved from an opening lead of a single shot to one of five strokes by the end of the third round. He shot 68s in the first two rounds, leading five players by a single stroke the first day and Barber and Peter Thomson, the great Australian, by the same margin after 36 holes. Then the man who found a new career as a TV golf commentator in America put on a premier performance for the Canadian networks Saturday. He birdied the first two holes and rolled to a 64 that broke the course and tournament record for 18 holes. His 200 total set new tournament and senior tour marks for that distance. He had four other birdies and holed from a bunker at the 13th for an eagle in his brilliant round over the 6,473-yard, par-72 course.

Littler shot a fine 67, yet still lost ground, ending the day in second place, five strokes off Goalby's pace. Goalby also had two of the other leading senior players — January and Barber — still within range at 206.

When Bob's game started sputtering Sunday, Littler and January did their best to take advantage of it. After 16 holes, Goalby's margin was down to two over Littler and was further jeopardized when Bob overshot the 17th green and

Gene put himself in birdie range. Goalby then showed the experience and ability of a pro who had won 11 times on the PGA Tour by saving par with a brilliant pitch to two feet. Littler made his birdie putt, but Goalby played the 18th perfectly to preserve the one-stroke victory margin with 73 for 273 and collect the $31,000 (Canadian) check.

Australian Kel Nagle posted a final-round 66 to tie for third at 277 with January (71) and Moe Norman (69), who might have been Canada's most talented pro had he chosen to play in America in his earlier years. Barber had a final-round 72 to place sixth at 278.

Goalby's winning total broke the Peter Jackson record for 72 holes and Arnold Palmer's three-week-old 276 mark for the senior tour, set at Marlboro, but it didn't remotely threaten the record of another Palmer, Johnny, set in that 1952 Canadian Open. Winning by 11 strokes, Johnny Palmer shot 263, still a Canadian Open record. They honored Palmer at the awards ceremony with an honorary membership to St. Charles, which must have made up for some of Johnny's disappointment with his play in the Peter Jackson. Only an occasional entrant in the senior events, the 64-year-old Palmer finished far down the standings with 317.

USGA Senior Open —$150,000
Winner: Miller Barber

Miller Barber is accomplishing in senior golf something that he just couldn't bring about on the PGA Tour during his long and lucrative career. In his more than two decades on the regular circuit, Barber never managed to land one of the game's major titles, coming closest at Houston, Texas, where a final-round collapse cost him the U.S. Open in 1969.

Now, in less than two years of senior campaigning, the 51-year-old Texan already has captured, among six victories, both the PGA and USGA Seniors championships, the titles of golf's two leading organizations. The latter win came in exciting fashion as national professional golf returned to the Northwest for the tournament at Portland Golf Club, a past venue for American tour and international events.

Saving the best for last, Barber put together the week's finest round on Sunday to move from a one-shot deficit into a runaway victory situation. He shot a six-under-par 65 and rolled to a four-stroke victory. His cards were 72–74–71–65—282.

Interestingly, Miller played that final round with Arnold Palmer, with whom he started the day at 217, two of four men a stroke behind third-round-leader Dan Sikes, and it was Palmer whom he succeeded as the USGA Seniors champion, just as it was Arnie he succeeded the previous December in Miami as the PGA Seniors king.

Like virtually all of his contemporaries, Barber has great respect for Palmer and what he means to senior golf and the game. Said Mr. X after the tournament: 'It's great just to be around the man. He has done so much to make the game what it is. I knew most of the fans wanted him to win. If I couldn't do it, I wanted him to win, too.' Bob Goalby had put it this way a few weeks earlier when Arnie won the Marlboro: 'Let's face it. He's still our saviour.'

The tight 6,439 yards of the sun-drenched Portland Golf Club course and the fast, undulating greens, which Gene Littler termed tougher than those at Augusta National, took a heavy toll on the scoring. Only three other 18-hole totals in the 60s were produced by the 98 pros and 52 amateurs all week.

The best anybody could do the first day was match par. As is so often the case, two little-known pros — Ken Towns and Joe Jimenez — led after the opening round. With even-par 71s, they were a stroke in front of Barber, Goalby, Freddie Haas and club pro Art Silvestrone and two ahead of a nine-man group that included Palmer, Littler and Gay Brewer, who remained in the hunt all the way.

Littler came up with one of the two 69s Friday and took a one-stroke lead at 142. Gene had five birdies on the first 11 holes, then had trouble, as most players did all week, on the back nine, giving back three of those strokes. Goalby and Brewer had similar experiences on the incoming nine, but shot 71 and 70, respectively, to tie for second at 143, while Sikes, with the other 69, and Palmer, with 71, were next at 144. Little noticed then was Barber, who probably saved his bid when he birdied the 16th and 18th holes for 74.

Sikes, one of the few who seemed able to handle the tough 13th-through-16th-hole stretch, discovered he could shoot a one-over 72 and advance into the lead Saturday, the toughest scoring day of all for the field. At 216, the Floridian had one shot on Palmer (73), Goalby (74), Towns (72) and Barber, whose 71 was the best of the day. Littler took a 76, but was just two behind at 218 with Brewer (75).

That set the stage for Barber to shoot 'one of the best rounds of golf in one of the biggest tournaments of my life, considering the conditions and what this title means.' He seemed genuinely surprised that he had shot 65. Driving mostly with his three-wood, Barber birdied the second, fifth and seventh holes to take a one-stroke lead over Littler and Sikes into the back nine, where he birdied 10 and 11 and widened his gap over Littler to two strokes. He capped the performance when he knocked an eight-iron approach two feet from the cup to set up his final birdie at No. 16 and breeze to his four-shot victory.

Littler closed with 68 and Sikes with 70 to tie for second at 286, Goalby had 72 for 289 and Palmer (74) and Brewer (73) fell back to 291 in a fifth-place deadlock. Towns, a Californian who played the tour for a few years in the early 1960s, hung on with a 75 that placed him seventh. Because four amateurs survived the cut, the prize money was juggled and Barber wound up with an unusual check for $28,648.

Denver Post Champions of Golf — $150,000
Winner: Arnold Palmer

When the seniors came to town for the new Denver Post Champions of Golf tournament in early August, a new generation of Colorado golf fans got a dose of the heady stuff that their elders have been reminiscing about for the last 22 years. In June of 1960 at Denver's Cherry Hills Country Club, Arnold Palmer scored probably the most memorable of the 84 victories that grace his great record, coming from seven strokes off the pace to win the U.S. Open Championship.

In the Champions of Golf event at Denver's Pinehurst Country Club, a considerably older Palmer demonstrated the technique again, though not as sensationally. He entered the final round of that tournament three strokes behind Art Wall and Bob Goalby, came up with his birdie flurry in a storm-interrupted stretch run and watched Goalby's stirring attempt to catch him fall one shot short. Palmer's cards were 68–67–73–67 for 275, five under par over Pinehurst's 6,908 yards. The victory, Palmer's fourth in senior golf, brought a $25,000 check.

The tournament built up to the final-round heroics this way:

Fred Hawkins, a journeyman player on the regular Tour for the better part of two decades, grabbed the first-round lead at 66 with a five-birdie, one-bogey round and a head cold. On his heels were Miller Barber at 67; Jack Fleck, Don January, Gay Brewer and Palmer at 68. As Hawkins faded with 72 the second day, Brewer (68–66) and Wall (69–65) moved in front at 134, a shot in front of Palmer (68–67) and two ahead of Fleck (68–68) and Goalby (70–66). Brewer shot the back nine in 30. January, who was to finish in a rush just two behind Palmer, probably did himself in Friday with a triple-bogey seven at the ninth hole, where he put two balls in the water.

Wall, who has been a frequent seniors contender but a winner only in the team Legends in 1980 and the off-tour extravaganza of Doug Sanders in Houston later in 1982, hung tough Saturday, his one-over 71 leaving him still tied for the lead after 54 holes, but then with Goalby, who had a 69 for his 205. For much of the day, Palmer had the tournament in his hands. He led by two strokes before encountering another of a string of bogeys that have caught him a few times in recent years. He drove out of bounds at the 11th hole, bogeyed that and four other of the next six holes for a back-nine 40 and the 73 that left him three strokes out. Brewer also faltered in the stretch after leading briefly, finishing the day a shot ahead of Palmer but two behind Wall and Goalby, one behind Gene Littler and tied with Barber and George Bayer.

Nobody did much in Sunday's early going. Palmer, for instance, turned in par 35 and was still even for the round after a birdie at the 11th and a bogey at the 13th. The first of two interruptions of play because of lightning-laced skies came after Arnie had birdied the 14th and 15th and moved into a five-way tie with Wall, Brewer, Barber and January at four under par. After that delay of some two hours, Palmer made his third straight birdie at the par-five 16th to take the lead for good, holing a clutch six-foot par putt at the 18th for the 67 after the second delay of an hour.

Only Goalby had a chance to catch Palmer at the 18th and how close he came. His approach hit the flagstick but didn't drop. Still, Bob's ensuing birdie was lucrative. It gave him second place to himself, a shot ahead of January, Barber, Brewer and Wall, and a $15,000 check. The four at 277 received $7,000 each. Goalby saluted Palmer at the closing ceremony. 'He's the king. I couldn't beat him for 30 years and I couldn't beat him today, damn it.'

Greater Syracuse Classic — $150,000
Winner: Bill Collins

It couldn't have been easy, Bill Collins' decision to give up his long-time position at Brae Burn Country Club in New York's wealthy Westchester County so he could play the senior circuit full-time. It wasn't just leaving the security and the friends he had at Brae Burn. He had not been a big winner when he played on the PGA Tour in the 1950s and early 1960s and was regularly subject to back problems that eventually required surgery. That is not the best kind of ailment for a full-time tournament player of 53 to have nagging him, even though the Senior Tour does permit its players to ride power carts.

But, Collins' confidence in his ability manifested itself in mid-August when he won the Greater Syracuse Classic 20 years after capturing his fourth and last title on the regular PGA Tour — the Buick Open at Flint, Michigan. The Buick, one of the richer events in 1962, paid him $8,000 compared to the $25,000 he picked up at Syracuse's Bellevue Country Club.

In a sense, the 6.4 native Pennsylvanian was an unlikely winner, considering the slick nature of the greens that had most of the pros grumbling and led Tour officials to raise the mowers after the first round — to little avail. Collins had three-putted 14 times the week before in Denver. Hardly the thing to bring to a course where putting was going to be so demanding. But he altered his stroke a bit and, perhaps more importantly, heeded the advice of the local amateurs familiar with the course with whom he played in the pro-am the first day. 'They told me that most every putt breaks towards the clubhouse and I finally believed them,' Bill remarked. 'Still, I only had one tap-in in the first three days.'

Collins snuck up on the lead during those first three rounds, all played in windy conditions that compounded the troubles on the greens. Freddie Haas jumped out in front the first day with a two-under-par 69 over the 6,572-yard Bellevue course, a design of noted architect Donald Ross, to lead Peter Thomson and Art Wall by two. After his 73 start, Collins climbed into a second-place tie Friday with Wolstenholme and Gene Littler at 144, two strokes off the pace, then being set by Haas (73) and Thomson (72). Not noted for long hot summers, Syracuse came up with a chill to go with the wind Saturday. A 71 by Collins and Don January's 69 gave them joint possession of the lead at 215, which was then two over par for the 54 holes. Their closest pursuers at that point were Wolstenholme (72), Goalby (70) and Thomson (74) at 216, Littler (73) at 217.

Calm, warmer weather Sunday seemed to open the door finally to some low scoring, but Collins collected the marbles with just a one-under 70, emerging from among several potential winners by handling Bellevue's difficult finishing hole better than the rest. Guy Wolstenholme, the transplanted Briton who has lived in Australia for many years, actually had the lead when he reached the 18th tee Sunday, but bogeyed the final hole when, after hitting a two-iron off the tee, his long-iron approach failed to hold the green, which slopes away from the player.

Following Guy in, Collins birdied the uphill 17th with a 15-footer and, ignoring the tightness of the 18th fairway that had daunted most others, hit a solid drive with his trusty No. 1 wood that left him with just a wedge to the green. His routine par brought him home with 70 and 285, one over par and a shot in front of Wolstenholme. Thomson and Goalby, with closing 71s, tied for third, while Bob Rosburg, with 68, surged into a fifth-place deadlock with Littler at 289.

Jeremy Ranch Shootout — $150,000
Winner: Bill Casper

The real Bill Casper finally stood up when the senior golfers visited his neighborhood for a new tournament on the outskirts of Salt Lake City, Utah. Much had been expected of Casper as soon as he officially became a senior in mid-1981, but those who did hadn't been paying attention. Casper had been in a deep slump for several years on the regular tour, rarely even making the cuts, and senior golf did not prove an immediate remedy.

Some intensive work with Phil Rodgers and sessions with two Utah hypnotists started turning things around in 1981, his victory in a slim-field U.S. National Seniors at Las Vegas and his playoff battle, though a losing effort, against Arnold Palmer in the USGA Senior Open, being the best indicators. Only once in the early stretch of the 1982 senior circuit did he seriously threaten, though, and he teed off at Jeremy Ranch only after spending two weeks in the care of a chiropractor at the expense of missing the Denver and Syracuse tournaments.

The scene of Casper's major re-arrival was a magnificent new course in the Rockies, a layout created by the Palmer Course Design duo of Arnold Palmer and Ed Seay that has drawn such raves in its short life that it is already thought of as a potential site for the first U.S. Open or PGA Championship in the Northwest in decades. Ironically, Jeremy Ranch did in its designer. Palmer had his worst senior tournament of the year, starting with 79, never breaking par and winding up at 300 in a tie for 21st place.

Casper, who moved to the Salt Lake City area in the mid-1970s, didn't start that strongly himself. His opening 74 Wednesday left him five strokes behind leader Don January and quite a few others in between, including Gene Littler at 70 and Paul Harney and Freddie Haas at 71. Littler took over Thursday with 71 and 141, as Jeremy Ranch proved a strong test for the seniors. January slipped to 75 and 144, falling behind Littler, Miller Barber (72–70) and Dean Lind (74–69), a senior who has played most of his national tournament golf recently in the Far East. Casper was still well back at 71—145. The tournament experienced its first weather problem late that day when late afternoon thunderstorms forced a third of the field to finish the round Friday morning.

The weather was perfect that day and when the shooting was over the challengers for the final round were in place. January, shooting for his second 1982 victory, moved back into a tie for first place with Littler, firing a bogey-free 67 to Gene's 70. They were at 211, Barber moved within a stroke with a 70 and Casper began his surge with a 69 for 214, actually taking the lead early in the round when he had three birdies, an eagle and a par on the first five holes before losing momentum. Nobody else finished that day under par.

The Casper of old really emerged in Saturday's final round, a finish reminiscent of many of those the Hall of Famer put on in winning 51 tournaments on the PGA Tour between 1956 and 1975. He broke the course record with 65, the product of seven birdies and 11 pars in among lightning storms that forced two suspensions of play during the afternoon totaling more than two hours. As it turned out, Casper needed every one of those birdies because Barber fashioned a 68 and January a 69 to finish at 280, a stroke off the winner's final score.

It was exciting down to the wire. Casper parred the last five holes, finishing ahead of January and Barber, who were tied with him at nine under with three holes to play. The par-three 17th cost January, where he overshot from 203 yards with a five-iron (up in the thin air of the high Rockies, remember), and Barber lost his bid for a tie at the final hole when he hit 'my worst drive of the week' into a fairway trap and ultimately just missed a 15-foot par putt. Littler, with 72, finished fourth at 283, then it was seven shots back to Julius Boros in fifth place. Said a gratified Casper in accepting the $25,000 check, 'Maybe Billy's finally back.'

Merrill Lynch/Golf Digest Commemorative Pro-Am — $125,000
Winner: Bill Casper

When you have to shoot 65 to win a tournament by a stroke, that's a tough assignment. When you come back in the next tournament and are taken four extra holes, you have worked just about as hard as possible to win two victories in a row. Which is exactly what Bill Casper accomplished in the mountains of Utah and on the coast of Rhode Island in becoming the year's first back-to-back winner on the PGA Senior Tour.

Casper had to come from behind again to score the second victory in the Merrill Lynch/Golf Digest Commemorative Pro-Am. Casper started the Sunday round at historic Newport Country Club two strokes off the lead of Dow Finsterwald and shot 68, enough to get him a stroke past Finsterwald. But, a match for Bill's 206 came from an unexpected source. Bob Toski, who does not play the regular PGA Senior Tour but does appear in a few selected events each year, gave Casper a dose of his own medicine to force the senior year's first playoff.

Toski, who has been a member of Golf Digest's professional instruction staff for many years, hence his appearances in that event each year, has not won a Tour title of any kind since 1958. He dropped off the circuit shortly thereafter, but showed how well he can still play the game earlier in 1982 when he and Chinese pro Chin Sei Ha (Chen Ching Po) tied for second in the Legends. He gave Casper all he could handle the first three extra holes at Newport. In fact, he missed a five-footer for a win at the first overtime hole. They halved the second (17th) and Casper left a 12-footer just short at the third (18th), letting Toski off the hook. It ended when they returned to the 16th hole as Casper sank from 22 feet after Toski had missed from 40 feet. The cash split was $22,500 for Bill, $14,300 for Bob, while Finsterwald got $9,000 for his third-place finish. Dow missed the playoff when he three-putted the 17th green while Casper was coming down the stretch with two birdies and two pars on the last four holes for the 68.

At 6,566 yards, Newport is not a particularly demanding course except that, being near the ocean, it gets plenty of wind. Casper and Gardner Dickinson handled it best in Friday's first round, shooting 68s to lead Finsterwald, Peter Thomson and 64-year-old Marty Furgol by a stroke. Five others in the select, 40-man field broke Newport's 72 par. Finsterwald followed his 69 with a five-under 67 Saturday and assumed a two-stroke lead over Bob Goalby, who shot 66, and Casper, who had a 70. Howie Johnson (70–69) and Dickinson (68–71) remained in the hunt, but never threatened the last two days.

World Seniors Invitational — $135,000
Winner: Gene Littler

Let's try an exercise in associations. Charlotte . . . rainy Sundays? Gene Littler? That's the way it has worked twice in the three-year history of the select World Seniors Invitational. The tournament sails along through excellent early fall weather in south-western North Carolina until the pre-dawn hours of the final day, the rain begins and it doesn't stop all day. Neither does Littler, who professes not to have any affinity for wet weather but obviously knows how to deal with it.

In 1980, he won a tough duel with Arnold Palmer in an all-day rain. In 1982, he shrugged off a shaky start, made an eagle deuce at the 14th hole and breezed home with a five-stroke victory, again in a crowd-dampening rain. Ironically, in perfect Sunday weather in 1981, Gene finished second to Miller Barber at Charlotte's respected Quail Hollow Country Club, venue of the Kemper Open for a decade in the 1970s. Barber switched places in 1982, nosing out Peter Thomson by a stroke for second place.

Although he had already banked $74,120 from senior golf in 1982, Littler had not maintained the pace that brought him $137,427 and ranking as senior golf's No. 1 money winner in 1981. Gene hadn't won since early that year when he took the Vintage riches and teamed with Bob Rosburg to capture the equally-lucrative Legends. It didn't look like his Charlotte magic was with him when he started the 1982 World Seniors with a double-bogey. Ever the cool professional, Littler decided 'to be patient and try to get it back to even par.' With a spurt on the back nine that included a 50-foot chip-in, he did even better than that, shooting a 71 that left him just two strokes behind leader Howie Johnson, who had a wild, 24-putt 69. Jack Fleck had a 70 and Gardner Dickinson and Art Wall were with Littler at 71.

Gene moved a step closer to the top Friday, posting a 70 that included an 80-foot eagle putt at the par-five fifth hole. At 141, he trailed only Jim Ferree, a native North Carolinian who plays the Senior Tour just part-time because of his summer/winter club jobs near Pittsburgh and at Hilton Head. Ferree, who had one of his rare good putting rounds (29, 'the first time I've had less than 30 putts in 1982'), shot 68 for his 140. Bob Goalby, who admittedly had never played well at Quail Hollow, shared second with Littler with 72–69 for his 141.

For all intents and purposes, Littler put it away Saturday. The 52-year-old shotmaker fired a solid 69, breaking to a five-stroke lead when he birdied the last hole and playing partner Ferree bogeyed the last two holes for 75, dropping into a four-way tie for second at 215 with Barber, Charley Sifford and Gay Brewer. Gene started somewhat shakily in the drizzle Sunday, bogeying the first and third holes and saving par after missing the second green. However, a birdie at No. 6 from 18 feet helped and when he holed 'a little, three-quarter nine-iron' for an eagle deuce at No. 14 'it was pretty well all over.' He birdied the 15th from 20 feet and parred in for 70 and an eight-under-par 280, five shots ahead of Barber, who also closed with a 70. Littler collected $23,000 for his fourth title in two years of senior campaigning.

Palmer was as disappointed with his golf as he was with the weather. Palmer, whose organization runs the World Seniors and who has a home and major business interests in Charlotte, never challenged seriously this time after finishing second in the inaugural and third in 1981. He didn't break par until the final round, shot 289 and tied for seventh place.

Suntree Classic — $135,000
Winner: Miller Barber

The 'horses for courses' principle that was displayed by Gene Littler in the previous seniors event at Charlotte, North Carolina, got another airing when the circuit of veteran pro stars performed at Melbourne, Florida, in mid-October in the Suntree Classic. Just as Littler has proven almost unbeatable (first-second-first) in his three appearances at the World Seniors Invitational's Quail Hollow Country Club, Miller Barber has found the Suntree Country Club at the mid-Florida coastal city very much to his liking.

In his first appearance at Suntree in 1981, the Senior Tour's hottest player came from behind with a final-round 65 to score a four-stroke victory. In 1982, it was a breeze — and a remarkable one. The 51-year-old Barber posted 66s on the scoreboard one after another through the entire tournament to finish five strokes in front of Don January and at least 13 shots ahead of everybody else in the field. If that is not impressive enough, realize that his 264 was a new Senior PGA Tour record by nine strokes.

Although his senior peers have never questioned Barber's abilities throughout his consistent career, his $22,500 performance at Suntree really had them shaking their heads. 'The course isn't that easy,' said January after his game but futile pursuit. 'You still have to put the ball in the fairway, on the green and in the hole, no matter where you play.'

The tournament was pretty much a Barber-January affair from the start. January, who had skipped the two previous senior events, got away winging on the 6,533-yard Suntree course with an eight-under-par 64, yet just had the two-shot lead over Miller. Barber's 132, the first of his important new Senior Tour records, vaulted him four shots into the lead as January mustered a mere par round. He fell back into a second-place tie with Sam Snead (68–68), who was to finish with a pair of 73s and place sixth. Barber's third 66 and January's 67 in Saturday's third round left everybody else behind and that was the margin of their finish Sunday — five strokes.

On two occasions Sunday, January pulled within three strokes of the steady

Barber, but bogeyed the final hole after the cause was lost. Gay Brewer, who played with Barber and January Sunday, started with an eagle, shot 68 and finished a distant third at 277, eight behind January.

Howie Johnson, who was enjoying a fine senior season, ran off six consecutive birdies — a Senior Tour record — en route to a 65 that pulled him into fourth place, a shot ahead of Jim Ferree. In his electrifying round, Johnson made putts ranging from five to 25 feet for the six birdies, starting at the fourth hole; canned a 35-footer to save par at the 10th, birdied the 11th from 40 feet and, after missing a birdie from five feet at the 12th, made his eighth and last birdie at No. 13. Yes, the record book took a beating at Melbourne.

Hilton Head International — $112,500
Winners: Miller Barber and Dan Sikes

It sounded like some sort of team event when they announced the winners of the Hilton Head Seniors International, but it was not a variation on the Legends of Golf theme. Miller Barber and Dan Sikes were adversaries, not partners in the new Seniors tournament on the famous resort island just off the South Carolina coast. It was just that heavy weather cut the tournament in half and Barber and Sikes, the leaders after 36 holes, were declared the winners.It was not feasible to extend the tournament into Monday.

Thus, Barber became a four-time winner in 1982, matching his total in his freshman senior season of 1981, and Sikes, who had been knocking on the door several times earlier in the year, finally joined the senior winners' ranks. Thirty-six-hole tournament finishes almost never happen in American golf, yet it was the second time Barber had won at that distance in his career. The first came on the regular tour back in 1969 when rain and cold bedeviled the Kaiser International at Napa, California, into a similar abbreviated finish, though not until Monday.

Thursday gave little hint of things to come in the skies. It was a perfect day and Don January shot the 6,603-yard Shipyard Golf Club course in four-under-par 68, taking a one-stroke lead over Barber, Sikes and Art Silvestrone, a former New York area club pro who used to play on the Tour's winter circuit and now winters in Florida. Eight players opened with 71s.

The weather turned cloudy, cool and misty Friday. Sikes and Barber matched their opening 69s to take a two-stroke advantage over January, who shot 72. At that point, Julius Boros (74–68), Bob Goalby (71–71), Ted Kroll (76–66) and Buck Adams (71–71), veteran pro at the Country Club of North Carolina, were next at 142. The 66 was Kroll's best ever as a senior.

They couldn't even start play until 11.20 Saturday because of heavy morning rain. Then, with the final group just reaching the eighth hole at 2.08, another downpour ended play for the day. Tour officials hoped to finish the third round and play the fourth off two tees Sunday, but nothing ever happened. It continued to rain heavily through the night and, faced with an unplayable course the next morning, officials called it a tournament. The purse was reduced 25 per cent across the board, Barber and Sikes getting $15,000 apiece and January collecting $7,500.

PGA Seniors' Championship — $150,000
Winner: Don January

When Don January won the PGA Seniors' Championship the first time he was eligible in 1979, it didn't create much of a stir. Senior golf in tour form was still a year away, sparked into existence by the exciting happenings in a couple of Legends of Golf team tournaments that had been on national television the previous couple of years rather than by January's victory. Furthermore, January was the first of his era of 'name' stars to enter senior competition, although the likes of older Sam Snead and Julius Boros had won the PGA title in earlier years.

When the lanky Texan, now 53, captured that championship again at the end of the 1982 season, it carried much more of both meaning and money — and did attract attention. The $150,000 purse and the prestige of the title drew all of the prominent seniors and 1982 winners except Gene Littler, and the most prominent of them all — Arnold Palmer — insured the attention with an ill-fated bid for his third seniors title of the year. In fact, January passed Palmer and Boros, the co-leaders after 54 holes, and two others as he came from four strokes off the pace Sunday to nip 62-year-old Julius by a stroke and capture this third 1982 title over the wind-swept 6,520 yards of the Champion course at the PGA National Golf Club in Palm Beach Gardens, Florida. A two-under-par 70 Sunday and his even-par 288 total did it, as both Boros and Palmer faded badly in the final round — acts that prompted January to remark that it was 'only the fifth of December and I just had Christmas Eve'.

Don was out of sight the first two days after scores of 74 and 75, although he had no trouble with the cut, which fell at 156 after two blustery days. Bob Goalby, one of senior golf's top players who was a consistent contender throughout the year, nailed the first-round lead with a solid 68, the product of five birdies and a bogey. He had two shots on Howie Johnson and Bob Stone, three on Palmer, Boros, Gay Brewer, Paul Runyan and Ken Mast, as more than a third of the field shot 80 or worse. Palmer overcame one ball in the water and made three early clutch putts Friday as he shot 70 and climbed into a first-place tie with the glib Johnson, 57, who had a good year on the Senior Tour with earnings of more than $43,000 in 12 starts and 24 years earlier had beaten Palmer in an Azalea Open playoff six days before Palmer won his first Masters. Goalby took a 75 and dropped two shots off the pace, sharing third position with Bob Toski, whose 70 matched Palmer's as the low of the day and included an eagle three.

Palmer retained his share of the lead Saturday, though taking a 73, with Boros, back in good form in senior golf despite serious heart surgery a year earlier, joining him there at 214 with a 70 when Arnie bogeyed the final hole. Art Wall was at 216 after a 71, Goalby at 217 after a 74. January, who had started the day eight strokes behind, cut the margin in half with a 69, the best score that round, and moved into a fifth-place tie with Stone and Toski at 218.

Surprisingly, it was Boros rather than Palmer who remained longest in the fight with January Sunday. 'My putting went south,' said Palmer of his short game that cost him three bogeys and a double-bogey in the middle of the round en route to a 76. A 25-foot birdie putt on the final green only helped him into a four-way tie for third with Brewer (69), Wall (74) and Goalby (73). Miller Barber, the four-time winner of 1982 who had opened the tournament with a 79, drew within two strokes of the lead before taking an eight at the par-four 16th, where Boros' bid also died with a bogey. By then, January had survived an out-of-bounds tee shot and double-bogey at the 14th by surrounding it with birdies — he had five in all Sunday — and making a great save from a pot bunker at the 17th hole. The win was his when Boros' bid for a tying birdie and 74 on the final green, a putt from 25 feet, rolled past the cup just six inches off line.

9. The European Tour

It took three years for Greg Norman to reach his goal of being No. 1 on the European Tour, but Norman claimed that pinnacle in 1982. The 27-year-old Australian, who now has geared his ambitions more towards the American Tour, won three tournaments — Dunlop Masters, State Express Classic and Benson & Hedges International Open — and was reasonably secure atop the Order of Merit with £66,405 when he left Europe in the early autumn to be with his expectant wife, Laura, in the United States. In previous attempts at the title, Norman was second on the Order of Merit in 1980 and fourth in 1981.

Several golfers took shots at Norman's No. 1 position in the closing weeks. The primary challenge was from Lyle, who was aiming to be first for the third time in four years. But Lyle was upstaged by a fellow Scot, Sam Torrance, who won both the Benson & Hedges Spanish Open and the season-ending Portuguese Open. In the Portuguese, Lyle had one-putt greens on the last two holes. Had Sandy missed either putt, Torrance would have replaced him in second. The final difference was £1.33 — about the cost of a golf ball — as Lyle won £61,517.84 to Torrance's £61,516.51.

Although playing consistently, Lyle won only one tournament for the year, that being his successful defense of the Lawrence Batley International title. The 1981 Order of Merit champion, Bernhard Langer, also had only one victory, and that also was a successful title defense, coming in the Lufthansa German Open. Langer was sixth on the Order of Merit with £43,847. In all, six titles were kept by the 1981 holders. Others were by Norman in the Dunlop Masters, Seve Ballesteros in the Suntory World Match Play Championship, David Graham in the Lancome Trophy and Peter Jacobsen in the Johnnie Walker Trophy, the last three falling on consecutive weeks.

Seventeen players had one or more victories — the same number as in 1981. Norman and Ballesteros had three each, although Seve was merely 10th on the Order of Merit because the £35,000 check from his World Match Play victory was unofficial money. Ballesteros earned £38,437 officially, including triumphs in two of the first four tournaments, the Madrid Open and French Open. Two victories each were scored by Torrance, Gordon Brand, Jr., Ian Woosnam, Bernard Gallacher and Mark James. Those with one victory, in addition to Lyle, included Tony Jacklin in the Sun Alliance PGA Championship, John O'Leary in the Carrolls Irish Open, Manuel Pinero in the European Open and Nick Faldo in the Haig Whisky Tournament Players Championship.

In reviewing the European Tour season, one must recognize, however, that several of the leading players — notably Norman, Ballesteros and Faldo — were essentially part-timers while playing the world's other major circuits. Norman and Ballesteros are acknowledged as international stars of the first rank. Faldo has proven to be particularly adaptable to playing in the United States, especially in comparison to his British rival, Lyle, whose game — much like Jerry Pate's on his trips from America to Britain — has not traveled well.

Gordon Brand, Jr., led the European Tour's impressive youth movement. In the Coral Classic, Brand became the first rookie winner of a major Tour event and later also won the prestigious Bob Hope British Classic. He placed seventh on the Order of Merit with £38,842. Another first-year player, Paul Way, was the Dutch Open champion although he was less often a contender than Brand, earning £17,249 for 30th place for the year.

There were other significant showings by rookies, aside from the victories by Brand and Way. Certainly, note must be made of Ronan Rafferty, who turned professional late in 1981 at age 17 with much fanfare, only to stumble at the start, failing in the Tour's qualifying tournament. Rafferty made his way onto the Tour through the South African Order of Merit and won £10,064 for 48th place in Europe. He later also gained his first victory in the Venezuelan Open.

Let's hope the same turn of fortune is due Wayne Player, Gary's son, who will set out on the European Tour in 1983, with plans to play primarily in the British events. He signed off as an amateur by leading the U.S. Open qualifying, and he and Gary became the first father and son entry in that championship's history. Wayne then made his professional debut in the Cacharel Under-25s and failed to qualify for the final 36 holes.

You may have noticed that many previously prominent names in European golf have not been mentioned. In a sense, Neil Coles' victory in the Sanyo Open was one of the year's more unusual. Like Miller Barber a while ago in America, Coles continues to prove to be more durable than his contemporaries. The 47-year-old Coles was 16th on the Order of Merit for the second successive year, although the win was his first since the 1977 Tournament Players Championship. Brian Barnes did not win in 1982, falling from 12th to 26th on the Order of Merit. Also remaining winless in Europe were Eamonn Darcy (since 1977), Ken Brown (1978), Howard Clark (1978), Tommy Horton (1978) and Hugh Baiocchi (1979). Those closing 1982 in Europe on the up scale included Bill Longmuir (from 52nd to 24th on the Order of Merit), Juan Anglada (74th to 27th) and Christy O'Connor, Jr. (75th to 40th).

Tunisian Open — £60,000
Winner: Antonio Garrido

Signs of the times included the Argentine military flag alongside the Union Jack as the European Tour began not on that continent but in Tunisia. And why were they in Africa? As recorded in the previous edition of this annual, the Tour officials decided to accept an invitation from Sousse Nord Development Company, which was interested in expanding Port El Kantaoui as a vacation resort, despite the fact that its South African members would necessarily be excluded. Talk of a boycott never materialized, and those passing Tunisian immigration without a hitch included British golfers who recently had participated in South Africa, thus violating the ban imposed by the Organization of African Unity. The championship resulted in an essentially Spanish affair, with Antonio Garrido winning on the fifth playoff hole over Manuel Calero, while Manuel Pinero shared third place with Des Smyth and Gordon Brand, Jr.

There was a distinct Tunisian flavor to the opening round. The joint leader, with Briton Keith Williams, was Mohamed Ben Nacr, his country's only native-born golf professional. Ben Nacr eventually tied for 19th place, while Ken Brown took over the leadership in the second round with his 67 for a 141 total, three strokes ahead of Garrido, who was then tied for fourth place. Brown, who had not won a tournament in four years, remained two strokes in front of Garrido and Calero through 54 holes, having 71 in the third round, then stumbled to 76 in the fourth. There was a fierce duel early in the third round between Brown and Sandy Lyle, but Sandy could not keep the pace and eventually tied for sixth.

On the last day, with eight golfers within two strokes of one another, the competition was such that no one seemed to notice the topless bathers on the beach along the 14th fairway. It was there that Garrido struck a 15-foot birdie putt to take the lead. Antonio walked to the 18th green certain that he would take the first prize of £10,000, because Calero was 50 feet from the hole with little prospect of a birdie to tie. But Calero holed the putt and they went on to the playoff, which was not decided until Garrido's eight-foot birdie at the fifth.

British followers took particular pleasure in the showing of Brand, who placed third in his first European Tour event. Brand, who shared the lead at one stage said, 'I am not surprised that I did well. I'm not afraid of winning. I kept my cool and I didn't see why I shouldn't finish well.'

Cespa Madrid Open — £42,900
Winner: Severiano Ballesteros

Even more so than in Tunisia, the Spaniards were the dominant nationality of the European Tour on their home ground in an exciting Cespa Madrid Open, won by Seve Ballesteros. Second place went to Jose-Maria Canizares and third to Antonio Garrido. It was Ballesteros' second victory in three years at Real Club Puerta de Hierro. The first, you may recall, marked his triumphant return from the 1980 Masters. Last year, Ballesteros did not play in the Madrid Open and instead went to Japan, creating the first of several conflicts with European officialdom during the season.

Garrido and Canizares were the leaders of the early rounds. Antonio shot 67, five under par, on the opening day for a one-stroke margin over Briton Carl Mason. Canizares covered the first nine holes of the second round in 30 strokes and finished with 64, one stroke off the course record set by Ballesteros two years earlier. That put Canizares at 134, and Garrido was second at 137, following his 70. Ballesteros was six strokes off the pace with rounds of 70 and 69. Seve posted 31 to start the third round and shared the lead at that stage, yet Canizares held a two-shot margin at the close of the round, having 69 to Seve's 66.

Ballesteros raced past Canizares on the final day, then almost gave back his advantage. He had to save par from a bunker on the last hole to win by one stroke with his 68 and 273 total, 15 under par. Canizares had 71 and 274 while Garrido had 69 and 275. Ballesteros was relieved at the finish. 'I wasn't really sure about winning until I got on the last green,' Seve said. 'Too many things have gone wrong this year. I felt the Masters slipped away from me and I thought it might happen here, too.'

Italian Open — £49,250
Winner: Mark James

It may be impossible for Mark James to completely live down his act of defiance in the 1978 Italian Open, when Mark took 111 strokes while playing with one hand after an injury in an absurd observance of a rule about being fined for walking off the course. Yet Mark has done much to mend his reputation since that time and his victory at Is Molas, Sardinia, served to underscore the fact.

James also has become a more accomplished golfer in the four-year span, as evidenced by his record-equalling 67 in windy conditions during the second round, enabling him to overtake the young American visitor, Bobby Clampett. With masterful club selection that day, Mark soared to a four-stroke margin and remained the leader for the rest of the championship. 'I am now more versatile,' James acknowledged. 'I can work the ball in either direction and I can drill it low when necessary.' The triumph also represented the first reward of a 'safety-first' policy. 'My coach, Gavin Christie at Kedlestone Park, Derby, reckons I'm a foolhardy so-and-so and ordered me to take no risks for three months,' Mark said. 'It seems to work.'

Clampett began the Italian Open with 68, standing one stroke clear of Ian Woosnam and Mark Thomas. While Clampett posted 73 in the second round, James carded his 67 for a 137 total. Mark added 71 on the third day and was three strokes in front of Woosnam. That margin went to six strokes after seven holes of the final round. It was a testing moment at the 17th hole when James realized that his lead had been cut to one shot by Clampett, who had a burst of five birdies in six holes. 'I don't like being that far in front. It makes me edgy and a bit negative,' said James, who then coolly flipped a wedge within six feet of the 17th hole for a birdie. He closed a level-par 72 for a three-stroke margin at 280 over Clampett and Woosnam, the small Welshman.

Also of note in the Italian Open was the first European appearance of the year by Bernhard Langer, the Order of Merit leader for 1981. Troubled with his putting, Langer tied for fourth place, five strokes behind, along with Florentino Molina, the Argentine who was then questioning (along with countryman Vicente Fernandez) whether to continue when the Tour reached Britain in two weeks. Both were popular figures across the Tour, but the fact remained that their countries were at war.

Paco Rabanne French Open — £43,220
Winner: Severiano Ballesteros

It was wet and cold at St. Nom-la-Breteche outside Paris during the second week of May but, in the aftermath of Seve Ballesteros' near-disastrous 1981 European season, the miserable weather could not dampen spirits. No mistake about it, Ballesteros was back with a vengeance and the initial continental segment of this circuit ended on an extremely high note, as Seve outdueled Sandy Lyle for first place in the Paco Rabanne French Open.

St. Nom-la-Breteche was the venue of one of Ballesteros' important earlier successes — when he won the Lancome Trophy in 1976 while establishing himself atop the European golf ladder — and this revival marked his fourth consecutive victory in Europe, including the Spanish Open and World Match Play titles of 1981 and the Madrid Open crown two weeks earlier. While producing the third Spanish victory in four weeks of the 1982 Tour, Ballesteros also captured public attention with the announcement that he would play challenge matches with Jack Nicklaus in Madrid and Paris on dates conflicting with the English Golf Classic and the Hennessy Cognac Cup matches. The announcement reflected a truce, perhaps uneasy, between Ballesteros and the Tour officials with whom he battled through most of 1981. Seve explained his way out of the Hennessy matches by saying, 'I'm no good in team events. They will do better without me'.

Ballesteros' announcement overshadowed the first-round efforts of Mark James, winner of the Italian Open the previous week. James, who later tied for third with Juan Anglada and Tommy Horton, began in the lead with 68, one stroke ahead of newcomer Paul Way, the 19-year-old Kent golfer. 'I was expecting an anti-climax after winning last week,' James said. 'It doesn't seem to have happened. I'm normally a slow starter to the season, so this year I began work a lot earlier and played more competitive golf before our season started.'

Lyle, the defending French Open champion, took a putting tip from his wife — the former Christine Drew, an accomplished golfer in her own right — and shot a course-record 64, eight under par, in the second round. Sandy needed only 29 putts in establishing a five-stroke lead over James and Ballesteros with his 136 total. To that stage, Ballesteros was playing faultlessly, but without Lyle's sort of putting touch. In the incessant rain of the third day, however, Ballesteros managed to shoot level-par 72 and went two strokes up on Lyle, who struggled around in 79, and Tommy Horton. Most significant in the third round was Ballesteros' resolve after a bogey-riddled opening nine. He dropped four strokes to par, then turned things around with birdies on the 10th, 13th and 15th holes. That surge left Ballesteros in position to leap past Lyle with a three-stroke swing at the par-five 17th, where Seve birdied and Sandy double-bogeyed.

Lyle was anxious to resume their match in the fourth round. Coming out of the clubhouse, Lyle saw two British reporters enjoying their customary morning glass of champagne. Sandy said in passing, 'Save some of that until after I've won'. Lyle proceeded to birdie three of the first four holes, but it was not to be. Ballesteros responded with an eagle-three at the fifth, hitting a wonderful five-iron second shot, and from there matched Lyle's every stroke until the 17th, where Seve expanded the lead with another birdie to Sandy's par. Ballesteros also birdied the 18th to win by four strokes, having 65 and 278 to Lyle's 67 and 282.

A closing note for the week concerns the unfortunate Argentines, who were advised by the Tour officials not to enter Britain the following week. Vicente Fernandez explained, 'We have not yet received visas and, anyway, we've been told by PGA officials not to go. It could be difficult for us'.

Martini International — £66,000
Winner: Bernard Gallacher

There was a striking similarity between Bernard Gallacher's two victories in the Martini International 11 years apart. At Norwich in 1971, Gallacher shot 80 on the opening day, yet won with rounds of 67, 68, and 67 as Bernard Hunt stumbled at the finish. This time, Gallacher's closing 67 coincided with Sandy Lyle's disastrous 80, after Lyle began the fourth round in the lead and with Gallacher three strokes deep in the pack. Gallacher won with earlier rounds of 71, 71, 68 and a 277 total, seven under par at Lindrick, and was three strokes ahead of the second-place finishers, Nick Faldo and Jose-Maria Canizares.

Bernard admitted, 'I am a bit surprised. I came here with no thoughts of victory, just determined to play well. I didn't want to know how the rest of the field was doing. I just played my own game. I wasn't going to change my tactics and didn't even look at a scoreboard. Somebody told me at the 18th tee that I was on my own in front.'

In recent years the Martini International had been dominated by Seve Ballesteros and Greg Norman, together accounting for five consecutive titles. Ballesteros was absent this year but Norman made his 1982 European debut as the defending champion. Nick Faldo, returning from the U.S. Tour, was also making his first European appearance and the field was the strongest thus far of the season.

Mark James' presence was again felt, as James led the first round, but Lyle emerged with the rounds of 68, 69, and 70 to be the pace-setter at both the 36-hole and 54-hole marks. Having squandered opportunities to win all four earlier tournaments with one poor round, Sandy was somewhat despondent, even with the lead. 'I just keep having a bad round and I can't seem to avoid it,' Lyle said. 'I am playing much better, but the disasters keep happening.' On the final day, that happened again. At the eighth hole, attempting to hit over a tree, Lyle hit into it for the first of two double-bogeys. Sandy eventually tied for 20th place. Veteran Neil Coles also made a serious challenge but at the close, Gallacher had only Canizares to contend with. That bid ended when the Spaniard hooked a shot into the trees at the 17th hole.

The 17th also provided for the demise of the defending champion. Norman took 17 strokes there — 10 over par — en route to placing 55th with a final-round 82. It wasn't the worst score ever recorded in Europe. That distinction still belongs to Philipe Porcquier, who took 20 in the 1978 French Open. Nevertheless, it was Norman's worst. Greg was distracted by a photographer and hooked his drive into a bush. He needed four penalty drops because each of his recovery shots went back into the foliage. He reached the fairway with his 10th stroke, then missed the green and two-putted. Norman commented, 'I'll know that photographer if I see him again'.

Car Care International — £60,000
Winner: Brian Waites

It has taken the better part of five years for club professional Brian Waites' ability to be recognized. That is not a long time, considering that Waites was approaching his 40th birthday before recognizing that ability himself. Then, in 1978, Brian won the Tournament Players Championship. He upstaged his touring counterparts four more times in Africa — twice in 1980 and twice earlier in 1982 — before claiming a second European Tour victory in the Car Care Plan International at Moor Allerton Golf Club in Leeds. Waites hoped that his second European victory would finally put to rest the notion that he was simply a 'lucky' club professional. 'I know they say I am a lucky winner because I've won only the Tournament Players Championship in four years in Europe,' Brian said. 'But now I've won another title and when you put this alongside my four overseas wins it proves I'm not such a bad player.'

Brazilian youngster Jaime Gonzalez, whose father Mario, an amateur, once played in the Masters, led the first round and eventually tied for 12th place. Gonzalez attended Oklahoma State University and, after trying unsuccessfully for the U.S. Tour, was making an effort in Europe. 'To tell the truth, I was unhappy in the States. I didn't have many friends,' Gonzalez said, 'But over here everybody is very friendly and ready to talk. I feel happier here and I can play better.'

In the second round, Manuel Calero took the lead with a course-record 66 while Ken Brown took the headlines with the revelation that he had prepared for the tournament by working for five hours in the garden of his friend, Mark James. 'I was pretty stiff afterwards,' said Brown, who then was two shots behind. 'But I think it helped me because I didn't try to hit the ball too hard.'

Another course-record score — 66 by Waites — was posted in the third round and Brian entered the final day with a four-stroke margin over Seve Ballesteros and Bernard Gallacher. 'If I play again like I did today, a one-stroke would be enough,' said Waites. His primary challengers in the fourth round were Brian Barnes and newcomer Paul Hoad. A playoff seemed unavoidable when Barnes and Hoad both finished with 69s and 277 totals. But Waites, after scoring a birdie at the 16th and saving par at the 17th, rolled in a 10-foot birdie at the 18th to complete his one-over-par 73 round and 276 total. Ballesteros was fourth with 71—278 and Gallacher fifth at 72—279.

Sun Alliance PGA Championship — £80,000
Winner: Tony Jacklin

'Oh, it does feel good to be back.'

Those were Tony Jacklin's words after winning the Sun Alliance PGA Championship, a victory which Jacklin acknowledged as his most significant since capturing Open championships on both sides of the Atlantic a decade earlier. 'I've had nine very turbulent years. To come through them and win a big one again somehow makes me a better person for it,' Jacklin said, following his playoff with Bernhard Langer at Hillside Golf Club in Southport. 'I've always felt that if I could just keep my concentration and confidence together, nobody could beat me. I've had a lot of downs and very few ups in the last few years. There have been the odd tournament wins, but none as important as this one. I feel now that I could win another British Open.'

Jacklin first served notice that this might be his week by shooting 69, three under par, in the second round to move within three strokes of the lead shared by Langer and Sam Torrance. Tony shot 73 in the third round while closing the gap to two strokes. On the last day, Jacklin's 70 forged the tie with Langer at 284, necessitating the one-hole playoff which Tony won with a birdie.

Torrance had some fatherly advice to account for his rapid start. His father told Sam that he was putting so much effort into his swing that he was on his toes when he struck the ball. With more of a flat-footed swing, Torrance shot 67 in the first round and was three strokes in front of Langer. They were tied for first place at 139 after 36 holes and at 212 after 54 holes. Torrance fell back quickly on the final day and eventually shot 76 to share fifth place at 288.

Langer and Jacklin continued in a duel, which the West German led until taking four putts from 30 feet at the 16th. Jacklin went ahead with a birdie at the 17th and when Langer drove into a bunker at the 18th, the title seemed to be Tony's. But Langer made a near-miraculous recovery, skimming the ball onto the green, and Jacklin three-putted after being distracted by a photographer. The playoff was at the 15th and Jacklin almost holed his second shot for an eagle before sinking the winning birdie. Tony then put a consoling arm around Langer's shoulders. 'It's always nice to win, but perhaps not when somebody makes that kind of mistake,' Jacklin said, later, referring to Langer's four-putt at the 16th. 'I feel genuinely sorry for Bernhard.'

Jersey Open — £42,000
Winner: Bernard Gallacher

Attention this week was focused more on the recent Sun Alliance PGA Championship than on the tournament in progress, the Jersey Open at La Moye. Tony Jacklin was home following his inspired victory and his telephone seldom stopped ringing. The calls, letters and telegrams were pouring in. 'I love being back as a winner, but it's not going to make things any easier this week,' said Jacklin, the defending Jersey Open champion. 'I tried to sneak onto a corner of the course for a bit of private practice, but within five minutes I was surrounded by people wanting to slap me on the back and shake my hand. The problem is, I badly want to win again. It means a lot to do it here in front of my own folks.' Perhaps Jacklin did well in scoring no higher than 71 and placing joint eighth, six strokes behind Bernard Gallacher, who went to a playoff against Eamonn Darcy and Des Smyth for his second victory of the season.

Another carry-over from the PGA Championship was the £125 fine imposed on Carl Mason for having sunk a one-inch putt snooker (or pool) style on the final hole. The prize money had been handed out before the infraction was discovered, so Mason was fined, according to his standing in the tournament, the equivalent of a two-stroke penalty. Mason explained, 'I was simply trying to give the crowd a laugh'.

Gallacher's victory put him atop the Order of Merit with £22,255. The Wentworth professional came from three strokes behind Smyth over the final round, chipping in from 60 feet on the last hole and shooting a two-under-par 70 for his 273 total. Darcy got into the playoff with 68 while Smyth shot 73. In the five-hole playoff, Darcy was the first to exit, failing to match the birdies of

Gallacher from 30 feet and Smyth from six feet at the second hole. Gallacher bunkered his approach at the third hole but saved his par, then won when Smyth three-putted the fifth hole.

Smyth and Darcy were the opening-round leaders with 65s. Because of fog, the second round was postponed to Saturday, when Smyth shot 68 to go one stroke ahead of Manuel Calero and two in front of Gallacher. Two rounds were played on Sunday. The most impressive move was by Sandy Lyle, who climbed to fourth place, two strokes behind, with 68 and 65 scores. Ian Woosnam posted 68 and 66 to place sixth, a stroke behind Ian Mosey.

Dunlop Masters — £85,000
Winner: Greg Norman

Greg Norman entered the Dunlop Masters intent upon putting his career back on track and did so in tremendous style, winning by eight strokes over Bernhard Langer. Norman's first victory of the year and his successful defense of the Dunlop Masters title was the result of Greg having broken two records and equalled one other. His eight-stroke margin and 267 total at St. Pierre in Chepstow were records for the tournament. The margin was the largest on the European Tour since his own 10-stroke victory in the 1980 French Open.

Norman tied the course record with his 65s in both the third and fourth rounds and was furious with himself for not having broken the record in the fourth round. 'I got my birdies at the start because I knew the pace would heat up,' Greg said. 'But then I let the record slip away.' Nevertheless, Norman was pleased to have regained his momentum. 'I lost confidence in my whole game earlier this year,' he said. 'The doubts were always hanging around my head. It was very worrying.' The difference, as Norman demonstrated from the third round onwards, was in his aggressive play. Norman explained, 'I had begun to have negative thoughts and play safe. But, really, I'm not that kind of player. I thrive on aggression. I love to attack. What I didn't realize until now is that an attacking player has these quiet periods when nothing seems to go right.'

The leaderboards for the first and second rounds reflected the largest deadlocks of the season. Six players were tied at 68 after the first round and seven were tied at 137 after the second day's play. Included in the 36-hole tie was Warren Humphreys, the former Walker Cup golfer, who confessed to an outrageously poor round, but only 23 putts. Quipped Norman, 'If I'd had 23 putts, I'd have shot 59'.

Coral Classic — £50,000
Winner: Gordon Brand, Jr.

On a couple of occasions earlier in the year, Gordon Brand, Jr., had demonstrated unusual ability for a first-year professional. He tied for second place behind Gary Player in South Africa's Lexington PGA and was joint third in the Tunisian Open, inaugural event of the European Tour. Thus, Brand's breakthrough to win the Coral Classic was just mildly surprising. The son of a club professional from Bristol, Brand merited a footnote in European Tour annals for his victory. He was the first European rookie to win a major tour event, if one can discount Peter Townsend's triumph in the 1967 Dutch Open and Sandy Lyle's victory in the 1978 Nigerian Open.

Before the tournament, the conversation was of Greg Norman's quest to replace Bernard Gallacher at the front of the Order of Merit. Since the Greater Manchester Open was cancelled, Norman had been the European Tour's last winner two weeks earlier in the Dunlop Masters and was ready for a 'Welsh Double' at Royal Porthcawl. Greg came close. His 276 total was three strokes off Brand's winning score. Third place at 278 went to Carl Mason, who was the leader until Brand shot 66 in the third round.

Mason 'did a Watson' in the first round, as they were saying in the days following Tom Watson's winning pitch in the United States Open. Mason's chip-in at the 16th hole for a birdie propelled him to 66, six under par. Most of the headlines went not to Mason but to Steve Martin, who declared after his 67 that he was junking his clubs, provided a replacement set arrived in time from his home in Dundee. 'I'm fed up with these. This is the first time I've broken 70 with them this year,' Martin said. 'It's not good enough and I need a change.' The British Rail service, however, could not produce such a speedy delivery and Martin continued with his original set.

Following his 66, Mason shot 70 and led Jeff Hall by one stroke. Then Brand posted 66 to go with his earlier scores of 69 and 70 and led by two strokes over Mason and Brian Barnes, who broke the course record with 65. Brand was caught only once in the fourth round, at the eighth hole by Mason, who then promptly dropped a shot. Brand continued around in 68 for his three-stroke margin. The victory, perhaps not incidentally, came under the guidance of caddy Peter Coleman, who has worked for Seve Ballesteros and Nancy Lopez. Coleman simply told Brand, 'I'll pick the club. You hit'.

Scandinavian Enterprise Open — £66,000
Winner: Bob Byman

What little success American Bob Byman has enjoyed has been primarily in Europe. Byman has won only the 1979 Bay Hill Classic in the United States, but has taken four continental Opens in a mere handful of appearances. He won the Scandinavian Enterprises Open for the second time in 1982 over Sam Torrance and an extremely disappointed Seve Ballesteros, and explained his record by saying, 'Playing in Europe is much easier. You don't have to be so aggressive'. Because of rain in the opening round, 36 holes were played on the last day. Byman overtook Ballesteros, the defending champion, with a flawless 66, then secured the championship with 71 for his 275 total, nine under par for the Linkoping, Sweden, course. Torrance shot a pair of 69s on the last day for his 278 total while Ballesteros shot 70 and 72 for third place at 279.

A straggler on the European Tour, Andrew Murray, also achieved a modest reversal of fortune with his share of 19th place, despite 76 in the final round. Murray was the opening-round leader with 66 and revealed that he was in debt £14,000 to his managers. In the second round, played on Saturday, Murray fell away with 74 while Ballesteros added 69 to his earlier 68, gaining the lead by one stroke over Byman and Brazilian Jaime Gonzalez. Byman went three strokes in front of the Spaniard with his five-birdie, no-bogey round which included no putts of more than six feet. 'It was the easiest 66 I ever had,' Byman said.

Ballesteros got within a stroke of Byman with three consecutive birdies from the fourth hole in the last round, but dropped two strokes in three holes after that. Frustrated, Ballesteros punctuated the remainder of his round with outbursts directed towards photographers. Later, Seve said, 'I've got no chance in the Open, unless things improve'. On the other hand, Torrance was encouraged by his best performance since winning the 1981 Carrolls Irish Open. Said Sam, 'It's nice to bounce back in time for the Open'.

The Scandinavian tournament was Ballesteros' last before the Open. 'I was planning to go to Troon a week early, but now I will return to Spain and relax before two matches with Jack Nicklaus,' Seve said. 'I will go to Scotland only on the Sunday.' He continued, 'I've never seen the course before, but I hadn't seen Royal Lytham when I won in 1979. In America (where he missed the cut in the United States Open with rounds of 81 and 79), I practiced for a week, and it was too long. The course was completely different when we started. If I don't win the Open, I will try to finish on top of the money list. It will be difficult, because I play only a few tournaments. But if I do well in the right ones, it is possible.'

State Express Classic — £80,000
Winner: Greg Norman

While there's no question that Shot-of-the-Year honors belong to Tom Watson for his chip-in at the United States Open, Greg Norman deserves a brief mention in that regard for driving the green on the celebrated 10th hole at the Belfry while winning the State Express Classic. The hole — a par four of 292 yards — was made famous in 1978 by Seve Ballesteros, who also drove the green against Nick Faldo in the Hennessy Cognac Cup matches. Said Norman, 'Seve had nothing to lose because he did it in match play. But I did it in stroke play. The risk was greater.'

Norman's first prize of £13,330 lifted the Australian to the top of the Order of Merit with £35,558. The triumph also prevented the embarrassment — at least in the view of the British press — of having a young American win for the second successive week. The top 25 finishers in the State Express Classic automatically qualified for the British Open and the field included a large number of men from the U.S. Tour, led by Danny Edwards, who earlier won the Greater Greensboro Open. The low amateur the last time the Open was held at Troon in 1973, Edwards held or shared the State Express lead for three rounds before placing joint fifth. The runner-up, one stroke off Norman's 13-under-par 279 pace, was young Scot Brian Marchbank, who posted 67 in the final round in a great effort.

Edwards and Manuel Pinero opened with 68s while Norman shot one of three consecutive 70s. After 36 holes, Edwards led by four strokes over Marchbank, with Norman standing five behind. Highlights of the early rounds were Edwards' two eagles on the 555-yard 17th hole, the first by holing a bunker shot, and, of course, Norman's drive on the 10th hole. Greg decided to go for the green at the 10th after noticing a tail wind at the seventh. When Ballesteros did it in 1978, he two-putted from 30 feet for a birdie. Norman holed his putt from about 100 feet for an eagle. But Steve Williams of South Africa out-performed both just minutes later with a drive so close that he required only a six-foot putt for an eagle.

Norman's third 70 and Edwards' 75 tied them at 210. Greg not only made up five strokes for the day, but also six strokes on the last six holes. He birdied four successive holes from the 13th, then Edwards birdied the 17th to push his margin back to two strokes. Danny then drove into the water at the 18th, taking a bogey, while Norman finished with a birdie to share the lead. In the fourth round, Norman shot 69 and Edwards faded with another 75.

Lawrence Batley International — £80,000
Winner: Sandy Lyle

After scoring 29 on the outward nine, Sandy Lyle's goal was to shoot 59 in the final round of the Lawrence Batley International. Although Lyle did not come remotely close to that target, the young British star did achieve his first victory since winning the Batley one year earlier. The triumph by two strokes over Manuel Pinero at Bingley St. Ives enabled Lyle to replace Greg Norman as No. 1 on the Order of Merit with earnings of £39,914 for the season.

Neither Norman, Seve Ballesteros nor Bernhard Langer were entered, but the field did include two American superstars, Arnold Palmer and Lee Trevino. The British press suggested that the presence of the latter, for large appearance fees, was the reason for the absence of the former. To that, Trevino responded, 'I don't know why they stayed away. You would have to ask them. But the game is too big for this sort of thing. We have given up a $400,000 event to play here. You will never stamp out appearance money. There are so many ways of paying, it will never be stopped.' Palmer and Trevino shot respectable scores, but were not contenders by the last round, having fallen victim to the multi-contoured Bingley greens which prompted Trevino to remark, 'If I had to putt on these all the time, I would end up in the nuthouse'.

Tony Johnstone spent four hours drawing maps of each green, and his preparation was rewarded by 10 one-putts and a share of the first-round lead at 66 with Eamonn Darcy and Brian Waites. All three faded after that, although Darcy tied for fourth place, five strokes behind, along with Nick Faldo, Bernard Gallacher and Paul Curry, who won a £4,000 mink coat for his mother by scoring a hole-in-one during the opening round. Waites and Gallacher, who shot 66, were the 36-hole leaders at 134. Then, Ken Brown posted 64 for the third-round lead at 201. Brown needed a par at the last hole to equal the course record and was so disgusted when he failed that he left without waving to the crowd, signing autographs or speaking with the press.

Three strokes ahead of Lyle starting the last round, Brown was seven strokes behind after just nine holes in the wake of Lyle's 29. Sandy's previous scores were 70, 66, and 67. He played the final nine in 37 for another 66 and his 269 total. Brown, who finished with 74, was left to encourage Lyle when Sandy hit into a bunker on the 18th hole. Said Brown, who had been so ill-mannered the previous day, 'Come on, Sandy, you can do it'. Lyle traced his victory to a mistake in the third round, when he hit a drive into a fir tree on the 15th hole. 'I hit it with a big cut and realized I wasn't taking the club back straight enough,' Sandy said. 'I corrected the fault and all my old confidence with the driver came back.' Lyle had four birdies on the outward nine and after holing an eagle putt from eight feet at the ninth, began thinking of 59.

That possibility was dimmed at the par-five 11th and 12th holes, where he merely scored birdies, not eagles. He encountered trouble at the 15th, 16th and 17th holes and narrowly came away with the victory. 'I wasn't going to let this one get away,' Lyle said. 'I've lost a few good chances, but I always told myself it was only a matter of time before it would all come together again for me.'

Lufthansa German Open — £45,720
Winner: Bernhard Langer

Before the Lufthansa German Open, Bernhard Langer had won nothing but money in 1982, nearly £30,000 without a victory, having finished second in the Sun Alliance PGA and Dunlop Masters. He had a change of fortune on home soil and successfully defended the championship while adding £7,620 to his bankroll and moving to third on the Order of Merit behind Sandy Lyle and Greg Norman.

The previous year at Hamburg, Langer was awarded a hero's welcome after his runner-up finish to Bill Rogers in the British Open and responded in marvelous fashion, becoming the first German to win the championship. The victory served the game well in his country and even was a factor in the continuation of the German Open itself, which came under the sponsorship of Lufthansa for the 1982 event at Solitude Club in Stuttgart. Langer was the focal point of the galleries, although he shared the limelight in the pro-am with soccer star Franz Beckenbaur.

Langer won over Bill Longmuir with a par on the first playoff hole after they tied with 179 totals, nine under par. Bernhard shot 66 on the final day to gain two strokes on Longmuir, who shared the 54-hole lead with Warren Humphreys and first-year professional Mark Thomas. Neither of the latter pair were factors in the final running, both having 74s to share fifth place at 285. Christy O'Connor, Jr., was third at 280, and Tony Jacklin, the 1981 runner-up, was fourth at 283.

Thomas was the first-round leader with 66, three strokes better than O'Connor, while Langer shot 73. O'Connor posted 68 in the second round, moving one stroke in front of Thomas. Langer then was seven strokes back, but cut the margin to two shots with his 69 in the third round. On the final day, Longmuir staged a last-minute challenge to Langer by scoring an eagle on the 18th hole. The threat was short-lived. Longmuir drove into the trees on the playoff hole and could not reach the green in two. Bernhard won with a routine par for the European Tour's third title defense of the year, following Norman at the Dunlop Masters and Lyle at the Lawrence Batley.

KLM Dutch Open — £42,375
Winner: Paul Way

Promoters of the KLM Dutch Open sought to establish a nostalgic tone by importing Sam Snead and Tommy Bolt for the championship, in view of the absence of 19 of Europe's 20 leading money winners. The impact of Snead's and Bolt's presence did not extend beyond pre-tournament publicity, however, as both failed to qualify for the final 36 holes. The championship instead ended on a youthful note, with Paul Way becoming the second first-year professional to win in Europe during 1982. The first to congratulate Way was the other rookie winner, Gordon Brand, Jr.

Starting the last round three strokes behind Mike Miller, Way equalled the course record set by Miller earlier in the week with 65, seven under par, at De Pan Golf Club in Utrecht and had 31 on the last nine, including an eagle and three birdies. Way had a 276 total for a two-stroke margin over David Feherty and Vicente Fernandez, while Miller dropped to share 10th place with his 75. Way's opening rounds were 71 and 73, then he began a streak of superb putting, requiring only 26 putts in his 67 on the third day and 27 putts in his winning 65. 'It came right out of the blue,' Way said. 'I had been playing rubbish.'

Way, 19 years old, is from Tonbridge, Kent. He is small (5 feet, 8 inches tall and weighing 140 pounds), built upon the lines of Gary Player, and says he follows Player's exercise routines. As an amateur, Way was a Walker Cup golfer. He said he 'never expected to win' in his first year. 'My goal was the top 60 money-winners.' He credited his success partly to the resemblance of the Utrecht course to his favorite in England, Sunningdale. 'I regularly traveled up from my home to play Sunningdale and the other Surrey courses, always with a card and pencil and sometimes when I should have been in school,' Way said. 'I liked the Utrecht course as soon as I saw it because it was so similar.'

While Way, whose best previous finish was 12th in the Tunisian Open, struggled in the first two rounds, the opening-day leaders with 69s were Jeff Hall and another rookie, Mark Thomas. Tienie Britz was among the 13 golfers with 70s and won a BMW automobile for his hole-in-one at the 15th. Miller set the course record with his 65 in the second round and led Hall by three strokes. Even with 73 in the third round, Miller clung to a one-stroke edge over Jeff Hawkes, but Way was beginning to make his move.

Carrolls Irish Open — £80,350
Winner: John O'Leary

A memory of failure in the Carrolls Irish Open haunted John O'Leary for four years, until O'Leary overcame the stigma in the best possible fashion — by winning under nearly identical circumstances. In 1978, John needed only a par at the last hole for victory, but he could not do it and Ken Brown became the surprised recipient of the title. Four strokes ahead with seven holes to play in this year's championship, O'Leary weathered several poor holes, then secured the closing par to win his national title by one stroke over Maurice Bembridge, who had shared the second and third-round leads. With his closing 73 and 287 total, one under par, O'Leary was the only golfer to break par for the week at Portmarnock.

The European Tour was back at full strength for the Irish Open after two tournaments which had missed many of the leading players. Also in the field were such Americans as Bobby Clampett, Tom Kite and Fuzzy Zoeller. The best showing from that group was Kite's share of seventh place. Greg Norman had predicted the lack of American success, taking the course and conditions into consideration and saying, 'It's going to be a bump-and-run week'. Norman took a share of third place, three strokes behind O'Leary, and claimed the Order of Merit lead from Sandy Lyle.

Gale-force winds struck Portmarnock for the opening round. O'Leary shot 74 while Bembridge led with 71, one under par. The most interesting reading was at the bottom of the scores that day. Tony Jacklin shot 83 and left the course with a smile. 'This is the kind of day when you've just got to laugh,' Tony said. 'It's not a day for stroke-making, but just prodding the ball forward.' New Dutch Open champion Paul Way, Mark James, and Brown all shot 80s.

Also on the first day, Christy O'Connor shot 74, the beginning of a remarkable performance for the 57-year-old Dubliner who shared third place at the close with Norman and Nick Faldo, a stroke ahead of Manuel Pinero. O'Connor would not have been in the tournament, had someone answered his telephone call to withdraw because of flu at 7.15 that morning. Once O'Connor got up and around, he felt better and continued to the club, where a doctor provided some tablets.

Bembridge repeated his 71 in the second round without much difficulty, while O'Leary shot 68 with five birdies around the turn to join him in first place at 142. Both shot 72s in the third round to remain tied at 214. This was the first tournament O'Leary played since withdrawing from the British Open with back problems. Although his back still was not fully recovered, O'Leary felt there was some advantage because the injury forced him to 'play within himself'.

O'Leary went ahead of Bembridge with a five-foot birdie on the first hole of the last round and was never caught. Bembridge dropped a stroke at the fifth and O'Leary lost one at the seventh, then there was a three-stroke swing at the eighth on O'Leary's birdie and Bembridge's double bogey, providing the Irishman with a four-shot margin. Beginning at the 12th hole, however, O'Leary started losing strokes and his lead was down to one with the 18th hole remaining. Yet John survived the test to post his first victory since the 1976 Greater Manchester Open.

Benson & Hedges International Open — £100,000
Winner: Greg Norman

Greg Norman's third victory of the year on the European Tour came in the Benson & Hedges International Open, where Norman again demonstrated that his talent and experience placed him a level above most other competitors. The triumph in only Norman's seventh European tournament secured first place in the Order of Merit with earnings of over £58,000 at that stage.

Before Norman could claim the first prize of £16,660, he had to withstand the challenges of Bob Charles, Graham Marsh, and Ian Woosnam. Greg once held a four-stroke lead. Charles and Marsh were finished with 284 totals when Norman and Woosnam went to the par-five 18th hole. If they made pars, there would be a four-way playoff. Greg reached the green with his second shot, a four iron, while Woosnam pushed his approach into the grandstand. Ian then chipped 10 feet short of the hole.

About that time, Norman began thinking of a similar situation when he lost the 1979 Australian Open. 'I was about the same distance away — just 25 feet — and I had two putts to force a playoff,' Greg recalled. 'But I decided to win the thing outright. The ball ran past about three feet and I missed the return.' This time, Norman lagged the ball close to the hole. When Woosnam left his putt on the lip, Greg became the winner with his 283 total, five under par at Fulford, York.

Except for the second round, when he shot 74, Norman was close to the lead all week. He began with 69 and was tied with four others, one stroke behind Ken Brown, who created another furore by refusing to speak to the press. Brown felt that he was having poor scores every time he had interviews after good rounds and was determined not to speak again until he won. Despite his silence, Brown followed with rounds of 73, 75 and 78. When Norman carded 74 in the second round, the lead was shared by Ian Mosey and Charles. Once regarded as a great putter, Charles surprisingly revealed that he now had to overcome the jitters with positive thinking. Another 69 by Norman in the third round lifted the Australian into the lead, one stroke ahead of Marsh, Woosnam, and Nick Faldo, who eventually settled for fifth place and remained without a victory for the year.

In the fourth round, Charles birdied two of the last four holes for 70 to set the target score at 284. Marsh had an eagle at the ninth, birdies at the 10th and 11th, but dropped a stroke at the 13th and could not birdie the 18th, finishing with 71 and 284 also. Norman, who was three strokes clear at the turn, got into trouble by pushing his tee shot into the trees at the 13th, where he faced a similar recovery to that which cost him a 14 earlier in the Martini International at Lindrick. 'I suddenly had this fear that I could be in those trees all day and never get out,' Greg said. He managed a double bogey which still let his rivals back into the contest. The young Welshman, Woosnam, took advantage by scoring birdies from 12 feet at the 16th and five feet at the 17th, but could not produce another birdie at the last. The second-place check of £7,453 was Woosnam's largest and his finish qualified him for the Hennessy Cognac Cup matches ahead of Gordon Brand, Jr. Norman was full of praise. 'He reminds me of myself a few years ago,' Norman said. 'He's very aggressive and a tremendous prospect, but he must learn to control that aggression. He should have taken me to a playoff.'

Ebel Swiss Open — £60,520
Winner: Ian Woosnam

When Ian Woosnam won the Ebel Swiss Open, one journalist wrote that Woosnam had taken six years to become an overnight success. That wasn't far off the mark. Woosnam's victory was his first as a professional and was deserved, if for no other reason than the fact he was second four times earlier in the year, including the previous week in the Benson & Hedges International Open. He also was a runner-up in the Italian Open and twice on the Safari Circuit in the Nigerian Open and Ivory Coast Open.

Woosnam, one of the smallest golfers at five feet, five inches tall, took the Swiss championship at Crans-sur-Sierre in a playoff when Bill Longmuir three-putted the third hole. He led the second and third rounds, then was tied at 272 by Longmuir, who made up four strokes on the last day with his 66. Woosnam's scores were 68, 68, 66 and 70. The first-round leader, one stroke ahead of Woosnam, was Jose-Maria Canizares, who eventually placed third, four strokes behind. Fourth place was shared by Juan Anglada and Hubert Green.

In his first-round 68, Woosnam sank no putt of more than 10 feet. He matched the score in the second round with a 25-foot birdie on the last green for a 136 total, one stroke ahead of Sandy Lyle and little-known American Matt Runge. Over the third round, Runge remained in second place, two strokes behind, while Longmuir shot 67 and advanced to third place, four strokes back. Runge shot 74 in the last round but earned over £2,000, an amount which was much needed by the struggling young man.

European Open — £120,000
Winner: Manuel Pinero

At Sunningdale during a qualifying round for the 1927 British Open, Bobby Jones played what was described as 'the perfect round of golf'. He shot 66 with 33 shots and 33 putts; nothing less than a three and nothing more than a four on his card. Under ideal conditions at Sunningdale during the European Open, Greg Norman tried to alter that description to a below-60 round. The closest that Norman came was his six-under-par 64 in the first round, but on the last day Manuel Pinero came one stroke nearer with his 63 to win the European title by two shots over Sam Torrance and by four shots over Norman. The winning score was 14 under par, 266.

Norman, who estimated that he plays Sunningdale 40 times a year, had an opening round that could stand comparison with Jones's 66. His 64 was equally divided between shots and putts. Greg was hardly satisfied. 'It could have been lower,' he said. 'I had 32 putts. If I cut down on that, I'm well below 60.' Norman had 70 in the second round and Sandy Lyle, who started with eagle-par-birdie, tied him for first place with 66 and a 134 total. Tony Jacklin also threatened to break 60 early in the second round. He holed a two-iron shot for a double eagle on the first hole, then birdied the next two. But Jacklin could do little else and finished with 68 for a 141 total.

The third round featured the emergence of Torrance, whose 64 gained a share of first place with Lyle, who had 67 for a 201 total. Norman shot 69 that day and was tied for third place, two strokes behind, with Pinero, whose rounds had been 68, 68, and 67. Torrance broke clear early on the last day, scoring three birdies on the first four holes, and shot 30 on the first nine to go five

om Watson secured Open championships on both sides of the Atlantic, a feat matched
ly by Bobby Jones (twice), Gene Sarazen, Ben Hogan and Lee Trevino.

The Walrus, Craig Stadler, won the Masters, three other American tournaments – Tucson Open, Kemper Open and World Series of Golf – and led the U.S. PGA Tour money list.

Regularly close to the pin and a
subject of interviews, Raymond
Floyd won the PGA Cham-
pionship, Memorial Tournament
and Memphis Classic, to place
second to Craig Stadler on the U.S.
PGA Tour money list. Floyd later
defeated Stadler in the Sun City
Challenge and claimed No. 1 on the
World money list.

Tom Watson began the year by yielding his Masters title to Craig Stadler. That was onl the beginning of great seasons for both.

Jack Nicklaus shot 69 in the first round of the Masters, which was extended to Friday morning because of rain. Nicklaus shot 77 in the afternoon, and Curtis Strange tied Craig Stadler for the lead at even-par 144.

On Saturday, Craig Stadler birdied the final three holes for 67 and a 211 total, leading Jerry Pate and Seve Ballesteros by three strokes. But Sunday, Stadler's bogey at the 18th dropped him into a tie with Dan Pohl.

Both Craig Stadler and Dan Pohl were somber after the tense playoff, waiting for the awards ceremony.

Dan Pohl contended for several titles, most importantly with his loss to Craig Stadler in the Masters.

Bruce Devlin and Bill Rogers were the leaders in the early rounds of the U.S. Open. They shared first place after the opening round, then Devlin went ahead after 36 holes. Through three rounds, Rogers shared the lead with Tom Watson.

om Watson didn't hole every shot from off the green, but he did save par here at the 10th route to his dramatic birdie at the 17th.

he shot of the year by Watson on the 17th deprived Jack Nicklaus of another major title.

atson received the coveted trophy from former President Gerald Ford and USGA esident William C. Campbell.

Bobby Clampett broke away from the pack in the first two rounds of the British Open. When Clampett faded in the fourth round, Nicky Price had a chance to win until missing this putt on the 18th green.

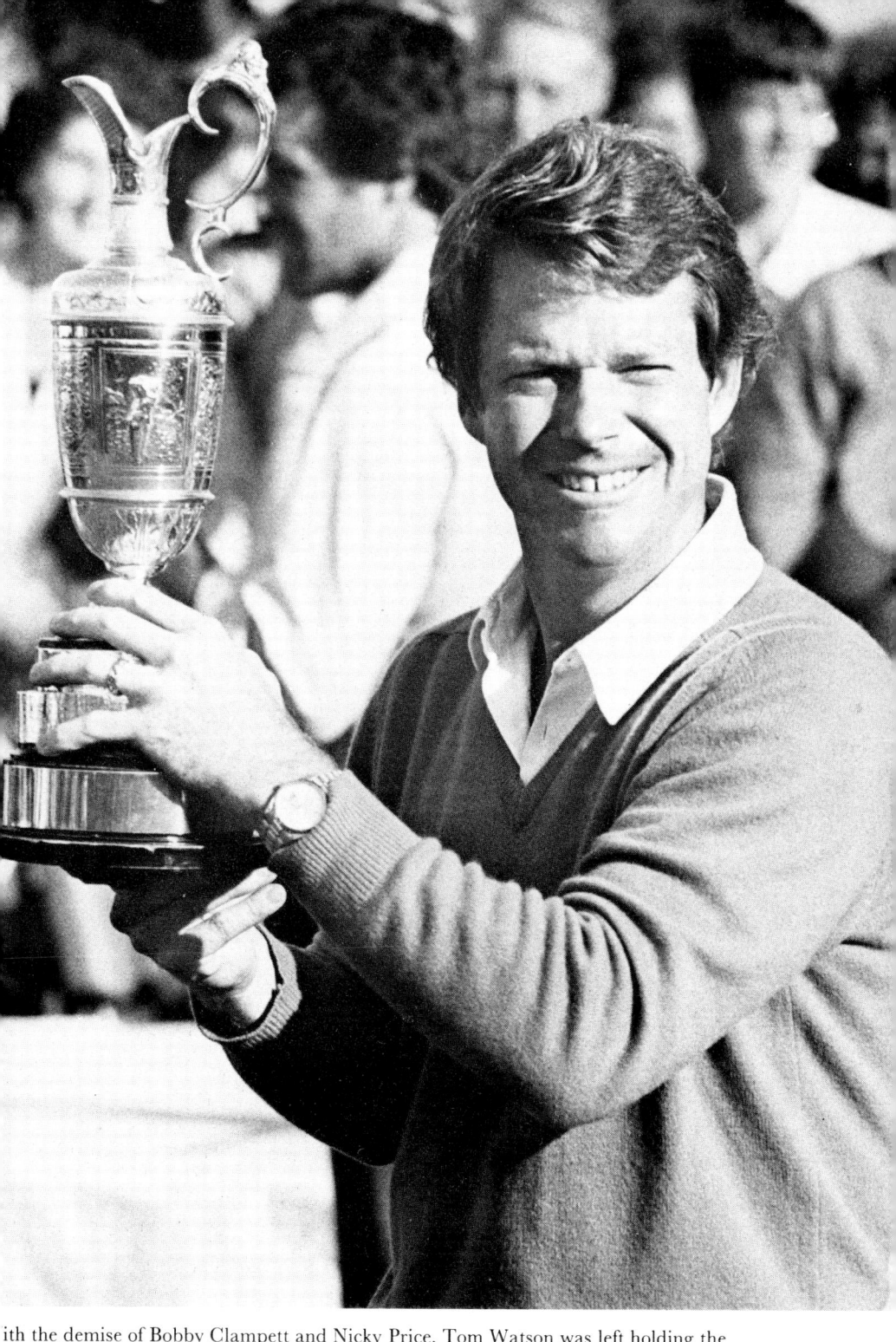

ith the demise of Bobby Clampett and Nicky Price, Tom Watson was left holding the
itish Open trophy for the fourth time.

In sweltering Tulsa, Raymond Floyd opened with a 63 and led wire-to-wire in the PGA Championship for the third major title of his career.

Seve Ballesteros won "a big one" in the Suntory World Match Play Championship, defeating Sandy Lyle at the 37th hole of the final match. In the first round, Lyle came from six down after 18 holes to defeat British rival Nick Faldo.

Semi-finalists in the Suntory World Match Play Championship were Seve Ballesteros, who defeated Lanny Wadkins, and Sandy Lyle, who beat Tom Kite. Third place in the consolation match went to Wadkins.

Gary Player made his 18th appearance in 19 years of the Suntory World Match Play Championship while newcomers included Masters champion Craig Stadler and Bobby Clampett.

The United States Amateur was won not by a youngster, but by insurance executive Jay Sigel of Philadelphia.

Spanish amateur Marta Figueras-Dotti won the British Women's Open.

Juli Inkster won her third consecutive United States Women's Amateur.

strokes ahead of Pinero. The Spaniard came back in 30 for his winning 63 and 266 total, while Torrance finished with 37 for a 67 round. Norman noted to a passing television interviewer that Torrance was playing protectively, and Torrance himself was asked that question between shots as he played (and bogeyed) the 17th hole. This interview drew much criticism, but Torrance said, 'I'm not blaming anybody. I gave permission for the interview before the round and just before the guy came up to talk to me. But I had not been playing defensively. I still wanted to win and I don't think I was put off by the talk.'

Hennessy Cognac Cup — £85,000
Winners: Great Britain and Ireland

The Hennessy Cognac Cup provided a break in the weekly routine of 72-hole stroke tournaments and proved to be an exciting competition for the surprisingly large galleries at Ferndown, near Bournemouth. There were three teams of 10 players each and the lowest eight scores from each team produced the daily team total. For four rounds the winning team was Great Britain and Ireland, having a score of 2,166 or 106 strokes under par. The Rest of the World was second at 86 under par and Europe, third at 67 under par. The low individual was Mark James with a 263 total, two strokes in front of Nick Faldo and Jose-Maria Canizares who broke the course record with 62 on the last day. James shot 64 in the first and fourth rounds to pace the British/Irish victory and generally the scoring was low, as might be expected in a relaxed atmosphere. Each day 23 or 24 of the 30 players broke par-71, and the British/Irish team took a nine-stroke lead, then expanded the margin to 12 strokes in the second round.

By the last day, the attention was focused only on the individual results, the outcome of the teams having been taken for granted. When Faldo birdied the 17th, he shared the lead. James birdied the 18th ahead of him, leaving Faldo to make another three to tie. He lost his chance at the 18th tee, hooking his drive into the trees. James won £5,000 for first place. Each member of the winning team also received £4,000. Members of the second-place team received £2,500 each and members of the third-place team, £1,500 each.

Haig Whisky Tournament Players Championship — £70,000
Winner: Nick Faldo

Winning the Haig Whisky Tournament Players Championship was a just reward for Nick Faldo, who had been winless during a very consistent year. 'What pleases me is that I set a standard this week to win and I made it,' Nick said, following his three-stroke triumph with a 270 total, 18 under par at Hollinwell, Nottinghamshire. 'I knew there was no way into the World Match Play event unless I won here.'

The previous week's Hennessy Cognac Cup put Faldo in a properly aggressive mood for the victory. He needed a birdie on the last hole to tie Mark James for the £5,000 first-place check, which was the only individual prize on offer. 'It was the perfect motivation,' Faldo said. 'We all had to attack and go for a win because there was absolutely no point in coming second. I made an error, but at least I had been attacking all the way in the final round and not trying to play safe.'

Even though Faldo had a successful year in America and, with the TPC victory, had reached third on the European Order of Merit, Nick was not overly conscious of his bank balance. 'That's not the name of the game,' he said. 'The accountant says I shouldn't worry about not winning as long as I keep bringing in hefty checks each week. I haven't been out of the top 10 in nine tournaments but I do seem to squander chances when they present themselves.'

John Bland set a course record at Hollinwell with 64 in the first round, having nine birdies. Sandy Lyle, having seven birdies, was second with 65, followed by Carl Mason and Tony Minshall with 68s, then came Faldo in the group with 69s. Two prizes were won the first day. Mason received a £14,000 Range Rover for his eagle-two at the 355-yard 16th and Steve Marr was later presented with a special bottle of Haig whisky for his hole-in-one at the 178-yard ninth. It was noted in the press that Marr's prize was either a reward or consolation, in that he shot 82, sharing the highest score of the day.

Faldo posted 67 in the second round, advancing within one stroke of Bland, who shot 71, and Manuel Calero, the eventual runner-up. Nick had to struggle for 12 holes, seemingly having half-shots to every green, but his grim scrambling and determination brought him through. He then completed the victory march with scores of 65 and 69, running his string to 10 consecutive rounds in the 60s beginning midway of the European Open. Faldo's most serious challenger in the last round was Calero, who made three birdies in four holes to cut the margin to one stroke with three to play. The crucial hole was the 16th. Calero duffed his approach into a bunker and Faldo followed suit. Nick came out of the bunker close to the hole for a priceless par while Calero made double bogey for a two-stroke swing. 'Manuel let me off twice,' Faldo admitted. 'I just told myself not to give in, but to stick with it.'

Bob Hope British Classic — £100,000
Winner: Gordon Brand, Jr.

The name of this Bob Hope production might be 'The Road to Rickmansworth' — not a very catchy title — but unquestionably the Bob Hope British Classic at Moor Park has become a highlight of the year, particularly among those followers who gather to see such celebrities as Gerald Ford, Telly Savalas, Ernest Borgnine and, of course, Mr. Hope himself. This, the third British Classic, provided a profit of £300,000 for the Stars Organization for Spastics and the Little Theatre at Eltham, Hope's birthplace. The previous two tournaments had operated with deficits, even though £133,000 was donated to those charities, and the final accounting for 1982 surely silenced any of the event's critics, including the Charity Commission, which had conducted a needless inquiry.

While James Garner won the pro-am, the £90,000 European Tour title went to Gordon Brand, Jr., who earned £15,000 to push his earnings over £35,000 with the second victory of his rookie season. Brand came from one stroke behind Mark James on the final day, shooting 69 for a 272 total to defeat James by three strokes. Bogeys at the fifth and sixth holes dropped James into second place and he couldn't recover. The championship was decided at the par-five 16th and 17th holes. James three-putted both holes for bogeys while Brand made a pair of birdies.

Brand was close to the lead throughout the rainy week. He shared opening-day honors at 65 with Bernard Gallacher and Vicente Fernandez, the Argentine who was making only his fourth appearance in Britain since the end of the Falklands war. Fernandez took 75 in the second round and eventually placed 10 strokes off the winning total. Gallacher was more of a contender, sharing fourth place with Howard Clark behind Brand, James and Bob Charles, who shot 68 in the last round. James was the 36 and 54-hole leader with rounds of 70, 66 and 66 before fading with his 73. Brand had a 73 in the second round, followed by another 65 in the third.

Benson & Hedges Spanish Open — £51,500
Winner: Sam Torrance

The way that Sam Torrance played in the Benson & Hedges Spanish Open, it was difficult to believe that Torrance had not won in more than a year, since the 1981 Irish Open. Torrance's putting, which had given him trouble in the past, was beautifully slow and Sam had an easy time, winning by eight strokes over Sandy Lyle, Ian Woosnam and Roger Chapman. His 273 total, 18 under par, represented excellent golf on the demanding 7,044-yard Club de Campo course near Madrid and the victory enabled Torrance to advance to third on the Order of Merit behind Greg Norman and Lyle.

Torrance's scores were 71, 65, 67 and 70. He described his 65 on the second day as 'the finest round of my life'. He had seven birdies, including three on the last three holes, to equal the course record and take a three-stroke lead. The opening-round leader with 69 and the eventual joint runner-up was Chapman, who previously had been overshadowed by fellow rookies Gordon Brand, Jr. and Paul Way. Torrance never trailed after the second round and, with nine holes remaining, held an eight-stroke margin after an outward 33. If Sam became a bit slack, it was understandable. He shot 37 on the last nine, being more interested in the progress of others, and was especially pleased that his friend, Chapman, managed a share of second place.

Sanyo Open — £60,000
Winner: Neil Coles

The European Tour went from one extreme to another while playing out the final weeks of the year in Spain. There could hardly have been greater contrast in moving from 7,044-yard Club de Campo near Madrid to the 5,662-yard Sant Cugat, on the hills above Barcelona, for the Sanyo Open. The professionals were driven almost to distraction and there was a spate of withdrawals, disqual-ifications and prominent names on the list of those failing to gain the last 36 holes: Seve Ballesteros, fellow Spaniards Antonio Garrido, Jose-Maria

Canizares and such Britons as Sandy Lyle, Gordon Brand, Jr., Paul Way and Irishman Des Smyth.

One of the shortest layouts ever used on the European Tour, Sant Cugat was a course to be played with irons. The two par-fives required two solid blows, conceivably all the par-fours could be played with wedge second shots and the four par-threes ranged from the flick of a wedge to a four-iron. Some people called Sant Cugat a pitch-and-putt course and certainly it was not to the liking of the professionals.

So much for the moans and groans. The pleasant result of the Sanyo Open was a victory for the veteran Neil Coles in this, a year highlighted by the play of the Tour's younger members including three triumphs by newcomers. Coles won by one stroke over Garry Cullen with a 266 total, 14 under par, after they had virtually identical day-by-day scores. The difference was Coles' 67 in the second round to Cullen's 68. They shot 71s in the first round and 64s on the last two days. Alone in the third place at 269 was Manuel Montes, who led the first round with 65. Warren Humphreys was the 36-hole leader by three strokes, but faded badly.

Lancome Trophy — £65,925
Winner: David Graham

David Graham had a chest infection and Seve Ballesteros was running a high temperature. Each contended that he felt worse than the other. Ballesteros was advised by a doctor that he would be better off in bed. 'But the trouble is,' Seve replied, 'you cannot play golf in bed.' The result in the Lancome Trophy was that Graham and Ballesteros underlined the truth of the old saying: Beware the ailing golfer. Graham repeated as champion at St. Nom la Breteche near Paris, leading from start to finish, while Ballesteros took second place, two strokes behind. Sandy Lyle put in a bid to replace Greg Norman as the Order of Merit leader with a victory but finished joint fourth with Arnold Palmer, one stroke behind Craig Stadler.

The Lancome Trophy featured a revised format and was virtually a European tournament of champions, rather than an exclusive invitational as it had been since 1970. Fifteen of the leading 16 players from the European Tour were on hand, the absentee being Norman, who returned to the United States to be with his wife, Laura, who gave birth to their first child. The 27-player entry also included Gary Player and Frenchmen Jean Garaialde and Gerry Watine, in addition to Palmer and Stadler.

Graham started with 66, then posted three 70s for his 276 total, 12 under par. Ballesteros remained two to three strokes behind with scores of 68, 71, 70 and 69 for his 278 total. Entering the last day, Graham was three ahead of Ballesteros, with Lyle poised in second place, one stroke off the lead, following Sandy's three-eagle round for 68. Lyle scored two quick birdies in the fourth round to catch Graham and Sandy went ahead at the fourth hole when the Australian bogeyed. David battled back with an eagle-three at No. 5 and a duel seemed to be developing. However Lyle, whose driving was erratic, hooked badly at the seventh and took a double bogey, including a hurriedly missed

12-inch putt. He dropped two more strokes on the par-three ninth and was out of contention. Then Ballesteros began to challenge. Seve had a triple-bogey seven at the fourth, where he lost a ball, and was out in 39 strokes. He came back in 30, passing Lyle, Stadler and Palmer, who played marvelously over the last two days with a pair of 68s, finishing each round with three birdies.

Cacharel Under-25s — £23,000
Winner: Ian Woosnam

The most experienced golfer in the field, and certainly the most successful during 1982, won the Cacharel Under-25s Championship in Nimes, France. That person was Ian Woosnam, winner of the Ebel Swiss Open earlier, with rounds of 71, 69, 74 and 76 for a 290 total, five strokes better than the runner-up, Keith Waters. Woosnam credited his victory, and his late-summer success, to the purchase of a second-hand driver for £17. 'I broke mine while playing in the Dutch Open,' Woosnam explained. 'I went to the professional to get another and there was only one in stock, so I decided that would have to do. I shot a last-round 66 to finish fourth there, then took second place behind Greg Norman in the Benson & Hedges International, and a week later I won the Swiss Open. I feel now that I can beat anyone.' On a less successful note, the Cacharel Under-25s marked the professional debut of Wayne Player, Gary's son, who failed to qualify for the last two days after rounds of 79 and 81.

Johnnie Walker Trophy — US$50,000
Winner: Peter Jacobsen

If Seve Ballesteros wondered what happened to the putting touch that deserted him in the final round of the Johnnie Walker Trophy, the Spaniard might have looked towards Peter Jacobsen, the young American who successfully defended the championship. Jacobsen admitted he had 'borrowed' Ballesteros' putting secret before the third round, when Jacobsen shot 64, one stroke off the course record at El Prat. 'I watched Seve putting and he gives the ball a sharp downward strike,' Jacobsen said. 'I tried it in the third round and had only 28 putts.' Jacobsen continued with 68 in the fourth round for a 274 total, 14 under par, and won by two strokes for the $16,000 first prize.

Ballesteros led by five strokes after 36 holes with scores of 67 and 69, then shot 69 and 71 over the last two rounds for his 276 total. Playing with Arnold Palmer before a huge gallery, Ballesteros had an erratic time on the first day. Despite six birdies, Seve failed to make fours on three par-fives and three-putted twice. Perhaps that was an indication of what was to come. Ballesteros was one stroke ahead, entering the final round. They juggled the lead for most of the day. Jacobsen tied Ballesteros on Seve's bogey at the 14th and went ahead with a chip-and-putt birdie at the next. Peter went two ahead when Ballesteros took three putts at the 17th and held that margin.

Portuguese Open — £42,000
Winner: Sam Torrance

Entering the final event of the European Tour, the Portuguese Open, Sandy Lyle had his sights on a victory which would have lifted the Scot ahead of Greg Norman and into first place on the Order of Merit for the third time in four years. That was not to be. In fact, Lyle remained in second place only by about the price of a golf ball. While Sandy finished 10th, Sam Torrance won the Portuguese title for his second triumph in five weeks.

The first-place check of £7,000 gave Torrance £61,516.51 for the year, only £1.33 short of Lyle's £61,517.84. Norman won the Order of Merit with £66,405.71. Rounding out the list of leaders were Nick Faldo, fourth with £56,844.21; Manuel Pinero, fifth with £54,211.00; 1981 winner Bernhard Langer, sixth with £43,847.70; rookie-of-the-year Gordon Brand, Jr., seventh with £38,842.24; Ian Woosnam, eighth with £38,819.66; Bernard Gallacher, ninth with £38,589.14; and Seve Ballesteros, 10th with £38,437.36.

It was said that the Portuguese Open confirmed the theory that golf clubs may also be used as divining rods, so adept are they at attracting rain. After a three-year drought on the Algarve, there was a 48-hour deluge starting on the second day which forced officials to reduce the tournament to three rounds.

Torrance's winning total was 207 on scores of 71, 67 and 69, four strokes better than Faldo, the runner-up. Jose-Maria Canizares shot 67 in the first round. The second round was carried over to Sunday morning. When it ended, Torrance was one stroke ahead of Faldo. On the final 18, Nick shot 72. Both Torrance and Faldo shot 35s on the opening nine of the last round, then Torrance pulled away with a trio of threes beginning at the 12th hole — two for birdies — while Faldo made three fours. Torrance could then free-wheel to the finish. He had one last flourish, covering the flag at No. 18 with a four-iron shot for another birdie to conclude the European golf season.

10. The African Tours

The African Tours — a total of 15 tournaments including two formally-structured circuits and independent events — featured victories by two of the most impressive golfers of our time (Gary Player and Raymond Floyd) plus the emergence of a new star on this continent (Mark McNulty). The most significant events took place in South Africa and in the newly independent nation of Bophutatswana, venue for the second $1,000,000 Sun City Challenge.

Early in the year, Player won his third South African PGA Championship, which turned out to be his only 1982 victory, breaking a skein in which Gary has gone 27 consecutive years winning two or more tournaments and amassing 123 career victories. At the same time, South Africa's new sensation, McNulty, was winning four of the Sunshine Circuit's seven tournaments just after a potentially fatal automobile crash in late 1981. McNulty won the Durban Open, SAB South African Masters, Sharp Electronics Open and Sun City Classic. Other Sunshine Circuit victories were by Nick Price in the Vaal Reefs Sigma Open and by Denis Watson in the Holiday Inns Pro-Am.

On the six-event Safari Tour, David Jagger and Brian Waites each won twice and Jagger led the Order of Merit by merely £403 after triumphing in the final event. Jagger's victories were in the Nigerian Open and the season-ending Kalahari Diamond Classic in Botswana. Waites won the Mufulira Open and Zambia Open on consecutive outings, while the other Safari champions were John Morgan in the Ivory Coast Open and Eamonn Darcy in the Benson & Hedges Kenya Open.

After a seven-month lull in African golf, the American professionals returned for the 12th annual Moroccan Grand Prix, won by Frank Conner. A few weeks later came the headline affair in Bophutatswana at the Gary Player Country Club, a part of Sol Kerzner's Sun City gambling resort. Raymond Floyd took away the first prize of $300,000 — as well as first place on the 1982 World Money List — after a four-hole playoff with Craig Stadler.

Two tournaments — the Datsun South African Open and ICL International (renamed the Tournament Players Classic) — were not played in 1982, but instead were scheduled in the six-event Sunshine Circuit for early 1983.

Durban Open — R100,000
Winner: Mark McNulty

Mark McNulty began the Sunshine Circuit with a bit of luck. Mark was lucky to be there, following an horrendous crash six weeks earlier while he was en route to the ICL International. He estimated that his car was traveling in excess of 100 miles an hour when it struck a bus head-on. The vehicle was totally destroyed, but McNulty came away with only multiple nose fractures and played the next week in the South African Open, where he took a share of ninth place with one 71 and three 69s. McNulty maintained that pace into 1982 and won first event, the Durban Open, with four 69s for a four-stroke victory with his 276 total, 12 under par at Royal Durban Golf Club.

The large British contingent, numbering about 80, was hardly noticeable in the final standings. Sharing second place were Hugh Baiocchi, Allen Henning, and Gavin Levinson, then came Simon Hobday and Teddie Webber at 281 and Mark McCann at 282. Des Smyth, Warren Humphreys and John Hawkes made the list in seventh place, along with American John McGough.

The leader for the first and second rounds was McCann, a former Transvaal Amateur champion who was returning from a stint on the mini-tours in the United States. The stepson of Phil Ritson, a teaching professional at the Walt Disney World complex in Florida, McCann said he intended to obtain American citizenship and try playing that tour.

The first day of the tournament coincided with a race meeting at the Greybill, a track which encircles the Durban course. McCann admitted to watching all seven races, each time stepping away from his ball until the horses had passed the winning post. He carded a 66, one stroke ahead of American Alan Pate and three ahead of a group including the eventual winner. In the second round, McCann shot 70 while McNulty advanced to second place, two strokes behind, with a round that included only four pars and none over the last 12 holes. Mark had nine birdies, one double-bogey and four bogeys.

McNulty's third 69 resulted in his two-stroke lead over Smyth and Levinson entering the final day. McCann lost his lead after just two holes and finished with 75, four strokes behind. The best score of the third round was 65 by Smyth, who was shaking off the effects of not having played a tournament since the Bob Hope British Classic the previous year. But Smyth closed with 74, and McNulty proved to be untouchable.

There were a few tense moments in the final round. McNulty three-putted the fourth hole, but drilled his three-wood approach to the fifth for an eagle. Mark got in trouble off the tee at the seventh, yet still scored his birdie after a brilliant five-iron shot. There was a two-stroke swing at the eighth, with Levinson's birdie and McNulty's bogey. They matched birdies at the ninth, and McNulty was still two strokes clear. When Levinson birdied the 11th, one stroke separated them. Levinson dropped a stroke at the 12th and, when McNulty birdied the 13th and saved par at the 14th, the others were too far behind to recover.

Lexington PGA — R100,000
Winner: Gary Player

The greater surprise in the Lexington PGA was not that Gary Player overcame a four-stroke deficit to defeat Mark McNulty, but that Gary also beat Bill Rogers in the final round at the Wanderers Golf Club in Johannesburg. The 1981 British Open champion, Rogers seemed to still be on his tear from the previous season, having won five of his last eight tournaments, while McNulty's brilliance of 1982 was not yet evident.

To win his third South African PGA title and secure his 123rd career victory,

Player had a closing round of 68 for a 272 total, 16 under par. McNulty shot 75 and Rogers 73. They shared second place at 275, three strokes behind, along with Gordon Brand, the former British Walker Cup player who was appearing in only his second professional tournament. South African newcomer David Frost was alone in fifth place at 277.

That 75 broke McNulty's string of 11 consecutive sub-par rounds. Mark had earlier scores of 67, 67 and 66 and was the leader after 36 and 54 holes. Denis Watson led the first day with 65. Much of the early attention was focused on David Feherty, a little-known Irishman who was then living in Orlando, Florida. Feherty was second with 66, one stroke ahead of McNulty and Rogers and two ahead of Player. He eventually took a share of seventh place, despite his 74 in the final round. McNulty's back-to-back 67s provided a two-stroke margin after 36 holes, and through the third round, Mark led by two over Rogers and by four over Player.

While McNulty was shooting 66 on that third day, Rogers carded 65 and Player 66. Gary has often said that 59 was possible at the Wanderers and he was certainly thinking in those terms when he had an eagle and four birdies in the first seven holes. He played the first nine in 30, his lowest-ever score there. He was jolted by a bogey at the 11th, however, and never regained the spark. Player made no more birdies and closed with another bogey.

McNulty led Player and Rogers by one stroke with nine holes remaining, having 39 after a double-bogey at the par-three ninth. Mark's adventurous start also included an eagle three at the fifth hole, a birdie at the fourth and bogeys at the second, sixth and eighth. He also birdied the 10th, but faded from there on. Rogers went out in 37 with bogeys at the eighth and ninth, then fell back after additional bogeys at the 14th and 17th.

Player's iron game was often ragged in the final round, but his chipping and putting were sensational. He sank birdie putts from the 15-foot range at the 10th and 11th holes and went ahead after McNulty's bogeys at the 11th and 12th. Gary holed a 45-foot birdie at the 16th to go four in front, and his bogey at the 18th did not matter.

SAB South African Masters — R100,000
Winner: Mark McNulty

If Mark McNulty's success on the Sunshine Circuit depended on one hole or one stroke, that would have been the 14th hole and his second tee shot in the final round of the SAB South African Masters.

Again, McNulty was on the verge of allowing a victory to slip away. Starting with a five-stroke lead, Mark was two ahead of Hugh Baiocchi when he drove out of bounds from the 14th tee. He had a long, lonely walk back to the tee, with plenty of time to think. He reflected that if he lost, it would not be a calamity and that he was fortunate to even be alive, considering his automobile accident in November.

By the time McNulty was ready to play, Baiocchi had already hit to the 14th green and was three feet from a near-certain birdie. If Mark played his second ball in four, for a total of six strokes, the lead would change hands on the double-bogey. With his newly-founded composure, a huge drive and a lucky bounce on his approach shot, McNulty scored a three on his second ball and still held a share of first place. He made three birdies on the remaining holes and won by two strokes over Denis Watson with a 74 and 275 total, 13 under par. Baiocchi was third at 278 and American David Ogrin fourth at 279.

'There comes a time in every man's life when you have to pull out all the stops to do something big,' McNulty said afterwards. 'I had come to the moment of truth. I just had to win, to score a victory over my negative thoughts. I even contemplated quitting the game if I had lost today. But I won and I'm happy with the way I did it.'

Nigel Burch, the Briton who lost a playoff in the 1981 Holiday Inns Pro-Am in Swaziland, shot 67 to lead the first round on Milnerton's windswept links. McNulty followed his opening 68 with a magnificent 64, including nine birdies and one bogey, to advance five strokes ahead of Ogrin. Mark had a 69 in the third round and was five strokes in front of Watson. 'I promise you I will not lose this one,' McNulty said at the time. 'I learned something then, and I am playing too well to let it happen again.' He almost did.

Sharp Electronics Open — R100,000
Winner: Mark McNulty

It seemed there would be no final-round drama in the Sharp Electronics Open, at least not involving Mark McNulty. He was six strokes off Tienie Britz' pace and Britz, who led by four, was probably thinking of Gavin Levinson and Nicky Price as the men to beat. All three were left with shares of second place, however, as McNulty stroked home a 15-foot birdie from the fringe of the 18th green, capping his four-under-par 66 and 274 total at Killarney for his third triumph in four weeks.

Through the tournament, McNulty was lurking, to use the popular American phrase for distant yet definite threats. He shot 69 in the first round, while Tertius Claassens had 67. Another 69 placed McNulty five strokes adrift of Denis Watson, whose 61 equalled Allan Henning's South African record score in the 1975 Rolux Toro Classic. (However, Henning then was 11 under par, while Watson was but nine under.) After 54 holes, Britz was in control by four strokes following his 65.

The finish was a heart-breaker for Price, among others, because Nicky's bogey at the 18th, after a stray drive, dropped him from a first-place tie. Britz maintained his lead for just nine holes, then Levinson took command for two holes before double-bogeying the 11th. McNulty entered the picture at that stage. He had birdied the first hole and was playing with true confidence. A 15-foot birdie at the 14th tied McNulty with Price. 'I was back in the game and then I knew I was going to win,' Mark said. 'But I believed that when I drove off and when I got that birdie on the first.'

There was a one-hour delay because of lightning. Minutes before, Price had a two-putt birdie at the 15th and was the sole leader. Returning to the course, McNulty encountered a six-foot putt to regain the tie. He missed it. 'That didn't throw me,' McNulty said. 'I knew I would birdie that last hole.' Mark's eight-iron approach to the 18th ran through the green. He had to sink a delicate 15-footer from the fringe. 'The ball was backed up against the fringe,' he related, 'and I had to change my stance. But as soon as I hit it, I knew it was going down.'

Price's route down the 18th was from tree to bunker to the green, where he still had a birdie opportunity from six feet. He watched Levinson and Britz putt out, but missed his, nevertheless. 'I knew what to do, but it just didn't come in from the left as I expected it to,' Nicky said. He could only shake his head about his play on that hole. Speaking of his drive, Price said, 'I mean there weren't more than three small trees within 70 meters, and I've got to find one. Even when I got in the bunker, I wasn't unduly perturbed. I've been playing some great bunker shots. I got out well only to muff the vital putt. Well, that's the way it goes.'

Sun City Classic — R100,000
Winner: Mark McNulty

When the Sunshine Circuit reached Sun City, Mark McNulty was playing as if he were six weeks late; that is, as if he belonged in the $1 Million Challenge over the 1981–82 New Year's holiday. Shades of Bobby Locke and Gary Player, McNulty made it three consecutive victories and four in five weeks with his one-stroke win in the Sun City Classic. McNulty played the last nine at Gary Player Country Club in 32, four under par, finishing off his 68 to turn back runner-up John Bland and the third-place contender, Nicky Price.

McNulty's total was 283, five under par and six strokes off Johnny Miller's winning Challenge score. The rough had grown considerably in those six weeks, and the lowest score of the tournament was 67 by Des Smyth, the Irish Ryder Cup player, in the last round. Smyth merely tied for ninth place, while the top finisher from the British Isles was Warren Humphreys, fourth behind the Zimbabwean and the two South Africans.

After Phil Simmons led the first two rounds with scores of 69 and 73, the three eventual challengers came forward and were tied at 215 after 54 holes. McNulty missed only one fairway and hit into just one bunker in the final round, while also having a sterling putting touch. 'I pitched and putted well all week,' Mark said. 'I was full of confidence.' Bland could not make the birdie he needed at the 18th and closed with 69. 'My putting has repeatedly let me down on this circuit,' John said. 'If you can't putt, you can't win tournaments, and that's been the story of my life over the last few months.'

Vaal Reefs Sigma Open — R40,000
Winner: Nicky Price

Mark McNulty and Gary Player were taking the week off and most of the British contingent had gone on to the Safari Tour. They all missed a fine tournament and an outstanding performance by Nicky Price in the Vaal Reefs Sigma Open. Price broke Bobby Cole's course record by one stroke with his 63, nine under par, in the third round and went on to a five-shot victory over Denis

Watson. It took 67 by Watson to come that close, as Price shot 71 on the last day for his 270 total. John Bland, who entered the last round in second place, eight strokes behind Price, placed third at 277.

British golfers Ian Mosey and Tony Bennett were struck by lightning in the first round at Orkney. Both had their umbrellas torn from their hands just as the siren was sounded to suspend play. They were not seriously injured. Mosey said, 'I felt the current flow down the metal shaft of my umbrella and it was ripped from my hand. I just saw sparks flying, but fortunately, I was holding the wooden handle. Otherwise, I could have been killed.'

Mosey was on the 14th fairway while Bennett was 250 yards away on the 10th fairway. 'It was like an electric shock,' Bennett said. 'My brolly was thrown five yards and my right arm is still throbbing. I have taken pain-killers.'

The performances of two black South Africans were of particular interest, especially in light of Price's runaway in which no one came closer than the final five-stroke margin in the last round. Vincent Tshabalala, the former French Open winner, had his best-ever finish in South Africa, sharing fourth place. And Joe Dlamini, the son of Swaziland's Minister of Finance, posted a 64 in the fourth round, his best-ever score, and was tied for 25th place.

Holiday Inns Pro-Am — R40,000
Winner: Denis Watson

A victory in the Holiday Inns Pro-Am was important to Denis Watson for more than the obvious reasons. The title and the prize money aside, Watson was most interested in gaining a top-three position on the Order of Merit and in qualifying for the World Series of Golf on the U.S. Tour. 'I have been building this year towards getting to the U.S. and getting a spot in the World Series, which will have a lot of pull with sponsors over there,' said Watson, who had not won in South Africa since the 1981 Asseng Champion of Champions.

Watson's triumph in the closing event of the 1981–82 Sunshine Circuit was by four strokes over Fulton Allem. He had rounds of 70, 64, 65 and 69 for his 268 total, 20 under par at the Swazi Spa Golf Club. Watson, who was second in the SAB South African Masters and Vaal Reefs tournaments, finished No. 2 on the final Order of Merit, between Mark McNulty and Gary Player.

McNulty had his worst performance of 1982, taking a share of fifth place despite his blistering 65 in the last round. 'I was upset by my poor third-round 73 and I tried to make amends,' said McNulty, who dropped two shots to par on the last four holes. 'I was going for too much, looking for the course record,' he said. 'But it would have been nice to make 62.'

British golfer David Williams shot 67, the best score of the first round, then Allem was the 36-hole leader with rounds of 69 and 63, the latter total setting the course record, for which McNulty was aiming. Watson's 64 in the second round and his 65 in the third round provided a 199 total, three strokes better than Allem. On the last day, Watson shot steady nines of 34 and 35, adding one stroke to his edge and never giving Allem a chance to break past him.

Nigerian Open — £41,050
Winner: David Jagger

At the conclusion of the Nigerian Open, champion David Jagger was carried off on the shoulders of the chanting, excited African caddies while Ian Woosnam was left to wonder how to ever win the tournament. The year before, Peter Tupling was the champion with a world-record 255 total. Woosnam possibly also set a record then, as the only golfer ever to shoot 61 in a tournament and not win. The 1982 title was decided on the second playoff hole, with a birdie by Jagger.

Other highlights of the four days at Ikoyi Golf Club, which by tradition is a venue for low scoring, included an opening-round lead by 1980 champion Bill Longmuir, who was second by six strokes to Tupling in 1981, and a second-round lead by a native Nigerian, Festus Makelemi, a past World Cup contestant.

In sweltering heat, the championship was left to be decided between Jagger and Woosnam. The third-place finisher, David Jones, was three strokes off their 274 totals, as both Jagger and Woosnam finished with 68s, three under par. Woosnam birdied the 18th hole to gain the playoff, but could not take advantage of Jagger's errant drives into bunkers on both extra holes. At the second, Woosnam found himself in worse difficulty, his tee shot resting in tall grass at the base of a palm tree, while Jagger was able to recover for the winning birdie.

The natives then took Jagger, who also won the Nigerian Open in 1975 and 1977, on a hair-raising jaunt half a mile back to the clubhouse. Along the way, Jagger had a gold chain torn loose, but he managed to hang on to it. David admitted, 'They were just happy for me, but it was a bit frightening.'

Ivory Coast Open — £36,200
Winner: John Morgan

Giving up his club professional job at Royal Liverpool to concentrate on a playing career, John Morgan could look with reasonable confidence towards the African warm-ups to the PGA European Tour. Morgan's only victories came on this continent in 1979, when he won both the Nigerian Open and Lusaka Open. His ambition was a top-three finish in the Order of Merit, which would result in an automatic qualifying exemption for the later events in Europe and Britain. Although Morgan later missed that objective by a narrow margin, his venture was a success by the second week, when he won the Ivory Coast Open, coming from five strokes behind the hapless Ian Woosnam and winning by two.

The toll of the Safari Tour was already having an effect by now as four players including David Jones, who was third in the Nigerian Open, were plagued by stomach disorders. Most of the contestants were taking special medication as well as salt and malaria tablets. Signing on a week late for this semi-hardship duty was Martin Poxon, who had been denied a visa by the Nigerians because he played in South Africa in 1979.

Morgan started off with 66, then relinquished the 36-hole lead to Poxon, who had 65 and a 135 total, including three birdies on the last four holes.

Woosnam posted rounds of 71, 65 and 67 to lead after 54 holes. Morgan opened the last round with an eagle three and was out in 31. He collected four more birdies and could afford a stroke when he bogeyed the 18th for his 64 and 272 total. He might have had 61 but for his final bogey, and missed the three-foot putts for birdies at the 13th and 14th.

Woosnam, who shot 71 for his 274 total, was a top-five finisher in an African tournament for the fifth time without a victory. He was two under par until bogeying the eighth. He scored two birdies after that, but bogeyed two par-three holes. Third place with 68 and 275 went to Nigerian champion David Jagger, who shot the rarest of birds by holing out his four-iron from 200 yards for a double eagle on the first. Jagger's round included four birdies, but also three bogeys.

Benson & Hedges Kenya Open — £38,470
Winner: Eamonn Darcy

Eamonn Darcy could not be faulted for regarding his victory in the Benson & Hedges Kenya Open as an especially good omen for 1982, for it was also in Africa that Darcy laid the foundation for his exceptional 1981 season. Eamonn held off a determined challenge from David Jagger to win by one stroke with a 274 total, 10 under par at Muthaiga Golf Club in Nairobi. Jagger equalled the course record twice, with 65s in the third and fourth rounds, but the 1974 Kenyan champion could not surpass the Irishman, who posted rounds of 72, 65, 67 and 70.

Early leaders were Trevor Powell and Tommy Horton, with 68s in the first rounds, followed by Peter Tupling, who shot 66 to command a 136 total after 36 holes. Of those three, only Tupling was among the top-10 finishers, gaining a share of seventh place. Rounding out the five behind Darcy and Jagger were Ken Brown, Gordon Brand and Ian Woosnam. Darcy had to sink a succession of putts in the 10-foot range after missing fairways and greens early in the final round. He steadied himself with a 20-foot birdie at the eighth and played home in pars. Jagger shot 31 on the final nine, although missing his birdie opportunity at the 18th and leaving Darcy to score three pars to win.

Mufulira Open – £48,396
Winner: Brian Waites

The jungle-variety rough around the Mufulira Golf Club is such that often a golfer's only hope of finding an errant ball is to step on it. That's precisely what happened to Brian Waites in the final round, and the chance discovery enabled Waites to retain his title in the Mufulira Open in this steamy copper-mining town in Zambia.

Waites, who trailed Martin Poxon by two strokes entering the last round, hit his tee shot into the jungle off the 15th fairway. The spectators looked for the ball for a while, then a woman stepped on it. With that, Waites successfully appealed for a free drop. His next shot was over the green, but he chipped within three feet of the hole and salvaged a par four. Waites' recovery seemed to deflate Poxon, who dropped two strokes behind with a bogey on the 17th. Then Waites birdied the 18th from 12 feet for his five-under-par 68 and 281 total, winning by three strokes from Poxon and Eamonn Darcy.

Brian had an astonishing bit of poor luck on the 18th in the third round. His tee shot on that par-three hole hit the flagstick and spun out into a bunker. Instead of winning £5,000 for a hole-in-one, Waites took a bogey four. That didn't bother Brian for long. He began the final 18 holes with three consecutive birdies, all with putts under five feet.

Zambia Open — £70,000
Winner: Brian Waites

The closest Brian Waites came to not winning the Zambia Open — for his second successive victory on the Safari Tour — was when he was almost struck by his own bunker shot in the final round. Four strokes ahead after 54 holes and five ahead midway through the last 18, Waites had a delicate shot from a bunker on the par-five 10th. He caught the ball on his follow-through and embarrassingly hit it backwards, over his shoulder. 'It narrowly missed hitting me,' said Waites, who scored a six on the hole, reducing the margin to three strokes. Had Waites been struck by the ball, there would have been an additional two-stroke penalty.

As things stood, Waites' bogey gave Ken Brown a spark of hope. But Brown missed a three-foot birdie opportunity at the 11th hole and double-bogeyed the 12th, while Waites went on to a four-shot triumph with his 72 and 276 total. The £12,000 first prize pushed Waites to the top of the Safari money list. Following Brown's 280 total were three golfers sharing third place at 281 — Tommy Horton, Howard Clark and Peter Tupling.

Waites was the wire-to-wire leader and almost won a £13,000 Range Rover as well. He nearly took that hole-in-one prize in the first round. His seven-iron tee shot on the 150-yard 11th hole struck the flag 10 inches above the cup and spun 12 feet away. He missed the birdie putt, in a twist of circumstances similar to that the previous week. Ian Woosnam won that Range Rover in the second round, however, holing his six-iron shot on the 184-yard 16th.

Kalahari Diamond Classic — £30,000
Winner: David Jagger

The only way David Jagger could finish atop of the Safari Tour money standings was by winning the final tournament of the circuit, the new Kalahari Diamond Classic at Gaborone Golf Club in Botswana. The young Englishman did just that, posting a five-stroke triumph over Peter Tupling to snatch the No. 1 position on the list from Brian Waites, the Tour's only other multiple-tournament winner.

Jagger completed the six-week circuit with £21,393, £403 more than Waites, and more than Jagger had earned in four years on the European Tour. Starting with a victory in the Nigerian Open, David was third in the Ivory Coast, second in Kenya, tied for fourth in Mufulira and tied for 11th in Zambia.

Few of the locals in Gaborone had ever heard of Jagger or any of the approximately 50 British and Irish professionals. They knew only the neighboring South Africans, who were barred from the tournament, as Botswana stepped in line with the other black African nations in establishing a boycott. The opening-round leader was little-known Mats Lanner of Sweden with 67, three ahead of Jagger. Roger Chapman posted a pair of 69s for the 36-hole lead at 138, then Jagger came through in the third round to share first place with young Scot Robert Craig. Jagger's rounds were 70, 70 and 69 while Craig had the same scores but with his 69 in the first round. Jagger shot 67 in the final round for a 276 total. Tupling closed with 69 and took second place at 281, and Craig shot 73 to tie John Morgan for fourth place at 282.

Moroccan Grand Prix — US$100,000
Winner: Frank Conner

'This makes up for a playoff earlier this year,' said Frank Conner, following his victory in the Moroccan Grand Prix over the tough Trent Jones course at Royal Dar-Es-Salaam. Conner's reference was to his loss to Tom Watson in the Heritage Classic, and Frank was delighted to have finished the year with a one-stroke triumph over Butch Baird and Lennie Clements. He shot 71 on three of the four days, along with 74 in the second round, for a 287 total, five under par on the 7,400-yard course. Defending champion Bob Eastwood had one of six sub-par scores with 70 in the first round. Morris Hatalsky's pair of 71s led after 36 holes. Through three rounds, the leaders at 214 were Hatalsky, Clements and Baird, with Conner two strokes behind. Baird and Clements both finished with 74s while Hatalsky shot 78 for seventh place.

Sun City Challenge — $1,000,000
Winner: Raymond Floyd

Once again, there was a finish to remember in golf's richest tournament, the $1,000,000 Sun City Challenge in Bophuthatswana. In the inaugural event, Johnny Miller went nine extra holes to defeat Seve Ballesteros. This time around, Raymond Floyd required four playoff holes and then, ironically, a mere one-foot putt to claim the $300,000 first prize from Craig Stadler, who missed from less than three feet. Whereas Stadler became the money leader of the U.S. Tour by edging Floyd in the World Series of Golf, Raymond took the honors on the World Money List with this victory.

The field for the second Sun City Challenge was doubled to 10 players, including the five originals — Miller, Ballesteros, Jack Nicklaus, Lee Trevino and host Gary Player — plus Floyd, Stadler, Greg Norman, Jerry Pate and Lanny Wadkins. A Calcutta in this gambling resort before the tournament raised almost $250,000, with Nicklaus going highest and Pate, lowest. Jerry was a great choice for three rounds, holding the lead, but shot 80 on the last day and tied for sixth place.

Pate shared the opening round lead with Ballesteros, both having 67s. Pate bogeyed the last hole while Ballesteros birdied as Seve, in a small way, settled an old score. He had lost the title there to Miller with a bogey. A typical escape by Ballesteros enabled the Spaniard to lead after 36 holes with 71 for a 138 total. At the 15th, Ballesteros lost all sight of the fairway with a spectacular hook. Yet, Seve managed to hit a wedge onto the fairway, another wedge to the green and sank a 12-foot putt for his par. Pate rebounded from his second-round 73 to shoot 66 in the third and lead with a 206 total. The highlight of Jerry's round was a 117-yard chip shot across water for an eagle at the ninth. Pate then led Wadkins by two strokes, and Floyd and Stadler by three. With three successive bogeys, Ballesteros was five strokes behind after his 73.

Floyd and Stadler shot 71s in the fourth round for 280 totals while Trevino charged into third place at 281 with his closing 67. Wadkins, whose disappointment was probably second to Pate's, had 74 to place fourth, two strokes behind. In the blistering heat, both playoff contestants made mistakes on the closing holes of regulation play. Floyd got ahead at the 14th with a birdie, then dropped the stroke by hitting through the green on the next. Stadler gave back the lead by hitting into a bunker on the 16th, and they were tied again when Floyd hooked his drive into deep rough on No. 17. On the last regulation hole, Stadler had to salvage par by hitting onto the green from beside a television tower.

The playoff nearly ended on the first hole, when Floyd exploded from a bunker to within inches of the hole. But Stadler sank a 22-foot putt to continue. They scored pars on the next two holes, then Stadler hit through the green at the 17th. He chipped back wonderfully to within a yard of the hole and Floyd, after a fine approach putt, was one foot away. They seemed headed for a fifth extra hole, then Stadler missed the short one, allowing Floyd to tap-in for the victory.

11. The Asia/Japan Tours

Young players had their days on the Asia and Japanese Circuits in 1982. Tsuneyuki Nakajima, a 28-year-old with seven years of domestic and international pro experience, dislodged Isao Aoki as Japan's leading money-winner during a season of almost constant contention in which he won a record Y68,220,640 (or $278,450) and five tournaments. Though his blazing pace slowed a bit, 27-year-old Masahiro Kuramoto, the 1981 rookie sensation, had a second successful season, adding two more victories and Y37,151,927 in prize money in Japan to his record and gaining international respect with his fourth-place finish in the British Open at Troon in July. Two young Americans— Denny Hepler (Malaysia) and Kurt Cox (Hong Kong)— and Kim Joo Heun, a 21-year-old Korean amateur (Korea Open), scored victories on the Asia Circuit.

By and large, though, 1982 was the year of the veteran in Asia. Hsu Sheng San, a regular campaigner since winning the Philippine Open in 1967, ran off a string of three victories on the Asia Circuit that led him easily to his third seasonal championship at age 40. His better known and even more accomplished compatriot, Hsieh Min Nan, 42, matched that streak months later on the tougher Japanese Tour after winning the venerable Philippine Open in late February. But, the most remarkable performance was staged by Teruo Sugihara, who had been expected to yield his position as Japan's top winner of tournaments during 1982 but instead, at 45, won five tournaments and equalled his age as his closest challengers — Aoki and Masashi (Jumbo) Ozaki — managed only a victory apiece during the year. Ozaki has 41 titles on his Japanese record, Aoki 40 and his prestigious World Match Play Championship. Both have considerably less longevity in pro golf than the quarter century of action of the gritty little Sugihara, who won his first big title, the Japan Open, in 1962.

Even with just the one win, the much-traveled Aoki still played strongly enough when he was home to nip Hsieh for the runnerup spot on the Japan money list, though both were more than Y20,000,000 behind Nakajima. It was the first time since 1976 that Aoki was not a multiple winner during the season. Ozaki's triumph in the Kanto Open was his first in almost two years. Hsieh, internationally noted for his World Cup victory in Australia in 1972, matched an eight-year-old Japanese Tour record with his successive victories in three of the more important events — Tokai, Golf Digest and Bridgestone — after often showing well in earlier tournaments. Sheng San's unprecedented string of three wins on the Asia Circuit — Thailand, India and Singapore Opens — was remarkable in a way, since he had blown the Philippine Open to Hsieh at the start of the season by shooting an 81 in the final round and losing a playoff by missing a two-foot putt.

Lu Hsi Chuen went winless in 1982, his first poor season in four as an Asian

NAKAJIMA'S RECORD YEAR IN JAPAN

Tournament	Position	Money
Shizuoka	T13	Y 470,000
Kuzuha Kokusai	T5	343,334
Hakuryuko	2	1,600,000
Bridgestone Aso	3	1,800,000
*Dunlop International	1	6,125,000
Chunichi Crowns	3	4,300,000
Fuji Sankei	1 (Playoff)	7,000,000
Japan Match Play	Lost 1st Rd	150,000
Pepsi Ube	MC	
Mitsubishi Galant	3	2,300,000
Tohoku	T2	1,875,000
Sapporo Tokyu	T4	1,180,000
Yomiuri	T2	1,800,000
Mizuno	T5	750,000
Nagano	1	3,000,000
Japan PGA	T3	1,270,000
Kanto PGA	6	800,000
Descente Cup	2	2,700,000
East-West Match Play	1 (Individual)	1,807,692
Kokudo Summers	DNP	
KBC Augusta	DNP	
Kanto Open	T5	775,000
Suntory	DNP	
ANA Sapporo	T3	1,775,000
Hiroshima	DNP	
Jun Classic	T6	1,400,000
Tokai	T8	900,000
Golf Digest	Y18	312,500
Bridgestone	T9	1,350,000
Japan Open	5	1,800,000
Goldwin Cup	10	4,900,000
Pacific Masters	T12	1,097,365
Dunlop Phoenix	MC	
Casio World	2	6,700,000
Japan Series	1	5,000,000

TOTAL . . . . . . †Y68.220,640

SUMMARY

Starts — 31 Complete tournaments — 28
Victories — 5 (Dunlop International, Fuji Sankei, Nagano, East-West Individual, Japan Series)
Seconds — 5   Top 5 — 20   Top 10 — 25

*Also Asia Circuit event.
†Official Japan PGA total; above figures total Y65,280,890

star, and was overshadowed by Chen Tze Ming, who joined the pro ranks with him in 1979 and had won just three times during the first three seasons. Chen took the China Open in his homeland and the KBC Augusta in Japan. His younger brother, Chen Tze Chung, didn't win in 1982, but impressed in America by qualifying in fourth position for the PGA Tour, something Cox, Hepler, the No. 2 performer on the 1982 Asia Circuit, and 1981's American star in Asia, Tom Sieckmann, failed to do. The other winners on the Asia Circuit in 1982 were Eleuterio Nival, the Philippines veteran, in the Indonesia Open and Nakajima, who started his finest season with his win in the Dunlop International, the final event on the Asia Circuit schedule which always ends in Japan. It was the only Japanese victory on the Asia Circuit, although it should be noted that few of Japan's leading players compete on that tour.

Overseas players again made a big dent in the victory column in Japan in 1982. Tour standouts from America swept the big November events, Scott Hoch taking the Pacific Masters and Casio World, Calvin Peete the Dunlop Phoenix and, with Bob Gilder, the individual championship in the Goldwin Cup Matches, the new version of the U.S. vs Japan competition. Gary Hallberg picked up his second foreign title when he won the rich Chunichi Crowns tournament in April, while Graham Marsh scored his 19th victory in Japan in the Mitsubishi Galant and fellow Aussie Terry Gale his first in the Yomiuri Open. Hoch took $122,000 out of Japan.

Four other Japanese pros — three veterans and a third-year pro — enjoyed 1982. Shigeru Uchida, a one-year-younger contemporary of Sugihara, picked off three of the circuit's lesser titles. Kikuo Arai, the No. 4 man on the final money list and a steady player throughout the season, also scored three victories, including the 72-hole Pepsi Ube and Descente Cup Hokkoku tournaments, and Norio Suzuki captured the ANA Sapporo and Kyushu Opens, finishing close behind Kuramoto on the money standings. Yutaka Hagawa had a financially-rewarding season, but the left-hander, who won the 1981 Japan Open in his sophomore season, had to settle for five second-place finishes and no new titles in 1982.

Here's how the season went in the Orient, starting at Manila with the

Philippine Open — US$150,000
Winner: Hsieh Min Nan

Long one of Asia's leading players, Hsieh Min Nan has compiled a distinguished record — three times the champion of the Asia Circuit, on which he has won five of his 13 titles. The Philippine Open, the oldest Asian tournament and long considered the crown jewel, had eluded him, however, until 1982. When it finally landed in his possession, it came when he least expected it.

Hsieh had no idea that he would wind up with the winner's trophy when he teed off in Sunday's final round, facing the tight fairways and unlikely prospects of low scoring at Wack Wack Golf and Country Club near Manila. He was nine strokes off the lead and that lead was held by able countryman Hsu Sheng San, who had launched his career 15 years earlier while still an amateur by winning the Philippine Open. It seemed that only a record-breaking round would give Hsieh any kind of a chance. Instead, the 41-year-old Chinese veteran found his patient par-72 round putting him into a sudden-death playoff against Hsu, when the smooth Taiwanese star, who had twice been the circuit champion himself, confounded everybody, himself more than anybody, by floundering to an unbelievable 81 and a matching 292, the highest winning score in the Philippine Open in 24 years.

As if that wasn't enough agony for one golfer, Hsu eventually lost the playoff at the third extra hole when he missed a two-foot par putt. That playoff pairing did insure one thing — continued domination of the Philippine Open by Taiwanese stars, Hsieh becoming the eighth different player from his country to win in the Philippines. It was Taiwan's 11th title in 18 years.

The unexpected should have been expected the way the tournament started. Gil Ababa, a 24-year-old amateur, who was ultimately to finish ahead of all except one Filipino pro in the field, seized the first-round lead at Wack Wack with a three-under-par 69, a shot ahead of Spaniard Manuel Calero and two in front of Hsu and Choi Sang Ho of South Korea. Ababa, who had practiced constantly at Wack Wack during the two months preceding the tournament, had four birdies and a bogey, but scrambled for five pars in becoming the first amateur since 1935 to lead the ancient tournament after the opening round. Hsieh was in a large group at 72, while John Mahaffey and Dave Hill were the best of the Americans in the field at 74.

When Ababa slipped to 76 Friday, Hsu took the lead with his second straight 71 for 142 and an American newcomer, Curt Byrum, a 23-year-old former basketball player from Naples, Florida, joined Hsieh in the runnerup slot at 144. A solid 69 Saturday opened a five-stroke lead for Hsu, who ran off nine pars on the front nine, then had four birdies and a bogey coming in for his 211. Byrum shot 72 for 216, while Hsieh appeared to have shot himself out of it with his 76—220. Ababa also was at that total after a 75.

Hsu had early warning signals Sunday of what was to come. He bogeyed the first two holes. He double-bogeyed the eighth, bogeyed the ninth and was out in 41. Birdies continued to escape him and he took another double-bogey at the 14th and a bogey at the 16th but still led by two as the pair and Mahaffey reached the 18th. Both Taiwanese missed the fairway, but Hsieh played a dazzling shot from the rough with his driver that stopped 10 feet from the cup. Hsu had no such opportunity from a fairway bunker and missed a fairly-long par putt before Hsieh rolled in his for the tying birdie.

They matched pars on the first two playoff holes (15th and 16th) before the star-crossed Hsu saw a spike mark knock his short putt for a half at the 17th off line to end the misery and bring a surprised 'Finally . . .' from Hsieh. Byrum, with 77, missed the playoff by a shot, bogeying the 18th hole. He tied another American, Alan Pate, at 293, a shot ahead of Mahaffey, Tsao Chien Teng and Eleuterio Nival. Fortunately for him, the humbling defeat did not shatter Hsu. His days were coming.

Cathay Pacific Hong Kong Open — US$130,000
Winner: Kurt Cox

Most players who had tried four times and failed to qualify for the U.S. Tour, as Kurt Cox did, would have turned to something else as a way of life. Cox turned to someWHERE else instead — the Asia Circuit. The decision continued to pay off in 1982 when Cox captured his third title on that Tour with victory in a three-man playoff in cold, blustery weather in the Cathay Pacific Hong Kong Open. It went with his 1980 triumphs in the Indian and Singapore Opens, but was perhaps more impressive, considering the strength of the Hong Kong field. The Cathy Pacific event drew leading players from Japan and Australia, who showed up just for that tournament, in addition to the full complement of regular competitors.

With all of the name stars, you might know how the tournament started — with a stranger at the top. Koichi Hirabayashi, 31, a hair stylist before turning pro in 1977, shot a three-under-par 67 over the composite course created for the tournament from Royal Hong Kong Golf Club's 36 holes. He only shared first place, though, and the other man, Terry Gale of Australia, was in the thick of it right into the playoff. Cox was among four players who had 68s, while Tom Sieckmann, who had won twice last year in Asia, began his move toward a spot in that eventual playoff with a par 70. The 'name' players were strung out behind Seickmann's group of five 70 shooters or were gone, as was Graham Marsh, who signed for a wrong score and was disqualified.

Another Australian, Stewart Ginn, the 1977 Malaysian Open winner in Asia, and Cox took over first place Friday. Between them they had shot four 68s, their 136s giving them a two-stroke lead over Seickmann (70–68) and Kikuo Arai, one of Japan's leading players, who had a pair of 69s. Gale was another shot back after his 72—139 in a group that included Greg Norman, Britain's able Brian Waites, Japan's young star Saburo Fujiki, Korea's circuit winner Kim Seung Hak and defending champion Chen Tze Ming.

The final battle lines were drawn in unusual fashion Saturday as the three players who were to fight it out in the playoff finished the third round in a three-way tie for the lead at 206. Gale had four consecutive birdies on the back nine en route to a 67, Seickmann had a 68 despite a ball out of bounds at the 16th hole and Cox had a 70. Ginn's bid failed when he bogeyed four of the last six holes. He dropped to 209, where he and three others — Kim, Chen and Fujiki — were closest to the top.

Nobody threatened the leading trio Sunday and they shot 70s in widely-varying fashions. Seickmann, for instance, eagled the par-five 12th and double-bogeyed the next hole when he whiffed trying to hit a shot out of a tree left-handed. He played the last five holes one under for his 70. Cox missed an eight-foot birdie putt for the win at the 18th, while Gale gained his spot in the playoff with a birdie on the last hole, where he played a skillful hooked approach around trees onto the green and dropped a 10-foot putt.

Gale exited the playoff quickly when he three-putted the first extra hole (16th), missing a short one after Cox failed on a short birdie try. Cox and Seickmann matched pars on the next two holes before Kurt nailed the $21,650 victory passively when Seickmann three-putted after Cox two-putted for his par.

Malaysian Open — US$150,000
Winner: Denny Hepler

The American impact on the Asia Circuit has been growing rapidly in recent years. In the 1960s and early 1970s, the straggle of little-known pros from the United States was no match for the Asian and Australian players, the only American victories coming twice when one of the U.S. Tour stars showed up for a single event. Since the mid-1970s, though, more talented young Americans, seeking experience for initial or return shots at the U.S. circuit, have gone to Asia. Starting with Howard Twitty's victory in Thailand in 1975, they have been winning, at least once every season since 1977.

One notable exception was at Kuala Lumpur, where no American had won in the 20-year history of the Malaysian Open, one of the four original tournaments on the Asia Circuit. That situation ended in 1982, although who knows what might have been if the tournament had run off on its normal pace and schedule. Denny Hepler, a 26-year-old native of Warsaw, Indiana, broke the ice for the U.S. when he won the circuit's third consecutive playoff after he, fellow American David Ogrin and Hsieh Min Nan, seeking his second 1982 win, tied at the end of 54 holes of the rain-shortened tournament at Royal Selangor Golf Club. Hepler, who had enrolled for Asia after twice failing to qualify for the U.S. Tour in 1981, grabbed the title on the second extra hole when he nudged in a 12-foot birdie putt after his two opponents had missed theirs, the veteran Hsieh from just slightly greater distance.

The tournament ended brightly for the survivors when Malaysian Open officials elected to award the full purse even though just 54 holes were played, but its start was clouded by heavy rains and ensuing controversial decisions. Even though more than half the field had finished and the final threesome was four holes on its way when Thursday's drenching rains made the course unplayable, tournament officials decided to wipe out all scores instead of finishing the next day, as is done on the American and other tours nowadays. They elected to go with a 54-hole tournament ending Sunday (the deadline for all Asia Circuit events because of the difficult travel situation), with a cut to the low 65 players after the replayed first round, the latter an unprecedented decision that was eventually to cost the tournament, among others, famous American Gene Littler, who missed that cut by a stroke with his 74.

The rain-out, which occurred despite the presence of Malaysia's famous elderly rain-chaser, was particularly painful to Graham Marsh, Masakatsu Sano of Japan and Chen Tze Ming, who had leading 69s cancelled by the weather and the committee edict. Sano Chen missed the cut the next day. The first round that counted Friday produced a home-grown leader for the first time in tournament history as Marimuthu Ramayah posted a four-under 67, an uncertain one because of driving problems that sent him to his three-wood, to share the top with amateur Frankie Minoza of the Philippines. Two of the three playoff protagonists moved into the picture Saturday. Hepler shot 68 for 138 to tie Terry Gale for the lead, while Hsieh's 68 for 139 deadlocked him with Minoza after the amateur's 72. Ramayah slipped to 74 and 141.

Ogrin, a 24-year-old, Chicago-born rookie pro from Texas, was still four back at 71–71—142. But the hefty newcomer to Asia carved out the week's best round Sunday, holing a 30-footer on the last green for 66, and watched as Hsieh finished with 69 and the 6.3, bespectacled Hepler with 70 to forge the three-way tie at 208, four shots better than the next in line — first-round leaders Ramayah and Minoza, Gale and Hung Wen Neng. Two playoff holes later, the elated Hoosier had his first national pro title.

Thailand Rattanakosin Bicentennial Open — US$100,000
Winner: Hsu Sheng San

Hsu Sheng San hadn't disappeared from view after his shattering loss in the Philippine Open, but the frightful finish at Manila had obviously shaken his confidence. His performances at Hong Kong and Kuala Lumpur were mediocre at best. As all winning athletes seem to do, though, he regained that confidence in the Thailand Rattanakosin Bicentennial Open in as positive a way as the defeat had been negative three weeks earlier. In that sad performance, Hsu had blown a big lead and lost a playoff. At Bangkok, the slender Taiwanese star roared from five strokes off the third-round pace and won the Asia Circuit's fourth consecutive playoff, an unprecedented occurrence. Adversity behind him, Hsu got his best of three circuit championship seasons in real motion there at the Royal Thai Army Golf Club course at Bang Khen. Interestingly, his victory in the Thailand Open was the high spot when he won his second season title in 1978.

The 40-year-old Chinese pro was not really visible through the first three rounds. In striking similarity to the start of the Malaysian Open the preceding week, a native Thai stirred the golfing masses by grabbing the first-round lead. As Malaysian Marimuthu Ramayah did on his home soil, Somsak Srisa Nga moved in front Thursday at Bang Khen with a five-under-par 67, two strokes ahead of American John McGough and Taiwan's Shen Chung Shyan. McGough, 25, a newcomer to Asia, had five consecutive birdies in his outgoing 31. Hsu opened with 70, then fell five shots off the lead the second day with a 73 as Chen Tze Ming ran off four front-nine birdies in a row and shot 67 for 138 and the lead. Sukree Onsham, Thailand's premier pro, took up the chase for the home fans when Somsak Srisa Nga began a slow slide with 73 for 140, where he was joined by Stewart Ginn (70–70). Onsham had 70–69—139.

Yet another switch transpired Saturday when Jerry Anderson, a 26-year-old Canadian from Toronto, who in his second season in Asia had not previously made a 36-hole cut, moved in front with a 68 for 210. That put him two better than Chen, who took a 74, as did Onsham, who joined six others, including Shen, McGough and Kurt Cox, the Hong Kong victor, at 213. At that point, Hsu was tied for 15th place at 215.

In striking contrast to his disaster in the Philippines, Hsu played flawlessly Sunday over the Royal Thai Army course's 7,023 yards, never driving out of the fairway and ticking off six birdies without a bogey for the week's best round — 66 — and the final 281. Shen, who, although a winner, has been the least successful of the young triumvirate of Lu Hsi Chuen, Chen Tze Ming and himself that joined the Asia Circuit in 1979, played nearly as well. He had five birdies, the final two coming on the 17th and 18th holes after he had taken his lone bogey at the 15th.

However, that tying birdie putt on the 18th green was to be his last gasp. After Hsu put his approach six feet from the pin on the short, par-four first hole in the playoff, his younger countryman badly missed his second shot, was still outside him with his pitch, missed the putt and conceded the victory, Hsu's fifth on the circuit. Shen's lone win came in the 1979 Korea Open. Onsham, making a brave bid to join the playoff, came within a foot of an eagle with his approach at the 17th hole and just missed a birdie putt for a tie on the final green. He shot 69, his 282 total putting him in a third-place tie with Ginn and ending unsuccessfully another bid for a win on the Asia Circuit. Ginn closed with a 68. Anderson was another stroke back after a 73 in the tightly-bunched finish.

Indian Open — US$75,000
Winner: Hsu Sheng San

A very hot shooter brought the American roll to an abrupt end in the Indian Open in 1982. Nowhere else had the growing presence of U.S. talent been more evident in recent years than in India. Starting with Bill Brask's victory in the 1978 Indian Open, Americans took the title four years running with Gaylord Burrows, Kurt Cox and Payne Stewart following Brask to titles. But neither the 1982 crop of pros from the U.S. nor those from anywhere else could stand up to the charge of Hsu Sheng San on his way to his second straight victory, a win that reversed another pattern, too. Well as the battery of brilliant Chinese pros from Taiwan has performed on the Asia Circuit over the years, India has been one of the soft spots. Hsu's triumph was just the third for Taiwan golfers in India and the first since Kuo Chi Hsiung won in 1974.

The tall, slender Chinese star lingered just off the pace during the first two rounds at Royal Calcutta Golf Club, the alternate-year venue for the Indian Open, as the players made a surprisingly strong assault on the 7,235-yard, par-73 course. Twenty-eight of the record 160 players broke par in the opening round, the veteran Hsieh Min Nan leading the attack with seven birdies and a five-under 68. Of the five 69 shooters, Japan's Ikuo Shirahama was to take the greatest advantage of the fast start over the week-end. Also at 69 were Hung Wen Neng of Taiwan, Priscillo Diniz of Brazil, Ray Arinno of the U.S. and Kyi Hla Han, a promising young Burmese pro, who had a five-under 32 on the back nine. Hsu opened with 70.

Another 70 amid an even-heavier barrage of scoring Friday moved Hsu into a second-place tie with Han (69–71), Lu Hsi Chuen (72–68) and Hsieh (68–72), as Shirahama surged to the fore with a six-under 67, a shot off the course record, his 136 giving him a four-stroke lead. No Japanese player had been in that position after 36 holes during the previous 12 years that the Indian Open has been a leg on the Asia Circuit. The tournament has not had a Japanese winner since Kenji Hosoishi took the title in 1967 and 1968 when it was an independent event.

Starting the day with two birdies, Hsu had overhauled Shirahama by the 10th hole Saturday, went on to a 68 and finished the round a shot ahead of the Japanese pro, 208 to 209. The field was strung out behind them with Hung, who also shot 68 on the strength of four consecutive birdies, at 210, Mya Aye at 212 and Hsieh and Lu at 213.

The final round focused almost totally on Hsu and Shirahama. The Chinese pro birdied the first and third holes and opened a three-stroke lead with his front-nine 32 to the Japanese player's 34. When Shirahama double-bogeyed the 10th hole, Hsu was home free, even though he three-putted the 12th and Ikuo eagled the par-five 15th to Hsu's following birdie. The two parred in, the winner shooting 69 for 277, the runner up 71 for 280. It was six strokes back to the third-place finishers — Han, Lu, Hung and Hsieh at 286. Hsu's $12,495 victory score set a new record for the redesigned Royal Calcutta course.

Singapore Open — US$100,000
Winner: Hsu Sheng San

Three in a row. Birdies, bogeys? Commonplace. Victories? Rare indeed . . . and usually the completion of the triple comes hard. When Hsu Sheng San captured the Singapore Open to become the first player in the history of the Asia Circuit to win three titles in successive weeks, though, the crowning victory was almost a breeze. Hsu, who had been close but had never before won in Singapore, coasted to a five-stroke victory with a par closing round, easily fending off Terry Gale, his only real challenger all week at Singapore Island Country Club's Bukit course.

The three wins in a single season themselves put Hsu in rather exclusive and all-Taiwanese company. Lu Liang Huan did it in 1974, Kuo Chi Hsiung in 1975 and Lu Hsi Chuen in 1979 and 1980. Hsu seemed as pleased to have won in Singapore as he was with his three-in-a-row achievement. 'It's a great feeling,' he remarked, recalling that in 1979 he had lost there in a playoff with Lu, until then a winless Tour rookie; had tied for second behind Kurt Cox in 1980 and finished third to Mya Aye in 1981.

Gale established himself as the major obstacle between the Chinese star and his third straight win when he opened the Singapore Open in late March with a record-matching 64 over the Bukit course's 6,645 yards. Still, Sheng San started with 68, which put him, countryman Chang Toang Liang and Ben Arda, the aging Philippine star, in a second-place deadlock. Hsu chopped a stroke off Gale's lead Friday with his 67 for 135 to the Australian's 68 for 132. Close observers noted a slight change in Hsu's swing during those first two rounds, which he later revealed was because he was favoring a sore hip. The somewhat outside-in action was costing him a little distance because of the resultant fade, but it did not prevent him from taking over first place Saturday. He shot 68 to go 10 under par for the distance and move two strokes ahead of Gale, who slipped to 73.

It was then clearly between those two men, since nobody else was within six shots even of Gale. And Terry had nothing in his arsenal to fire at Hsu Sunday. The impending winner parred the first five holes and held his margin as the 35-year-old bogeyed the second and birdied the fourth. Then Gale bogeyed the sixth, seventh and eighth, falling a helpless five behind as Hsu offset a three-putt bogey at the seventh with a chip-in birdie at the eighth. The back nine was uneventful for both as Hsu posted his par 71 for his winning, 10-under-par 274. Gale struggled to 74 for 279, still good enough for second place, a comfortable three shots ahead of Chen Tze Chung, who charged through the rest of the field with 68s in the final two rounds.

Indonesia Open — US$60,000
Winner: Eleuterio Nival

Nobody was happier than Eleuterio Nival when Hsu Sheng San elected to pass up the Indonesia Open rather than shoot for his fourth victory in as many weeks. The veteran pro from the Philippines had been looking for an opening for a victory on the Asia Circuit for eight years, an up-and-down period that followed his Tour victories in Taiwain in 1973 and Singapore in 1974 and solid play that had stamped him as the Filipino to succeed Ben Arda as his country's No. 1 player. He has never donned that mantle, although remaining one of the leading pros in the Philippines.

The husky Nival had given little hint of his upcoming success in Indonesia at the earlier circuit stops, his only high finish coming with a fifth-place tie at Manila. However, he had played well in the past in Jakarta and had finished second to Kuo Chi Hsiung in the 1978 Indonesia Open at Jaya Ancol Golf Course, the 1982 venue. In 1981, he was in contention until a third-round 76.

So, the 42-year-old pro was comfortable with his 69 start at Ancol on April 1st. Nival was bunched with four others a stroke behind co-leaders Chang Chung Fa of Taiwan and Jeff Jones of the U.S. Three other Americans mounted bids in the second round to succeed fellow Yank Payne Stewart as the Indonesia champion. Denny Hepler (71–69), Ray Arinno (69–71) and John McGough (71–69) shared the lead when Jones skied to 81 and Chang to 77. Nival's 72 kept him close and a stroke in front of two other U.S. pros — Jimmy Paschal and John Hamarik, the 1981 Chilean Open winner — and Canadian Ray Stewart.

The picture changed only slightly Saturday as Hepler, Arinno and Nival all shot par 71s. So, the Malaysian Open winner and Arinno led at 211, Nival was at 212 and McGough fell back into a tie at 213 with Australia's Rodger Davis. The final round developed into a three-way fight among Nival, Hepler and Davis, as Arinno was unable to keep pace and McGough was ultimately disqualified. Eleuterio had the strongest finishing kick. He was still even par for the day after 13 holes, then birdied the 14th and 17th for a 69 and a three-under-par total of 281, enough to edge Hepler, who had a par final round, and Davis, who had a second straight 69 for his matching 282. Arinno took a 73, dropping into a tie for fourth with Aussie Brian Jones. Nival's victory was the first Tour win for a Filipino since Arda won his ninth Asia Circuit title in the 1979 Philippine Open.

China Open — US$100,000
Winner: Chen Tze Ming

The situation seemed ripe for Hsu Sheng San. After playing in the first six tournaments on the Asia Circuit and winning the last three of them in a row, he had skipped the Indonesia Open to return home to Taiwan, rest a bothersome hip and await the tour's arrival for the 17th China Open. Furthermore, the powerful Taiwanese pros dominate their home tournament more than they do anywhere else. They had won the last eight years, back to Eleuterio Nival's victory in 1973, and 13 times in those previous 16 China Opens. Every one of the country's veteran stars had won in Taiwan at least once — except Hsu Sheng San. Surely, he was due. But it was not to be.

Instead, the 1982 China Open turned into a family affair, yet still one that followed form with a Taiwanese winner of considerable repute. For the first two days at the venerable Taiwan Golf and Country Club at Tamsui, the stage was commanded by young Chen Tze Chung. Then, he yielded to older brother Chen Tze Ming, who didn't exactly play the final rounds with any flourish but handled matters well enough to nail his fourth Asia Circuit title in as many years as a pro and salvage what had been a struggling season up to that point. His winning 289, produced by rounds of 69, 72, 75 and 73, was the highest victory total since the tournament was launched in 1965 with Hsu Chi San's 290 triumph.

Chen Tze Chung fashioned the only really impressive score of the week when he opened with a wind-blown 66 that gave him a three-stroke lead over his 28-year-old brother and Taiwan's two winningest veterans — Hsieh Yung Yo and Lu Liang Huan, who have 21 circuit victories between them. There was nary a 70, but eight 71s. The 24-year-old came back to earth Friday, shot 74 and found his brother just a stroke behind him after his 72 for 141. Lu also slipped to 74 and Hsieh to 77 on a sunny day with gusting winds. Normally, a 75 does little but cost a player ground, but at Tamsui Saturday it jacked Chen Tze Ming into first place by a stroke. At 216, even par, he had a shot on Lu, twice a winner and three times a runnerup in past China Opens, and Hsu, charging up his bid for a fourth straight circuit victory with a third-round 71. Amateur Lai Chung Jen also shot 71. That put him at 218 with Chen Tze Chung after his fading 78, while another amateur, Lu Chien Shun, joined Kuo Chi Hsiung, a three-time champion, and Chen Chien Chung at 219.

Conditions were so difficult Sunday that Hsieh Yung Yo's 70 was the best score of the day. In those circumstances, Chen's 73 — 17 pars and a bogey — handled the victory as Kuo and amateur Lu shot par 72s for 291 and joint second place. Lai was the only other player close. He shot 74 for 292, three strokes in front of American David Ogrin, Chen Chien Chung, Mr. Lu, amateur Lee Wen Sheng — and Hsu, whose hopes for No. 4 crashed with a 78. The win was particularly satisfying for Chen Tze Ming, who had only a single top 10 finish on his 1982 record and had even missed two cuts, something that rarely happens to the better players on the Asia Circuit.

Korea Maekyung Open — US$90,000
Winner: Kim Joo Heun

The Asia Circuit turned the calendar back to the mid-1960s at its ninth stop of the 1982 season in Seoul, Korea, when it put the Korea Maekyung Open title in the hands of an amateur, a highly unlikely occurrence in national and international tour golf these days. It hadn't happened on the Asia Circuit since 1982's leading player, Hsu Sheng San, won the 1967 Philippine Open. Doug Sanders was the last to accomplish it on the American Tour when he took the 1956 Canadian Open before turning pro. It has happened only a handful of times on the other world circuits in the interim.

What occurs more often is that contending amateurs fade in the pressure of the final round, lacking the experience and poise of the professionals. That's what figured to happen at Seoul Country Club in mid-April when 21-year-old Korean amateur Kim Joo Heun wound up the third round tied for the lead with Lu Hsi Chuen, the Taiwanese star who had won seven Asia Circuit titles in the three previous seasons. Master Lu had been looking for just such an opportunity after experiencing his first disappointing pro season, one in which his best finish has been a distant tie for third in India.

But it was Lu who cracked in the final round over the 6,995-yard course, turning over the lead to Kim when he bogeyed the sixth and eighth holes en route to 74. The young Korean went on to a two-under-par 70, a 285 total and a three-stroke victory margin over Mexico's Rafael Alarcon, who closed with a par 72 to edge Lu by a shot for second place. More importantly, that single shot gave the 23-year-old native of Guadalajara first money of $15,000 because of Kim's amateur status. It was Alarcon's best showing in his two-year pro career as he produced three back-nine bogeys to grab the runnerup slot and his biggest check.

Kim's victory, while quite unexpected, should not have been overly surprising, since he was completing his college education at the time at Tokyo's Nihon University, which has a standout golf program that has produced several young stars on the Japanese circuit the last few years. Besides, until Chen Tze Ming won in Korea in 1980 and 1981, Koreans usually have taken the tournament titles despite the presence of strong international players. That had been the case six times in the previous 12 tournaments that span the event's existence on the Asia Circuit.

Tom Seickmann, twice a winner on the 1981 circuit, jumped off in front at Seoul Thursday with a five-birdie 67, staking out a two-stroke lead over Lu and Japan's Yoshiyuki Isomura. Kim was back where amateurs usually reside with his opening 74. One Yank replaced another as Californian Brad Sherfy, with 71–70, took a one-shot lead over Lu, Isomura and Alarcon after 36 holes. Kim began his move that day when, on the strength of a seventh-hole eagle, he climbed into a fifth-place tie with Sieckmann, who fell back with 76 for his 143 on his way out of contention. The young Korean then joined Lu in the co-leadership spot Saturday with his par 72 as the Taiwanese pro scored his second straight 73 for 215. Their 74s kept Isomura and Alarcon close, but Sherfy shot himself out with 82.

Thus, the stage was set for Kim's strong finish and the rare amateur triumph. Although Hsu Sheng San was never in contention, he clinched the Asia Circuit championship (Order of Merit) with his tie-for-eighth finish.

Dunlop International — US$150,000
Winner: Tsuneyuki Nakajima

Another form of 'three in a row' happened when the Asia Circuit wound up the

1982 season with its usual final stop in Japan, where the Dunlop International not only closes that Tour but shifts the fledgling Japanese season into high gear. The string that the Dunlop extended to three was the matching nationalities of the champions. A Chinese player had won the China Open and a Korean had won the Korea Open during the two previous weeks. Then, at Ibaraki Golf Club's 7,006-yard west course, Tsuneyuki Nakajima maintained his country's hold on that final leg of the Asia Circuit by scoring an easy, five-stroke victory. The Dunlop had fallen to other Japanese pros in each of the preceding three years.

The victory no doubt meant more to Nakajima from a personal standpoint, though. It broke a win drought of almost two years for the bespectacled, 27-year-old pro, who had burst upon the Japanese Tour scene at age 21 after a brief but flashy amateur career and won six tournaments in his first two pro seasons of 1976 and 1977, one of them the 1977 Japan PGA Championship. Since 1977, though, Tsuneyuki, or Tommy, as he is sometimes called in golfing circles, had dropped back into the group of heavy money-winners but infrequent tournament-winners, taking only that one Tour title in 1980 until the Dunlop victory came along. His acclaim during the dry spell had been primarily negative — the disastrous single-hole scores he had in the Masters and British Open of 1978.

Because of its sizeable purse and its position on the two schedules, particularly coming right ahead of the rich Chunichi Crowns and several other important spring events on the Japanese Tour, the Dunlop attracts a strong international field. Greg Norman, Graham Marsh and Craig Stadler, who had just won the Master two weeks earlier, joined the best of the Asia and Japanese Tour players in the run for the $25,000 first prize. Norman made the strongest start of the stars, linking up with four others just a stroke behind the first-round leaders, Toshiharu Kawada of Japan and Hsieh Min Nan, the veteran Taiwanese star who had scored six of his 11 Far East victories on the Japanese Tour. They shot 68s. Nakajima had a 71, Marsh a 72 and Stadler a 73.

But, when Tsuneyuki came up with an eagle-spurred 66 as the weather warmed up and dried out Friday, he took charge of the tournament, staking out a two-stroke lead over Norman (69–70) and three over Marsh, fellow Aussie Brian Jones and Hsieh, who settled for a par round and his 140. Although he only moved within four shots of the top, Stadler showed the Japanese fans why he had won the Masters, running off six consecutive birdies until three-putting the 15th green and finishing with a 68.

Nakajima widened his margin to six strokes with a 68 Saturday, eagling the par-five 14th hole for a second day in a row. His 205 gave him that edge on Saburo Fujiki, who shot 66, and Liao Kuo Chi and Satsuki Takahashi, who had 68s. The more prominent challengers fell back, Norman to 212 and Marsh and Stadler to 213. Nakajima was never in jeopardy Sunday, at one point opening an eight-stroke lead before settling for 71, 276 and a five-shot victory over Fujiki, landing his eighth Japanese Tour title. Marsh and Isao Aoki moved up into a four-way tie for third place with Yoshikazu Yokoshima and Liao. Hsu Sheng San posted a steady 283 to wrap up his Asia Circuit championship by 238 points over America's Denny Hepler, one of nine players at 285 in the Dunlop final standings.

JAPAN TOUR

Actually, the Dunlop International occupied the sixth position on the official US$7,585,000 Japan PGA Tour, being played more than a month after the opening event, one of three preceding 72-hole tournaments:

Shizuoka Open — Y30,510,000
Winner: Eitaro Deguchi

Appropriately, the new season was launched in Japan by a winner brandishing a new idea. Though it probably had no real bearing on the achievement, Eitaro Deguchi became the first pro to win a Japanese tournament playing with golf balls of other than traditional white. Deguchi, who had come into his 12th pro season without a victory on his record, maneuvered his optic orange golf balls to a closing 68 that carried him four shots off the third-round pace to a two-stroke triumph. The 68 followed earlier rounds of 74, 69 and 71 for a six-under-par 282 score over the 6,859-yard Hamaoka course of Shizuoka Country Club, bringing the 33-year-old Deguchi the largest single collection of his career. The Y6,000,000 check was almost double his 1981 earnings that had placed him 60th on the Tour's money list.

Until heavy overnight rains soaked the course for Sunday's final round, it appeared the year's first title would fall to one of the country's popular veterans long out of the winner's circle. After 25-year-old Nobumitsu Yuhara sported the lead for the first two days with rounds of 67 and 70, he yielded the top spot to 41-year-old Takaaki Kono, a Japanese star of the 1960s and early 1970s; and 37-year-old Takashi Murakami, another of his country's winningest players with 24 titles to his credit, who shared the lead at 211 with Yasuhiro Funatogawa. All three fell under Deguchi's charge Sunday, Murakami taking a 78, Kono and Funatogawa 75s. Instead, Eitaro battled Yuhara and Akira Yabe, the 1981 playoff loser at Shizuoka, through the stretch, going ahead to stay after his only bogey at the 14th hole that created a three-way tie. First Yuhara, then Yabe bogeyed the next two holes and Deguchi wrapped it up by holing an 18-foot birdie putt on the final green.

Veteran champions did win the next two events on the schedule, both abbreviated types. Shigeru Uchida, who has been campaigning for a quarter-century in Asian circles, put together week-end rounds of 68 and 71 to capture the Kagawa Open by a stroke over Kikuo Arai at Shido Country Club. It was the 16th career victory for the 44-year-old Uchida. Weather brought about a 27-hole tournament the next week-end, when rain and powerful winds led officials to shorten the opening round of the 54-player Kuzuha International at Osaka's Kuzuha public course to nine holes. Yet another long-time Japanese ace, Teruo Sugihara, 45, and Toshiharu Kawada shared that strange lead with 34s with Namio Takasu among five players at 35. The 38-year-old Takasu emerged from that pack Sunday with a three-under-par 67 to claim victory and the Y3,000,000 first prize, a shot in front of Yoshikazu Yokoshima.

Hakuryuko Open — Y15,000,000
Winner: Toshimitsu Kai

Toshimitsu Kai, whose only previous Tour victory had come barely a year earlier in the 36-hole Kagawa Open, handled the 72-hole variety in style with a four-stroke triumph in the Hakuryuko Open in Hiroshima in early April. The win was impressive as the 26-year-old Kai stood off two of Japan's leading players in the final round, holding the lead through the final three rounds. He took over from first-day leader Yoshio Fumiyama (67) when he tacked a four-under 66 onto his opening 73. He then led by three and maintained that margin Saturday even though managing just a 74 for 213. Still, lined up to challenge were Masahiro Kuramoto at 216, Toru Nakamura at 217 and three others, including Tsuneyuki Nakajima, at 218. Kai pushed aside any threats with an outgoing 32 Sunday and breezed to the four-stroke victory with 70 for 283. It paid Y3,000,000. Nakajima produced a 69 for 287 and claimed the runnerup spot from Kuramoto, who finished with a par round.

Bridgestone Aso Open — Y30,000,000
Winner: Toru Nakamura

The tournament at Aso Kogen Hotel's Golf Club in Kumamoto Prefecture in southern Japan reached full maturity in 1982 when it attracted sponsorship of the Bridgestone tire company and was played at 72 holes for the first time. The full test produced a solid winner — Toru Nakamura, a strong player who has represented Japan in international events and had scored 14 previous victories on the Japanese Tour. The 31-year-old Nakamura broke from a three-way tie after 54 holes to score a three-stroke victory. His rounds were 74–72–68–69 for 283, bringing him a Y5,000,000 check. Shigeru Uchida, 44, who had won the 36-hole Kagawa Open two weeks earlier, made a serious bid for a second 1982 victory. The veteran was in first place for three days, sharing the position Thursday with Motomasa Aoki at 69, moving a stroke in front of Kikuo Arai at 141 Friday and dropping back into a tie with Nakamura and Seiichi Kanai Saturday. Shigeru shot 73 as Nakamura moved up with his 68 and Kanai with his 70.

Kanai fell back early Sunday and the other two traded the lead in a stretch duel. Uchida went in front for the last time when he birdied the par-five 14th to Toru's bogey, then Shigeru bogeyed the next two holes and dropped to a final three-stroke deficit with a third bogey at the 18th as Nakamura scored his sixth birdie of the round. Nakajima pushed past Kanai into third place with a closing 69 for 287, the only other man to break Aso's par.

Chunichi Crowns — Y70,000,000
Winner: Gary Hallberg

Gary Hallberg's victory in the rich Chunichi Crowns tournament the first weekend of May clearly defied most odds and logic. Not that the 23-year-old American doesn't have the talent of a winner. He had certainly shown it during a brilliant collegiate career, but it had submerged on the U.S. Tour when he played so poorly that he failed to win exempt-from-qualifying status after a struggling 1981 season that continued into 1982. Then, he elected to play in the Chunichi Crowns at Nagoya Golf Club even though that important event has a remarkably continuous list of prominent champions, always draws a potent international field and had never been won by an American. Finally, his travel plans, whether by design or otherwise, put him into Nagoya on the eve of the tournament, denying him a practice round on the course.

Against all of that, Hallberg performed amazingly well throughout the tournament. The former Wake Forest All-American (four times) started with a one-under-par 69, took the lead the second day and was never headed after that, heading off the only real challenge from Shigeru Uchida, at 44 truly old enough to be Gary's father. Hallberg's opening 69 put him just a stroke behind leaders Namio Takasu and Koichi Inoue. Then, with a four-birdie, one-bogey round of 67, he moved two strokes in front Friday, leading Takasu by two and Uchida by three. Now on a tear, Gary ripped off six birdies, posted a 66 and widened his lead to five strokes Saturday. At 202, he led Uchida (70–69–68) by five and everybody else by at least eight.

In Sunday's final round, he allowed Uchida to close the gap to two strokes with a 16th-hole birdie, but forged a final 70 and 272 for a three-shot win when he birdied the final hole to land the Y14,000,000 cash prize and one of the sponsor's cars. The impressive Uchida added a closing 68 for second place at 275, a shot ahead of the previous week's Dunlop International winner, Tsuneyuki Nakajima, who finished with 65, the week's best round, and 276. So, in the fashion of U.S. contemporary Bobby Clampett, Hallberg had two foreign titles as the first entries on his pro record. Now, would he emulate Clampett and land a U.S. title to add to the Chunichi Crowns and his 1981 Argentine Open victory?

Fuji-Sankei Classic — Y40,000,000
Winner: Tsuneyuki Nakajima

The Americans went home, but the international cast remained strong as the Japanese Tour moved on to Ito in nearby Shizuoka Prefecture for the Fuji-Sankei Classic on the Fuji course at the Kawana Hotel. One of them — the steady Australian Graham Marsh, who has won 18 times in Japan, more than any other non-Japanese pro — made a strong run at the Fuji-Sankei title, but it fell to the hot-shooting Tsuneyuki Nakajima after the two wound up in the season's first playoff. Nakajima picked up his second win in three weeks when he two-putt-parred the first extra hole as Marsh, who took the first two Fuki-Sankei tournaments in 1973 and 1974, failed to save par from a trap on the 185-yard 17th hole. Graham has had almost as many seconds as he has had firsts in Japan — six in 1980 alone — so the role was not new to him.

The two men had stayed at or near the top through the early rounds. Nakajima shared the first-round lead with Taiwan's Lu Hsi Chuen at 67, then regained it Saturday at 206 (67–73–66) after Masaru Amano held it with a 36-hole 137. Tsuneyuki entered the final round with a two-shot lead over Marsh and Toru Nakamura, and Sunday became a seesawing fight between the ultimate playoff opponents after the Aussie shook off the shock of a first-hole double-bogey. With four birdies on the front nine and another at the par-three 11th, he took the lead and went two ahead when Nakajima bogeyed the 13th. Tsuneyuki bounced back with birdies at the 14th and 16th and seemed to have the victory in hand when he hit the 18th green in regulation as Marsh bunkered. Graham bogeyed, but Nakajima three-putted and then needed the playoff to score his ninth victory on the Japanese Tour.

Japan Match Play Championship — Y32,000,000
Winner: Isao Aoki

The setting was proper and Isao Aoki was ready. Japan's No. 1 star of major world stature had campaigned with fair success in America in March and early April, then returned home for the first of the big events on the Japanese Tour. In succession, the 39-year-old Aoki placed third, eighth and fourth in the Dunlop, Chunichi Crowns and Fuji-Sankei — no bad rounds, no hot ones. Then, what has to be one of his favorite tournaments came up on the schedule — the Japan Match Play, which he had won three of the previous years. The brilliant match-play exponent made it four out of five as he swept through five opponents, climaxing the week with a 4-and-2 triumph over left-hander Yutaka Hagawa in the Y7,000,000 finale.

His first victim was Seiichi Kanai, 2 and 1, when the opening round's biggest surprise was Masaji Kusakabe's 2-and-1 win over Tsuneyuki Nakajima, who was coming off his second victory in three weeks when the Match Play began at Totsuka Country Club's West course at Yokohama. Aoki followed with victories over Saburo Fujiki, 5 and 4; Nobumitsu Yuhara, 3 and 2, and Hsieh Min Nan, 3 and 2, in the 36-hole semi-finals. Hagawa captured his semi-final match over veteran Takaaki Kono, 2 and 1, after scoring earlier wins over Haruo Yasuda, the 1980 Match Play champion, on the first extra hole of their first-round match; Teruo Sugihara, 2 and 1, and Toru Nakamura, 3 and 2.

The 24-year-old southpaw, who won the 1981 Japan Open, took advantage of some erratic play by Aoki during the morning round Sunday and led by three at the lunch break. But, the veteran Isao smoothed his brilliant putting stroke in the afternoon. He caught up once at the sixth hole, then put it away with a spree of four birdies, beginning at the 11th hole. His 30-footer at the 12th pulled him even and putts of 14 and 10 feet at the next two holes put him two in front. He won the 15th with a par and the match by concession on the 16th green when Hagawa took five strokes to reach the green Aoki had found in three.

Pepsi Ube — Y30,000,000
Winner: Kikuo Arai

Victories have been hard to come by for Kikuo Arai over his long pro career dating back to 1966, when he became the circuit's first university graduate. The 39-year-old Arai, a man of many hats, had won just twice coming into the 1982 season, even though he has long been a consistent money-winner. The previous year, for instance, he was the 48th-positioned player on the World Money List with more than $130,000. He picked up his third title in late May, parlaying an in-and-out final round of par 72 into a two-stroke victory in the Pepsi Ube tournament at Ube Country Club in western Japan.

Arai, who reportedly has more than 100 hats in his wardrobe, was in the picture virtually from start to finish. He took the lead after Friday's second round with his 67–68—135, supplanting Thursday front-runner Radao Nakamura. He headed into the third round two shots in front of Katsuji Hasegawa, three ahead of Shinsaku Maeda and four on top of Isao Aoki and Graham Marsh, among others. At day's end, Kikuo still had his two-stroke lead, now over Hsieh Min Nan, who shot 65, and Motomasa Aoki. Arai shot 70 for his 205, still three strokes ahead of Marsh and four in front of Isao Aoki, who is not related to the younger Motomasa.

Arai started off Sunday as if to run away from the contenders, going out in 33 to lead Marsh and Motomasa Aoki by four shots at the turn. Then, he came back to the field when he drove out of bounds and double-hogeyed the 11th hole and bogeyed the 13th, at that point leading Marsh and the Aokis by just a shot. He clung to that lead for two holes, then eased his burden with a par at the 16th as the other three all took bogeys and maintained his par pace to the clubhouse. His final-round 72 gave him a 277 total. Motomasa Aoki birdied the final hole to snatch second place from Isao Aoki, Marsh and Yasuhiro Funatogawa.

Mitsubishi Galant — Y40,000,000
Winner: Graham Marsh

Graham Marsh found himself trying to win tournaments the hard way in the early stages of the 1982 Japanese season, encountering one playoff after another. The first time, he came off second best to Tsuneyuki Nakajima in the Fuji-Sankei Classic, but he made amends three weeks later in the Mitsubishi Galant when he bested Teruo Sugihara in another overtime match, scoring his 19th victory in his favorite foraging pasture away from home. In accepting the Y7,000,000 check put up by sponsor, Marsh quipped: 'The Mitsubishi people are making money in Australia and I'm happy to help balance the trade between the two countries.'

Graham had to break from a pack of contenders in the stretch to claim that money. Kume Country Club was yielding low scores — Masami Nishiyama and veteran Haruo Yasuda had 64s the first day and Saburo Fujiki a 66–65—131 start over the par-71 course's 6,679 yards. The omnipresent Tsuneyuki Naka-jima then pieced together the best round of them all — a 63 — to jump into a three-way tie for the lead with Sugihara (68–68–67) and Takaaki Kono (67–71–65) at 203. They had just a stroke on Fujiki (73), Marsh (66–69–69), Isao Aoki (66–73–65) and Fujio Kobayashi (69–68–67). Marsh and Sugihara surged ahead of the rest at the same hole in the final round. Graham holed a long eagle putt at the par-five 14th to go 13 under par and Teruo followed with a birdie there to match that score. Both then parred in, missing makeable birdie putts on the final green.

The playoff lasted just one hole as Sugihara came up short of the green with his five-iron tee shot on the 168-yard 15th hole. Teruo's chip was six feet long and he missed the putt after Marsh had holed out his routine par. A note about the international integrity of the game: Yasuda disqualified himself when he learned that he may have played a shot from out of bounds during the second round.

Tohoku Classic — Y30,000,000
Winner: Shinsaku Maeda

Graham Marsh made a strong run at a second consecutive circuit victory when the tour moved north for the Tohoku Classic at Nishi Sendai Country Club in Miyagi Prefecture, but he ran into a hot round and out of time. The hot round came off the clubs of Shinsaku Maeda, who nailed the victory, his first in six years, with a 66 on the final day. It was only the third round played in the tournament, though, as heavy rains wiped out the first day and forced shortening of the event to 54 holes — to Maeda's obvious benefit. The 66 brought Maeda from three strokes off the pace to a two-shot victory at 208, eight under par for the 6,993-yard course. Marsh was one of four players in a second-place tie at 210.

After the opening-day washout, Takashi Murakami, the long-time Tour standout, and young Saburo Fujiki took the initial lead Friday with 69s over the soggy course. Following a rare 18-hole cut that fell at 76, Marsh established his bid for two in a row with 67 for 139, joining Toshiyuki Tsuchiyama and Norio Suzuki at that score. At that point, Maeda was at 142 after rounds of 72 and 70. But, he didn't trail for long Sunday. He clicked off six birdies on the front nine for an outgoing 30 that put him a shot ahead of Marsh. He birdied twice more but took two bogeys on the back nine, posted the 208 and awaited word from the course. Marsh's bid ended when he bogeyed the par-three 16th and his birdie at the 17th merely put him into the four-man deadlock with Fujiki, Tsuchiyama and Tsuneyuki Nakajima, once again in strong contention. Marsh might have known he was in trouble in the Tohoku. It is one of the few tournaments on the Japanese circuit that has never been won by a foreigner.

Sapporo Tokyu Open — Y30,000,000
Winner: Yasuhiro Funatogawa

The season's first real runaway victory was authored by an unlikely member of the Japanese Tour — Yasuhiro Funatogawa, who had only one previous win on his seven-year career. Bolstered by the advice of Isao Aoki, 'my golf teacher' to play at his own pace in the pressure of the final round, the 27-year-old pro nursed his five-stroke margin after 54 holes to a seven-shot triumph in the Sapporo Tokyu Open at Hokkaido's Sapporo International Country Club in Northern Japan in early June. Funatogawa built the five-shot lead with rounds of 68–69–67 for 204 and needed just a par 72 for a seven-stroke margin at 12-under-par 276 and a companion title for his 1980 triumph in the Nihon Kokudo Keikaku Summers.

Yasuhiro was in the picture from the start. He trailed first-round leader Toru Nakamura (67) by just a stroke and at the midway point was tied for first with Tsuneyuki Nakajima at 137, shooting a 69 while the year's leading player had a

67. It was Funatogawa's turn for 67 Saturday and, when Nakajima took a par 72, Yasahiro had his five-shot lead. The win was even easier than the scores indicate because Funatogawa bogeyed the last two holes for the 72. None of the stars in the field could mount a challenge, the strongest threat coming from 36-year-old amateur Kazuhiko Kato, who picked off second place with a closing 69, the day's lowest score. Naomichi Ozaki took third and Nakajima dropped into a five-way tie for fourth when he slumped to 77 Sunday, tied at 286 with Aoki, Nakamura, Koichi Uehara and Taiwanese veteran Hsieh Yung Yo.

Yomiuri Open — Y30,000,000
Winner: Terry Gale

Terry Gale joined the company of some highly-distinguished countrymen when he won the Yomiuri Open in Osaka in mid-June, a victor in Japan as had been Graham Marsh, Peter Thomson, David Graham, Greg Norman and Billy Dunk, among others, before him. It came, too, in the midst of the 36-year-old Western Australian's finest season, one in which Gale also had a victory in Australia and two in New Zealand on the Australasian Tour.

Gale's triumphant performance varied greatly from that of Yasuhiro Funatogawa in the previous Japanese tournament. He surged from a four-shot deficit after 54 holes to score a three-stroke victory with a 68 on the par-73 Yomiuri Country Club course, where the first two rounds of the season-ending Japan Series is played. His start certainly was inconspicuous. He shot 70 and was confused in at least one account with American Terry Diehl. Nobumitsu Yuhara's second-round 65 shot him past Akio Toyoda and amateur Isamu Kanamoto, the first-day leaders at 68, and into a four-stroke advantage at 134. Another 70 left Gale six shots off the pace and he was still four back despite a 68 Saturday as the 24-year-old Yuhara added a 70 for 204 and Tsuneyuki Nakajima contended once again with a course-record 64 and 207.

Alone at 208, Gale became the third member of the final threesome for Sunday's finale. The Aussie made up ground on the faltering Yuhara with four birdies and a bogey on the front nine, had the lead momentarily with a birdie at the par-five 16th and went to the final tee tied for first after his young opponent birdied the 17th. However, Yuhara's bid died when he sliced his tee shot with a metal driver out of bounds. Gale birdied the final hole for his 68 and three-shot win over Nakajima and Yuhara, as well as Masahiro Kuramoto and Namio Takasu, who closed with a 66. Kuramoto shot 70, Nakajima 72 and Yuhara 75 Sunday.

Mizuno — Y21,000,000
Winner: Teruo Sugihara

The start of Teruo Sugihara's startling run of 1982 victories followed a pattern that preceded the win of Graham Marsh a month earlier in Japan. Marsh had scored in a playoff after losing in an earlier one. So did Sugihara in the Mizuno, in which 179 pros started on the two courses of Tokinodai Country Club in

Western Japan. Loser to Marsh in that late May playoff in the Mitsubishi Galant, the 45-year-old Sugihara bounced back when he went two holes into overtime against lefthander Yutaka Hagawa, the reigning Japan Open champion, sinking a two-foot birdie putt for his 40th career victory and first in more than a year.

With a round played the first two days on each course, the Bijodai at par 72 and Nosudai at par 71, a true leader wasn't established until Friday night. Actually, three leaders — Sugihara (70–68), Hagawa (69–69) and Toru Nakamura (70–68). Southpaw Hagawa, one of Japan's outstanding young college-trained pros, jumped three shots in front Saturday with a six-birdie, two-bogey 68. Sugihara was second with 71—209, two strokes in front of four others. Nobody broke 70 Sunday, fortunately for Sugihara and Hagawa, who had their problems as they fumbled into the dead-lock after 72 holes. Hagawa struggled to 76 for his 282, five under par, and Teruo caught him with a 73.

The Japanese Tour traditionally switches to several weeks of shorter tournaments, two or three at a time, in late June and July. In 1982, one 54-hole event, six 36-hole tournaments and another that was scheduled for 36 were run off in three weeks, producing a variety of winners, including the season's two most frequent ones — Tsuneyuki Nakajima and Teruo Sugihara.

Nakajima, who had been in position to win time and again after his triumphs in the Dunlop International in April (the Asia Circuit finale in Japan) and the Fuji-Sankei in May, finally nailed his third 1982 title in early July in the Nagano Open. Tsuneyuki came from two shots off the first-round pace with a five-under-par 67 at the Suwako Country Club course in Nagano Prefecture to post a 137 and a one-shot victory over Yoshiharu Takai. Sugihara's victory was a bit tainted, since it came on just an 18-hole effort. Still, Teruo put together an excellent 68 in the first round of the Descente Osaka Open at the par-72 Ibaraki Kogen Country Club course, running off five birdies against a single bogey for a two-stroke lead. Then, when heavy rains swamped the course the next day and a postponement was not in order, Sugihara was declared the winner — No. 41.

Akio Toyoda prevailed over a strong field in the Y15,000,000 Kanagawa Open in the first week of the multiple tournaments. His 72–68—140 gave him his third tournament victory in 16 pro seasons. Toyoda, 41, won by two over the likes of Isao Aoki, Sugihara and Namio Takasu, the first-round leader who was still in front until driving out of bounds at the 15th hole of the final round.

Shigeru Uchida scored his second 36-hole-tournament victory among three events the following week. The veteran of a quarter-century of competitive golf in Japan came from behind in the Toyama Open with a second-round 67 that caught Masaru Amano at 136 and Uchida won the subsequent sudden-death playoff. Both of the other events that week also were decided in overtime. Hisashi Kaji, scoring his first win in eight years of trying, beat Shiro Kubo (72–66) and Yuji Takagi (69–69) with a three-foot par putt on the first extra hole in the Wakayama Open after shooting a pair of 69s at Kunikihara Golf Club. Yoshitaka Yamamoto registered his 11th career win when he defeated Hsieh Min Nan at the fourth hole of a sudden-death playoff in the Niigata Open. Yamamoto overtook Hsieh in regulation with rounds of 69–69 against

68–70, then took the title when he dropped a three-foot par putt on that fourth extra hole.

Fujio Kobayashi picked up his only 1982 title in the 54-hole Gunma Open at the Ikaho International Country Club, rolling to an easy four-stroke victory. He matched 68s the first two days and coasted with a 75 in the third round for 211 and the four-shot edge over Hiroshi Ishii. At the same time, Kazuo Kanayama ended a seven-year drought with a one-shot win in the Hyogo Open. He shot 65–71—136 as his strongest competitor, Hisashi Morioka, posted 65–72—137.

Japan PGA Championship — Y32,000,000
Winner: Masahiro Kuramoto

Perhaps it took new challenges to re-ignite Masahiro Kuramoto, the dazzling 1981 rookie who had been less than sparkling during the early months of the 1982 season. His best effort had put him in a four-way tie for second place three strokes off Terry Gale's winning pace in the Yomiuri Open in June. Then, he went to Scotland for his first British Open and tied for fourth amid that classy field at Royal Troon. Back in Japan, Kuramoto teed off in his first Japan PGA Championship, was the dominant figure throughout the week at Meishin Yokaichi Country Club with four rounds in the 60s and scored a four-stroke victory. It duplicated the feat of Tsuneyuki Nakajima, who landed the prestigious PGA title in his sophomore season five years earlier.

The strong and sprightly Kuramoto, who had two valuable years of college in America before turning pro, started toward his initial 1982 win with a five-under-par 67, just a shot off the pace of Fujio Kobayashi, moved into a tie for first at 136 with little-known Yoshimi Niizeki the second day following a 67 and went in front to stay with another 69 for 205. He had 18 birdies during the first 54 holes, at which point he led veteran Haruo Yasuda by two strokes and Hsieh Min Nan and Yutaka Hagawa by four.

The weather turned sour Sunday, but, with one exception, Kuramoto seemed to thrive in the steady downpour. He picked up seven more birdies, faltering only when he drove out of bounds and double-bogeyed the par-four 13th. Even then, he had three strokes on Hsieh and he matched birdies with the Taiwanese star on the next two holes, chipped in for a third straight birdie at the 16th and coasted home with 69 for his 14-under-par 274. Hsieh also shot 69 for 278, taking second place by three strokes over Kobayashi, Saburo Fujiki, Toru Nakamura and Nakajima. Yasuda, who has never won the PGA in his long career, tumbled to 76 in the wet weather Sunday, finishing at 283 with Teruo Sugihara, a stroke behind Isao Aoki.

Kanto PGA Championship — Y20,000,000
Winner: Motomasa Aoki

The name Aoki went into the record books of the Japanese Tour once again at the conclusion of the Kanto PGA Championship, but the familiarity ended there. The victory belonged, not to Isao, but to his taller, younger and less experienced unrelated namesake — 32-year-old Motomasa, who, at 6.2, is the tallest Japanese regular on the circuit. It was his first win in six years of pro campaigning; in fact, until 1982 he never even came close to making expenses on the Tour. It also was a case of the pupil beating the teacher. Kikuo Arai, who had worked with Aoki in getting his game on track, was one of two veterans who unsuccessfully challenged Motomasa in the rain in Sunday's final round.

Aoki had taken the lead Saturday, when he shot a five-under-par 67 at the Kanuma Koryo Country Club to move three strokes ahead of Arai with 202 to Kikuo's 205. Equally important to that move had been Aoki's second-round 65, which matched that of Hsieh Min Nan, who took the lead then at 134 after Michiyuki Kawanami topped the first-day standings with 67. Aoki never lost the lead Sunday, but Arai and Kenji Mori had their chances. Mori, who had started the day five shots back, came up with a 69 in the wet weather, finishing ahead of the leader with a bogey on the last hole. Aoki bogeyed the 17th, leading Arai and Mori then by two strokes, and made a steady par for a 72—274 to hold that margin over Mori. Arai bogeyed the 18th to slip to third place at 277. So, Motomasa Aoki was the 1982 Kanto PGA champion, a title Isao Aoki had previously won five times.

Kansai PGA Championship — Y13,000,000
Winner: Hideto Shigenobu

The news of the first round of the Kansai PGA Championship, played at the same time as the Kanto PGA, focused on the disaster of Masahiro Kuramoto, the new young Japanese star who had arrived at the Ogori Country Club with the national PGA Championship in hand and promptly shot an 80. Far less attention was paid to the tournament leader that day. After all, Hideto Shigenobu, whose 68 was the day's best by two strokes, had won only once since turning pro in 1979 and that was in a small, unofficial event. However, Shigenobu forced the attention the rest of the week as he raced to a four-stroke, wire-to-wire victory, the first of the season in Japan. He held his two-stroke lead after his second-round 70 for 138 and doubled it with his third-round 68 for 206. Tadami Ueno was in second place through the two middle rounds and was the only player with any real chance entering Sunday's concluding action. Four players, including Teruo Sugihara, were next in line a distant eight strokes off the pace.

As it turned out, the skillful veteran Sugihara fashioned a 67 Sunday, but it merely gave him the runnerup spot as Shigenobu eased home with a one-under-par 71 for 277 and the four-shot triumph. Kuramoto's week deserves notice, as he showed one of the most important traits of a championship golfer. Instead of withdrawing after the 80 or going through the motions Friday to miss the cut, Masahiro went full blast through the remaining three rounds, shot 66–70–70 and tied for fourth place with 286.

Descente Cup Hokkoku Open — Y30,000,000
Winner: Kikuo Arai

One of the peaks in Kikuo Arai's excellent season in Japan came in early August when he became the second double winner of full-length tournaments at that point of the Japanese year, scoring a come-from-behind victory in the Descente Cup Hokkoku Open at Katayamazu Golf Club, then followed with a mid-week win in the 36-hole Saitama Open. He picked up Y8,000,000 for those efforts and trailed only Tsuneyuki Nakajima on Japan's money list at the time. As it turned out, Nakajima started out as the man to beat at Katayamazu. He jumped in front with a near-flawless 66 Thursday, reeling off an eagle and four birdies, but led Norio Suzuki by just a stroke. Arai moved into position Friday, his 71–67—138 leaving him only a stroke behind Nakajima, who had a double-bogey en route to 71 for 137.

Haruo Yasuda supplanted Nakajima at the top Saturday when he mustered seven birdies and shot 66 for 205. Nakajima's 69 put him at 206, Tateo (Jet) Ozaki had 69 for 208 and Arai lost ground with 71 for 209. The veteran Yasuda didn't have it Sunday, eventually shooting 79. That left the door open for the other contenders and Arai jumped at the opportunity. He posted an eagle and two birdies on the front nine to take the lead, then made two more birdies with a bogey coming home for 67—276 and a two-shot victory over Nakajima, who closed with a par 72.

The 39-year-old Arai also came from off the lead to win the Saitama, a Y10,000 tournament at Kasumigaseki Country Club played the next Wednesday and Thursday. He trailed Mitsuo Watanabe and Hideo Kishiro by three with his par 72 opening round, then landed his third 1982 title and 10th of his 16-year pro career with a 67 for 139. The round, a combination of seven birdies and a double-bogey, gave him a three-shot win over Yutaka Hagawa, Takashi Kurihara and Watanabe.

East-West Match Play Championship — Y18,000,000
Winners: Team — West (Kansai); Individual — Tsuneyuki Nakajima

Tsuneyuki Nakajima's consistently-challenging play continued in the East-West (Kanto-Kansai) Match Play Championship, but it wasn't enough to prevent the 12-man Kansai group from winning its fourth straight team title in the 33rd renewal of the event. The West has now won 10 of the last 17 tournaments after the East won the first 15. They tied in 1965.

The 1982 victory was a narrow one for the Kansai players — 26 points to 22. The Western pros mustered one more victory each of the two days to garner the margin, getting two wins from Toru Nakamura and Akio Kanamoto. Nakajima, with scores of 65 and 62 in the stroke-scoring matches, was a double-winner for the Kanto team, as were Kikuo Arai, completing a hot two-week period, and Motomasa Aoki. Nakajima's 17-under-par 127, a record for the first-36-hole efforts in Japan, gave him a six-stroke victory in the individual competition over Suzuki, who had 65–68—133. It was his fourth overall title of 1982. Arai shot 66–69 in his two matches for 135 and third place. The venue was Asahigaoka Country Club in Tochigi Prefecture, a relatively-short course of 6,639 yards.

Nihon Kokudo Keikaku Summers — Y30,000,000
Winner: Teruo Sugihara

After one victory via a playoff and a second in a rain-shortened tournament, Teruo Sugihara went the normal route in annexing his third title of 1982 in the Nihon Kokudo Keikaku Summers tournament. He won in regulation time — and going away. The final round, in which he widened a three-stroke lead to a final five-shot margin, was a testimony to the skills of the 45-year-old pro, who at 5.4 and 122 pounds, would be expected to be at a definite disadvantage in the windy weather that greeted the field Sunday. Instead, he outplayed his two closest pursuers, primarily because of his talent with his extra-long fairway woods, and scored the five-shot win with a closing 71 for 275, 13 under par.

Sugihara started the tournament strongly and never slowed down. His opening 65 over the 7,035 yards of Budo Country Club in Ishihara put him just a stroke behind leader Isao Isozaki and he drew even with Isozaki and Norio Suzuki Friday at 134 with his 69. A third-round 70 gave Teruo a three-stroke lead as both Isozaki and Suzuki took 73s. Sugihara had a few anxious moments Sunday when Isozaki closed within two strokes on the front nine, but Isao then bogeyed No. 10 and 11, Teruo birdied the 10th and was on easy street from there in. Suzuki had double-bogeyed the fourth hole, but birdied the last two holes to again post matching 73s with Isozaki and tie for second. Norio Mikami and Chen Tze Ming had final-round 68s to occupy the next two slots in the standings. The victory was Sugihara's 42nd of a 25-year career.

KBC Augusta — Y32,000,000
Winner: Chen Tze Ming

Other than the frequent challenges of Hsieh Min Nan, the mid-summer portion of the Japanese Tour had the homeland pros in the domineering roles. That changed in late August when the circuit reached Fukuoka Country Club for the KBC Augusta tournament. Chen Tze Ming joined a sizeable number of his Taiwanese countrymen as a winner in Japan and stood off the bid of Hal Sutton, the 24-year-old winner of the 1980 U.S. Amateur Championship to do so. The one-stroke victory was achieved over 54 holes, the second time in the 1982 season that weather had wiped out a round. Ironically, one of Chen's four victories during his four seasons on the Asia Circuit came when rain washed out a round of the 1980 Korea Open.

The 29-year-old Chen shared the first-round lead at 68 with Yurio Akitomi, Keichi Kobayashi and Minoru Kawakami before the tournament got unlucky with the arrival Friday of a typhoon weathermen had numbered 13. When play resumed Saturday, Chen took a two-stroke lead over Sutton, Akitomi, Kawakami and Shigeru Uchida with his 71 for 139, making four birdies and two bogeys on the windy day. The wind had subsided Sunday and a duel between the Taiwanese and the American developed. Sutton birdied the 13th hole to catch Chen, dropped a stroke behind when Chen birdied the 15th hole and reforged the deadlock when he sank a 20-foot par putt at the 17th after a bad chip and Chen missed his from just three feet. However, the Taiwanese pro dropped a six-footer for a birdie and 70—209 at the final hole for the win after

Sutton had missed from nine feet. It was a fine showing for Sutton in his first trip to Japan and signaled his forthcoming first victory on the U.S. Tour two months later in Florida.

Kanto Open — Y20,000,000
Winner: Masashi Ozaki

There's nothing like playing in a tournament in which one has a winning history to shake oneself out of a slump. That's what happened to Masashi (Jumbo) Ozaki when he went to Fujioyama Golf Club in Shizuoka Prefecture to compete in the Kanto Open, a tournament in which he had scored three of his 40 victories — in 1972, 1976 and 1977. His fourth Kanto Open title, one he captured by a stroke over lefty Yutaka Hagawa, ended the longest winless period of his outstanding career. Ozaki had not won since capturing the season-ending Japan Series in early December of 1980.

In high winds most of the weekend, high scores were the rule. Ozaki's winning two-over-par score — 73–72–73–72—290 — was the highest among the more important events of the season. The 69 Hagawa shot the last day in his bid to catch Ozaki was one of three 69s posted all week and none was lower. Par 72s recorded by Hideyo Sugimoto and Shoji Kikuchi, the 1980 Japan Open champion, were the best scores on opening day, Ozaki placing among 11 men who shot 73. Kikuchi edged a stroke ahead of Sugimoto Friday, adding 70 to his first round for 142 as Sugimoto had a 71 for 143. Ozaki's 72 that day left him three off the pace but in a tie for fifth place. The wind took a heavy toll Saturday. Ozaki had three birdies, two bogeys and a double-bogey for 73, yet took a share of the lead with Fujio Kobayashi at 218, Kobayashi shooting 74 with three birdies and five bogeys. Kikuchi and Sugimoto took 77s. The powerful Jumbo played steadily in the wind Sunday, running off 16 pars, a birdie and a bogey. He avoided a playoff with Hagawa when he dug his third shot out of the rough at the par-five 18th and two-putted for the victory. Kobayashi and Isao Isozaki tied for third three behind Hagawa.

Kansai Open — Y15,000,000
Winner: Teruo Sugihara

Circumstances were quite similar that same week when the Kansai Open was played in the western part of the country — with one major exception. Teruo Sugihara was having no problems with anything even resembling a slump. But, in the Kansai Open at Rokko International Golf Club at Kobe, he was competing in a tournament that he had won seven previous times, starting in 1964 and 1965. Like Ozaki, he found that to his liking and rolled to another victory in the event. His win came much more easily than Ozaki's, Sugihara taking the lead in the second round and winding up a four-stroke victor on rounds of 72–68–75–70 for 285

Hiromi Watanabe, a former bank clerk, was the first-round leader with his two-under-par 70 before Sugihara took over Friday with his 72–68—140. That round, the day's best, jumped him four strokes ahead of Toru Nakamura, who had rounds of 75 and 69. Watanabe, with 75, slipped to 145 and into a three-way tie at that score. Sugihara had six birdies Friday, but, when the winds came up strong Saturday, he managed only one and took four bogeys on the back nine. Still, he held onto first place despite the 75 as Nakamura took a 73 and nobody else stirred a threat. It was easy Sunday. Sugihara carded three birdies and a bogey for his 70 and widened the gap to four again as Nakamura closed with a par 72. Again, no other player got anything going. In fact, just as was the case across the country in the Kanto Open, only three scores in the 60s were posted — the winner's 68 and Nakamura's 69 in the second round and one other 69 Sunday.

The Kansai and Kanto Opens headed the busiest week of the Japanese season — or any tour season, for that matter. Four other 72-hole tournaments with smaller purses were played that week and, remarkably, all four of them followed much the same pattern that existed in the Kansai and Kanto. Former winners prevailed in all of them, in two cases succeeding as defending champions. It went this way:

CHUBU OPEN — Shigeru Uchida led from the second round on, shooting scores of 69–68–75–70 for 282 and a six-stroke victory over Masahiko Yamamoto and Teruo Suzumura. The veteran Uchida, who had won the 36-hole Kagawa and Toyama Opens earlier in the season, had captured the Chubu Open in 1971 and 1981.

CHUGOKU OPEN — Masahiro Kuramoto, who got his career off to a winning start in that tournament while still an amateur and launched his great freshman pro season of six victories there in 1981, made it three in a row in the Chugoku Open. Kuramoto, nailing his second 1982 title to go with his Japan PGA Championship, also won handily. With rounds of 67–70–73–68—278, he finished four strokes ahead of Norio Mikami.

KYUSHU OPEN — This tournament 'belongs' to two men — Norio Suzuki and Yurio Akitomi. Starting in 1974, Suzuki won it five years in a row. Then in 1979, Akitomi took over for three seasons befor Suzuki captured his sixth Kyushu title. Norio's 71–72–77–71—291 was the highest 72-hole winning score of the year in Japan. Suzuki won by two over Kaneya Yoshimura with amateur Kiyotaka Oke next at 296. A third-round 79 headed Akitomi toward a 13th-place finish this time.

HOKKAIDO OPEN — Koichi Uehara won the Hokkaido Open for the fifth time in seven years, in 1982 by five strokes over Katsunari Takahashi. Only Soichi Sato in 1979 and Mitsuyushi Goto in 1981 have interrupted Uehara's dominance of the tournament. His fifth victory came on rounds of 71–72–76–70 for 289. Not a player broke 70 during the tournament.

Suntory Open — Y50,000,000
Winner: Pete Izumigawa

Wet weather and typhoons continued to plague the Japanese Tour as it moved through the month of September and this time Pete Izumigawa was the beneficiary. The approaching Typhoon No. 18 dumped rain on the second and third rounds of the Suntory Open at Narashino Country Club in Chiba Prefecture and the deluge finally got so heavy that Sunday's final round had to be cancelled and Izumigawa, who had led after the second and third rounds, was declared the winner. It was an impressive victory for the long-hitting, 26-year-old pro, nonetheless, since the strong domestic field had been strengthened with the presence of Bill Rogers (the defending champion), Tom Kite and Scott Simpson from America.

In the lull before the storm Thursday, Narashino yielded good scores. Norio Suzuki took the lead with a 65, Rogers shot 66 and Izumigawa was at 67 with Kikuo Arai and Yoshimi Niizeki. Suzuki, a late starter, didn't finish Friday because of the first of the rain and a lightning delay, but Izumigawa had taken over the lead hours earlier. Pete, whose only previous win on the circuit had been in the 1981 Kanagawa Open, shot 68 Friday and at 135 had a one-stroke lead over Tadami Ueno, as Suzuki was on his way to 73, the same score posted by Rogers. The two-time winner bounced back in the wet and windy weather Saturday with a 70 for 209, moving within two strokes of Izumigawa, who had 72 for 207. Also challenging at that point were Suzuki, Masahiro Kuramoto and Tateo Ozaki at 210, but they had no chance to do anything about it when the round was cancelled Sunday.

ANA Sapporo Open — Y40,000,000
Winner: Norio Suzuki

Even a poor starting round had little effect on the hot streak of Norio Suzuki when the circuit moved north for the All-Nipon Airway Sapporo Open on the Watsu course of Sapporo Golf Club at Hokkaido. The veteran Suzuki, who had scored his 18th career victory two weeks earlier in the Kyushu Open and was in strong contention in the rain-shortened Suntory Open the previous week, was back in 46th position when he opened with 74 at Sapporo. Then, he vaulted all the way into the lead with a course-record 63 Friday and rode that impetus to his second 1982 triumph. Norio had closing rounds of 69 and 72 for 278 and a one-stroke victory over fast-closing Isao Aoki, making his presence seriously felt in Japan for the first time in months. Aoki had weekend rounds of 67 and 69 and jumped into second place, his nine-under-par score of 279 giving him a one-shot edge in turn over Jumbo Ozaki, Tsuneyuki Nakajima, Akira Yabe and the luckless Yutaka Hagawa.

A collegiate amateur grabbed the first-round lead for the second time in the season when Satoshi Azuma, of Nihon University, opened with 68, leading four pros by a stroke. Suzuki even had a bogey in his 63 round Friday as the eagle, eight-birdie effort not only gave him first place but a three-stroke margin over Hagawa, Nakajima, Hsieh Yung Yo and Toshiaki Sekimizu. Norio had another eagle Saturday, but when he could do no better than 69, he lost most of his lead as Hagawa shot 67 and Yabe came into the picture with 65. Suzuki had problems Sunday, going out in 37, but his incoming 35 for 72 was just enough to outlast Aoki, who had six birdies but cancelled out half of them with bogeys. What of amateur Azuma? He wound up in a tie for 55th place with erratic rounds following his first-day glory of 78, 70 and 82.

Hiroshima Open — Y30,000,000
Winner: Takashi Kurihara

Time and again during the earlier months of the season, Yutaka Hagawa had fallen short in his bid for victories to uphold his credentials as the reigning Japan Open champion. It happened again in the Hiroshima Open at the Hiroshima Country Club when Hagawa had no defense against a man with a blazing putter in the final round. Takashi Kurihara, a 34-year-old who had won just three times in his previous 13 years on the Japanese Tour, obliterated Hagawa's three-stroke lead after 54 holes with a 29-putt 66 Sunday that stroke victory in the six-year-old tournament. His cards were 69–70–70–66 for under-par 272. Hagawa abetted Takashi's strong finish with a feeble 73 Sunday.

The lead changed hands each day during the tournament, which now has had seven straight Japanese winners. Taiwan's Lu Hsi Chuen, who had a disappointing overall season in 1982, opened the Hiroshima Open in a three-way tie for the lead at 67 with Masaji Kusakabe and Toshiharu Kawada. Then, they all gave way to Fujio Kobayashi in the second round, Kobayashi shooting 69–65—134 to take a two-shot lead over Kurihara. Hagawa had begun his move that day with his first of two 66s. The second on Saturday — a flawless five-birdie effort — vaulted Yutaka into the three-shot advantage over Kobayashi and Kurihara, although the biggest stir of the day was created by Hsieh Min Nan, who scored a Y1,000,000 hole-in-one. In Sunday's final round, Kurihara took command with an outgoing 32 and held it on the incoming nine with eight pars and a birdie.

Gene Sarazen Jun Classic — Y50,000,000
Winner: Teruo Sugihara

The Gene Sarazen Jun Classic, first of the big-money events on the fall segment of the Japanese Tour, attracted the initial influx of foreign players, but they proved no threat to the remarkable Teruo Sugihara, who ran his record to 45 victories with a sensational finish belieing his 45 years. Sugihara, scoring the fifth victory of his incredible season, fired a six-under-par 66 in Sunday's final round at the Jun Classic Country Club in Tochigi Prefecture to post a three-stroke victory in the six-year-old tournament. His cards were 69–70–70–66 for 275, 13 under par for the distance.

Australia's Terry Gale, who had won the Yomiuri Open earlier in the year, returned to Japan and promptly tied the Jun Classic course record in the first round. His 65 gave him a one-stroke lead over Koichi Uehara and at least four over everybody else, Sugihara included. However, Gale managed only a par 72 Friday and was overtaken in first place at 137 by Norio Suzuki, who had rounds of 69–68. At that point, Sugihara was just two shots behind. Suzuki opened a four-stroke gap Saturday, making seven birdies en route to a 67 for his 204, 12 under par, that left Sugihara five shots in the lurch after his 70. Toru Nakamura was then second at 208, as Gale slipped back to 211 after a 74.

Nobody was a match for Sugihara Sunday. Teruo opened with birdies on the first four holes to take the lead and ran off another string with three birdies on the back nine starting at the 10th hole. He took his only bogey at the last hole, merely reducing his margin over runnerup Suzuki. Obscured by Sugihara's great round and victory was the finish of Tateo (Jet) Ozaki, just back from America. Ozaki finished third, primarily on the strength of a stretch in the round in which he made five birdies and an eagle in six holes shooting 67.

Tokai Classic — Y40,000,000
Winner: Hsieh Min Nan

The third star of the 1982 season in Japan moved center stage in the Tokai Classic after hovering impatiently in the wings through much of the earlier year. Hsieh Min Nan, the 42-year-old Taiwanese veteran, began his run of victories in resounding fashion with a five-stroke victory at Miyoshi Country Club in Nagoya. He never trailed after tying the course record with his opening-round 64, although he gave the field a chance through the middle rounds before salting the title away Sunday.

Hsieh ran off eight birdies in an error-free round Thursday, taking a two-stroke lead over Kosaku Shimada, who had a front-nine 30 as part of his 66. The Chinese pro widened the margin to three Friday, though shooting just a one-under-par 71. Tsuneyuki Nakajima and Masaji Kusakabe were at 138 after rounds of 71 and 69, respectively. Compatriot Chen Tze Ming caught Hsieh Saturday, firing a 68 while his older countryman had posted a par round. Nakajima closed to within a stroke with his 70, joined at 208 by Hideto Shigenobu. Hsieh went one way and the rest of the contenders went the other Sunday. He made three birdies on the front nine to break it open and coasted to a 67 and the winning 274, his sixth in Japan and 25th of his career. The failures of the others opened the door for America's Larry Nelson, who won the Tokai in 1980. Nelson also shot 67 Sunday and jumped up into second place.

Golf Digest — Y30,000,000
Winner: Hsieh Min Nan

Even though his start in the Golf Digest tournament was a carbon copy of his opening round the week before, Hsieh Min Nan reached his second win in a row through a much different route. In reality, he staggered to a one-stroke victory at Tomei Country Club in Shizuoka Prefecture with a final-round 75 that almost wiped out a domineering margin off the lowest 54-hole score of the season. When he finally got in with his 274 and one-shot win over Akira Yabe, Hsieh's gallery of friends and neighbors from the area breathed easier.

The second consecutive 64 in an opening round — eight birdies, no bogeys just as in the Tokai the previous week — merely put Hsieh in a first-place tie with Seiichi Kanai and a shot ahead of Teruo Suzumura. He took a one-stroke lead over Kanai and two over Suzumura Friday when he shot 70 and Kanai and Suzumura had 71s. The runaway loomed Saturday when Hsieh, who didn't have a bogey during the first three rounds, ran off seven birdies for a 65. The 199 shot him eight strokes in front, American Bruce Lietzke and Kikuo Arai moving into a second place with 67s. The bogeys emerged to plague Hsieh

Sunday. He had five of them while shooting the 75 and barely hung on. Yabe came from far back with a 66 in his unsuccessful bid to catch the Taiwanese pro. Lietzke, with 69, finished third, another stroke back at 276.

Bridgestone — Y50,000,000
Winner: Hsieh Min Nan

Even more remarkable than Hsieh Min Nan's achievement of winning three straight tournaments on the Japanese Tour was his opening round in the Bridgestone. While many fine pros go entire careers without shooting 64, Hsieh opened the Bridgestone with 64, just as he did the two previous weeks. Even though he never trailed over the 12 rounds, Hsieh found it kept getting tougher for him. He had to go extra holes against Kikuo Arai before putting away that third victory at Sodegaura Country Club in Chiba Prefecture. The competition also was becoming deeper as more leading American pros played and two of them — Lee Trevino and Tom Weiskopf — were factors in the finish.

The opening 64 over Sodegaura's 7,151 yards put Hsieh four strokes on top of the field Thursday and set a new course record in the process. Weiskopf, Saburo Fujiki and Norio Mikami were at 68, with five others, including Hale Irwin, at 69. Hsieh had an eagle, seven birdies and a bogey in the record round. His second-round 70 added another stroke to his margin as Weiskopf shot 71 and was alone in second place at 139. Hsieh's edge remained five Saturday, his 71—205 giving him that margin over Weiskopf, Arai, Fujiki and Tadami Ueno. It turned into a two-man fight Sunday, though, as Arai closed in on the back nine. Hsieh's three-shot lead dissolved on the last five holes as he bogeyed the 14th and 17th and Arai birdied the 15th. He missed a birdie chance from 12 feet for the win, halved the first playoff hole, then three-putted the next one to lose to Hsieh's routine par. Weiskopf and Trevino tied with Seiichi Kanai and Motomasa Aoki for third place, three back at 282. The win, which gave Hsieh winnings of Y23,000,000 (more than $90,000) for the three tournaments, came 10 years after an earlier victory in the Bridgestone.

Japan Open — Y50,000,000
Winner: Akira Yabe

Akira Yabe, who had been trying to put it all together all season, picked an excellent time to do so. Two weeks after falling just a stroke short of breaking Hsieh Min Nan's three-tournament winning streak in half, the slender Yabe blended four solid rounds into victory in the Japan Open Championship, the 36-year-old pro's first important title among the seven he had won during an 18-year career. He stepped in front with a third-round 67 and raced to a five-shot victory with his closing 69. He shot 277 over the 6,678 yards of Musashi Country Club's Toyooka course the final week of October. While the triumph ended a year of frustration for Yabe, it added another chapter to that of Yutaka Hagawa, the defending champion, who finished second for the fifth time and remained winless in 1982.

In the early jockeying for position, Hideo Ishii took the first-round lead, shooting 67 to go one shot ahead of Tsuneyuki Nakajima, Jumbo Ozaki, Hideyo Sugimoto and Toyotake Nakao. Then, they all yielded Friday to Masahiro Kuramoto, the second-year pro who was bidding to add the Open title to his PGA championship. Kuramoto started with a pair of 70s to gain a one-stroke lead after 36 holes over six players, among them Yabe, who had shot 71–70. The big news that day, though, was the departure of Hsieh Min Nan, who finally ran out of gas after his great run of low scores and victories. Hsieh shot 76–73 and missed the cut, while Japan's No. 1 player, Isao Aoki, who has never won the Open, muddled along at 145.

With six birdies and two bogeys, Yabe grabbed the third-round lead by a stroke over Isuo Shirahama, who also had a 67 for his 209. Still close, too, were Chen Tze Ming at 210 and Nakajima and Ozaki at 211. But, Yabe was not to be denied. He shot a solid outgoing par 35, birdied the 10th and 11th holes and rolled home with the five-shot victory Sunday.

Goldwin Cup (U.S. vs Japan) — US$440,000
Winners: Team — United States
     Individual — Bob Gilder, Calvin Peete

Under the old format for the annual confrontation between the professionals of the U.S. and Japan, the outcome was unpredictable. Japan won six times, the U.S. four and once a deadlock occurred. Japan always fielded its best available players, while the American team, though always potent, did not usually include a full group of the leading players of the time, since the team was assembled by invitation. It was a different matter in 1982. In forming the replacing Goldwin Cup Matches, the PGA Tour selected its eight-man team straight off the top of its current money list and that group of Americans that competed at Sobu Country Club near Tokyo was just too much for the Japanese. Bob Gilder and Calvin Peete led the U.S. to a 33-to-15 point team victory and tied for individual honors with eight-under-par 134s with their scores from the singles matches of the last two days. As Raymond Floyd, the captain and oldest member of the U.S. squad, said afterward: 'We brought our strongest team here and it would have been embarrassing if we had not won.'

The competition was close only through the first two days of better-ball doubles matches when just 16 of the 48 points were at stake, the U.S. winning four, Japan three and one ending in a tie. The rout came in the singles as the U.S. won 10, halved four and lost only single matches to Isao Aoki and Kikuo Arai, who was involved in five of Japan's 15 points. Gilder, Peete, Tom Watson and Tom Kite all swept their singles matches and had a victory apiece in doubles. Craig Stadler won both of his singles matches, Lanny Wadkins both of his doubles, Floyd had a win and a half in both singles and doubles and Jerry Pate a win and two draws in his efforts. Gilder birdied his last hole to tie Peete for the individual honors. Bob shot 65–69 and Calvin 66–68, finishing four shots ahead of Stadler (68–70). Even though he lost both singles matches, Masahiro Kuramoto led the Japanese in the individual competition, placing fourth with 68–71—139, a stroke ahead of Aoki and Watson.

Taiheiyo Club Masters— Y80,000,000
Winner: Scott Hoch

The strength of America's pro golfers was flexed the first week of November in the Goldwin Cup Matches. The depth of the U.S. talent was demonstrated by comparison the next week in the Taiheiyo Club (Pacific) Masters, when Scott Hoch, who hadn't qualified as a member of the U.S. team at Sobu, captured the title in Japan's second-richest individual tournament. Hoch, another in a long list of Tour winners out of Wake Forest, overcame a one-shot deficit in the final round to score his second 1982 victory and first abroad. He had won the New Orleans Open in April. Scott had rounds of 73–70–66–69 for 278, a 10-under-par total at the Gotemba course of the Taiheiyo Club in Shizuoka Prefecture, and won by three over Masahiro Kuramoto, who made Japan's best showing against the foreign competition for the second week in a row.

At first, it appeared that Norio Suzuki would come up with another of his prime performances in that tournament. The 31-year-old Suzuki, who had won the Pacific Masters in 1979 and 1980, jumped off in front Thursday with 67 as Japanese players held the first eight places. Suzuki remained in front Friday, shooting 71 for 138, but the picture changed drastically behind him. Wayne Levi fired 67 for 139, Chen Tze Chung 68 for 140 and Hoch began his move with 70 for 143. Danny Edwards, the 1981 winner, exited with 152. Suzuki faded from contention Saturday with 74, Levi taking over with 69 for 208 and Hoch soaring into second place with 66 for 209. Kuramoto's 69 put him at 210. Levi, in turn, came up with a poor round Sunday, leaving things open for the 26-year-old North Carolinian, who fashioned his winning 69 with four birdies and a bogey. Kuramoto had 71 for his 281 and Levi dropped into a third-place tie with Calvin Peete after his 75. Peete closed with 71. Americans have now won eight of the 11 Pacific Masters.

Dunlop Phoenix — Y90,000,000
Winner: Calvin Peete

Foreign domination of the Dunlop Phoenix tournament continued in 1982. Since it was transformed into one of the prime events on the Japanese circuit in 1974 and into the Tour's richest in recent seasons, the Dunlop Phoenix has attracted many of the best international players from the U.S. and other parts of the world. One or another of the invaders has captured the title every year since then — Americans Johnny Miller, Hubert Green, Andy Bean, Bobby Wadkins and Tom Watson, Australia's Graham Marsh and, in 1977 and 1981, Spain's Severiano Ballesteros. Calvin Peete extended the Japanese drought in a proper climax to his brilliant season, taking the lead with a third-round 67 at the resort Phoenix Country Club in southern Japan and carrying on to a three-stroke victory over Ballesteros and Larry Nelson Sunday. Peete, who had shared the individual title with Bob Gilder in the Goldwin Cup Matches and finished a solid third the week before in the Pacific Masters, posted rounds of 73–69–67–72 for his seven-under-par 281 and sixth title of his brilliant 1982 season.

Peete's American compatriots were in the forefront the first two days.

Danny Edwards, who had missed the cut in defense of his Pacific Masters title the previous week, rebounded with a 69 Thursday at Phoenix Country Club, taking a one-stroke lead over Nelson and Shinsaku Maeda in the choice field of 84 pros. Seven of them, including Tom Watson and Ballesteros, were at 71. Nelson, the 1981 PGA champion, had a rather wild 70 Friday, carding six birdies, two bogeys and a double-bogey as he took a one-stroke lead over Tom Purtzer and two over six players, Peete among them. Edwards was, too, after a 73. The cut, though only reducing the field from 84 to 60, took a heavy toll of Japan's top players, as well as Jim Simons and Vance Heafner of the U.S. Tsuneyuki Nakajima, Isao Aoki, Masahiro Kuramoto and Yutaka Hagawa all missed the 151 cutoff score. With six birdies and a bogey Saturday, the 39-year-old Peete seized first place by a five-stroke margin over Nelson, 1979 winner Wadkins and Hsieh Min Nan. Peete was at 209, seven under par, the other three at 214. The steady American pro was never in danger Sunday with his finishing round of 72. Even with 67, the day's best round, Ballesteros could only get within three of the winner and catch Nelson, who closed with a 70. Seve finished birdie-birdie-eagle.

Casio World Open — Y65,000,000
Winner: Scott Hoch

Scott Hoch completed America's November sweep of four of Japan's most important and rewarding events just when it appeared it wouldn't happen. The way he had played throughout the season, who would have thought that Tsuneyuki Nakajima, the leading money-winner in Japan, would blow a four-stroke lead in the final round of the Casio World Open, the two-year-old tournament at Ibusuki Golf Club in Kagoshima Prefecture, the last event of the season drawing international players? But, blow it he did. Nakajima soared to 76 in Sunday's final round and Hoch slipped past him by a stroke with his closing 70, two under par on the 6,966-yard course. The win for Hoch came two Sundays after he took the Pacific Masters title and four days after his 27th birthday.

After Taiwan's Chen Tze Ming, the KBC Augusta winner in August, held the first-round lead in the Casio with his 67 (followed by Fred Couples at 68 and Lu Hsi Chuen at 69), Nakajima took over, seemingly headed for his fifth win of the year in Japan. He grabbed the lead with his second-round 66 for 137, followed by Lu at 138 and Seve Ballesteros at 139 as Chen shot 74 for 141. With 72–71—143, Hoch was then in a 12th-place tie. When Nakajima followed with 70 Saturday, it gave him a four-stroke lead over Kikuo Arai, who had shot 69, and a five-shot margin over Chen and Hoch, who had 71 and 69, respectively, that day. Heavy winds made playing difficult Sunday, the 70s of Hoch, Ballesteros and Isao Aoki being the best rounds of the day. The finish had Hoch at 282, Nakajima at 283 and Ballesteros and Aoki at 284 as the young U.S. Tour became the first American ever to win twice in Japan in a single season. Scott went ahead to stay with a birdie at the 13th, Nakajima salvaging second place with a birdie at the last hole after a bogey at the 14th hole.

Japan Series — Y17,000,000
Winner: Tsuneyuki Nakajima

Tsuneyuki Nakajima made amends for his collapse in the Casio World when the Japanese Tour wrapped up its official 1982 season as usual with the Japan Series, that circuit's counterpart of America's World Series of Golf, though one that included only the domestic stars of its year of golf. Nakajima waited until the select group of 18 pros moved to Tokyo for the last two rounds of the Series before making his move and stashing his fifth victory of 1982 and 13th of his career.

As is always the format, the 17 Japanese pros and Hsieh Min Nan — winners of seven major tournaments and leading sums of money during 1982 — played the first two rounds at Osaka's Yomiuri Country Club, a 7,079-yard layout that has a 73 par. Motomasa Aoki, the Kanto PGA champion, took the first-round lead there with a bogey-less 67, then shot a bogey-laden 80 and yielded the lead and other contending positions as well. Fujio Kobayashi, who barely qualified for the Series, took over the lead with 69–71—140, leading Japan Open champion Akira Yabe by a stroke and Hsieh and Masahiro Kuramoto by two.

Nakajima, who had shot a pair of 72s in Osaka, improved measurably at Tokyo's Yomiuri, a par-72 course of 7,017 yards. He had seven birdies and a bogey Saturday for 66, jumping into a one-stroke advantage over Kobayashi and at least four over the rest of the field. For a while Sunday, it appeared Nakajima might be on the verge of repeating his last-round disaster of the previous week when winds came up again. He eventually shot 73, but few did much better in the conditions and his 283, which was seven under par, gave him a two-stroke triumph over Kobayashi. Masahiro Kuramoto and Jumbo Ozaki finished another shot back.

12.   The Australasian Tour

When Bob Shearer captured the Order of Merit of the Australasian Tour in 1981, the achievement was significant and impressive. He came from the clouds with victories in the final two events in New Zealand to do it. His second Order of Merit triumph in 1982 carried far greater prestige, however. The burly Victorian won it on the strength of fulfillment of a lifelong ambition with a decisive victory in the Australian Open championship. The success back home, particularly the determined and dedicated way Shearer went about winning the Australian Open, crowned an invigorating season in America, where his victory at Tallahassee secured his status on 1983's all-exempt U.S. Tour and his future in America. It delighted his followers in Australia, who saw in him a much quieter and more mature player with a now-solid game than the hell-raiser he was tabbed during the first 10 years of his career.

Shearer managed to avoid becoming entangled in the complex matter of appearance money on the Australasian Tour. When Greg Norman and Graham Marsh traded verbal barbs prior to the Mayne Nickless PGA, Shearer calmly went his own way. When Bruce Devlin, David Graham and Norman again were involved in appearance money controversy before the Australian Open in Sydney, Shearer locked himself away and concentrated harder than ever on his golf.

Of the younger players in Australia, Mike Clayton was Rookie of the Year, and deservedly so after his Victorian Open win, while the tremendous competitive nature of Terry Gale, an underrated golfer in Australia, was emphasized when he won the last two events in New Zealand and lifted himself to fourth place in the Order of Merit. He won once earlier in the year in Australia and took the Yomiuri Open in Japan.

Slow play once again came under intense fire from both amateur and professional organizations but the players still seemed to find the problem insurmountable. Appearance money remained a controversial question, with sponsors genuinely disturbed that their tournaments would be downgraded if they are not permitted to bring in leading overseas players, either on the course or through television, radio and newspapers. It is not clear whether they had any bearing on the decision, but the Australasian Tour suffered a severe jolt in December when Mayne Nickless, one of the major sponsors in Australia, announced it was withdrawing from golf and redirecting its sponsorship allocations for future years. Tour officials will have difficulty finding another sponsor of equal enthusiasm and financial strength.

Few gestures in recent years in Australian golf have been better received than that of Jack Nicklaus, who put the $50,000 appearance money that had been designated for him into the prize money pool of the Australian Open. It sweetened first prize pickings for Shearer, but was no match for his winning of the event, a moment of such intense pleasure that the normally unflappable Shearer was noticeably emotional.

Tooth Illawarra Open — A$25,000
Winner: Bob Shaw

Bob Shaw started the New Year in fine style by taking the Tooth Illawarra Open by a shot, even though heavy rain and a fluctuating last-round 75 almost cost him the first prize of $4,500. There was no indication the first day that Shaw was likely to challenge for the championship, with Ted Ball shooting a magnificent 66 and Stewart Ginn and Chris Tickner holding down second place with 67s. Shaw really got it going in the second round with a wonderful 64, in the course of which he putted as well for 18 holes as he ever has in his life.

Two shots in the lead in just about perfect weather, Shaw had every right to be confident about starting 1982 with a victory. He felt even better after the third round when he finished six shots ahead of Col Bishop and Vic Bennetts after firing a 67, a round bettered by a single shot by Queensland professional Vaughan Somers.

Bishop made his charge the last day, having played consistently on the second and third days with 67 and 69. Overcast and humid conditions brought a mid-morning thunderstorm and this undoubtedly upset the rhythm Shaw had shown in the early part of the tournament. He hung in grimly, however, and became almost a two-man event. Ball shot 74 to finish five strokes in arrears.

Many Australians, Peter Thomson among them, feel Shaw still has time to translate his playing talents into thoughtful performances, which will take him to the top of the Australasian Order of Merit. There is no doubting his skill, but too often he fails to capitalize on three good rounds in a tournament.

Ford Dealers' South Australian Open — A$25,000
Winner: Graham Marsh

At 38 years of age, Graham Marsh has won well in excess of 30 golf tournaments around the world, many of them on the Asian and Japanese circuits, some in Europe, plus the Sea Pines Heritage Classic in 1977 in the United States. He has never produced a victory in a major tournament on the Australasian circuit. That, to his friends and fellow-competitors, is quite astonishing and, although it was a rather 'minor' major, Marsh broke through in the South Australian Open at the Kooyonga Golf Club in Adelaide. It was as clear-cut as many of his other victories around the world, eight shots over Billy Dunk.

He had taken the lead the second day with rounds of 71 and 67, then moved smoothly into a four-stroke lead the third day. 'I'll remember this tournament for two main reasons,' he said afterwards. 'It is the first event listed as a major I have won in Australia and I've certainly never played in such heat for all four days of a tournament anywhere in the world.' The temperature was in excess of 100 degrees every day. It took a toll of the players, although they had the advantage of playing on a golf course with immaculate fairways and greens.

Marsh really won the tournament on the third day, when he started four shots behind the leader and, after Dunk had birdied the first two holes of the third round and gone to 10 under for the tournament, effected a five-stroke swing. Graham birdied the third, fourth and fifth holes, Dunk had two bogeys and a par and Marsh was two strokes ahead.

He is no stranger to the lead and increased his margin from four to eight shots over the final 18 holes. At the end, only three players had managed to break par — 288 — for the event.

Tattersalls' Tasmanian Open — A$30,000
Winner: Col Bishop

Six times a bridesmaid in five years as a tournament professional. That was Col Bishop's fate before victory was handed to him in the $30,000 Tasmanian Open in Hobart. Bishop made his charge in the third round with a splendid 68, which was one of only eight scores better than 70 posted during the event.

The second and third days provided pleasant conditions — the weather was hot with light breezes — but the first and last days tested the players with strong, blustery winds. In fact, only on the third day did Bishop appear on the short leaderboard, his first two rounds of 73 and 74 having him six shots behind the leader and potential winner, Stewart Ginn.

Ginn had won the Tasmanian championship on three previous occasions and, when he moved to a three-shot lead at the end of the third round, it seemed as though another one was in the bag. Rodger Davis had fluctuating rounds of 75, 66 (a course record) and 74, following his non-participation in the South Australian Open at Kooyonga. Davis incurred two bogeys in the record round, which was one stroke better than the previous mark held jointly by Bob Shearer and Ted Ball. When the pressure was on Ginn in the third round, he played very solid golf for his 71. Some of his competitors fell away and made things tough for themselves on the final day.

All went well for Ginn through much of the last day. Bishop was in the clubhouse with a 71 for 286 and Cahill, Newton and Davis, having shot 67, 69 and 72, respectively, were at 287. Ginn knew all he had to do was par the last two holes but he collapsed with two disastrous bogeys. At the par-four 17th his second shot drifted right and found a greenside bunker. Even though he blasted out to 10 feet, he was unable to save par. Now the pressure was really on. At 18 he hooked his tee shot into another bunker and again was faced with a 10-foot putt, this time to tie Bishop for a playoff. Sadly, he missed, but it provided a great moment for the 26-year-old Bishop.

There was joy also for Victorian professional Mike Clayton, who had only turned pro six months previously. Not that his four rounds of 76–76–75–76 were anything to produce a beaming smile . . . nor his check for $189. But, on the last hole of the tournament, Clayton hit a four-iron which landed in the center of the green, bounced and went in for a hole-in-one and $5,000.

Victorian Open — A$100,000
Winner: Mike Clayton

Skill is all-important in winning golf tournaments, but a little bit of luck comes in handy occasionally as well. Take Mike Clayton, for example. On the last hole of the preceding Tasmanian Open, he holed in one and picked up $5,000. At the Metropolitan Club in Melbourne he collected another $20,000 for a hole-in-one at the 200-yard 13th and then, buoyed by this success, raced away with the Victorian Open itself, winning by three strokes over Bob Shearer and taking another $18,000. Collecting $43,000 in one week was almost like winning a major tournament on the American circuit as far as the Australian rookie was concerned.

Clayton had set himself for the event. Metropolitan is his home course and, even though he was down to his last few dollars and playing with borrowed cash, he felt confident he would put up a good showing in front of his supporters.

The Victorian Open is a magnificent event. This year it attracted a record entry of 369 players, beating the previous figure of 339 entries for the 1981 Australian Open. Golfers came from all over the world to play in it and three pre-qualifying courses were needed to determine which men would comprise the eventual 160-player field. Lee Trevino was one of the American players. He hadn't been to Melbourne since leaving Royal Melbourne in 1974, declaring he wouldn't be back because the greens were 'the biggest joke since Watergate.'

Although Super Mex was in good form, having cancelled two weeks of U.S. Tour engagements before the tournament to prepare for the Victorian Open, he needed to break a precedent to carry off first prize. No guest celebrity had ever won the Victorian Open and some big names graced the field over the years. In 1977 Johnny Miller missed, in 1978 Arnold Palmer was a playoff loser to Guy Wolstenholme, in 1979 Rodger Davis defeated Gary Player and in 1980 and 1981 Wolstenholme and Billy Dunk accounted for players like Ben Crenshaw, Bobby Clampett and Curtis Strange.

Now, in 1982, at different ends of the age scale, 42-year-old Trevino and 15-year-old Brad Hughes competed in the championship. Hughes, who needed permission from his school to play in the tournament, shot a 77 at the Kingswood Club to snatch one of the 53 vacant spots from the 270 who tried to qualify. In the end he didn't get past the second round, but it was a brave effort from the youngster.

In the pro-am the day before the main event, Chris Tickner, the New South Wales professional, shot an astonishing 62 from near the back tees, Trevino was in form with 69 and Terry Gale, Bob Shearer and Greg Norman all turned in solid practice rounds.

All these players were keen to win, to balance the end of the 1981 Australasian tour, which had been a disaster as far as Australia's top golfers were concerned. Five consecutive wins by overseas stars the previous October and November in Australia were galling to the local professionals.

Clayton shot a splendid 67 the first day for a one-stroke lead over Lithgow professional Ken Dukes, with Shearer and Dunk the only prominent names among those within two strokes of the lead. Disappointing starts were made by Graham Marsh and Greg Norman, who had 73s; Bob Shaw 72 and Rodger Davis 74. Trevino fired a solid 70 and came in the second day with a brilliant 68 for a one-stroke lead, Clayton having fallen back to equal second with a par 72 and 139.

Clayton had his hole-in-one Saturday in the course of what might have been a disastrous 74. Those two strokes saved were to be of enormous importance in the context of the final day. At that point Shearer and Trevino were looking ominously solid, on top with 211, and Canadian Jerry Anderson, at 212, was pressing them hard.

Clayton began the day two shots behind Trevino and Shearer and in hot, humid conditions played some magnificent golf, carding only 33 strokes on the front nine. Defending champion Dunk said at the turn he thought Clayton was striking the ball like a winner. Clayton was in the third-from-last group, posted his score of 281 and left Trevino, Shearer, Anderson, Somers, Stanley and Norman to get on with it. None were able to break 70 and it was left to Garry Merrick, 68, and Graham Marsh, with a one-under-par 71, to edge their way into the top six money-winners.

It had been a marvelous week for Clayton. Three months earlier he had gone to Tweed Heads to play in the Tooth Classic with a little less than $300 in the bank. A family loan had increased that to $1,300. Now, suddenly, an extra $43,000 was in the kitty.

As an amateur, Clayton had been regarded as slightly temperamental but he played it very, very cool, even in the heat, although when he began the last day he wasn't at all convinced he could win.

'There was no way I thought I could give Trevino two strokes coming into a final round,' he said. 'Although I desperately wanted to win, I didn't think it would be possible. Once I got pumped up, though, with a six-foot putt at the eighth hole and then the 10-footer at the ninth, I reckoned I was in with a good chance. It is a great thrill to win on my home course, particularly when I hadn't really expected a tournament victory in the first year where I was intending to concentrate solely on trying to build up a good, solid swing for a professional career.'

His swing was solid enough over the last 18 holes and so was his tempera-ment. To beat players like Shearer, Trevino, Anderson, Marsh and Norman in such convincing style was undoubtedly the highlight of his young but promising career.

Australian Masters — A$100,000
Winner: Graham Marsh

Having won his 'mini' major in South Australia earlier on the circuit, Graham Marsh finally won a top-class event in his home country when he took the Australian Masters at Huntingdale by one shot from Stewart Ginn. Marsh collected the $18,000 first prize despite shooting 75 in the last round. The par 73, 7,000-yard course and its greens have a habit of boosting the scores of even the best players, who had to cope the first and third days with unpleasant, blustery winds. Conditions were so difficult that nobody broke 70 in any round except the second.

The tournament organizers had a shock before the event started when Jack Newton withdrew, but the field still was an impressive one, with overseas stars Bernhard Langer, Tony Jacklin, Arnold Palmer and four top Japanese players adding strength to the Australian entry. Bob Shearer, the Melbourne star and favorite, headed the first-round scores with a three-under-par 70, joined there by Lyndsay Stephen and Peter McWhinney. Shearer kept up the pace on the second day. Another three-under-par round kept him three strokes ahead of the pack.

The players were less than complimentary about the condition of the greens at this famous course. From the point of view of diplomacy, Shearer said he did not wish to make any comment about them, but did remark 'All I will say, though, is today I putted the best I have for 10 years — and never made one. I can't say any more than that because what I would like to say would almost certainly produce a fine from the PGA.'

More outgoing were Stephen and Greg Norman, the latter saying he had never known a tournament venue anywhere in the world to have such poor quality putting surfaces in tournaments over a two-year span. 'I've seen greens around the world that have been bad one year, but never anything like this where we've come back a second year and they are just as disappointing.'

Shearer's second-round 70 was a patient effort with 15 pars and three birdies, but the highlight of that day was Tsuneyuki Nakajima, the 28-year-old Japanese champion who shot a record-equalling round of 66. Through an interpreter, Nakajima said he had been spurred on by an autograph from Arnold Palmer he had carried in his pocket throughout the round, Palmer having been his hero throughout his professional career. It didn't help him two days later, though, when he was disqualified for incorrectly signing his card.

With the cut at 153, not many players were threatening to break par for the four rounds and Graham Marsh, with a steady 71 to go with his 71–72, led the field into the last day. Shearer blew up with a disastrous 80, starting in miserable fashion by hitting into the trees and taking a bogey at the first, another bogey at the second, and a triple-bogey six at the third, when he failed three times to get out of a bunker. To shoot 71 in the blustery conditions was a fine performance and March well deserved his three-stroke lead over Stewart Ginn, whose 70, shared with Vaughan Somers, was the finest golf of the day. So strong was the wind that spectators were looking anxiously at television towers and tents for fear they might blow away. Officially, the day was described as 'gale conditions in the afternoon.'

Marsh felt he needed to shoot 70 in the last round to prevent anybody from catching him. 'It is the first time I have led a tournament in Australia going into the last round, and I shall be very disappointed if I don't finish it off now,' he remarked. Graham just made it. Although there was no sudden charge from the players behind him, Marsh played the seventh hole in such uncharacteristic style that he threw away a three-stroke advantage. Having pushed his drive far to the right and finding it with a bush lying between him and the hole, he tried to hit a sand wedge over the bush to get back on the fairway. He didn't make it, had to take a penalty drop and finished with a double-bogey seven. Now he was back with Akira Yabe, Mike Ferguson, Stewart Ginn and Rob McNaughton. He settled down and played some of the most patient golf seen in a long time on that difficult course.

From the eighth hole to the 18th, he was one under par and the birdie he picked up at the 14th put him back in a leadership tie with Ginn. Then Stewart bogeyed 17 and, although he then parred the final hole, left Marsh needing only to make his own par to win his first major event in Australia. His drive was a good one, his second shot finished 63 feet from the flag and his approach putt was a magnificent piece of judgment, finishing only a foot past the hole.

It was bad luck for television viewers around Australia that the ABC, who were covering the event, managed to cut off the last putt for viewers other than in Melbourne, so Marsh's close victory was not recorded around the country.

'I didn't think I would feel so good about winning my first big one in Australia,' Marsh said afterwards, 'but it is, in fact, a tremendous thrill, even though I have won lots of tournaments around the world. I believe now that I've managed it once, I'll be able to win a lot more because the pressure has gone. I'd love to win the Australian Open and the Australian PGA titles. I think I have a few more years left to try and to win other events overseas, too. In particular, I would like to top the Australasian Order of Merit because it means such a lot around the world in exemptions from qualifying for events like the U.S. Open Championship and the Open Championship in Great Britain.'

Halls Head Western Open — A$35,000
Winner: Mike Cahill

There are many ways to win golf tournaments. Generally, the skill of the winner carries him to the top but, occasionally, a slice of monumental luck plays a hand in the drama of the final 18 holes. It was this type of good fortune which helped Mike Cahill win the Halls Head Western Open at the Mandurah Country Club.

On the last hole Cahill snapped a vicious hook into the trees lining the fairway but managed to miss the timber, hit the side of a parked car and bounce back onto the edge of the fairway. Such good luck should not be spurned and Cahill didn't. He registered a solid par four to complete a round of 70 and become the clubhouse leader with 279. It put him one stroke ahead of Wayne Grady, who had fired a fine 69, the best score of the day. Then it was a matter of waiting for Terry Gale and Bob Shaw to come in with the last group. However, Gale sliced his final drive into the trees and then, trying to play a controlled hook, he finished on the 16th green. His wedge left him a 45-foot putt to force a sudden-death playoff with Cahill. He didn't make it. Nor did Shaw overtake Cahill.

It was quite a slump for Gale, who invariably plays well in his home state, Western Australia. He had gone into the fourth day five strokes ahead after firing 18 birdies on the three previous days. But that last-round 76 meant a difference of almost $4,000 in prize money.

It was a welcome return to form, though, for Cahill, who had not won a tournament since 1978 when he took the Gold Coast Classic. It was also a welcome tonic for Cahill's father, who was ill in a Melbourne hospital and had been urging his son to get down to some serious practice to try to win an event as a present for him. The present was worth $6,300 to Cahill and an uplifting phone call to his father.

Cahill credited his improved finish to the extra practice which had had a good effect on his driving. At Mandurah he was rarely far from the center of the fairway and that provided him with the chance to play some bold shots into the greens.

His winning check here gave him the confidence to try the European circuit later in the year. He qualified for the Open Championship at Troon and made both cuts, having a place in the stirring events of the final day.

Town and Country Channel Nine Western Australian Open — A$25,000
Winner: Terry Gale

Terry Gale is king of Western Australian golf, outdoing even Graham Marsh in local events, and it had been a surprise when, in the tournament prior to the Western Australian Open, he slumped and lost on the last day. However, Gale was back in his accustomed position at Mount Lawley, but only after going through a sudden-death playoff, which he won on the first hole over Vaughan Somers, the Queensland professional.

Gale was not in the headlines the first day when he shot 71, but he was back on the second and third days in fine style, shooting 68 and 65 to seize a six-shot lead. A strong north-easterly breeze and rain on the fourth day made life difficult for nearly everyone, but Somers took it in stride. He estimated before he started that he needed something like a 65 or 66 to have a chance in the tournament and he played some blazing golf all the way round. Somers birdied the third hole and suddenly Gale's lead of six strokes had been cut to three. Then came a crucial shot, which rescued Gale from trouble on the par-five sixth hole. Somers had played a delicate chip to within seven feet of the pin and Gale was in a bunker 60 yards short. But a magnificent sand wedge to 15 inches gave Gale his birdie, while Somers missed the putt and had to be content with par.

From that point on, Gale's play was consistent, although Somers never stopped trying. Probably the 14th hole saved Gale. He sliced into the rough and hit a rather weak shot into some longish grass near the green. He then stopped a superb high, floating pitch three feet from the hole and made his birdie. To Somers' credit he never gave up and his performance on the 18th hole was typical of the way he played the final round. He was on the par-five hole for three, facing a 60-foot putt to force a playoff. He rocketed the ball into the back of the hole. The playoff lasted only minutes, with Gale getting his par at the short 17th and Somers bogeying after his tee shot landed in a bunker.

C.I.G. Channel Nine Nedlands Masters — A$40,000
Winner: Mike Cahill

Mike Cahill became the season's second double winner when he took the first prize of $7,200 in th Nedlands Masters to go with the Halls Head prize money he had won just a fortnight earlier. For a man who had been quoted as wondering if he had been wasting his time over the previous three years with the golf he had been playing, Cahill certainly had provided his own answer.

In fact, he came from nowhere to tie John Clifford at the last hole and force a playoff, shooting 68–68, by far the best two final rounds. Clifford dominated the tournament everywhere but on the playoff hole, carding 68, 71 and then a steady 70 in the third round to give him a one-stroke lead over Bob Shaw and a two-stroke lead over Cahill, Terry Gale and Wayne Grady. Rain squalls and stiff winds had made conditions unpleasant on the first three days, but day four was fine and sunny, with a moderate breeze providing ideal conditions for the competitors.

Clifford started the fourth round at seven under par, but dropped three shots at the ninth, 12th and 13th to give Cahill a chance. Mike had dropped two strokes on the front nine, but played some superb golf on the way back, notching birdies at 10, 11 and 12. This was a big turn-around and two more birdies gave him his 68 and the matching low score with Clifford.

When the players went to the first hole for the sudden-death playoff, Cahill took a long look down the fairway and made a snap decision to try to drive the green. Three years ago he had done the same thing on this 298-yard hole. This time he landed his ball 45 feet short of the pin to give himself a very good chance of a birdie, which he achieved with a good lag putt and a tap-in. Clifford, who had hit a three-wood down the center of the fairway and played his chip shot 12 feet past the flag, could only make par and the tournament belonged to Cahill. Wayne Grady and Bob Shaw were three strokes away in third place but the middle part of this Australasian circuit had been a triumph for Mike Cahill.

His two victories provided a welcome change for the professionals who visit Perth each year to observe at first hand Terry Gale's dominance of the local scene. Wayne Grady quipped to the gallery at the start of the Western Australian circuit, 'Here goes the start of another Terry Gale benefit month.' This time, though, it was Mike Cahill's turn. Two 72-hole tour victories and a 36-hole win in the Royal Fremantle Open gave him a total of $15,000 in his own benefit month.

Resch's New South Wales PGA Championship — A$25,000
Winner: Frank Nobilo

At the close of the New South Wales PGA the only thing to match the joy of 22-year-old Frank Nobilo was the despair of 26-year-old Lyndsay Stephen. Stephen took four to get down from the edge of the green at the final hole of the tournament and Nobilo's safe par gave him his first win since turning professional. The young New Zealander shot 67, 66 on the last two days and his fourth round was a great putting exhibition. At the start of the day he was at 213, four shots behind Wayne Grady and two strokes in arrears of Stephen. Grady's putting let him down badly during the next four-and-a-half hours, but Nobilo was delighted with his work on the greens. He was five under par on the first nine holes, starting with a splendid putt on the first and following with birdies at the second, fourth, fifth, seventh and eighth. A bogey at the sixth put him out in 31, although Stephen was challenging with some putting that was almost as good.

Nobilo's recent experience on the European circuit was proving valuable to him and he showed no sign at all of wavering under the pressure despite dropping a shot at the 15th. Birdies at 13 and 17 and a magnificent shot at the 16th which finished 14 inches from the hole and saved a par brought him in with a 66 and 279. Stephen came to the 18th tee one stroke ahead and seemingly with the tournament safely in his keeping. A fine drive and a great second shot alongside the green gave him the task of getting down in three, but his chip shot was hit far too thin and skated past the hole, leaving him two putts for the win. He couldn't manage it and dejectedly left the green shaking his head, muttering over and over, 'It was terrible — simply terrible'. Stephen was correct in his assessment. For Nobilo, though, it completed an upturn in fortune, as he had only a short time earlier been named to New Zealand's World Cup team.

Kooralbyn Valley Golf Classic — A$30,000
Winner: Col Bishop

When it rains in Queensland, it is not your ordinary English garden type of rain. No sir! It comes down like stair-rods, with visibility reduced to 50 yards. Floods are the norm rather than the exception. So it was at the magnificent Kooralbyn Valley course on the final day when Col Bishop won what was eventually reduced to a 54-hole event. For some of the rookies it was a strange introduction to the professional ranks. A week earlier at the PGA players' school in New South Wales, 12 of them had been through weather so fierce the first round of their examination had been abandoned.

On the first three days, the weather was fine at Kooralbyn, a superb American-style resort with a testing golf course designed by Desmond Muirhead, playing to every one of its 72 strokes for par. You would hardly have thought that, however, when burly Col Bishop put together a 66, two strokes clear of the field. Bob Shaw matched this on the second day to join Bishop in the lead at 137.

Bishop had a 73 Saturday and moved two strokes in front of Shaw, whose 75 put him at 212. Little did they expect that they would finish that way. Officials started the fourth round, but got in only four holes before the wind became too fierce and the rain too heavy. Play was abandoned that day, then Monday as well. Bishop was declared the winner and given the A$5,400 check. 'I'm sorry it wasn't a victory in a 72-hole event,' he said. 'But, in the absence of anything better, it will have to do.'

Dunhill Queensland Open — A$30,000
Winner: Graham Marsh

'This could finish up as one of my best years' — Graham Marsh. Not a bad quote from a golfer before the tournament when asked to comment on his chance of winning the Dunhill-sponsored Queensland Open and later topping the Order of Merit. Marsh won his first major Australian tournament earlier in the year at Huntingdale when he took the Australian Masters. Before the Queensland, Marsh had won $175,000 around the world, but only $27,000 of that in Australia. The event was originally to be played for A$50,000 but, when the television coverage did not materialize, it was reduced to A$30,000.

Marsh was using new Japanese clubs after discarding a set which had served him well for 12 years. The first round with them was a mixture. He had a one-over-par 73, but declared himself satisfied being within four shots of the four leaders at 69. Marsh began to get the feel of his new clubs the second day on the difficult, 6,951-yard Royal Queensland Golf Club course. He matched the best round of the day and moved within a shot of local pro John Victorsen, Stewart Ginn and Wayne Grady who were at 141.

Grady, who confessed that at times in the past he worked 'only half as hard as I should' at his game, spent the three days before the event hitting 500 balls a day, double his usual ration. He followed his second-round 71 with a 70, which thrust him into the lead at 211, one shot ahead of Marsh after three rounds.

Conditions for the fourth day were unpleasant and not one player broke par. Only one, Jeff Senior, equalled it. Marsh and Grady quickly established that first money would go to one or the other, even though they could not find the answer to the stiff westerly wind which blasted across the course. Marsh only needed par on the 72nd hole for a 72 and 285 to beat Grady, but bogeyed, then made certain of the title at the first extra hole of the sudden-death playoff.

National Panasonic New South Wales Open Championship—A$100,000
Winner: Bob Shearer

The early tournaments of the second part of the Australasian circuit provide a valuable lead-up to the main events, the most important of which are the Westpac Classic, the Mayne Nickless PGA and the Australian Open championships. The final tune-up tournament, the New South Wales Open, produced a splendid field, with Bob Shearer back from America, Texan Bill Rogers defending his title, along with New Zealander John Lister and a host of other top-line players, including Jack Newton and Americans Payne Stewart, who had victories in 1982 in the Magnolia Classic and the Quad Cities Open and two the year before in Asia, and Denny Hepler, who had missed the U.S. player's card by one shot after a fine season on the Asia circuit.

With the Manly Golf Club course playing at only 6,433 yards in pleasant conditions, some excellent scoring occurred on opening day, Roger Stephens setting the pace with 65. An Adelaide-based professional making a name for himself as a consistent player, Stephens had been using a new metal driver and his tee shots showed the benefit. He was one shot ahead of Bill Rogers, whose 66 pleased him but didn't satisfy him.

Denny shot to the lead with a magnificent second-round 66 that included seven birdies. His play from tee to green was immaculate. Shearer, playing with Rogers, sank all the putts the American champion would have liked and, after his 71–66—137, he was widely regarded as the main threat, though three shots off the lead. Shearer added to that impression on the third day with another 66, taking a one-stroke lead over Chris Tickner.

The frustrating round of the day was that of Graham Marsh, who could hardly get a putt to drop and had to be content with a 69, which left him six shots off the pace. It also meant he would play Sunday three groups ahead of Shearer and therefore, when he shot his blazing 64 on the last day, he set the target for Shearer, who then knew he had to fire 69 to win by a shot. Marsh was in marvelous form. His image for years has been one of solid dependability with an occasional touch of brilliance, but now it was a different matter. His storming 64 gave Shearer a mild attack of nerves and it all happened on the last nine holes. At the turn, there was still a six-shot difference, then the leaderboard changed dramatically as Marsh birdied five times on the back nine.

Shearer's biggest shock came when a roar from the 18th signaled yet another birdie for Marsh. It was then a matter for Shearer not to drop any more shots or otherwise face a playoff situation. He had saved a valuable par with a nasty, curling, 40-foot putt at the seventh, but the key to his success was at the 12th after the leaderboard had revealed Marsh's challenge. A weak chip left Bob with a sidehill putt of 12 feet. When he rolled it in, he thought it was to be his day. 'When you make putts of that kind as I did on those two holes, you reckon it could be the omen for a win,' he said.

Westpac Golf Classic — A$100,000
Winner: Ian Stanley

Very few winners of golf tournaments around the world are unpopular. Occasionally, though, a victory occurs which not only delights the spectators and television viewers but also is received with pleasure by the player's fellow professionals. This happened in the Westpac Golf Classic at the splendid Royal Adelaide Club in South Australia, when Ian Stanley fired two magnificent opening rounds and managed to hang on and notch his first victory of the summer. Runner-up Stewart Ginn was thrilled. So were other professionals who congratulated Stanley on what was not only a triumph in often difficult conditions but also one of concentration, an attribute not always part of Stanley's repertoire.

Excellent conditions on the first day allowed Stanley to come in with 69 and say he thought his game might be just coming together. Even so, he was still two strokes of the pace of Ginn. Having dispensed with the plus-twos he's worn for six years and now garbed in jeans and shirt-sweater, Ginn came in with 67, one stroke ahead of American Payne Stewart, who played some magnificant golf for his 68.

Ginn wasn't the only one to change his style. As mentioned before, Stanley is something of a 'joker' and one of the most outgoing personalities on the Australasian Tour. When he's in this kind of mood, his concentration often suffers, though. It was the new-look Stanley in Adelaide. He had practiced hard in Adelaide . . . and had not talked to anyone on the course during his first-round 69. Whatever mental application he had decided on definitely worked the second day, when he fired 67 in conditions far more difficult than those prevailing on Thursday.

Thirty-knot westerly winds on Saturday made life extremely difficult for the field and, astonishingly, Stanley was able to keep his three-stroke lead despite shooting 77. Jack Newton was the only one to beat par that day with 72. The rest of the field slipped away and left it, seemingly, a battle between Stanley and Newton on the final day. At 213, Stanley led Newton by three strokes. Stewart and Bob Charles, another two shots back, needed to turn in some extraordinary golf if they were to challenge.

The last 18 holes proved a day of fluctuating golf, Newton falling out of contention with 78 and Ginn, the first-round leader, coming back with some magnificent play to card 69 and put pressure on Stanley over the back nine. Strong westerlies again made life tough for the players and Stanley concentrated throughout on holding his lead rather than in doing anything spectacular. Although Ginn threatened him with a fine four-under-par 33 on the front nine, Stewart bogeyed the 18th hole, giving Stanley a little padding for what turned out to be a splendid victory. Ian finished in style, chipping in for 72 and 285 after playing his second stroke too firmly into the 18th.

Mayne Nickless PGA Championship — A$175,000
Winner: Graham Marsh

There was never a dull moment in the Mayne Nickless PGA Championship of Australia. It was played on one of the great golf courses in the world, the composite at Royal Melbourne Golf Club in Victoria, and because of the nature of the event it attracted every good Australasian player and some from overseas as well, including Americans Ben Crenshaw and Bill Rogers. As always, it produced its share of controversy. Some might say more than its share. In a celebrated incident last year, Jack Newton was at the Melbourne Cup when he should have been registering for the tournament and was subsequently disqualified. This led to a debate between Seve Ballesteros and Peter Thomson on whether or not Newton should have been disqualified. Eventually Graham Marsh won the event in more than grim-faced fashion.

The battle of words in 1982 erupted between Marsh, the Australasian TPS chairman, and young superstar Greg Norman. It seems Marsh had obligations in Japan for the same dates as the Australian Open, scheduled in two weeks at the Kensington course in Sydney. Norman said he was staggered to learn that Marsh had decided to play in Japan instead of in the major event on the Australasian Tour. 'I thought playing the Open would have been one of the Chairman's priorities,' he said. 'It all adds up to the huge mess which has developed in this country over the running of the major golf events.' Marsh came back with a strongly-worded statement.

So, even before a ball had been struck in anger or frustration, the tournament had once again taken the lead positions on the back pages of newspapers. Although the sponsors may not have been over-delighted by the incidents that brought this about, it was certainly the talking point of Australian sport 24 hours before the first round began. When it became action, rather than words, Norman won the first round handsomely with a 68, even though he reckoned he was playing only to about 70 percent capacity. He tied John Clifford in the lead. With a marvelous burst of five birdies and an eagle, Crenshaw took the lead by two shots from Shearer the second day and Norman, although he had 69, dropped back to three strokes behind Crenshaw. Ben shot 65 for 134, Shearer 67 for 136.

The worst wind for Royal Melbourne course is a hot northerly. It came up that way the third day and almost blew Crenshaw out of contention. It couldn't have been blamed, though, for his poor tee shots into bushes at the first hole, where he ran up a double-bogey six, but his eventual three-over-par 75 left him just one shot behind the leaders, Clifford and Shearer, and a stroke ahead of Norman and Marsh.

Marsh came through on the final day with a steady round of 72, which proved too much for his immediate competitors and, in fact, was bettered by only a handful of players, including Payne Stewart, who shot 69, and Texan Art Russell, who had an excellent 71 to ease himself into ninth place with Ian Stanley. But it was Marsh's event and he has never shown more delight on a golf course than when the last putt went in. He said, 'I'm absolutely thrilled at winning this national PGA, and I think I can say now that it really is the first proper major I've ever won in Australia'.

Resch's Pilsener Golf Classic — A$150,000
Winner: Payne Stewart

Over the last 10 years many young American golfers have used the Australasian Tour as a springboard to greater things. The latest of these is Payne Stewart, a talented 25-year-old from Springfield, Missouri, who, by the time he arrived in Australia in the autumn, had already won two events on the 1982 U.S. Tour, the Quad Cities Open and the unofficial Magnolia Classic. The year before, Stewart had victories in Southeast Asia in the Indian and Indonesian Open Championships and finished third in the Asian Order of Merit. At the end of 1981 he cemented ties with Australia when he married Tracey Ferguson, sister of Queensland professional Mike Ferguson. Now he plays the full U.S. and Australasian Tours.

The first day's golf was played in difficult conditions with a very strong wind whipping across the course. But Kyi Hla Han, putting excellently, took a three-stroke advantage with a 66. Local players were unable to come to terms with the greens, but the Burmese pro was magnificent once he reached for the putter. At 5.3 and 141 pounds, there is not much of him, but he was not overawed by the big-hitting giants in the field.

Stewart grabbed the headlines Friday with a blazing, course-record 65 to bring him even with Han and six shots clear of the field with their 136s. Not a bad way to celebrate the week of your first wedding anniversary. Stewart had the benefit of playing early before the gusty southerly wind arrived to make life difficult for the late starters. But his putting was the main reason for his sensational round. An eagle and seven birdies came from the superb putting stroke which let him down only at the 13th and 15th holes. Han managed to hang on well in the third round, played in far pleasanter conditions, but his par 72 dropped him one stroke behind Stewart, who picked up three birdies over the last five holes en route to his 71 and 207.

Stewart began with a birdie at the easy opening hole, a 536-yard par-five, but then his game slipped. A missed three-foot putt at the fourth hole was followed by a bogey and then a triple-bogey at the 390-yard, par-four seventh. Han was then in the lead, although he was unaware of the disasters behind him. As soon as the news filtered through, though, he abandoned his attacking strategy and his game deteriorated. On 10, 11 and 12 he missed putts, had two bogeys and Stewart was able to pull ahead again. The young American made no further mistakes, playing the last 11 holes in three under par for the two-stroke victory.

Australian Open Championship — A$225,000
Winner: Bob Shearer

Bob Shearer won the Australian Open by four shots on the Australian Golf Club course redesigned by Jack Nicklaus. At 287, Shearer was the only man to break par. Nicklaus won the event on the same course in 1978 with a winning score of 284. Those bare facts convey the statistical part of the 1982 Australian Open championship, but emotion and drama filled four splendid days at Kensington. It was a tournament lacking both overseas stars (other than Nicklaus and Bill Rogers) and decent weather as scores soared in high winds the first two days. But it had character and was played on a marvelous golf course prepared specifically for a top championship.

The drama began in a battle of words two weeks prior to the start when Greg Norman's request for appearance money of A$12,500 was turned down. Colin Phillips, executive director of the Australian Golf Union, said, 'Our policy in which we pay appearance money only to winners of the world's major championships remains unchanged'. Ah! 'But,' said David Graham from Dallas, 'where does this leave me, having won the U.S. Open in 1981 and the U.S. PGA in 1979?' It left him with an offer of two airline tickets and a hurried, unsourced statement that the original quote about winners of major championships applied only to non-Australians. It also left him with a slightly bitter taste in his mouth. Aussies, even those with a record as great as Graham's, were apparently expected to play for nothing. Graham issued a statement that he wouldn't be at Kensington and, coinciding with that, Greg Norman announced he would play in the tournament minus appearance money.

Kerry Packer, the golf entrepreneur, had spoken to Nicklaus during the Crosby at Pebble Beach in February and told him he would love to see him playing in the Open at the Australian. Packer financed the course redesigning and he and Nicklaus have been friends for a long time. When Nicklaus arrived, he found the prize money for the tournament was only $175,000 — $25,000 less than when Packer ran the event several years before. The Australian Golf Union had originally contacted Nicklaus and offered him a $50,000 fee for playing. He talked to Packer in Sydney that evening and announced he would put that fee into the tournament purse.

While all this was being settled, Norman was rushed to hospital in great pain for an operation to remove a kidney stone. That happened at midnight, seven hours before the start, but Norman insisted that he be left in the field to try to make his late starting time of 2.05. Accompanied by two doctors and as courageous as they come, Norman made that starting time and lasted 16 holes. He was 11 over par when eventually he had to call it quits. He knew he really shouldn't be playing, but he had hoped to fire well enough to make the cut for the last two days when he would have been stronger and in a position to make a charge. But not even brave, strappingly-built Queenslanders can defy nature and beat the debilitating effects of an operation.

Besides, conditions definitely weren't in his favor. The fierce westerly wind that whipped across the demanding course Thursday prevented any player from breaking par, although Bill Rogers managed to equal it and lead the field. Shearer had a 75, although he took only 73 shots. He called a two-stroke penalty on himself for a bunker violation on the 15th hole. He blasted out of the sand, but the ball only made it to the top of the grassy edge. Shearer thumped the sand in frustration and was horrified to see the ball roll back into the sand.

Shearer's plan of campaign for the week was to lock himself away from friends and well-wishers and concentrate solely on his golf. That dedication worked Friday when he shot 70 to dash into the lead with Nicklaus, who had the same two scores.

On Saturday Shearer stode to a two-stroke lead over Nicklaus and Grady the latter playing a superb back nine of 31 to leap onto the leaderboard at 219 with a 70. Payne Stewart should have been with them at 219 but, late in the evening, incurred a two-stroke penalty for having removed a crossover pole to play a shot on the 16th. He had not read his Local Rules card carefully enough Much the same thing had happened to Keith Fergus at Augusta in 1981.

Jack Newton, with par 72 and 221, was right in the picture and so, too, was Bob Shaw with another par round, but, going into the drama-charged final day in the lead, Shearer was the only player within easy range of par. Shearer, Nicklaus and Newton were in the last group. In front of them were Grady, Shaw and Stewart. Shearer, who had been so methodical in his approach all week, set out to make the others catch him and played steady par golf to the 13th hole. He was still two shots clear of Nicklaus, who had birdied the 12th. Faced with a nasty 40-foot putt from the front edge of the 13th green, Shearer holed it and, with Nicklaus making just a par, the gap widened to three. Then came the crucial par-five 14th and a blow for Nicklaus along the lines of the one he suffered at Pebble Beach when Tom Watson pitched in at the 17th. Upset by photographers snapping a branch, Shearer hit a poor second into the trees, was unable to get a clear shot to the green and had to settle for advancing the ball to some 50 yards short of the pin. He then chipped in to turn a probable bogey into a birdie. The championship was almost his.

With a four-stroke lead, Shearer could afford the luxury of trying to match Nicklaus as the latter hit a magnificent second onto the par-five 18th green. Shearer could have played safe but instead hit an equally exciting shot which gave him, as well as Nicklaus, the chance for an eagle. They settled for birdies which gave Shearer a 70 and 287 and left Nicklaus tied for second place with Stewart at 291.

New Zealand BP Open — NZ$80,000
Winner: Terry Gale

Terry Gale, known to his fellow-professionals as 'Stormy', won the New Zealand BP Open at the Christchurch Golf Club in Shirley with a magnificent exhibition of fighting golf in conditions blustery enough to be a facsimile of his nickname. He defeated Bob Charles by two strokes on the delightful course where the New Zealander is now a life member and won the first of his four Open championships as an 18-year-old amateur in 1954. Australian Open winner Bob Shearer was in the field and increased slightly his lead over Graham Marsh in the Australasian Order of Merit. Marsh had returned to Australia from Japan, but remained at home in Perth, where his wife Julie was giving birth to their fourth child. Shearer was never in serious contention and tied for 10th, 12 strokes off Gale's winning, four-under-par 284.

Hot conditions on the opening day made life difficult for the players with a strong northwesterly wind, at times at gale force, sending the scores soaring. Only six players bettered par and veteran New Zealander Bob Charles shared the lead with Texan Art Russell and the promising 18-year-old New Zealand amateur, Grant Waite, at the close of the first day with two-under 70s.

Early starters on the second day had delightful conditions but the northwesterly wind returned late in the afternoon to provide those still on the course with plenty of problems. Art Russell began his round in brilliant fashion with seven birdies in the first eight holes for a six-stroke lead over his rivals. He was nine under par for 26 holes. Then came the ferocious wind and swirling dust, which sent the scores rocketing and troubled those players wearing contact lenses, among them Russell. A double-bogey at the ninth and bogeys at 12, 13, 14 and 15 hurt him badly — but he birdied No. 16 and, by parring the last two holes for 70 and 140, finished one stroke ahead of Gale and three better than left-handed American Robert Michael and Englishman Maurice Bembridge. Waite hung in well to finish at 144 with American Mike Colandro and Bob Charles. Gale's superb 66 was the best round of the tournament. After his opening 75, he had taken full advantage of the calm conditions in the morning to set the pace for those hitting off late.

On Saturday Gale slipped back with a 74 for 215 to put him even with Art Russell, who described his three-over-par 75 as 'horrible'. It was a two-horse race between Charles and Gale on Sunday, with Gale coming out on top by two shots. The other players fell away rapidly and Mike Colandro's 71, which placed him third at 290, six strokes adrift of Gale, was one of only four sub-par rounds. Charles lost his two-shot lead over Gale and Art Russell after only two holes. Gale birdied the first and second while Charles bogeyed the first, but by the turn Charles had drawn even and went ahead with a birdie at the 10th. Gale dropped a shot at the 12th and Charles seemed to have victory secured. But the 15th and 16th brought his downfall. He missed the fairway at 15, chipped a gum tree with his second into a bunker and his long putt for par failed. A cut drive into the willows at 16 cost him another shot. Meanwhile, Gale had birdied Nos. 16 and 18, in the clubhouse with 284. Charles needed birdies on the last two holes to force a playoff, but found the task beyond him.

Air New Zealand-Shell Open — NZ$100,000
Winner: Terry Gale

The Air New Zealand-Shell Open, the last official tournament on the Australasian circuit, was an exciting event at the Titirangi Golf Club in Auckland, where Terry Gale triumphed over Wayne Grady at the second extra hole in a nail-biting, sudden-death playoff. The field for the $100,000 tournament had been strengthened by the arrival of American Bruce Lietzke, fresh from a trout fishing trip on Lake Tarawera; Britain's Sandy Lyle and Australians David Graham, Bruce Devlin and Graham Marsh.

Gale was 11 under par at the beginning Sunday and held a six-stroke lead over fellow-Australian Grady. But Gale was sometimes tentative and the 36-year-old golfer from Perth saw his lead dwindle away as he slipped to a 74. Meanwhile Grady, playing in the same group as Gale and Lietzke, was showing fine touch on the greens and, as they reached the 71st tee, Gale and Grady were both eight under par. Grady then fell behind with a bogey at the 17th and Gale could breathe again. Briefly. His approach shot to the 18th found the deep trap in front of the green and Grady hit a superb shot straight over the flagstick. It spun back to within five feet of the hole. The drama was only beginning. Gale left his bunker shot in the sand. He exploded his fourth to seven feet and holed the downhill putt for a bogey. Grady watched wistfully as what would have been a winning putt slipped by the hole, leaving him a nerve-wracking 18-inch one back to force the playoff.

They halved the first extra hole with par fours. At the next one, Grady pushed his second shot wide of the green into short rough while Gale's magnificent four-wood approach finished seven yards past the pin and he sank the birdie putt. It was the 847th birdie during the tournament and there were 30 eagles recorded during the four days on the splendid course designed by the immortal golf course architect, Dr. Alister Mackenzie.

New Zealand PGA Championship — NZ$25,000
Winner: Stuart Reese

Any golfer equalling a course record with a magnificent 63 and then losing a tournament would have every right to feel aggrieved. In such a situation, Stuart Reese, the 28-year-old New Zealand professional, managed to hang on for a one-stroke victory in the New Zealand PGA Championship. His wonderful second-round 63, matching the record of John Sheargold, made it all possible. Sadly, the field for the prestigious tournament was depleted, because the prize money failed to reach a modest $25,000 Australian, the requirement for an Order of Merit event. It was a blow for organizers and players alike. With one of Australia's outstanding sponsors, Mayne Nickless, pulling out of golf the same week, it was seven days of financial misery for the Australasian tournament circuit.

No one paid much attention to Reese before the tournament — nor did he capture the headlines with a first-round 70 that placed him only on the fourth line behind Simon Owen, Art Russell and Bob Charles, all of them trailing the brilliant 67 shot by rookie Sydney professional Wayne Riley. The second day was all Reese with his astonishing front nine of 28 which contained eight successive birdies. With a good chance to break the 60 mark, he managed 'only' a one-under 35 for the home nine. Owen, with 66, finished the day just a stroke behind at 134. Owen caught Reese on Saturday, both men bogeying the 18th and finishing 12 under, with Newton one stroke behind.

Rain and strong winds came Sunday and Reese hung on grimly as Owen fell away, then Lister and Wolstenholme were unable to sink vital birdie putts. Newton matched Reese with a last-round 73, but it wasn't good enough and the popular Hamilton professional won by one stroke.

13. The LPGA Tour

JoAnne Carner. When reviewing the 1982 LPGA season, the first two words written must be JoAnne Carner. Golf's 'Big Momma,' at age 43, was living proof that the LPGA is not getting older, just better. She may have won her way into the Hall of Fame but is hardly ready to be placed on a pedestal and immortalized yet. 'I'm going to keep my nose to the grindstone,' declared Carner. 'I don't see any reason why I can't keep on winning. In fact, I want to be the leading money winner again in 1983.' It is difficult to image what 1983 could be like for Carner if it is to top or even equal 1982. She won her entry into the LPGA Hall of Fame by running away with the Chevrolet World Championship of Women's Golf, her 35th career victory. And she went on to win the Henredon Classic and Rail Classic in the next two weeks before taking a two-week vacation to catch salmon in Alaska with her husband, Don. With five Tour victories, plus sharing the JC Penney Mixed Team Championship with John Mahaffey, JoAnne was the Tour's leading winner of official money with $310,400 and total money with about $430,000 — both all-time records. And, naturally enough, she had the low scoring average of 1982 at 71.49, plus the most top-10 finishes at 21. She also had 25 rounds in the 60s, the most for the year.

All this in a season which should have been devoted to transition. Carner changed her putting stance, copying the upright style of the Tour's No. 1 putter, Sally Little. And, according to Carner, she had trouble with her iron game all season. 'I have never worked harder in my life,' she said. And that's why she deserves all the accolades we can muster.

Despite her accomplishments, however, Carner did not commandeer all the glory in 1982. For one thing, the Chevrolet World Championship was her only major title and no other golfer was able to win two of the major events.

Another Hall of Famer, Sandra Haynie, won the Peter Jackson Classic and finished second in official earnings at $245,432. Haynie won two individual titles to increase her total to 42 in 21 years, plus the Ping Team Championship with first-time winner Kathy McMullen. For Haynie, who dropped out of Tour golf for four years, 1982 was the second year of the most remarkable comeback in LPGA history.

Little won the Dinah Shore and three other tournaments to finish third on the money list at $228,941. She also took the J&B Putter Award with a stroke average of 29.34 and had the lowest 72-hole total, 275 at the Mayflower, of the year. And she made the biggest comeback of the season at the UVB Classic, starting the final round six shots back but winning with a closing 64.

Jan Stephenson, despite personal problems, displayed her courage and talent by winning the LPGA Championship and the Lady Keystone in successive weeks. Easily the surprise of the year was Janet Alex's victory in the U.S. Open. Beth Daniel led Carner by one shot at the start of the last round, but Alex, a non-winner out of Slippery Rock Teachers College, pulled out to win by six shots.

Daniel did not win a major tournament and finished fifth in official earnings at $223,635 after leading the Tour in earnings the previous two seasons. But 1982 could hardly be called an 'off year' as she did win five events, won an extra $125,000 by taking the Mazda Series title and another $50,000 for the J&B Gold Putter competition in Las Vegas, Nevada. In both the Mazda and J&B competitions, Daniel edged Carner for the top prizes.

A late charge was put on by Patty Sheehan, the 1981 Rookie of the Year. She won the Safeco and Inamori, the last two events in the United States, along with the Orlando Classic earlier in the year, to finish fourth in earnings at $225,022 and establish herself as one of the bright young stars of the future.

Another bright newcomer was Patti Rizzo, the 1982 Rookie of the Year. Rizzo finished in the top 10 in five events and finished 31st in the standings at $46,441. 'My career is just beginning,' she said. 'I had to grow up quickly but now I think I know my way around.'

Nancy Lopez would have thought of 1982 as a disappointing year if it had not been for her victory in the final event of the season, the Mazda Classic in Japan. Her two wins gave her 25 total for five seasons. She finished seventh in winnings at $166,474 despite changing her swing due to a dramatic weight loss and despite the pleasant distraction of marriage to Houston Astros' third baseman Ray Knight.

The year was disappointing for some. Donna Caponi fell from fourth in 1981 to 16th in 1982 in earnings. Pat Bradley, Jane Blalock and Sandra Post were three other proven performers who would just as well forget 1982 and concentrate on 1983.

One all-time LPGA record was broken and another tied in 1982. Joan Joyce broke the fewest putts record with 17 in one round of the Michelob Classic, while Daniel tied the record for most birdies in a round with 10 at Columbia.

Besides Alex winning the U.S. Open and McMullen sharing victory in the Ping Team Championship, other first time winners were Cathy Morse in the Chrysler and, to everyone's delight, Ayako Okamoto of Japan in the Arizona Copper Classic.

In all, it was a thrilling year, but we can see more excitement ahead in 1983. For one thing, Carner, Kathy Whitworth and Caponi are the only three women with more than $1 million in official earnings for their careers. But Lopez, Blalock, Bradley, Amy Alcott, Little, Haynie and Daniel are all in reach of the $1 million plateau in 1983. That's prosperity.

Whirlpool Championship — $125,000
Winner: Hollis Stacy

Ray Volpe began the 1982 LPGA season by announcing his resignation as tour commissioner on the eve of the $125,000 Whirlpool Championship of Deer Creek at Deerfield Beach, Florida. Administrative concerns were quickly forgotten when Hollis Stacy and JoAnne Carner, 1981 Player of the Year, staged a 77-hole battle for the first tournament victory of the season. With a birdie to Carner's bogey on the fifth playoff hole, Stacy earned her ninth career win in 200 tournaments played.

Until Sunday's showdown, however, most of the publicity was aimed at the 'new' Nancy Lopez, who turned out for 1982 weighing 135 pounds, 26 pounds less than the season before. 'I feel good about my game and, for the first time in a long time, I feel healthy,' said Lopez, who then proved it by finishing third at 284, just two shots out of the playoff.

The on-course drama belonged to Stacy and Carner. Leading from the beginning, Stacy had rounds of 67–70–72 before closing with a one-over-par 74 for a six-under 282. Carner, always a fast starter who won here two years ago on the 6,079-yard course, had rounds of 73 and 71 before catching Stacy with weekend scores of 67 and 71. Carner thought she had won with a closing birdie in regulation play but her 12-foot putt rimmed the right edge and hung on the back of the cup to send the twosome into match-play overtime.

What a match they were, each shooting par on the 10th, 11th, 12th and 10th hole again as they and a crowd of thousands traveled a circular route away from and back to the clubhouse. But it finally became too much golf, especially for Carner. She faced No. 11, a 161-yard par three, for the third time that day and her muscles betrayed her. 'My legs went out just as I started to swing,' she said. 'My legs just wouldn't work.'

The result was a tee shot that drifted into a bunker to the left of the green, about 60 feet from the cup. Her blast was too strong, rolling 12 feet past the cup and her putt was short. Stacy, meanwhile, had driven just eight feet to the left of the cup and watched Carner bogey before having to two-putt to win. 'It was quite nice to have a lag situation after having to make six-footers all day,' she said. With the pressure off, she drilled the putt for a bird and first prize of $18,750.

Carner did not have to feel bad, however, as she and Stacy were destined to dominate the tour for two more weeks before letting anyone else share the winners' circle.

Elizabeth Arden Classic — $125,000
Winner: JoAnne Carner

For JoAnne Carner, 43 years old, entry into the LPGA Hall of Fame was her driving goal as she began the 1982 season. It didn't take her long to move a step closer, as she won the second tournament, the Elizabeth Arden Classic, after losing a playoff in the first. 'You had better believe that is my major goal this year,' said Carner about entering the Hall.

Carner began the season needing either three more tour titles or a victory in either the LPGA Championship or Peter Jackson Classic. She was striving to be the first inductee into the Hall of Fame since Sandra Haynie and Carol Mann in 1977. She took a step closer with a rugged, five-under-par 283 on the demanding Turnberry Isle course in North Miami, Florida.

Carner's score was just enough to hold off the late charge of Jo Ann of a different spelling. Jo Ann Washam shot a closing 68 to move from 16th to second on the final day, finishing at 284. 'I'm back' said Washam, who tore a cartilage on her right side in June of 1981, then suffered seven broken ribs on her left side in an automobile accident later in the year.

Still, no player worked any harder than Carner to conquer one of the more deceptively difficult courses on the tour. Turnberry Isle is building a reputation based on its champions. Since the Miami LPGA Tour stop moved there in 1979, the tournament has been won by Amy Alcott, Jane Blalock, Sally Little and now Carner. And the PGA Seniors have played there too for the last three years, with Don January, Arnold Palmer and Miller Barber taking the honors.

Admitting she was still exhausted after losing a five-hole playoff to Hollis Stacy on the previous Sunday, Carner struggled in with a 70 in the first round, two shots behind Betsy King. Carner shot another 70 and lost a stroke to new leader Vicki Singleton, who had shot 66. Carner shot 71 in the third round and trailed Singleton by a shot.

Singleton never got started in the final round, shooting 75 on three bogeys and no birdies to tie with Little, the defending champion, for third at 285. Carner led by two shots at the turn and coasted home with an even-par 72 as Washam simply had too much ground to cover in too little time. Carner's check of $18,750 gave her a total of $31,000 for two weeks' work. But for the 1981 Player of the Year, it was the win itself that counted more than anything else.

S&H Classic — $125,000
Winner: Hollis Stacy

If it seemed that Hollis Stacy and JoAnne Carner were trying to turn 1982 into a personal match-play season during the first two weeks, it became obvious that was their intention in the third tournament of the season, the S&H Classic at the Pasadena Golf Club in St. Petersburg, Florida. But 1981 Rookie of the Year Patty Sheehan crashed the party and turned the final round into one of the most thrilling days of the year.

Stacy telephoned her younger sister, Laurie, on the eve of the final round and mentioned that she would be playing in the final pairing with Carner and Sheehan. 'Great, you must be in the hunt,' said the younger Stacy. 'Laurie, I *am* the hunt,' replied Hollis. Indeed she was. The third and final round began with Stacy holding a one-shot lead at six-under-par 138 over both of her challengers. When it was over, Stacy had shot 67, still leading Sheehan (67) by one shot and Carner (70) by four. Her 11-under total of 204 was a record for the oldest stop (29 years) on the tour.

Between the three, 18 birdies were shot down in that final round as each freely admitted they had given all they had to give. 'You might get one or two players doing well, but rarely do you find all three playing as good as we did,' said Carner. 'It was the best round of golf I ever played,' said young Sheehan. 'I think I play better with some heat on me,' understated Stacy, who had a first, fifth and first in three weeks of play.

Stacy led all three rounds but could never shake the other two. She shot 66 on the first day, while Sheehan shot 67 and Carner 68. Both Stacy and Sheehan posted 71s in the second round as Carner shot 70 to move into a tie for second. Then came the showdown that saw Stacy still leading the other two by just a stroke when they came to No. 16, the turning point.

Stacy birdied the 380-yard, par-four hole from 16 feet, while Sheehan lipped out a 12-foot birdie putt to settle for par and Carner missed the green for a bogey. That gave Stacy a two-shot lead on Sheehan and three shots on Carner. Sheehan wouldn't quit however, as she fell just two feet short of an ace on the

145-yard, par-three 17th and tapped in the birdie to close within a stroke again. But Stacy closed the door on the easy, par-five finishing hole when she chipped up within two feet for a birdie. Sheehan birdied, too, but it wasn't enough to stop Stacy from collecting her second check for $18,750 in three weeks. Sheehan took second and $12,250, while Carner earned $8,750 after finishing second, first and third to open the year.

Bent Tree Ladies Classic — $150,000
Winner: Beth Daniel

Perhaps the truest test of awesome talent is when an athlete is not at his or her best, but still is good enough to win. Such was the case with Beth Daniel when she came to the Bent Tree Classic to 'work on my game' and left as champion with a 12-under-par total of 276 that tied the tournament record. 'I'm not at my best right now, and I'm not ashamed to admit it,' said Daniel, who did not have to be at her best.

Defending champion Amy Alcott tried to make a tournament out of it, as she was still within one shot of Daniel with two holes to play. But Daniel calmly sank birdie putts of 14 and 10 feet on the last holes, while Alcott faded with a par and bogey. The result was a four-shot victory and $22,500 for the 'struggling' Daniel, the LPGA top money winner for the previous two years.

In the first tournament of the year, Daniel said 'It was the worst I have ever hit the ball in competition,' even though she tied for sixth at just one over par. She withdrew after one round of the second tournament because of the death of her grandmother and then skipped the third, trying to get her game into order back home in Charleston, South Carolina.

Apparently one thing she did not have to touch up was her putting, which really carried her all week on the Bent Tree Golf and Raquet Club course in Sarasota, Florida. 'I cannot ever remember making so many putts in one tournament,' she said. 'I averaged just 26 putts a round and a lot of them were long ones.'

Daniel's return to competitive action, if not competive form, put an end to the early domination of the tour by Hollis Stacy and JoAnne Carner. For Carner, who had a first, second and third in the first three weeks, the best she could come up with was a tie for sixth at 284, eight shots behind Daniel. Stacy tied for ninth at 285 after two victories and a fifth. 'I'm burned out,' laughed Stacy. 'I'm stretcher material.'

Veteran Kathy Postlewait led the first two days with rounds of 66 and 71, then held on to finish third at 281. Rookie Pam Gietzen was fourth at 282 and Barbara Moxness was fifth at 283. Tied with Carner were Sally Little and the happiest golfer on the course, rookie Sue Ertl. She lives at Bent Tree and represents it on the tour. More than that, one year ago she was selling beer in a concessions tent near the clubhouse instead of taking bows on the 18th green.

Arizona Copper Classic — $125,000
Winner: Ayako Okamoto

The game of golf took on an unexpected but delightful international flavor in the Arizona Copper Classic when Ayako Okamoto of Japan took the title in a playoff with Sally Little of South Africa after both had held off the challenges of Americans Amy Alcott and Patti Rizzo.

Ayako Okamoto was hardly a well-known name around the Randolph Park North course in Tucson until the end of the final round. She had shot rounds of 70–72–70–69 for a seven-under-par total of 281, but Little had fashioned a closing 66 by playing the last six holes in five under to tie. After each parred the first playoff hole, Okamoto sank a 20-foot putt on the second hole for her first American victory and a prize of $18,750.

Okamoto's victory was not surprising to anyone who has followed the women's tour in Japan. In 1981, the 30-year-old star became the first lady professional in Japan to win more than 30 million yen or about $139,000 in American money. In 28 tournaments the year before, she won eight, was second six times and third twice.

Little certainly did not underestimate her opponent. She and Okamoto had become friends on the tour and frequently went out to dinner together. Reporters asked Okamoto if it was difficult to be in a playoff with a friend. She displayed her professionalism by replying, 'It is her business; it is my business.'

So Okamoto took care of business, while Little had many fine days ahead of her. But the tournament was a major disappointment for Rizzo and Alcott. Playing in her first tournament as a professional, Rizzo looked like she was going to be an instant winner. After Okamoto and Janet Coles shared the first-round lead of 70, Rizzo shot a course-record 65 in the second round to take a five-shot lead over Alcott. And despite a 73 in the third round, Rizzo still led Alcott by two and Okamoto by three going into the final round.

The rookie had lost her touch, however. Three bogeys on each side resulted in a closing 76 for Rizzo, who had to settle for a tie for fourth with Lynn Adams. Alcott was even more distressed. Tied for the lead with two holes to play, she bogeyed No. 17 from two feet, then double bogeyed the last hole. 'Maybe I should putt with my eyes closed,' she said.

Little, meanwhile, made an incredible run. She played the last six holes birdie, eagle, bogey, birdie, birdie, birdie to tie Okamoto. But it wasn't quite enough, for this was Okamoto's day to shine in the Arizona sun.

Sun City Classic — $100,000
Winner: Beth Daniel

After Ayako Okamoto won at Tucson the week before, it appeared Tatsuko Ohsako was going to give back-to-back victories to Japan as she had a four-stroke lead with eight holes to play in the American Express-Sun City Classic, the second Arizona stop on the LPGA Tour. But a disastrous quadruple bogey, including two penalty strokes, ruined Ohsako's chances and left the door open for Beth Daniel to claim her second win of the year in a playoff with Carole Jo Callison.

Despite some putting miseries, Daniel and Callison (the former Carole Jo Skala, who married Verne Callison, an American public links champion) tied at 10-under-par 278 on the Hillcrest Golf Course in Sun City West, a retirement center. 'Carole Jo and I were joking on the back nine,' said Daniel, 'that we were having a contest to see who would miss the most putts and still win the tournament.'

What happened to Ohsako was no joke, however. She entered the final round four shots ahead of Daniel and five ahead of Callison. She still held that margin before teeing off on No. 11, a 359-yard par four. Her errant tee shot landed in a tree well, leaving her without a shot. She tried anyway and her second shot hit the tree and rebounded against the shaft of her club, drawing an automatic two-stroke penalty. Six shots plus the penalty gave her a quadruple bogey eight and she limped in for a 78 that dropped her into a tie for sixth at 282.

'I hate to see someone fall apart,' said Daniel about Ohsako's misfortune. 'She had pure bad luck.' Daniel had problems of her own. She held a one-shot lead on Callison when she prepared to sink a one-foot par putt on No. 17 — and missed it. 'To tell the truth, it wasn't even a foot,' she admitted. 'It was ridiculous and I couldn't believe it.'

Believe it or not, the bogey dropped Daniel into a tie with Callison that lasted for two extra holes. Daniel had her chance to end it on No. 11, the hole that destroyed Ohsako's chances, and did not fail, sinking a five-foot birdie putt for the win. Daniel had fashioned her 278 on rounds of 70–67–71–70, while Callison shot 68–71–70–69.

An amateur from Arizona State University, Lauri Merten-Peterson took the first-round lead with a five-under 67 but faded on the second day with a five-over 77. Ohsako and Daniel shot 67 each in the second round to share the lead, while Ohsako followed with another 67 for what seemed like a commanding, four-shot lead going into the final round before the sun set on Japan's hopes for an Arizona sweep.

Olympia Gold Classic — $150,000
Winner: Sally Little

Sally Little was the first to admit it. When the Olympia Gold Classic in 1981 was stopped after just 36 holes because of rain, she felt like half a winner. 'I didn't want to win it this way,' she said then. She proved her point and proved herself a complete champion one year later by going the distance for another Olympia Gold title.

It was hardly easy. Nothing comes easily on the Eisenhower and Zaharias courses that wind around and through a hill in the Industry Hills complex of California. With both courses playing to par 73, Little had little to cheer about after opening rounds of 75 and 74, but closing efforts of 69 and 70 were good enough for a four-under-par 288 and two-shot win over Donna White, who lost the lead with a 76 on the final round.

Ironically, Little almost lost the same way she won the year before. The final round was rained out on Sunday, but the skies cleared on Monday. The year before, rain kept the players in the clubhouse on Saturday, Sunday and Monday. 'It would have been ironic to lose it, or at least not have the chance to win it this year because of rain,' said Little. 'It's an incredible feeling to win here again for a number of reasons. First of all, to prove that I could do it over four rounds.'

Little did not seem like a contender at first. Janet Coles took the first-round lead with a three-under 70 but faded steadily after that. White, after a year away from the tour to give birth to her daughter, was back with young Kristin. Feedings in the middle of the night did not keep Donna from shooting a course-record 68 on the Eisenhower in the second round to take the lead. She shot par in the third round to lead Japanese star Ayako Okamoto by three shots and Little by four.

The day's delay seemed to take something out of White. Little tied her on the 11th hole and took a two-shot lead when Little birdied and White bogeyed the 12th. Little increased her lead to four shots before giving back two with a double bogey on No. 17. Nancy Lopez caused excitement by shooting a closing 68 that lifted her into a tie for third with Okamoto at 291, three shots behind the winner. But it was Little's week to prove she could go the distance.

J&B Scotch Pro-Am — $200,000
Winner: Nancy Lopez

The 'old' Nancy Lopez felt she gave away the title in dazzling Las Vegas in 1981, so the 'new' Nancy simply ran away with it in 1982, taking the newly-named J&B Scotch Pro-Am by five shots with a record-shattering 10-under-par total of 279.

As was the case everywhere she played in '82, Lopez was drawing the immediate attention of fans, reporters and especially photographers without picking up a club. Thirty pounds lighter than the year before, her appearance was as stunning as her game. 'I feel the weight loss has helped my swing considerably,' she said. 'I'm able to get through the ball quicker and smoother, and I think I'm hitting it farther.'

She got no argument in Las Vegas. The year before, in what was then called the Desert Inn Pro-Am, she led for three rounds but shot 76 in the last round to tie for fourth. Lopez won this tournament in 1979, but Donna Caponi won it in 1980 and '81. With Lopez's victory in '82, a rubber-match showdown might be anticipated for next year.

Concentration is not easy anywhere on the LPGA Tour, but especially not here. The event begins with two rounds on the par-73 Las Vegas Country Club course with 88 pros and 264 amateurs, including many celebrities from the entertainment and sporting worlds. Then the survivors play the last two rounds on the par 72 Desert Inn course. And this year nearly freezing temperatures added to the challenge.

Nothing detered Lopez. She opened with a 70, one shot behind early leaders Judy Clark and Alice Ritzman. Nancy tied the course record in the second round with a six-under 67, taking the lead by two shots over Sandra Haynie. Lopez moved over to the Desert Inn and shot a 69 on Saturday to widen her lead over Haynie to five shots.

The final round was no contest. After nine holes, Lopez had a nine-shot lead. She faltered a bit on the back nine, but everyone knew it hardly mattered. 'I almost congratulated Nancy when she made the turn,' said Haynie, who took second at 284, one shot ahead of Mathy Whitworth and Alice Miller.

The victory was worth 30,000 silver dollars, but, for the new Nancy Lopez, it meant much more than that. 'My confidence level is the highest it has been since 1979,' Nancy said. And she never looked better, either.

Women's Kemper Open — $175,000
Winner: Amy Alcott

When the Women's Kemper Open moved to the Hawaiian isle of Maui this year, it was obvious that the LPGA's biggest hitters would dominate on the rolling fairways at the Royal Kaanapali North Course. That's exactly what took place as Amy Alcott held off JoAnne Carner and Nancy Lopez in a battle of titans.

'The par fives,' predicted Nancy, 'they should make the difference with three players who can really go for it.' Lopez was right, but it was Alcott who proved it by playing the par fives in 10 under par en route to a 72-hole total of 286, six under par for the course. Carner finished a shot back and Lopez one more in a final-round battle that turned into a three-way match play.

'I thrive on competition and I wished I was matched like this every time,' said Alcott after her first win of the season. 'And I knew this would be a good week for me because you always play better in places you enjoy.'

The competition was fierce from the start. Lopez, trying for back-to-back wins after taking the J&B Scotch Pro-Am in Las Vegas the week before, shot 70 to share the first-round lead with Kathy Young. But a second-round 70 by Carner gave her the lead after two rounds, while Lopez and Carner held first going into the final round with Alcott just a shot behind.

Lopez then discovered that her putter had deserted her. After 13 holes on the final day, Alcott and Carner were at six under with Lopez three shots behind. But Lopez got her first birdie of the day on the next hole to close within two shots of the leaders. And on No. 16, both Alcott and Carner bogeyed, allowing Nancy to get another shot back with a par.

The next-to-last hole, a par three, was the difference. All three hit their tee shots within 15 feet of the cup, but only Alcott sank the birdie putt. Each shot par on the final hole, giving Alcott a two-under 71 and first prize of $26,250, while Carner shot 73 and Lopez 74.

Nabisco-Dinah Shore Invitational — $300,000
Winner: Sally Little

After 12 years of striving for Sally Little and 11 years of the Dinah Shore tournament, both achieved superstar status at the same time when Little shot her career-best round of eight-under-par 64 to move from five back to a three-shot win in the richest tournament on the Tour.

Actually, major status for the tournament came later in the season when the LPGA officially declared that the Dinah Shore was one of its major events. But Little, 30, proved her position among the elite with that brilliant closing round that gave her 12 career wins and two for the year. 'This is a very special event to me,' said Little. 'In my heart, I feel this is a major.'

And so was she, even though she received little attention until the final round. Hollis Stacy, already a two-time winner this season, held a four-shot lead over two other attention getters — vivacious Jan Stephenson and vibrant JoAnne Carner, who was celebrating her 43rd birthday on the closing Sunday at the Mission Hills Country Club. And Nancy Lopez, even though six shots behind, was holding her large gallery after shooting a 67 in the third round.

Nobody was taking much notice of Little, except Little. In cold, bitter weather, she had opened with a 76. But the weather changed for the best and so did her game as she shot 67 in the second round. 'I feel like I played myself back into contention,' she said at the time if anyone was listening.

After a third-round 71, Little was not invited into the press tent as she was still five shots behind Stacy. Then came the final round . . . Little, who never sank a putt longer than 20 feet, took birdies on Nos. 2, 4, 5, and 8 to close within one shot of Stacy at the turn. She tied for the lead with a two-inch birdie tap-in on No. 10, a 350-yard par four that she drilled with an eight-iron approach. The lead was hers with another birdie on No. 11, then she sealed the outcome with her seventh and eighth birdies on Nos. 14 and 16.

Stacy went through the frustration of making 18 pars while watching Little erode her lead. Almost lost in the excitement was a 65 by Sandra Haynie that lifted her into a tie for second with Stacy at 281, three shots behind Little, who vaulted into first place among the money leaders on a check for $45,000.

CPC International — $150,000
Winner: Kathy Whitworth

Your last victory is usually the sweetest, but one of the more historic victories of this or any season seemed to embarrass Kathy Whitworth more than anything else. It was if she was not quite ready to assume her role in golfing's archives despite tying Mickey Wright's all-time LPGA total of 82 wins by running away with the CPC International at Moss Creek Plantation at Hilton Head Island, South Carolina. 'The 82nd win is great, I'm not putting it down,' Whitworth said to the slightly puzzled media. 'But as far as Mickey is concerned, that doesn't demean her or her record at all. So many times we played together, going head to head. I think she respects me and Mickey knows how much I respect her.'

That was the problem. Whitworth was concerned about disturbing Wright's rightful place in golf history. That won't happen, of course, but room must be made for Whitworth. At age 42, she has proven she remains one of the great competitors in the game. But to be truthful, she received little competition during the CPC International as she won by a stunning nine shots on rounds of 73–68–73–67 for 281. Patty Sheehan was a distant second at 290. Amazingly, it was not a wire-to-wire win. Whitworth's opening 73 left her three shots behind Sandra Post. But Post soared to an 82 in the second round, while Whitworth shot 68 to take the lead. Despite high winds and another 73, she expanded her lead to four shots after the third round.

The final round was never a contest. Whitworth shot 33 on the front side to take an eight-shot lead with nine holes to play. She's the only player on the

LPGA Tour using an orange ball and it is a good thing she had it, or else everyone would have lost sight of her. She admitted that even while she was putting the finishing touches on her closing 67, the low round of the tournament, she was thinking about both the past and the future. 'When you first start, you think you have got forever. Forever isn't forever anymore. I'm going to miss it bad when I have to quit. And, you never know, this could be the last one.'

It wasn't.

Orlando Classic — $150,000
Winner: Patty Sheehan

Patty Sheehan gave up a chance for her first LPGA win at Orlando in 1981 when she bogeyed the first hole in a five-way playoff that Beth Daniel eventually won. But Sheehan still ran all the way to the clubhouse to call her parents and tell them how close she had come. And when she did win last year in Japan, she did a somersault. Sheehan returned to Orlando in 1982 and posted her second Tour victory in overtime but without any running or jumping.

'I thought about making a somersault, but I just couldn't,' Patty said. 'I'm exhausted, sick and extremely happy, not necessarily in that order.' If Sheehan was all those things, Kathy Postlewait was everything but happy. At age 32, she came so close to earning her first LPGA win in her home town but saw the dream end when she bogeyed the fourth playoff hole of the Orlando Classic at the Rio Pinar Country Club. 'Well, at least I learned I can play golf in Orlando,' Postlewait said. 'I made some good shots to get into the playoff and made some good shots in the playoff. That can't be choking.'

The tournament learned a lot, too. Without a sponsor in its fourth year, the tournament survived as a civic event and also served as an experiment for the Tour by going to a 54-hole format with two pro-ams preceding it. The LPGA is considering this format as a way to ensure profits through the funds derived from the pro-ams. Unfortunately, the tournament received little help from the weather. Winds were gusting to 30 miles per hour on the first day, bothering everyone but Postlewait, who shot a 66 for a quick, four-stroke lead. It rained the second day and the top 21 golfers were unable to finish their rounds until Sunday. Postlewait came in with a 71 that left her one shot ahead of Janet Coles and two ahead of Sheehan.

Postlewait still had a one-shot edge on Sheehan with three holes left in the regulation span. But Postlewait bogeyed the tricky 16th, a 187-yard, par-three over water, while Sheehan birdied it. Sheehan then bogeyed the next hole, setting up the playoff that began on No. 16 and ended on No. 16. Both had shot seven-under-par 209. When the twosome came to No. 16 for the second time in the playoff, it was the fourth time they had played that hole on the final day and their 26th hole for Sunday. Neither could reach the green, but Sheehan chipped to within three feet. After Postlewait missed a 15-foot par putt, Sheehan sank hers — and sank to the ground in what amounted to a 'victory collapse.'

Birmingham Classic — $100,000
Winner: Beth Daniel

Numbers can be deceiving, such as knowing Beth Daniel took a four-shot lead after one round of the Birmingham Classic and then won by four shots. That makes it sound routine, which was hardly the case as Daniel reenacted the hare's role in 'The Tortoise and the Hare' by running away and then waiting for someone to catch up. The only competitor who came close was torrid Patty Sheehan. The 1981 Rookie of the Year finished second, giving her three consecutive weeks of second, first and second. 'I've quit worrying about poor shots,' said Sheehan, revealing her secret. 'I just tell myself, "Relax, Bozo. If you can't have fun, you shouldn't be out here".'

No player was having as much fun as Daniel, especially in the opening round, although a touch of frustration was evident, too. To say that Daniel shot a course record, eight-under-par 64 is impressive enough, but the effort becomes stunning when you consider she was eight under after just 13 holes. She already had her four-shot lead then but could do no more, playing the last five holes in par to finish four shots ahead of Bonnie Lauer. Then came the slowdown in the second round when Daniel played the front in two over. And Sandra Haynie actually took the lead with an eagle on the 11th hole. You could almost hear Daniel cut in the after-burners as she birdied five times on the back nine for a 70, regaining the lead by two shots over Sheehan as Haynie faded.

In the final round, Sheehan birdied the first hole to close within one shot, but once again, Daniel took off with birdies on the next three holes to regain her two-shot margin. It stayed that way until Sheehan bogeyed No. 15 to give Daniel a three-shot lead with three to play. 'When Patty bogeyed there,' said Daniel, 'I knew I had it won.' Daniel went on to birdie the final hole for a 13-under-par 203 on rounds of 64–70–69 and to end up winning by the four shots she had earned after just 13 holes on Friday. Sheehan was second at 207, while Haynie and Lauer tied for third at 209. And Lauer put the weekend into perspective, saying, 'Chasing Beth is like swimming upstream against the current.'

United Virginia Bank Classic — $125,000
Winner: Sally Little

Kathy Whitworth was ready to sign her name to another page in LPGA history, but Sally Little forced a delay with another of her stunning charges as she made up six strokes on the final round and won a one-hole playoff with Whitworth in the United Virginia Bank Classic over the Sleepy Hole Course in Suffolk, Virginia. There was nothing sleepy about Little as she fashioned a six-under-par 67 for an 11-under-par 208. Little then birdied the first playoff hole for her third win of the season. It was almost Whitworth's second win of the year and, far more importantly, 83rd of her career, which would have broken the LPGA record she shared with Mickey Wright after winning the CPC International three weeks earlier.

'I don't feel like I lost the tournament,' said Whitworth. 'Sally just plain won it. She took charge of the whole day. When Sally gets on a roll, she can shoot nothing. Remember her 64 in the last round to win the Dinah Shore?' Jan Stephenson probably remembered. She had been one of the leaders in the final day of the Dinah Shore when Little closed from five shots back to win by two. This time Stephenson was the sole leader going into the final round, despite some severe personal problems at the time. After brilliant rounds of 68 and 67, she faded to a 74 and settled for a tie for third with Beth Daniel at 209, one shot out of the playoff.

Stephenson and Whitworth had shared the first-round lead at 68, while Little had shot 72. Then Stephenson took a two-shot lead on Whitworth and six on Little after the second round. But Little waited no longer. In the final round, she birdied No. 4, eagled the par-5 fifth with a five-foot putt and birdied No. 6 to pick up four strokes in three holes. Still, she didn't catch Whitworth until she birdied the 17th. Whitworth needed a birdie on the final hole but settled for a par. And she could do no better than par the first playoff hole, while Little used an eight-iron approach to set up a two-foot birdie.

'I don't feel I've taken anything away from Kathy,' said Little. 'She's a true champion and has proven it many times. She'll win again — and it may not be too many days away.' With that remark, Little proved to be a prophet, along with a champion.

Lady Michelob — $150,000
Winner: Kathy Whitworth

It was this simple: Kathy Whitworth did not want to wait any longer. 'I told myself that if I didn't do it here, I'd have all this to go through again. It's not the pressure that I put on myself that was difficult, it was trying to do something that everyone expected me to do.'

After losing to Sally Little in a playoff the week before, Whitworth ran away with a four-shot win in the Lady Michelob Classic and established a niche in LPGA history that may never be disturbed. It was her 83rd win, one more than the long-standing record of Mickey Wright, and it is an accomplishment that no woman golfer, other than Whitworth, may ever surpass. At the time Whitworth won her 83rd, Sandra Haynie was next among active golfers with 40. JoAnne Carner had 33, followed by Nancy Lopez with 24. 'These kinds of numbers may be out of reach,' admitted Whitworth. 'But there's an awful lot of talented girls out here. Whether the record is broken depends on how long some of them play.'

Whitworth has been playing pro golf 23 years and her 83rd victory was typical of her style, steady and determined. As it turned out, her competition at Brookfield West in Atlanta, Georgia, came from three youngsters each seeking their first win on Tour. Kelly Fuiks and Julie Stanger Pyne, teammates in high school and college in Phoenix, Arizona, shot 68 each to share the first-round lead, one shot ahead of Whitworth. Whitworth shot a 68 in the middle round to lead Fuiks by one and Stanger-Pyne by two. 'Just think,' said Fuiks, 'we'll be part of history. Either Kathy will win her 83rd, or Julie or I will win our first.' Fuiks was the first to go as she was five over par on her first four holes, ending with a 78. Stanger-Pyne had a slower fade to a 74.

Barbara Moxness rose up to actually take a two-shot lead over Whitworth with a birdie on No. 13. When her turn came, Whitworth birdied No. 13, too, while Moxness was taking a bogey on No. 15, placing the two in a tie. The competition ended when Moxness hit into trees on No. 16 and suffered a double bogey. She finished with a 71 to tie Sharon Barrett for second at 211.

Whitworth coasted home for her closing 70 and 207 total. She underplayed her accomplishment with a philisophical thought that could be used by every man, woman and child who attempts to master the game of golf. 'I guess it just goes to prove that if you stay with anything long enough, have good health and a fair-to-middling golf swing, good things will happen.'

Chrysler-Plymouth Charity Classic — $125,000
Winner: Cathy Morse

Some victories transcend the game of golf and have a meaning never found in the statistics. Such victories are triumphs for the heart. When Cathy Morse won the Chrysler-Plymouth Charity Classic for her first LPGA triumph, it was a victory for the heart. On Christmas Eve, 1981, Morse was engaged to Jim Meyer. But on January 4, he underwent open-heart surgery and died on the operating table. Morse skipped the start of the Tour and searched for a way to put her life back together. 'Jim would always tell me, no matter how badly I'd played or how badly I felt, "You're a winner, Cathy." He would walk behind the ropes for most of my rounds and he never stopped telling me, "You're a winner".'

Her fiancé was proven right on the Wykagyl Country Club course in New Rochelle, New York, as Morse ignored cold and steady rain to shoot rounds of 70-72-74 for an even-par 216. That was good enough for the first-place cheque of $18,750, which more than doubled her earnings to nearly $30,000. Good fortune was on Morse's side as she started the final round three shots behind Sally Little, the Tour's leading money winner at the time. But Little, seeking her fourth win of the year, took a stunning 80 to finish second, three shots behind Morse.

Little, who had held the lead for two days on rounds of 68 and 71, lost part of it in just one hole of the final round. She double-bogeyed the first hole, while Morse sank a 20-foot putt for a birdie and a share of the lead. Little went on to bogey four straight holes from the fourth to the seventh, giving Morse a four-shot lead at the turn. It was never a contest after that. 'I only wish Jim was here to see me win, something I never did while he was alive,' said Morse, rain and tears flowing down her face. 'I could feel him this afternoon, could almost hear him say again, "You're a winner, Cathy, you're a winner".'

Corning Classic — $125,000
Winner: Sandra Spuzich

In many ways, the 1982 season was a tribute to dedication and determination. Before the Corning Classic, Kathy Whitworth had set an all-time record with her 83rd win. And later in the year, JoAnne Carner would win her way into the Hall of Fame. Sandra Spuzich added her contribution in Corning, New York, by becoming the oldest player to win an LPGA event at age 45. Spuzich said, 'Well, I've always thought it was a complete myth that once someone reaches a certain age, they can't do something they set out to do. As long as you have your wits about you, a solid game and dedication, you can do it. I've always believed that or I wouldn't be out here in the first place.'

Even with her wisdom, Spuzich did not have an easy time. She had to catch young Patty Sheehan on the last two holes of regulation and then defeat her in the first hole of a playoff after both tied at eight-under-par 280. Sheehan did not take the lead until after a birdie on No. 15 on the final day. And, with two holes to play, Spuzich trailed her by three. But Sheehan took a bogey on No. 17, while Spuzich dropped a pair of 15-foot birdies to tie. Sheehan could have won by sinking a five-foot birdie putt on the 18th but left it outside the cup.

Even so, Sheehan appeared to have the upper hand on the first playoff hole. She was on the green in regulation, while Spuzich was short and in heavy grass. But the veteran chipped to within a foot of the cup and tapped in for a par. Sheehan then pushed a 35-foot putt four feet past the cup and missed coming back.

It was anybody's tournament for most of the week. Sheehan and Nancy Lopez shared the first round lead at 67 each, but a 74 on Friday and 76 on Sunday knocked Lopez out of contention. Defending champion Kathy Hite shot a 67 on the second day to go with her opening 70 for a three-shot lead. Hite had a two-shot lead after a 71 on Saturday but fell back into the pack with a 75 in the closing round.

McDonald's Kids Classic — $250,000
Winner: JoAnne Carner

'I'm going to win. I need two wins and I've got to have this one.' JoAnne Carner made it that simple on the morning of the final round of the McDonald's Kids Classic, then proceeded to glide to a six-stroke victory that left her just one triumph short of the LPGA Hall of Fame. Thirty-five victories qualifies for the Hall. This was Carner's second of the season and 34th of her career. 'It is something you really want, and I've been thinking about it since the season began,' said the ever-popular Big Mama. 'Right now I want to get it over with.'

Carner certainly took little time handling the difficult White Manor Country Club course in Malvern, Pennsylvania, just outside of Philadelphia, and the field that included nine of the top ten money winners. When Carner's game and confidence are equally high, she becomes an indestructible force. 'I never expected a runaway — but I was feeling so confident.' Opening with a 68, Carner took a one-shot lead. But she proved herself human on the second round, taking a 73 to fall four shots behind Kathy Postlewait, a veteran who never won and admits to playing without the confidence she needs. Postlewait lost a playoff to Patty Sheehan in her home town, Orlando, Florida, earlier in the year and said she still had not regained her composure despite her opening rounds of 69–68.

In a reversal of scores, Carner returned to 68 and Postlewait shot 73 on Saturday to give a one-shot lead to Carner. Sandra Haynie rallied with a 66 and was just two back going into the final round. But Carner just smiled and repeated, 'I'm going to win it.' Haynie, Postlewait and the hard-charging Sheehan stayed close until after the turn for home in the final round. But Carner sank birdie putts on Nos. 12, 16 and 17, while the three contenders fell back. Closing with a 67, Carner's 12-under-par total of 276 was worth $37,500. Haynie took second at 282, followed by Sheehan at 283 and Postlewait at 284.

As for Carner, the next one would be the big one, but it was still 11 weeks away in the Chevrolet World Championship.

LPGA Championship — $200,000
Winner: Jan Stephenson

Few seasons have produced so many stories of individual courage overcoming adversity as the 1982 LPGA season. And the LPGA Championship was no exception. Jan Stephenson put aside enough personal adversity to script a television soap opera in order to play brilliant golf and capture one of the year's major events. What should be remembered is Stephenson's solid, nine-under-par 279 on the grizzly course at Kings Island, fashioned on rounds of 69–69–70–71. It was enough to hold off sizzling JoAnne Carner by two strokes and was worth $30,000 to Stephenson. 'Unfortunately,' said the champion, 'I hate to think where this money will go.'

Probably into lawyers' fees. Stephenson had been making headlines all season but not about her golf. Charges and counter-charges between her and her third husband were receiving almost lurid attention by the press and, subsequently, the public. And, not surprisingly, her golf had suffered because it is difficult to concentrate on your game when your world is falling apart. Stephenson decided to fight back. Her parents came up from Australia for support. She checked out of her hotel and refused to let the press — or her lawyers — know how to reach her off the course. She stayed in her room, ate salads and practiced her putting. It paid off. 'The more trouble Jan's in, the better she plays,' said Carner.

Stephenson shot an opening 69 to share the lead with Beth Daniel and Therese Hession. After two rounds and another 69, Stephenson was a shot ahead of Daniel. Playing in the rain on the third day, Stephenson had a five-shot lead with two holes to play. But she bogeyed No. 18, while Daniel got birdies on the last two holes to close within two shots. Carner, Pam Gietzen and Hollis Stacy were four shots back. The expected fireworks on the final day never really materialized. Stephenson remained steady, while Daniel bowed out with four straight bogeys to start the back side. Carner made a late move, but it was too little from too far back. Gietzen and Janet Alex tied for third at 283, four shots behind. Alex shot a closing 67 to forewarn the competition about how she would play six weeks later in the U.S. Open. But this week and this championship belonged to Jan Stephenson, who proved that even some soap operas can have happy endings.

Lady Keystone — $200,000
Winner: Jan Stephenson

After winning the LPGA Championship for herself, Jan Stephenson came right back and won the Lady Keystone for her father to prove that you do not have to go through a letdown after taking a major title. Actually, the Lady Keystone was more of a thriller than Stephenson's win in the Association's championship the week before. Stephenson began the final round five shots behind Barbara Moxness — and bogeyed the first two holes. 'My system was in shock after those bogeys at the start,' she said, 'but five birdies straightened that out.'

Make that five straight birdies, from Nos. 7 to 11, that began with a 30-foot putt. 'That putt gave me a boost,' said Stephenson, still embroiled in some off-course dramas concerning her marriage and her finances. Still, it was her father-caddie who may have made the difference. 'My daddy said he'd like for me to win for a Father's Day present. But I still can't believe I came from that far back.' Neither could Moxness, who was chasing her first win in five years on the Tour. Vickie Fergon had taken the first-day lead with a 67, but rounds of 69–68 had given Moxness a three-shot advantage with one round to play on the Hershey, Pennsylvania, Country Club course.

Stephenson took the lead when she birdied No. 15 but gave a share of it back to Moxness when she bogeyed No. 17. With Stephenson in the clubhouse at five-under-par 211 on rounds of 71–71–69, Moxness needed a par on the final hole to tie and a birdie to win. But she got a bogey instead, three-putting for the fourth time to take a closing 75 and 212 total. And Alexandra Reinhardt chipped in on the final hole to tie for second, while Sandra Haynie was third at 213 and slump-ridden Pat Bradley fourth at 214.

Rochester International — $200,000
Winner: Sandra Haynie

The Rochester International produced one of the great closing rounds of the season and, at the time, one of the most surprising winners. It was a showdown between 'hometown' favorite Nancy Lopez, soon-to-be Hall of Famer JoAnne Carner and veteran Sandra Haynie. Not even Haynie thought she would end up winning by six strokes.

The final round at the Locust Hill Country Club in the Rochester suburb of Pittsford, New York, drew a crowd estimated at 24,000. And at least 20,000 were openly rooting for Lopez, who had played here on three occasions and won every time. More than anywhere else in the world, Lopez is queen in Rochester. If she ever runs for mayor there, it won't even be close. But, after three rounds, the tournament was close. Haynie held a one-stroke lead on Lopez and Carner. Truthfully, few gave Haynie a chance. But she changed opinions quickly with birdies on the first, fourth and eighth holes to take a three-shot lead on Lopez. Carner had faded from contention.

The crowd went crazy, however, when Lopez sank birdie putts on the 10th and 11th holes to close within a shot again. The drama lessened somewhat when Lopez suffered a bogey, while Haynie sank a six-foot birdie putt on No. 12 to extend her lead to three again. The drama ended on an ironic note when the two reached No. 16, a 331-yard par four. Haynie hooked her drive, which appeared destined to stop deep in the rough. But the ball struck the arm of a Lopez follower and stayed just in the fairway. She went on to drop an eight-foot birdie putt, while Lopez missed the green and took another bogey to give Haynie a five-shot margin with two holes to play.

'I'm not disappointed for myself that I didn't win,' said Lopez with tears in her eyes. 'But I'm disappointed for the people of the city, whom I love dearly. I wanted to win it for them and I felt I let them down a little bit.'

Haynie had rounds of 72–68–69–67 for a 12-under-par 276, worth $30,000. After three 70s, Lopez had a closing 72 to tie Hollis Stacy (69 on the last round) for second at 282. Carner, who had led Haynie by five shots after opening rounds of 67 and 68, slipped to rounds of 75 and 73 for fourth place at 283. And Jan Stephenson, after winning the previous two events, set a course record of 66 in the final round to take fifth at 284.

Peter Jackson Classic — $200,000
Winner: Sandra Haynie

Only a fortunate few can be a success at two careers. Sandra Haynie is among the fortunate and, in her case, both careers centered around playing golf. She capped the second career on the Fourth of July by winning the Peter Jackson Classic, one of the LPGA's major events. Haynie, 39, began her first career in 1961. It lasted 16 years and included 39 victories before injuries forced her into a premature retirement that lasted four years. Career No. 2 began last year with one victory and blossomed this season with consecutive wins at Rochester and the Peter Jackson at St. George's Golf and Country Club in Toronto. The Jackson win was her fourth major and 42nd career title, moving her past Patty Berg into fourth place on the all-time LPGA victory list.

'I was afraid that the pin had gotten to my balloon,' said Haynie. 'But, right now, I feel as if I'm playing as good as any time in my life. Winning on a tough course, against a class field, is what every player strives for.'

It was not easy. Haynie had to make a curling, 10-foot par putt on the final hole to avoid a playoff with deadly Beth Daniel. Haynie had solid rounds of 71–71–70–68 for an eight-under-par 289 to edge Daniel by a stroke for the $30,000 first-place prize. JoAnne Carner and Donna Caponi tied for third at 283. Nancy Lopez finished in a tie for ninth at 290 but was thrilled anyway. She recorded the first hole-in-one of her six-year professional career.

The first-round thrills and lead belonged to Daniel, who shot 67. Then the Canadian crowd became excited when their own Sandra Post took a three-shot lead at the midway point on rounds of 70–69. Post entered the tournament just 69th on the money list because of back problems that have thrown her into the worst slump of her 14-year career. And her back went out with three holes left in the third round as she finished triple-bogey, bogey, bogey before a sympathetic audience for a 77. She limped home on the final day with an 81.

Nothing was wrong with Haynie on the final day. After playing the front in one under, she birdied Nos. 11 and 13, both par-fives, to take a three-shot lead. But Daniel rallied with birdies on Nos. 15 and 16 to close within one shot. Then she cost herself a playoff chance by missing a four-foot birdie putt on No. 17, allowing Haynie to avoid the risk of sudden death by sinking that tough, 10-foot twister on the last hole.

West Virginia Classic — $125,000
Winner: Hollis Stacy

Golf fans around Wheeling love the West Virginia Classic because they can always count on a playoff. Hollis Stacy loves the Speidel Golf Club course because she usually can count on winning. And Kathy Postlewait is weary of losing playoffs and losing to Stacy. Like it or not, the 1982 Classic followed the usual script as Stacy defeated Postlewait on the first hole of a playoff for $18,750 and her third win of the season. Stacy won the year before in a playoff against Postlewait, Penny Pulz, Alice Ritzman and Susie McAllister.

Fans have come to expect it as this was the fourth straight West Virginia Classic to be determined by a playoff. Postlewait is beginning to hate the sudden-death affairs. Never a tournament winner in nine years on the Tour, she has lost the two playoffs here to Stacy plus one to Patty Sheehan in Orlando earlier in 1982. Postlewait caused this playoff by sinking birdie putts on the final two holes of regulation play in the 54-hole event to catch Stacy at seven-under-par 209. But she was never out of trouble on the first playoff hole, traveling from behind a tree to inside a bunker to just the fringe of the green, two-putting for a bogey. Stacy two-putted for a regulation par and victory.

'When I got here last year, I was like a swimmer in quicksand,' said Stacy. 'Victory was a lifesaver. If you can play Speidel, you can play anywhere.'

Many of the tour's stars skipped the three days on the rolling public course designed by Trent Jones. But that was forgotten once the event began and comely Janet Coles took the lead with a 69. Stacy took command after two rounds of 71–66, going into the final round with a one-shot lead on Postlewait and Cathy Morse. Thirteen players were within six shots of the lead with 18 holes to play. Stacy bogeyed the first hole on the final day, allowing Postlewait to move up with two quick birdies. But two bogeys came almost as quickly on the front, allowing beautiful Cathy Reynolds to hold the lead briefly at the turn. While everyone else started to fade, however, Stacy played the back nine in two under par for an even-par 72 and 209. Postlewait closed with her two birdies for a 71 to tie. Morse and Alice Miller finished a shot out at 210, while Reynolds was fifth at 211.

Mayflower Classic — $200,000
Winner: Sally Little

Normally, Sally Little wins by making an incredible rally at the end to pass the field. Perhaps that's why she hardly knew how to finish in the Mayflower Classic as she uncomfortably coasted to a five-shot victory over Beth Daniel on rounds of 71–66–70–68 for a 13-under-par 275. Little, the 30-year-old native South African who passed her U.S. citizenship test a few weeks before, had a six-shot lead with nine holes to play on the Country Club of Indianapolis

(Indiana) course. She had to chip-and-putt five times on the back nine to shoot an even-par 36. 'I started aggressively,' said Little after her fourth 'win of the year. 'But then I started missing some greens and had to get up and down all day on the back nine. My putter saved me.' She used just 22 putts in her closing 68.

The final round began as a shootout between Little and Sandra Haynie, who were tied for the lead and five shots ahead of anybody else. Haynie birdied the first hole but then quickly bogeyed three holes, three-putting each of them, as her putter doomed her. 'I birdied the first hole and I birdied the last,' said Haynie. 'In between, it was murder.' Meanwhile, Little birdied three of the first four holes to quickly pull away. While Daniel, who started the last round eight shots back, could never hope to catch Little, she put on a show. She eagled the first hole with a 20-foot putt and went on to shoot a seven-under 65 to take second place at 280.

'I felt really competitive toward Sandra for seven holes and then she kind of let go,' said Little, who had to endure a 95-minute rain delay before she could collect her $30,000. 'Then I looked at the board and saw Beth was seven under. It shocked me.' Perhaps, but the shock was hardly enough to matter. Haynie struggled in with a 75 but still took third at 282, seven behind Little and two behind Daniel. Donna Caponi and Amy Alcott shot non-contending 72s to tie for fifth at 284 as the field geared up for what would be a real shock outcome in the U.S. Open the following week.

U.S. Open — $175,400
Winner: Janet Alex

United States Open golf tournaments, whether for male or female, have always lived up to the democratic principles inherent in the name. You do not have to be a superstar to win. You do not even have to be a previous winner. And in the grand tradition of the U.S. Open, Janet Alex rose from relative obscurity to claim one of the major titles of 1982.

Going into the final round at the Del Paso Country Club in Sacramento, Beth Daniel led JoAnne Carner by one stroke. The final twosome was a classic match of two generations of golfing excellence. And their motivation could not have been greater. Daniel, for all her quick success, had yet to win a 'major' tournament, while Carner was still trying for that 35th win to gain her long overdue admission into the LPGA Hall of Fame. What about Alex? At age 26, she was in her fifth season on the Tour and still looking for her first win. Perhaps there was a clue to her performance in that she charged on the final round of the LPGA Championship to finish in a tie for third. But even though she was just two shots behind Daniel going into the final 18 holes, she was lost in the ballyhoo around the Carner–Daniel shootout.

When the smoke cleared, however, it was Alex who had shot the Open's lowest round of 68 to win by an incredible six shots over Daniel, Carner, Sandra Haynie and Donna White — all former USGA champions. For the record, Alex had rounds of 70–73–72–68 for a five-under-par 283, meaning she was also the only competitor to break par for the week.

Carner had shot an opening 69 to lead by a stroke, then led by three after a second-round 70. But she slipped to 75 in the third round, allowing Daniel to take the front-runner position after three 71s. Another 71 or better would have made Daniel the first woman to shoot below par in all four rounds of an U.S. Open. Daniel began as if it would be no problem, making birdies on the first and third holes to take a three-shot lead on Carner. Alex, playing just ahead of the favored twosome, had birdied the same two holes to stay within two shots of Daniel but nobody really noticed. After seven holes, Carner had fought back to be just a shot behind Daniel, while Alex was still two back.

Daniel will never forget No. 8, a 511-yard par five. As she addressed a 10-foot birdie putt, the ball moved. Nobody else saw it, but she immediately called a one-stroke penalty on herself, then missed the putt for a bogey. 'It just shows you what a fine person Beth is,' said Carner. 'She never really recovered from that.' Daniel just gradually faded after that, shooting a 76. Alex now had her chance and didn't waste it. She birdied No. 9 from five feet to take the lead for the first time. Carner didn't quit, however. She birdied Nos. 10 and 12, while Alex bogeyed No. 11 to give Carner a brief, one-shot lead. Momentum swung back to Alex on No. 13, which she birdied and Carner bogeyed. Another bird on No. 15 gave Alex a two-shot lead.

The final four holes at Del Paso are the toughest on the course and absolutely the last place where you would want to play catch-up. Carner had no choice and tried to gamble. The result was a bogey on all four holes, allowing Alex to stroll down the 18th fairway knowing her first victory was the U.S. Open. Carner finished with a 75, one shot better than Daniel. Haynie shot 71 and White 72 to move into the tie for second. Susie McAllister was sixth, another four shots back at 293. Nancy Lopez, Vicki Tabor and Carole Jo Callison tied for seventh at 294. Besides the closing 68 by Alex, Lopez was the only golfer to break 70 on the final day with a three-under 69.

Columbia Savings Classic — $200,000
Winner: Beth Daniel

One week earlier, in the U.S. Open, Beth Daniel had led by one stroke going into the final round but let victory slip away with a closing 76. Proving that kind of play would not become a habit, she shot a final 64 in the Columbia Savings Classic to catch and pass Sally Little for her fourth win of the year. Little, known now as 'Sunday Sal' because of her frequent charges in the final round, seemed in a solid position. Three rounds of 68–69–72 had given her a two-shot lead on Patty Sheehan, Sandra Haynie and Pat Bradley, plus a three-stroke advantage over Daniel. And Little, with four wins already, practically owned Sundays. 'They call me the "Sunday Gal". I love Sundays,' she said. 'It's a day of do or die. It's competition at its highest.'

Nobody had to tell Daniel after her collapse the week before. And she knew she was playing well after rounds of 72–68–72 at the mile-high Columbine Country Club in Denver, Colorado. Everything was working perfectly except her putter. The putter woke up Sunday. Daniel came out swinging, scoring six birds for a six-under 30 on the front side. At the turn, she had a three-shot lead on Little and Sheehan. A bogey on No. 11 was only a momentary delay as

Daniel birdied four of the next five holes to clinch the win despite a bogey on No. 17.

Daniel finished at 276, 12 under par, to collect $30,000. The real frustration belonged to Sheehan, who shot 67 but had to settle for second at 278, worth $19,600. Little shot 71 and took third at 280. She had some consolation in that her check for $14,000 was just enough to make her the first LPGA player to top $200,000 and the earliest to break that barrier in Tour history.

Boston Five Classic — $175,000
Winner: Sandra Palmer

One of the finest aspects of golf tournaments is how often they provide a heart-warming lesson in courage defeating adversity. The Boston Five Classic was blessed with two such stories concerning winner Sandra Palmer and runnerup Terri Moody.

For Palmer, 41, the victory provided the confidence to continue one of the great careers in LPGA history. She had not won in 18 months and admitted 1982 probably would have been her final season if not for the win at the Radisson Ferncroft Hotel and Country Club course in suburban Danvers, Massachusetts. 'I've been close to quitting a lot of times in the last two years,' said Palmer after winning on rounds of 74–67–71–69 for a seven-under-par 281. 'But now I feel I've enjoyed playing this year more than ever.'

And don't cry for rookie Terri Moody. Even though she finished a stroke behind Palmer, her mere presence was a triumph in itself. On May 18, her boyfriend Mick Luckhurst, the Atlanta Falcons' placekicker in the National Football League, was driving Moody to the Atlanta airport when they were in an accident. Moody had to spend eight hours in surgery and required 180 sutures to close the wounds on her body. The worst was the left side of her face, which was torn open from the front to her ear. Less than three months after the accident, Moody was back on the tour, playing in her 10th event as a professional and fighting Palmer for victory all the way.

M.J. Smith took the first-round lead with a 68, six shots ahead of Palmer. But Palmer's 67 in the second round placed her in a leading tie with Jane Blalock, Muffin Spencer-Devlin and Vivian Brownlee. Palmer shot 71 and Moody shot 70 on Saturday to tie Judy Clark, who shot 67, for the lead going into the last 18 holes. The final day was a Palmer-Moody battle all the way. With three holes to play, they were tied and facing a 156-yard, uphill par three. Palmer two-putted for par, while Moody put her tee shot in a bunker and then missed a five-foot par putt. That proved to be the difference as Palmer birdied No. 17 from five feet for a two-shot edge. Moody never gave up, however, as her 91-yard wedge on the last hole missed being an eagle by six inches.

There were no losers in Boston.

WUI Classic — $125,000
Winner: Beth Daniel

One trait of a true star is the capacity to be awesome. Beth Daniel has that capacity and demonstrated it in the WUI Classic when she coasted to her fifth victory of the season, shooting a closing 73 and still winning by eight shots over Martha Hansen and Japan's Ayako Okamoto.

Obviously, Daniel won in the first three rounds. After shooting 68–68–67 on the long Meadow Brook Club course in Long Island, New York, Daniel had a seven-shot lead over Diane Dailey, who closed with an unfortunate 80. 'Momentum seems to be in my favor,' observed Daniel going into the last round. She had two bogeys and one birdie in the first five holes of the final round, then decided playing for par was the smartest course of action. And she proceded to par the last 13 holes, while everyone else fought for second. Even Daniel admitted to watching the leader boards on the back nine to see how the fight for second was going.

'Both Martha and Ayako are good players,' said Daniel. 'Ayako is the best in Japan and I know Martha is going to get a taste of victory soon if she keeps up her progress.' This time, however, Hansen had to settle for a taste of second as she shot a closing 69 and Okamoto a 68 to tie at 284. As for Daniel, tournament-sponsoring Western Union International admitted it had made out the first-place check of $18,750 in the name of Beth Daniel — on the night before the final round.

Chevrolet World Championship of Women's Golf — $150,000
Winner: JoAnne Carner

It is common for an athlete to feel honored by winning a prestigious event. But there are times, too, when the event feels honored to have been won by a prestigious athlete. So it is that every person connected with the Chevrolet World Championship of Women's Golf will never forget that JoAnne Carner made LPGA history here.

As Carner reached the final green to a standing ovation by a gallery of more than 15,000, best in the tournament's three-year history, she stopped long enough to hug the Waterford crystal trophy that sat in a display case next to the fairway. The symbolism was obvious. By winning the World Championship, her 35th career LPGA victory, Carner had created a display case of her own that will be shown for all time in the LPGA Hall of Fame. 'If you could write the script, you'd like to do it the way I did, by winning here,' said Carner. 'Most of the time, I don't play well in the prestige events. It was a hard, tough victory with all the pressure that surrounds it. It's one victory I'll remember for a long time.'

Carner shot steady rounds of 72–70–71–71 for a four-under-par 284 to take the first-place prize of $50,000. And with that check, she also broke the LPGA's single-season, money-winning record of $231,000, set by Beth Daniel (when she won here, too) in 1980. The victory placed Carner at $248,109, well on her way to the new record of $310,400 she established at the end of the season.

By finishing second, Ayako Okamoto of Japan, gave the tournament cause for pride, too, because she proved it is truly a World Championship. She shot a one-over-par 289, worth $26,000, at the demanding Shaker Heights Country Club in suburban Cleveland.

As always, the field consisted of 12 of the world's best women golfers. Amy Alcott was third at 290, while Jan Stephenson and Patty Sheehan tied for fourth at 292. Tied for sixth at 294 were Hollis Stacy and Janet Alex, while Sandra Haynie was eighth at 297. Nancy Lopez finished next at 298, followed by amateur Marta Figueras Dotti at 302. Daniel, who had won the first two World Championships, never got started in her defense and finished at 304, one shot ahead of Sally Little.

'After the first day I played here,' said Daniel, 'I predicted Carner would win because she's the only player in the field strong enough to get out of the rough.'

Carner, who set the course record for women with a 66 on the final round of 1981, was a wire-to-wire winner in 1982 on the 6,225-yard, Donald Ross-designed course. She and Stacy shared the first-round lead with even-par 72, marking the first round in tournament history that no player has broken par.

While it was windy the first day, rain fell on the second as did most of Carner's competition. With three straight birds from Nos. 12 to 14, she shot a 70 to pull one shot ahead of Alcott, who shot 69 and praised the greens. 'The minute the ball comes off the blade,' said Alcott, 'you know if you've made the putt or not.'

More wind in the third round bothered everyone except Carner, who shot 71 and opened up a five-shot lead on Alcott after her 75. Okamoto provided some drama early in the fourth round, however, when she shot a two-under 33 on the front and pulled within two shots of Carner. But Big Momma rose to the challenge with birds on Nos. 11, 12, 14 and 17 before taking that unforgettable walk down the last fairway into the Hall of Fame.

'It makes for a good obituary,' laughed Carner, who then sipped champagne and added with a gentle smile, 'It's a wonderful feeling. I'm happy, very happy.' And the first lady to earn her way into the Hall of Fame since 1977 was exactly where she belonged — at the top of the best in the world.

Henredon Classic — $165,000
Winner: JoAnne Carner

JoAnne Carner won her way into the LPGA Hall of Fame the week before by winning the Chevrolet World Championship of Women's Golf. Instead of an ending, that turned out to be just the beginning of an emotional string of victories. The second was the hardest as Carner had hold off another Hall of Famer, Sandra Haynie, through five playoff holes before winning the second Henredon Classic in High Point, North Carolina.

'Last week was the greatest win; this was the hardest,' said Carner, who had to battle Haynie, a severe cold and a mental letdown after her historic Chevrolet World Championship victory. 'But I never quit. I'd have to die to withdraw.'

Haynie, who began one of golf's great comebacks by winning the initial Henredon in 1982, never quit either. But an unplanned dive into a water hazard led to her defeat. Haynie's drive on the fifth playoff hole at the Willow

Creek Golf Club almost rolled into a pond. She took a baseball swing to hit her next shot, resulting in a half gainer into the water. 'When I took that dive, I lost both my concentration and composure,' said Haynie. 'It's hard to concentrate when you're sloshing up the fairway and you're wet up to your . . . waist.' Haynie, her ball short of the green, fluffed her approach, then was too strong with the next and had to sink a 15-foot putt for a bogey.

Meanwhile, Carner was on the green in regulation, sitting 12 feet short of a bird. She easily two-putted for victory and another $24,750 added onto her No. 1 money standing. Haynie collected $16,170. Haynie thought she had won on the second playoff hole when she made a three-foot putt for a birdie. But Carner, who had hit a tree with her drive and then flew the green, pitched 64 feet downhill for a bird of her own. 'That's when I began to get the message,' said Haynie.

Spectators were calling it the Hayniedon Classic after Haynie shot a nine-birdie, one-bogey 64 in the second round for a two-shot lead over Hollis Stacy. Four shots back with two rounds left, Carner cut two shots each day from Haynie's lead to force the playoff. Stacy, Kathy Whitworth and Janet Coles finished one shot out at 283, while Nancy Lopez and Patti Rizzo tied for sixth at 284.

Rail Charity Classic — $125,000
Winner: JoAnne Carner

While the Chevrolet World Championship was the greatest and the Henredon Classic the hardest, the Rail Charity Classic was the easiest as JoAnne Carner continued her winning binge for the third straight week. Shooting the lowest 54-hole total of the LPGA season, a 14-under-par 202, she ran away with a six-shot victory.

Entering the final round with a three-shot lead, Carner was her own worst enemy for a while. Even though no other player was making a move, she cut her own lead to one shot with a bogey on the 10th hole. As it turned out, that bogey may have been responsible for the win as she birdied six of the next seven holes. 'I couldn't really get fired up until I bogeyed No. 10,' said Carner. 'Then I got mad at myself and started making some birdies. A lot of times you have to excite yourself, and I wasn't doing anything exciting.'

The excitement began with a short birdie putt on No. 11. Then she kept on going through the 17th hole, her only par on No. 14 when she narrowly missed a 12-foot birdie try. If she had made it, she would have tied Carol Mann's all-time record of seven straight birdies. As it was, Carner 'settled' for her third straight win, fifth of the season, 37th of her career and second straight at the Rail Golf Club in Springfield, Illinois. Her check of $18,750 placed her seasonal winnings at $291,609 and put her on the brink of becoming the first woman to win $300,000 in a season on the LPGA Tour.

'Don't ask me about $300,000,' laughed Carner. 'I just got rid of worrying about making the Hall of Fame and now you're trying to give me something else to worry about.' Carner announced that she was going to spend the next two weeks fishing in Alaska with her husband, Don, which must have been good news for the rest of the Tour players. Now they could start shooting for something other than second.

Carner's rounds of 69–66–67 at the Rail prevented anyone else from thinking about first. Susie McAllister took second at 208. Jo Ann Washam opened the tournament by tying the season's low round of 64 and held on to tie Cathy Morse for third at 209.

Mary Kay Classic — $155,000
Winner: Sandra Spuzich

With JoAnne Carner 'gone fishin',' 45-year-old Sandra Spuzich added to her own footnote in LPGA history. When she won the Corning Classic in May, she became the oldest player to ever win an LPGA event. And she was four months older when she became the oldest player to win two tournaments in one season with a victory in the Mary Kay Classic at the Bent Tree Country Club in Dallas.

Amazingly, in a career that began in 1962 and includes winning the USGA Women's Open in 1966, this was the first season that Spuzich had earned more than one win. Instead of thinking of her age as a handicap she felt it was the key to her success. 'Now I know how to keep my wits and I've learned how to score,' said Spuzich. 'I know what my nerves are going to do to me under extreme pressure. You learn to enjoy that feeling of tautness because it means you are in contention. And that beats going out and working for a check.'

There was more than enough pressure in the last round of the Mary Kay. Spuzich shot a closing 67 after rounds of 70–69 for a 10-under 206, barely holding off the charge of 26-year-old Carole Charbonnier. Born in the African Congo and living in Switzerland, Charbonnier has won junior national championships in France, Spain and Switzerland, along with the amateur championship of Switzerland. Charbonnier, who has been bothered by injuries since she joined the LPGA Tour in 1980, shot a closing 68 to finish second at 207.

Finishing a disappointed third at 209 was 24-year-old Chris Johnson. She took the first-round lead with a 66, made easy by some incredible drives including one measured at 328 yards. The former collegiate All-American shot a 69 in the second round, stretching her lead to three strokes. But she couldn't make a putt in the final round and faded to a 74, while Spuzich taught her that good things do come to those who wait.

Portland Ping Team Championship — $120,000
Winners: Sandra Haynie and Kathy McMullen

As Sandra Haynie poured champagne on her head, Kathy McMullen just sat there and grinned. After all, nobody ever gets doused with champagne immediately after losing. It's the drink (and shampoo?) of champions and McMullen, along with partner Haynie, had just won the Portland Ping Team Championship. It was McMullen's first victory in 13 years on the LPGA Tour. 'Actually, 'said McMullen, wiping the champagne out of her eyes, 'it feels awfully good. I see no reason why I can't have the same positive feelings now when I play alone. My problems have been mostly tension, being uptight.'

'I hope this helps Kathy's career,' said Haynie, no stranger to success. 'Getting that first victory is a hurdle but, once you get over it, there can be more.' Haynie should know. She entered the team tournament at Columbia-Edgewater Country Club in Portland, Oregon, as the second leading winner of the year. And the Hall of Famer had 42 individual titles in 21 years on the Tour.

McMullen entered 102nd on the money list and with no career wins. But she was the one who actually predicted victory after the first round. 'I felt different than I'd ever felt before,' she said. 'I just knew I was going to play well and, of course, I knew that Sandy always plays well.'

McMullen was right. In three rounds of best-ball play, McMullen had 12 birdies and Haynie 11 to shoot a 20-under-par 196 for a two-shot win over the teams of Sharon Barrett–Nancy Rubin and Lori Garbacz–Patti Rizzo. On rounds of 67–64–65, each winner earned $10,800. Three teams tied for fourth at 200. They were Nancy Lopez and Jo Ann Washam, Chris Johnson and Robin Walton, and Donna Caponi and Kathy Whitworth, the annual favorites here. In the six years of the tournament's existence, Caponi and Whitworth have won three times and never finished worse than fifth.

But this was Haynie and McMullen's week. They trailed by two shots after the first round, then just a shot after the second. They took the lead for good on the third hole of the final round when McMullen sank a 15-foot birdie putt. Garbacz and Rizzo stayed within one shot until the 17th, when McMullen sank a 20-foot birdie for a two-shot lead with one to play.

Safeco Classic — $175,000
Winner: Patty Sheehan

It was hometown heroine JoAnne Carner that the 34,000 fans turned out to see in the inaugural Safeco Classic in Kent, Washington, 20 miles outside of Seattle. But it was pert Patty Sheehan who took the first Safeco championship and captured at least part of the admiration of the crowd.

Carner's presence made the tournament a success. After two weeks of hauling in salmon in Alaska with her husband, Don, she was back on the tournament trail trying to extend her string of three victories in her last three events. Counting Safeco, there were three tournaments left in the LPGA season, just enough time to break the seemingly unbreakable record of five straight wins set by Nancy Lopez in 1978.

And despite near exhaustion from the salmon fishing, Carner would have had her fourth straight win — except for Sheehan, the 1981 Rookie of the Year. Sheehan had rounds of 68–69–69–70 for a 12-under-par 276, one shot better than Carner. The win was worth $26,250 for Sheehan, while Carner took $17,150, not a bad catch itself. Carner did have the satisfaction of becoming the first woman golfer to earn more than $300,000 in an official season, hitting $308,759.

Playing at the Meridian Valley Country Club, Donna White and rookie Cindy Lincoln shared the first-round lead with 67 each, while Sheehan and Carner were a shot back. Kathy Whitworth took the midway lead with 69–67, while Sheehan held her position and Carner fell three shots off the pace. But a

67 by Carner and 69 by Sheehan put them into a tie for first after the third round, setting the stage for the fourth.

And with one hole to play, they were still tied for the lead. But, despite the encouragement of the crowd, it was obvious that Carner was struggling. Carner hit a fat wedge that buried into a greenside bunker, while Sheehan was on the fringe for an easy two-putt par. Carner's blast sailed 20 feet past the pin and she had to make the putt to send the twosome into overtime. She didn't make it.

One victory string had ended — and another had begun.

Inamori Classic — $150,000
Winner: Patty Sheehan

Pretty Patty Sheehan had won the previous week's Safeco Classic by beating JoAnne Carner in Carner's home town. Considering that the final Tour event in the United States was the Inamori Classic in San Jose, California, which happens to be Sheehan's adopted home town, it was no wonder that she was the favorite to win. And she didn't let her fans down, shooting 277 for her second straight win and third of the season.

After shooting 68–69–69–70 the week before for a 12-under-par 276, Sheehan displayed stunning consistency by adding rounds of 69–70–69–69 for a 15-under 277 on the par 73 Almaden Golf Club in San Jose. And her consistent checks of $26,250 and $22,500 boosted her into fourth place on the money list at $223,032 in just her second complete season.

Just as she had done the week before, Sheehan seemed content to sit back just behind the leaders until the race was in the back stretch. Beth Daniel and amateur Juli Inkster shared the first-round lead at 68, while Sheehan was a shot back. Sandra Haynie took the lead in the second round at 70–67, while Sheehan was two shots behind. The young star made her move in the third round when four straight birdies gave her another 69 and a three-shot lead on Joyce Kazmierski. And that's exactly how it finished as both shot 69 in the fourth round to maintain the three-shot difference. Dale Eggeling took third at 282, two shots behind Kazmierski.

Mazda Classic — $200,000
Winner: Nancy Lopez

Nancy Lopez was not happy with the 1982 LPGA season even though she realized it was a year of adjustment for her, both on and off the course. But prospects for 1983 became considerably brighter when she easily won the Mazda Classic in Japan, the last official event of the 1982 season.

Lopez was at her best on the Meishin Yokaichi Country Club course in Kibjauchi, leading all the way. It was vintage Lopez as she shot 66–70–71 for a nine-under-par 207 and six-shot win over Amy Alcott, her only real competitor. After two 69s, Alcott was just two shots behind Lopez going into the final round but soared to a 75 on the final day, allowing Lopez to coast home.

The $30,000 victory was the second of the season for Lopez. She finished seventh on the money list, just $3,000 behind Alcott. A fine finish for most, but still not satisfying for Lopez. A weight loss of 30 pounds altered her golf swing, along with intensifying her already immense appeal on the Tour. And a divorce was followed in late October by marriage to Ray Knight, third baseman for the Houston Astros of the National baseball League. Then came the Mazda victory as a fitting wedding present from Nancy to herself — as a promise for the future.

Lopez was not the only golfer to find year-end success at Mazda. Beth Daniel finished third at 214 but was the biggest financial winner of the week. She birdied the final hole to edge JoAnne Carner for first in the 34-tournament Mazda Series. The Series win was worth $125,000 to Daniel.

A few weeks earlier, Daniel was a surprise winner in the J&B Gold Putter competition in Las Vegas, beating Carner in the championship round. That extracuricular win was worth $50,000 for Daniel. Still, nothing or nobody could detract from the season that Carner will remember as her greatest — at least to date. Five victories, including the World Championship win that put her into the LPGA Hall of Fame, plus an all-time seasonal money-earning record of $310,400.

And with the Mixed Team Championship to be played, the fun for Carner wasn't quite over in 1982.

JC Penney Mixed Team Classic — $500,000
Winners: JoAnne Carner and John Mahaffey.

JoAnne Carner had never had any luck just keeping a partner, much less winning in the JC Penney Mixed Team Classic that ends each season on an unofficial but rich note. And she considered not even playing in 1982 when her scheduled partner, Raymond Floyd, pulled out to seek a fortune in the Sun City Challenge in Africa. Carner couldn't blame Floyd, especially considering he won. Besides, she found John Mahaffey.

'Who needs Raymond Floyd?' said Carner after she and Mahaffey shot a 20-under-par 268 on rounds of 68–67–63–70 to win the Mixed Team by a shot over Hollis Stacy and Jay Haas. 'John told me before the tournament that he was going to keep me laughing and relaxed all week. I told him the only thing that keeps me feeling like that is a lot of birdies. He made them, too.'

For Carner, the check for $46,500 was a pleasant addition to her record breaking year. Her official earnings were an all-time record of $310,400, while her total earnings for the season were somewhere around $430,000, certainly an all-time record, too.

For Mahaffey, the identical check for $46,500 was a salvation as he had won just $77,047 on the men's Tour to finish 56th. He candidly told the media that his problems on the course had been caused by a drinking problem off the course. It's a problem he no longer has.

A major problem for both Carner and Mahaffey was finding a way to win at the Bardmoor Country Club in Largo, Florida. Their opening 68 left them three shots behind the teams of Carole Charbonnier and Leonard Thompson and Lynn Adams and Chi Chi Rodriguez. The spectators were supporting Rodriguez, who had finished 182nd on the men's list with $7,119 in earnings. 'The year was so bad that the Internal Revenue Service sent me a get-well card,' said Rodriguez.

Four teams were tied for the midway lead at 133, while Carner and Mahaffey were in a tie for sixth place, two shots back. That's when they unleashed their nine-under-par 63 to take a three-shot lead going into the final round. They still had a two-shot edge on Stacy and Haas going into the final hole — and almost were forced into overtime. Carner made a tricky three-foot par putt, while Stacy's chip for an eagle three missed by just inches, leaving her one shot short.

Special mention should go to Betsy King, teamed with Ed Fiori. Just before the tournament began, she was giving a lesson and was hit in the head by a nine-year-old's club. King needed 30 sutures to close the wound but teamed with Fiori to finish third at 271.

APPENDIXES

World Money List

This listing of the 200 leading money winners in the world of professional golf in 1982 was compiled from the results of all tournaments carried in the Appendixes of this edition, along with such other non-tour and international events for which accurate figures could be obtained and in which the players competed for prize money provided by someone other than the competitors themselves. In the 17 years during which World Money Lists have been compiled, the earnings of the player in the 200th position have risen from a total of $3,326 in 1966 to $40,064 in 1982. Raymond Floyd's $738,699 in 1982 was a new high. The top 200 players in 1966 earned a total of $4,680,287. In 1982, the comparable total was $23,363,579.

Because of the unsettled state of money throughout the world in 1982, it was necessary to determine an average value of non-American currency to U.S. dollars to prepare this listing. The conversion rates are: British pound = US$1.70; South African rand = US$1.02; Australian dollar = US$1.00; 245 Japanese yen = US$1.00; New Zealand dollar = US$.75.

POS.	PLAYER, COUNTRY	TOTAL MONEY
1	Ray Floyd, U.S.	$738,699
2	Craig Stadler, U.S.	664,372
3	Calvin Peete, U.S.	455,140
4	Lanny Wadkins, U.S.	445,227
5	Tom Watson, U.S.	417,048
6	Tom Kite, U.S.	400,018
7	Jerry Pate, U.S.	380,759
8	Bob Gilder, U.S.	372,387
9	Severiano Ballesteros, Spain	352,312
10	Jack Nicklaus, U.S.	321,052
11	Scott Hoch, U.S.	319,019
12	Wayne Levi, U.S.	311,903
13	Curtis Strange, U.S.	293,209
14	Tsuneyuki Nakajima, Japan	287,202
15	Jay Haas, U.S.	274,966
16	Johnny Miller, U.S.	262,853
17	Isao Aoki, Japan	255,771
18	Hal Sutton, U.S.	252,903
19	Bruce Lietzke, U.S.	233,264
20	Bobby Clampett, U.S.	232,877
21	Hsieh Min Nan, Taiwan	231,293
22	Bob Shearer, Australia	227,759
23	Greg Norman, Australia	226,059
24	Larry Nelson, U.S.	215,533
25	Andy Bean, U.S.	212,986
26	Masahiro Kuramoto, Japan	194,303
27	Graham Marsh, Australia	191,363
28	George Burns, U.S.	190,114
29	Hale Irwin, U.S.	189,233
30	Miller Barber, U.S.	187,678
31	Peter Jacobsen, U.S.	183,850
32	Tom Weiskopf, U.S.	183,657

POS.	PLAYER, COUNTRY	TOTAL MONEY
33	Kikuo Arai, Japan	178,886
34	Teruo Sugihara, Japan	178,259
35	Don January, U.S.	177,684
36	Bill Rogers, U.S.	172,839
37	Nick Faldo, Great Britain	171,420
38	Fuzzy Zoeller, U.S.	161,484
39	Lee Trevino, U.S.	160,241
40	Sandy Lyle, Great Britain	160,209
41	Payne Stewart, U.S.	159,810
42	Scott Simpson, U.S.	159,579
43	Peter Oosterhuis, Great Britain	159,266
44	Ed Sneed, U.S.	152,933
45	Toru Nakamura, Japan	148,134
46	Norio Suzuki, Japan	146,753
47	Danny Edwards, U.S.	145,019
48	Yutaka Hagawa, Japan	143,953
49	Gil Morgan, U.S.	143,203
50	Tom Purtzer, U.S.	139,361
51	John Mahaffey, U.S.	136,672
52	David Graham, U.S.	132,920
53	Terry Gale, Australia	131,442
54	Sam Torrance, Great Britain	130,741
55	Mark McNulty, South Africa	128,441
56	Keith Fergus, U.S.	128,058
57	Jim Simons, U.S.	126,876
58	Arnold Palmer, U.S.	126,756
59	D.A. Weibring, U.S.	126,445
60	Bob Goalby, U.S.	120,974
61	Vance Heafner, U.S.	120,945
62	Gene Littler, U.S.	120,825
63	Dan Halldorson, Canada	117,105
64	Manuel Pinero, Spain	114,663
65	Saburo Fujiki, Japan	111,577
66	Gary Player, South Africa	110,844
67	Denis Watson, South Africa	108,826
68	Ed Fiori, U.S.	108,339
69	Chen Tze Ming, Taiwan	105,649
70	Bernhard Langer, West Germany	105,318
71	Akira Yabe, Japan	103,592
72	Billy Casper, U.S.	102,622
73	Brad Bryant, U.S.	102,418
74	Dan Pohl, U.S.	101,279
75	Jack Renner, U.S.	99,289
76	Gary Hallberg, U.S.	98,223
77	Bob Eastwood, U.S.	97,433
78	J.C. Snead, U.S.	96,756
79	Ian Woosnam, Great Britain	96,540
80	Steve Melnyk, U.S.	94,831
81	Hubert Green, U.S.	94,373
82	Bobby Wadkins, U.S.	93,945
83	Doug Tewell, U.S.	93,863
84	Naomichi Ozaki, Japan	93,794
85	Brian Waites, Great Britain	93,750
86	Shigeru Uchida, Japan	93,718
87	Andy North, U.S.	93,341
88	Frank Conner, U.S.	92,181
89	Fred Couples, U.S.	91,912
90	George Archer, U.S.	89,618

POS.	PLAYER, COUNTRY	TOTAL MONEY
91	Don Pooley U.S.	88,929
92	Dan Sikes, U.S.	85,706
93	Shinsaku Maeda, Japan	84,341
94	Jim Colbert, U.S.	83,646
95	Rex Caldwell, U.S.	83,502
96	Mike Reid, U.S.	82,767
97	Mark James, Great Britain	82,613
98	Hsu Sheng San, Taiwan	82,608
99	Jim Thorpe, U.S.	82,379
100	Fujio Kobayashi, Japan	82,369
101	Jose-Maria Canizares, Spain	80,924
102	Sam Snead, U.S.	80,041
103	Ben Crenshaw, U.S.	79,537
104	Bernard Gallacher, Great Britain	78,916
105	Roger Maltbie, U.S.	78,167
106	Bill Britton, U.S.	75,328
107	Gordon Brand, Jr, Great Britain	74,929
108	Tateo Ozaki, Japan	73,989
109	Ron Streck, U.S.	73,962
110	Lu Hsi Chuen, Taiwan	73,036
111	Des Smyth, Ireland	72,148
112	Morris Hatalsky, U.S.	71,146
113	Mark Lye, U.S.	71,033
114	John Bland, South Africa	69,503
115	Tom Jenkins, U.S.	69,253
116	Leonard Thompson, U.S.	68,787
117	Masashi Ozaki, Japan	68,160
118	Tommy Valentine, U.S.	67,759
119	Charles Coody, U.S.	66,737
120	Motomasa Aoki, Japan	66,397
121	Mike Holland, U.S.	66,310
122	Bob Charles, New Zealand	65,987
123	Tim Norris, U.S.	65,643
124	Nobomitsu Yuhara, Japan	65,550
125	Namio Takasu, Japan	65,336
126	Mark Pfeil, U.S.	64,883
127	Barry Jaeckel, U.S.	64,824
128	Pete Izumikawa, Japan	64,808
129	Yoshitaka Yamamoto, Japan	64,573
130	Tim Simpson, U.S.	63,753
131	Chip Beck, U.S.	63,721
132	Nick Price, Zimbabwe	62,677
133	Pat McGowan, U.S.	61,573
134	Seiichi Kanai, Japan	61,515
135	Art Wall, U.S.	61,025
136	Lon Hinkle, U.S.	59,956
137	Howard Twitty, U.S.	59,376
138	Bob Byman, U.S.	58,699
139	John Cook, U.S.	58,599
140	Dave Eichelberger, U.S.	58,233
141	Victor Regalado, Mexico	57,481
142	Stewart Ginn, Australia	57,029
143	Eamonn Darcy, Ireland	56,811
144	Ken Brown, Great Britain	55,827
145	Gay Brewer, U.S.	55,424
146	Jim Dent, U.S.	55,095
147	Lennie Clements, U.S.	54,796
148	Manuel Calero, Spain	54,189

POS.	PLAYER, COUNTRY	TOTAL MONEY
149	Woody Blackburn, U.S.	54,165
150	Bill Collins, U.S.	54,125
151	David Edwards, U.S.	54,035
152	John Adams, U.S.	54,014
153	Bob Rosburg, U.S.	53,746
154	Takashi Kurihara, Japan	53,723
155	Joe Inman, U.S.	53,683
156	Julius Boros, U.S.	53,537
157	Denny Hepler, U.S.	53,316
158	Koichi Inoue, Japan	53,278
159	Dow Finsterwald, U.S.	53,097
160	Yasuhiro Funatogawa, Japan	52,988
161	Thomas Gray, U.S.	52,574
162	John O'Leary, Ireland	52,177
163	Jim Booros, U.S.	51,933
164	Eitaro Deguchi, Japan	51,750
165	Larry Ziegler, U.S.	50,289
166	Jim Nelford, Canada	50,008
167	Antonio Garrido, Spain	49,846
168	Gary Koch, U.S.	49,727
169	Mark Hayes, U.S.	49,508
170	Tony Jacklin, Great Britain	48,984
171	Allen Miller, U.S.	48,301
172	Neil Coles, Great Britain	48,093
173	Hideto Shigenobu, Japan	47,373
174	Peter Thomson, Australia	46,891
175	Ian Mosey, Great Britain	46,653
176	Greg Powers, U.S.	46,148
177	Lou Graham, U.S.	46,042
178	Pat Lindsey, U.S.	45,979
179	Jack Newton, Australia	45,882
180	Mike McCullough, U.S.	45,407
181	Guy Wolstenholme, Australia	45,234
182	Teruo Suzumura, Japan	44,799
183	Lee Elder, U.S.	43,980
184	Gavin Levenson, South Africa	43,936
185	Koichi Uehara, Japan	43,721
186	Howie Johnson, U.S.	43,651
187	Pal Harney, U.S.	43,025
188	Bill Longmuir, Great Britain	42,576
189	Wayne Grady, Australia	42,494
190	Hugh Baiocchi, South Africa	42,232
191	Gibby Gilbert, U.S.	41,464
192	Satsuki Takahashi, Japan	41,261
193	Howard Clark, Great Britain	41,252
194	Clarence Rose, U.S.	41,075
195	Tommy Horton, Great Britain	41,022
196	Bob Toski, U.S.	40,650
197	Mike Clayton, Australia	40,629
198	Maurice Bembridge, Great Britain	40,117
199	Isao Isozaki, Japan	40,084
200	Al Geiberger, U.S.	40,064

World Stroke Averages List

The World Stroke Averages which follow were compiled from the results of all tournaments carried in this Appendix for the year 1982 with the exceptions of the match play and team events, senior tournaments and the LPGA Tour. It includes only those players who competed in at least 60 rounds during the year.

POS.	PLAYER	ROUNDS	STROKES	AVERAGE
1	Calvin Peete, U.S.	108	7,590	70.28
2	Curtis Strange, U.S.	113	7,964	70.48
3	Tom Kite, U.S.	111	7,833	70.57
4	Tom Watson, U.S.	92	6,496	70.61
5	Wayne Levi, U.S.	105	7,425	70.71
6	Scott Hoch, U.S.	112	7,931	70.81
T7	Raymond Floyd, U.S.	97	6,870	70.82
	Steve Melnyk, U.S.	83	5,878	70.82
9	Tsuneyuki Nakajima, Japan	113.5	8,047	70.90
T10	Peter Jacobsen, U.S.	107	7,587	70.91
	Severiano Ballesteros, Spain	86	6,098	70.91
12	Craig Stadler, U.S.	124	8,794	70.92
13	Sandy Lyle, Great Britain	113	8,016	70.94
T14	Andy Bean, U.S.	109	7,738	70.99
	Bob Gilder, U.S.	115	8,164	70.99
16	Jim Colbert, U.S.	94	6,674	71.00
17	Jay Haas, U.S.	116	8,238	71.02
T18	Jerry Pate, U.S.	90	6,393	71.03
	Johnny Miller, U.S.	78	5,540	71.03
	Nick Faldo, Great Britain	120	8,524	71.03
T21	Graham Marsh, Australia	95	6,753	71.08
	Bernard Gallacher, Great Britain	72	5,118	71.08
23	Scott Simpson, U.S.	105	7,465	71.10
24	Hal Sutton, U.S.	113	8,037	71.12
25	Jack Nicklaus, U.S.	64	4,553	71.14
26	Lanny Wadkins, U.S.	99	7,045	71.16
27	David Graham, Australia	93	6,622	71.20
28	Bobby Clampett, U.S.	112	7,976	71.21
29	Larry Nelson, U.S.	105	7,478	71.22
30	D.A. Weibring, U.S.	121	8,619	71.23
31	Bruce Lietzke, U.S.	105	7,480	71.24
32	Tom Purtzer, U.S.	116	8,267	71.27
33	Sam Torrance, Great Britain	115	8,198	71.29
34	Fuzzy Zoeller, U.S.	102	7,276	71.32
T35	George Burns, U.S.	122	8,702	71.33
	Jose-Maria Canizares, Spain	93	6,634	71.33
37	Gil Morgan, U.S.	96	6,849	71.34
38	J.C. Snead, U.S.	112	7,992	71.36
T39	Bob Eastwood, U.S.	113	8,069	71.41
	Dan Halldorson, Canada	99	7,070	71.41
41	Hale Irwin, U.S.	89	6,356	71.42
42	Brian Waites, Great Britain	96	6,858	71.44
43	George Archer, U.S.	118	8,431	71.45

POS.	PLAYER	ROUNDS	STROKES	AVERAGE
44	Greg Norman, Australia	96	6,860	71.46
45	Isao Aoki, Japan	135	9,654	71.51
46	Peter Oosterhuis, Great Britain	110	7,868	71.53
47	Chen Tze Ming, Taiwan	89	6,368	71.55
48	Ed Sneed, U.S.	108	7,730	71.57
49	Vance Heafner, U.S.	126	9,021	71.60
50	Bill Rogers, U.S.	108	7,736	71.63

Multiple Winners of 1982

PLAYER	WINS
Calvin Peete, U.S.	6
Graham Marsh, Australia	5
Tsuneyuki Nakajima, Japan	5
Teruo Sugihara, Japan	5
Craig Stadler, U.S.	4
Tom Watson, U.S.	4
Bob Gilder, U.S.	4
Raymond Floyd, U.S.	4
Mark McNulty, South Africa	4
Hsieh Min Nan, Taiwan	4
Terry Gale, Australia	4
Miller Barber, U.S.	4
Lanny Wadkins, U.S.	3
Payne Stewart, U.S.	3
Bob Shearer, Australia	3
Scott Hoch, U.S.	3
Severiano Ballesteros, Spain	3
Brian Waites, Great Britain	3
Greg Norman, Australia	3
Hsu Sheng San, Taiwan	3
Shigeru Uchida, Japan	3
Kikuo Arai, Japan	3
Don January, U.S.	3
Wayne Levi, U.S.	2
Hale Irwin, U.S.	2
Jay Haas, U.S.	2
Gary Hallberg, U.S.	2
Mark James, Great Britain	2
Bernard Gallacher, Great Britain	2
Gordon Brand Jr., Great Britain	2
Manuel Pinero, Spain	2
Sam Torrance, Great Britain	2
David Jagger, Great Britain	2
Chen Tze Ming, Taiwan	2
Masahiro Kuramoto, Japan	2
Norio Suzuki, Japan	2
Col Bishop, Australia	2
Mike Cahill, Australia	2
Arnold Palmer, U.S.	2
Bill Casper, U.S.	2

World's Winners of 1982

U.S. TOUR

Tucson Open	Craig Stadler
Bob Hope	Ed Fiori
Phoenix Open	Lanny Wadkins
San Diego Open	Johnny Miller
Bing Crosby	Jim Simons
Hawaiian Open	Wayne Levi
Los Angeles Open	Tom Watson
Doral Open	Andy Bean
Bay Hill Classic	Tom Kite
Inverrary Classic	Hale Irwin
Tournament Players Championship	Jerry Pate
Heritage Classic	Tom Watson
Greensboro Open	Danny Edwards
Masters	Craig Stadler
Magnolia Classic	Payne Stewart
Tournament of Champions	Lanny Wadkins
Tallahassee Open	Bob Shearer
USF&G (New Orleans) Classic	Scott Hoch
Byron Nelson	Bob Gilder
Houston Open	Ed Sneed
Colonial National Invitation	Jack Nicklaus
Atlanta Classic	Keith Fergus
Memorial Tournament	Raymond Floyd
Kemper Open	Craig Stadler
Memphis Classic	Raymond Floyd
U.S. Open Championship	Tom Watson
Westchester Classic	Bob Gilder
Western Open	Tom Weiskopf
Milwaukee Open	Calvin Peete
Quad Cities Open	Payne Stewart
Anheuser-Busch Classic	Calvin Peete
Canadian Open	Bruce Lietzke
PGA Championship	Raymond Floyd
Hartford Open	Tim Norris
Buick Open	Lanny Wadkins
World Series of Golf	Craig Stadler
B.C. Open	Calvin Peete
Bank of Boston Classic	Bob Gilder
Hall of Fame	Jay Haas
Southern Open	Bobby Clampett
Texas Open	Jay Haas
LaJet Classic	Wayne Levi
Pensacola Open	Calvin Peete
Walt Disney World Classic	Hall Sutton

EUROPEAN TOUR

Tunisian Open	Antonio Garrido
Madrid Open	Severiano Ballesteros

Italian Open	Mark James
French Open	Severiano Ballesteros
Martini International	Bernard Gallacher
Car Care Plan International	Brian Waites
PGA Championship	Tony Jacklin
Jersey Open	Bernard Gallacher
Dunlop Masters	Greg Norman
Coral Classic	Gordon Brand Jr.
Scandinavian Open	Bob Byman
State Express Classic	Greg Norman
British Open	Tom Watson
Lawrence Batley International	Sandy Lyle
German Open	Bernhard Langer
Dutch Open	Paul Way
Irish Open	John O'Leary
Benson & Hedges International	Greg Norman
Swiss Open	Ian Woosnam
European Open	Manuel Pinero
Hennessy Cognac Cup	Britain/Ireland (team)
	Mark James (individual)
Tournament Players Championship	Nick Faldo
Bob Hope British Classic	Gordon Brand Jr.
Spanish Open	Sam Torrance
Sanyo Open	Neil Coles
World Match Play Championship	Severiano Ballesteros
Lancome Trophy	David Graham
Johnnie Walker Trophy	Peter Jacobsen
Portuguese Open	Sam Torrance

AFRICAN TOURS

S.I.S.A. Classic	Mark McNulty
S. African PGA Championship	Gary Player
S.A.B. Masters	Mark McNulty
Sharp Electronics Open	Mark McNulty
Sun City Classic	Mark McNulty
Vaal Reefs Sigma Open	Nick Price
Holiday Inns Pro-Am	Denis Watson
Nigerian Open	David Jagger
Ivory Coast Open	John Morgan
Zambia Open	Brian Waites
Kenya Open	Eamonn Darcy
Mufulira Open	Brian Waites
Kalahari Diamond Classic	David Jagger
Moroccan Grand Prix	Frank Conner
Sun City Challenge	Raymond Floyd

ASIA/JAPAN TOURS

Philippine Open	Hsieh Min Nan
Hong Kong Open	Kurt Cox
Malaysian Open	Denny Hepler
Thailand Open	Hsu Sheng San
Indian Open	Hsu Sheng San
Singapore Open	Hsu Sheng San
Indonesia Open	Eleuterio Nival
China Open	Chen Tze Ming
Korea Open	*Kim Joo Heun
Dunlop International	Tsuneyuki Nakajima
Shizuoka Open	Eitaro Deguchi
Kagawa Open	Shigeru Uchida

Kuzuha Kokusai	Namio Takasu
Hakuryuko Open	Toshimitsu Kai
Bridgestone Aso Open	Toru Nakamura
Chunichi Crowns	Gary Hallberg
Fuji Sankei Classic	Tsuneyuki Nakajima
Japan Match Play Championship	Isao Aoki
Pepsi Ube	Kikuo Arai
Mitsubishi Galant	Graham Marsh
Tohoku Classic	Shinsaku Maeda
Sapporo Tokyu Open	Yasuhiro Funatogawa
Yomiuri Open	Terry Gale
Mizuno	Teruo Sugihara
Nagano Open	Tsuneyuki Nakajima
Kanagawa Open	Akio Toyoda
Toyama Open	Shigeru Uchida
Wakayama Open	Hisashi Kaji
Niigata Open	Yoshitaka Yamamoto
Hyogo Open	Kazuo Kanayama
Gunma Open	Fujio Kobayashi
Descente Osaka Open	Teruo Sugihara
Japan PGA Championship	Masahiro Kuramoto
Kanto PGA Championship	Motomasa Aoki
Kansai PGA Championship	Hideto Shigenobu
Descente Cup Hokkoku Open	Kikuo Arai
Saitama Open	Kikuo Arai
East-West Match Play	West (team)
	Tsuneyuki Nakajima (individual)
Kokudo Keikaku Summers	Teruo Sugihara
KBC Augusta	Chen Tze Ming
Kyushu Open	Norio Suzuki
Kansai Open	Teruo Sugihara
Kanto Open	Masashi Ozaki
Chubu Open	Shigeru Uchida
Chugoku Open	Masahiro Kuramoto
Hokkaido Open	Koichi Uehara
Suntory Open	Pete Izumikawa
ANA Sapporo Open	Norio Suzuki
Hiroshima Open	Takashi Kurihara
Gene Sarazen Jun Classic	Teruo Sugihara
Tokai Classic	Hsieh Min Nan
Golf Digest	Hsieh Min Nan
Bridgestone	Hsieh Min Nan
Japan Open	Akira Yabe
Goldwin Cup (U.S. vs Japan)	U.S. (team)
	Bob Gilder–Calvin Peete (individual)
Taiheiyo Club (Pacific) Masters	Scott Hoch
Dunlop Phoenix	Calvin Peete
Casio World Open	Scott Hoch
Japan Series	Tsuneyuki Nakajima

AUSTRALASIA TOUR

Tooth Illawarra Open	Bob Shaw
South Australian Open	Graham Marsh
Tasmanian Open	Col Bishop
Victorian Open	Mike Clayton
Australian Masters	Graham Marsh
Halls Head Western Open	Mike Cahill
Western Australian Open	Terry Gale
Nedlands Masters	Mike Cahill

New South Wales PGA Championship	Frank Nobilo
Kooralbyn Valley Classic	Col Bishop
Queensland Open	Graham Marsh
New South Wales Open	Bob Shearer
Westpac Classic	Ian Stanley
Australian PGA Championship	Graham Marsh
Resch's Pilsener Classic	Payne Stewart
Australian Open	Bob Shearer
New Zealand Open	Terry Gale
Air New Zealand-Shell Open	Terry Gale
New Zealand PGA Championship	Stuart Reese

MISCELLANEOUS NON-TOUR EVENTS

Canadian PGA Championship	Jim Thorpe
Venezuelan Open	Ronan Rafferty
Preservatrice Fonciere Open	Gary Hallberg
World Cup/International Trophy	Spain (team)
	Manuel Pinero (individual)
Sao Paulo Open	John Cook
Brazilian Open	Hale Irwin
Marcos Invitational	George Archer

SENIOR TOUR

Vintage Invitational	Miller Barber
Tampa Classic	Don January
Legends of Golf	Sam Snead–Don January
Marlboro Classic	Arnold Palmer
Peter Jackson Champions	Bob Goalby
USGA Senior Open	Miller Barber
Denver Post Champions	Arnold Palmer
Syracuse Classic	Bill Collins
Jeremy Ranch Shootout	Bill Casper
Golf Digest Commemorative	Bill Casper
World Seniors Invitational	Gene Littler
Suntree Classic	Miller Barber
Hilton Head International	Miller Barber
	Dan Sikes
PGA Seniors Championship	Don January

LPGA TOUR

Whirlpool	Hollis Stacy
Elizabeth Arden	JoAnne Carner
S&H Classic	Hollis Stacy
Bent Tree	Beth Daniel
Arizona Copper	Ayako Okamoto
Sun City	Beth Daniel
Olympia Gold	Sally Little
J&B Scotch	Nancy Lopez
Kemper	Amy Alcott
Dinah Shore	Sally Little
CPC International	Kathy Whitworth
Orlando Classic	Patty Sheehan
Birmingham	Beth Daniel
UVB Classic	Sally Little
Lady Michelob	Kathy Whitworth
Chrysler Classic	Cathy Morse
Corning Classic	Sandra Spuzich
McDonalds Kids	JoAnne Carner

LPGA Championship	Jan Stephenson
Lady Keystone	Jan Stephenson
Rochester	Sandra Haynie
Peter Jackson Classic	Sandra Haynie
West Virginia	Hollis Stacy
Mayflower	Sally Little
U.S. Open Championship	Janet Alex
Columbia Savings	Beth Daniel
Boston Five	Sandra Palmer
WUI Classic	Beth Daniel
World Championship	JoAnne Carner
Henredon Classic	JoAnne Carner
Rail Classic	JoAnne Carner
Mary Kay	Sandra Spuzich
Ping Team Championship	Sandra Haynie–Kathy McMullen
Safeco	Patty Sheehan
Inamori	Patty Sheehan
Japan Mazda	Nancy Lopez
Pioneer Cup	U.S. (team)
	Nayoko Yoshikwa (individual)
JC Penney Classic	JoAnne Carner/John Mahaffey

Career World Money List
The following is a listing of the 50 leading money-winners of the world for their careers through the 1982 season. The World Money List totals from this and the 16 previous editions of this annual and a table prepared for a companion book, *The Wonderful World of Professional Golf* (Atheneum, 1973), form the basis for this compilation. Additional figures were taken from official records of major golf associations, although shortcomings in records-keeping in professional golf outside the United States in the 1950s and 1960s and exclusions from U.S. records in a few cases during those years prevent these figures from being totally complete and accurate. Conversions of foreign currency figures to U.S. dollars are based on average values during the particular years involved.

POS.	PLAYER, COUNTRY	TOTAL MONEY
1	Jack Nicklaus, U.S.	$4,915,568
2	Lee Trevino, U.S.	3,499,470
3	Tom Watson, U.S.	3,352,489
4	Gary Player, South Africa	2,887,820
5	Raymond Floyd, U.S.	2,853,581
6	Johnny Miller, U.S.	2,568,002
7	Tom Weiskopf, U.S.	2,550,514
8	Hale Irwin, U.S.	2,462,929
9	Arnold Palmer, U.S.	2,454,431
10	Bill Casper, U.S.	2,306,555
11	Gene Littler, U.S.	2,257,602
12	Isao Aoki, Japan	2,244,467
13	Miller Barber, U.S.	2,068,608
14	Hubert Green, U.S.	1,949,478
15	Tom Kite, U.S.	1,926,953
16	Graham Marsh, Australia	1,867,709
17	Jerry Pate, U.S.	1,815,247
18	Lanny Wadkins, U.S.	1,791,454
19	David Graham, Australia	1,753,762
20	Severiano Ballesteros, Spain	1,727,824
21	Ben Crenshaw, U.S.	1,721,752
22	Don January, U.S.	1,649,629
23	Bill Rogers, U.S.	1,551,587
24	Bruce Crampton, Australia	1,499,554
25	George Archer, U.S.	1,467,848
26	Al Geiberger, U.S.	1,480,338
27	Bruce Lietzke, U.S.	1,445,076
28	Lou Graham, U.S.	1,388,882
29	J.C. Snead, U.S.	1,384,499
30	Dave Stockton, U.S.	1,367,571
31	Craig Stadler, U.S.	1,366,692
32	Andy Bean, U.S.	1,345,159
33	Charles Coody, U.S.	1,331,422
34	Julius Boros, U.S.	1,292,836
35	Bob Murphy, U.S.	1,283,784
36	John Mahaffey, U.S.	1,280,196
37	Larry Nelson, U.S.	1,271,039
38	Dave Hill, U.S.	1,267,279

POS.	PLAYER, COUNTRY	TOTAL MONEY
39	Masashi Ozaki, Japan	1,251,115
40	Gil Morgan, U.S.	1,200,760
41	Bob Charles, New Zealand	1,173,020
42	Gay Brewer, U.S.	1,172,555
43	Bruce Devlin, Australia	1,167,921
44	Curtis Strange, U.S.	1,148,622
45	Jim Colbert, U.S.	1,141,008
46	Bobby Nichols, U.S.	1,128,951
47	Frank Beard, U.S.	1,112,966
48	Tommy Aaron, U.S.	1,074,475
49	Lee Elder, U.S.	1,069,039
50	Chi Chi Rodriquez, U.S.	1,057,953

Senior World Money List

POS.	PLAYER	TOURNAMENTS	MONEY
1	Miller Barber	13	$171,390
2	Don January	10	158,508
3	Bob Goalby	13	119,474
4	Arnold Palmer	10	108,448
5	Gene Littler	10	97,120
6	Bill Casper	11	91,479
7	Dan Sikes	12	84,946
8	Sam Snead	12	80,041
9	Art Wall	10	61,025
10	Bill Collins	11	54,125
11	Julius Boros	12	53,746
12	Bob Rosburg	10	53,537
13	Gay Brewer	9	51,511
14	Dow Finsterwald	11	47,036
15	Peter Thomson	9	46,891
16	Howie Johnson	12	43,183
17	Paul Harney	11	43,025
18	Bob Toski	5	40,650
19	Roberto De Vicenzo	5	39,833
20	Charles Sifford	13	37,185
21	Gardner Dickinson	11	36,385
22	Kel Nagle	9	33,415
23	Guy Wolstenholme	7	32,860
24	Jerry Barber	14	31,816
25	Tom Nieporte	11	30,030
26	George Bayer	11	28,446
27	Jack Fleck	12	27,729
28	Fred Hawkins	13	26,724
29	Mike Fetchick	12	25,058
30	Fred Haas	12	24,517
31	Lionel Hebert	13	24,227
32	Doug Ford	11	22,613
33	Bob Erickson	10	22,547
34	Al Balding	13	22,456
35	Bill Johnston	12	21,755
36	Jim Ferree	8	20,455
37	Billy Maxwell	11	17,905
38	Mike Souchak	9	17,613
39	Ted Kroll	10	16,703
40	Harvie Ward	6	15,639
41	Dick Mayer	4	15,393
42	Bob Stone	5	14,069
43	Henry Ransom	9	13,948
44	Denis Hutchinson	7	13,857
45	Tommy Bolt	4	13,005
46	Bob Hamilton	7	12,734
47	Al Besselink	10	12,585
48	Marty Furgol	10	12,023

POS.	PLAYER	TOURNAMENTS	MONEY
49	Jack Burke	2	12,000
50	Pete Cooper	11	11,540

TOURNAMENTS INCLUDED: Vintage, Tampa, Legends of Golf, Marlboro Classic, Peter Jackson (Winnipeg), USGA Senior Open, Denver, Syracuse, Jeremy Ranch (Salt Lake City), Golf Digest, World Invitational, Suntree (Melbourne, Florida), Hilton Head, PGA Seniors. TOTAL PRIZE MONEY: $2,497,437.50.

LPGA World Money List

POS.	PLAYER	TOTAL MONEY
1	JoAnne Carner	$356,899.75
2	Sandra Haynie	264,073.97
3	Beth Daniel	242,263.33
4	Patty Sheehan	241,083.80
5	Sally Little	238,214.44
6	Hollis Stacy	193,816.96
7	Nancy Lopez	173,800.87
8	Amy Alcott	169,581.81
9	Jan Stephenson	150,674.11
10	Kathy Whitworth	148,749.75
11	Pat Bradley	127,033.27
12	Kathy Postlewait	92,682.09
13	Sandra Spuzich	92,310.81
14	Barbara Moxness	90,268.91
15	Janet Alex	89,104.56
16	Ayako Okamoto	87,767.60
17	Donna Caponi	84,778.31
18	Donna H. White	80,648.21
19	Sandra Palmer	80,411.46
20	Janet Coles	79,221.34
21	Cathy Morse	73,193.65
22	Lynn Adams	68,125.17
23	Betsy King	67,303.83
24	Chris Johnson	66,257.37
25	Jo Ann Washam	65,786.15
26	Alexandra Reinhardt	64,716.59
27	Dale Eggeling	59,772.97
28	Patti Rizzo	56,200.75
29	Vickie Tabor	55,566.47
30	Myra Van Hoose	49,649.24
31	Dot Germain	49,246.33
32	Judy Clark	48,959.16
33	Dianne Dailey	48,556.99
34	Carole Charbonnier	47,904.95
35	Silvia Bertolaccini	47,529.96
36	Jane Blalock	43,969.44
37	Carole Jo Callison	43,806.70
38	Bonnie Lauer	43,674.18
39	Beverly Klass	42,458.81
40	Susie McAllister	41,185.99
41	Alice Miller	38,661.34
42	Alice Ritzman	37,683.50
43	Pam Gietzen	37,054.61
44	Sharon Barrett	36,517.74
45	Cindy Hill	35,729.55
46	Lori Garbacz	35,073.42
47	Barbara Barrow	34,915.99
48	Penny Pulz	33,838.71

POS.	PLAYER	TOTAL MONEY
49	Debbie Austin	33,105.75
50	Shelley Hamlin	32,878.48
51	Jeannette Kerr	32,655.16
52	Beverley Davis-Cooper	30,427.71
53	Terri Moody	30,203.24
54	Jerilyn Britz	29,540.35
55	Gail Hirata	28,919.80
56	Martha Hansen	28,736.62
57	Kathy Hite	28,570.78
58	Beth Solomon	27,140.14
59	Joyce Kazmierski	27,114.03
60	Yuko Moriguchi	26,326.47
61	Muffin Spencer-Devlin	26,066.93
62	Sandra Post	24,865.33
63	M.J. Smith	24,190.06
64	Nancy Rubin	24,156.13
65	Vicki Fergon	22,865.43
66	Kathy McMullen	21,831.18
67	Julie Pyne	21,697.14
68	Vicki Singleton	20,949.85
69	Mary Dwyer	20,376.62
70	Kathryn Young	19,978.07
71	Sue Ertl	19,772.15
72	Marlene Floyd-DeArman	18,358.75
73	Cathy Sherk	18,342.26
74	Joan Joyce	18,193.56
75	Pat Meyers	18,117.42
76	Vivian Brownlee	17,958.89
77	Kathy Martin	17,791.24
78	Lori Huxhold	17,580.45
79	Cathy Reynolds	17,448.52
80	Becky Pearson	17,400.45
81	Judy Rankin	16,568.19
82	Jan Ferraris	16,511.81
83	Therese Hession	16,250.18
84	Tatsuko Ohsako	15,745.00
85	Debbie Massey	15,310.91
86	Robin Walton	15,196.86
87	Mardell Wilkins	14,908.72
88	Patty Hayes	13,602.41
89	Stephanie Farwig	13,331.87
90	Marlene Hagge	12,405.20
91	Carolyn Hill	12,304.33
92	Holly Hartley	12,085.67
93	Mindy Moore	11,706.00
94	Lenore Muraoka	11,692.43
95	Kyle O'Brien	11,651.52
96	Connie Chillemi	11,110.59
97	Jane Lock	10,491.84
98	Marty Dickerson	10,395.46
99	Lynn Stroney	10,121.53
100	Alison Sheard	9,757.33

(Above list includes LPGA official money, Portland Ping, J.C. Penney and Pioneer Cup. Tu Ai Yu of Taiwan won $159,183.67 on the Japanese Women's Tour plus $4,600 on the LPGA Tour.)

LPGA World Stroke Averages

PLAYER	ROUNDS	STROKES	AVERAGE
JoAnne Carner	95	6,792	71.49
Beth Daniel	96	6,879	71.66
Patty Sheehan	94	6,742	71.72
Sandra Haynie	107	7,689	71.86
Sally Little	100	7,206	72.06
Nancy Lopez	83	5,988	72.14
Amy Alcott	96	6,938	72.27
Kathy Whitworth	93	6,722	72.28
Pat Bradley	106	7,663	72.29
Jan Stephenson	74	5,350	72.30
Hollis Stacy	102	7,395	72.50
Donna Caponi	86	6,235	72.50
Ayako Okamoto	52	3,775	72.60
Donna H. White	84	6,113	72.77
Janet Coles	96	6,996	72.88
Sandra Spuzich	78	5,699	73.06
Cathy Morse	86	6,296	73.21
Barbara A. Moxness	95	6,957	73.23
Janet Alex	89	6,518	73.24
Lynn Adams	108	7,920	73.33
Sandra Palmer	91	6,675	73.35
Terri Moody	47	3,451	73.43
Dot Germain	79	5,802	73.44
Jane Blalock	83	6,098	73.47

The U.S. Tour

Joe Garagiola Tucson Open

Randolph Park North Course, Tucson, Arizona
Par 35–35—70; 6,797 yards

January 7–10
purse, $300,000

	SCORES				TOTAL	MONEY
Craig Stadler	65	64	66	71	266	$54,000
Vance Heafner	68	68	69	64	269	26,400
John Mahaffey	71	66	67	65	269	26,400
Bob Gilder	68	70	67	65	270	14,400
Jay Haas	67	68	67	69	271	12,000
Joe Hager	69	72	66	65	272	8,764.29
Andy Bean	70	65	70	67	272	8,764.29
Leonard Thompson	67	69	69	67	272	8,764.29
Peter Jacobsen	68	70	67	67	272	8,764.29
Keith Fergus	71	69	65	67	272	8,764.28
John Jackson	71	68	66	67	272	8,764.28
Greg Powers	69	69	65	69	272	8,764.28
Pat McGowan	71	69	68	65	273	6,000
Mike McCullough	73	66	65	69	273	6,000
Jim Booros	71	68	69	66	274	4,500
Scott Hoch	73	69	66	66	274	4,500
Bobby Clampett	68	70	69	67	274	4,500
Tim Simpson	72	69	68	65	274	4,500
Ed Fiori	71	70	65	68	274	4,500
Tom Purtzer	69	69	67	69	274	4,500
Scott Simpson	67	67	70	70	274	4,500
Mike Reid	72	67	68	68	275	3,000
Calvin Peete	68	72	67	68	275	3,000
Forrest Fezler	70	69	67	69	275	3,000
Bob Eastwood	70	67	67	71	275	3,000
Gary Trivisonno	73	66	69	68	276	2,265
Jeff Mitchell	73	67	69	67	276	2,265
Bill Kratzert	71	71	64	70	276	2,265
David Edwards	71	67	68	70	276	2,265
Don January	71	67	70	69	277	1,602.50
Skeeter Heath	69	68	70	70	277	1,602.50
Joe Inman	70	71	68	68	277	1,602.50
Woody Fitzhugh	70	71	66	70	277	1,602.50
Al Geiberger	66	69	71	71	277	1,602.50
Alan Tapie	67	66	73	71	277	1,602.50
Johnny Miller	70	70	70	67	277	1,602.50
Allen Miller	69	72	69	67	277	1,602.50
Mike Sullivan	68	69	69	71	277	1,602.50
Mike Donald	71	66	69	71	277	1,602.50
Barry Jaeckel	69	70	67	71	277	1,602.50
Jeff Sanders	72	70	69	66	277	1,602.50
Dana Quigley	73	68	67	70	278	965.25
Terry Mauney	71	69	68	70	278	965.25

*DENOTES AMATEUR IN ALL APPENDIXES

	SCORES				TOTAL	MONEY
Jim Colbert	69	72	66	71	278	965.25
Curtis Strange	70	72	66	70	278	965.25
Lanny Wadkins	70	70	71	67	278	965.25
Bob Byman	74	68	69	67	278	965.25
Victor Regalado	71	71	69	67	278	965.25
Dan Halldorson	71	70	71	66	278	965.25
John Schroeder	71	70	68	70	279	723.60
John Cook	70	72	67	70	279	723.60
Peter Oosterhuis	71	70	65	73	279	723.60
Bruce Douglass	69	71	71	68	279	723.60
George Burns	72	70	69	68	279	723.60

Bob Hope Desert Classic

January 13–17
purse, $304,500

Bermuda Dunes Country Club
Bermuda Dunes, California
Par 36–36—72; 6,793 yards

Indian Wells Country Club
Palm Desert, California
Par 36–36—72; 6,455 yards

Eldorado Country Club
Palm Desert, California
Par 36–36—72; 6,840 yards

LaQuinta Country Club
LaQuinta, California
Par 36–36—72; 6,855 yards

	SCORES					TOTAL	MONEY
Ed Fiori	70	65	66	67	67	335	$50,000
Tom Kite	68	66	66	69	66	335	29,700
(Fiori defeated Kite on second hole of sudden-death playoff.)							
Rex Caldwell	64	69	70	66	68	337	18,700
Scott Hoch	68	69	69	67	65	338	13,200
Curtis Strange	67	70	69	68	65	339	11,000
Wayne Levi	68	68	73	67	64	340	9,537.50
Mark O'Meara	71	70	65	64	70	340	9,537.50
Mike Reid	70	71	68	65	67	341	8,525
Calvin Peete	69	65	71	68	69	342	7,975
Forrest Fezler	66	70	67	67	73	343	7,425
Jim Booros	72	66	66	73	67	344	6,875
Jerry Pate	70	73	65	72	65	345	6,325
Barry Harwell	68	70	73	69	66	346	5,500
Keith Fergus	69	67	71	69	70	346	5,500
Tom Jenkins	70	72	70	68	67	347	4,675
Jim Simons	72	68	70	70	67	347	4,675
Jack Renner	70	70	69	70	68	347	4,675
John Cook	67	72	70	72	67	348	3,465
Bobby Wadkins	70	71	70	70	67	348	3,465
Dan Halldorson	72	68	71	70	67	348	3,465
Jay Haas	71	73	66	69	69	348	3,465
J.C. Snead	69	67	71	72	69	348	3,465
Lanny Wadkins	65	69	72	72	70	348	3,465
Fred Couples	71	67	72	71	68	349	2,292
Jim Colbert	69	70	71	72	67	349	2,292
Lee Elder	67	69	72	72	69	349	2,292
Scott Simpson	69	69	71	71	69	349	2,292
Jet Ozaki	64	68	70	76	71	349	2,292
Terry Mauney	70	70	74	67	69	350	1880
Greg Powers	73	70	71	69	67	350	1880
Bob Byman	70	68	69	72	71	350	1880

	SCORES				TOTAL	MONEY
Morris Hatalsky	70	71	66	74	70	351	1433.34
Peter Oosterhuis	69	71	67	74	70	351	1433.34
Tim Simpson	72	69	71	69	70	351	1433.34
Fuzzy Zoeller	71	70	69	72	69	351	1433.33
Ron Streck	71	67	72	69	72	351	1433.33
Dave Eichelberger	73	73	66	71	68	351	1433.33
George Archer	70	68	72	73	68	351	1433.33
Skeeter Heath	67	67	69	74	74	351	1433.33
Ed Sneed	72	73	69	71	66	351	1433.33
Bruce Lietzke	73	68	72	68	71	352	1060
John Mahaffey	70	75	69	68	70	352	1060
Mike Sullivan	69	74	71	70	68	352	1060
Don Pooley	71	69	72	70	71	353	828.34
Bill Britton	72	69	70	72	70	353	828.34
Peter Jacobsen	76	70	64	73	70	353	828.33
David Graham	67	71	77	68	70	353	828.33
Mark Hayes	77	73	68	66	69	353	828.33
Mike Morley	74	67	69	68	75	353	828.33
Dale Douglass	68	71	73	70	72	354	654.29
D.A. Weibring	70	70	70	70	74	354	654.29
Rod Curl	66	70	73	70	75	354	654.29
Miller Barber	69	69	69	76	71	354	654.29
Bill Kratzer	71	73	69	70	71	354	654.28
Bud Allin	68	74	70	73	69	354	654.28
Joe Hager	70	73	71	71	69	354	654.28

Phoenix Open

Phoenix Country Club, Phoenix, Arizona
Par 36-35—71; 6,726 yards

January 21–25
purse, $300,000

	SCORES				TOTAL	MONEY
Lanny Wadkins	65	70	63	65	263	$54,000
Jerry Pate	71	69	64	65	269	32,400
Mike Reid	70	68	66	66	270	20,400
Andy Bean	70	67	69	65	271	12,400
Larry Nelson	63	70	71	67	271	12,400
Morris Hatalsky	67	67	68	69	271	12,400
Fuzzy Zoeller	76	65	65	66	272	9,675
D.A. Weibring	71	69	65	67	272	9,675
Jim Simons	67	71	69	66	273	7,800
Tom Purtzer	66	69	70	68	273	7,800
Scott Simpson	75	66	63	69	273	7,800
John Cook	70	66	67	70	273	7,800
Craig Stadler	69	67	72	66	274	6,000
Tom Kite	71	67	68	68	274	6,000
Gibby Gilbert	71	68	69	67	275	5,400
Jay Haas	69	69	66	73	277	3,810
George Archer	72	71	66	68	277	3,810
Scott Hoch	71	69	69	68	277	3,810
Hale Irwin	73	67	69	68	277	3,810
Fred Couples	69	65	73	70	277	3,810
Terry Mauney	70	71	66	70	277	3,810
Bob Gilder	69	71	67	70	277	3,810
Bill Kratzert	70	69	68	70	277	3,810
Mike Donald	71	69	66	71	277	3,810
Bruce Lietzke	71	69	66	71	277	3,810

	SCORES				TOTAL	MONEY
Curtis Strange	69	70	70	69	278	2,085
Rex Caldwell	71	70	68	69	278	2,085
Homero Blancas	72	68	71	67	278	2,085
Calvin Peete	74	67	68	69	278	2,085
Dan Halldorson	70	70	71	67	278	2,085
Tom Weiskopf	70	67	71	70	278	2,085
Jack Renner	71	70	71	66	278	2,085
Ben Crenshaw	70	71	66	71	278	2,085
Wayne Levi	72	68	70	69	279	1,620
Jim Dent	69	71	69	70	279	1,620
David Graham	67	68	76	68	279	1,620
Jim Colbert	69	71	70	70	280	1,350
Bob Byman	73	68	70	69	280	1,350
Lon Nielsen	69	66	73	72	280	1,350
J.C. Snead	73	70	68	69	280	1,350
Dave Eichelberger	70	72	65	73	280	1,350
Barry Harwell	68	75	66	72	281	1,050
Keith Fergus	70	70	69	72	281	1,050
Allen Miller	74	68	69	70	281	1,050
Bill Calfee	71	68	73	69	281	1,050
Don January	69	69	74	69	281	1,050
Bob Eastwood	66	70	73	73	282	781
Mike Sullivan	71	69	69	73	282	781
Gary Hallberg	70	70	73	69	282	781
Roger Maltbie	72	70	72	68	282	781
Victor Regalado	74	68	72	68	282	781
Tom Jenkins	74	69	71	68	282	781

Wickes-Andy Williams San Diego Open

Torrey Pines Golf Club, LaJolla, California

January 28–31
purse, $300,000

North Course (Thursday, Friday only)
Par 36–36—72; 6,667 yards

South Course (all four days)
Par 36–36—72; 7,002 yards

	SCORES				TOTAL	MONEY
Johnny Miller	65	67	68	70	270	$54,000
Jack Nicklaus	69	68	70	64	271	32,400
Tom Kite	72	65	66	70	273	17,400
Tom Weiskopf	69	67	68	69	273	17,400
Curtis Strange	68	67	71	68	274	12,000
Andy Bean	70	66	71	68	275	10,800
Hale Irwin	70	67	74	65	276	8,730
Gary Hallberg	70	67	71	68	276	8,730
Tom Watson	67	69	69	71	276	8,730
Fuzzy Zoeller	65	70	70	71	276	8,730
Gil Morgan	66	71	69	70	276	8,730
Hal Sutton	70	72	67	68	277	6,075
Bill Rogers	71	69	68	69	277	6,075
Al Geiberger	72	68	68	69	277	6,075
George Burns	71	65	70	71	277	6,075
John Lister	73	67	71	67	278	4,500
Morris Hatalsky	67	68	74	69	278	4,500
Vance Heafner	69	71	70	68	278	4,500
J.C. Snead	73	69	70	66	278	4,500
Jeff Mitchell	68	69	72	69	278	4,500
Jim Dent	70	71	70	68	279	3,360

	SCORES				TOTAL	MONEY
Forrest Fezler	69	72	71	67	279	3,360
Tom Purtzer	72	68	68	71	279	3,360
Bruce Fleisher	67	70	75	68	280	2,374.29
John Adams	70	69	74	67	280	2,374.29
Howard Twitty	71	70	68	71	280	2,374.29
Jerry Pate	74	67	72	67	280	2,374.29
Bobby Clampett	72	66	70	72	280	2,374.28
Nick Faldo	69	69	69	73	280	2,374.28
Raymond Floyd	70	70	67	73	280	2,374.28
Phil Hancock	68	70	73	70	281	1,596
Don January	68	70	72	71	281	1,596
Bob Byman	73	67	72	69	281	1,596
Mark Pfeil	73	67	70	71	281	1,596
Craig Stadler	68	70	74	69	281	1,596
John Cook	72	68	70	71	281	1,596
Dan Halldorson	69	68	72	72	281	1,596
Dan Pohl	72	66	75	68	281	1,596
Mark Lye	66	70	72	73	281	1,596
Peter Jacobsen	69	70	69	73	281	1,596
Mike Sullivan	70	68	73	71	282	1,140
Mark O'Meara	71	68	72	71	282	1,140
Dave Eichelberger	71	67	72	72	282	1,140
Scott Hoch	70	72	72	68	282	1,140
Ron Streck	71	67	73	72	283	930
Peter Oosterhuis	70	67	72	74	283	930
Danny Edwards	70	70	73	70	283	930
Jet Ozaki	73	67	70	74	284	763.20
Rex Caldwell	69	72	71	72	284	763.20
Dave Barr	69	71	69	75	284	763.20
Fred Couples	72	70	71	71	284	763.20
Chi Chi Rodriguez	72	64	77	71	284	763.20

Bing Crosby National Pro-Am

Pebble Beach, California

February 4–7
purse, $300,000

Pebble Beach Golf Links
Par 36–36—72, 6,806 yards

Cypress Point Golf Club
Par 36–36—72; 6,464 yards

Spyglass Hill Golf Club
Par 36–36—72, 6,810 yards

	SCORES				TOTAL	MONEY
Jim Simons	71	66	71	66	274	$54,000
Craig Stadler	71	71	64	70	276	32,400
Johnny Miller	71	71	71	67	280	13,530
Mike Morley	72	76	65	67	280	13,530
Rex Caldwell	73	67	73	67	280	13,530
Joe Inman	73	69	69	69	280	13,530
Jack Nicklaus	69	70	71	70	280	13,530
Tommy Valentine	70	71	73	67	281	8,400
Gene Littler	70	71	71	69	281	8,400
George Burns	67	69	77	68	281	8,400
Dave Stockton	71	70	70	70	281	8,400
George Archer	76	69	70	67	282	6,300
Tom Watson	69	73	72	68	282	6,300
Bob Gilder	71	70	72	69	282	6,300

	SCORES				TOTAL	MONEY
Tim Simpson	73	67	74	69	283	5,100
Chip Beck	69	73	69	72	283	5,100
Scott Simpson	69	73	69	72	283	5,100
Bob Eastwood	75	66	72	71	284	4,500
Hubert Green	71	69	74	71	285	3,765
Gibby Gilbert	72	70	71	72	285	3,765
Bobby Wadkins	71	68	71	75	285	3,765
Hal Sutton	70	67	72	76	285	3,765
Mark Hayes	75	70	69	72	286	2,760
Mark O'Meara	71	70	75	70	286	2,760
Scott Hoch	71	75	71	69	286	2,760
Ben Crenshaw	69	74	75	68	286	2,760
Vance Heafner	73	73	73	68	287	2,040
Fuzzy Zoeller	73	73	72	69	287	2,040
Mark Pfeil	73	75	70	69	287	2,040
Curtis Strange	71	70	75	71	287	2,040
Jay Haas	73	68	73	73	287	2,040
Greg Powers	72	70	72	73	287	2,040
Jeff Mitchell	70	72	71	74	287	2,040
Mike Reid	74	68	74	72	288	1,515
Roger Maltbie	75	69	71	73	288	1,515
John Cook	73	75	68	72	288	1,515
Bruce Lietzke	66	72	79	71	288	1,515
David Graham	75	71	71	71	288	1,515
John Mahaffey	75	72	71	70	288	1,515
Lanny Wadkins	72	72	72	73	289	1,110
Fred Couples	72	69	74	74	289	1,110
Peter Jacobsen	71	74	70	74	289	1,110
Tom Kite	73	70	73	73	289	1,110
Dave Eichelberger	70	76	72	71	289	1,110
D.A. Weibring	72	73	73	71	289	1,110
Forrest Fezler	66	75	71	77	289	1,110
Tom Weiskopf	72	72	72	74	290	870
Morris Hatalsky	70	70	76	75	291	738.75
Dan Pohl	73	71	71	76	291	738.75
Jim Booros	71	72	71	77	291	738.75
Doug Tewell	73	73	71	74	291	738.75
John Lister	74	71	72	74	291	738.75
Eric Batten	74	71	74	72	291	738.75
Barney Thompson	73	71	74	73	291	738.75
Danny Edwards	72	67	79	73	291	738.75

Hawaiian Open

Waialae Country Club, Honolulu, Hawaii   February 11–14
Par 36–36—72; 6,881 yards   purse, $325,000

	SCORES				TOTAL	MONEY
Wayne Levi	72	68	67	70	277	$58,500
Scott Simpson	70	69	70	69	278	35,100
Chip Beck	72	68	71	68	279	22,100
Ben Crenshaw	70	72	68	70	280	13,433.34
Bobby Clampett	67	72	70	71	280	13,433.33
Andy North	69	69	69	73	280	13,433.33
Jim Booros	72	72	70	67	281	10,133.34
Nick Faldo	73	67	73	68	281	10,133.33
Bruce Lietzke	77	68	68	68	281	10,133.33

	SCORES				TOTAL	MONEY
Dan Halldorson	75	66	71	70	282	8,775
John Mahaffey	72	68	74	69	283	6,910
Rocky Thompson	71	73	70	69	283	6,910
Jeff Sanders	68	72	73	70	283	6,910
Al Geiberger	72	74	66	71	283	6,910
Forrest Fezler	72	70	70	71	283	6,910
Ed Sneed	69	76	69	70	284	4,712.50
Bruce Douglass	74	72	69	69	284	4,712.50
Larry Nelson	74	71	71	68	284	4,712.50
Greg Powers	72	66	74	72	284	4,712.50
Jim Nelford	73	69	69	73	284	4,712.49
Charles Coody	72	69	68	75	284	4,712.49
Terry Diehl	72	71	72	70	285	2,853.75
Pete Izumigawa	70	70	74	71	285	2,853.75
Tom Purtzer	72	73	69	71	285	2,853.75
Bob Proben	68	72	73	72	285	2,853.75
George Cadle	73	70	74	68	285	2,853.75
Arnold Palmer	71	73	69	72	285	2,853.75
Fred Couples	74	72	72	67	285	2,853.75
Tom Watson	70	69	70	76	285	2,853.75
Gary Hallberg	73	70	72	71	286	1,877.50
Mike Reid	74	70	71	71	286	1,877.50
Allen Miller	72	70	72	72	286	1,877.50
Roger Maltbie	77	69	70	70	286	1,877.50
Bill Rogers	75	70	68	73	286	1,877.50
Scott Stager	75	71	72	68	286	1,877.50
Bob Gilder	71	73	76	66	286	1,877.50
Mark Lye	69	71	71	75	286	1,877.50
Ray Floyd	73	69	73	72	287	1,330.72
John Schroeder	69	73	73	72	287	1,330.72
Gary Koch	78	68	70	71	287	1,330.72
Isao Aoki	74	71	72	70	287	1,330.71
Rex Caldwell	71	70	72	74	287	1,330.71
Mark Hayes	72	72	75	68	287	1,330.71
Tommy Valentine	69	73	70	75	287	1,330.71
Doug Campbell	76	68	72	72	288	929.17
Howard Twitty	73	73	70	72	288	929.17
Mark Pfeil	75	71	70	72	288	929.17
Mark O'Meara	73	71	73	71	288	929.17
George Burns	74	69	70	75	288	929.16
Lee Elder	69	72	71	76	288	929.16

Glen Campbell Los Angeles Open

Riviera Country Club, Los Angeles, California   February 18–21
Par 35–36—72; 7,029 yards   purse, $300,000

	SCORES				TOTAL	MONEY
Tom Watson	69	67	68	67	271	$54,000
Johnny Miller	68	68	66	69	271	32,400
(Watson defeated Miller on third hole of sudden-death playoff.)						
Tom Weiskopf	67	67	68	73	275	20,400
Lennie Clements	74	68	68	66	276	13,200
Bill Rogers	70	68	68	70	276	13,200
Tim Simpson	73	66	70	68	277	10,800
Jim Nelford	70	70	70	68	278	9,350
Jay Haas	69	69	69	71	278	9,350

	SCORES				TOTAL	MONEY
Vance Heafner	68	68	71	71	278	9,350
Jack Ferenz	74	69	69	67	279	7,500
Mike Morley	67	69	70	73	279	7,500
Tom Kite	71	70	66	72	279	7,500
Eric Batten	69	69	74	68	280	4,987.50
Gene Littler	73	68	71	68	280	4,987.50
Curtis Strange	73	71	68	68	280	4,987.50
Fred Couples	72	71	73	64	280	4,987.50
Wayne Levi	67	69	73	71	280	4,987.50
Woody Blackburn	71	68	70	71	280	4,987.50
John Cook	73	68	67	72	280	4,987.50
Jack Renner	70	67	70	73	280	4,987.50
Don January	73	71	69	68	281	3,240
Craig Stadler	71	72	71	67	281	3,240
Rod Funseth	73	70	71	67	281	3,240
Bob Gilder	75	70	66	70	281	3,240
Barry Jaeckel	73	71	69	69	282	2,193.75
Jerry Pate	70	71	71	70	282	2,193.75
Ed Sneed	73	67	71	71	282	2,193.75
Danny Edwards	71	71	69	71	282	2,193.75
Terry Mauney	63	73	74	72	282	2,193.75
Rex Caldwell	70	68	71	73	282	2,193.75
John Schroeder	70	71	68	73	282	2,193.75
Tom Purtzer	70	71	68	73	282	2,193.75
Mark O'Meara	71	68	71	73	283	1,695
John Adams	74	69	68	72	283	1,695
Gil Morgan	74	71	70	68	283	1,695
Morris Hatalsky	68	76	69	71	284	1,352.15
Andy North	73	70	71	70	284	1,352.15
Hale Irwin	74	68	70	72	284	1,352.14
George Archer	75	70	69	70	284	1,352.14
Don Bies	72	70	73	69	284	1,352.14
Isao Aoki	69	73	69	73	284	1,352.14
Skip Dunaway	72	69	70	73	284	1,352.14
Mark Pfeil	73	68	72	72	285	936
Tom Jenkins	74	69	70	72	285	936
Jim Simons	71	68	73	73	285	936
Scott Simpson	73	70	71	71	285	936
Jim Colbert	73	70	72	70	285	936
Gary Koch	74	70	71	70	285	936
Jim Dent	71	74	74	66	285	936

Doral-Eastern Open

Doral Country Club, Miami, Florida
Par 36–36—72; 7,065 yards

February 25–28
purse, $300,000

	SCORES				TOTAL	MONEY
Andy Bean	68	69	72	69	278	$54,000
Scott Hoch	69	70	71	69	279	22,400
Mike Nicolette	68	70	71	70	279	22,400
Jerry Pate	70	70	69	70	279	22,400
Curtis Strange	70	76	68	67	281	10,950
Calvin Peete	68	72	70	71	281	10,950
Craig Stadler	66	69	73	73	281	10,950
Jim Dent	71	72	72	67	282	9,000
Eric Batten	67	72	72	71	282	9,000

		SCORES			TOTAL	MONEY
Seve Ballesteros	69	71	75	68	283	8,100
Ed Sneed	70	73	73	68	284	6,150
Tom Weiskopf	69	71	75	69	284	6,150
Barry Jaeckel	70	71	73	70	284	6,150
Bobby Wadkins	67	74	72	71	284	6,150
Nick Faldo	68	72	73	71	284	6,150
Jack Nicklaus	67	71	72	74	284	6,150
Rick Pearson	70	74	74	67	285	4,200
Woody Blackburn	72	74	70	69	285	4,200
Barney Thompson	72	72	71	70	285	4,200
Isao Aoki	70	72	72	71	285	4,200
Ed Fiori	72	70	71	72	285	4,200
Leonard Thompson	70	74	73	69	286	2,785
Ray Floyd	71	70	75	70	286	2,785
Tom Jenkins	72	71	73	70	286	2,785
Bill Britton	70	75	71	70	286	2,785
Jim Nelford	72	70	72	72	286	2,785
Hubert Green	72	69	72	73	286	2,785
Larry Nelson	75	71	71	70	287	2,130
Bob Eastwood	72	68	75	72	287	2,130
Phil Hancock	71	73	76	67	287	2,130
Vance Heafner	72	75	74	67	288	1,860
George Burns	70	73	74	71	288	1,860
Wayne Levi	69	71	73	75	288	1,860
Jim Colbert	70	73	75	71	289	1,620
John Fought	69	74	74	72	289	1,620
Tom McGinnis	72	69	74	74	289	1,620
Bobby Nichols	74	73	74	69	290	1,290
Bobby Cole	71	74	74	71	290	1,290
Gibby Gilbert	70	71	77	72	290	1,290
Dave Eichelberger	73	74	72	71	290	1,290
Jim Albus	71	69	76	74	290	1,290
Tom Shaw	70	75	71	74	290	1,290
Jim Booros	68	73	74	75	290	1,290
Steve Benson	68	75	76	72	291	932.40
Mike Sullivan	72	73	74	72	291	932.40
Scott Watkins	72	73	74	72	291	932.40
Jeff Sanders	74	72	71	74	291	932.40
Bruce Fleisher	71	73	71	76	291	932.40
Perry Arthur	74	71	75	72	292	733
Skeeter Heath	73	73	73	73	292	733
Mike McCullough	70	75	73	74	292	733
Hal Sutton	70	75	73	74	292	733
Bill Sander	71	71	75	75	292	733
Bruce Douglas	72	75	71	74	292	733

Bay Hill Classic

Bay Hill Club and Lodge, Orlando, Florida   March 4–7
Par 36–35—71; 7,089 yards   purse, $300,000

		SCORES			TOTAL	MONEY
Tom Kite	69	70	70	69	278	$54,000
Jack Nicklaus T.2	69	67	67	75	278	26,400
Denis Watson T.2	69	68	69	72	278	26,400
(Kite defeated Nicklaus and Watson on first hole of sudden-death playoff.)						
Craig Stadler	66	70	73	70	279	13,200

	SCORES				TOTAL	MONEY
Lanny Wadkins	69	69	70	71	279	13,200
Fuzzy Zoeller	67	74	72	67	280	10,425
Ray Floyd	68	70	66	76	280	10,425
Gil Morgan	67	74	72	68	281	8,700
Tom Jenkins	69	73	70	69	281	8,700
Scott Hoch	65	71	73	72	281	8,700
Manuel Pinero	71	68	74	69	282	6,150
Hale Irwin	68	74	70	70	282	6,150
Frank Conner	69	70	70	73	282	6,150
Dave Eichelberger	68	72	67	75	282	6,150
Larry Nelson	69	69	69	75	282	6,150
Woody Blackburn	70	70	68	74	282	6,150
Nick Faldo	72	67	73	71	283	4,800
Howard Clark	71	69	75	69	284	4,200
Scott Watkins	67	73	70	74	284	4,200
Curtis Strange	72	68	71	73	284	4,200
Andy Bean	72	71	73	69	285	3,240
Barry Jaeckel	72	67	73	73	285	3,240
Jay Haas	67	71	71	76	285	3,240
Jerry Pate	70	68	70	77	285	3,240
Bill Britton	68	72	72	74	286	2,640
Mark McNulty	68	73	74	72	287	2,220
Phil Hancock	70	69	75	73	287	2,220
Bobby Clampett	76	67	71	73	287	2,220
Mike McCullough	71	68	74	74	287	2,220
David Graham	73	67	71	76	287	2,220
Isao Aoki	70	73	75	70	288	1,740
Danny Talbot	69	74	74	71	288	1,740
Paul Azinger	71	72	73	72	288	1,740
Gary Hallberg	70	73	72	73	288	1,740
Gary Koch	74	68	71	75	288	1,740
Johnny Miller	72	68	72	76	288	1,740
Mark Calcavecchia	73	69	74	73	289	1,290
Ed Sneed	69	73	73	74	289	1,290
John Cook	73	70	72	74	289	1,290
Mark O'Meara	69	73	73	74	289	1,290
Mick Soli	65	73	76	75	289	1,290
Bruce Lietzke	71	72	71	75	289	1,290
Mark McCumber	69	72	72	76	289	1,290
Jim Simons	71	71	74	74	290	960
John Fought	68	75	73	74	290	960
Bobby Cole	68	73	73	76	290	960
Mike Brannan	71	71	72	76	290	960
Ben Crenshaw	70	72	78	71	291	786
Tom Shaw	74	69	74	74	291	786
Mike Smith	71	71	70	79	291	786

Honda Inverrary Classic

Inverrary Golf and Country Club, Lauderhill, Florida
Par 36-36—72; 7,129 yards

March 11–14
purse, $400,000

	SCORES				TOTAL	MONEY
Hale Irwin	65	71	67	66	269	$72,000
Tom Kite	65	67	71	67	270	35,200
George Burns	66	67	67	70	270	35,200
Bobby Clampett	68	70	67	66	271	19,200

	SCORES				TOTAL	MONEY
Calvin Peete	70	66	67	69	272	16,000
Ray Floyd	68	69	69	68	274	14,400
Ed Sneed	68	71	69	67	275	13,400
Peter Oosterhuis	70	67	68	71	276	12,400
Andy Bean	68	68	73	68	277	11,200
David Graham	67	74	69	67	277	11,200
Andy North	68	70	69	71	278	8,480
Scott Simpson	71	67	68	72	278	8,480
Johnny Miller	69	71	72	66	278	8,480
Seve Ballesteros	68	72	68	70	278	8,480
Denis Watson	73	68	66	71	278	8,480
Bob Gilder	70	68	69	72	279	6,200
Lee Trevino	69	71	66	73	279	6,200
Don Pooley	72	71	67	69	279	6,200
Bill Britton	74	68	69	68	279	6,200
Bobby Wadkins	70	68	70	72	280	4,035
Mark McNulty	68	71	69	72	280	4,035
Gil Morgan	70	68	69	73	280	4,035
Isao Aoki	68	71	71	70	280	4,035
Bruce Lietzke	69	71	70	70	280	4,035
Greg Powers	73	70	69	68	280	4,035
Tom Watson	71	69	69	71	280	4,035
Mark McCumber	71	70	70	69	280	4,035
Mike McCullough	69	70	73	69	281	2,720
George Archer	68	66	74	73	281	2,720
Howard Twitty	71	70	69	71	281	2,720
Larry Ziegler	70	71	70	70	281	2,720
Morris Hatalsky	72	69	69	71	281	2,720
Bill Rogers	68	70	73	71	282	2,068.58
Jim Simons	70	70	73	69	282	2,068.57
Bud Allin	72	70	70	70	282	2,068.57
Brad Bryant	68	74	70	70	282	2,068.57
J.C. Snead	73	70	70	69	282	2,068.57
Tom Purtzer	71	72	67	72	282	2,068.57
Mark Hayes	71	70	73	68	282	2,068.57
Gary Hallberg	68	69	74	72	283	1,680
Mark Lye	70	70	70	73	283	1,680
Bill Kratzert	68	71	74	71	284	1,322.29
Hal Sutton	70	67	74	73	284	1,322.29
Woody Blackburn	70	70	70	74	284	1,322.29
Doug Tewell	70	70	71	73	284	1,322.29
D.A. Weibring	72	71	67	74	284	1,322.28
Charles Coody	70	73	69	72	284	1,322.28
Payne Stewart	69	74	70	71	284	1,322.28
Mark James	69	70	73	73	285	998
Dan Pohl	68	70	77	70	285	998
Mick Soli	68	72	75	70	285	998
Leonard Thompson	74	69	70	72	285	998

Tournament Players Championship

Tournament Players Club, Ponte Vedra, Florida
Par 36–36—72; 6,857 yards

March 18–21
purse, $500,000

	SCORES				TOTAL	MONEY
Jerry Pate	70	73	70	67	280	$90,000
Scott Simpson	68	70	73	71	282	44,000

	SCORES			TOTAL	MONEY
Brad Bryant	70	69 71	72	282	44,000
Bruce Lietzke	69	72 69	73	283	24,000
Roger Maltbie	69	72 73	70	284	20,000
Hubert Green	73	75 70	68	286	16,187.50
Craig Stadler	71	68 75	72	286	16,187.50
Tom Watson	70	76 68	72	286	16,187.50
Seve Ballesteros	73	72 69	72	286	16,187.50
Jim Booros	73	72 71	71	287	12,500
Larry Nelson	67	72 77	71	287	12,500
Ed Sneed	68	71 74	74	287	12,500
J.C. Snead	72	76 70	70	288	9,100
George Burns	67	73 75	73	288	9,100
Scott Hoch	72	70 72	74	288	9,100
Tim Simpson	72	66 75	75	288	9,100
Vance Heafner	68	70 73	77	288	9,100
Bill Rogers	73	70 75	71	289	7,500
Bob Eastwood	69	72 74	75	290	6,500
Don January	69	73 72	76	290	6,500
Hale Irwin	70	68 75	77	290	6,500
Ray Floyd	78	70 71	72	291	4,800
Bob Byman	71	75 73	72	291	4,800
Tom Weiskopf	73	68 74	76	291	4,800
Gibby Gilbert	69	71 74	77	291	4,800
George Archer	69	73 70	79	291	4,800
Mike Reid	71	74 77	70	292	3,550
Peter Jacobsen	72	72 77	71	292	3,550
Tom Kite	71	71 75	75	292	3,550
D.A. Weibring	74	73 70	75	292	3,550
Jay Haas	72	66 77	77	292	3,550
Andy North	76	70 76	71	293	2,958.67
Bill Britton	71	76 70	76	293	2,958.67
Jim Thorpe	69	76 71	77	293	2,958.66
Nick Faldo	75	70 75	74	294	2,412.34
John Mahaffey	73	72 74	75	294	2,412.34
Bobby Cole	72	75 72	75	294	2,412.33
Bruce Fleisher	69	73 77	75	294	2,412.33
Andy Bean	77	69 73	75	294	2,412.33
Jim Simons	69	77 72	76	294	2,412.33
Calvin Peete	73	73 79	70	295	1,800
Jim Dent	73	73 78	71	295	1,800
Lee Elder	71	76 74	74	295	1,800
John Cook	72	75 73	75	295	1,800
Denis Watson	72	74 73	76	295	1,800
Bruce Douglass	77	69 73	76	295	1,800
Gil Morgan	70	76 78	72	296	1,345
George Cadle	74	74 74	74	296	1,345
Allen Miller	73	75 74	74	296	1,345
Mike McCullough	76	71 74	75	296	1,345

Sea Pines Heritage Classic

Harbour Town Golf Links, Hilton Head Island, South Carolina March 25–28
Par 36–35—71; 6,804 yards   purse, $300,000

	SCORES			TOTAL	MONEY
Tom Watson	69	68 72	71	280	$54,000

	SCORES				TOTAL	MONEY
Frank Conner	71	66	70	73	280	32,400
(Watson defeated Conner on third hole of sudden-death playoff.)						
D.A. Weibring	69	73	70	70	282	20,400
Bobby Clampett	70	71	72	70	283	12,400
Bob Shearer	69	71	71	72	283	12,400
Doug Tewell	68	71	71	73	283	12,400
Ed Sneed	74	69	68	73	284	9,350
Craig Stadler	69	70	71	74	284	9,350
Fred Couples	69	68	71	76	284	9,350
Gil Morgan	72	71	72	70	285	8,100
Gary Player	73	69	73	71	286	6,900
Mike Donald	64	75	76	71	286	6,900
*Jodie Mudd	72	74	66	74	286	
Scott Hoch	68	72	69	77	286	6,900
J.C. Snead	73	67	77	70	287	4,950
Fuzzy Zoeller	69	74	73	71	287	4,950
Mike McCullough	67	70	78	72	287	4,950
Peter Oosterhuis	74	70	71	72	287	4,950
George Archer	70	69	74	74	287	4,950
John Mahaffey	68	71	73	75	287	4,950
Nick Faldo	69	73	74	72	288	3,372
David Edwards	67	74	75	72	288	3,372
George Burns	68	75	73	72	288	3,372
Bill Rogers	72	71	72	73	288	3,372
Bobby Wadkins	68	76	70	74	288	3,372
Bob Gilder	71	72	73	73	289	2,520
Tom Purtzer	71	71	70	77	289	2,520
Tom Jenkins	69	73	77	71	290	2,085
Gibby Gilbert	67	74	78	71	290	2,085
Jay Cudd	72	70	76	72	290	2,085
Mark McCumber	72	72	72	74	290	2,085
Woody Blackburn	76	70	69	75	290	2,085
Larry Nelson	72	68	73	77	290	2,085
Peter Jacobsen	71	74	74	72	291	1,585
Mark Lye	72	71	76	72	291	1,585
Lyn Lott	71	75	73	72	291	1,585
Wally Armstrong	70	76	73	72	291	1,585
Jim Colbert	69	74	74	74	291	1,585
Chip Beck	70	72	72	77	291	1,585
Miller Barber	73	73	73	73	292	1,230
Tim Simpson	72	74	72	74	292	1,230
Mike Reid	69	74	74	75	292	1,230
Dan Pohl	70	69	78	75	292	1,230
Mike Sullivan	71	73	72	76	292	1,230
Jerry Pate	68	76	76	73	293	932.40
Bruce Devlin	73	72	74	74	293	932.40
Lanny Wadkins	73	68	77	75	293	932.40
Tommy Valentine	68	69	79	77	293	932.40
Tom Kite	69	73	73	78	293	932.40
Rex Caldwell	71	70	80	73	294	733
Jeff Mitchell	71	74	75	74	294	733
Lou Graham	72	74	74	74	294	733
John Cook	71	72	74	77	294	733
Keith Fergus	71	71	74	78	294	733
Bud Allin	64	75	75	80	294	733

Greater Greensboro Open

Forest Oaks Country Club, Greensboro, North Carolina   April 1–4
Par 36–36—72; 6,984 yards   purse, $300,000

		SCORES			TOTAL	MONEY
Danny Edwards	66	72	72	75	285	$54,000
Bobby Clampett	69	72	72	73	286	32,400
Jack Renner	73	72	72	70	287	20,400
Woody Blackburn	70	70	75	73	288	14,400
Ben Crenshaw	68	73	78	69	289	11,400
Bill Rogers	69	74	74	72	289	11,400
D.A. Weibring	71	68	75	76	290	9,037.50
Denis Watson	72	65	76	77	290	9,037.50
Doug Black	69	70	75	76	290	9,037.50
Lanny Wadkins	69	71	73	77	290	9,037.50
Bobby Wadkins	72	67	78	74	291	7,200
Wayne Levi	75	69	72	75	291	7,200
Yutaka Hagawa	69	76	78	69	292	6,000
Andy North	73	72	73	74	292	6,000
Ray Floyd	72	74	72	75	293	5,100
J.C. Snead	71	69	76	77	293	5,100
Peter Oosterhuis	67	74	73	79	293	5,100
Gary Player	72	73	76	73	294	4,050
Nick Faldo	75	71	74	74	294	4,050
Jack Newton	70	74	75	75	294	4,050
Gary Hallberg	70	71	77	76	294	4,050
Mark Pfeil	69	75	76	75	295	2,785
George Burns	72	74	73	76	295	2,785
Mike Sullivan	69	76	74	76	295	2,785
Leonard Thompson	70	70	78	77	295	2,785
Keith Fergus	66	73	77	79	295	2,785
Pat McGowan	69	74	73	79	295	2,785
Skeeter Heath	74	72	76	74	296	1,995
Wally Armstrong	77	69	75	75	296	1,995
Jim Dent	73	73	75	75	296	1,995
Bobby Nichols	73	73	74	76	296	1,995
Mark Lye	70	73	76	77	296	1,995
Peter Jacobsen	72	69	78	77	296	1,995
Pat Lindsay	74	70	77	76	297	1,515
George Archer	70	71	79	77	297	1,515
Bruce Douglass	71	71	76	79	297	1,515
George Cadle	67	73	77	80	297	1,515
Jim Booros	76	70	71	80	297	1,515
Mark Calcavecchia	70	76	71	80	297	1,515
Mark McCumber	71	69	82	76	298	1,080
Phil Hancock	76	70	77	75	298	1,080
Howard Twitty	73	72	76	77	298	1,080
Don Reese	72	73	76	77	298	1,080
Tom Purtzer	70	71	79	78	298	1,080
Bruce Lietzke	72	72	76	78	298	1,080
Jay Haas	71	75	74	78	298	1,080
Fuzzy Zoeller	71	68	75	84	298	1,080
Bob Shearer	73	73	79	74	299	754
Allen Miller	70	76	80	73	299	754
John Mazza	70	73	81	75	299	754
Jay Cudd	69	75	79	76	299	754
Roger Maltbie	70	75	78	76	299	754
Jim Thorpe	71	68	79	81	299	754

The Masters

Augusta National Golf Club, Augusta, Georgia   April 8–11
Par 36–36—72; 6,905 yards   purse, $368,652

	SCORES				TOTAL	MONEY
Craig Stadler	75	69	67	73	284	$64,000
Dan Pohl	75	75	67	67	284	39,000
(Stadler defeated Pohl on first hole of sudden-death playoff.)						
Severiano Ballesteros	73	73	68	71	285	21,000
Jerry Pate	74	73	67	71	285	21,000
Tom Kite	76	69	73	69	287	13,500
Tom Watson	77	69	70	71	287	13,500
Larry Nelson	79	71	70	69	289	11,067
Curtis Strange	74	70	73	72	289	11,067
Ray Floyd	74	72	69	74	289	11,067
Andy Bean	75	72	73	70	290	8,550
Mark Hayes	74	73	73	70	290	8,550
Fuzzy Zoeller	72	76	70	72	290	8,550
Tom Weiskopf	75	72	68	75	290	8,550
Bob Gilder	79	71	66	75	291	6,700
Yutaka Hagawa	75	74	71	72	292	5,850
Jim Simons	77	74	69	72	292	5,850
Gary Player	74	73	71	74	292	5,850
Jack Nicklaus	69	77	71	75	292	5,850
David Graham	73	77	70	73	293	5,000
Peter Jacobsen	78	75	70	71	294	4,300
Bruce Lietzke	76	75	69	74	294	4,300
Jack Renner	72	75	76	71	294	4,300
*Jodie Mudd	77	74	67	76	294	
Morris Hatalsky	73	77	75	70	295	3,075
Wayne Levi	77	76	72	70	295	3,075
Ben Crenshaw	74	80	70	71	295	3,075
Danny Edwards	75	74	74	72	295	3,075
Peter Oosterhuis	73	74	75	73	295	3,075
John Schroeder	77	71	70	77	295	3,075
George Archer	79	74	72	71	296	2,475
Calvin Peete	77	72	73	74	296	2,475
Ron Streck	74	76	75	73	298	2,300
Lanny Wadkins	75	78	72	74	299	2,100
George Burns	75	79	71	74	299	2,100
Keith Fergus	76	74	72	77	299	2,100
Tommy Aaron	78	72	77	73	300	1,875
Greg Norman	73	75	73	79	300	1,875
Bill Rogers	77	77	77	70	301	1,667
Lee Trevino	75	78	75	73	301	1,667
Juan Rodriguez	78	75	73	75	301	1,667
*Willard Wood	78	75	73	76	302	
*Jim Holtgrieve	74	76	72	80	302	
Hubert Green	76	72	77	78	303	1,500
Jay Haas	76	74	76	78	304	1,500
Gay Brewer	73	80	72	80	305	1,500
Bob Goalby	81	72	78	77	308	1,500
Arnold Palmer	75	76	78	80	309	1,500
Out of final 36 holes						
Isao Aoki	75	80			155	1,500
Bernhard Langer	77	78			155	1,500
*Jay Sigel	80	75			155	

	SCORES			TOTAL	MONEY
Charles Coody	75	81		156	1,500
John Cook	82	74		156	1,500
Dave Eichelberger	79	77		156	1,500
Ed Fiori	76	80		156	1,500
Lon Hinkle	81	75		156	1,500
John Mahaffey	76	80		156	1,500
Gil Morgan	78	78		156	1,500
Dave Barr	75	82		157	1,500
Art Wall	75	82		157	1,500
Hale Irwin	80	78		158	1,500
*Brian Lindley	80	78		158	
Andy North	86	72		158	1,500
*Corey Pavin	79	79		158	
Bill Casper	85	74		159	1,500
Don Pooley	79	80		159	1,500
*Robert Lewis, Jr.	83	78		161	
Johnny Miller	81	80		161	1,500
Jim Thorpe	88	74		162	1,500
*Nathaniel Crosby	85	78		163	
*Philippe Ploujoux	81	82		163	
*Frank Fuhrer, III	86	79		165	
Doug Ford	86	83		169	1,500
Frank Conner	89	82		171	1,500
Herman Keiser		WD			1,500
Sam Snead	82	WD			1,500
J.C. Snead	78	DQ			1,500

Magnolia Classic

Hattiesburg Country Club, Hattiesburg, Mississippi
Par 35–35—70; 6,594 yards

April 8–11
purse, $75,000

	SCORES				TOTAL	MONEY
Payne Stewart	65	67	71	67	270	$13,500
Jay Cudd	70	66	71	66	273	6,600
Bruce Douglass	68	69	63	73	273	6,600
Jim Dent	69	71	66	68	274	3,350
Charles Krenkel	70	70	67	67	274	3,350
Robert Thompson	69	70	69	66	274	3,350
Mark Calcavecchia	69	67	70	69	275	2,400
Ron Commans	69	69	68	69	275	2,400
Paul Azinger	66	70	70	69	275	2,400
Mike Smith	68	66	69	72	275	2,400
Terry Anton	68	70	70	68	276	1,687.50
Lennie Clements	68	71	70	67	276	1,687.50
Tom Woodard	67	68	69	72	276	1,687.50
Jim Kiely	69	70	66	71	276	1,687.50
Nick Faldo	68	71	70	68	277	1,300
Buddy Gardner	71	69	69	68	277	1,300
Don Levin	64	68	73	72	277	1,300
Roger Calvin	70	68	69	71	278	933.34
John Mazza	71	67	69	71	278	933.34
DeWitt Weaver	69	68	71	70	278	933.34
Bill Buttner	71	70	69	68	278	933.33
Dave Hill	71	65	73	69	278	933.33
Mike Donald	69	72	69	68	278	933.33
Jeff Thomsen	66	68	69	76	279	675

	SCORES				TOTAL	MONEY
Steven Liebler	72	69	66	72	279	675
Scott Steger	69	66	71	73	279	675
Allen Miller	71	65	71	72	279	675
Barney Thompson	68	73	69	69	279	675
Lance Ten Broeck	70	69	67	73	279	675
Jack Slocum	71	69	71	69	280	555
Eric Batten	73	67	71	69	280	555
Rick Borg	66	72	72	71	281	497.50
Bruce Fleisher	71	69	70	71	281	497.50
John Adams	71	67	72	72	282	450
Lindy Miller	72	69	69	72	282	450
Hal Sutton	71	69	66	76	282	450
Blaine McCallister	69	69	74	71	283	393
Jerry Heard	72	68	73	70	283	393
Jeff Sanders	70	71	71	71	283	393
Dave Lundstrom	73	68	71	71	283	393
Stan Altgelt	72	69	68	74	283	393
Tommy McGinnis	70	71	75	68	284	345
Bill Sander	69	70	75	70	284	345
Johnny Elam	72	69	70	73	284	345
Richard Zokol	71	69	70	74	284	345
Butch Baird	69	71	77	68	285	317.50
Bobby Cole	72	68	72	73	285	317.50
Ed Selser	69	71	74	72	286	310
David Thore	70	70	74	74	288	302.50
Gene George	71	70	72	75	288	302.50

MONY Tournament of Champions

LaCosta Country Club, Carlsbad, California
Par 36-36—72; 6,911 yards

April 15–18
purse, $350,000

	SCORES				TOTAL	MONEY
Lanny Wadkins	67	72	68	73	280	$63,000
Craig Stadler	74	72	73	64	283	26,162.50
Andy Bean	70	72	71	70	283	26,162.50
David Graham	70	72	70	71	283	26,162.50
Ron Streck	72	70	68	73	283	26,162.50
Johnny Miller	74	70	73	67	284	12,840
Danny Edwards	73	72	71	68	284	12,840
Wayne Levi	71	72	71	70	284	12,840
Tom Kite	72	74	65	73	284	12,840
Tom Watson	69	68	72	75	284	12,840
Lee Trevino	71	72	74	68	285	9,033.34
Dave Eichelberger	73	71	71	70	285	9,033.34
Fuzzy Zoeller	70	72	70	73	285	9,033.34
Ray Floyd	71	71	72	72	286	7,900
Hale Irwin	69	74	70	74	287	7,400
Keith Fergus	73	77	71	67	288	6,400
Bruce Lietzke	70	74	72	72	288	6,400
J.C. Snead	71	71	72	74	288	6,400
Peter Oosterhuis	72	66	76	75	289	5,450
John Mahaffey	73	73	75	69	290	4,775
Ed Fiori	70	73	76	71	290	4,775
Larry Nelson	74	73	71	72	290	4,775
Jay Haas	73	73	70	74	290	4,775
Morris Hatalsky	74	74	72	71	291	4,300

	SCORES				TOTAL	MONEY
Jerry Pate	72	72	71	76	291	4,300
Tom Weiskopf	70	72	75	75	292	4,100
Bill Rogers	69	76	72	75	292	4,100
Dave Barr	74	73	72	74	293	3,950
Jim Simons	70	73	78	76	297	3,850
Jack Renner	77	72	75	74	298	3,750
Hubert Green	73	75	75	76	299	3,650

Tallahassee Open

Killearn Golf & Country Club, Tallahassee, Florida
Par 36–36—72; 7,024 yards

April 15–18
purse, $100,000

	SCORES				TOTAL	MONEY
Bob Shearer	69	69	68	66	272	$18,000
Hal Sutton	66	69	72	66	273	8,800
Denis Watson	69	68	69	67	273	8,800
Tim Simpson	69	68	69	68	274	4,950
Rik Massengale	71	67	71	66	275	3,825
John Adams	68	70	70	67	275	3,825
Mark Lye	72	69	67	67	275	3,825
Bob Murphy	70	67	68	70	275	3,825
Bobby Wadkins	68	71	67	70	276	2,900
Bob Byman	67	69	66	74	276	2,900
Pat McGowan	69	72	67	69	277	2,600
Ed Sneed	67	70	71	70	278	2,300
Rod Curl	73	68	65	72	278	2,300
Leonard Thompson	70	70	70	69	279	1,720
Roger Calvin	71	69	69	70	279	1,720
Pat Lindsey	67	73	69	70	279	1,720
Jim Dent	67	70	71	71	279	1,720
Antonio Cerda	69	72	67	71	279	1,720
Bobby Cole	74	67	71	68	280	1,142.86
Mark Calcavecchia	70	69	72	69	280	1,142.86
Mark Pfeil	69	71	71	69	280	1,142.86
Joe Inman	70	68	72	70	280	1,142.86
Woody Blackburn	71	70	67	72	280	1,142.86
Bob Duval	70	69	67	74	280	1,142.85
Mark O'Meara	69	69	67	75	280	1,142.85
Tommy Aaron	73	68	71	69	281	900
Wally Armstrong	71	68	72	71	282	816.67
Mike Donald	70	71	70	71	282	816.67
Larry Rinker	62	75	71	74	282	816.66
Lennie Clements	72	69	72	70	283	675
Ed Dougherty	72	68	72	71	283	675
Jodie Mudd	71	69	70	73	283	675
Barry Jaeckel	71	69	70	73	283	675
Tommy Armour III	66	71	72	74	283	675
Tommy McGinnis	71	70	69	73	283	675
Roger Maltbie	72	68	73	71	284	550
Rex Caldwell	71	68	72	73	284	550
Jim Thorpe	67	71	73	73	284	550
Tim Graham	72	69	69	74	284	550
Jim Bertoncino	70	71	72	72	285	485
Jim Booros	69	72	70	74	285	485
Brad Bryant	70	71	70	74	285	485

	SCORES			TOTAL	MONEY
Bob Eastwood	69	69	72	75	285	485
Beau Baugh	69	71	70	76	286	460
Tim Norris	67	74	73	74	288	435
DeWitt Weaver	66	75	73	74	288	435
Gavin Levenson	67	69	76	76	288	435
David Thore	69	70	72	77	288	435
Gary Hallberg	73	67	74	75	289	410
Mike Hill	72	69	76	79	296	400

USF & G Classic

Lakewood Country Club, New Orleans, Louisiana   April 22–26
Par 36–36—72; 7,080 yards   purse, $300,000
(Tournament extended to Monday, shortened to three rounds because of rain.)

	SCORES			TOTAL	MONEY
Scott Hoch	67	69	70	206	$54,000
Tom Watson	71	70	67	208	26,400
Bob Shearer	66	71	71	208	26,400
Steve Melnyk	69	72	68	209	14,400
Vance Heafner	72	70	68	210	10,537.50
Jodie Mudd	72	71	67	210	10,537.50
Don Pooley	72	68	70	210	10,537.50
Lon Hinkle	70	69	71	210	10,537.50
Jay Haas	69	73	69	211	7,200
Chip Beck	71	70	70	211	7,200
Bruce Fleisher	71	69	71	211	7,200
Bob Eastwood	71	69	71	211	7,200
Gil Morgan	71	69	71	211	7,200
Larry Ziegler	68	71	72	211	7,200
Tommy Valentine	75	68	69	212	4,086
Dave Eichelberger	69	75	68	212	4,086
Lanny Wadkins	72	72	68	212	4,086
Lou Graham	71	73	68	212	4,086
Barry Jaeckel	70	72	70	212	4,086
Curtis Strange	72	70	70	212	4,086
Mike Reid	72	70	70	212	4,086
Wally Armstrong	71	71	70	212	4,086
Gary Koch	71	68	73	212	4,086
Tom Jenkins	69	69	74	212	4,086
Allen Miller	72	72	69	213	2,450
Lennie Clements	72	70	71	213	2,450
Jim Simons	68	71	74	213	2,450
Lindy Miller	71	73	70	214	1,952.15
Bill Kratzert	70	72	72	214	1,952.15
Jeff Sanders	73	72	69	214	1,952.14
Wayne Levi	75	67	72	214	1,952.14
George Burns	75	70	69	214	1,952.14
Jim Colbert	67	73	74	214	1,952.14
Doug Tewell	75	71	68	214	1,952.14
*Tommy Moore	73	70	71	214	
David Edwards	72	72	71	215	1,355
Phil Hancock	71	72	72	215	1,355
Mark Pfeil	71	72	72	215	1,355
Joe Inman	73	69	73	215	1,355
Jay Cudd	72	73	70	215	1,355
Lance Ten Broeck	72	73	70	215	1,355

	SCORES			TOTAL	MONEY
Dan Pohl	71	74	70	215	1,355
Steve Thomas	72	74	69	215	1,355
Leonard Thompson	73	73	69	215	1,355
Danny Edwards	73	70	73	216	990
George Archer	68	76	72	216	990
Ed Dougherty	74	71	71	216	990
Roger Calvin	71	73	73	217	793.20
Bobby Wadkins	73	71	73	217	793.20
Tim Graham	73	71	73	217	793.20
Tom McGinnis	74	72	71	217	793.20
Greg Powers	69	74	74	217	793.20

Byron Nelson Classic

Preston Trail Golf Club, Dallas, Texas   April 29–May 2
Par 35–35—70; 6,993 yards   purse, $350,000

	SCORES				TOTAL	MONEY
Bob Gilder	67	65	67	67	266	$63,000
Curtis Strange	65	72	65	69	271	37,800
Tom Watson	71	68	67	67	273	18,200
Dan Halldorson	68	68	69	68	273	18,200
David Graham	68	69	66	70	273	18,200
Bruce Lietzke	69	69	70	66	274	11,331.25
Bob Shearer	68	68	71	67	274	11,331.25
Phil Hancock	70	68	66	70	274	11,331.25
George Archer	65	68	71	70	274	11,331.25
Pat Lindsey	70	72	69	65	276	7,758.34
Lon Hinkle	69	68	72	67	276	7,758.34
Scott Hoch	72	68	68	68	276	7,758.33
Bobby Wadkins	68	69	70	69	276	7,758.33
Jack Newton	71	69	67	69	276	7,758.33
Jim Colbert	68	72	66	70	276	7,758.33
Mike Reid	70	73	67	67	277	5,600
Vance Heafner	66	70	72	69	277	5,600
Bruce Fleisher	66	73	67	71	277	5,600
Tim Graham	68	74	67	69	278	4,725
D.A. Weibring	68	68	69	73	278	4,725
Steve Melnyk	71	71	71	66	279	4,060
Bob Eastwood	69	70	71	69	279	4,060
Ray Floyd	72	70	72	66	280	3,027.50
Jay Cudd	70	71	70	69	280	3,027.50
Lance Ten Broeck	72	68	70	70	280	3,027.50
Ron Streck	70	71	69	70	280	3,027.50
Tom Jones	71	66	71	72	280	3,027.50
Mike Holland	67	73	68	72	280	3,027.50
Jerry Heard	72	70	73	66	281	2,432.50
Barry Harwell	68	74	72	67	281	2,432.50
Tom Kite	72	69	73	68	282	1,942.50
Scott Simpson	69	69	75	69	282	1,942.50
Antonio Cerda	72	69	72	69	282	1,942.50
Don Reese	71	70	72	69	282	1,942.50
Howard Twitty	71	71	70	70	282	1,942.50
Thomas Gray	71	70	71	70	282	1,942.50
Calvin Peete	69	72	70	71	282	1,942.50
Woody Blackburn	71	70	68	73	282	1,942.50
George Burns	71	70	74	68	283	1,261.40

	SCORES				TOTAL	MONEY
Forrest Fezler	70	69	74	70	283	1,261.40
Mark Hayes	70	71	70	72	283	1,261.40
Mike Nicolette	69	73	69	72	283	1,261.40
Jack Renner	72	70	69	72	283	1,261.40
Mark Lye	71	69	70	73	283	1,261.40
Leonard Thompson	69	70	70	74	283	1,261.40
Eric Batten	66	75	68	74	283	1,261.40
Tom Purtzer	70	71	67	75	283	1,261.40
Morris Hatalsky	67	72	68	76	283	1,261.40

Michelob — Houston Open

Woodlands Country Club, Woodlands, Texas   May 6–9
Par 36–35—71; 7,031 yards   purse, $350,000

	SCORES				TOTAL	MONEY
Ed Sneed	64	70	71	70	275	$63,000
Bob Shearer	69	67	64	75	275	37,800
(Sneed defeated Shearer on first hole of sudden-death playoff.)						
Danny Edwards	71	68	69	68	276	23,800
George Burns	73	68	69	67	277	16,800
Tom Kite	70	69	73	66	278	13,300
Tommy Valentine	68	71	72	67	278	13,300
Peter Oosterhuis	68	68	72	71	279	11,287.50
Scott Hoch	65	73	69	72	279	11,287.50
Jim Dent	73	67	71	69	280	9,450
Jay Haas	72	69	69	70	280	9,450
Ron Streck	70	69	67	74	280	9,450
Lennie Clements	74	70	67	70	281	7,700
Peter Jacobsen	70	70	68	73	281	7,700
Antonio Cerda	69	73	70	70	282	6,125
Pat McGowan	71	71	69	71	282	6,125
David Graham	70	72	68	72	282	6,125
Woody Blackburn	69	73	68	72	282	6,125
Payne Stewart	73	71	71	68	283	4,260
Ed Dougherty	67	75	72	69	283	4,260
Mike Sullivan	73	71	70	69	283	4,260
Jack Renner	71	69	72	71	283	4,260
Fred Couples	71	66	74	72	283	4,260
Bobby Clampett	67	74	69	73	283	4,260
Dan Halldorson	71	73	67	72	283	4,260
Hal Sutton	74	69	72	69	284	2,671.67
Dave Eichelberger	71	71	72	70	284	2,671.67
Bob Gilder	70	73	71	70	284	2,671.67
Thomas Gray	70	74	70	70	284	2,671.67
Allen Miller	71	69	72	72	284	2,671.66
Steve Melnyk	68	75	69	72	284	2,671.66
Ken Green	70	72	74	69	285	2,075.60
Mike Nicolette	71	71	72	71	285	2,075.60
Bruce Lietzke	71	72	69	73	285	2,075.60
Hubert Green	70	69	72	74	285	2,075.60
Hale Irwin	67	71	73	74	285	2,075.60
Scott Simpson	71	73	72	70	286	1,542.13
Gibby Gilbert	68	76	70	72	286	1,542.13
Jodie Mudd	67	74	72	73	286	1,542.13
Victor Regalado	73	68	72	73	286	1,542.13
Andy North	71	70	71	74	286	1,542.12

	SCORES				TOTAL	MONEY
Tom Purtzer	69	69	73	75	286	1,542.12
Wally Armstrong	71	72	68	75	286	1,542.12
Gil Morgan	72	67	70	77	286	1,542.12
D.A. Weibring	68	72	77	70	287	1,087.80
Gavin Levenson	72	72	72	71	287	1,087.80
Curtis Strange	70	70	73	74	287	1,087.80
Leonard Thompson	72	72	68	75	287	1,087.80
Mike Reid	69	74	68	76	287	1,087.80

Colonial National Invitation

Colonial Country Club, Fort Worth, Texas   May 13–16
Par 35–35—70; 7,190 yards   purse, $350,000

	SCORES				TOTAL	MONEY
Jack Nicklaus	66	70	70	67	273	$63,000
Andy North	68	69	67	72	276	37,800
Jerry Pate	69	68	69	71	277	23,800
Tom Kite	68	68	74	68	278	16,800
Bob Eastwood	74	71	70	65	280	12,293.75
Joe Inman	69	73	70	68	280	12,293.75
Lennie Clements	66	69	75	70	280	12,293.75
Tom Purtzer	69	74	67	70	280	12,293.75
Lee Trevino	72	74	67	68	281	9,800
Danny Edwards	72	68	66	75	281	9,800
Hubert Green	73	66	76	67	282	7,700
Curtis Strange	72	71	69	70	282	7,700
Steve Melnyk	74	69	69	70	282	7,700
Frank Conner	71	70	69	72	282	7,700
George Burns	73	72	71	67	283	5,600
Chip Beck	73	74	69	67	283	5,600
Bruce Lietzke	71	74	69	69	283	5,600
Bobby Wadkins	70	72	70	71	283	5,600
Roger Maltbie	73	69	68	73	283	5,600
Peter Oosterhuis	69	70	76	69	284	3,530.63
John Mahaffey	70	70	74	70	284	3,530.63
John Cook	71	73	70	70	284	3,530.63
Bruce Fleisher	72	70	72	70	284	3,530.63
Mike Reid	73	72	69	70	284	3,530.62
Ben Crenshaw	72	72	70	70	284	3,530.62
Don January	70	74	69	71	284	3,530.62
Bob Murphy	69	71	71	73	284	3,530.62
Jim Booros	68	77	74	66	285	2,327.50
Greg Powers	70	75	71	69	285	2,327.50
Scott Hoch	69	72	73	71	285	2,327.50
John Schroeder	74	70	70	71	285	2,327.50
Mike Donald	71	70	72	72	285	2,327.50
George Archer	68	72	73	72	285	2,327.50
Barry Jaeckel	68	77	72	69	286	1,890
Tommy Valentine	73	72	70	71	286	1,890
Bobby Clampett	70	73	71	72	286	1,890
Jay Haas	71	74	74	68	287	1,575
Gene Littler	70	73	73	71	287	1,575
Tom Jenkins	72	75	68	72	287	1,575
Fuzzy Zoeller	69	72	72	74	287	1,575
Vance Heafner	65	76	70	76	287	1,575
Al Geiberger	73	72	73	70	288	1,017.70

	SCORES				TOTAL	MONEY
Fred Couples	77	70	71	70	288	1,017.70
Doug Tewell	69	76	72	71	288	1,017.70
Brad Bryant	68	73	75	72	288	1,107.69
Ed Sneed	71	76	70	71	288	1,107.69
Dan Pohl	72	73	72	71	288	1,017.69
Mike Sullivan	72	73	71	72	288	1,017.69
Larry Nelson	68	76	72	72	288	1,017.69
Gil Morgan	74	71	71	72	288	1,017.69

Georgia Pacific-Atlanta Classic

Atlanta Country Club, Marietta, Georgia   May 20–23
Par 36–36—72; 7,007 yards   purse, $300,000

	SCORES				TOTAL	MONEY
Keith Fergus	66	72	66	69	273	$54,000
Ray Floyd	72	69	64	68	273	32,400
(Fergus defeated Floyd on first hole of sudden-death playoff.)						
Wayne Levi	69	68	69	68	274	20,400
Larry Nelson	66	67	68	74	275	14,400
David Edwards	72	69	68	67	276	10,170
Scott Hoch	67	67	74	68	276	10,170
Steve Melnyk	70	73	66	67	276	10,170
Gibby Gilbert	69	69	69	69	276	10,170
Peter Jacobsen	68	69	67	72	276	10,170
Joe Inman	67	72	71	67	277	8,100
Hubert Green	68	71	71	68	278	7,500
George Cadle	72	72	67	68	279	6,075
Calvin Peete	69	70	71	69	279	6,075
Tommy Valentine	71	69	68	71	279	6,075
Tom Watson	68	70	69	72	279	6,075
Payne Stewart	70	71	72	67	280	4,800
Dan Halldorson	70	72	69	69	280	4,800
Mike Nicolette	70	71	69	70	280	4,800
Mark Pfeil	70	71	71	69	281	3,636
Jim Barber	71	72	69	69	281	3,636
Dave Eichelberger	74	66	70	71	281	3,636
Lee Elder	70	69	68	74	281	3,636
Roger Maltbie	70	67	69	75	281	3,636
Clarence Rose	67	72	73	70	282	2,640
Allen Miller	71	70	69	72	282	2,640
Vance Heafner	73	70	66	73	282	2,640
Danny Edwards	72	72	72	67	283	2,130
Doug Tewell	72	70	74	67	283	2,130
Tom Gray	73	72	69	69	283	2,130
Charles Coody	71	68	73	71	283	2,130
Lanny Wadkins	72	64	74	73	283	2,130
Richard Zokol	73	69	72	70	284	1,736.25
Lyn Lott	71	71	71	71	284	1,736.25
Peter Oosterhuis	67	71	73	73	284	1,736.25
Jack Newton	70	71	70	73	284	1,736.25
Gavin Levenson	71	73	73	68	285	1,321.88
Jay Haas	74	70	72	69	285	1,321.88
Wally Armstrong	69	72	74	70	285	1,321.88
Bill Rogers	71	70	73	71	285	1,321.88
Al Geiberger	76	69	68	72	285	1,321.87
Tom Jenkins	74	70	69	72	285	1,321.87

	SCORES				TOTAL	MONEY
Rod Nuckolls	73	68	70	74	285	1,321.87
Doug Black	69	70	71	75	285	1,321.87
Larry Ziegler	75	69	75	67	286	885.43
Andy Bean	72	73	71	70	286	885.43
Chip Beck	75	68	72	71	286	885.43
Lennie Clements	70	71	73	72	286	885.43
Beau Baugh	70	71	73	72	286	885.43
Frank Conner	74	71	69	72	286	885.43
Fuzzy Zoeller	71	69	71	75	286	885.42

Memorial Tournament

Muirfield Village Golf Club, Dublin, Ohio
Par 36–36—72; 7,116 yards

May 27–30
purse, $380,445

	SCORES				TOTAL	MONEY
Ray Floyd	74	69	67	71	281	$63,000
Wayne Levi	74	70	69	70	283	23,100
Peter Jacobsen	74	69	68	72	283	23,100
Gil Morgan	72	70	67	74	283	23,100
Roger Maltbie	68	66	75	74	283	23,100
Bruce Lietzke	73	70	71	70	284	12,162.50
Dan Pohl	70	72	70	72	284	12,162.50
Jay Haas	70	72	70	73	285	10,150
Scott Simpson	71	69·	71	74	285	10,150
Tom Purtzer	74	69	68	74	285	10,150
Jack Nicklaus	74	68	72	72	286	7,420
Fred Couples	71	71	73	71	286	7,420
Howard Twitty	73	70	70	73	286	7,420
Bobby Clampett	74	68	70	74	286	7,420
Hale Irwin	70	70	71	75	286	7,420
Tom Watson	74	73	70	70	287	5,075
Hal Sutton	71	69	75	72	287	5,075
Don Pooley	73	68	73	73	287	5,075
Fuzzy Zoeller	76	72	66	73	287	5,075
Peter Oosterhuis	71	69	72	75	287	5,075
Bob Gilder	72	70	69	76	287	5,075
Mike Sullivan	71	72	73	72	288	3,404
Tom Jenkins	71	73	71	73	288	3,404
Mike Holland	75	71	68	74	288	3,404
Johnny Miller	70	72	71	75	288	3,404
Calvin Peete	72	72	69	75	288	3,404
Lou Graham	70	74	73	72	289	2,642.86
Keith Fergus	69	76	72	72	289	2,642.86
Andy Bean	75	68	73	73	289	2,542.86
Tom Kite	70	75	70	74	289	2,642.86
Gary Player	75	72	68	74	289	2,642.86
Bruce Fleisher	69	73	70	77	289	2,642.85
Lon Hinkle	72	72	68	77	289	2,642.85
Ed Sneed	74	72	72	72	290	2,275
George Archer	78	68	71	73	290	2,275
Dan Halldorson	74	75	68	73	290	2,275
Jim Colbert	71	71	73	75	290	2,275
Jerry Pate	74	73	68	75	290	2,275
Scott Hoch	73	68	73	76	290	2,275
D.A. Weibring	76	72	73	70	291	2,000
Mark McNulty	73	74	73	71	291	2,000

		SCORES			TOTAL	MONEY
Danny Edwards	72	73	73	74	291	2,000
J.C. Snead	76	69	71	75	291	2,000
Steve Melnyk	69	74	71	77	291	2,000
Frank Conner	69	72	72	78	291	2,000
Skeeter Heath	73	76	71	72	292	1,850
John Cook	70	72	76	74	292	1,850
John Schroeder	76	69	73	74	292	1,850
Bob Eastwood	71	72	74	75	292	1,850
Mike Reid	72	74	74	73	293	1,760
Bobby Wadkins	76	73	70	74	293	1,760
Seve Ballesteros	72	73	73	75	293	1,760
Mark Hayes	71	78	70	74	293	1,760
Greg Powers	70	74	71	78	293	1,760

Kemper Open

Congressional Country Club, Bethesda, Maryland
Par 36-36—72; 7,113 yards

June 3–6
purse, $400,000

		SCORES			TOTAL	MONEY
Craig Stadler	72	67	67	69	275	$72,000
Seve Ballesteros	72	69	72	69	282	43,200
Jack Nicklaus	72	65	72	74	283	23,200
Gil Morgan	68	72	70	73	283	23,200
George Burns	75	66	73	70	284	16,000
Steve Melnyk	72	71	71	72	286	14,400
Jim Nelford	77	69	73	68	287	12,050
Calvin Peete	69	74	73	71	287	12,050
Bob Eastwood	71	72	72	72	287	12,050
Dan Halldorson	74	69	69	75	287	12,050
Jodie Mudd	74	71	69	74	288	9,600
Lon Hinkle	70	74	70	74	288	9,600
Leonard Thompson	73	73	73	70	289	7,500
Mark Lye	73	72	73	71	289	7,500
Gavin Levenson	68	73	76	72	289	7,500
Charles Coody	72	73	70	74	289	7,500
Clarence Rose	70	74	75	71	290	5,060
D.A. Weibring	76	72	71	71	290	5,060
Lance Ten Broeck	74	73	71	72	290	5,060
Jim Colbert	74	72	71	73	290	5,060
Mark McNulty	72	73	72	73	290	5,060
Bob Byman	73	71	72	74	290	5,060
Mike Reid	73	71	71	75	290	5,060
Wayne Levi	72	71	68	79	290	5,060
Hal Sutton	75	70	75	71	291	3,266.67
Bill Britton	71	76	73	71	291	3,266.67
George Archer	76	66	71	78	291	3,266.66
Dave Eichelberger	72	72	79	69	292	2,660
Andy Bean	71	73	77	71	292	2,660
Phil Hancock	73	76	72	71	292	2,660
Lee Elder	76	71	73	72	292	2,660
Greg Powers	76	70	72	74	292	2,660
Bob Gilder	73	75	68	76	292	2,660
Bob Tway	74	75	73	71	293	1,935
Pat McGowan	72	76	74	71	293	1,935
Fred Couples	71	74	76	72	293	1,935
Gary Player	74	73	73	73	293	1,935

	SCORES				TOTAL	MONEY
George Cadle	71	77	72	73	293	1,935
Ronnie Black	75	70	74	74	293	1,935
Ron Commans	71	75	73	74	293	1,935
Gibby Gilbert	70	72	74	77	293	1,935
Mark McCumber	74	75	75	70	294	1,322.29
Don January	73	72	75	74	294	1,322.29
Doug Tewell	71	76	73	74	294	1,322.29
Steven Liebler	72	73	75	74	294	1,322.29
Payne Stewart	76	73	71	74	294	1,322.28
Andy North	76	73	71	74	294	1,322.28
Tom Purtzer	77	70	70	77	294	1,322.28
Ed Dougherty	74	74	73	74	295	1,024
J.C. Snead	74	71	74	76	295	1,024

Danny Thomas — Memphis Classic

Colonial Country Club, Cordova, Tennessee
Par 36-36—72; 7,249 yards

June 10–13
purse, $400,000

	SCORES				TOTAL	MONEY
Ray Floyd	67	68	67	69	271	$72,000
Mike Holland	72	67	68	70	277	43,200
Curtis Strange	72	70	67	69	278	27,200
Mark McNulty	74	67	67	71	279	19,200
Mark Lye	67	71	71	71	280	16,000
Scott Hoch	73	71	68	69	281	14,400
J.C. Snead	70	72	68	72	282	12,900
Tom Purtzer	72	67	69	74	282	12,900
Larry Nelson	72	69	72	70	283	10,400
Payne Stewart	75	72	67	69	283	10,400
Bob Murphy	70	74	69	70	283	10,400
Hal Sutton	72	67	70	74	283	10,400
Wayne Levi	71	71	73	69	284	7,733.34
Gil Morgan	75	71	69	69	284	7,733.33
Tom Kite	70	73	71	70	284	7,733.33
Bob Eastwood	73	74	71	67	285	6,600
Dave Hill	71	70	71	73	285	6,600
Lon Hinkle	73	69	75	69	286	5,216
Pat McGowan	74	68	74	70	286	5,216
Frank Conner	71	72	71	72	286	5,216
Larry Ziegler	70	74	70	72	286	5,216
Hale Irwin	72	74	67	73	286	5,216
Lindy Miller	72	74	72	69	287	3,680
Charles Coody	71	74	69	73	287	3,680
Don Pooley	72	72	69	74	287	3,680
Bobby Cole	71	72	70	74	287	3,680
Chuck Thorpe	72	75	70	71	288	2,720
Fred Couples	72	71	73	72	288	2,720
Perry Arthur	72	70	74	72	288	2,720
Ron Streck	70	73	73	72	288	2,720
Bill Sander	74	70	71	73	288	2,720
Mark McCumber	68	76	70	74	288	2,720
Jim Nelford	76	63	72	77	288	2,720
Gibby Gilbert	74	72	73	70	289	1,977.15
Dave Eichelberger	73	73	72	71	289	1,977.15
Peter Jacobsen	73	71	72	73	289	1,977.14
George Cadle	72	74	70	73	289	1,977.14

	SCORES				TOTAL	MONEY
Phil Hancock	74	72	70	73	289	1,977.14
Rod Curl	73	71	70	75	289	1,977.14
Lance Ten Broeck	70	70	73	76	289	1,977.14
Mark Pfeil	72	74	70	74	290	1,520
Roger Maltbie	74	71	71	74	290	1,520
Bill Britton	71	73	72	74	290	1,520
Mike Gove	74	73	68	75	290	1,520
Jeff Mitchell	74	71	77	69	291	1,204
Bob Byman	76	71	72	72	291	1,204
Doug Tewell	70	74	74	73	291	1,204
Lon Nielsen	74	70	74	73	291	1,204
Alan Tapie	76	71	74	71	292	998
Gene Littler	74	72	74	72	292	998
John Mahaffey	74	73	73	72	292	998
Gary Koch	69	74	74	75	292	998

U.S. Open

Pebble Beach Golf Links, Pebble Beach, California   June 17–20
Par 36–36—72; 6,825 yards   purse, $375,000

	SCORES				TOTAL	MONEY
Tom Watson	72	72	68	70	282	$60,000
Jack Nicklaus	74	70	71	69	284	34,506
Bobby Clampett	71	73	72	70	286	14,967
Dan Pohl	72	74	70	70	286	14,967
Bill Rogers	70	73	69	74	286	14,967
Gary Koch	78	73	69	67	287	8,011
Jay Haas	75	74	70	68	287	8,011
Lanny Wadkins	73	76	67	71	287	8,011
David Graham	73	72	69	73	287	8,011
Calvin Peete	71	72	72	73	288	6,332
Bruce Devlin	70	69	75	74	288	6,332
Charles Beck	76	75	69	69	289	5,510.67
Danny Edwards	71	75	73	70	289	5,510.67
Lyn Lott	72	71	75	71	289	5,510.66
Fuzzy Zoeller	72	76	71	71	290	4,661
J.C. Snead	73	75	71	71	290	4,661
Larry Rinker	74	67	75	74	290	4,661
Scott Simpson	73	69	72	76	290	4,661
Hal Sutton	73	76	72	70	291	4,008.34
Larry Nelson	74	72	74	71	291	4,008.33
Ben Crenshaw	76	74	68	73	291	4,008.33
Joe Hager	78	72	72	70	292	3,403.72
Gene Littler	74	75	72	71	292	3,403.72
Andy North	72	71	77	72	292	3,403.72
Mike Brannan	75	74	71	72	292	3,403.71
John Mahaffey	77	72	70	73	292	3,403.71
Gil Morgan	75	75	68	74	292	3,403.71
Craig Stadler	76	70	70	76	292	3,403.71
Tom Kite	73	71	75	74	293	3,006
Isao Aoki	77	74	72	71	294	2,718
Jack Renner	74	71	77	72	294	2,718
Greg Powers	77	71	74	72	294	2,718
Don Bies	73	74	74	73	294	2,718
Peter Oosterhuis	73	78	67	76	294	2,718
Jim Thorpe	72	73	72	77	294	2,718

	SCORES				TOTAL	MONEY
George Burns	72	72	70	80	294	2,718
Terry Diehl	71	77	75	72	295	2,430.50
Bob Gilder	73	76	74	72	295	2,430.50
Tom Weiskopf	74	77	73	72	296	2,175
Lou Graham	75	73	74	74	296	2,175
Curtis Strange	74	73	74	75	296	2,175
Rod Nuckolls	78	73	69	76	296	2,175
Hale Irwin	76	75	68	77	296	2,175
Kermit Zarley	75	74	69	78	296	2,175
Johnny Miller	78	69	78	72	297	1,855
Dave Stockton	79	71	73	74	297	1,855
Woody Blackburn	75	73	73	76	297	1,855
Lon Hinkle	73	75	69	80	297	1,855
Ray Floyd	78	73	75	72	298	1,599
Clarence Rose	73	78	73	74	298	1,599
Bob Shearer	75	75	72	76	298	1,599
Skeeter Heath	73	74	74	77	298	1,599
Butch Baird	72	75	78	74	299	1,409.34
Larry Ziegler	77	74	73	75	299	1,409.33
Vance Heafner	75	74	74	76	299	1,409.33
Tom Sieckmann	77	73	75	76	301	1,358
Ron Streck	72	77	75	77	301	1,358
Mark O'Meara	77	74	77	74	302	1,336
*Nathaniel Crosby	77	73	76	77	303	
Bobby Wadkins	73	74	82	75	304	1,319
*Corey Pavin	77	74	78	75	304	
Jim King	71	77	80	77	305	1,300
Kenny Knox	76	75	77	77	305	1,300
Lloyd Monroe	79	70	78	78	305	1,300
William Israelson	76	69	80	83	308	1,300
Doug Tewell	75	75	79	90	319	1,300

Out of final 36 holes

	SCORES		TOTAL
*Gary Marlowe	79	73	152
Joe Inman	75	77	152
Frank Conner	83	69	152
Mike Reid	75	77	152
Bruce Lietzke	76	76	152
Bobby Heins	73	79	152
Keith Fergus	73	79	152
Hubert Green	78	74	152
Bill Bergin	73	79	152
Bob Mann	75	78	153
Scott Spence	79	74	153
Arthur Russell	78	75	153
Donnie Hammond	80	73	153
*Jeff Wilson	78	75	153
Mark Hayes	78	75	153
Jerry Pate	79	74	153
*Brad Faxon	79	74	153
John McNaney	81	72	153
Mark McCumber	79	75	154
Chi Chi Rodriguez	80	74	154
Don Pooley	79	75	154
Lee Trevino	78	76	154
John Calabria	77	77	154
Ronnie Black	76	78	154

	SCORES		TOTAL
Tom Purtzer	74	80	154
Keith Killmeyer	77	77	154
Jay Don Black	78	76	154
John Traub	81	74	155
John Cook	79	76	155
Ralph Landrum	78	77	155
Bobby Nichols	81	74	155
Jack Ferenz	76	79	155
Joey Sindelar	80	75	155
Stan Stopa	78	77	155
*David Nelson	79	76	155
Gary Player	78	78	156
*Willie Wood	78	78	156
Tom Jenkins	75	81	156
Arnold Palmer	81	75	156
Larry Mize	82	74	156
Gary Pinns	74	82	156
Tim Norris	86	71	157
Rod Funseth	80	77	157
Daniel Forsman	79	78	157
Eugene Tredway	76	81	157
Ron Vlosich	78	79	157
*Brian Fogt	79	78	157
Bradley Sherfy	78	79	157
*Frank Fuhrer	78	79	157
Mark McNulty	82	75	157
*Chris Perry	76	81	157
Mike Stubblefield	76	81	157
Scott Stegner	81	77	158
John Schroeder	80	78	158
Bill Britton	81	77	158
Bob Hoyt	79	79	158
Jim Simons	81	78	159
Jim Albus	82	77	159
Bernhard Langer	80	79	159
Richard Gilstad	81	78	159
Jeff Gryfiel	81	78	159
*Wayne Player	81	79	160
Morris Hatalsky	79	81	160
Seve Ballesteros	81	79	160
Bill Schumaker	81	79	160
Don Robertson	78	82	160
Jon Chaffee	84	76	160
Mel Buam	83	78	161
Ken Green	78	83	161
*Guy Bill	79	82	161
Steve Spray	80	81	161
Dick Crosby	82	80	162
Al Chandler	81	81	162
Mike Malaska	89	74	163
Griff Moody	83	81	164
Fred Couples	83	81	164
Jimmy Wright	79	86	165
Johnny Elam	83	82	165
Lynn Janson	84	82	166
*David Dupre	83	83	166
*Donald Bliss	83	83	166
Bob E. Smith	91	76	167

	SCORES	TOTAL
Bill Brodell	88 79	167
Scott Hoch	74 WD	
Andy Bean	78 WD	
Walter Zembriski	88 WD	

(All professional contestants who missed cut received $600.)

Manufacturers Hanover Westchester Classic

Westchester Country Club, Harrison, New York   June 24–27
Par 35-35—70; 6,329 yards   purse, $400,000

	SCORES				TOTAL	MONEY
Bob Gilder	64	63	65	69	261	$72,000
Tom Kite	66	64	68	68	266	35,200
Peter Jacobsen	68	62	70	66	266	35,200
Wayne Levi	70	65	67	68	270	17,600
Don Pooley	69	66	68	67	270	17,600
Jerry Pate	72	68	68	64	272	14,400
J.C. Snead	67	70	69	67	273	12,900
Jim Colbert	69	65	68	71	273	12,900
D.A. Weibring	67	68	71	68	274	11,200
Bill Rogers	69	69	67	69	274	11,200
Doug Tewell	67	70	70	68	275	8,200
Mark Hayes	68	69	70	68	275	8,200
Isao Aoki	67	72	67	69	275	8,200
Jack Renner	69	69	68	69	275	8,200
Ray Floyd	69	71	66	69	275	8,200
George Burns	71	67	66	71	275	8,200
Kermit Zarley	68	68	71	69	276	6,200
Curtis Strange	70	67	70	69	276	6,200
Charles Coody	67	71	71	68	277	4,514.29
Craig Stadler	71	67	71	68	277	4,514.29
Ben Crenshaw	68	72	68	69	277	4,514.29
Dave Eichelberger	65	73	69	70	277	4,514.29
Bruce Devlin	72	69	66	70	277	4,514.28
Mark Pfeil	70	70	66	71	277	4,514.28
Lee Elder	69	70	67	71	277	4,514.28
Larry Ziegler	68	73	71	66	278	2,960
Howard Twitty	71	68	72	67	278	2,960
Jim Albus	72	69	69	68	278	2,960
Scott Watkins	70	69	69	70	278	2,960
Mark Lye	68	66	71	73	278	2,960
Jay Haas	69	70	72	68	279	2,425
Rex Caldwell	69	68	72	70	279	2,425
Gary McCord	72	66	71	70	279	2,425
Tom Jenkins	71	69	67	72	279	2,425
Scott Simpson	70	70	73	67	280	1,888.58
Chi Chi Rodriguez	70	69	73	68	280	1,888.57
Gil Morgan	69	70	72	69	280	1,888.57
Clarence Rose	68	71	70	71	280	1,888.57
Bobby Wadkins	72	69	68	71	280	1,888.57
Leonard Thompson	69	71	68	72	280	1,888.57
Jim Simons	69	69	69	73	280	1,888.57
Bill Israelson	70	68	73	70	281	1,400
Lanny Wadkins	66	74	70	71	281	1,400
Mike Hill	68	70	71	72	281	1,400

	SCORES				TOTAL	MONEY
Tom Shaw	70	69	69	73	281	1,400
Tim Simpson	71	69	68	73	281	1,400
George Cadle	70	70	73	69	282	995.20
Jodie Mudd	69	72	71	70	282	995.20
Frank Conner	69	70	72	71	282	995.20
Larry Rinker	75	65	71	71	282	995.20
Bruce Douglass	71	70	70	71	282	995.20
Lindy Miller	68	71	71	72	282	995.20
Lance Ten Broeck	69	70	71	72	282	995.20
Bob Murphy	72	67	71	72	282	995.20
Victor Regalado	72	68	70	72	282	995.20
Hubert Green	68	68	72	74	282	995.20

Western Open

Butler National Golf Club, Oak Brook, Illinois   July 1–4
Par 36–36—72; 7,097 yards   purse, $350,000

	SCORES				TOTAL	MONEY
Tom Weiskopf	69	67	70	70	276	$63,000
Larry Nelson	66	72	68	71	277	37,800
Bob Gilder	64	71	74	69	278	23,800
Jim Thorpe	67	75	68	70	280	15,400
Bill Rogers	69	72	69	60	280	15,400
Curtis Strange	69	72	72	69	282	12,600
Mark Pfeil	70	72	69	72	283	11,725
Lanny Wadkins	76	72	68	68	284	9,800
Tom Jenkins	69	72	73	70	284	9,800
George Burns	68	74	71	71	284	9,800
Doug Tewell	70	76	68	70	284	9,800
Keith Fergus	70	73	70	72	285	8,050
Rex Caldwell	76	71	71	68	286	7,000
Jim Booros	66	73	75	72	286	7,000
Tom Purtzer	74	76	68	70	287	5,950
Andy Bean	71	73	71	72	287	5,950
Kermit Zarley	68	71	73	75	287	5,950
Lon Hinkle	73	72	72	71	288	4,260
Larry Rinker	76	71	71	70	288	4,260
Wayne Levi	76	71	70	71	288	4,260
Bobby Clampett	73	73	70	72	288	4,260
Ben Crenshaw	74	74	68	72	288	4,260
Leonard Thompson	73	67	75	73	288	4,260
Billy Glisson	72	72	69	75	288	4,260
Bob Murphy	73	72	77	67	289	2,559.38
Steve Melnyk	73	76	71	69	289	2,559.38
Ed Sneed	74	73	72	70	289	2,559.38
J.C. Snead	72	75	72	70	289	2,559.38
Gibby Gilbert	77	71	71	70	289	2,559.37
Calvin Peete	70	75	73	71	289	2,559.37
Bruce Lietzke	68	73	75	73	289	2,559.37
Bobby Wadkins	70	75	73	71	289	2,559.37
Hal Sutton	74	74	72	70	290	1,933.75
Alan Tapie	73	72	74	71	290	1,933.75
Peter Jacobsen	75	72	72	71	290	1,933.75
D.A. Weibring	76	72	71	71	290	1,933.75
Don Pooley	73	76	73	69	291	1,610

	SCORES				TOTAL	MONEY
Jim Barber	75	71	72	73	291	1,610
Mark Calcavecchia	72	76	68	75	291	1,610
Barry Jaeckel	74	70	71	76	291	1,610
John Schroeder	76	72	76	68	292	1,295
Mark McNulty	80	69	71	72	292	1,295
Jack Renner	69	76	74	73	292	1,295
Gil Morgan	71	77	71	73	292	1,295
Wally Armstrong	73	75	69	75	292	1,295
Lee Elder	77	72	73	71	293	922.25
Lindy Miller	78	71	73	71	293	922.25
Mark McCumber	75	70	75	73	293	922.25
Vance Heafner	73	73	74	73	293	922.25
Ron Streck	74	74	72	73	293	922.25
Michael Brannan	76	73	71	73	293	922.25
Mike Holland	72	75	72	74	293	922.25
Dave Barr	69	77	71	76	293	922.25

Greater Milwaukee Open

Tuckaway Country Club, Franklin, Wisconsin   July 8–11
Par 36–36—72; 7,010 yards   purse, $250,000

	SCORES				TOTAL	MONEY
Calvin Peete	70	66	69	69	274	$45,000
Victor Regalado	71	66	68	71	276	27,000
Terry Diehl	65	69	72	71	277	17,000
Jim Colbert	67	69	70	72	278	12,000
Larry Ziegler	72	69	68	70	279	9,125
Morris Hatalsky	68	70	70	71	279	9,125
Richard Zokol	65	69	70	75	279	9,125
David Edwards	65	72	71	72	280	7,500
Wayne Levi	68	68	68	76	280	7,500
Dan Pohl	70	71	71	69	281	6,000
Howard Twitty	71	71	68	71	281	6,000
Dave Stockton	70	68	70	73	281	6,000
Andy Bean	68	70	69	74	281	6,000
Clarence Rose	73	69	72	68	282	4,625
Scott Simpson	65	70	75	72	282	4,625
Ed Dougherty	70	71	73	69	283	3,625
Mark Lye	69	67	76	71	283	3,625
Phil Hancock	71	69	72	71	283	3,625
Jim Dent	71	71	69	72	283	3,625
Mark Calcavecchia	70	70	70	73	283	3,625
Bob Tway	66	73	70	74	283	3,625
Bruce Fleisher	68	73	75	68	284	2,253.58
Mike Morley	69	71	74	70	284	2,253.57
Mike Hill	72	71	71	70	284	2,253.57
Michael Brannan	74	67	70	73	284	2,253.57
Andy North	68	71	71	74	284	2,253.57
Bill Sander	72	70	67	75	284	2,253.57
Roger Maltbie	68	70	69	77	284	2,253.57
Charles Coody	70	72	72	71	285	1,555.43
Mark McCumber	68	71	74	72	285	1,555.43
Ed Fiori	73	68	72	72	285	1,555.43
Gary McCord	74	68	70	73	285	1,555.43
George Cadle	71	69	71	74	285	1,555.43
Dale Douglass	71	71	69	74	285	1,555.43

	SCORES				TOTAL	MONEY
Charles Krenkel	69	74	67	75	285	1,555.42
Jack Renner	69	73	73	71	286	1,152
Gary Koch	69	72	74	71	286	1,152
Dave Eichelberger	72	71	72	71	286	1,152
Ronnie Black	67	76	71	72	286	1,152
Jay Haas	69	70	72	75	286	1,152
Lon Nielsen	72	71	68	75	286	1,152
Lee Elder	68	74	73	72	287	785
Steve Melnyk	72	68	74	73	287	785
Frank Conner	71	71	72	73	287	785
Jeff Thomson	70	67	76	74	287	785
Mark Pfeil	68	72	73	74	287	785
Tim Morris	67	74	72	74	287	785
Brad Bryant	67	72	72	76	287	785
Bill Calfee	67	70	74	76	287	785
Jay Cudd	65	73	72	77	287	785

Quad Cities Open

Oakwood Country Club, Coal Valley, Illinois
Par 35–35—70; 6,514 yards

July 15–18
purse, $200,000

	SCORES				TOTAL	MONEY
Payne Stewart	66	71	68	63	268	$36,000
Brad Bryant	69	67	68	66	270	17,600
Pat McGowan	71	67	65	67	270	17,600
Jim Thorpe	72	67	66	66	271	9,600
Allen Miller	68	70	71	64	273	7,300
Barry Jaeckel	72	63	71	67	273	7,300
Jeff Mitchell	69	63	71	70	273	7,300
Gary McCord	70	67	70	67	274	4,825
Jim Dent	74	66	67	67	274	4,825
Rod Curl	69	69	68	68	274	4,825
Lyn Lott	68	66	71	69	274	4,825
Bob Eastwood	72	68	66	68	274	4,825
Don Pooley	72	67	67	68	274	4,825
Vance Heafner	69	66	70	69	274	4,825
Dave Eichelberger	68	69	68	69	274	4,825
Bobby Cole	69	65	73	68	275	3,100
Dan Halldorson	66	69	70	70	275	3,100
Jodie Mudd	69	68	68	70	275	3,100
Calvin Peete	67	67	69	72	275	3,100
Rod Nuckolls	70	68	70	68	276	2,330
Victor Regalado	69	67	71	69	276	2,330
Tim Norris	69	69	68	70	276	2,330
Howard Twitty	67	69	69	71	276	2,330
Pat Lindsey	71	68	69	69	277	1,582.86
Leonard Thompson	69	66	73	69	277	1,582.86
Gavin Levenson	69	71	67	70	277	1,582.86
Larry Rinker	69	68	70	70	277	1,582.86
Beau Baugh	68	67	71	71	277	1,582.86
Tom Woodard	70	68	68	71	277	1,582.85
Jim Barber	72	68	72	65	277	1,582.85
Bob Byman	67	68	72	71	278	1,134.29
John Adams	69	66	72	71	278	1,134.29
Jack Newton, Jr	69	65	72	72	278	1,134.29
Bob Mann	70	66	70	72	278	1,134.29

	SCORES				TOTAL	MONEY
Miller Barber	67	67	75	69	278	1,134.28
Butch Baird	71	63	75	69	278	1,134.28
D.A. Weibring	68	67	70	73	278	1,134.28
Ed Dougherty	69	71	68	71	279	880
Gary Koch	75	64	69	71	279	880
Thomas Gray	71	66	72	70	279	880
Charles Krenkel	69	66	71	73	279	880
Bob Murphy	66	70	73	71	280	740
Bruce Douglass	73	67	71	69	280	740
Bill Britton	71	69	72	68	280	740
Bruce Fleisher	71	67	70	73	281	541.78
Bob Tway	67	68	73	73	281	541.78
Lon Nielsen	75	65	69	72	281	541.78
Paul Azinger	71	67	71	72	281	541.78
John Schroeder	68	67	74	72	281	541.78
David Sann	71	69	71	70	281	541.78
Buzz Fly	71	69	71	70	281	541.78
Steven Liebler	73	66	73	69	281	541.77
Mark McCumber	69	70	74	68	281	541.77

Anheuser-Busch Golf Classic

Kingsmill Golf Club, Williamsburg, Virginia   July 22–25
Par 36-35—71; 6,684 yards   purse, $350,000
(Tournament reduced to 54 holes because of weather.)

	SCORES			TOTAL	MONEY
Calvin Peete	66	68	69	203	$63,000
Bruce Lietzke	65	74	66	205	37,800
Hal Sutton	68	69	69	206	20,300
Rik Massengale	68	68	70	206	20,300
Bill Rogers	66	70	71	207	14,000
Doug Tewell	72	69	67	208	11,331.45
Victor Regalado	70	71	67	208	11,331.25
Peter Oosterhuis	71	69	68	208	11,331.25
David Edwards	68	70	70	208	11,331.25
Ed Dougherty	72	68	69	209	9,100
Pat McGowan	69	71	69	209	9,100
Jim Colbert	76	68	66	210	6,650
Hale Irwin	73	69	68	210	6,650
George Burns	73	68	69	210	6,650
Lanny Wadkins	73	67	70	210	6,650
Mark Hayes	72	67	71	210	6,650
Lee Elder	72	66	72	210	6,650
Forrest Fezler	72	72	67	211	4,410
Mike Sullivan	69	74	68	211	4,410
Curtis Strange	73	68	70	211	4,410
Terry Diehl	70	70	71	211	4,410
John Mahaffey	68	71	72	211	4,410
Payne Stewart	69	68	74	211	4,410
Jim Thorpe	73	71	68	212	2,480.67
Don Pooley	72	70	70	212	2,480.67
John Fought	73	69	70	212	2,480.67
Tom Chain	71	71	70	212	2,480.67
Mike Donald	70	72	70	212	2,480.67
Beau Baugh	71	71	70	212	2,480.67
Jack Newton	73	68	71	212	2,480.67

	SCORES			TOTAL	MONEY
Larry Mize	69	72	71	212	2,480.67
Jack Renner	72	69	71	212	2,480.66
Clarence Rose	73	68	71	212	2,480.66
Dan Pohl	72	66	74	212	2,480.66
Doug Black	72	66	74	212	2,480.66
Mike Reid	72	72	69	213	1,612.84
Bobby Wadkins	69	73	71	213	1,612.84
George Cadle	72	69	72	213	1,612.83
Phil Hancock	75	66	72	213	1,612.83
J.C. Snead	71	69	63	213	1,612.83
Barry Jaeckel	68	71	74	213	1,612.83
Miller Barber	72	72	70	214	1,126.13
Fred Couples	76	68	70	214	1,126.13
Bill Buttner	71	72	71	214	1,126.13
Vance Heafner	69	74	71	214	1,126.13
Steve Melnyk	75	67	72	214	1,126.12
Lance Ten Broeck	72	70	72	214	1,126.12
Andy North	72	70	72	214	1,126.12
Bill Kratzert	71	70	73	214	1,126.12
Eric Battan	72	72	71	215	832
Larry Rinker	75	69	71	215	832
Fred Funk	72	71	72	215	832
Mike Holland	72	71	72	215	832
Jim Nelford	74	69	72	215	832
Paul Azinger	70	70	75	215	832
Allen Miller	69	71	75	215	832

Canadian Open

Glen Abbey Golf Club, Oakville, Ontario   July 29–August 1
Par 35–36—71; 7,060 yards   purse, $425,000 (Canadian)

	SCORES				TOTAL	MONEY (Canadian)
Bruce Lietzke	68	68	68	73	277	$76,500
Hal Sutton	68	68	72	71	279	45,900
Charles Coody	71	70	72	67	280	24,650
Tommy Valentine	70	68	68	74	280	24,650
Lou Graham	68	70	75	68	281	13,919.17
Johnny Miller	71	71	70	69	281	13,919.17
Nick Faldo	68	70	73	70	281	13,919.17
Larry Nelson	73	71	67	70	281	13,919.17
Vance Heafner	71	72	67	71	281	13,919.16
Andy Bean	70	71	69	71	281	13,919.16
Steve Melnyk	71	71	75	66	283	9,350
Tom Weiskopf	72	70	76	66	283	9,350
Wayne Levi	68	70	75	70	283	9,350
Peter Oosterhuis	69	73	69	72	283	9,350
Pat Lindsey	68	71	75	70	284	7,012.50
Morris Hatalsky	71	71	70	72	284	7,012.50
Mark Pfeil	71	70	71	72	284	7,012.50
Jerry Anderson	73	70	69	72	284	7,012.50
Dan Pohl	73	67	74	71	285	4,796.43
Barry Jaeckel	70	73	70	72	285	4,796.43
George Burns	72	73	68	72	285	4,796.43
Keith Fergus	68	75	70	72	285	4,796.43
Bobby Wadkins	71	72	70	72	285	4,796.43

	SCORES				TOTAL	MONEY
Clarence Rose	71	72	69	73	285	4,796.43
Greg Norman	67	71	71	76	285	4,796.42
Jim Rutledge	72	72	73	69	286	3,081.17
David Graham	68	74	73	71	286	3,081.17
Dan Halldorson	70	73	72	71	286	3,081.17
Bill Calfee	75	70	70	71	286	3,081.17
Jack Newton, Jr	70	72	70	74	286	3,081.16
Mike Nicolette	71	68	71	76	286	3,081.16
Tom Jenkins	73	70	74	70	287	2,252.63
Blaine McCallister	75	69	72	71	287	2,252.63
David Edwards	71	74	72	70	287	2,252.63
Perry Arthur	71	73	72	71	287	2,252.63
Brad Bryant	67	75	73	72	287	2,252.62
Ron Streck	71	70	72	74	287	2,252.62
Wally Armstrong	71	72	69	75	287	2,252.62
Denis Watson	71	69	71	76	287	2,252.62
Bruce Devlin	71	70	76	71	288	1,699.50
Allen Miller	71	72	74	71	288	1,699.50
Bob Murphy	72	73	71	72	288	1,699.50
Bob Shearer	74	70	70	74	288	1,699.50
Mike Reid	71	70	76	72	289	1,284.50
Jim Thorpe	69	75	73	72	289	1,284.50
Mark Lye	72	70	74	73	289	1,284.50
Scott Simpson	71	74	71	73	289	1,284.50
Fred Couples	71	72	72	74	289	1,284.50
J.C. Snead	69	75	71	74	289	1,284.50
Dave Barr	71	69	80	70	290	1,044.67
Bobby Clampett	69	73	76	72	290	1,044.67
Gary Koch	69	75	71	75	290	1,044.66

PGA Championship

Southern Hills Country Club, Tulsa, Oklahoma
Par 35-35—70; 6,862 yards

August 5–8
purse, $450,000

	SCORES				TOTAL	MONEY
Raymond Floyd	63	69	68	72	272	$65,000
Lanny Wadkins	71	68	69	67	275	45,000
Fred Couples	67	71	72	66	276	27,500
Calvin Peete	69	70	68	69	276	27,500
Jim Simons	68	67	73	69	277	16,000
Jay Haas	71	66	68	72	277	16,000
Greg Norman	66	69	70	72	277	16,000
Bob Gilder	66	68	72	72	278	11,000
Tom Kite	73	70	70	67	280	7,918.75
Tom Watson	72	69	71	68	280	7,918.75
Jerry Pate	72	69	70	69	280	7,918.75
Lon Hinkle	70	68	71	71	280	7,918.75
Seve Ballesteros	71	68	69	73	281	6,500
Curtis Strange	72	70	71	69	282	5,750
Nick Faldo	67	70	73	72	282	5,750
Jack Nicklaus	74	70	72	67	283	4,625
Tom Purtzer	73	69	73	68	283	4,625
Jim Colbert	70	72	72	69	283	4,625
Bruce Lietzke	73	71	70	69	283	4,625
Dan Halldorson	69	71	72	71	283	4,625
Craig Stadler	71	70	70	72	283	4,625

	SCORES				TOTAL	MONEY
Peter Oosterhuis	72	72	74	66	284	3,600
Mark Pfeil	68	73	76	67	284	3,600
Leonard Thompson	72	72	71	69	284	3,600
Doug Tewell	72	70	72	70	284	3,600
Ron Streck	71	72	71	70	284	3,600
Danny Edwards	71	71	68	74	284	3,600
Gil Morgan	76	66	68	74	284	3,600
Mike Holland	71	73	70	71	285	3,100
Bill Rogers	73	71	70	71	285	3,100
Hal Sutton	72	68	70	75	285	3,100
Scott Simpson	71	71	75	69	286	2,850
Johnny Miller	76	67	73	70	286	2,850
Bobby Nichols	73	69	74	71	287	2,350
Jim Thorpe	72	71	73	71	287	2,350
Miller Barber	71	74	70	72	287	2,350
John Cook	71	72	71	73	287	2,350
Bob Murphy	71	74	68	74	287	2,350
George Archer	71	70	71	75	287	2,350
Mark Hayes	69	72	70	76	287	2,350
Peter Jacobsen	73	70	69	75	287	2,350
Mike Reid	71	72	73	72	288	1,642.86
John Mahaffey	74	70	72	72	288	1,642.86
Barry Jaeckel	72	69	74	73	288	1,642.86
Hale Irwin	73	69	73	73	288	1,642.86
George Burns	72	72	71	73	288	1,642.86
Dave Barr	71	72	71	74	288	1,642.85
Masahiro Kuramoto	71	70	70	77	288	1,642.85
Bobby Wadkins	71	71	75	72	289	1,315
Isao Aoki	69	75	71	74	289	1,315
David Graham	68	71	74	76	289	1,315
Gene Littler	73	72	67	77	289	1,315
Tom Valentine	73	68	70	78	289	1,315
Mark McNulty	76	69	76	69	290	1,182.15
Ed Fiori	72	71	76	71	290	1,182.15
Roger Maltbie	71	73	72	74	290	1,182.14
Vance Heafner	68	71	76	75	290	1,182.14
Lyn Lott	70	73	72	75	290	1,182.14
Gibby Gilbert	72	73	69	76	290	1,182.14
Morris Hatalsky	72	73	69	76	290	1,182.14
Jim Nelford	73	71	73	74	291	1,137.50
Brad Bryant	74	70	71	76	291	1,137.50
Ed Sneed	72	72	70	77	291	1,137.50
Rex Caldwell	67	76	70	78	291	1,137.50
Jeff Mitchell	73	72	73	74	292	1,122.50
Tom Jenkins	69	71	75	77	292	1,122.50
Bill Casper	72	73	75	73	293	1,110
Don Pooley	73	71	72	77	293	1,110
Mark Lye	72	73	70	78	293	1,110
Andy North	72	72	77	73	294	1,100
Dan Pohl	71	71	73	79	294	1,100
Don Padgett	72	72	74	77	295	1,100
Woody Blackburn	74	71	78	77	300	1,100
Lennie Clements	75	69	82	78	304	1,100

Out of the final 36 holes

Tim Simpson	72	74		146
Don January	73	73		146

	SCORES		TOTAL
Dave Stockton	73	73	146
Chip Beck	73	73	146
John Jackson	68	78	146
Joe Inman	73	73	146
Gary Player	76	70	146
Jim Kiely	72	75	147
Buddy Whitten	73	74	147
Richard Crawford	75	72	147
Jim Logue	77	70	147
Denis Watson	72	75	147
D.A. Weibring	75	72	147
Jim Booros	69	79	148
Fuzzy Zoeller	74	74	148
Steve Melnyk	72	76	148
Mike Sullivan	71	77	148
Dave Eichelberger	75	73	148
Payne Stewart	76	72	148
Dave Barber	76	73	149
Greg Powers	75	74	149
Keith Fergus	76	73	149
Lee Harper	72	77	149
Richard Bassett	73	76	149
Mike Wynn	74	75	149
Gary Hallberg	77	72	149
Larry Nelson	74	75	149
Ben Crenshaw	73	76	149
Hubert Green	77	72	149
Tom Weiskopf	76	73	149
Wayne Levi	76	73	149
Jim Dent	73	76	149
Jim Albus	77	72	149
Bob Menne	75	74	149
Arnold Palmer	74	76	150
Al Geiberger	75	75	150
Bill Kratzert	74	76	150
Jack Renner	73	77	150
Rodney Loesch	75	75	150
Jim King	74	76	150
Gary Robinson	77	73	150
Mark McCumber	74	76	150
J.C. Snead	77	73	150
Don Massengale	76	75	151
Frank Conner	73	79	152
Andy Bean	71	81	152
Bobby Clampett	76	76	152
Bill Britton	74	78	152
John Calabria	79	74	153
Jim Marshall	77	76	153
Larry Gilbert	78	75	153
Benny Passons	79	74	153
Ross Randall	77	77	154
Bob Eastwood	77	77	154
Roger Kennedy	80	75	155
Bruce Ashworth	74	81	155
Dick Hendrickson	76	79	155
Howard Twitty	76	79	155
Jack Sommers	76	79	155
Gene Ferrell	80	76	156

	SCORES	TOTAL
Robbie Gilmore	79 77	156
Russell Helwig	77 79	156
Vince Bizik	81 76	157
Dave Philo	82 75	157
Bob Moreland	80 77	157
Dick Smith	77 80	157
Dwight Nevil	80 78	158
Dave Ragan	80 78	158
Jim Lucius	78 82	160
Joe McDermott	77 84	161
Kevin Morris	84 77	161
James Dolan	82 82	164
Gary Gant	82 83	165
Jimmy Wright	81 85	166
Tony Wallin	78 WD	
Bob Shearer	79 (Injury)	

(Each player who finished 36 holes received $650.)

Sammy Davis Jr. — Greater Hartford Open

Wethersfield Country Club, Hartford, Connecticut   August 12–15
Par 35-36—71; 6,534 yards   purse, $300,000

	SCORES				TOTAL	MONEY
Tim Norris	63	64	66	66	259	$54,000
Hubert Green	66	66	66	67	265	26,400
Raymond Floyd	65	65	67	68	265	26,400
Curtis Strange	68	66	69	63	266	11,310
Gavin Levenson	66	64	69	67	266	11,310
Mark McNulty	66	65	68	67	266	11,310
D.A. Weibring	66	65	68	67	266	11,310
Peter Jacobsen	65	67	67	67	266	11,310
Dana Quigley	70	69	61	67	267	8,400
David Edwards	68	64	67	68	267	8,400
Terry Diehl	69	69	66	64	268	6,600
Beau Baugh	70	67	66	65	268	6,600
Andy Bean	68	67	67	66	268	6,600
Clarence Rose	70	63	67	68	268	6,600
Jodie Mudd	66	66	71	66	269	5,100
Steve Melnyk	67	67	67	68	269	5,100
Isao Aoki	71	65	66	67	269	5,100
Bill Britton	64	68	70	68	270	4,050
Howard Twitty	68	67	67	68	270	4,050
Mark O'Meara	70	68	63	69	270	4,050
Barry Jaeckel	67	69	64	70	270	4,050
Jim Simons	69	67	67	68	271	2,785
Jack Renner	69	70	64	68	271	2,785
Roger Maltbie	67	67	68	69	271	2,785
Lennie Clements	71	68	63	69	271	2,785
Thomas Gray	66	67	68	70	271	2,785
Mark Calcavecchia	64	68	65	74	271	2,785
Don Pooley	68	70	68	66	272	1,791.82
Bob Byman	70	68	68	66	272	1,791.82
Rod Curl	67	68	70	67	272	1,791.82
Jeff Mitchell	70	67	68	67	272	1,791.82
Bill Calfee	71	68	66	67	272	1,791.82
Larry Mize	71	66	67	68	272	1,791.82

	SCORES				TOTAL	MONEY
Mark Pfeil	65	72	66	69	272	1,791.82
Mick Soli	66	67	68	71	272	1,791.82
Larry Nelson	70	69	65	68	272	1,791.82
Rex Caldwell	66	66	68	72	272	1,791.81
Bob Eastwood	68	66	65	73	272	1,791.81
J.C. Snead	70	68	67	68	273	1,230
Perry Arthur	70	68	66	69	273	1,230
John Adams	66	66	72	69	273	1,230
Richard Zokol	67	67	68	71	273	1,230
Jim Dent	67	69	66	71	273	1,230
Mike Donald	71	67	68	68	274	990
Mike Nicolette	69	70	67	68	274	990
Jay Cudd	69	68	66	71	274	990
Scott Simpson	66	72	71	66	275	770.58
Lon Nielsen	68	69	69	69	275	770.57
Pat Lindsey	66	68	71	70	275	770.57
George Archer	67	69	69	70	275	770.57
Tim Simpson	70	68	67	70	275	770.57
Jim Booros	69	66	68	72	275	770.57
David Graham	68	65	68	74	275	770.57

Buick Open

Warwick Hills Country Club, Grand Blanc, Michigan
Par 36–36—72; 7,001 yards

August 19–22
purse, $350,000

	SCORES				TOTAL	MONEY
Lanny Wadkins	66	71	71	65	273	$63,000
Tom Kite	71	67	69	67	274	37,800
George Archer	74	67	69	66	276	18,200
Curtis Strange	66	69	69	72	276	18,200
Payne Stewart	68	69	67	72	276	18,200
Jack Renner	73	68	69	68	278	12,162.50
Hale Irwin	70	68	69	71	278	12,162.50
John Cook	65	72	71	71	279	10,150
Bob Eastwood	67	71	69	72	279	10,150
Peter Jacobsen	72	67	68	72	279	10,150
Rex Caldwell	71	68	72	70	281	7,175
Calvin Peete	72	70	69	70	281	7,175
John Adams	68	74	69	70	281	7,175
Lou Graham	70	72	68	71	281	7,175
Larry Ziegler	74	66	68	73	281	7,175
Mike Donald	71	68	69	73	281	7,175
Bill Calfee	73	70	71	68	282	5,075
Barry Jaeckel	73	69	70	70	282	5,075
Victor Regalado	69	69	73	71	282	5,075
Scott Simpson	69	69	73	71	282	5,075
Andy Bean	72	71	70	70	283	3,500
Mike Reid	70	68	73	72	283	3,500
Tim Simpson	70	69	72	72	283	3,500
Clarence Rose	72	69	69	73	283	3,500
Fred Couples	71	66	72	74	283	3,500
Craig Stadler	69	68	71	75	283	3,500
Morris Hatalsky	73	71	72	68	284	2,432.50
Bobby Clampett	70	73	71	70	284	2,432.50
Dave Eichelberger	72	71	70	71	284	2,432.50
Fuzzy Zoeller	70	72	70	72	284	2,432.50

	SCORES				TOTAL	MONEY
Dana Quigley	70	70	71	73	284	2,432.50
Gavin Levenson	70	69	70	75	284	2,432.50
Peter Oosterhuis	72	72	72	69	285	1,660.91
Paul Azinger	74	70	71	70	285	1,660.91
Ed Fiori	71	71	71	72	285	1,660.91
Tim Norris	72	71	71	71	285	1,660.91
Steve Melnyk	71	72	70	72	285	1,660.91
Tom Purtzer	70	69	73	73	285	1,660.91
Ed Sneed	70	72	70	73	285	1,660.91
Rod Curl	72	71	73	69	285	1,660.91
Jeff Mitchell	70	72	69	74	285	1,660.91
Dan Halldorson	69	71	71	74	285	1,660.91
Ed Dougherty	71	69	70	75	285	1,660.91
Jim Colbert	72	69	72	73	286	1,058.17
Bruce Devlin	72	69	71	74	286	1,058.17
Mark Pfeil	71	68	73	74	286	1,058.17
Lon Nielsen	72	70	70	74	286	1,058.17
Wayne Levi	71	69	69	77	286	1,058.16
Phil Hancock	73	66	72	75	286	1,058.16
Mike Sullivan	71	72	75	69	287	826.88
Mark Lye	72	72	72	71	287	826.88
D.A. Wiebring	73	71	72	71	287	826.88
Frank Conner	72	70	73	72	287	826.88
Jack Ferenz	74	68	72	73	287	826.87
Chip Beck	74	70	71	72	287	826.87
Mark Calcavecchia	70	73	71	73	287	826.87
Mark Hayes	76	66	70	75	287	826.87

World Series of Golf

Firestone Country Club, Akron, Ohio
Par 35–35—70; 7,173 yards

August 26–29
purse, $400,000

	SCORES				TOTAL	MONEY
Craig Stadler	70	68	75	65	278	$100,000
Raymond Floyd	69	71	68	70	278	55,000
(Stadler defeated Floyd on fourth hole of sudden-death playoff.)						
Isao Aoki	77	66	70	67	280	34,500
Bob Shearer	69	69	73	71	282	19,600
Curtis Strange	71	71	72	68	282	19,600
Tom Kite	75	68	73	71	285	15,000
Jack Nicklaus	71	75	72	67	285	15,000
Lanny Wadkins	70	72	72	71	285	15,000
Bill Rogers	76	72	71	67	286	13,000
Tom Watson	75	74	69	69	287	11,500
Jerry Pate	76	72	70	69	287	11,500
Tom Weiskopf	71	76	69	72	288	10,000
Tsuneyuki Nakajima	74	71	72	73	290	8,750
Calvin Peete	72	72	73	73	290	8,750
Andy Bean	73	73	74	72	292	7,500
Scott Hoch	76	70	74	72	292	7,500
Denis Watson	74	71	76	71	292	7,500
Mark McNulty	73	76	74	70	293	6,500
Terry Gale	77	72	76	70	295	6,000
Masahiro Kuramoto	69	74	76	77	296	5,500
Bob Gilder	74	77	75	72	298	5,000
George Burns	78	73	78	71	300	4,550

	SCORES				TOTAL	MONEY
Sam Torrance	79	70	78	73	300	4,550
*Nathaniel Crosby	73	77	74	78	302	
Larry Gilbert	79	81	71	73	304	4,200
Bruce Lietzke	81	WD				4,000

B.C. Open

EnJoie Golf Club, Endicott, New York
Par 37–34—71; 6,966 yards

September 2–5
purse, $275,000

	SCORES				TOTAL	MONEY
Calvin Peete	69	63	64	69	265	$49,500
Jerry Pate	67	66	66	73	272	29,700
Fuzzy Zoeller	68	62	67	76	273	18,700
Craig Stadler	71	68	69	66	274	13,200
Michael Brannan	68	70	70	67	275	10,450
Tom Kite	67	67	68	73	275	10,450
Antonio Cerda	70	72	67	67	276	8,850
Doug Tewell	69	67	67	73	276	8,850
Don Pooley	68	71	69	69	277	7,700
Gary McCord	70	70	70	67	277	7,700
Bob Gilder	70	73	68	67	278	6,600
Mark Calcavecchia	71	69	70	68	278	6,600
Beau Baugh	74	67	73	65	279	5,005
Barry Jaeckel	68	72	70	69	279	5,005
Peter Jacobsen	68	72	69	70	279	5,005
Tom Purtzer	70	72	67	70	279	5,005
Jim Simons	68	72	67	72	279	5,005
Bobby Clampett	74	66	71	69	280	3,347.15
Jeff Mitchell	69	71	71	69	280	3,347.15
Mike Sullivan	72	70	69	69	280	3,347.14
Frank Conner	68	71	71	70	280	3,347.14
Gil Morgan	68	70	71	71	280	3,347.14
Ed Sneed	70	71	68	71	280	3,347.14
Wayne Levi	69	70	68	73	280	3,347.14
George Archer	72	70	71	68	281	2,260
Scott Simpson	69	72	69	71	281	2,260
Jim Colbert	68	68	71	74	281	2,260
Bob Eastwood	73	66	73	70	282	1,800
D.A. Weibring	72	70	70	70	282	1,880
Rex Caldwell	69	73	69	71	282	1,880
Bruce Devlin	69	71	69	73	282	1,880
Leonard Thompson	70	71	68	73	282	1,880
Tom Jenkins	71	72	71	69	283	1,525
Mike Smith	65	74	71	73	283	1,525
Scott Hoch	68	68	73	74	283	1,525
Vance Heafner	71	70	69	73	283	1,525
Terry Diehl	70	72	72	70	284	1,270
Denis Watson	72	68	74	70	284	1,270
Tim Simpson	70	70	71	73	284	1,270
Larry Nelson	69	72	70	73	284	1,270
Thomas Gray	71	68	75	71	285	1,032.50
Kenny Knox	70	73	71	71	285	1,032.50
Ed Dougherty	72	71	70	72	285	1,032.50
Mark O'Meara	70	73	68	74	285	1,032.50
Mick Soli	68	73	75	70	286	850
Pat McGowan	68	73	72	73	286	850

	SCORES			TOTAL	MONEY
Forrest Fezler	72 71 68 75			286	850
Larry Mize	75 67 74 71			287	712.50
Joe Inman	72 70 73 72			287	712.50
Mike Holland	69 71 73 74			287	712.50
Ed Fiori	71 71 69 76			287	712.50

Bank of Boston Classic

Pleasant Valley Country Club, Sutton, Massachusetts
Par 36–35—71; 7,119 yards

September 9–12
purse, $300,000

	SCORES			TOTAL	MONEY
Bob Gilder	67 67 70 67			271	$54,000
Fuzzy Zoeller	69 69 68 67			273	32,400
Gil Morgan	72 66 68 68			274	17,400
Mike McCullough	72 64 66 72			274	17,400
Ed Sneed	66 72 68 69			275	10,170
John Cook	73 67 66 69			275	10,170
Brad Bryant	68 72 64 71			275	10,170
David Graham	69 69 68 69			275	10,170
Peter Jacobsen	70 67 66 72			275	10,170
Tom Jenkins	69 70 68 69			276	7,800
George Archer	66 68 69 73			276	7,800
Mike Donald	68 69 72 68			277	6,075
Barry Jaeckel	71 68 70 68			277	6,075
Jim Colbert	72 71 66 68			277	6,075
Mick Soli	68 69 70 70			277	6,075
Mark Lye	71 67 72 68			278	4,650
Lon Hinkle	68 72 69 69			278	4,650
Jack Newton	69 68 70 71			278	4,650
Wayne Levi	70 68 68 72			278	4,650
Joe Inman	72 68 70 69			279	3,495
Jack Renner	69 70 70 70			279	3,495
John Fought	67 76 65 71			279	3,495
Forrest Fezler	70 69 68 72			279	3,495
George Cadle	73 70 70 67			280	2,374.29
Blaine McCallister	77 66 69 68			280	2,374.29
Terry Mauney	73 67 71 69			280	2,374.29
Tom Shaw	72 70 69 69			280	2,374.29
Jack Ferenz	70 69 71 70			280	2,374.28
Mark McCumber	69 69 71 71			280	2,374.28
Michael Brennan	71 68 69 72			280	2,374.28
Ron Streck	68 73 73 67			281	1,701.43
Jeff Sanders	70 68 74 69			281	1,701.43
Lindy Miller	72 65 73 71			281	1,701.43
Allen Miller	70 70 70 71			281	1,701.43
Mike Holland	72 66 71 72			281	1,701.43
Frank Conner	72 69 68 72			281	1,701.43
Jim Simons	71 70 67 73			281	1,701.42
Lee Elder	73 68 69 72			282	1,410
Bill Britton	69 72 71 71			283	1,230
Bruce Fleisher	72 71 69 71			283	1,230
Bob Eastwood	69 72 70 72			283	1,230
Kenny Knox	72 67 70 74			283	1,230
Bill Buttner	69 70 66 78			283	1,230
Mark O'Meara	74 68 72 70			284	867
Lou Graham	71 71 71 71			284	867

	SCORES				TOTAL	MONEY
Howard Twitty	70	72	70	72	284	867
Bobby Wadkins	69	73	70	72	284	867
John Mahaffey	71	67	73	73	284	867
Peter Oosterhuis	70	73	69	72	284	867
Steve Melnyk	68	71	72	73	284	867
Larry Rinker	71	71	69	73	284	867

Hall of Fame Tournament

Pinehurst Country Club, Pinehurst, North Carolina   September 16–19
Par 35–36—72; 7,020 yards   purse, $250,000

	SCORES				TOTAL	MONEY
Jay Haas	70	70	70	68	276	$45,000
John Adams	67	69	71	69	276	27,000
(Haas defeated Adams on second hole of sudden-death playoff.)						
Curtis Strange	69	70	69	69	277	17,000
Morris Hatalsky	70	68	73	68	279	10,333.34
Allen Miller	69	72	71	67	279	10,333.33
Bobby Clampett	69	71	70	69	279	10,333.33
Mike Reid	70	69	70	71	280	8,062.50
D.A. Weibring	73	71	66	70	280	8,062.50
Roger Maltbie	71	72	71	67	281	7,000
Jack Renner	72	64	71	74	281	7,000
Jim Dent	73	69	70	70	282	6,250
Mike Holland	70	69	74	70	283	4,605.15
Leonard Thompson	73	69	71	70	283	4,607.15
Bob Byman	69	74	70	70	283	4,607.14
Larry Mize	69	70	73	71	283	4,607.14
Jim Barber	68	73	71	71	283	4,607.14
Bruce Fleisher	74	67	69	73	283	4,607.14
Lance Ten Broeck	68	68	73	74	283	4,607.14
Jerry Heard	70	73	72	69	284	2,925
Tim Norris	70	74	70	70	284	2,925
Charles Coody	72	70	71	71	284	2,925
Lee Elder	70	71	72	71	284	2,925
Jim Thorpe	72	71	70	71	284	2,925
Lindy Miller	68	72	70	74	284	2,925
Eric Batten	71	71	73	70	285	1,950
Peter Oosterhuis	72	72	71	70	285	1,950
Don Pooley	69	76	69	71	285	1,950
Scott Hoch	71	71	71	72	285	1,950
Mark McCumber	74	67	72	72	285	1,950
Vance Heafner	74	69	73	70	286	1,552.60
Bobby Cole	72	71	72	71	286	1,552.60
Beau Baugh	75	70	70	71	286	1,552.60
Kenny Knox	76	69	70	71	286	1,552.60
Charles Krenkel	71	69	74	72	286	1,552.60
Tom Purtzer	72	72	72	71	287	1,259.25
Steve Melnyk	70	73	72	72	287	1,259.25
Gary McCord	71	72	71	73	287	1,259.25
Hal Sutton	69	72	71	75	287	1,259.25
Wally Armstrong	74	70	75	69	288	1,050
Mike Sullivan	73	70	74	71	288	1,050
Chip Beck	72	73	73	70	288	1,050
Denis Watson	70	75	70	73	288	1,050
John Fought	74	71	75	69	289	850

	SCORES				TOTAL	MONEY
Mark Hayes	72	72	72	73	289	850
Ed Fiori	69	76	71	73	289	850
Bruce Devlin	73	70	73	73	289	850
Bobby Wadkins	72	73	75	70	290	686.67
George Burns	72	72	74	72	290	686.67
Jim Nelford	71	73	71	75	290	686.66
Bill Calfee	77	68	76	70	291	608.75
Jeff Sanders	71	74	72	74	291	608.75
Richard Zokol	71	72	74	74	291	608.75
Tommy Valentine	68	78	71	78	291	608.75

Southern Open

Green Island Country Club, Columbus, Georgia
Par 35–35—70; 6,791 yards

September 23–26
purse, $250,000

	SCORES				TOTAL	MONEY
Bobby Clampett	65	69	68	64	266	$45,000
Hale Irwin	67	72	68	61	268	27,000
George Burns	67	68	66	68	269	17,000
Hal Sutton	69	68	67	66	270	12,000
Andy Bean	69	67	69	66	271	10,000
Jim Thorpe	70	67	69	66	272	8,687.50
Gary Hallberg	69	68	68	67	272	8,687.50
Jim Rinker	67	72	66	68	273	7,500
Vance Heafner	69	70	66	68	273	7,500
John Mahaffey	71	71	66	66	274	6,500
John Fought	67	66	70	71	274	6,500
Joe Inman	68	70	70	67	275	5,500
Mike McCullough	67	70	70	68	275	5,500
Wally Armstrong	66	70	69	72	277	4,625
John Adams	71	67	67	72	277	4,625
Tim Simpson	66	69	75	68	278	3,507.15
Howard Twitty	72	71	68	67	278	3,507.15
Lindy Miller	68	70	72	68	278	3,507.14
Larry Nelson	72	67	70	69	278	3,507.14
Joe Hager	72	71	66	69	278	3,507.14
Chip Beck	69	67	72	70	278	3,507.14
Tim Norris	70	69	69	70	278	3,507.14
Dave Eichelberger	74	68	68	69	279	2,225
Forrest Fezler	68	70	71	70	279	2,225
Terry Anton	69	69	70	71	279	2,225
Lance Ten Broeck	65	73	68	73	279	2,225
Lon Nielsen	70	67	67	75	279	2,225
Rod Curl	67	73	71	69	280	1,626.86
Larry Mize	70	68	73	69	280	1,626.86
Bill Britton	71	71	69	69	280	1,626.86
Scott Hoch	69	72	70	69	280	1,626.86
Antonio Cerda	72	67	71	70	280	1,626.86
Dick Mast	71	70	69	70	280	1,626.85
Bill Calfee	69	70	67	74	280	1,626.85
Bobby Cole	74	67	75	65	281	1,027.85
Clarence Rose	73	69	72	67	281	1,027.85
Buddy Gardner	72	71	71	67	281	1,027.85
Tommy Armour	71	71	71	68	281	1,027.85
Hubert Green	68	70	74	69	281	1,027.85
J.C. Snead	71	70	71	69	281	1,027.85

	SCORES			TOTAL	MONEY
Dan Pohl	70	72	70	69	281	1,027.85
Allen Miller	72	69	70	70	281	1,027.85
Charles Krenkel	70	68	72	71	281	1,027.84
George Cadle	72	69	69	71	281	1,027.84
Doug Tewell	71	71	68	71	281	1,027.84
John Cook	66	71	71	73	281	1,027.84
Lou Graham	70	71	68	72	281	1,027.84
Tom Jenkins	67	75	73	67	282	621.43
Gary McCord	75	68	70	69	282	621.43
Frank Conner	70	70	72	70	282	621.43
Gary Koch	72	67	73	70	282	621.43
Mark O'Meara	71	70	71	70	282	621.43
Sammy Rachels	71	69	71	71	282	621.43
Mark McNulty	71	70	70	71	282	621.42

Texas Open

Oak Hills Country Club, San Antonio, Texas   September 30–October 3
Par 35-35—70; 6,525 yards   purse, $250,000

	SCORES			TOTAL	MONEY
Jay Haas	63	67	67	65	262	$45,000
Curtis Strange	65	66	66	68	265	27,000
Keith Fergus	65	66	69	67	267	17,000
Larry Ziegler	66	68	67	68	269	12,000
D.A. Weibring	67	64	69	70	270	9,500
Leonard Thompson	68	67	64	71	270	9,500
Tim Simpson	71	69	69	63	272	6,767.86
Steve Veriato	68	70	70	64	272	6,767.86
Tom Kite	74	65	68	65	272	6,767.86
Gary McCord	70	65	71	66	272	6,767.86
Peter Oosterhuis	68	69	67	68	272	6,767.86
David Graham	71	68	65	68	272	6,767.85
Bill Calfee	67	68	67	70	272	6,767.85
John Mahaffey	72	68	68	65	273	4,375
Jim Colbert	71	68	67	67	273	4,375
Jim Thorpe	69	66	69	69	273	4,375
Tom Purtzer	66	68	68	71	273	4,375
Lee Trevino	69	69	72	64	274	2,519.24
Bobby Wadkins	70	68	70	66	274	2,519.23
Gary Koch	71	67	68	68	274	2,519.23
Clarence Rose	70	69	67	68	274	2,519.23
Hal Sutton	67	72	67	68	274	2,519.23
Hubert Green	67	68	69	70	274	2,519.23
Charles Coody	67	72	66	69	274	2,519.23
J.C. Snead	70	66	69	69	274	2,519.23
Doug Tewell	74	65	65	70	274	2,519.23
Gil Morgan	67	72	64	71	274	2,519.23
Craig Stadler	65	71	67	71	274	2,519.23
Bruce Lietzke	69	67	67	71	274	2,519.23
Allen Miller	67	67	68	72	274	2,519.23
Jeff Sanders	68	70	71	66	275	1,450
Bill Bergin	68	68	72	67	275	1,450
Johnny Miller	66	70	70	69	275	1,450
Beau Baugh	70	69	67	69	275	1,450
Stanton Altgelt	68	68	69	70	275	1,450
Bill Kratzert	68	69	67	71	275	1,450

	SCORES				TOTAL	MONEY
George Archer	70	70	68	68	276	1,175
Mike Donald	71	68	68	69	276	1,175
Pat Lindsey	68	67	71	70	276	1,175
Forrest Fezler	70	67	73	67	277	925
Mark O'Meara	68	69	72	68	277	925
Ron Streck	70	70	69	68	277	925
Mike Nicolette	66	74	69	68	277	925
Tom Jenkins	69	68	70	70	277	925
Lee Elder	70	66	71	70	277	925
Ben Crenshaw	66	71	69	71	277	925
Dan Halldorson	70	70	71	67	278	634.38
Brad Bryant	70	69	71	68	278	634.38
Tommy Armour	69	71	70	68	278	634.38
Bob Murphy	67	70	72	69	278	634.38
Antonio Cerda	72	68	69	69	278	634.37
Mark McCumber	71	67	70	70	278	634.37
Steve Liebler	68	71	68	71	278	634.37
Bob Eastwood	69	66	68	75	278	634.37

LaJet Classic

Fairway Oaks Country Club, Abilene, Texas
Par 36–36—72; 7,166 yards

October 7–10
purse, $350,000

	SCORES				TOTAL	MONEY
Wayne Levi	64	71	68	68	271	$63,000
Thomas Gray	73	71	66	67	277	37,800
Bobby Cole	67	71	69	71	278	20,300
Johnny Miller	68	74	69	67	278	20,300
Gary Koch	67	71	70	71	279	14,000
Bruce Devlin	67	70	72	71	280	12,600
Steven Liebler	68	71	72	70	281	11,287.50
Hal Sutton	71	72	71	67	281	11,287.50
Gil Morgan	71	73	67	71	282	9,800
Ed Fiori	68	73	69	72	282	9,800
Doug Tewell	70	71	72	70	283	7,700
Brad Bryant	70	73	72	68	283	7,700
J.C. Snead	69	71	72	71	283	7,700
Jay Haas	67	75	69	72	283	7,700
Jack Renner	70	72	72	70	284	5,600
Mark Pfeil	69	71	72	72	284	5,600
Mike Smith	72	70	71	71	284	5,600
D.A. Weibring	69	72	69	74	284	5,600
Ron Streck	70	72	70	72	284	5,600
Jim Thorpe	67	72	72	74	285	3,650
John Fought	66	76	70	73	285	3,650
Gary Hallberg	70	75	70	70	285	3,650
Lee Trevino	71	71	74	69	285	3,650
Tom Purtzer	69	73	72	71	285	3,650
Robert Hoyt	69	75	71	70	285	3,650
Mark McCumber	68	73	69	75	285	3,650
Frank Conner	70	74	67	76	287	2,642.50
Craig Stadler	66	74	70	77	287	2,642.50
Howard Twitty	71	69	69	79	288	2,225.50
Andy Bean	67	74	69	78	288	2,225.50
Pat Lindsey	72	73	72	71	288	2,225.50
Bill Britton	67	77	74	70	288	2,225.50

	SCORES				TOTAL	MONEY
Fuzzy Zoeller	67	75	73	73	288	2,225.50
Tom Weiskopf	70	75	73	70	288	2,225.50
Vance Heafner	66	77	72	74	289	1,688.67
Lanny Wadkins	71	74	73	71	289	1,688.67
Roger Maltbie	73	70	73	73	289	1,688.67
Jeff Mitchell	71	73	72	73	289	1,688.67
Allen Miller	71	72	74	72	289	1,688.66
Jeff Sanders	71	71	76	71	289	1,688.66
Mark McNulty	75	71	72	72	290	1,191.75
Keith Fergus	69	75	74	72	290	1,191.75
Bob Murphy	68	78	70	74	290	1,191.75
Phil Hancock	72	71	75	72	290	1,191.75
George Archer	74	71	72	73	290	1,191.75
Bob Eastwood	73	70	74	73	290	1,191.75
Bill Kratzert	72	73	74	71	290	1,191.75
Jim Dent	72	73	71	74	290	1,191.75
Tom Jenkins	71	75	73	72	291	884.34
Mike Morley	65	79	76	71	291	884.33
Rod Nuckolls	78	67	71	75	291	884.33

Pensacola Open

Perdido Bay Country Club, Pensacola, Florida
Par 35–36—71; 7,093 yards

October 21–24
purse, $200,000

	SCORES				TOTAL	MONEY
Calvin Peete	65	66	72	65	268	$36,000
Hal Sutton	66	67	68	74	275	17,600
Dan Halldorson	69	73	66	67	275	17,600
George Burns	66	68	70	72	276	7,540
John Fought	68	67	75	66	276	7,540
Mike Sullivan	68	69	66	73	276	7,540
Tom Watson	69	67	70	70	276	7,540
Brad Bryant	64	73	71	68	276	7,540
J.C. Snead	68	68	72	69	277	4,800
Jerry Pate	71	68	66	72	277	4,800
Larry Mize	66	68	71	72	277	4,800
Pat Lindsey	69	69	70	69	277	4,800
Steven Liebler	64	66	74	73	277	4,800
Mark McCumber	71	69	69	68	277	4,800
Charles Coody	67	67	73	71	278	3,400
Bill Kratzert	65	68	74	71	278	3,400
Tom Purtzer	69	71	65	73	278	3,400
Mark Hayes	69	73	70	67	279	2,700
Jim Colbert	67	68	68	76	279	2,700
George Cadle	72	68	69	70	279	2,700
Scott Hoch	72	67	71	69	279	2,700
D.A. Weibring	67	67	68	78	280	2,000
Woody Blackburn	69	68	73	70	280	2,000
Mark Pfeil	71	70	70	69	280	2,000
Steve Melnyk	67	70	67	76	280	2,000
Clarence Rose	69	73	69	70	281	1,390
Forrest Fezler	65	71	72	73	281	1,390
Bruce Fleisher	70	70	70	71	281	1,390
Gary Koch	68	71	72	70	281	1,390
Mark Lye	70	71	74	66	281	1,390
Jim Simons	68	68	71	74	281	1,390

	SCORES				TOTAL	MONEY
Allen Miller	65	73	73	70	281	1,390
Mike Donald	72	70	70	69	281	1,390
Frank Conner	70	69	68	75	282	1,055
Ed Dougherty	70	71	68	73	282	1,055
Bobby Wadkins	70	70	68	74	282	1,055
Lindy Miller	70	72	70	70	282	1,055
Jeff Mitchell	70	71	73	69	283	820
Kenny Knox	69	71	73	70	283	820
Dan Pohl	74	67	71	71	283	820
Don Pooley	71	70	73	69	283	820
Mike Smith	70	71	71	71	283	820
Bill Calfee	73	67	71	72	283	820
Greg Powers	75	67	73	68	283	820
Jim Nelford	68	70	69	77	284	585.60
Bob Murphy	71	71	74	68	284	585.60
Keith Fergus	67	70	72	75	284	585.60
Jerry Heard	69	65	75	75	284	585.60
Jay Cudd	75	66	75	68	284	585.60
Pat McGowan	71	70	73	71	285	504

Walt Disney World Classic

Walt Disney World, Lake Buena Vista, Florida
Magnolia Course: Par 36–36—72; 7,170 yards
Palm Course: Par 36–36—72; 6,856 yards
Lake Buena Vista Course: Par 36–36—72; 6,642 yards

October 28–31
purse, $400,000

	SCORES				TOTAL	MONEY
Hal Sutton	71	63	68	67	269	$72,000
Bill Britton	69	67	69	64	269	43,200
(Sutton defeated Britton on fourth hole of sudden-death playoff.)						
Jay Haas	66	66	65	73	270	27,200
Don Pooley	71	66	68	66	271	19,200
Larry Nelson	71	64	67	71	273	15,200
Howard Twitty	67	66	70	70	273	15,200
Mark Lye	72	67	65	70	274	12,050
Bob Gilder	73	69	64	68	274	12,050
Wayne Levi	70	67	70	67	274	12,050
Pat Lindsey	70	67	70	67	274	12,050
Jim Nelford	72	68	70	65	275	9,200
Steve Melnyk	68	72	65	70	275	9,200
Larry Mize	68	71	69	67	275	9,200
Ed Sneed	70	66	69	71	276	6,400
Antonio Cerda	73	66	70	67	276	6,400
Andy Bean	73	68	67	68	276	6,400
Mark Pfeil	73	63	70	70	276	6,400
Tom Jenkins	69	69	72	66	276	6,400
Ken Green	71	71	68	66	276	6,400
Bob Eastwood	69	71	69	67	276	6,400
Keith Fergus	69	71	67	70	277	4,480
Dan Pohl	68	67	69	73	277	4,480
Barry Harwell	68	74	66	69	277	4,480
George Burns	69	70	69	70	278	3,165.72
D.A. Weibring	69	69	72	68	278	3,165.72
Ed Fiori	72	66	71	69	278	3,165.72
Barry Jaeckel	67	70	71	70	278	3,165.71
Scott Hoch	70	71	66	71	278	3,165.71

	SCORES				TOTAL	MONEY
Larry Rinker	68	68	71	71	278	3,165.71
Tom Purtzer	72	72	66	68	278	3,165.71
Gary Koch	70	66	72	71	279	2,600
Jim Thorpe	74	67	71	68	280	2,366.67
Greg Powers	72	72	68	68	280	2,366.67
Jim Colbert	72	68	71	69	280	2,366.66
Roger Maltbie	68	71	73	69	281	1,725.46
Mark Hayes	75	70	66	70	281	1,725.46
George Archer	72	69	71	69	281	1,725.46
J.C. Snead	67	68	72	74	281	1,725.46
Mike Holland	72	70	69	70	281	1,725.46
Jim Simons	74	67	71	69	281	1,725.45
Woody Blackburn	70	74	67	70	281	1,725.45
Danny Edwards	68	73	70	70	281	1,725.45
Forrest Fezler	73	67	70	71	281	1,725.45
Tim Simpson	74	68	71	68	281	1,725.45
Pat McGowan	69	73	66	73	281	1,725.45
Tom Jones	68	69	74	71	282	1,108.80
Rex Caldwell	72	69	71	70	282	1,108.80
Calvin Peete	66	74	70	72	282	1,108.80
Ron Streck	71	68	68	75	282	1,108.80
John Fought	70	71	70	71	282	1,108.80

World Cup and International Trophy Championships

Pierre Marques Golf Club, Acapulco, Mexico   December 2–5
Par 35-36—71; 6,870 yards   purse, US$64,500

World Cup

	SCORES				TOTAL
Spain	139	140	138	146	563
United States	144	144	140	138	566
Italy	143	144	141	146	574
England	146	144	142	143	575
Korea	143	145	144	146	578
Mexico	134	148	148	140	579
Scotland	145	146	146	144	581
Ireland	146	143	148	148	585
Canada	141	148	150	147	586
Argentina	150	144	149	144	587
Brazil	149	148	148	142	587
Japan	146	148	150	148	592
Australia	151	144	144	155	594
Philippines	146	147	142	169	595
Thailand	151	148	148	150	597
Colombia	150	154	146	149	599
Chile	152	148	147	155	602
New Zealand	146	151	154	152	603
Malaysia	153	154	150	147	604
France	153	156	149	146	604
Morocco	150	151	154	153	608
Germany	149	152	156	152	609
Wales	155	152	150	152	609
Pakistan	152	148	153	159	612
Singapore	159	148	149	156	612
Venezuela	151	155	152	154	612
Holland	159	146	155	152	612
Austria	154	155	154	155	618
Zimbabwe	158	155	162	149	624
Belgium	155	159	153	158	625
Uruguay	167	165	167	169	668

PRIZE MONEY: Pinero, Canizares $10,000 each; Gilder, Clampett $6,000 each; Dassu, Molteni $4,000 each; James, Waites $1,500 each.

International Trophy

	SCORES				TOTAL
Manuel Pinero, Spain	72	65	71	73	281
Jose-Maria Canizares, Spain	67	75	67	73	282
Bob Gilder, U.S.	71	74	69	68	282
Baldovino Dassu, Italy	69	70	70	74	283
Bobby Clampett, U.S.	73	70	71	70	284
Bernard Gallacher, Scotland	68	72	74	73	287

	SCORES			TOTAL
Dan Halldorson, Canada	68	72	74	73	287
Choi Sang Ho, Korea	72	71	71	73	287
Mark James, England	74	72	70	71	287
Brian Waites, England	72	72	72	72	288
Tony Cerda, Mexico	72	75	74	67	288
Uthai Thabpavibul, Thailand	72	74	70	74	290
Hahn Chang Sang, Korea	71	74	73	73	291
Victor Regalado, Mexico	71	73	74	73	291
Florentino Molina, Argentina	72	72	75	72	291
Jose Diniz, Brazil	73	74	74	70	291
Pietro Molteni, Italy	74	74	71	72	291
Michael Clayton, Australia	73	70	71	78	292
John O'Leary, Ireland	73	73	72	74	292
Des Smyth, Ireland	73	70	76	74	293
Oswald Gartenmaier, Austria	72	75	74	73	294
Sam Torrance, Scotland	77	74	72	71	294
Pete Izumigawa, Japan	73	74	73	76	296
Eleuterio Nival, Philippines	72	73	71	80	296
Ian Woosnam, Wales	74	73	75	74	296
Namio Takasu, Japan	73	74	77	72	296
Adan Domingo Sowa, Argentina	78	72	74	72	296
Federico German, Brazil	76	74	74	72	296
Frank Nobilo, New Zealand	72	75	77	73	297
Francisco Cerda, Chile	76	75	72	74	297
Gery Watine, France	74	76	74	74	298
Mario Siodina, Philippines	74	74	71	80	299
Marimuthu Ramayah, Malaysia	73	77	77	72	299
Alberto Rivadeneira, Colombia	75	78	73	73	299
Dave Barr, Canada	73	76	76	74	299
Lim Kian Tiong, Singapore	78	71	74	77	300
Mohammed Shafique, Pakistan	75	71	77	77	300
Luis Arevelo, Colombia	75	76	73	76	300
Ramon Munoz, Venezuela	74	79	77	71	301
Michael Cahill, Australia	78	74	73	77	302
Fatmi Moussa, Morocco	75	74	77	77	303
Cees Renders, Holland	77	74	79	73	303
Heinz-Peter Thuel, Germany	73	78	77	76	304
Luis Cabrera, Chile	76	73	75	81	305
Philippe Toussaint, Belgium	73	78	75	79	305
Torsten Giedeon, Germany	76	74	79	76	305
Mohammed Makrounne, Morocco	75	77	77	76	305
Nazamuddin Yusoff, Malaysia	80	77	73	75	305
Jean Garaialde, France	79	80	75	72	306
Richard Coombes, New Zealand	74	76	77	79	306
Suthep Messawad, Thailand	79	74	78	76	307
Jan Dorrestein, Holland	82	72	76	79	309
Freddy Acevedo, Venezuela	77	76	75	83	311
Ghulam Nabi, Pakistan	77	77	76	82	312
Fung Hee Kwan, Singapore	81	77	75	79	312
Don Gammon, Zimbabwe	81	76	81	74	312
Tim Price, Zimbabwe	77	79	81	75	312
Keith Williams, Wales	81	79	75	78	313
Andre Van Damme, Belgium	82	81	78	79	320
Franz Laimer, Austria	82	80	80	82	324
Juan R. Aguirre, Uruguay	84	82	81	83	330
Hugo Santurio, Uruguay	83	83	86	86	338

PRIZE MONEY: Pinero $10,000; Gilder, Canizares $5,000 each; Dassu $1,500.

The U.S. Seniors Tour

The Vintage Invitational

Vintage Club, Indian Wells, California
Par 36–36—72; 6,682 yards

March 11–14
purse, $300,000

	SCORES				TOTAL	MONEY
Miller Barber	74	69	66	73	282	$40,000
Arnold Palmer	69	72	72	70	283	18,666.66
Dan Sikes	70	71	69	73	283	18,666.66
Art Wall	74	70	69	70	283	18,666.66
Roberto DeVicenzo	75	70	74	68	287	12,000
Billy Casper	71	74	70	74	289	10,000
Don January	76	70	69	75	290	9,000
Tom Nieporte	74	74	73	71	292	7,750
Bob Rosburg	75	69	75	73	292	7,750
Kel Nagle	72	74	71	76	293	6,500
Guy Wolstenholme	78	71	70	74	293	6,500
Paul Harney	76	75	67	75	293	6,500
Jack Burke	73	73	75	73	294	5,000
Gene Littler	72	70	78	74	294	5,000
Jerry Barber	76	76	69	73	294	5,000
Sam Snead	74	78	71	72	295	4,000
Harvie Ward	75	76	75	71	297	4,000
Mike Souchak	76	78	73	71	298	4,000
George Bayer	77	74	69	78	298	4,000
Tommy Bolt	74	73	80	72	299	4,000
Dow Finsterwald	80	72	74	73	299	4,000
Don Fairfield	74	75	74	76	299	4,000
Bob Stone	78	80	72	70	300	4,000
Lionel Hebert	76	75	76	73	300	4,000
Bob Goalby	81	75	68	76	300	4,000
Bob Toski	76	73	77	75	301	4,000
Al Balding	74	75	76	76	301	4,000
Gardner Dickinson	78	75	74	76	303	4,000
Flory Van Donck	77	73	77	77	304	4,000
Paul Runyan	77	73	75	79	304	4,000
Doug Ford	78	73	75	82	304	4,000
Christy O'Connor	76	84	75	78	313	4,000
Bobby Locke	86	85	843	85	339	4,000
Ken Venturi	80	82	73	WD		
Julius Boros	79	82	74	WD		

Michelob Seniors Classic

Carrollwood Village Golf and Tennis Club, Tampa, Florida
Par 36–36—72; 6,529 yards

April 1–4
purse, $125,000

	SCORES				TOTAL	MONEY
Don January	73	69	67	69	278	$20,000
Dow Finsterwald	70	72	71	68	281	11,600

	SCORES				TOTAL	MONEY
Paul Harney	69	72	71	70	282	8,000
Bill Collins	70	70	73	70	283	5,150
Miller Barber	68	74	71	70	283	5,150
Dan Sikes	70	72	73	69	284	4,000
Arnold Palmer	74	69	72	71	286	3,450
Art Wall, Jr.	72	67	74	73	286	3,450
Gene Littler	72	72	73	70	287	3,000
Tom Nieporte	74	73	72	70	289	2,520
Jim Ferree	74	71	74	70	289	2,520
Sam Snead	74	72	70	73	289	2,520
J.C. Goosie	68	71	75	75	289	2,520
Billy Casper	73	69	71	76	289	2,520
Jerry Barber	70	75	76	69	290	2,150
Howie Johnson	72	74	73	71	290	2,150
Tommy Bolt	73	71	76	71	291	2,000
Ken Mast	77	75	70	70	292	1,900
Bob Erickson	72	74	75	74	295	1,750
Charles Sifford	75	73	73	74	295	1,750
Ed Causey	74	76	76	70	296	1,650
George Bayer	80	73	71	73	297	1,525
Doug Ford	75	74	75	73	297	1,525
Mike Fetchick	71	75	75	76	297	1,525
Charles Malchaski	74	70	73	80	297	1,525
Lionel Hebert	75	77	72	74	298	1,390
Jack Fleck	72	73	79	74	298	1,390
Fred Hawkins	75	72	75	76	298	1,390
Bob Rosburg	71	79	77	72	299	1,330
Mike Souchak	74	75	78	73	300	1,300
Bill Johnston	76	72	73	80	301	1,270
Bob Hamilton	74	78	74	75	301	1,270
Ted Dorius	81	74	73	74	302	1,230
Gordon Jones	79	71	76	76	302	1,230
Billy Maxwell	75	75	80	73	303	1,200
Ted Kroll	76	77	76	75	304	1,180
Roland Stafford	78	74	77	76	305	1,160
Al Balding	79	75	76	76	306	1,130
Ed Furgol	77	77	76	76	306	1,130
Chick Harbert	77	80	76	74	307	1,085
Marty Furgol	74	77	79	77	307	1,085
Al Besselink	77	76	77	77	307	1,085
Julius Boros	77	74	78	78	307	1,085
Freddie Haas	79	77	73	79	308	1,060
Pete Cooper	78	76	80	76	310	1,050
Bob Hamrich	77	83	81	73	314	1,040
Dick Metz	81	79	82	77	319	1,030
Henry Ransom	81	84	78	80	323	1,020
Johnny Palmer	84	77	81	82	324	1,010
Herman Keiser	88	77	84	80	329	1,000

Legends of Golf

Onion Creek Club, Austin, Texas
Par 35–35—70; 6,584 yards

April 22–25
purse, $464,000

	SCORES			TOTAL	MONEY (each)
Sam Snead–Don January	62	60	61	183	$50,000

	SCORES			TOTAL	MONEY
Bob Toski–Chin Sei Ha	68	62	65	195	17,500
Gene Littler–Bob Rosburg	63	68	64	195	17,500
Bob Goalby–Roberto DeVicenzo	68	63	64	195	17,500
Arnold Palmer–Dow Finsterwald	68	65	63	196	11,500
Julius Boros–Miller Barber	65	65	68	198	10,500
Dan Sikes–Gardner Dickinson	66	68	65	199	9,000
Freddie Haas–Dick Mayer	67	64	68	199	9,000
Jack Fleck–Fred Hawkins	68	67	65	200	8,000
George Bayer–Charles Sifford	68	67	65	200	8,000
Jack Burke–Paul Harney	70	65	66	201	7,000
Harvie Ward–Bill Collins	66	67	68	201	7,000
Jerry Barber–Doug Ford	67	65	70	202	6,000
Billy Casper–Gay Brewer	70	65	67	202	6,000
Peter Thomson–Kel Nagle	68	65	70	203	5,500
Lionel Hebert–Jay Hebert	69	65	70	204	5,500
Tommy Bolt–Art Wall	66	71	68	205	5,500
Mike Souchak–Tom Nieporte	73	66	68	207	5,500
*Dale Morey–*Ed Updegraff	74	68	68	210	
Bob Hamilton–George Fazio	75	68	68	211	5,500
Stan Leonard–Ralph Guldahl	70	74	71	215	5,000
Chick Harbert–Al Balding	72	72	75	219	5,000
Henry Ransom–Walter Burkemo	76	74	71	221	5,000
Gene Sarazen–Jimmy Demaret	75	77	78	230	5,000

Marlboro Classic

Marlboro Country Club, Marlboro, Massachusetts
Par 35–36—71; 6,174 yards

June 10–13
purse, $150,000

	SCORES				TOTAL	MONEY
Arnold Palmer	68	70	69	69	276	$25,000
Billy Casper	73	68	70	69	280	12,500
Bob Rosburg	71	74	65	70	280	12,500
Peter Thomson	72	70	70	69	281	6,750
Dan Sikes	76	70	67	68	281	6,750
Art Wall	72	66	72	72	282	4,500
Bob Goalby	73	69	76	66	284	4,000
Bob Erickson	75	68	71	72	286	3,750
Charles Owens	69	72	76	70	287	3,250
Miller Barber	73	71	73	70	287	3,250
Bill Johnston	69	73	73	72	287	3,250
Doug Ford	70	73	74	72	289	2,900
George Bayer	71	74	76	71	292	2,600
Tom Nieporte	72	74	76	70	292	2,600
Charles Sifford	73	75	73	71	292	2,600
Howie Johnson	72	74	74	72	292	2,600
Denis Hutchinson	73	74	71	74	292	2,600
Pete Hessemer	79	73	72	69	293	2,250
Don Hoenig	72	73	76	72	293	2,250
Bill Collins	76	74	70	74	294	2,100
Pete Cooper	78	72	73	72	295	1,985
Mike Fetchick	72	74	74	75	295	1,985
Gardner Dickinson	75	75	74	72	296	1,875
Roland Stafford	76	74	71	75	296	1,875
Kel Nagle	75	74	77	71	297	1,775
Fred Hawkins	73	78	75	71	297	1,775
Ed Causey	78	74	75	72	299	1,675

	SCORES				TOTAL	MONEY
Billy Maxwell	74	74	76	75	299	1,675
Lionel Hebert	76	78	76	70	300	1,575
Chandler Harper	74	79	75	72	300	1,575
Paul Runyan	80	76	72	73	301	1,500
Bob Crowley	73	81	71	77	302	1,450
Freddie Haas	76	74	73	80	303	1,390
Marty Furgol	74	75	74	80	303	1,390
Herman Keiser	76	77	76	75	304	1,310
Bill Ezinicki	80	72	75	77	304	1,310
Eddie Rubis	73	76	77	78	304	1,310
Ed Furgol	81	77	71	76	305	1,235
Jimmy Clark	75	79	74	77	305	1,235
Al Besselink	76	77	73	80	306	1,190
Ted Kroll	76	75	74	81	306	1,190
Charles Malchaski	72	76	75	84	307	1,160
Stan Leonard	79	73	79	78	309	1,130
Al Balding	78	78	77	76	309	1,130
Jerry Barber	80	74	83	74	311	1,100
John Kalinka	79	76	81	76	312	1,080
Henry Ransom	80	86	77	77	320	1,060
Johnny Palmer	81	79	82	83	325	1,040
Jack Fleck	73	75	DQ			1,010
Sam Snead	68	DQ				1,010

Peter Jackson Champions

St. Charles Country Club, Winnipeg, Manitoba   June 24–27
Par 36–36—72; 6,473 yards   purse, Can$200,000

	SCORES				TOTAL	MONEY
Bob Goalby	68	68	64	73	273	Can$31,500
Gene Littler	70	68	67	69	274	18,000
Don January	72	66	68	71	277	10,133.33
Kel Nagle	69	70	72	66	277	10,133.34
Moe Norman	70	69	69	69	277	10,133.33
Miller Barber	69	68	69	72	278	6,500
Sam Snead	71	72	69	68	280	5,500
Peter Thomson	70	67	72	73	282	4,700
Denis Hutchinson	73	68	72	70	283	4,000
Charley Sifford	69	70	71	73	283	4,000
Dan Sikes	76	68	68	71	283	4,000
Jerry Barber	71	69	70	74	284	3,650
Howie Johnson	71	68	70	75	284	3,650
Julius Boros	71	71	68	75	285	3,500
Billy Casper	73	68	76	69	286	3,350
Art Wall	69	75	69	73	286	3,350
Gardner Dickinson	75	67	71	74	287	3,200
Ted Kroll	73	71	73	71	288	3,050
Bob Rosburg	70	70	75	73	288	3,050
Dow Finsterwald	74	70	72	74	290	2,850
Bill Collins	75	69	71	75	290	2,850
Doug Ford	74	69	75	74	292	2,700
Bill Johnston	72	70	76	76	294	2,550
John Henrick	75	71	73	75	294	2,550
Michael Fetchick	74	77	70	74	295	2,350
Bill Mawhinney	75	71	72	77	295	2,350
Billy Maxwell	74	73	73	76	296	2,240

	SCORES				TOTAL	MONEY
John Davis	75	78	71	73	297	2,140
Gay Brewer	72	73	77	75	297	2,140
*Nick Weslock	74	74	73	76	297	
Stan Kolar	71	72	75	79	297	2,140
Lionel Hebert	78	72	72	76	298	2,040
Ted Dorius	70	77	79	72	298	2,040
Bill Kozak	75	74	75	75	299	1,960
Jack Fleck	75	73	75	76	299	1,960
Pete Cooper	77	77	74	72	300	1,900
Freddie Haas	77	77	74	73	301	1,840
Marty Furgol	69	76	76	80	301	1,840
Al Besselink	75	74	79	74	302	1,780
Fred Hawkins	78	81	70	74	303	1,720
Jimmy Clark	74	72	78	79	303	1,720
Henry Ransom	78	75	75	76	304	1,680
Don Fairfield	78	77	77	73	305	1,650
Herman Keiser	77	71	78	79	305	1,650
Ed Furgol	76	74	74	83	307	1,620
Al Balding	79	75	77	78	309	1,600
Don Whitt	75	76	83	77	311	1,580
Stan Leonard	76	81	77	78	312	1,550
Pat Fletcher	71	78	81	82	312	1,550
Johnny Palmer	85	76	79	77	317	1,530
Bill Kerr	79	86	77	78	320	1,520
Norm Smith	80	WD				1,505
Tommy Bolt	78	73	WD			1,505

USGA Senior Open

Portland Golf Club, Portland, Oregon
Par 35–36—71; 6,439 yards

July 8–11
purse, $150,000

	SCORES				TOTAL	MONEY
Miller Barber	72	74	71	65	282	$28,648
Gene Littler	73	69	76	68	286	12,519.50
Dan Sikes	75	69	72	70	286	12,519.50
Bob Goalby	72	71	74	72	289	6,532
Gay Brewer	73	70	75	73	291	4,813
Arnold Palmer	73	71	73	74	291	4,813
Ken Towns	71	74	72	75	292	3,942
Charles Sifford	76	71	77	69	293	3,572
Jack Fleck	73	72	75	74	294	3,282
Bob Gajda	75	74	72	74	295	2,890
Howie Johnson	74	73	72	76	295	2,890
Art Wall	75	74	74	74	297	2,608
Billy Casper	77	76	72	73	298	2,409
Joe Jimenez	71	78	72	77	298	2,409
Bob Rosburg	74	74	74	77	299	2,223
Art Silvestrone	72	77	80	71	300	2,058
Joe Sodd	77	74	74	75	300	2,058
Doug Higgins	81	73	74	73	301	1,865.50
Peter Thomson	74	77	74	76	301	1,865.50
Billy Maxwell	78	73	78	73	302	1,714.50
Don Fairfield	76	76	76	74	302	1,714.50
Dean Lind	77	76	78	72	303	1,468
John Langford	78	76	77	72	303	1,468
Stan Thirsk	78	73	76	76	303	1,468

	SCORES				TOTAL	MONEY
Mike Fetchick	78	74	75	76	303	1,468
Tom Nieporte	73	79	74	77	303	1,468
Bob Erickson	78	75	72	78	303	1,468
Bob Stone	77	74	73	79	303	1,468
Lionel Hebert	77	76	80	71	304	1,249
Mac Main	73	76	82	73	304	1,249
Denis Hutchinson	78	72	80	84	304	1,249
Fred Hawkins	75	78	79	73	305	1,146
George Bayer	75	76	77	77	305	1,146
Jerry Barber	73	80	77	76	306	1,043
John Zontek	73	80	77	76	306	1,043
George Thomas	77	76	77	76	306	1,043
Hampton Auld	76	78	79	74	307	960
Don Hoenig	77	77	77	77	308	919
Everett Vinzant	78	74	82	75	309	864.34
Fred Wampler	79	75	78	77	309	864.33
Jack Webb	79	75	77	78	309	864.33
*John Harbottle	79	72	80	79	310	
Freddie Haas	72	76	77	86	311	809
*Arthur Ellis	73	78	74	77	312	
Tommy Williams	77	73	84	78	312	768
Stan Jawor	74	75	81	82	312	768
*Howard Slocum	77	77	77	81	312	
Dick Sarta	79	75	76	83	313	727
*Ted Richards	74	80	81	79	314	
Chico Miartuz	74	77	82	82	315	

Denver Post Champions of Golf

Pinehurst Country Club, Denver, Colorado
Par 35–35—70; 6,908 yards

August 12–15
purse, $150,000

	SCORES				TOTAL	MONEY
Arnold Palmer	68	67	73	67	275	$25,000
Bob Goalby	70	66	69	71	276	15,000
Don January	68	74	70	65	277	7,000
Miller Barber	67	70	70	70	277	7,000
Gay Brewer	68	66	73	70	277	7,000
Art Wall	69	65	71	72	277	7,000
Dan Sikes	70	69	71	68	278	4,000
Gene Littler	70	68	68	73	279	3,750
George Bayer	68	69	70	75	282	3,375
Fred Hawkins	66	72	73	71	282	3,375
Jack Fleck	68	68	72	75	283	2,900
Charles Sifford	72	69	72	70	283	2,900
Guy Wolstenholme	69	69	72	73	283	2,900
Dow Finsterwald	69	68	75	72	284	2,650
Paul Harney	70	71	69	74	284	2,650
Robert Erickson	71	71	72	72	286	2,350
Howie Johnson	69	77	72	68	286	2,350
Billy Maxwell	72	71	75	68	286	2,350
Peter Thomson	74	75	67	70	286	2,350
Julius Boros	76	72	72	67	287	2,060
Bill Johnston	73	73	70	71	287	2,060
Bill Collins	74	75	71	68	288	1,900
Mike Fetchick	71	74	73	70	288	1,900
Sam Snead	75	73	73	67	288	1,900

	SCORES				TOTAL	MONEY
*Larry Eaton	75	74	70	70	289	
Dick Mayer	70	70	75	76	291	1,800
Hulen Coker	74	71	75	72	292	1,700
Gardner Dickinson	74	72	73	73	292	1,700
Freddie Haas	71	72	71	78	292	1,700
Denis Hutchinson	74	75	72	72	293	1,575
Kel Nagle	75	73	68	77	293	1,575
Jack Harden	74	74	70	76	294	1,475
Pat Rea	73	72	72	77	294	1,475
Bob Ellsworth	78	74	73	70	295	1,373.34
Lionel Hebert	82	70	72	71	295	1,373.33
Warren Smith	73	78	71	73	295	1,373.33
Al Balding	73	78	76	70	297	1,310
Jerry Barber	72	77	77	72	298	1,280
Bill Metier	70	76	77	77	300	1,235
Paul Runyan	74	79	75	72	300	1,235
Pete Cooper	74	74	76	77	301	1,180
Ed Furgol	74	77	74	76	301	1,180
Henry Ransom	80	75	75	71	301	1,180
Ted Kroll	73	77	79	75	304	1,140
Al Besselink	79	76	74	76	305	1,110
Marty Furgol	75	78	75	77	305	1,110
Tony Novitsky	77	78	75	76	306	1,080
Donald Whitt	79	77	73	78	307	1,060
Herman Keiser	76	78	82	75	311	1,030
Stan Leonard	73	79	82	77	311	1,030
Jim Ferrier	89	90	92	91	362	1,000

Greater Syracuse Classic

Bellevue Country Club, Syracuse, New York   August 19–22
Par 35–36—71; 6, 572 yards   purse, $150,000

	SCORES				TOTAL	MONEY
Bill Collins	73	71	71	70	285	$25,000
Guy Wolstenholme	71	73	72	70	286	15,000
Peter Thomson	70	72	74	71	287	9,000
Bob Goalby	70	76	70	71	287	9,000
Bob Rosburg	73	73	75	68	289	5,000
Gene Littler	72	72	73	72	298	5,000
Paul Harney	71	74	78	69	292	3,875
Don January	72	74	69	77	292	3,875
Bob Erickson	72	77	75	69	293	3,250
Sam Snead	78	70	75	70	293	3,250
Bill Johnston	74	71	77	71	293	3,250
Freddie Haas	69	73	76	76	294	2,800
Gardner Dickinson	77	69	74	74	294	2,800
Art Wall	71	76	74	73	294	2,800
Jim Ferree	75	74	78	68	295	2,500
George Bayer	72	73	78	72	295	2,500
Art Silvestrone	73	75	75	72	295	2,500
Howie Johnson	71	74	78	73	296	2,300
Kel Nagle	73	76	75	73	297	2,106.67
Don Hoenig	75	73	75	74	297	2,106.67
Marty Furgol	73	76	74	74	297	2,106.66
Gordon Jones	75	73	76	74	298	1,950
Billy Maxwell	80	72	72	75	299	1,900

	SCORES				TOTAL	MONEY
Mac Main	77	75	75	72	300	1,800
Al Balding	77	75	76	72	300	1,800
Dan Sikes	75	79	73	73	300	1,800
Charles Sifford	77	71	76	77	301	1,700
Denis Hutchinson	78	76	74	74	302	1,600
Chandler Harper	78	74	75	75	302	1,600
Mike Fetchick	77	72	78	75	302	1,600
Tom Nieporte	79	80	75	69	303	1,475
Harvie Ward	76	75	80	72	303	1,475
Miller Barber	75	74	77	78	304	1,342
Jack Fleck	76	80	73	75	304	1,342
Julius Boros	75	76	78	75	304	1,342
Fred Hawkins	76	77	75	76	304	1,342
Jerry Barber	75	74	78	77	304	1,342
Milon Marusic	81	76	75	73	305	1,250
Ed Causey	73	78	77	78	306	1,210
Al Besselink	79	71	78	78	306	1,210
Ted Kroll	82	76	74	75	307	1,160
Lionel Hebert	81	73	75	78	307	1,160
Jimmy Clark	73	82	72	79	307	1,160
Pete Cooper	79	72	80	77	308	1,120
Bob Hamilton	77	78	79	75	309	1,100
Paul Runyan	80	78	76	77	311	1,070
Donald Whitt	82	78	78	73	311	1,070
Ed Rubis	78	79	77	78	312	1,040
Ed Furgol	81	79	81	81	322	1,020
Herman Keiser	80	80	85	80	325	1,000
*Joe Russo, Sr.	93	79	89	81	342	

Jeremy Ranch Seniors

Jeremy Ranch Golf Club, Park City, Utah — August 25–28
Par 36–36—72; 6,947 yards — purse, $150,000

	SCORES				TOTAL	MONEY
Billy Casper	74	71	69	65	279	$25,000
Don January	69	75	67	69	280	12,500
Miller Barber	72	70	70	68	280	12,500
Gene Littler	70	71	70	72	283	8,000
Julius Boros	73	73	72	72	290	5,500
Paul Harney	71	75	71	74	291	4,250
Bob Goalby	74	79	70	68	291	4,250
Gay Brewer	77	70	71	75	293	3,625
Peter Thomson	74	75	71	73	293	3,625
Dick Mayer	72	76	71	75	294	3,125
Jerry Barber	72	76	74	72	294	3,125
Guy Wolstenholme	76	74	73	72	295	2,900
Sam Snead	74	71	78	73	296	2,800
Bill Collins	76	79	74	68	297	2,500
Mike Fetchick	78	75	74	70	297	2,500
Bill Johnston	75	74	77	71	297	2,500
Dean Lind	74	69	80	74	297	2,500
Howie Johnson	72	78	73	74	297	2,500
Kel Nagle	76	77	72	74	299	2,150
Charles Sifford	75	76	74	74	299	2,150
Arnold Palmer	79	76	72	73	300	1,985
Jack Fleck	74	77	73	76	300	1,985

	SCORES			TOTAL	MONEY
Tommy Williams	73	73	77 78	301	1,900
Pete Hessemer	75	75	78 74	302	1,800
Freddie Haas	71	79	76 76	302	1,800
Billy Maxwell	75	77	74 76	302	1,800
Bob Rosburg	74	77	79 73	303	1,675
Mike Souchak	76	72	77 78	303	1,675
Al Besselink	77	74	77 76	304	1,550
Gordon Jones	72	76	80 76	304	1,550
Jack Harden	76	73	76 79	304	1,550
Bob Hamilton	77	78	75 77	307	1,450
Ed Furgol	78	77	79 75	309	1,373.34
Al Balding	78	78	77 76	309	1,373.33
Bob Erickson	75	73	80 81	309	1,373.33
Pete Cooper	76	76	78 80	310	1,295
Denis Hutchinson	76	74	77 83	310	1,295
Fred Hawkins	74	81	79 77	311	1,250
George Schneiter	77	81	77 77	312	1,200
Harvie Ward	81	77	79 75	312	1,200
Ralph Emery	76	79	82 75	312	1,200
Henry Ransom	76	77	82 78	313	1,140
Don Collett	75	79	79 80	313	1,140
Don Whitt	78	77	78 80	313	1,140
Ted Kroll	73	78	82 81	314	1,100
Mark Hipkins	76	83	81 76	316	1,080
Marty Furgol	81	78	81 78	318	1,050
Lionel Hebert	83	82	79 74	318	1,050
Paul Runyan	79	83	83 78	323	1,020
Jimmy Clark	84	83	79 80	326	1,000
Herman Keiser	83	83	82 83	331	1,000

Merrill Lynch/Golf Digest Commemorative

Newport Country Club, Newport, Rhode Island
Par 36–36—72; 6,566 yards

September 17–19
purse, $125,000

	SCORES			TOTAL	MONEY
Billy Casper	68	70	68	206	$22,500
Bob Toski	72	69	65	206	14,300
(Casper defeated Toski on fourth hole of sudden-death playoff.)					
Dow Finsterwald	69	67	71	207	9,000
Howie Johnson	70	69	69	208	6,500
Gardner Dickinson	68	71	70	209	5,550
Mike Fetchick	73	69	67	209	5,550
Bob Goalby	72	66	72	210	4,550
Dan Sikes	71	72	67	210	4,550
Sam Snead	72	72	67	211	3,700
Julius Boros	72	69	70	211	3,700
Peter Thomson	69	71	72	212	3,100
Paul Harney	71	73	70	214	2,550
Roberto DeVicenzo	74	70	70	214	2,550
Al Balding	71	72	73	216	1,775
Bill Collins	72	72	72	216	1,775
Kel Nagle	73	73	70	216	1,775
Bill Johnston	72	73	71	216	1,775
Jim Ferree	75	74	67	216	1,775
Pete Cooper	72	76	68	216	1,775
Bob Rosburg	70	72	75	217	1,467.50

	SCORES			TOTAL	MONEY
Freddie Haas	72	73	72	217	1,467.50
Dick Mayer	72	75	70	217	1,467.50
Doug Ford	74	73	70	217	1,467.50
George Bayer	73	78	67	218	1,400
Marty Furgol	69	75	75	219	1,350
Gene Littler	77	70	72	219	1,350
Jerry Barber	76	73	70	219	1,350
Charley Sifford	74	72	74	220	1,300
Tom Nieporte	80	70	71	221	1,275
Ted Kroll	72	73	77	222	1,237.50
Chandler Harper	76	74	72	222	1,237.50
Billy Maxwell	76	76	71	223	1,200
Lionel Hebert	77	76	71	224	1,175
Paul Runyan	79	77	71	227	1,150
Ed Furgol	74	80	75	229	1,125
Fred Hawkins	78	75	77	230	1,100
Herman Keiser	83	77	74	234	1,075
Al Besselink	84	75	77	236	1,050
Henry Ransom	77	84	78	239	1,025
Jim Ferrier	85	92	84	261	1,000

World Seniors Invitational

Quail Hollow Country Club, Charlotte, North Carolina   September 23–26
Par 36–36—72; 6,894 yards   purse, $135,000

	SCORES				TOTAL	MONEY
Gene Littler	71	70	69	70	280	$23,000
Miller Barber	74	71	70	70	285	14,000
Peter Thomson	72	73	73	68	286	10,000
Roberto De Vicenzo	73	73	73	69	288	6,333.34
Howie Johnson	69	76	71	72	288	6,333.33
Gay Brewer	73	74	68	73	288	6,333.33
Arnold Palmer	72	73	73	71	289	4,433.34
Tom Nieporte	73	71	73	72	289	4,433.33
Bob Goalby	72	69	75	73	289	4,433.33
Jim Ferree	72	68	75	75	290	4,000
Charles Sifford	73	73	69	76	291	3,800
Paul Harney	72	74	75	71	292	3,500
Billy Casper	73	77	71	71	292	3,500
Mike Souchak	77	72	70	75	294	3,100
Bob Toski	72	76	72	74	294	3,100
Bob Erickson	79	70	75	72	296	2,600
Bill Collins	72	76	73	75	296	2,600
Jack Fleck	70	74	76	76	296	2,600
Guy Wolstenholme	72	77	77	71	297	1,900
Mike Fetchick	75	77	72	73	297	1,900
Kel Nagle	73	76	74	74	297	1,900
Art Wall	71	74	74	78	297	1,900
Julius Boros	78	75	73	72	298	1,375
Doug Ford	77	76	71	74	298	1,375
*Ed Tutwiler	72	78	74	75	299	
Bill Johnston	75	72	77	75	299	1,350
Fred Hawkins	73	75	79	74	301	1,300
*Bill Hyndman	79	77	73	73	302	
Jerry Barber	74	74	77	77	302	1,300
Al Mengert	75	82	71	75	303	1,300

	SCORES				TOTAL	MONEY
Billy Maxwell	75	76	77	75	303	1,300
Al Balding	78	74	79	74	305	1,250
Gardner Dickinson	71	77	79	79	306	1,250
Bob Rosburg	81	74	73	78	306	1,250
Dow Finsterwald	74	77	79	77	307	1,250
George Bayer	74	78	76	80	308	1,250
Pete Hessemer	79	72	81	77	309	1,250
Lionel Hebert	77	73	81	79	310	1,250
*Lew Oehmig	78	77	81	75	311	
Don Cherry	77	78	77	79	311	1,250
*Dale Morey	83	79	76	80	318	
Harvie Ward	78	75	76	WD	(Injury)	937.50

Suntree Seniors Classic

Suntree Country Club, Melbourne, Florida
Par 36–36—72; 6,533 yards

October 14–17
purse, $135,000

	SCORES				TOTAL	MONEY
Miller Barber	66	66	66	66	264	$22,500
Don January	64	72	67	66	269	13,500
Gay Brewer	71	69	69	68	277	9,000
Howie Johnson	71	71	73	65	280	7,200
Jim Ferree	73	71	68	69	281	4,950
Sam Snead	68	68	73	73	282	4,050
Charles Sifford	75	68	71	69	283	3,333.34
Dan Sikes	69	74	70	70	283	3,333.33
Bob Goalby	67	77	68	71	283	3,333.33
Paul Harney	72	70	71	71	284	2,800
Gardner Dickinson	68	71	74	71	284	2,800
Fred Hawkins	74	75	69	68	286	2,600
Julius Boros	77	69	71	70	287	2,350
Arnold Palmer	71	70	74	72	287	2,350
Dow Finsterwald	69	72	72	74	287	2,350
Mike Fetchick	72	72	69	74	287	2,350
Ted Kroll	75	70	71	72	288	2,050
Bob Stone	72	73	68	75	288	2,050
Freddie Haas	73	72	73	71	289	1,900
Bill Johnston	74	74	73	69	290	1,800
Billy Maxwell	74	72	75	70	291	1,625
Lionel Hebert	76	74	69	72	291	1,625
Jack Fleck	67	75	73	76	291	1,625
Denis Hutchinson	70	72	74	76	292	1,537.50
Bob Erickson	71	72	72	77	292	1,537.50
Art Silvestrone	76	70	74	73	293	1,475
Jerry Barber	73	67	77	76	293	1,475
Doug Ford	74	71	72	76	293	1,475
Gordon Waldespuhl	73	77	72	72	294	1,425
J.C. Goosie	78	73	72	72	295	1,400
Ed Causey	73	75	72	77	297	1,375
Bob Ross	78	72	74	74	298	1,337.50
Tom Nieporte	78	74	72	74	298	1,337.50
George Bayer	73	77	73	76	299	1,300
Al Balding	73	75	75	77	300	1,262.50
Bob Hamilton	77	73	74	76	300	1,262.50
Paul Runyan	76	78	75	72	301	1,225
Guy Wolstenholme	79	74	70	79	302	1,200

	SCORES				TOTAL	MONEY
Walter Burkemo	80	77	68	79	304	1,175
Al Besselink	75	77	76	77	305	1,150
Ed Furgol	78	80	74	74	306	1,125
Herman Keiser	74	81	76	77	308	1,090
Bert Weaver	76	76	79	77	308	1,090
Pete Cooper	76	77	77	79	309	1,065
Marty Furgol	77	78	76	78	309	1,065
Mike Souchak	76	85	72	78	311	1,050
Henry Ransom	77	81	81	77	316	1,040
Johnny Palmer	82	84	81	85	332	1,030
Jim Ferrier	86	91	94	93	364	1,020
Bill Collins	73	WD				

Hilton Head Seniors International

Shipyard Golf Club, Hilton Head, South Carolina October 21–24
Par 36–36—72; 6,603 yards purse, $112,500

(Tournament reduced to 36 holes because of rain, purse reduced 25% from $150,000.)

	SCORES		TOTAL	MONEY
Co-Winners:				
Miller Barber	69	69	138	$15,000
Dan Sikes	69	69	138	15,000
Don January	68	72	140	7,500
Julius Boros	74	68	142	4,125
Bob Goalby	71	71	142	4,125
Ted Kroll	76	66	142	4,125
Buck Adams	71	71	142	4,125
Guy Wolstenholme	73	70	143	2,460
G. Dickinson	71	72	143	2,460
Howie Johnson	71	72	143	2,460
Jim Ferree	72	71	143	2,460
Al Besselink	71	72	143	2,460
Bill Johnston	74	70	144	1,950
Gordon Jones	74	70	144	1,950
Paul Harney	73	71	144	1,950
Art Silvestrone	69	75	144	1,950
Billy Casper	71	73	144	1,950
Charles Sifford	73	72	145	1,725
Bob Stone	72	74	146	1,550.63
Jerry Barber	71	75	146	1,550.63
Dow Finsterwald	74	72	146	1,550.63
Mac Main	73	73	146	1,550.63
George Bayer	73	74	147	1,350
Pete Cooper	76	71	147	1,350
Jack Fleck	74	73	147	1,350
Gay Brewer	73	74	147	1,350
Mike Fetchick	72	75	147	1,350
Bob Erickson	75	73	148	1,218.75
Ed Furgol	75	73	148	1,218.75
Walter Burkemo	73	76	149	1,026
Bert Weaver	71	78	149	1,026
Andrew Gard	78	71	149	1,026
Dean Lind	74	75	149	1,026

	SCORES	TOTAL	MONEY
Hulen Coker	74 75	149	1,026
Bob Hamilton	72 77	149	1,026
Sam Snead	73 76	149	1,026
Marty Furgol	73 76	149	1,026
Fred Hawkins	74 75	149	1,026
E. Harvie Ward	73 76	149	1,026
Billy Maxwell	76 74	150	900
Doug Ford	74 77	151	885
Tom Nieporte	74 78	152	862.50
Johnny Palmer	80 72	152	862.50
Lionel Hebert	76 77	153	840
Al Balding	77 77	154	825
Mike Souchak	77 78	155	802.50
Henry Ransom	79 76	155	802.50
Herman Keiser	76 82	158	780
Dick Metz	82 79	161	765
Freddie Haas	77 WD (unofficial money)		750

PGA Seniors' Championship

PGA National Golf Club, Champion Course, Palm Beach Gardens, Florida
December 2–5
Par 36–36—72; 6,520 yards
purse $150,000

	SCORES				TOTAL	MONEY
Don January	74	75	69	70	288	$25,000
Julius Boros	71	73	70	75	289	18,000
Gay Brewer	71	76	74	69	290	11,250
Arnold Palmer	71	70	73	76	290	11,250
Art Wall	72	73	71	74	290	11,250
Bob Goalby	68	75	74	73	290	11,250
Miller Barber	79	72	70	72	293	5,000
Bob Stone	70	74	74	75	293	5,000
Bob Erickson	73	75	76	71	295	3,250
Bill Collins	75	74	74	72	295	3,250
Jim Ferree	75	72	76	73	296	2,250
Howie Johnson	70	71	78	77	296	2,250
Gardner Dickinson	77	71	78	71	297	1,750
Auggie Navarro	73	73	76	75	297	1,750
Bill Casper	73	71	78	75	297	1,750
Bob Toski	73	70	75	79	297	1,750
Roberto De Vicenzo	72	80	70	76	298	1,450
Jerry Barber	74	74	72	78	298	1,450
Dan Sikes	76	78	76	69	299	1,325
Pat Rea	72	77	75	75	299	1,325
Stan Mosel	77	72	80	71	300	1,250
Bob Hamilton	74	77	78	72	301	1,125
Bob Duden	73	75	76	77	301	1,125
Joe Moresco	75	74	74	78	301	1,125
Richard Lotz	73	73	75	80	301	1,125
Paul Harney	74	78	74	76	302	950
Joe Jimenez	77	74	74	77	302	950
Ken Mast	71	77	75	79	302	950
Joe Taylor	72	74	84	73	303	808.34
Charlie Owens	77	75	77	74	303	808.33
Tom Nieporte	80	73	74	76	303	808.33
Fred Hawkins	76	77	81	70	304	700

	SCORES				TOTAL	MONEY
Stan Thirsk	81	73	76	74	304	700
John Cook	75	76	76	77	304	700
Mal McMullen	74	76	75	79	304	700
Dean Lind	76	74	76	78	304	700
Dick Sarta	76	75	80	74	305	625
Bill Davis	72	80	77	77	306	580
Mike Fetchick	74	78	75	79	306	580
Roland Stafford	75	76	76	79	306	580
John Kalinka	74	79	78	76	307	530
Eddie Rubis	77	78	75	77	307	530
George Thomas	77	78	76	77	308	500
Ken Towns	75	81	75	77	308	500
Buck Adams	76	73	78	81	308	500
Bert Weaver	78	78	78	75	309	470
Ted Kroll	79	76	79	75	309	470
Andy Borkovich	76	78	76	79	309	470
Mac Main	76	79	78	77	310	430
Kyle Burton	78	77	78	77	310	430
Tony Clecak	79	77	75	79	310	430
Ray Montgomery	77	78	74	81	310	430
Gordon Jones	72	75	79	84	310	430

The European Tour

Tunisian Open

El Kantaoui Golf Course, Sousse, Tunisia
Par 36–36—72; 6,570 yards

April 15–19
purse, £60,000

	SCORES				TOTAL	MONEY
Antonio Garrido	71	73	70	72	286	£10,000
Manuel Calero	75	69	70	72	286	6,660
(Garrido defeated Calero on fifth hole of sudden-death playoff.)						
Manuel Pinero	73	70	75	69	287	3,100
Des Smyth	71	74	71	71	287	3,100
Gordon Brand, Jr	76	72	68	71	287	3,100
Sandy Lyle	74	69	73	72	288	1,950
Ken Brown	74	67	71	76	288	1,950
Ian Mosey	74	72	73	70	289	1,500
Sam Torrance	76	71	69	74	290	1,213.33
Carl Mason	72	73	71	74	290	1,213.33
Keith Williams	70	74	73	73	290	1,213.33
Brian Barnes	73	76	68	74	291	983.33
Paul Way	74	74	70	73	291	983.33
Martin Poxon	78	72	71	70	291	983.33
Mark James	71	75	73	73	292	880
Trevor Powell	81	70	72	70	293	806.67
Mark Thomas	76	74	72	71	293	806.67
Mats Lanner	74	75	70	74	293	806.67
Keith Waters	75	71	76	72	294	700
Denis Durnian	76	75	71	72	294	700
Brian Waites	71	76	74	73	294	700
Bill Longmuir	74	75	72	73	294	700
Ronan Rafferty	73	74	72	75	294	700
Gordon Brand	72	72	74	76	294	700
Mohamed Ben Nacr	70	74	72	78	294	700
Howard Clark	76	72	74	73	295	610
Michel Tapia	74	73	74	74	295	610
Warren Humphreys	81	70	74	71	296	550
Peter Thomas	73	75	75	73	296	550
John Morgan	75	76	72	73	296	550
Juan Anglada	75	73	73	75	296	550
Andrew Murray	75	75	73	74	297	470
Anders Forsbrand	77	74	72	74	297	470
Ewen Murray	72	77	73	75	297	470
Christy O'Connor, Jr	74	74	72	77	297	470
Peter Teravainen	74	77	74	73	298	415
Baldovino Dassu	79	71	74	74	298	415
Manuel Ballesteros	77	75	71	75	298	415
Eamonn Darcy	77	69	74	78	298	415
Philip Elson	77	73	74	75	299	370
Tony Johnstone	73	77	74	75	299	370
Joe Higgins	80	69	74	76	299	370
David Jones	75	74	73	77	299	370
Roger Chapman	76	70	75	78	299	370

	SCORES				TOTAL	MONEY
Rafe Botts	75	74	78	73	300	330
Jose Cabo	74	77	73	76	300	330
Garry Logan	73	76	74	77	300	330
Steve Martin	73	77	77	74	301	280
John Hay	77	73	76	75	301	280
Mike Miller	74	78	74	75	301	280
Graham Burroughs	76	74	76	75	301	280
Gery Watine	74	78	74	75	301	280
Mac O'Grady	78	74	72	77	301	280
Robert Craig	78	73	67	83	301	280

Cespa Madrid Open

Puerta De Hierro, Madrid
Par 36–36—72; 6,968 yards

April 22–25
purse, £42,900

	SCORES				TOTAL	MONEY
Severiano Ballesteros	70	69	66	68	273	£7,147.46
Jose-Maria Canizares	70	64	69	71	274	4,766.76
Antonio Garrido	67	70	69	69	275	2,680.97
Vicente Fernandez	69	71	71	67	278	2,144.77
Sam Torrance	71	67	68	74	280	1,823.06
Sandy Lyle	71	67	68	76	282	1,501.34
Jose Rivero	72	72	68	71	283	1,286.86
Ian Mosey	72	75	69	68	284	922.25
Joey Rassett	72	69	72	71	284	922.25
Des Smyth	71	71	68	74	284	922.25
Jerry Anderson	70	69	70	75	284	922.25
Juan Anglada	72	69	72	72	285	729.22
Jose Davila	70	69	72	74	285	729.22
Jeff Hall	77	72	70	67	286	608.58
John O'Leary	69	73	74	70	286	608.58
Tony Johnstone	74	71	70	71	286	608.58
Manuel Calero	72	70	73	71	286	608.58
Carl Mason	68	71	74	73	286	608.58
Michel Tapia	69	69	73	75	286	·608.58
Philip Elson	71	73	72	71	287	501.34
Paul Way	73	72	71	71	287	501.34
Peter Teravainen	73	73	71	71	288	461.13
Manuel Pinero	73	70	73	72	288	461.13
Garry Logan	75	70	68	75	288	461.13
Garry Harvey	70	74	75	70	289	412.87
Manuel Garcia	72	73	73	71	289	412.87
Baldovino Dassu	69	74	74	72	289	412.87
Howard Clark	74	74	68	73	289	412.87
Ronan Rafferty	75	70	69	75	289	412.87
Jimmy Heggarty	73	71	69	76	289	412.87
Ross Drummond	72	76	72	70	290	364.61
Angel Macias	75	70	74	71	290	364.61
Garry Cullen	73	69	74	74	290	364.61
Tony Jacklin	75	72	75	69	291	332.44
Michael McLean	73	71	74	73	291	332.44
Gordon Brand	77	71	69	74	291	332.44
Gordon Brand Jr	74	72	77	69	292	310.99
*Jesus Lopez Moreno	73	71	70	78	292	
Andrew Murray	72	77	72	72	293	273.46
Jose Luis Blas	73	75	72	73	293	273.46

	SCORES			TOTAL	MONEY
Manuel Montes	73	71	75	74	293	273.46
Ian Woosnam	76	73	70	74	293	273.46
Hugh Baiocchi	72	75	70	76	293	273.46
Michael King	72	71	71	79	293	273.46
Anders Forsbrand	73	75	76	70	294	220.91
Angel Gallardo	74	74	73	73	294	220.91
Warren Humphreys	77	71	72	74	294	220.91
Ewen Murray	74	72	72	76	294	220.91
Keith Waters	70	75	71	78	294	220.91
Steve Martin	73	76	76	70	295	187.67
Harold Henning	73	73	77	72	295	187.67
Fulton Allem	71	71	80	73	295	187.67
John Bland	72	74	75	74	295	187.67
John Morgan	75	73	74	73	295	187.67
Charles Cox	74	73	74	74	295	187.67
Philip Harrison	73	74	72	76	295	187.67

Italian Open

Is Molas, Sardinia
Par 35–37—72; 6,980 yards

April 29–May 2
purse, £49,250

	SCORES			TOTAL	MONEY
Mark James	70	67	71	72	280	£8,205.57
Ian Woosnam	69	74	68	72	283	4,274.09
Bobby Clampett	68	73	72	70	283	4,274.09
Florentino Molina	72	76	68	69	285	2,276.23
Bernhard Langer	70	74	70	71	285	2,276.23
Manuel Pinero	73	74	66	74	287	1,476.80
Juan Anglada	73	70	70	74	287	1,476.80
Ronan Rafferty	71	75	71	70	287	1,476.80
Jose-Maria Canizares	73	75	71	69	288	961.46
Manuel Montes	71	77	67	73	288	961.46
John Bland	71	74	72	71	288	961.46
Antonio Garrido	70	71	71	76	288	961.46
Manuel Calero	75	72	72	70	289	792.29
Gordon Brand	76	75	70	69	290	708.99
Andy North	74	75	71	70	290	708.99
Brian Waites	72	76	67	75	290	708.99
John Morgan	73	71	72	74	290	708.99
Paul Hoad	74	74	71	72	291	623.13
Joey Rassett	70	76	70	75	291	623.13
Ross Drummond	74	77	69	72	292	576.02
Roger Chapman	72	78	70	72	292	576.02
Jeremy Bennett	75	70	74	73	292	576.02
Joe Higgins	71	76	72	74	293	546.04
David Feherty	75	75	71	73	294	531.91
Trevor Powell	75	78	71	71	295	502.21
Martin Poxon	74	75	72	74	295	502.21
Aldo Trillini	71	76	75	73	295	502.21
David A. Russell	74	77	74	71	296	443.25
Pietro Molteni	73	77	74	72	296	443.25
Mac O'Grady	74	76	71	75	296	443.25
Peter Teravainen	73	73	75	75	296	443.25
David J. Russell	73	68	78	77	296	443.25
David Jones	72	76	73	76	297	399.36
Angel Gallardo	70	76	73	78	297	399.36

	SCORES			TOTAL	MONEY
Joe Purcell	78	70	74	76	298	364.28
Ken Brown	76	77	71	74	298	364.28
Jerry Anderson	74	77	75	72	298	364.28
Garry Logan	70	78	70	80	298	364.28
Mark Thomas	69	75	77	77	298	364.28
Baldovino Dassu	76	77	72	74	299	320.34
Bill Longmuir	75	76	71	77	299	320.34
Michael McLean	74	76	76	73	299	320.34
Stephen Bennett	74	73	76	76	299	320.34
Mike Miller	76	75	75	74	300	285.51
Charles Cox	75	75	73	77	300	285.51
Jimmy Heggarty	75	73	79	73	300	285.51
Keith Waters	71	82	73	75	301	241.26
Andrew Murray	79	74	75	73	301	241.26
*Andrea Canessa	77	75	74	75	301	
Jan Sonnevi	74	77	77	73	301	241.26
Garry Cullen	77	74	81	69	301	241.26
Angelo Croce	76	74	73	78	301	241.26
Danny Goodman	73	73	76	79	301	241.26

Paco Rabanne French Open

St. Nom-La-Breteche (Red Course), Paris
Par 36–36—72; 6,715 yards

May 6–9
purse, £43,220

	SCORES			TOTAL	MONEY
Severiano Ballesteros	71	70	72	65	278	£7,206.55
Sandy Lyle	72	64	79	67	282	4,804.37
Juan Anglada	73	75	71	68	287	2,236.88
Mark James	68	73	75	71	287	2,236.88
Tommy Horton	73	69	73	72	287	2,236.88
Manuel Pinero	69	76	73	71	289	1,215.42
Jerry Anderson	75	71	71	72	289	1,215.42
Antonio Garrido	71	71	74	73	289	1,215.42
Paul Hoad	75	71	70	73	289	1,215.42
Manuel Calero	73	70	74	73	290	846.22
Jose-Maria Canizares	74	74	72	71	291	711.56
Bernhard Langer	69	74	76	72	291	711.56
Steve Martin	71	73	74	73	291	711.56
Des Smyth	71	77	70	73	291	711.56
Matt Runge	72	73	71	75	291	711.56
Brian Barnes	74	72	74	72	292	614.19
Jeff Hall	77	74	73	69	293	568.70
Tony Charnley	73	76	73	71	293	568.70
Baldovino Dassu	72	72	76	73	293	568.70
John Bland	74	76	73	71	294	494.09
Sam Torrance	76	71	74	73	294	494.09
Howard Clark	74	76	70	74	294	494.09
Brian Waites	75	74	71	74	294	494.09
Mac O'Grady	70	74	75	75	294	494.09
Simon Bishop	74	72	78	71	295	443.51
Ian Woosnam	74	72	73	76	295	443.51
Trevor Powell	74	77	74	71	296	381.03
Angel Gallardo	75	73	76	72	296	381.03
Ken Brown	72	73	78	73	296	381.03
Bernard Gallacher	73	73	77	73	296	381.03
John O'Leary	71	75	76	74	296	381.03

Driving and diving remained two specialties of Jerry Pate, who shoved U.S. PGA Tour commissioner Deane Beman into a lake after winning the Tournament Players Championship.

On a putting streak. Lanny Wadkins won three times in 1982, in the Phoenix Open, Tournament of Champions and Buick Open.

With help from caddy Creamy Carolin, and a double eagle, Bob Gilder equalled a Tour record for 54 holes with 192 in the Westchester Classic. He won by five strokes. Gilder had two other 1982 titles.

In his most successful year, Calvin Peete won four U.S. titles – Great Milwaukee Open, Anheuser Busch Classic, B.C. Open and Pensacola Open.

Although Curtis Strange did not win in America, Fila and Spalding got plenty of advertisement benefit from his tour-record earnings without a victory.

Bruce Lietzke posted three consecutive 68s in winning the prestigious Canadian Open.

It was a sad year for some, particularly Ben Crenshaw, who finished 83rd on the U.S. PGA Tour money list.

After winning the Doral Eastern Open, Andy Bean had more success with his favorite pastime, fishing, than on the golf course. He is shown here with his wife Debbie, near their Florida home.

Warming up for Troon, Tom Weiskopf won the Western Open. He also won the unofficial Jerry Ford Invitational, a charity event in Colorado.

Johnny Miller walked off with an early-season victory at San Diego.

The highlight of Hale Irwin's season was his victory in the Inverrary Classic.

The son of Clayton, young Vance Heafner won over $100,000.

Bay Hill Classic host Arnold Palmer and executive director Alastair Johnston watch the concluding holes on a television monitor with champion Tom Kite, who later won the title in a playoff with Jack Nicklaus and Denis Watson of South Africa.

Bay Hill featured the pairing of two of golf's young stars, Bobby Clampett and Germany's Bernhard Langer, pictured beside caddy Andy Martinez. Palmer's event included 18 international players from nine countries.

Australia's Greg Norman ranked
No. 1 on the European Tour with
victories in the Benson & Hedges
International (pictured here), Dunlop
Masters and State Express English
Classic.

Sandy Lyle won the Lawrence Batley International and was second on the European
Order of Merit, while fellow Scot Sam Torrance was third.

Occasional bouts with the "yips" dropped Germany's Bernhard Langer from No. 1 on the European Order of Merit, although Langer retained his German Open title.

Playing in America and Europe, Nick Faldo was without a victory until the Haig Whisky Tournament Players Championship in September.

Tony Jacklin's one victory was significant – the Sun Alliance PGA Championship.

Spain's Manuel Pinero led his countrymen on the Order of Merit and won the European Open.

Jose-Maria Canizares of Spain had a strong performance in the British Open and was a top-10 finisher on the Order of Merit.

Severiano Ballesteros won the Madrid Open and French Open.

Brian Waites won two Safari Tour championships and the Car Care Plan International
on the European Tour.

Wentworth professional Bernard Gallacher won
two of the first eight European Tour events.

In his first professional tour, Ian Woosnam won
the Swiss Open and placed among the Order of
Merit leaders.

Mark McNulty was the star of the South African circuit, with four victories in five tournaments to start the year.

The other early-season South African titles were claimed by who else but Gary Player, winning his 13th South African Open and his third PGA championship.

Japan, Isao Aoki continued as a dominant player, and also made a strong challenge in
e World Series of Golf in the United States.

ter winning six tournaments in his first six months, new Japanese star Masahiro
uramoto continued his fine play in 1982 and was joint fourth in the British Open.

Major LPGA victories were posted by Janet Alex in the U.S. Open and Jan Stephenson in the LPGA Championship.

JoAnne Carner won the Chevrolet World Championship of Women's Golf and joined the LPGA Hall of Fame with 35 career victories.

hn D. Laupheimer took over as LPGA commissioner, while Nancy Lopez and Beth
aniel remained the Tour's best drawing cards and Sandra Haynie staged a successful
omeback.

Gary Player and Arnold Palmer joined Sam Snead for his 70th birthday at the Memorial Tournament. Palmer and Snead also were on the Seniors Tour with leaders Miller Barber, Don January and Gene Littler.

	SCORES				TOTAL	MONEY
Philip Harrison	73	75	74	74	296	381.03
Eddie Polland	74	74	74	74	296	381.03
Martin Poxon	74	72	75	75	296	381.03
Ian Mosey	74	77	77	69	297	332.12
David J. Russell	74	75	76	72	297	332.12
Manuel Montes	69	77	78	74	298	309.37
Marc Farry	70	78	76	74	298	309.37
Paul Way	69	75	76	78	298	309.37
Gordon Brand	74	74	79	72	299	272.98
Carl Mason	76	75	74	74	299	272.98
Ross Drummond	74	72	78	75	299	272.98
Florentino Molina	75	73	76	75	299	272.98
Jose Cabo	78	68	77	76	299	272.98
Manuel Garcia	79	72	76	73	300	232.03
Joey Rassett	72	79	76	73	300	232.03
Peter Tupling	77	72	77	74	300	232.03
Peter Teravainen	73	74	76	77	300	232.03
Christian Bonardi	74	76	79	72	301	193.27
Mike Steadman	76	75	77	73	301	193.27
Garry Logan	76	71	80	74	301	193.27
Michel Tapia	75	73	78	75	301	193.27
David Feherty	75	76	75	75	301	193.27

Martini International

Lindrick Golf Club, Yorkshire
Par 35–36—71; 6,633 yards

May 13–16
purse, £66,000

	SCORES				TOTAL	MONEY
Bernard Gallacher	71	71	68	67	277	£11,000
Nick Faldo	69	74	68	69	280	5,739
Jose-Maria Canizares	71	67	72	70	280	5,730
Antonio Garrido	72	70	72	67	281	2,803.33
Des Smyth	72	70	71	68	281	2,803.33
Neil Coles	71	69	68	73	281	2,803.33
Mark James	67	73	69	73	282	1,980
Gordon Brand	72	72	72	67	283	1,565
John Bland	75	69	67	72	283	1,565
John Morgan	73	69	77	65	284	1,197.50
Tony Johnstone	79	69	68	68	284	1,197.50
Tienie Britz	71	70	74	69	284	1,197.50
Ian Mosey	74	71	68	71	284	1,197.50
Tommy Horton	70	76	68	71	285	1,030
Michael McLean	73	69	75	69	286	892
Denis Durnian	74	72	70	70	286	892
Manuel Pinero	75	70	70	71	286	892
Jaime Gonzalez	72	69	73	72	286	892
Eamonn Darcy	73	69	71	73	286	892
Ian Woosnam	71	74	70	72	287	770
Ken Brown	70	71	71	75	287	770
Sandy Lyle	68	69	70	80	287	770
John O'Leary	73	72	70	73	288	730
Brian Waites	73	74	71	71	289	710
Joey Rassett	72	73	74	71	290	640
Jeff Hawkes	71	75	72	72	290	640
Michael King	72	70	74	74	290	640
Manuel Ballesteros	71	73	73	73	290	640

	SCORES				TOTAL	MONEY
Paul Hoad	72	70	74	74	290	640
Manuel Calero	72	72	72	74	290	640
Emilio Rodriguez	76	71	76	68	291	522.50
Sam Torrance	75	70	76	70	291	522.50
Maurice Bembridge	70	75	75	71	291	522.50
Christy O'Connor	72	75	72	72	291	522.50
Hugh Baiocchi	74	71	74	72	291	522.50
Angel Gallardo	72	71	75	73	291	522.50
Craig Defoy	69	73	73	76	291	522.50
Bernhard Langer	73	72	68	78	291	522.50
Arnold O'Connor	73	72	74	73	292	432.50
Trevor Powell	72	74	72	74	292	432.50
Brian Barnes	73	73	71	75	292	432.50
Mac O'Grady	71	73	73	75	292	432.50
Gery Watine	74	72	75	72	293	366
David Feherty	73	74	72	74	293	366
Jeremy Bennett	72	75	72	74	293	366
Peter Teravainen	73	72	72	76	293	366
Nick Job	74	71	70	78	293	366
Paul Way	72	75	77	70	294	315
Rodger Davis	78	70	76	70	294	315
Tony Jacklin	70	74	77	73	294	315
Howard Clark	73	74	70	77	294	315

Car Care Plan International

Moor Allerton Golf Club, Leeds
Par 35–36—71; 6,834 yards

May 20–23
purse, £60,000

	SCORES				TOTAL	MONEY
Brian Waites	68	69	66	73	276	£10,000
Paul Hoad	70	69	69	69	277	5,210
Brian Barnes	68	72	68	69	277	5,210
Severiano Ballesteros	70	70	67	71	278	3,000
Bernard Gallacher	70	68	69	72	279	2,540
John O'Leary	72	74	69	65	280	1,800
Nick Faldo	72	70	72	66	280	1,800
Manuel Calero	68	66	76	70	280	1,800
Sandy Lyle	72	73	69	68	282	1,213.33
Greg Norman	72	68	73	69	282	1,213.33
Ken Brown	69	67	71	75	282	1,213.33
Carl Mason	70	70	69	74	283	983.33
Sam Torrance	71	68	71	73	283	983.33
Jaime Gonzalez	67	68	72	76	283	983.33
Ronan Rafferty	69	71	72	72	284	860
Tony Minshall	73	70	68	73	284	860
David Jones	72	72	70	72	286	800
Mark James	75	71	72	69	287	780
Eamonn Darcy	70	75	75	68	288	720
Manuel Pinero	73	73	72	70	288	720
Ian Mosey	73	73	72	70	288	720
Howard Clark	71	77	69	71	288	720
David J. Russell	71	70	72	75	288	720
John Bland	74	72	72	71	289	630
Ian Woosnam	73	74	70	72	289	630
Eddie Polland	75	69	72	73	289	630
Harold Henning	72	71	73	73	289	630

	SCORES				TOTAL	MONEY
Des Smyth	74	75	72	69	290	520
Garry Cullen	73	73	74	70	290	520
Tony Johnstone	72	74	72	72	290	520
Andrew Payne	74	71	72	73	290	520
Noel Ratcliffe	72	72	73	73	290	520
Denis Durnian	69	74	73	74	290	520
Gordon Brand Jr	73	73	69	75	290	520
Craig Defoy	73	76	73	69	291	420
David Feherty	71	74	76	70	291	420
Massimo Mannelli	75	71	72	73	291	420
Tommy Horton	72	73	73	73	291	420
Michael McLean	73	73	70	75	291	420
Peter Highmoor	71	76	74	71	292	370
Joe Higgins	72	75	74	71	292	370
Jeff Hawkes	71	77	73	71	292	370
Jerry Anderson	77	70	73	72	292	370
Jimmy Heggarty	72	69	75	76	292	370
Emilio Rodriguez	73	72	76	72	293	330
Manuel Ballesteros	70	75	75	73	293	330
John Morgan	73	73	73	74	293	330
Hugh Baiocchi	73	76	73	72	294	290
Mac O'Grady	72	74	75	73	294	290
David Jagger	72	77	72	73	294	290
Martin Foster	75	74	71	74	294	290
Noel Hunt	70	74	73	77	294	290

Sun Alliance PGA Championship

Hillside Golf Club, Southport
Par 36–36—72; 6,951 yards

May 28–31
purse, £80,000

	SCORES				TOTAL	MONEY
Tony Jacklin	72	69	73	70	284	£13,330
Bernhard Langer	69	70	73	72	284	8,890
(Jacklin defeated Langer on first hole of sudden-death playoff.)						
John Bland	69	74	74	70	287	4,500
Mac O'Grady	77	74	70	66	287	4,500
Rodger Davis	72	74	75	67	288	2,866.66
Jose-Maria Canizares	76	72	70	70	288	2,866.66
Sam Torrance	67	72	73	76	288	2,866.66
Harold Henning	73	73	75	68	289	1,900
Brian Barnes	71	76	71	71	289	1,900
Mark James	71	78	71	70	290	1,600
John O'Leary	77	71	72	71	291	1,334
Nick Faldo	73	73	73	72	291	1,334
Eddie Polland	75	73	70	73	291	1,334
Bernard Gallacher	71	70	75	75	291	1,334
Gordon Brand Jr	78	73	67	73	291	1,334
Greg Norman	78	73	73	68	292	1,085
Angel Gallardo	75	74	71	72	292	1,085
Tommy Horton	74	69	75	74	292	1,085
Howard Clark	72	72	75	73	292	1,085
Sandy Lyle	81	68	73	71	293	916.66
Ken Brown	73	73	75	72	293	916.66
Martin Poxon	74	73	74	72	293	916.66
Manuel Calero	76	71	77	70	294	830
Guy Wolstenholme	74	73	77	70	294	830

388

	SCORES				TOTAL	MONEY
Jerry Anderson	74	71	78	71	294	830
Paul Hoad	73	73	74	74	294	830
Robert Craig	73	76	80	66	295	730
Neil Coles	78	73	75	69	295	730
Michael McLean	76	72	75	72	295	730
Brian Waites	78	71	73	73	295	730
Ross Drummond	73	75	73	74	295	730
Graham Burroughs	69	78	74	74	295	730
Philip Elson	76	73	75	72	296	650
Baldovino Dassu	74	71	74	77	296	650
Tony Minshall	74	78	75	70	297	600
Glenn Ralph	76	75	74	72	297	600
Jeff Hawkes	79	70	71	77	297	600
Warren Humphreys	77	75	76	70	298	500
Ian Collins	76	72	79	71	298	500
Joe Higgins	73	75	79	71	298	500
Maurice Bembridge	75	74	75	74	298	500
Jaime Gonzalez	76	75	72	75	298	500
Carl Mason	74	74	74	76	298	500
Tienie Britz	73	76	73	76	298	500
Eamonn Darcy	78	74	73	74	299	410
Mark Thomas	75	75	74	75	299	410
Des Smyth	72	74	73	80	299	410
Martin Foster	79	73	76	72	300	375
Hugh Baiocchi	75	72	80	73	300	375
Steve Martin	72	80	73	75	300	375
Peter Thomas	75	76	73	76	300	375

Jersey Open

La Moye, Jersey
Par 36–36—72; 6,647 yards

June 3–6
purse, £42,000

	SCORES				TOTAL	MONEY
Bernard Gallacher	69	66	68	70	273	£7,000
Eamonn Darcy	65	71	69	68	273	3,912.50
Des Smyth	65	68	67	73	273	3,912.50
(Gallacher won sudden-death playoff, defeating Darcy on second and Smith on fifth extra hole.)						
Sandy Lyle	72	70	68	65	275	2,100
Ian Mosey	69	68	68	71	276	1,780
Ian Woosnam	73	70	68	66	277	1,470
Eddie Polland	73	65	70	70	278	1,260
Tony Jacklin	71	69	71	68	279	943.33
Simon Bishop	69	69	70	71	279	943.33
Noel Ratcliffe	68	69	70	72	279	943.33
Hugh Baiocchi	70	69	70	71	280	760
Brian Waites	67	71	70	72	280	760
Garry Logan	73	70	71	67	281	670
Emilio Rodriguez	69	68	72	72	281	670
Jerry Anderson	69	68	73	72	282	610
Warren Humphreys	72	68	71	72	283	570
Sam Torrance	72	71	70	70	283	570
Jose-Maria Canizares	74	71	71	67	283	570
Peter Tupling	71	70	71	72	284	520
Manuel Calero	68	66	75	75	284	520
Noel Hunt	71	70	73	71	285	423.18

	SCORES				TOTAL	MONEY
Mac O'Grady	71	71	73	70	285	423.18
Carl Mason	71	70	70	74	285	423.18
Howard Clark	71	69	73	72	285	423.18
Jeremy Bennett	72	68	73	72	285	423.18
John Bland	68	75	70	72	285	423.18
Tommy Horton	68	71	72	74	285	423.18
Jeff Hawkes	72	68	73	72	285	423.18
Gordon Manson	72	71	71	71	285	423.18
John Wilkinson	66	72	74	73	285	423.18
Paul Hoad	67	70	72	76	285	423.18
Manuel Pinero	71	73	68	74	286	345
Brian Marchbank	66	73	76	71	286	345
Jaime Gonzalez	67	72	75	72	286	345
Peter Dawson	72	72	76	66	286	345
Christy O'Connor Jr	70	72	73	72	287	305
Kim Swan	74	69	73	71	287	305
Tienie Britz	68	70	75	74	287	305
Michael King	71	74	70	72	287	305
Garry Cullen	71	72	72	73	288	265
Tony Minshall	71	72	74	71	288	265
Andrew Chandler	69	69	77	73	288	265
Martin Poxon	71	73	70	74	288	265
Gordon Brand Jr	69	74	75	71	289	225
John O'Leary	70	70	72	77	289	225
David Jones	76	67	76	70	298	225
Ewen Murray	70	74	71	74	289	225
Philip Elson	70	71	74	75	290	200
Maurice Bembridge	74	71	71	75	291	192.50
Ross Drummond	71	74	71	75	291	192.50

Dunlop Masters

St. Pierre Golf & Country Club, Chepstow
Par 35–36—71; 6,700 yards

June 10–13
purse, £85,000

	SCORES				TOTAL	MONEY
Greg Norman	68	69	65	65	267	£14,160
Bernhard Langer	70	70	67	68	275	9,400
Graham Marsh	71	68	68	69	276	3,967.50
Tommy Horton	70	67	68	71	276	3,967.50
Manuel Pinero	68	71	67	70	276	3,967.50
Hubert Green	68	69	68	71	276	3,967.50
Brian Barnes	71	69	69	68	277	2,246.66
Fuzzy Zoeller	69	70	69	69	277	2,246.66
Nick Faldo	72	68	68	69	277	2,246.66
Tony Jacklin	69	69	71	70	279	1,715
Warren Humphreys	71	66	70	72	279	1,715
Eddie Polland	69	69	73	69	280	1,417.51
Bob Charles	69	68	72	71	280	1,417.51
Antonio Garrido	69	71	69	71	280	1,417.51
Eamonn Darcy	69	70	69	72	280	1,417.51
Carl Mason	69	72	72	68	281	1,310
Harold Henning	72	69	68	72	281	1,310
Noel Ratcliffe	70	71	71	70	282	1,190
John Morgan	69	69	72	72	282	1,190
John Bland	68	69	72	73	282	1,190
Hugh Baiocchi	69	68	71	74	282	1,190

	SCORES			TOTAL	MONEY
Rodger Davis	71	72	72	68	283	1,055
Ken Brown	72	73	70	68	283	1,055
Sandy Lyle	71	71	70	71	283	1,055
Bernard Gallacher	72	72	66	73	283	1,055
Des Smyth	73	71	68	72	284	965
Michael King	75	70	67	72	284	965
Maurice Bembridge	76	70	71	68	285	875
Brian Waites	69	73	72	71	285	875
Gery Watine	73	70	70	72	285	875
Nick Price	68	70	73	74	285	875
Sam Torrance	77	70	68	71	286	790
Angel Gallardo	70	70	73	73	286	790
Gordon Brand	74	70	69	73	286	790
Manuel Calero	72	75	74	66	287	732.50
Ian Mosey	73	73	72	69	287	732.50
John O'Leary	71	74	70	72	287	732.50
Baldovino Dassu	72	73	70	72	287	732.50
David Jones	73	75	69	71	288	687.50
Neil Coles	69	73	73	73	288	687.50
Tony Johnstone	75	70	72	72	289	657.50
David Jagger	78	70	70	71	289	657.50
Mark James	75	68	76	72	291	635
Guy Hunt	75	73	72	73	293	620
Ian Woosnam	76	74	74	71	295	605
Jose-Maria Canizares	73	73	76	74	296	585
Ewen Murray	72	75	72	77	296	585
Howard Clark	72	71	77	77	297	570
Nick Job	68	76	76	78	298	560
Steve Martin	73	76	74	76	299	550

Coral Classic

Royal Porthcawl, Mid-Glamorgan
Par 36–36—72; 6,605 yards

June 24–27
purse, £50,000

	SCORES			TOTAL	MONEY
Gordon Brand Jr	69	70	66	68	273	£8,330
Greg Norman	67	72	70	67	276	5,550
Carl Mason	66	70	71	71	278	3,130
Tony Johnstone	68	70	72	70	280	2,310
Jeff Hawkes	68	72	70	70	280	2,310
Ken Brown	71	70	67	73	281	1,750
Nick Faldo	70	75	66	71	282	1,500
Sandy Lyle	73	70	72	68	283	1,072.50
Jeff Hall	68	69	74	72	283	1,072.50
David Robertson	68	71	69	75	283	1,072.50
Brian Barnes	71	71	65	76	283	1,072.50
Ross Drummond	72	72	73	67	284	810
Rafael Alarcon	68	73	69	74	284	810
Brian Waites	71	71	68	74	284	810
Vaughan Somers	69	73	73	70	285	705
Eamonn Darcy	70	72	72	71	285	705
Ian Mosey	70	68	74	73	285	705
Ronan Rafferty	73	69	71	73	286	645
Jeremy Bennett	72	69	73	73	287	578.33
Garry Cullen	71	70	73	73	287	578.33
Martin Poxon	70	72	71	74	287	578.33

	SCORES				TOTAL	MONEY
Philip Elson	71	70	71	75	287	578.33
Rodger Davis	69	73	70	75	287	578.33
Manuel Ballesteros	71	68	72	76	287	578.33
Peter Tupling	70	72	75	71	288	495
David Feherty	71	74	72	71	288	495
Chris Moody	68	75	74	71	288	495
Harold Henning	71	73	71	73	288	495
Stephen Bennett	71	69	72	76	288	495
Mark James	75	68	76	70	289	428.75
Clive Tucker	72	71	74	72	289	428.75
Des Smyth	71	75	70	73	289	428.75
Craig Defoy	70	74	70	75	289	428.75
David A. Russell	71	75	73	71	290	375
Mike Cahill	69	75	74	72	290	375
Paul Way	74	72	71	73	290	375
David Vaughan	72	73	72	73	290	375
Malcolm Gregson	70	75	71	74	290	375
Simon Bishop	69	75	72	74	290	375
Mike Miller	71	72	76	72	291	320
Warren Humphreys	74	70	72	75	291	320
Christy O'Connor Jr	73	72	71	75	291	320
Mark Johnson	73	71	71	76	291	320
Steve Martin	67	72	74	78	291	320
Mac O'Grady	72	74	72	74	292	275
Andrew Murray	75	67	74	76	292	275
Gordon Manson	70	72	74	76	292	275
Joey Rassett	76	68	69	79	292	275
David J. Russell	72	72	76	73	293	220
John Morgan	74	70	76	73	293	220
John Fowler	76	70	74	73	293	220
David Jagger	71	74	74	74	293	220
Lawrence Farmer	71	71	76	75	293	220
Ian Woosnam	72	73	73	75	293	220
Garry Hay	70	74	71	78	293	220

Scandinavian Enterprise Open

Linkoping Golf Club, Sweden
Par 35–36—71; 6,503 yards

June 31–July 3
purse, £66,000

	SCORES				TOTAL	MONEY
Bob Byman	69	69	66	71	275	£11,000
Sam Torrance	71	69	69	69	278	7,330
Severiano Ballesteros	68	69	70	72	279	4,130
Garry Cullen	73	73	66	69	281	3,050
Tom Sieckmann	73	70	65	73	281	3,050
Mark James	71	74	69	69	283	2,145
Jaime Gonzalez	69	69	74	71	283	2,145
Des Smyth	71	73	71	69	284	1,483.33
Ian Mosey	73	70	72	69	284	1,483.33
John Morgan	75	66	70	73	284	1,483.33
*Krister Kinell	68	72	70	74	284	
Gordon Brand Jr	72	73	69	71	285	1,190
Bernhard Langer	71	74	72	68	285	1,190
Mac O'Grady	72	72	73	69	286	1,005
Bill Longmuir	72	73	68	73	286	1,005
Graham Marsh	74	69	74	69	286	1,005

	SCORES				TOTAL	MONEY
Jeremy Bennett	69	72	72	73	286	1,005
Tony Jacklin	71	71	72	73	287	870
Mike Cahill	71	75	70	71	287	870
Sandy Lyle	70	74	72	72	288	751.43
Ian Woosnam	72	72	74	70	288	751.43
Graham Burroughs	69	75	70	74	288	751.43
Paul Curry	72	71	75	70	288	751.43
Philip Harrison	72	71	74	71	288	751.43
Tony Johnstone	72	74	72	70	288	751.43
Andrew Murray	66	74	72	76	288	751.43
Tony Price	71	75	76	67	289	650
Eddie Polland	70	73	71	75	289	650
Peter Tupling	67	73	76	73	289	650
Bill McColl	74	71	73	72	290	583.75
Ross Drummond	71	74	70	75	290	583.75
Tony Charnley	72	74	73	71	290	583.75
Baldovino Dassu	74	69	72	75	290	583.75
Danny Goodman	72	74	76	69	291	545
Noel Ratcliffe	70	73	77	72	292	522.50
Ronan Rafferty	75	71	72	74	292	522.50
Maurice Bembridge	72	72	71	78	293	470
Bob Charles	75	70	77	71	293	470
David J. Russell	70	73	77	73	293	470
Garry Hay	74	72	72	75	293	470
John Hay	71	71	81	70	293	470
Keith Waters	72	71	71	80	294	395
John O'Leary	75	70	72	77	294	395
Mike Preston	72	69	75	78	294	395
Mats Lanner	74	72	72	76	294	395
Hugh Baiocchi	71	75	74	74	294	395
Simon Owen	74	71	78	73	296	345
Simon Bishop	74	72	74	76	296	345
Rafael Alarcon	72	73	78	75	298	330
Clive Tucker	72	72	76	79	299	315
David Frost	72	74	77	76	299	315

State Express Classic

Brabazon Course, The Belfry, Sutton Coldfield
Par 37–36—73; 6,823 yards

July 7–10
purse, £80,000

	SCORES				TOTAL	MONEY
Greg Norman	70	70	70	69	279	£13,330
Brian Marchbank	70	69	74	67	280	8,890
Josie-Maria Canizares	75	65	72	69	281	5,000
Sam Torrance	74	70	72	68	284	4,000
Chip Beck	73	69	73	70	285	2,866.66
Jaime Gonzalez	73	71	70	71	285	2,866.66
Danny Edwards	68	67	75	75	285	2,866.66
Rex Caldwell	71	73	68	74	286	2,000
Mark James	71	71	74	71	287	1,700
Sandy Lyle	72	68	76	71	287	1,700
Eamonn Darcy	72	71	72	73	288	1,480
Roger Chapman	72	77	70	70	289	1,297.50
Bill Longmuir	72	77	69	71	289	1,297.50
Brian Waites	73	76	68	72	289	1,297.50
John Fowler	72	70	71	76	289	1,297.50

	SCORES				TOTAL	MONEY
Ian Woosnam	71	71	78	70	290	1,110
John Bland	75	73	70	72	290	1,110
Denny Hepler	71	71	73	75	290	1,110
David Feherty	70	76	72	73	291	910
Ken Brown	72	71	74	74	291	910
Tony Minshall	69	73	75	74	291	910
Steve Martin	69	78	71	73	291	910
Neil Coles	72	69	74	76	291	910
Graham Marsh	71	72	72	76	291	910
Howard Clark	76	72	74	70	292	740
Michael King	71	76	74	71	292	740
Hugh Baiocchi	74	75	72	71	292	740
Michael McLean	73	71	75	73	292	740
Nick Price	73	75	72	72	292	740
Bernard Gallacher	71	75	73	73	292	740
Manuel Pinero	68	74	75	75	292	740
Bernhard Langer	70	72	73	77	292	740
John O'Leary	71	73	70	78	292	740
Mats Lanner	73	74	75	71	293	620
Joey Rassett	77	71	73	72	293	620
David J. Russell	73	71	75	74	293	620
Greg Powers	73	75	76	70	294	550
Jeff Hall	74	71	75	74	294	550
Philip Elson	73	70	76	75	294	550
David Frost	74	73	72	75	294	550
John Morgan	74	73	74	74	295	480
Rafael Alarcon	73	75	73	74	295	480
Peter Tupling	74	72	74	75	295	480
Brian Jones	74	73	79	70	296	417.50
Tommy Horton	70	78	76	72	296	417.50
Mike Cahill	70	75	77	74	296	417.50
Maurice Bembridge	72	74	76	74	296	417.50
Tony Price	75	74	75	73	297	375
Philip Harrison	74	73	73	77	297	375
Garry Cullen	74	69	76	78	297	375
Peter Teravainen	73	72	74	78	297	375

British Open

Royal Troon, Ayrshire
Par 36–36—72; 7,067 yards

July 15–18
purse, £261,500

	SCORES				TOTAL	MONEY
Tom Watson	69	71	74	70	284	£32,000
Peter Oosterhuis	74	67	74	70	285	19,300
Nick Price	69	69	74	73	285	19,300
Nick Faldo	73	73	71	69	286	11,000
Des Smyth	70	69	74	73	286	11,000
Thomas Purtzer	76	66	75	69	286	11,000
Masahiro Kuramoto	71	73	71	71	286	11,000
Fuzzy Zoeller	73	71	73	70	287	8,750
Sandy Lyle	74	66	73	74	287	8,750
Jack Nicklaus	77	70	72	69	288	7,350
Bobby Clampett	67	66	78	77	288	7,350
Sam Torrance	73	72	73	71	289	6,300
Severiano Ballesteros	71	75	73	71	290	5,400
Bernhard Langer	70	69	78	73	290	5,400

	SCORES				TOTAL	MONEY
Raymond Floyd	74	73	77	67	291	3,900
Curtis Strange	72	73	76	70	291	3,900
Ben Crenshaw	74	75	72	70	291	3,900
Denis Watson	75	69	73	74	291	3,900
Ken Brown	70	71	79	72	292	2,900
Toru Nakamura	77	68	77	71	293	2,500
Isao Aoki	75	69	75	74	293	2,500
Jose-Maria Canizares	71	72	79	72	294	2,200
Johnny Miller	71	76	75	72	294	2,200
Bill Rogers	73	70	76	75	294	2,200
Graham Marsh	76	76	72	71	295	1,950
Bernard Gallacher	75	71	74	75	295	1,950
Jay Haas	78	72	75	71	296	1,600
Greg Norman	73	75	76	72	296	1,600
Arnold Palmer	71	73	78	74	296	1,600
Lee Trevino	78	72	71	75	296	1,600
David Graham	73	70	76	77	296	1,600
Mike Miller	74	72	78	73	297	1,200
Larry Nelson	77	69	77	74	297	1,200
Mark Thomas	72	74	75	76	297	1,200
Eamonn Darcy	75	73	78	72	298	833.33
Jack Ferenz	76	69	80	73	298	833.33
Paul Way	72	75	78	73	298	833.33
Craig Stadler	71	74	79	74	298	833.33
Brian Barnes	75	69	76	78	298	833.33
David J. Russell	72	72	76	78	298	833.33
Harold Henning	74	74	76	75	299	650
Bob Shearer	73	72	81	74	300	650
*Malcolm Lewis	74	74	77	75	300	
Gary Player	75	74	76	75	300	650
Terry Gale	76	74	75	75	300	650
Neil Coles	73	73	72	82	300	650
Bill Longmuir	77	72	77	75	301	650
Tienie Britz	81	70	74	76	301	650
Roger Chapman	75	76	74	76	301	650
Brian Waites	75	77	73	76	301	650
Mark James	74	73	79	76	302	650
Hsu Sheng San	75	75	75	77	302	650
Manuel Pinero	75	75	74	78	302	650
Mark McNulty	76	74	76	77	303	600
Peter Townsend	76	73	76	78	303	600
Martin Poxon	74	70	78	81	303	600
Keith Waters	73	78	71	81	303	600
Philip Harrison	78	74	74	78	304	600
Michael King	73	78	74	80	305	600
Michael Cahill	73	76	77	80	306	600

Out of final 18 holes

	SCORES			TOTAL	MONEY
Jeff Hawkes	79	73	75	227	440
Tom Weiskopf	79	73	75	227	440
Rex Caldwell	84	68	75	227	440
Peter Dawson	78	73	76	227	440
Warren Humphreys	76	75	76	227	440
Brian Jones	81	71	76	228	400
John Bland	80	72	76	228	400
Paul Hoad	73	79	76	228	400
Joey Rassett	76	76	76	228	400

	SCORES			TOTAL	MONEY
Tom Kite	73	76	79	228	400
Chip Beck	75	73	80	228	400
Hugh Baiocchi	77	75	77	229	375
Antonio Garrido	75	77	77	229	375
Vaughan Somers	78	73	78	229	375
Tommy Horton	77	73	79	229	375
Gil Morgan	74	74	81	229	375
Jeremy Bennett	74	73	82	229	375
Hubert Green	76	75	79	230	375
David Matthew	76	76	78	230	375
Brian Evans	77	72	81	230	375
Simon Owen	73	77	81	231	375
Gordon Brand	77	75	79	231	375
Ian Woosnam	78	73	80	231	375
Tony Johnstone	75	77	80	232	375
Peter Tupling	75	77	81	233	375
Simon Bishop	76	75	83	234	375
Danny Edwards	71	81	86	238	375

Out of final 36 holes

	SCORES		TOTAL	MONEY
Tony Jacklin	77	76	153	225
Steve Cipa	75	78	153	225
*Jonathan Plaxton	77	76	153	
Mark Johnson	76	77	153	225
*Andrew Oldcorn	79	74	153	
Brian Marchbank	76	77	153	225
Denis Scanlan	78	75	153	225
Ed Sneed	76	77	153	225
Hal Sutton	80	73	153	225
Denny Hepler	78	75	153	225
Carl Mason	78	75	153	225
Bob Charles	79	74	153	225
Gordon Brand Jr	75	79	154	225
Jaime Gonzalez	78	76	154	225
Robert Jamieson	74	80	154	225
Mike Ferguson	76	78	154	225
Ian Stanley	77	77	154	225
*Andrew Stubbs	74	80	154	
Steve Rooke	76	78	154	225
Peter Berry	79	75	154	225
*Martin Thompson	78	76	154	
Joe Inman Jr	79	76	155	225
John Wilkinson	83	72	155	225
J. McAlister	79	76	155	225
Christy O'Connor Jr	76	79	155	225
Graham Walker	80	75	155	225
Greg Powers	77	78	155	225
Maurice Bembridge	79	76	155	225
Philip Elson	79	76	155	225
Bruce Lietzke	77	78	155	225
*Andy Rose	79	77	156	
David Jagger	75	81	156	225
Michael McLean	81	75	156	225
*Magnus Persson	83	73	156	
David Feherty	81	75	156	225
*Gary Broadbent	80	76	156	
*John Thompson	79	77	156	

	SCORES	TOTAL	MONEY
Paul Bradley	75 81	156	225
Bill Pelham	78 79	157	225
*David Ray	84 73	157	
John Fowler	76 81	157	225
Ross Whitehead	78 79	157	225
Manuel Calero	83 74	157	225
Andrew Murray	78 80	158	225
Peter Cowen	83 75	158	225
Rodger Davis	79 79	158	225
Steve Martin	81 78	159	225
Howard Clark	79 80	159	225
Hedley Muscroft	81 79	160	225
*Per Andersson	81 79	160	
Denis Durnian	82 78	160	225
Keith Lobban	81 80	161	225
Carlo Knauss	79 82	161	225
*Ian Young	82 79	161	
David Williams	81 81	162	225
Jimmy Heggarty	81 82	163	225
*Chris Poxon	80 83	163	
*Michael Higgins	83 80	163	
Nick Job	83 80	163	225
*Nathaniel Crosby	82 84	166	
Garry Hay	75 WD		225
John O'Leary	80 WD		225
Jerry Pate	81 WD		225

Lawrence Batley International

Bingley St. Ives, Bradford
Par 35–36—71; 6,429 yards

July 22–25
purse, £80,000

	SCORES				TOTAL	MONEY
Sandy Lyle	70	66	67	66	269	£13,330
Manuel Pinero	71	66	69	65	271	8,890
Rex Caldwell	68	70	66	69	273	5,000
Eamonn Darcy	66	69	69	70	274	3,150
Nick Faldo	68	71	64	71	274	3,150
Paul Curry	69	67	67	71	274	3,150
Bernard Gallacher	68	66	68	72	274	3,150
Joey Rassett	68	72	67	68	275	1,900
Ken Brown	67	70	64	74	275	1,900
Brian Waites	66	68	70	72	276	1,600
Hugh Baiocchi	69	69	70	69	277	1,440
Jose-Maria Canizares	73	69	63	72	277	1,440
Juan Anglada	69	71	70	68	278	1,263.33
Manuel Ballesteros	69	68	70	71	278	1,263.33
Manuel Montes	71	71	64	72	278	1,263.33
Rodger Davis	69	70	74	66	279	1,035
Neil Coles	72	66	73	68	279	1,035
Lee Trevino	69	71	70	69	279	1,035
Sam Torrance	70	70	69	70	279	1,035
Michael King	72	70	67	70	279	1,035
Keith Waters	69	70	69	71	279	1,035
David Ogrin	70	69	70	71	280	870
Philip Harrison	72	69	68	71	280	870
Tony Johnstone	66	71	71	73	281	830

	SCORES				TOTAL	MONEY
John Hay	70	66	72	73	281	830
Tony Minshall	68	76	70	68	282	720
Mark Thomas	71	71	71	69	282	720
Gordon Brand Jr	73	71	69	69	282	720
Tommy Horton	71	73	68	70	282	720
Martin Poxon	75	69	68	70	282	720
Mike Miller	72	71	69	70	282	720
Arnold Palmer	70	68	71	73	282	720
Denny Hepler	70	72	67	73	282	720
David Jones	68	70	70	74	282	720
Bob Charles	68	73	72	70	283	580
John Bland	71	71	69	72	283	580
Vaughan Somers	69	72	68	74	283	580
John Fowler	74	69	66	74	283	580
Garry Cullen	70	70	67	76	283	580
Jeremy Bennett	72	69	73	70	284	453.75
Simon Owen	70	71	72	71	284	453.75
Paul Way	72	69	72	71	284	453.75
Steve Martin	70	69	74	71	284	453.75
Jaime Gonzalez	74	69	70	71	284	453.75
Paul Hoad	67	73	71	73	284	453.75
David Jagger	71	71	69	73	284	453.75
Harold Henning	67	69	73	75	284	453.75
Jeff Hall	74	69	70	72	285	380
Brian Barnes	72	68	71	74	285	380
Carl Mason	68	69	71	77	285	380
Philip Elson	69	70	73	74	286	345
Mike Ingham	70	68	74	74	286	345
Tienie Britz	74	68	70	74	286	345
Ian Mosey	69	74	66	77	286	345
Greg Powers	67	72	75	73	287	315

Lufthansa German Open

Solitude Club, Stuttgart
Par 36–36—72; 6,834 yards

July 27–August 1
purse, £45,720

	SCORES				TOTAL	MONEY
Bernhard Langer	73	71	69	66	279	£7,620.16
Bill Longmuir	69	72	70	68	279	5,099.65
(Langer defeated Longmuir on first hole of sudden-death playoff.)						
Christy O'Connor Jr	69	68	74	69	280	2,883.94
Tony Jacklin	72	71	70	70	283	2,241.50
Bernard Gallacher	71	74	70	70	285	1,608.44
Warren Humphreys	72	68	71	74	285	1,608.44
Mark Thomas	66	72	73	74	285	1,608.44
Gordon Brand Jr	72	71	73	70	286	1,066.82
Eamonn Darcy	71	70	71	74	286	1,066.82
David Frost	72	70	75	70	287	869.70
Bob Charles	73	69	72	73	287	869.70
Jeff Hall	75	72	72	69	288	767.88
Neil Coles	69	74	73	72	288	767.88
Ian Mosey	74	71	75	69	289	713.95
Clive Tucker	72	74	76	78	290	654.55
Martin Poxon	78	71	73	68	290	654.55
Stephen Bennett	72	72	74	72	290	654.55
Vicente Fernandez	73	73	77	78	291	561.55

	SCORES				TOTAL	MONEY
John Bland	74	73	72	72	291	561.55
John Hoskison	74	74	70	73	291	561.55
Keith Waters	70	76	69	76	291	561.55
Garry Logan	75	73	74	70	292	500.59
Brian Marchbank	72	73	76	71	292	500.59
Paul Way	75	73	74	71	293	453.69
Eddie Polland	71	77	74	71	293	453.69
Tienie Britz	75	73	74	71	293	453.69
Peter Tupling	73	73	75	72	293	453.69
Carl Mason	78	68	74	73	293	453.69
Peter Teravainen	72	73	72	76	293	453.69
Torsten Giedion	76	72	79	67	294	396.83
Jeremy Bennett	72	74	75	73	294	396.83
Ross Drummond	75	74	72	73	294	396.83
Rafael Alarcon	74	77	70	73	294	396.83
Michael Clayton	75	72	76	72	295	368.11
Mike Miller	75	74	71	75	295	368.11
Gordon Brand	74	70	80	72	296	344.67
Sam Torrance	73	75	72	76	296	344.67
Joey Rassett	71	76	72	77	296	344.67
Steven Cipa	77	73	77	70	297	316.53
David J. Russell	74	76	76	71	297	316.53
Philip Harrison	77	72	75	73	297	316.53
Alan Pate	76	72	72	78	298	297.77
Jaime Gonzalez	71	72	85	71	299	274.33
Paul Curry	73	77	75	74	299	274.33
David Williams	75	74	75	75	299	274.33
Vaughan Somers	74	76	73	76	299	274.33
Roman Krause	76	73	79	72	300	241.50
Bruno Dupont	70	81	77	72	300	241.50
Manfred Kessler	73	77	74	76	300	241.50

KLM Dutch Open Championship

De Pan Golf Club, Utrecht, Holland
Par 36–36—72; 6,699 yards

August 5–8
purse, £42,375

	SCORES				TOTAL	MONEY
Paul Way	71	73	67	65	276	£7,059.32
David Feherty	74	69	68	67	278	3,677.97
Vicente Fernandez	72	69	69	68	278	3,677.97
Eddie Polland	70	74	69	66	279	1,957.63
Ian Woosnam	70	70	73	66	279	1,957.63
Jeff Hawkes	72	70	67	71	280	1,483.05
Vaughan Somers	71	71	69	70	281	1,271.19
Gordon Brand Jr.	70	75	69	68	282	1,004.24
Jan Dorrestein	72	71	70	69	282	1,004.24
Howard Clark	71	71	69	72	283	785.31
Manuel Garcia	74	68	69	72	283	785.31
Mike Miller	70	65	73	75	283	785.31
Roger Chapman	72	70	72	70	284	665.25
Michael King	72	74	69	69	284	665.25
Craig Defoy	70	69	71	75	285	597.46
Jaime Gonzalez	71	70	71	73	285	597.46
Martin Poxon	71	72	71	71	285	597.46
Juan Anglada	73	73	72	68	286	498.18
Gordon Brand	70	73	71	72	286	498.18

	SCORES			TOTAL	MONEY
Ian Mosey	72	73	73	68	286	498.18
David Ogrin	70	73	73	70	286	498.18
Emilio Rodriguez	71	73	70	72	286	498.18
Matt Runge	70	72	70	74	286	498.18
Gery Watine	70	70	72	74	286	498.18
Rafael Alarcon	71	70	70	76	287	419.49
Tienie Britz	70	77	72	68	287	419.49
Michael Clayton	74	70	71	72	287	419.49
Danny Goodman	75	70	72	70	287	419.49
Mark Thomas	69	73	71	74	287	419.49
Joe Higgins	72	71	73	72	288	363.35
Larry Mowry	70	74	71	73	288	363.35
Peter Teravainen	75	69	73	71	288	363.35
Peter Tupling	72	69	74	73	288	363.35
Ross Drummond	72	72	73	72	289	322.03
Philip Harrison	75	70	73	71	289	322.03
Bill McColl	70	73	73	73	289	322.03
Chris Moody	70	73	74	72	289	322.03
Mac O'Grady	73	73	69	74	289	322.03
*Bart Nolte	73	75	71	71	290	
David J. Russell	71	72	74	73	290	288.14
Tom Sieckmann	74	70	76	70	290	288.14
Clive Tucker	75	71	71	73	290	288.14
Keith Waters	70	71	72	78	291	271.19
Russell Fischer	77	70	73	72	292	245.76
David Frost	73	71	72	76	292	245.76
Jeff Hall	69	69	75	79	292	245.76
Harold Henning	74	72	73	73	292	245.76
John Hoskison	76	69	75	72	292	245.76
Mats Lanner	72	74	74	73	293	211.86
Brian Marchbank	73	72	73	75	293	211.86
Manuel Montes	72	73	76	72	293	211.86

Carrolls Irish Open

Portmarnock, Dublin
Par 36–36—72; 7,104 yards

August 12–15
purse, £80,350

	SCORES			TOTAL	MONEY
John O'Leary	74	68	72	73	287	£13,386.90
Maurice Bembridge	71	71	72	74	288	8,919.24
Greg Norman	79	73	71	67	290	4,151.60
Nick Faldo	78	70	73	69	290	4,151.60
Christy O'Connor	74	74	70	72	290	4,151.60
Manuel Pinero	75	70	74	72	291	2,812.37
Martin Poxon	75	72	75	70	292	2,073.12
Eamonn Darcy	76	70	72	74	292	2,073.12
Tom Kite	76	70	71	75	292	2,073.12
Gordon Brand Jr	78	75	69	71	293	1,489.22
Carl Mason	78	72	71	72	293	1,489.22
Warren Humphreys	75	71	74	73	293	1,489.22
David Ogrin	74	73	76	71	294	1,234.76
David Jones	76	74	73	71	294	1,234.76
Manuel Garcia	78	68	75	73	294	1,234.76
Howard Clark	77	75	72	71	295	1,042.99
Eddie Polland	76	70	77	72	295	1,042.99
Tommy Horton	77	70	73	75	295	1,042.99

	SCORES			TOTAL	MONEY
Bob Charles	79	70	70	76	295	1,042.99
Ian Woosnam	74	70	74	77	295	1,042.99
John Morgan	76	77	75	68	296	867.82
Graham Marsh	75	77	74	70	296	867.82
Nick Price	78	75	71	72	296	867.82
Sam Torrance	77	74	72	73	296	867.82
Terry Gale	80	71	72	73	296	867.82
Ken Brown	80	73	69	74	296	867.82
Des Smyth	75	69	75	77	296	867.82
Brian Barnes	76	73	78	70	297	666.14
Ross Drummond	76	71	78	72	297	666.14
Sandy Lyle	76	74	75	72	297	666.14
Bill Longmuir	76	75	74	72	297	666.14
Vaugham Somers	76	74	74	73	297	666.14
Jeff Hawkes	72	76	76	73	297	666.14
Christy O'Connor Jr	76	73	74	74	297	666.14
Jeff Hall	76	71	76	74	297	666.14
Michael Clayton	80	71	72	74	297	666.14
Brian Waites	77	71	74	75	297	666.14
Bobby Clampett	76	75	70	76	297	666.14
Peter Teravainen	82	71	73	72	298	546.40
Philip Harrison	79	74	73	72	298	546.40
David Frost	77	76	70	75	298	546.40
Ewen Murray	81	71	76	71	299	490.16
Leonard Owens	76	72	78	73	299	490.16
Paul Way	80	73	72	74	299	490.16
Manuel Calero	77	71	76	75	299	490.16
David Jagger	81	68	79	72	300	425.87
Chris Moody	78	71	76	75	300	425.87
Bill McColl	77	72	76	75	300	425.87
Jerry Anderson	76	74	73	77	300	425.87
Bernhard Langer	76	75	79	71	301	337.48
Jose-Maria Canizares	76	76	79	70	301	337.48
Philip Elson	78	74	77	72	301	337.48
Paul Carrigill	78	75	76	72	301	337.48
David A. Russell	78	71	77	75	301	337.48
Tienie Britz	80	71	75	75	301	337.48

Benson & Hedges International Open

Fulford, York
Par 36–36—72; 6,787 yards

August 19–22
purse, £100,000

	SCORES			TOTAL	MONEY
Greg Norman	69	74	69	71	283	£16,660
Bob Charles	71	69	74	70	284	7,453.33
Graham Marsh	72	69	72	71	284	7,453.33
Ian Woosnam	71	71	71	71	284	7,453.33
Carl Mason	70	74	70	71	285	3,870
Nick Faldo	70	72	71	72	285	3,870
Denis Durnian	72	72	72	71	287	3,000
Vaughan Somers	74	71	72	71	288	2,145
John Bland	72	70	75	71	288	2,145
Neil Coles	69	75	71	73	288	2,145
Bernard Gallacher	71	71	72	74	288	2,145
Ian Mosey	71	69	77	72	289	1,620
Brian Waites	72	76	70	71	289	1,620

	SCORES				TOTAL	MONEY
Howard Clark	72	72	72	73	289	1,620
Sandy Lyle	72	76	71	71	290	1,440
Bill Longmuir	69	78	70	73	290	1,440
Bernhard Langer	75	71	76	69	291	1,165
Christy O'Connor Jr	72	74	74	71	291	1,165
Stewart Ginn	70	76	74	71	291	1,165
Ronan Rafferty	72	73	74	72	291	1,165
Philip Elson	72	74	73	72	291	1,165
Jesus Lopez	76	74	69	72	291	1,165
Michael King	74	69	73	75	291	1,165
Brian Barnes	73	73	70	75	291	1,165
Manuel Calero	70	74	71	76	291	1,165
Brian Marchbank	73	73	69	76	291	1,165
Jose-Maria Canizares	71	75	75	71	292	960
Tony Jacklin	73	76	72	71	292	960
Manuel Garcia	71	75	73	73	292	960
Keith Waters	74	76	72	71	293	857.50
Michael Clayton	77	73	70	73	293	857.50
Antonio Garrido	71	76	72	74	293	857.50
Jerry Anderson	75	74	70	74	293	857.50
Tom Sieckmann	72	74	75	73	294	780
Ewen Murray	74	71	73	76	294	780
Ken Brown	68	73	75	78	294	780
Maurice Bembridge	71	79	73	72	295	710
Jeff Hall	76	72	74	73	295	710
Des Smyth	70	76	73	76	295	710
Gordon Brand	72	73	73	77	295	710
Noel Ratcliffe	73	75	76	72	296	580
*Haydn Green	77	73	74	72	296	
Joe Purcell	75	73	74	74	296	580
Mark James	75	71	76	74	296	580
Philip Harrison	72	77	73	74	296	580
Paul Way	73	73	75	75	296	580
Manuel Pinero	74	74	73	75	296	580
Richard Masters	73	74	74	75	296	580
Ross Drummond	74	72	74	76	296	580
David Jones	69	76	74	77	296	580

Ebel Swiss Open

Crans-Sur-Sierre Golf Club
Par 36–36—72; 6,811 yards

August 26–29
purse, £60,520

	SCORES				TOTAL	MONEY
Ian Woosnam	68	68	66	70	272	£10,085.28
Bill Longmuir	69	70	67	66	272	6,718.02
(Woosnam defeated Longmuir on third hole of sudden-death playoff.)						
Jose-Maria Canizares	67	72	70	67	276	3,790.92
Hubert Green	69	71	70	67	277	2,792.30
Juan Anglada	71	72	66	68	277	2,792.30
Matt Runge	69	68	67	74	278	2,118.29
Brian Waites	72	74	66	67	279	1,706.64
Jerry Anderson	73	67	70	69	279	1,706.64
Joe Higgins	71	70	67	72	280	1,251.72
Silvano Locatelli	70	71	72	67	280	1,251.72
Tony Johnstone	70	70	70	71	281	1,024.76
Sandy Lyle	68	69	73	79	281	1,024.76

	SCORES				TOTAL	MONEY
Dave Eichelberger	73	71	68	70	282	905.78
Ross Drummond	74	68	73	67	282	905.78
Greg Norman	71	69	74	68	282	905.78
John Bland	70	68	74	70	282	905.78
Peter Thomas	73	71	69	70	283	781.29
Keith Waters	71	71	75	66	283	781.29
Alberto Croce	73	67	70	73	283	781.29
Peter Tupling	73	69	71	70	283	781.29
Mac O'Grady	76	70	66	71	283	781.29
Manuel Calero	73	70	69	72	284	671.25
Brian Marchbank	70	76	64	74	284	671.25
Ewen Murray	72	70	69	73	284	671.25
Mike Miller	74	67	72	71	284	671.25
Hugh Baiocchi	74	67	72	71	284	671.25
Clive Tucker	73	71	70	71	285	561.21
Bob Charles	70	72	73	70	285	561.21
Tienie Britz	73	69	73	70	285	561.21
Christy O'Connor Jr	72	73	73	67	285	561.21
Baldovino Dassu	71	73	69	72	285	561.21
Harold Henning	72	72	69	73	285	470.98
Andrew Murray	76	69	69	72	286	470.98
Antonio Garrido	69	69	73	75	286	470.98
Jesus Lopez	75	70	69	72	286	470.98
Paul Curry	74	71	72	69	286	470.98
Russell Fischer	74	72	71	70	287	418.16
Paul Way	71	70	74	72	287	418.16
Giuseppe Cali	71	73	70	73	287	418.16
Maurice Bembridge	68	76	75	68	287	418.16
Jaime Gonzales	75	71	70	72	288	368.64
Pietro Molteni	74	72	75	67	288	368.64
Peter Teravainen	74	71	70	73	288	368.64
Eddie Polland	77	67	73	71	288	368.64
Tom Sieckmann	74	70	73	71	288	368.64
Vaughan Somers	74	72	71	72	289	302.61
Gary Player	74	72	73	70	289	302.61
Manuel Montes	72	71	72	74	289	302.61
Manuel Pinero	73	70	75	71	289	302.61
Angel Gallardo	73	73	70	73	289	302.61
Rafael Alarcon	76	70	71	76	289	302.61
*Johnny Storjohann	72	70	71	76	289	
Patrick Bagnoud	74	71	70	74	289	302.61

European Open

Sunningdale, Berkshire
Par 35–35—70; 6,563 yards

September 2–5
purse, £120,000

	SCORES				TOTAL	MONEY
Manuel Pinero	68	68	67	63	266	£20,000
Sam Torrance	67	70	64	67	268	13,320
Greg Norman	64	70	69	67	270	6,760
Sandy Lyle	68	66	67	69	270	6,760
Neil Coles	69	68	70	64	271	5,080
John Bland	68	72	66	67	273	4,200
Vicente Fernandez	70	71	69	66	276	3,300
John O'Leary	69	69	69	69	276	3,300
Rodger Davis	69	67	74	67	277	2,540

	SCORES				TOTAL	MONEY
Nick Faldo	70	72	67	68	277	2,540
Des Smyth	71	69	70	68	278	2,025
Christy O'Connor Jr	70	69	71	68	278	2,025
Brian Waites	68	72	69	69	278	2,025
Manuel Calero	68	69	71	70	278	2,025
Noel Ratcliffe	70	71	72	66	279	1,720
Graham Marsh	68	70	71	70	279	1,720
Antonio Garrido	73	68	71	68	280	1,560
Paul Way	72	70	69	69	280	1,560
Ken Brown	68	70	70	72	280	1,560
Maurice Bembridge	72	69	70	70	281	1,480
Chris Moody	71	70	72	69	282	1,380
Bill McColl	69	71	73	69	282	1,380
Ian Mosey	69	70	71	72	282	1,380
Harold Henning	71	68	70	73	282	1,380
Vaughan Somers	71	72	74	66	283	1,220
Eamonn Darcy	68	74	73	68	283	1,220
Garry Cullen	72	74	69	68	283	1,220
Juan Anglada	68	69	75	71	283	1,220
Paul Hoad	70	70	76	68	284	982.50
Ewen Murray	72	73	70	69	284	982.50
Danny Goodman	70	68	75	71	284	982.50
Malcolm Gregson	72	70	72	70	284	982.50
Bob Charles	73	70	71	70	284	982.50
Eddie Polland	69	70	72	73	284	982.50
Mark James	73	69	70	72	284	982.50
Manuel Ballesteros	72	67	72	73	284	982.50
Severiano Ballesteros	72	73	73	67	285	830
Hugh Baiocchi	75	70	72	68	285	830
Jose-Maria Canizares	70	73	75	68	286	760
Ross Drummond	74	70	73	69	286	760
Tony Johnstone	74	71	70	71	286	760
Bernhard Langer	74	71	70	71	286	760
Tony Jacklin	73	68	71	74	286	760
Philip Elson	74	71	73	69	287	680
Ian Woosnam	70	72	72	73	287	680
Tony Charnley	75	69	69	74	287	680
Peter Townsend	72	73	73	70	288	580
Simon Owen	76	70	71	71	288	580
Graham Burroughs	70	71	75	72	288	580
Gordon Brand Jr	72	70	74	72	288	580
Clive Tucker	73	71	71	73	288	580
David Jones	76	67	73	72	288	580
Ronan Rafferty	71	69	74	74	288	580

Hennessy Cognac Cup

Ferndown Golf Club, Ferndown
Par 71; 6,442 yards

September 9–12
purse, £85,000

FINAL RESULTS: Great Britain & Ireland: −106, Rest of the World: −86
Continent of Europe: −67

	SCORES				TOTAL	MONEY
Mark James	64	66	69	64	263	*9,000

*includes individual prize of £5,000

	SCORES				TOTAL	MONEY
Jose-Maria Canizares	68	68	67	62	265	1,500
Nick Faldo	67	65	66	67	265	4,000
John Bland	67	65	68	67	267	2,500
Bob Charles	67	68	66	69	270	2,500
John O'Leary	71	68	66	66	271	4,000
Sam Torrance	67	71	69	66	273	4,000
Hugh Baiocchi	69	70	69	65	273	2,500
Juan Anglada	66	71	69	67	273	1,500
Bernard Gallacher	68	70	69	67	274	4,000
Greg Norman	68	73	66	67	274	2,500
Brian Waites	67	70	69	68	274	4,000
Antonio Garrido	70	69	69	67	275	1,500
Vaughan Somers	69	67	70	70	276	2,500
Bernhard Langer	69	69	70	68	276	1,500
Sandy Lyle	70	71	70	66	277	4,000
Tony Johnstone	70	69	70	68	277	2,500
Vicente Fernandez	71	70	68	69	278	2,500
Ian Woosnam	69	66	70	73	278	4,000
Tony Jacklin	69	67	72	71	279	4,000
Jeff Hawkes	72	69	69	71	281	2,500
Manuel Ballesteros	70	71	71	69	281	1,500
Manuel Montes	72	70	70	69	281	1,500
Manuel Calero	70	70	70	71	281	1,500
Mac O'Grady	68	70	74	70	282	2,500
Jaime Gonzalez	74	68	71	70	283	2,500
Manuel Pinero	72	67	75	69	283	1,500
Des Smyth	69	71	73	71	284	4,000
Baldovino Dassu	69	74	70	72	285	1,500
Manuel Garcia	73	73	69	74	289	1,500

Teams: GB & I — James, Faldo, O'Leary, Torrance, Gallacher, Waites, Lyle, Woosnam, Jacklin, Smyth; R of W — Bland, Charles, Baiocchi, Norman, Somers, Johnstone, Fernandez, Hawkes, O'Grady, Gonzalez; C of E — Canizares, Anglada, Garrido, Langer, Ballesteros, Montes, Calero, Pinero, Dassu, Garcia.

Haig Whisky Tournament Players' Championship

Notts Golf Club, Hollinwell   September 16–19
Par 36-36—72; 7,017 yards   purse, £70,000

	SCORES				TOTAL	MONEY
Nick Faldo	69	67	65	69	270	£11,660
Manuel Calero	69	66	70	68	273	7,780
John Bland	64	71	72	69	276	3,940
Hugh Baiocchi	74	67	70	65	276	3,940
Jose-Maria Canizares	70	70	67	70	277	2,970
Bernhard Langer	69	68	72	69	278	2,450
Brian Waites	72	71	68	68	279	1,703.75
Des Smyth	71	71	68	69	279	1,703.75
Sandy Lyle	65	74	71	69	279	1,703.75
Eamonn Darcy	69	72	66	72	279	1,703.75
Ken Brown	69	74	70	67	280	1,195
Denis Durnian	71	70	70	69	280	1,195
Christy O'Connor Jr.	70	72	69	69	280	1,195
David Feherty	70	68	70	72	280	1,195
Neil Coles	72	70	71	68	281	962.50
Brian Barnes	77	69	67	68	281	962.50

	SCORES				TOTAL	MONEY
Ian Mosey	69	72	69	71	281	962.50
Howard Clark	69	70	70	72	281	962.50
Steve Martin	73	70	72	67	282	832.50
Harold Henning	70	69	72	71	282	832.50
Juan Anglada	70	73	68	71	282	832.50
Sam Torrance	74	69	66	73	282	832.50
Michael King	71	71	73	68	283	740
Simon Bishop	74	71	69	69	283	740
Ewen Murray	73	72	68	70	283	740
Mark James	75	71	67	70	283	740
Tony Johnstone	72	67	71	73	283	740
Philip Morley	72	71	73	68	284	640
Garry Cullen	75	71	71	67	284	640
Carl Mason	68	69	78	69	284	640
Vicente Fernandez	75	69	70	70	284	640
John Hoskison	73	73	68	70	284	640
Ian Woosnam	70	72	74	69	285	520
Bill Longmuir	73	71	72	69	285	520
Rodger Davis	75	71	70	69	285	520
Martin Foster	74	69	72	70	285	520
Ross Drummond	74	69	72	70	285	520
Philip Elson	71	69	74	71	285	520
Paul Hoad	70	69	74	72	285	520
Ronan Rafferty	74	68	73	71	286	402.14
Steve Cipa	73	70	72	71	286	402.14
Graham Burroughs	72	72	71	71	286	402.14
Martin Poxon	71	72	72	71	286	402.14
Gordon Brand Jr	74	70	71	71	286	402.14
David Jagger	72	71	70	73	286	402.14
Bobby Mitchell	70	71	70	75	286	402.14
Russell Fischer	74	70	74	69	287	340
Tom Sieckmann	77	69	72	69	287	340
Tony Minshall	68	72	75	72	287	340
Bob Charles	72	72	71	72	287	340
John O'Leary	73	67	73	74	287	340

Bob Hope British Classic

Moor Park, Rickmansworth
Par 36–36—72; 6,907 yards

September 23–26
purse, £100,000

	SCORES				TOTAL	MONEY
Gordon Brand Jr	65	73	65	69	272	£15,000
Mark James	70	66	66	73	275	10,000
Bob Charles	68	69	71	68	276	5,670
Howard Clark	72	72	67	66	277	3,700
Bernard Gallacher	65	72	69	71	277	3,700
Brian Barnes	68	70	65	75	278	2,500
David Feherty	66	73	68	72	279	2,250
Sandy Lyle	73	69	65	73	280	2,000
Michael King	72	72	69	69	282	1,580
Severiano Ballesteros	70	70	72	70	282	1,580
Tommy Horton	72	73	66	71	282	1,580
Ewen Murray	73	71	66	72	282	1,580
Jose-Maria Canizares	69	71	70	72	282	1,580
Vicente Fernandez	65	75	69	73	282	1,580
Ken Brown	70	74	65	74	283	1,370

	SCORES				TOTAL	MONEY
Brian Waites	72	73	69	70	284	1,220
Vaughan Somers	68	72	72	72	284	1,220
Tom Sieckmann	72	69	71	72	284	1,220
Paul Hoad	69	71	69	75	284	1,220
Ross Drummond	68	75	71	70	284	1,220
Hugh Baiocchi	74	76	69	67	286	982
Christy O'Connor Jr	69	73	70	74	286	982
Nick Faldo	70	72	75	69	286	982
Chi Chi Rodriguez	74	72	70	70	286	982
Antonio Garrido	74	73	67	72	286	982
Jeff Hall	67	74	72	74	287	865
Warren Humphreys	71	76	68	72	287	865
Bill Longmuir	71	73	76	68	288	800
John O'Leary	68	77	73	70	288	800
John Bland	71	72	69	76	288	800
Tony Johnstone	74	70	71	73	288	800
Juan Anglada	74	76	70	69	289	740
Greg Norman	69	73	72	75	289	740
Philip Elson	74	75	71	70	290	690
Ian Woosnam	74	74	71	71	290	690
Bernhard Langer	73	72	68	77	290	690
Neil Coles	69	76	79	67	291	620
Eamonn Darcy	70	74	74	73	291	620
Manuel Pinero	74	74	70	73	291	620
Malcolm Gregson	71	76	70	74	291	620
Noel Ratcliffe	76	69	73	74	292	542.50
Ronan Rafferty	72	69	76	75	292	542.50
Des Smyth	71	69	72	80	292	542.50
Gordon Brand	75	71	69	77	292	542.50
Steve Martin	70	74	75	74	293	490
Maurice Bembridge	70	71	76	76	293	490
Sam Torrance	69	74	74	76	293	490
Carl Mason	72	73	72	76	293	490
Eddie Polland	70	76	71	76	293	490
Harold Henning	73	74	75	72	294	455
Jaime Gonzalez	73	73	73	75	294	455

Benson & Hedges Spanish Open

R.S.H.E. Club De Campo, Madrid
Par 36–36—72; 7,044 yards

September 30–October 3
purse, £51,500

	SCORES				TOTAL	MONEY
Sam Torrance	71	65	67	70	273	8,578.78
Ian Woosnam	71	69	69	72	281	3,837.80
Sandy Lyle	71	68	70	72	281	3,837.80
Roger Chapman	69	71	67	74	281	3,837.80
Howard Clark	70	69	69	74	282	1,992.79
Manuel Pinero	69	70	69	74	282	1,992.79
Garry Cullen	74	68	71	70	283	1,328.53
Paul Hoad	71	70	68	74	283	1,328.53
Juan Anglada	73	68	68	74	283	1,328.53
Jose-Maria Canizares	71	76	67	70	284	988.67
Michael King	71	70	72	71	284	988.67
Ronan Rafferty	70	72	74	69	285	814.88
Severiano Ballesteros	73	70	72	70	285	814.88
Eddie Polland	74	70	69	72	285	814.88

	SCORES			TOTAL	MONEY
Ewen Murray	73	70	68	74	285	814.88
Ross Drummond	73	70	76	67	286	710.61
Peter Tupling	75	72	70	69	286	710.61
Martin Poxon	73	69	79	66	287	651.39
Philip Elson	73	72	71	71	287	651.39
Paul Way	73	74	72	69	288	587.02
Gordon Brand Jr	73	71	74	70	288	587.02
Manuel Calero	73	74	69	72	288	587.02
Antonio Garrido	75	71	69	73	288	587.02
Neil Coles	72	69	73	74	288	587.02
Tom Sieckmann	74	74	72	69	289	509.78
Eamonn Darcy	74	73	72	70	289	509.78
Manuel Montes	72	76	72	70	289	509.78
Des Smyth	73	74	70	72	289	509.78
Steve Martin	71	74	69	75	289	509.78
Mark James	76	71	71	72	290	455.72
Bernard Gallacher	70	75	71	74	290	455.72
Philip Harrison	74	75	75	67	291	422.25
Jesus Lopez	71	72	75	73	291	422.25
Bill Longmuir	71	70	75	75	291	422.25
Ken Brown	77	71	73	71	292	375.90
Michael McLean	76	73	72	71	292	375.90
Jose Cabo	73	71	76	72	292	375.90
Christopher Moody	74	74	72	72	292	375.90
Jose Davila	74	69	74	75	292	375.90
John Hoskison	74	71	71	76	282	375.90
Brian Barnes	71	74	76	72	283	319.26
Bobby Mitchell	75	72	73	73	293	319.26
Juan Quiros	77	71	72	73	293	319.26
German Garrido	76	73	71	73	293	319.26
Russell Fischer	75	74	69	75	293	219.26
Tienie Britz	75	69	78	72	294	283.21
Mark Thomas	78	71	73	72	294	283.21
Valentine Barrios	76	73	74	72	295	262.62
Gordon Brand	71	76	73	75	295	262.62
Juan Cruz	76	72	76	72	296	231.72
Jose Rivero	73	75	74	74	296	231.72
Simon Bishop	77	71	73	75	296	231.72
Joe Higgins	73	73	74	76	296	231.72

Sanyo Open

Sant Cugat, Barcelona
Par 34–36—70; 5,662 yards

October 7–10
purse, £60,000

	SCORES			TOTAL	MONEY
Neil Coles	71	67	64	64	266	£10,000
Garry Cullen	71	68	64	64	267	6,660
Manuel Montes	65	70	64	70	269	3,760
Manuel Pinero	69	66	68	67	270	3,000
Keith Waters	70	67	69	65	271	2,320
Juan Anglada	66	69	68	68	271	2,320
David Jones	68	69	70	65	272	1,800
Warren Humphreys	67	65	72	69	273	1,420
Tommy Horton	68	70	64	71	273	1,420
Manuel Calero	66	70	72	66	274	1,150
David J. Russell	71	64	71	68	274	1,150

	SCORES				TOTAL	MONEY
Tom Sieckmann	74	68	70	63	275	957.50
Garry Logan	70	71	69	65	275	957.50
Ronan Rafferty	70	67	72	66	275	957.50
Andrew Chandler	74	66	66	69	275	957.50
Tony Charnley	68	69	72	67	276	806.66
Tienie Britz	69	72	67	68	276	806.66
John Morgan	71	69	67	69	276	806.66
David A. Russell	68	74	71	64	277	730
Nick Faldo	69	72	69	67	277	730
Eamonn Darcy	72	69	68	68	277	730
Chris Moody	70	68	69	70	277	730
Roger Chapman	70	72	70	66	278	620
Andrew Murray	73	69	69	67	278	620
Manuel Garcia	69	71	70	68	278	620
Jeremy Bennett	73	67	70	68	278	620
Jose Rivero	72	68	69	69	278	620
Paul Hoad	69	72	68	69	278	620
Eddie Polland	69	68	70	71	278	620
Steve Hadfield	71	72	69	67	279	520
Juan Miguel Hurtado	68	73	70	68	279	520
*Alfonso Vidaor	71	65	73	70	279	
Russell Fischer	69	68	71	71	279	520
Francisco Hurtado	67	75	71	67	280	460
German Garrido	72	67	71	70	280	460
*Haydn Green	71	69	68	72	280	
Gordon Brand	70	70	68	72	280	460
Rafael Gallardo	70	66	76	69	281	415
Miguel Angel Martin	73	66	73	69	281	415
Tony Johnstone	71	70	71	69	281	415
Craig Maltman	71	71	69	70	281	415
Jose Roca	69	74	71	68	282	375
Juan Cruz	73	67	71	71	282	375
Mohamed Ben Nacr	69	73	69	71	282	375
Charles Cox	68	74	69	71	282	375
Martin Foster	73	69	75	66	283	325
Steve Martin	70	71	75	67	283	325
Mark Thomas	72	70	73	68	283	325
Simon Bishop	68	71	74	70	283	325
Manuel Ramos	70	71	71	71	283	325
Nigel Burch	69	69	73	72	283	325
Santiago Sota	66	75	70	73	284	285
Jose Cabo	73	68	70	73	284	285

Suntory World Match Play Championship

Wentworth Club, West Course, Virginia Water, Surrey, England October 14–17
Par 434 534 444—35; 345 434 455—37 — 72
6,945 yards   purse, £125,000

FIRST ROUND

Bobby Clampett defeated Masahiro Kuramoto, 5 and 4.

Kuramoto	444	544	434—36	445	345	455—39—75
Clampett	435	434	543—35	355	535	454—39—74

  Clampett leads, 2 up.

| Kuramoto | 435 | 434 | 545—37 | 34c | 43 | |

Clampett	434	334	445—34	354	43	

Lanny Wadkins defeated Gary Player, 2 and 1.

Wadkins	524	434	435—34	344	435	544—36—70
Player	534	333	444—33	344	424	454—34—67

  Player leads, 3 up.

Wadkins •	434	424	444—33	w44	433	45
Player	435	435	344—35	c45	43c	45

Sandy Lyle defeated Nick Faldo, 2 and 1.

Lyle	4c4	444	545—x	345	444	454—37—x
Faldo	425	444	444—35	354	334	353—33—68

  Faldo leads, 6 up.

Lyle	424	433	443—31	334	334	44
Faldo	435	534	445—37	344	435	35

Tom Kite defeated Curtis Strange, 2 and 1.

Kite	534	534	456—39	344	434	444—34—73
Strange	434	543	444—35	354	524	454—36—71

  Strange leads, 1 up.

Kite	525	434	444—35	344	434	45
Strange	534	444	634—37	345	534	45

SECOND ROUND

Severiano Ballesteros defeated Clampett, 2 and 1.

Ballesteros	5w5	434	455—x	444	434	454—36—x
Clampett	454	444	544—38	435	435	444—36—74

  Clampett leads, 1 up.

Ballesteros	434	334	434—32	344	433	44
Clampett	43c	434	434—x	344	434	44

Wadkins defeated Greg Norman, 6 and 5.

Norman	535	544	543—38	445	434	444—36—74
Wadkins	425	534	444—35	335	434	445—35—70

  Wadkins leads, 4 up.

Norman	534	424	533—33	345	4	
Wadkins	423	434	444—32	343	4	

Lyle defeated Raymond Floyd, 3 and 1.

Floyd	534	433	344—33	344	434	554—36—69
Lyle	434	434	535—35	344	433	444—33—68

  Lyle leads, 2 up.

Floyd	435	434	444—35	444	344	4c
Lyle	434	434	543—34	345	435	44

Kite defeated Craig Stadler, 4 and 3.

Stadler	434	434	544—35	445	434	544—37—72
Kite	434	435	334—33	345	435	445—37—70

  Kite leads, 1 up.

Stadler	436	533	545—38	245	424	
Kite	535	533	434—35	344	334	

SEMI-FINALS

Ballesteros defeated Wadkins, 3 and 1.

Ballesteros	425	443	454—35	354	434	445—36—71
Wadkins	434	434	445—35	344	533	354—34—69

Wadkins leads, 2 up.

Ballesteros	435	433	544—35	346	445	ww
Wadkins	435	544	445—38	346	445	cc

Lyle defeated Kite, 8 and 7.

Lyle	434	434	444—34	345	334	455—36—70
Kite	545	434	445—38	445	434	455—38—76

Lyle leads, 6 up.

Lyle	544	434	434—35	43
Kite	428	434	544—38	44

FINAL

Ballesteros defeated Lyle, 1 up, 37 holes.

Ballesteros	444	625	433—35	345	434	354—35—70
Lyle	435	433	453—34	245	534	465—38—72

Ballesteros leads, 3 up.

Ballesteros	535	444	543—37	353	434	454—35—72
Lyle	444	434	555—38	344	324	354—32—70

Match even

Ballesteros	3
Lyle	4

Wadkins defeated Kite, 3 and 1, in playoff for third place.

PRIZE MONEY: Ballesteros £35,000; Lyle £18,000; Wadkins £12,000; Kite £10,000; Clampett, Norman, Floyd, Stadler £7,000 each; Kuramoto, Player, Faldo, Strange £5,500 each.

LEGEND: c – conceded hole to opponent; w – won hole by concession without holing out; x – no total score.

Lancome Trophy

St. Nom La Breteche, Paris
Par 36–36—72; 6,714 yards

October 21–24
purse, £65,925

	SCORES				TOTAL	MONEY
David Graham	66	70	70	70	276	£13,272.85
Severiano Ballesteros	68	71	70	69	278	8,328.47
Craig Stadler	69	74	70	67	280	5,032.22
Sandy Lyle	69	70	68	74	281	3,384.10
Arnold Palmer	73	72	68	68	281	3,384.10
Des Smyth	75	68	74	66	283	2,312.81
Gery Watine	72	72	71	68	283	2,312.81
Gordon Brand, Jr	71	73	70	69	283	2,312.81
Mark McNulty	73	71	72	67	283	2,312.81
Peter Jacobsen	74	69	70	71	284	1,900.78
Manuel Pinero	71	72	70	72	285	1,818.38

	SCORES				TOTAL	MONEY
Sam Torrance	72	70	69	75	286	1,694.77
Bernhard Langer	71	73	73	69	286	1,694.77
Bernard Gallacher	72	68	74	73	287	1,529.95
Nick Faldo	70	71	71	75	287	1,529.95
Ian Woosnam	73	73	73	70	289	1,365.14
Manuel Calero	73	69	74	73	289	1,365.14
Jose-Maria Canizares	72	73	75	71	291	1,241.53
Jean Garaialde	70	71	76	75	292	1,159.13
Tony Jacklin	74	75	71	73	283	1,117.92
Neil Coles	78	73	74	69	294	1,076.72
Brian Waites	74	76	77	69	296	997.06
John O'Leary	74	76	74	72	296	997.06
Paul Way	70	79	74	73	296	997.06
Antonio Garrido	75	75	75	72	297	944.87
Gary Player	76	71	77	75	299	928.39
Mark James	72	78	72	78	300	913.39

Johnnie Walker Trophy

Real Club de Golf El Prat,
Barcelona
Par 35-37—72; 6,476 yards

October 28–31
purse, US$50,000

	SCORES				TOTAL	MONEY
Peter Jacobsen	69	73	64	68	274	$16,000
Severiano Ballesteros	67	69	69	71	276	11,000
Sandy Lyle	76	67	70	68	281	5,500
Bernhard Langer	69	72	68	72	281	5,500
David Graham	72	70	69	74	285	3,000
Manuel Pinero	73	72	70	71	286	2,400
Nick Faldo	74	71	73	72	290	1,900
Manuel Calero	71	73	75	71	290	1,900
Gary Player	71	75	73	72	291	1,500
Arnold Palmer	71	75	77	74	297	1,300

Portuguese Open

Penina, Algarve
Par 35-38—73; 7,010 yards
(Tournament reduced to 54 holes because of rain.)

November 4–7
purse, £42,000

	SCORES			TOTAL	MONEY
Sam Torrance	71	67	69	207	£7,000
Nick Faldo	70	69	72	211	4,660
Jeff Hall	69	72	72	213	2,630
Juan Anglada	69	71	74	214	2,100
Howard Clark	75	69	71	215	1,780
Tommy Horton	74	71	71	216	1,365
Antonio Garrido	72	73	71	216	1,365
Christy O'Connor Jr	70	74	73	217	995
Ken Brown	72	70	75	217	995
Carl Mason	70	77	71	218	786.66
Sandy Lyle	73	71	74	218	786.66
Glenn Ralph	73	70	75	218	286.66
Mike Miller	72	75	72	219	635
Des Smyth	74	73	72	219	635
David J. Russell	73	76	70	219	635

	SCORES			TOTAL	MONEY
Keith Waters	68	75	76	219	635
Peter Harrison	72	75	73	220	530
John Hoskison	74	72	74	220	530
Andrew Chandler	71	73	76	220	530
John Morgan	73	77	70	220	530
Jose-Maria Canizares	67	76	77	220	530
Paul Way	74	75	72	221	448.75
Bill McColl	76	73	72	221	448.75
Mark James	71	76	74	221	448.75
Eddie Polland	75	74	72	221	448.75
Mark Thomas	77	71	74	222	415
Peter Barber	70	75	77	222	415
Warren Humphreys	77	71	75	223	380
Chris Moody	76	73	74	223	380
German Garrido	73	74	76	223	380
Eamonn Darcy	73	76	74	223	380
Steve Martin	75	74	74	223	380
Ewen Murray	73	75	76	224	350
Clive Tucker	77	71	77	225	320
Jesus Lopez	73	75	77	225	320
Michael King	77	73	75	225	320
Ronan Rafferty	75	75	75	225	320
Roger Chapman	72	79	74	225	320
Philip Elson	71	78	77	226	265
Anders Forsbrand	75	75	76	226	265
Brian Barnes	74	75	77	226	265
John Woof	77	73	76	226	265
Peter Jones	74	77	75	226	265
Ian Woosnam	74	77	75	226	265
Noel Hunt	74	76	77	227	225
Gordon Brand Jr	75	76	76	227	225
Simon Bishop	72	76	80	228	205
Philip Morley	76	75	77	228	205
Danny Goodman	72	78	79	229	195
Michael McLean	77	71	82	230	190

The African Tours

Durban Open

Royal Durban Golf Club, Durban

January 6–9
purse, R50,000

	SCORES				TOTAL	MONEY
Mark McNulty	69	69	69	69	276	R8,000
Allan Henning	71	72	67	70	280	3,933.34
Hugh Baiocchi	71	70	70	69	280	3,933.34
Gavin Levenson	73	69	67	71	280	3,933.34
Teddie Webber	72	71	70	68	281	2,000
Simon Hobday	71	69	72	69	281	2,000
Mark McCann	66	70	75	71	282	1,600
John McGough	69	74	71	69	283	1,107.50
Jeff Hawkes	71	71	71	70	283	1,107.50
Warren Humphreys	71	74	67	71	283	1,107.50
Des Smyth	72	72	65	74	283	1,107.50
Nigel Burch	75	70	69	71	285	870
Tertius Claassens	73	70	72	71	286	778.34
John Fourie	72	70	73	71	286	778.34
John Bland	71	72	68	75	286	778.34
Denis Watson	75	67	73	72	287	685
Bobby Lincoln	71	72	71	73	287	685
David Feherty	69	74	71	73	287	685
Ian Mosey	71	75	73	70	289	588
Dale Hayes	72	73	74	70	289	588
David Frost	69	76	74	70	289	588
Graham Henning	72	75	72	70	289	588
Anthony Johnstone	77	71	71	70	289	588
Gordon Brand	76	73	71	70	290	532.50
Sam Torrance	74	70	71	75	290	532.50
Nick Price	78	71	75	67	291	502.50
D. Gammon	71	75	74	71	291	502.50
Tienie Britz	77	71	71	73	292	465
Fred Beaver	74	73	71	74	292	465
S. Van Vuuren	70	75	71	76	292	465
Chris Moody	75	72	75	71	293	405.84
S. Williams	69	76	74	74	293	405.84
Philip Harrison	75	72	72	74	293	405.84
John Heggarty	69	73	74	77	293	405.84
Ian Palmer	71	74	72	76	293	405.84
Alan Pate	67	74	74	78	293	405.84
D. Cooper	72	74	76	72	294	345
Stephen Bennett	72	75	73	74	294	345
Brian Sharrock	74	74	71	75	294	345
Andrew Payne	72	76	71	75	294	345
Ronan Rafferty	73	74	71	76	294	345
Phil Simmons	71	71	76	76	294	345
Harold Henning	72	72	78	74	296	295
Peter Thomas	75	74	73	74	296	295
V. Karatzias	75	70	76	75	296	295

	SCORES			TOTAL	MONEY
T. Bennett	75	73	72	76	296	295
Carlo Knauss	74	71	78	74	297	250
Fulton Allem	74	73	75	75	297	250
Keith Waters	75	74	72	76	297	250
Peter Barber	72	76	72	77	297	250
Andrew Murray	71	69	77	80	297	250

Lexington PGA

Wanderers Golf Club, Johannesburg
Par 36–34—70; 6,906 yards

January 13–16
purse, R100,000

	SCORES				TOTAL	MONEY
Gary Player	68	70	66	68	272	R16,000
Gordon Brand	72	68	67	67	275	7,866.67
Bill Rogers	67	70	65	73	275	7,866.67
Mark McNulty	67	67	66	75	275	7,866.67
David Frost	68	71	67	76	277	4,400
Denis Watson	65	71	69	74	279	3,600
Allan Henning	70	74	69	67	280	2,412
Andries Oosthuizen	73	65	72	70	280	2,412
Sam Torrance	68	71	71	70	280	2,412
Nick Price	68	73	68	71	280	2,412
David Feherty	66	70	70	74	280	2,412
Mark McCann	71	66	75	69	281	1,535
S. Williams	75	69	68	69	281	1,535
Graham Henning	66	72	71	72	281	1,535
Simon Hobday	68	72	68	73	281	1,535
Phil Simmons	71	68	66	73	281	1,535
Fulton Allem	72	67	70	72	281	1,535
Tienie Britz	70	68	72	72	282	1,256.67
Jeff Hawkes	68	71	71	72	282	1,256.67
Hugh Baiocchi	70	70	70	72	282	1,256.67
Gert Van Biljon	71	73	72	67	283	1,000
John Fourie	72	71	71	69	283	1,000
Alan Pate	71	71	71	70	283	1,000
Paul Way	70	75	67	71	283	1,000
Martin Barton	68	71	73	71	283	1,000
David Robertson	67	71	78	68	284	930
Tertius Claassens	69	74	68	73	284	930
John McComish	70	69	71	74	284	930
Anthony Johnstone	70	72	68	74	284	930
Richie Adham	72	69	76	68	285	850
John Bland	71	74	70	70	285	850
Nigel Burch	74	70	69	72	285	850
Ian Mosey	69	75	69	72	285	850
Philip Harrison	72	69	68	76	285	850
Warren Humphreys	71	72	75	68	286	730
J. O'Flynn	71	70	75	70	286	730
Tom Weiskopf	70	70	76	70	286	730
Mark James	75	70	71	70	286	730
John Heggarty	69	73	75	70	287	680
Des Smyth	68	73	74	72	287	680
Ronan Rafferty	71	71	73	72	287	680
Brian Sharrock	70	72	75	71	288	630
Jeremy Bennett	73	69	71	75	288	630
Andrew Chandler	71	74	74	70	289	550

	SCORES			TOTAL	MONEY
T. Bennett	68	76	70	75	289	550
Henry Trevena	70	75	73	71	289	550
Chris Moody	74	71	72	72	289	550
Bobby Lincoln	70	73	73	73	289	550
G. Pearson	70	72	74	73	289	550

SAB South African Masters

Milnerton Golf Club, Cape Town
Par 36–36—72

January 20–23
purse, R100,000

	SCORES			TOTAL	MONEY
Mark McNulty	68	64	69	74	275	R16,000
Denis Watson	69	69	68	71	277	11,600
Hugh Baiocchi	70	70	67	71	278	7,000
David Ogrin	70	67	72	70	279	5,000
Allan Henning	70	70	73	67	280	4,400
Gary Player	71	70	71	69	281	3,400
Gery Watine	70	70	70	71	281	3,400
Jimmy Johnson	71	69	73	69	282	2,038.34
Nigel Burch	67	71	72	72	282	2,038.34
Alan Pate	69	70	71	72	282	2,038.33
Warren Humphreys	74	64	72	72	282	2,038.33
Phil Simmons	70	72	68	72	282	2,038.33
Ian Mosey	72	69	69	72	282	2,038.33
Simon Hobday	70	76	69	68	283	1,520
Gavin Levenson	69	69	74	71	283	1,520
Sam Torrance	72	73	69	70	284	1,370
Teddie Webber	70	72	71	71	284	1,370
David Frost	74	68	71	71	284	1,370
Philip Harrison	72	69	74	70	285	1,160
Fulton Allem	72	70	72	71	285	1,160
S. Williams	70	71	73	71	285	1,160
David Robertson	72	70	71	72	285	1,160
Mark McCann	72	68	72	73	285	1,160
Noel Hunt	72	67	72	74	285	1,160
Ronan Rafferty	74	72	68	72	286	1,035
Robin Mann	75	69	68	74	286	1,035
Keith Waters	70	74	74	69	287	945
John Bland	73	74	70	70	287	945
Nick Job	72	72	72	71	287	945
John McComish	72	72	71	72	287	945
Jeff Hawkes	73	74	71	70	288	822
David Feherty	70	71	75	72	288	822
D. Cooper	69	73	73	73	288	822
Gordon Brand	70	76	67	75	288	822
Harold Henning	73	71	69	75	288	822
Richie Adham	73	70	75	71	289	740
Ian Palmer	72	74	71	72	289	740
Tienie Britz	71	71	72	75	289	740
Bill Brask	76	68	77	69	290	650
G. Pearson	73	73	72	72	290	650
Stephen Bennett	70	73	74	73	290	650
John Heggarty	70	72	74	74	290	650
T. Bennett	74	69	72	75	290	650
Bobby Lincoln	73	72	70	75	290	650
Dale Hayes	72	73	75	71	291	560

	SCORES				TOTAL	MONEY
David Stratton	72	70	74	75	291	560
John McGough	72	72	72	75	291	560
Andrew Chandler	72	74	74	72	292	520
Nick Price	71	74	76	72	293	490
Tertius Claassens	74	71	72	76	293	490

Sharp Electronics Open

Killarney Golf Club
Par 70

January 27–30
purse, R100,000

	SCORES				TOTAL	MONEY
Mark McNulty	69	69	70	66	274	R16,000
Tienie Britz	69	68	65	73	275	7,866.67
Gavin Levenson	71	67	68	69	275	7,866.67
Nick Price	68	68	70	69	275	7,866.67
John Bland	69	68	71	68	276	4,400
Sam Torrance	68	71	73	65	277	2,925
Gary Player	74	68	68	67	277	2,925
Denis Watson	72	61	75	69	277	2,925
Phil Simmons	69	71	69	68	277	2,925
Anthony Johnstone	72	72	67	67	278	2,100
John Fourie	71	67	71	70	279	1,800
Tertius Claassens	67	72	69	71	279	1,800
Ian Mosey	74	67	69	70	280	1,525
Mark James	69	70	70	71	280	1,525
Simon Hobday	73	69	67	71	280	1,525
Des Smyth	72	69	66	73	280	1,525
C. Bolling	72	71	68	70	281	1,285
Nigel Burch	74	69	67	71	281	1,285
Jimmy Heggarty	70	68	69	74	281	1,285
Chris Williams	70	67	70	74	281	1,285
Gordon Brand	71	69	79	63	282	1,155
Ian Palmer	70	70	79	73	282	1,155
Brian Marchbank	73	71	70	69	283	1,035
Peter Thomas	68	76	66	73	283	1,035
Bernhard Langer	69	70	73	71	283	1,035
D. Cooper	70	70	71	72	283	1,035
George Harvey	72	69	69	73	283	1,035
Allan Henning	70	68	72	73	283	1,035
Richie Adham	71	66	73	74	284	930
Mark McCann	75	69	72	69	285	846
Hugh Baiocchi	70	72	73	70	285	846
Paul Way	74	70	70	71	285	846
Peter Harrison	72	71	70	72	285	846
Warren Humphreys	71	73	68	73	285	846
David Stratton	69	72	74	71	286	730
Mark Bright	74	68	73	71	286	730
Gery Watine	69	73	72	72	286	730
David Frost	71	68	73	74	286	730
Teddie Webber	72	72	67	75	286	730
Ronan Rafferty	70	68	72	76	286	730
R. Richardson	71	71	76	69	287	610
Bob Charles	76	68	75	76	287	610
B. Jacobs	71	70	72	74	287	610
Jeremy Bennett	75	68	73	71	287	610
Alan Pate	71	69	74	73	287	610

	SCORES				TOTAL	MONEY
Michael King	72	71	71	73	287	610
Mitch Adcock	71	70	76	71	288	490
G. Pearson	75	69	69	75	288	490
John McGough	71	71	74	72	288	490
Fulton Allem	72	71	72	73	288	490
Joe Dlamini	73	69	72	74	288	490
Vincent Tshabalala	71	72	71	74	288	490

Sun City Classic

Gary Player Country Club, Bophuthatswana
Par 36–36—72; 7,693 yards

February 3–6
purse, R100,000

	SCORES				TOTAL	MONEY
Mark McNulty	73	72	70	68	283	R16,000
John Bland	71	74	70	70	284	11,600
Nick Price	70	73	72	71	286	7,000
Warren Humphreys	73	74	70	70	287	5,000
Allan Henning	74	71	73	70	288	4,400
Anthony Johnstone	72	73	75	70	290	3,133.34
Denis Watson	74	70	74	72	290	3,133.34
Jeff Hawkes	72	75	69	74	290	3,133.34
Des Smyth	74	77	73	67	291	1,926
Gary Player	71	74	76	70	291	1,926
Chris Moody	76	73	71	71	291	1,926
Mitch Adcock	70	78	72	71	291	1,926
David Feherty	71	74	73	73	291	1,926
Harold Henning	70	75	75	72	292	1,490
Bernhard Langer	70	77	72	73	292	1,490
Mark Bright	71	75	70	76	292	1,490
Mark James	72	77	74	70	293	1,340
Hugh Baiocchi	73	74	69	77	293	1,340
C. Bolling	71	74	73	78	296	1,250
Tienie Britz	77	74	78	68	297	1,157.50
David Ogrin	71	74	76	76	297	1,157.50
Tertius Claassens	70	75	75	77	297	1,157.50
Phil Simmons	69	73	77	78	297	1,157.50
Teddie Webber	78	73	78	70	299	1,080
Paul Way	76	78	71	75	300	1,035
Jimmy Heggarty	74	79	70	77	300	1,035
David Frost	73	70	76	74	302	888.75
Matt Runge	76	73	76	77	302	888.75
Andrew Murray	80	74	74	74	302	888.75
Simon Hobday	76	75	74	77	302	888.75
David Whitfield	73	75	77	77	302	888.75
Robbie Stewart	77	74	74	77	302	888.75
John McGough	73	79	75	75	302	888.75
Mark McCann	76	72	80	74	302	888.75
Vincent Tshabalala	75	79	77	72	303	750
Alan Pate	73	70	76	75	303	750
Philip Harrison	78	72	75	78	303	750
Bill Brask	74	72	76	81	303	750
John Fourie	77	75	78	74	304	690
Bob Charles	80	74	75	75	304	690
Stephen Bennett	77	74	80	74	305	630
Gary Harvey	71	78	80	76	305	630
N. Roe	76	76	75	78	305	630

	SCORES				TOTAL	MONEY
Andrew Chandler	73	76	76	77	305	630
Michael McLean	74	80	78	74	306	530
Noel Hunt	73	77	75	81	306	530
Dale Hayes	72	80	77	77	306	530
V. Karatzias	77	77	75	77	306	530
Gavin Levenson	70	82	75	79	306	530
Graham Henning	77	71	80	78	306	530

Vaal Reefs Sigma Open

Orkney Golf Club, Orkney   February 10–13
Par 36–36—72   purse, R40,000

	SCORES				TOTAL	MONEY
Nick Price	70	66	63	71	270	R6,400
Denis Watson	69	67	72	67	275	4,640
John Bland	67	71	69	70	277	2,800
Vincent Tshabalala	72	71	68	68	279	1,880
Anthony Johnstone	71	67	70	71	279	1,880
Warren Humphreys	73	69	71	68	281	1,440
Michael King	66	73	74	69	282	1,160
Matt Runge	73	72	70	67	282	1,160
Fulton Allem	73	67	73	70	283	880
Tertius Claassens	69	73	66	75	283	880
Ronan Rafferty	73	71	69	71	284	727
Gavin Levenson	70	71	71	72	284	727
Andrew Chandler	70	71	74	70	285	617
Ian Palmer	72	68	75	70	285	617
David Frost	69	73	73	70	285	617
Dale Hayes	72	72	69	72	285	617
Joe Dlamini	79	71	72	64	286	511.80
Hugh Baiocchi	68	72	71	75	286	511.80
Paul van Zyl	65	74	71	76	286	511.80
Phil Simmons	67	74	70	75	286	511.80
Gary Birch	71	70	69	76	286	511.80
Philip Harrison	71	73	72	71	287	445
Mark Bright	70	71	76	70	287	445
Andries Oosthuizen	69	72	72	74	287	445
Andrew Murray	72	71	70	74	287	445
J. Ackerman	71	74	75	68	288	397
Tienie Britz	74	74	70	70	288	397
John Fourie	71	75	70	72	288	397
John O'Leary	73	73	69	74	288	397
Simon Hobday	72	72	77	69	290	344.75
David Stratton	71	76	71	72	290	344.75
Paul Way	77	72	65	76	290	344.75
Nick Job	71	71	71	77	290	344.75
Keith Waters	73	75	72	71	291	320
J. O'Flynn	76	75	72	69	292	312
S. Van Vuuren	73	73	76	71	293	284
Vin Baker	72	69	74	78	293	284
Carlo Knauss	73	72	77	71	293	284
Jeff Hawkes	73	74	75	71	293	284
David Robertson	74	70	76	73	293	284
Stephen Bennett	72	73	72	76	293	284
Allan Henning	80	70	72	72	294	252
Bobby Lincoln	71	80	71	72	294	252

	SCORES				TOTAL	MONEY
Graham Henning	70	75	78	72	295	224
David Whitfield	77	73	71	74	295	224
Paul Carrigill	76	72	73	74	295	224
M. Roe	72	73	74	76	295	224
R. Molt	71	78	69	77	295	224
M. Palmer	74	76	73	73	296	196
Robin Mann	72	76	74	74	296	196

Holiday Inns Pro-Am

Swazi Spa Golf Club, Swaziland February 16–20
purse, R40,000

	SCORES				TOTAL	MONEY
Denis Watson	70	64	65	69	268	R6,400
Fulton Allem	69	63	70	70	272	4,640
Phil Simmons	67	70	70	68	275	2,400
John Fourie	68	66	69	72	275	2,400
Mark McNulty	70	68	73	65	276	1,493.34
John Bland	67	71	70	68	276	1,493.34
Jeff Hawkes	69	69	67	71	276	1,493.34
Hugh Baiocchi	70	67	70	71	278	1,040
Ronan Rafferty	71	73	69	66	279	920
Bobby Lincoln	71	73	67	70	281	764.67
John O'Leary	70	68	70	73	281	764.67
D. Cooper	70	70	68	73	281	764.67
Gavin Levenson	71	71	70	70	282	643
J. Cockayne	71	68	71	72	282	643
Warren Humphreys	71	70	72	70	283	591
Ian Mosey	73	70	70	70	283	591
Stephen Bennett	72	69	72	71	284	543
Tertius Claassens	72	73	68	71	284	543
Anthony Johnstone	74	67	75	69	285	491
Carlo Knauss	72	70	72	71	285	491
Michael McLean	73	69	71	72	285	491
Chris Williams	71	69	74	72	286	463
S. Van Vuuren	73	73	72	69	287	445
David Williams	67	71	73	76	287	445
Peter Barber	75	70	74	69	288	397
G. Pearson	79	69	68	72	288	397
Joe Dlamini	73	73	71	71	288	397
Theo Manyama	71	71	73	73	288	397
T. Bennett	73	70	72	73	288	397
Nigel Burch	71	68	74	75	288	397
David Frost	75	73	74	67	289	324.67
Ian Palmer	71	73	73	72	289	324.67
Paul Carrigill	69	71	77	72	289	324.67
Robbie Stewart	69	72	75	73	289	324.67
J. O'Flynn	70	71	74	74	289	324.67
Richard Mogoerane	74	70	71	74	289	324.67
R. Richardson	73	73	72	72	290	284
Vincent Tshabalala	73	71	73	73	290	284
Andries Oosthuizen	67	76	73	74	290	284
R. Adham	72	69	74	75	290	284
R. Molt	74	75	73	69	291	260
Paul Way	72	71	72	76	291	260
Andrew Murray	69	75	77	71	292	248

	SCORES				TOTAL	MONEY
Peter Harrison	71	78	75	69	293	228
Fred Beaver	73	73	74	73	293	228
Tienie Britz	73	75	70	75	293	228
Keith Waters	70	71	74	78	293	228
D. Whitfield	75	72	76	71	294	200
Paul Van Zyl	74	71	75	74	294	200
S. Williams	71	74	74	75	294	200

Nigerian Open

Ikoyi Golf Club, Lagos
Par 35-36—71; 6,255 yards

February 4–7
purse, £41,050

	SCORES				TOTAL	MONEY
David Jagger	71	69	66	68	274	£6,838.93
Ian Woosnam	67	71	68	68	274	4,556.65
(Jagger defeated Woosnam on second hole of sudden-death playoff.)						
David Jones	67	75	65	68	275	2,569.73
John Morgan	69	71	68	71	279	1,894.45
Steve Martin	70	68	70	71	279	1,894.45
Malcolm Gregson	69	70	71	70	280	1,486.01
Tony Uduimoh	71	69	74	67	281	1,047.80
Gordon Brand	72	69	72	68	281	1,047.80
Bill Longmuir	66	72	69	74	281	1,047.80
Peter Tupling	68	72	69	72	281	1,047.80
Ewen Murray	68	72	71	71	282	800.47
Peter Cowen	72	69	73	69	283	721.10
Philip Elson	73	72	69	69	283	721.10
Tommy Horton	69	70	71	73	283	721.10
Tony Charnley	73	72	69	70	284	648.59
Joe Higgins	69	73	74	71	287	609.59
Mohammed Moussa	71	72	72	72	287	609.59
Mike Steadman	73	75	71	69	288	582.91
Andrew Brooks	76	72	69	72	289	554.17
John Hay	70	70	75	74	289	554.17
David Oweyemi	74	72	70	73	289	554.17
Festus Makelemi	68	69	79	74	290	525.44
Clifford Maudesley	72	74	76	69	291	492.60
Arnold O'Connor	74	76	69	72	291	492.60
Paul Osanebi	71	72	74	74	291	492.60
Mike Inglis	72	73	71	75	291	492.60
Peter Dawson	76	71	73	72	292	451.55
Peter Akakasiaka	75	72	70	75	292	451.55
Tim Rastall	75	76	75	68	294	424.86
Garry Harvey	73	76	70	75	294	424.86
Usman Yesup	69	76	74	77	296	402.29
Robert Craig	80	79	68	70	297	369.45
Cletus Iriaka	78	71	78	70	297	369.45
David Barton	73	73	76	75	297	369.45
Anthony Higgins	78	72	74	73	297	369.45
Mark Thomas	76	75	71	76	298	340.71
Bello Seibidor	81	72	74	73	300	328.40
Mark Vickery	72	74	76	78	300	328.40
Bachery Samateh	73	73	75	79	300	328.40
Tony Price	72	70	78	81	301	316.08
Peter Berry	77	74	77	74	302	303.77
Jones Esioyibo	77	71	75	79	302	303.77

	SCORES			TOTAL	MONEY
Chris Okwu	72	75	74	82	303	295.56
*Pendar Umuebo	74	79	78	74	305	
Friday Amadi	77	72	78	78	305	287.35
*Henry George	78	74	78	76	306	
Jeff Quarshie	77	72	76	83	308	279.14
Emmanuel Lawrence	76	76	79	79	310	270.93
Patrick Okpomu	75	75	80	80	310	270.93
Christopher Gray	79	76	76	81	312	258.61
Stephen James	76	79	75	85	315	254.51
Mike Miller	71	71	75	Retd		254.51

Ivory Coast Open

President Golf Club, Yamoussoukro
Par 36–36—72; 6,715 yards

February 11–14
purse, £36,200

	SCORES			TOTAL	MONEY
John Morgan	66	72	70	64	272	£6,030.76
Ian Woosnam	71	65	67	71	274	4,018.09
David Jagger	70	66	71	68	275	2,266.06
Tommy Horton	70	69	67	70	276	1,561.08
Tsao Chien Teng	71	68	67	70	276	1,561.08
Martin Poxon	70	65	73	68	276	1,561.08
Robert Craig	68	71	71	67	277	1,158.37
Peter Tupling	71	68	69	70	278	941.17
David Jones	68	71	70	69	278	941.17
Chen Tze Ming	68	70	72	69	279	760.18
Mike Steadman	68	71	71	69	279	760.18
Tony Charnley	68	69	73	70	280	669.68
Peter Dawson	73	68	72	69	282	633.48
Gordon Brand	71	71	73	68	283	597.28
Mark Thomas	71	70	70	74	285	561.08
Garry Harvey	70	68	75	72	285	561.08
Mike Inglis	72	71	74	69	286	521.26
Joe Higgins	71	70	70	75	286	521.26
Bill Longmuir	73	70	71	72	286	521.26
Gary Stubbington	69	74	69	75	287	485.06
Philip Elson	69	73	74	71	287	485.06
Peter Cowen	71	74	71	73	289	448.86
Clifford Maudesley	70	72	71	76	289	448,86
John Hay	72	71	72	74	289	448.86
Tim Rastall	69	76	71	74	290	419.90
Andrew Brooks	77	73	70	71	291	390.95
Peter Berry	71	77	70	73	291	390.95
Ossie Gartenmaier	70	73	75	73	291	390.95
Mohammed Moussa	76	70	74	74	292	356.56
Mark Vickery	69	70	73	80	292	356.56
James Lebbie	73	75	77	70	295	336.65
Tony Price	73	74	75	73	295	336.65
David Barton	76	75	73	73	297	318.55
Georges Leven	70	76	77	74	297	318.55
Arnold O'Connor	74	72	72	79	297	318.55
Christopher Gray	74	78	72	74	298	304.07
*Marc Pendaries	77	75	77	72	301	
Bachary Samateh	74	76	77	75	302	296.83
Anthony Higgins	73	73	77	81	304	289.59
*Didier Villard	76	81	73	81	311	

	SCORES				TOTAL	MONEY
Graham Walker	81	73	83	76	313	278.73
Jean-Baptiste Ahoule	83	76	76	78	313	278.73
Jeff Doe	79	77	77	81	314	267.87
Desire Djibi	76	78	83	78	315	260.63
Blaise Adje	78	82	80	76	316	253.39
Guy Gomon	75	80	84	79	318	246.15
*Christophe Djoman	80	77	81	83	321	
Jean-Claud Querrien	84	76	78	84	322	238.91
Pierre Nandjui	89	77	79	81	326	231.67
Mohammed Mahrous	86	86	80	75	327	224.43
Belghiti Ahmed	80	83	85	80	328	217.19
*Y.T. Kim	82	84	83	81	330	
Ladji Cisse	88	79	81	88	336	209.95
*Guy Olson	80	77	80	101	338	
Henri Doudjon	85	89	80	86	340	202.71

Benson & Hedges Kenya Open

Muthaiga Golf Club, Nairobi
Par 36–35—71; 6,765 yards

March 11–14
purse, £38,470

	SCORES				TOTAL	MONEY
Eamonn Darcy	72	65	67	70	274	£6,102.56
David Jagger	71	74	65	65	275	3,897.44
Ken Brown	70	69	70	68	277	2,064.10
Gordon Brand	71	67	70	69	277	2,064.10
Ian Woosnam	74	68	72	66	280	1,564.10
Bernard Gallacher	72	71	67	71	281	1,333.33
Peter Tupling	70	66	74	72	282	1,083.33
Paul Hoad	76	67	69	72	282	1,083.33
Brian Barnes	73	74	68	68	283	865.38
Philip Elson	71	70	72	70	283	865.38
Brian Waites	70	74	70	70	284	719.23
Tony Jacklin	75	68	70	71	284	719.23
Tommy Horton	68	74	68	74	284	719.23
Peter Cowen	73	74	71	67	285	646.41
Roger Chapman	72	72	73	70	287	558.65
John Morgan	73	72	72	70	287	558.65
Bill Longmuir	70	69	76	72	287	558.65
Steve Martin	72	73	70	72	287	558.65
Trevor Powell	68	73	73	73	287	558.65
Garry Harvey	72	71	71	73	287	558.65
Martin Foster	76	71	66	74	287	558.65
Simon Bishop	73	71	67	76	287	558.65
Maurice Bembridge	74	72	70	73	289	501.28
Tony Payne	73	72	76	69	290	477.35
Bobby Mitchell	74	73	68	75	290	477.35
David Jones	72	77	65	76	290	477.35
Brian Gunson	76	71	75	69	291	429.49
David Vaughan	73	75	72	71	291	429.49
Gary Smith	77	72	72	70	291	429.49
Joe Higgins	72	75	72	72	291	429.49
Tony Charnley	74	71	72	74	291	429.49
Bob Cameron	75	72	75	70	292	372
Garry Cullen	72	73	73	74	292	372
Ross Drummond	71	75	72	74	292	372
Mark Thomas	71	73	73	75	292	372

	SCORES				TOTAL	MONEY
John Fowler	76	71	68	77	292	372
Stephen Harrison	77	73	72	71	293	341.88
Mike Steadman	76	74	70	73	293	341.88
Donald Stirling	77	70	70	76	293	341.88
Craig Maltman	79	65	73	77	294	331.03
John Garner	78	72	73	72	295	323.08
Peter Berry	76	72	75	74	297	311.97
John Hay	73	80	68	76	297	311.97
Mike Miller	73	76	71	77	297	311.97
David Thorp	76	74	73	76	299	295.30
Matts Lanner	72	76	74	77	299	295.30
Roger Yates	75	76	71	77	299	295.30
Charles Farrar	73	72	78	77	300	280.51
Steven Kelly	72	72	77	81	302	277.18
David Barton	75	75	72	81	303	275.64

Mufulira Open

Mufulira Golf Club, Mufulira, Kenya   March 18–21
Par 36–37—73; 6,928 yards   purse, £48,396

	SCORES				TOTAL	MONEY
Brian Waites	73	70	70	68	281	£8,076.22
Eamonn Darcy	73	72	72	67	284	4,234.72
Martin Poxon	72	68	71	73	284	4,234.72
Roger Chapman	74	71	71	69	285	2,077.03
David Jagger	73	73	70	69	285	2,077.03
Brian Barnes	69	76	70	70	285	2,077.03
Peter Tupling	71	71	75	69	286	1,310.74
Ken Brown	73	75	69	69	286	1,310.74
Ewen Murray	74	69	71	72	286	1,310.74
Ian Woosnam	76	72	72	67	287	989.11
John Fowler	69	73	72	73	287	989.11
Tommy Horton	74	75	69	70	288	824.25
David Vaughan	69	74	74	71	288	824.25
Simon Bishop	72	69	74	73	288	824.25
Steve Martin	70	75	69	74	288	824.25
John Morgan	70	71	76	72	289	744.10
Tony Charnley	69	73	74	73	289	744.10
David Jones	76	73	73	68	290	660.61
David Thorp	73	76	72	69	290	660.61
Mike Steadman	74	72	72	72	290	660.61
Bill Longmuir	70	74	72	74	290	660.61
Carl Mason	70	70	74	76	290	660.61
Martin Foster	70	73	75	73	291	598.91
Craig Maltman	77	74	72	70	293	562.61
Paul Hoad	72	77	71	73	293	562.61
Charles Ray	74	70	74	75	293	562.61
Philip Elson	75	72	75	72	294	517.24
Paul Tembo	72	75	72	75	294	517.24
Gary Cullen	78	78	70	69	295	454.72
Malcolm Gregson	74	75	74	72	295	454.72
Mike Inglis	74	76	71	74	295	454.72
Gordon Brand	73	74	73	75	295	454.72
Maurice Bembridge	73	75	72	75	295	454.72
Mats Lanner	70	73	78	74	295	454.72
Peter Cowen	76	76	70	74	296	409.86

	SCORES				TOTAL	MONEY
Jose-Maria Canizares	74	73	73	76	296	409.86
Robert Mitchell	73	77	74	73	297	391.71
Mike Ingham	77	71	75	74	297	391.71
Peter Dawson	75	78	72	73	298	364.48
Seiichi Numazawa	73	75	75	75	298	364.48
Mark Thomas	75	73	75	75	298	364.48
Trevor Powell	75	72	75	76	298	364.48
Arnold O'Connor	79	74	72	75	300	337.26
Gordon Manson	75	77	72	76	300	337.26
Peter Harrison	75	74	74	78	301	319.11
Robert Craig	73	75	73	80	301	319.11
John Garner	75	73	78	76	302	302.48
Gary Smith	79	74	72	77	302	302.48
Hideo Ishii	75	77	71	79	302	302.48
Joe Higgins	73	77	75	78	303	145.19
Graham Walker	78	73	74	78	303	145.19

Zambia Open

Lusaka Golf Club, Lusaka
Par 35–38—73; 6,599 yards

March 25–28
purse, £70,000

	SCORES				TOTAL	MONEY
Brian Waites	68	68	68	72	276	£12,195.12
Ken Brown	72	65	73	70	280	8,140.24
Tommy Horton	69	69	73	70	281	3,851.62
Howard Clark	71	68	71	71	281	3,851.62
Peter Tupling	71	68	70	72	281	3,851.62
Mike Miller	70	69	69	74	282	2,652.44
Bernard Gallacher	70	69	72	72	283	2,286.59
Ewen Murray	73	69	74	68	284	1,820.12
Jose-Maria Canizares	73	73	67	71	284	1,820.12
Ian Woosnam	74	70	70	71	285	1,542.68
David Jones	73	73	73	67	286	1,314.02
David Jagger	75	73	71	67	286	1,314.02
David Vaughan	77	67	74	68	286	1,314.02
Carl Mason	73	71	73	69	286	1,314.02
John Morgan	72	73	72	71	288	1,069.51
Gordon Brand	75	65	75	73	288	1,069.51
John Fowler	72	72	71	73	288	1,069.51
Roger Chapman	69	69	76	74	288	1,069.51
Brian Barnes	71	74	67	76	288	1,069.51
Pip Elson	72	77	71	69	289	969.51
Mike Steadman	74	69	73	73	289	969.51
Gary Smith	73	69	80	68	290	859.76
John Garner	74	74	73	69	290	859.76
Steve Martin	74	71	74	71	290	859.76
Joe Higgins	76	72	71	71	290	859.76
Eamonn Darcy	68	76	75	71	290	859.76
Trevor Powell	76	72	71	71	290	859.76
Mark Thomas	74	69	74	73	290	859.76
Tony Charnley	75	75	70	71	291	737.80
Bill McColl	72	76	71	72	291	737.80
Seichii Numazawa	72	72	74	73	291	737.80
Bill Longmuir	71	75	74	72	292	652.44
Craig Maltman	71	77	71	73	292	652.44
Robert Cameron	69	72	74	77	292	652.44

	SCORES			TOTAL	MONEY
Peter Cowen	76	72	68	76	292	652.44
David Matthew	73	71	75	74	293	603.66
Martin Poxon	72	72	78	72	294	560.98
Arnold O'Connor	77	72	73	72	294	560.98
Malcolm Gregson	76	76	70	72	294	560.98
Hideo Ishii	74	69	76	75	294	560.98
Garry Cullen	69	74	74	77	294	560.98
Mike Inglis	71	73	73	77	294	560.98
Garry Harvey	73	73	75	74	295	512.20
Robert Craig	69	75	74	77	295	512.20
Simon Bishop	72	73	78	74	297	475.61
Charles Ray	74	74	74	75	297	475.61
Paul Tembo	72	74	75	76	297	475.61
David J. Russell	70	74	75	78	297	475.61
Gordon Manson	71	74	78	75	298	439.02
Maurice Bembridge	71	75	76	76	298	439.02

Kalahari Diamond Golf Classic

Gaborone Golf Club, Gaborone, Botswana   April 1–4
Par 36–36—72; 6,813 yards   purse, £30,000

	SCORES			TOTAL	MONEY
David Jagger	70	70	69	67	276	£5,000
Peter Tupling	70	70	72	69	281	3,330
John Morgan	70	71	71	70	282	1,715
Robert Craig	69	70	70	73	282	1,715
Ian Woosnam	71	72	68	72	283	1,300
Craig Maltman	72	73	69	70	284	1,025
Roger Chapman	69	69	74	72	284	1,025
Mike Inglis	73	70	71	71	285	760
Bobby Mitchell	69	72	72	72	285	760
David Vaughan	72	72	72	70	286	650
Tony Charnley	75	71	70	72	288	600
Bob Cameron	75	74	68	72	289	530
Peter Cowen	72	70	74	73	289	530
Bill Longmuir	74	71	71	73	289	530
Simon Bishop	75	68	74	73	290	460
Bill McColl	74	74	71	71	290	460
Paul Tembo	71	74	76	70	291	420
Mike Steadman	72	75	72	72	291	420
David Thorp	71	72	71	77	291	420
David J. Russell	73	76	72	71	292	390
Mats Lanner	67	77	76	72	292	390
Gordon Manson	75	70	74	73	292	390
David Hunter	72	74	75	72	293	365
Paul Hoad	75	74	72	72	293	365
John Fowler	71	76	76	71	294	350
Tim Rastall	75	76	76	68	295	330
Joe Higgins	71	76	76	72	295	330
Nick Brown	70	78	74	73	295	330
Graham Walker	73	76	77	71	296	290
Steve Hadfield	73	76	75	72	296	290
Mike Ingham	82	68	72	74	296	290
Peter Carr	75	73	73	75	296	290
Mark Mouland	73	74	74	75	296	290
Bryan Malone	76	75	73	74	298	260

	SCORES			TOTAL	MONEY
Martin Foster	73	79	77	70	299	245
Gary Stubbington	76	72	78	73	299	245
Peter Berry	74	72	79	74	299	245
Tony Price	74	77	74	75	300	232.50
Peter Sinyama	74	77	74	75	300	232.50
Mark Vickery	79	73	76	73	301	222.50
David Barton	77	73	73	78	301	222.50
Peter Dawson	80	76	73	73	302	215
Charles Ray	78	78	71	78	305	210
*Steve Mahtson	81	75	78	72	306	
Clifford Maudesley	77	77	82	71	307	205
Anthony Higgins	80	76	78	76	310	197.50
Christopher Gray	72	76	85	77	310	197.50
John Grant	79	79	75	79	312	190
Steven Kelly	79	79	76	80	314	185
Kevin Barnes	82	79	75	80	316	180
*Joe Marudu	80	79	76	82	317	
*Keith Munger	81	80	82	75	318	
*Jake Sibiya	81	75	86	77	319	
Peter Harrison	78	81	85	76	320	175

Moroccan Grand Prix

Dar-es-Salaam Royal Golf Club, Rabat, Morocco
Par 73, 7,400 yards   purse, US$88,000

	SCORES			TOTAL	MONEY
Frank Conner	71	74	71	71	287	US$20,000
Butch Baird	72	72	70	74	288	10,000
Lennie Clements	70	73	71	74	288	10,000
Ron Streck	73	70	72	74	289	6,000
Bob Eastwood	70	73	77	70	290	4,500
Tom Jenkins	75	74	70	71	290	4,500
Morris Hatalsky	71	71	72	78	292	3,500
Pat McGowan	72	73	75	73	293	2,900
Angel Gallardo	74	76	72	71	293	2,900
Mike Reid	74	72	73	76	295	2,600
Greg Powers	74	76	74	72	296	2,400
Mike McCullough	75	75	73	74	297	2,200
Lou Graham	75	73	73	77	298	1,900
Bill Casper	75	72	75	76	298	1,900
Bruce Fleisher	76	76	73	73	298	1,900
Victor Regalado	76	74	76	74	300	1,700
Tim Simpson	72	77	81	72	302	1,600
Gery Watine	80	80	70	73	303	1,500
Fatmi Moussa	78	78	75	75	306	1,400
George Burns	83	77	73	77	310	1,250
Mohamed Makroune	76	79	76	79	310	1,250
Roger Maltbie	79	80	73	79	311	1,100
Barbra Benaceur	77	76	80	82	315	1,000

Sun City Challenge

Gary Player Country Club
Sun City, Bophuthatswana
Par 36–36—72; 7,693 yards

December 2–5
purse, US$1,000,000

	SCORES				TOTAL	MONEY
Raymond Floyd	72	69	68	71	280	$300,000
Craig Stadler	72	67	70	71	280	150,000
(Floyd defeated Stadler on fourth hole of sudden death playoff.)						
Lee Trevino	71	73	70	67	281	105,000
Lanny Wadkins	70	70	68	74	282	85,000
Johnny Miller	72	68	71	72	283	75,000
Jerry Pate	67	73	66	80	286	63,500
Severiano Ballesteros	67	71	73	75	286	63,500
Jack Nicklaus	70	71	72	74	287	56,000
Greg Norman	71	72	78	70	291	52,000
Gary Player	71	75	72	76	294	50,000

The Asia/Japan Tours

Philippine Open

Wack Wack Golf and Country Club,
East Course, Manila
Par 36–36—72; 7,046 yards

February 18–21
purse, US$150,000

	SCORES				TOTAL	MONEY
Hsieh Min Nan	72	72	76	72	292	US$24,900
Hsu Sheng San	71	71	69	81	292	16,665
(Hsieh defeated Hsu on third hole of sudden-death playoff.)						
Curt Byrum	73	72	71	77	293	8,445
Alan Pate	72	78	71	72	293	8,445
John Mahaffey	74	75	72	73	294	5,370
Tsao Chien Teng	73	77	72	72	294	5,370
Eleuterio Nival	76	75	71	72	294	5,370
*Gil Ababa	69	76	75	75	295	
Jose Rates	72	75	75	74	296	3,370
Fuzzy Zoeller	78	73	73	72	296	3,370
Ben Arda	72	76	76	72	296	3,370
Paterno Braza	75	77	72	73	297	2,700
Yasushi Taki	76	70	77	74	297	2,700
Lu Hsi Chuen	77	71	75	75	298	2,490
*Frankie Minoza	73	74	74	77	298	
Robert Michael	77	76	73	73	299	2,230
Ireneo Legaspi	74	77	76	72	299	2,230
Jaime Gonzalez	77	74	72	76	299	2,230
Chen Tze Chung	78	70	74	78	300	1,869
Robert Wrenn	75	72	75	78	300	1,869
Hsieh Yung Yo	76	75	72	77	300	1,869
Denny Hepler	78	74	71	71	300	1,869
Sadatoshi Makimura	74	74	76	76	300	1,869
Sukree Onsham	74	77	72	78	301	1,650
Raphael Alarcon	74	76	74	77	301	1,650
Sonny Orquiza	78	72	75	76	301	1,650
Hahn Chang Sang	78	72	75	76	301	1,650
Choi Sang Ho	71	75	77	79	302	1,391.25
Dan Pohl	75	78	72	77	302	1,391.25
Hideto Shigenobu	76	73	74	79	302	1,391.25
Hung Wen Neng	79	72	76	75	302	1,391.25
Manuel Calero	70	77	76	79	302	1,391.25
Norio Adachi	75	74	78	75	302	1,391.25
Lu Ho Tsai	74	75	73	80	302	1,391.25
Chang Chen Hsiung	77	74	77	74	302	1,391.25
Kurt Cox	77	73	79	74	303	1,014
Gaylord Burrows	74	72	78	79	303	1,014
Bob Henderson	76	76	74	77	303	1,014
Peter Townsend	72	79	75	77	303	1,014
Pastor Domingo	72	77	77	77	303	1,014
Yasutomo Ishii	73	75	78	77	303	1,014
Mike Robles	76	75	76	76	303	1,014
Priscillo Diniz	76	74	78	75	303	1,014

	SCORES				TOTAL	MONEY
Tom Sieckmann	75	74	79	75	303	1,014
Don Klenk	76	77	78	72	303	1,014
Hiroshi Yamada	78	75	75	76	304	815
Shen Chung Shyan	76	76	77	75	304	815
Shen Kun Yen	77	75	77	75	304	815
*Mario Manubay	76	79	76	73	304	
Lai Chum Hui	76	75	76	78	305	765
Dean Lind	72	81	72	81	306	697.50
Tadao Koide	77	73	77	79	306	697.50
Kesahiko Uchida	79	72	71	84	306	697.50
Chang Toang Liang	78	74	76	78	306	697.50
Lin Chia	73	80	76	77	306	697.50
Hsu Chi San	78	75	77	76	306	697.50

Cathay Pacific Hong Kong Open

Royal Hong Kong Golf Club (Composite Course), Fanling   February 25–28
Par 34–36—70; 6,691 yards   purse, US$130,000

	SCORES				TOTAL	MONEY
Kurt Cox	68	68	70	70	276	US$21,650
Terry Gale	67	72	67	70	276	11,290
Tom Sieckmann	70	68	68	70	276	11,290

(Cox defeated Gale and Sieckmann in sudden-death playoff, Gale on first hole
and Sieckmann on fourth hole.)

	SCORES				TOTAL	MONEY
Saburo Fujiki	71	68	70	69	278	6,005
Stewart Ginn	68	68	73	69	278	6,005
Lu Hsi Chuen	72	72	66	69	279	4,550
Norio Suzuki	71	70	69	70	280	3,900
Greg Norman	71	68	72	70	281	2,920
Chen Tze Ming	70	69	70	72	281	2,920
Kim Seung Hack	68	71	70	72	281	2,920
Choi Youn Soo	74	70	68	70	282	2,340
Brian Waites	70	69	71	72	282	2,340
Pete Izumigawa	75	71	71	68	285	1,895
Cho Ho Sang	74	73	69	69	285	1,895
Lai Chum Hui	71	73	72	69	285	1,895
Nobumitsu Yuhara	73	71	70	71	285	1,895
Hsieh Yung Yo	70	72	71	72	285	1,895
Kikuo Arai	69	69	73	74	285	1,895
Hsu Chi San	74	70	73	69	286	1,542
Hsu Sheng San	73	68	75	70	286	1,542
Mike Clayton	74	70	69	73	286	1,542
Tommy Horton	73	67	72	74	286	1,542
Tom Anton	74	72	74	67	287	1,430
Peter Townsend	73	72	73	69	287	1,430
Mike Miller	69	75	73	71	288	1,320
Liao Kuo Chih	70	74	70	74	288	1,320
Alan Pate	74	69	71	74	288	1,320
Chen Tze Chung	72	73	68	75	288	1,320
Hahn Chang Sang	77	69	70	73	289	1,200
Ray Arrino	73	73	70	73	289	1,200
Lee Kang Sun	77	71	74	68	290	1,022
Brian Barnes	75	70	74	71	290	1,022
Jim Blair	73	75	70	72	290	1,022
Curt Byrum	71	72	75	72	290	1,022
Sukree Onsham	71	74	72	73	290	1,022

	SCORES			TOTAL	MONEY
Hung Wen Neng	68	74	74	74	290	1,022
Denny Hepler	74	69	71	76	290	1,022
Tsao Chien Teng	70	77	67	76	290	1,022
Naomichi Ozaki	73	75	72	71	291	784
Kuo Chirahama	73	74	71	73	291	784
Lee Booker	71	75	72	73	291	784
Chas Bolling	74	73	70	73	291	784
Don Klenk	71	76	70	74	291	784
Chang Ming Tsung	76	72	68	75	291	784
Kim Suck Bong	72	75	72	73	292	650
Kyihla Han	72	75	72	73	292	650
Hajime Meshiai	72	74	72	74	292	650
Masashi Ozaki	74	71	73	74	292	650
Rafael Alarcon	74	71	73	74	292	650
Hsieh Min Nan	72	71	75	74	292	650
Paterno Braza	72	71	74	75	292	650

Malaysian Open

Royal Selangor Golf Club, Old Course, Kuala Lumpur   March 4–7
Par 35–36—71; 6,843 yards   purse, US$150,000

	SCORES			TOTAL	MONEY
Denny Hepler	70	68	70	208	US$25,000
Hsieh Min Nan	71	68	69	208	13,028
David Ogrin	71	71	66	208	13,028
(Hepler defeated Hsieh and Ogrin on second hole of sudden-death playoff.)					
Marimuthu Ramayah	67	74	71	212	6,370
Hung Wen Neng	73	71	68	212	6,370
Terry Gale	70	68	74	212	6,370
*Frankie Minoza	67	72	73	212	
Robert Michael	70	73	70	213	3,335
Cho Ho Sang	71	72	70	213	3,335
Stewart Ginn	70	71	72	213	3,335
Sukree Onsham	71	69	73	213	3,335
Ray Stewart	73	71	69	213	3,335
John Benda	71	70	72	213	3,335
John McGough	68	74	72	214	2,185
Yasutomo Ishii	73	73	68	214	2,185
Robert Wrenn	71	70	73	214	2,185
Chris Moody	70	74	70	214	2,185
Ryoichi Furugori	70	71	73	214	2,185
Curt Byrum	70	70	74	214	2,185
Mike Clayton	71	71	73	215	1,758
Don Klenk	68	73	74	215	1,758
Ray Arinno	71	74	70	215	1,758
Jim Blair	71	70	74	215	1,758
Rodger Davis	71	73	71	215	1,758
Rafael Alarcon	71	73	72	216	1,436
John Hamarik	71	72	73	216	1,436
Kurt Cox	73	70	73	216	1,436
Gaylord Burrows	73	70	73	216	1,436
Eleuterio Nival	71	71	74	216	1,436
Graham Marsh	71	71	74	216	1,436
Lu Hsi Chuen	72	70	74	216	1,436
Shen Chung Shyan	71	74	71	216	1,436
Brad Sherfy	70	71	75	216	1,436

	SCORES			TOTAL	MONEY
Toshiaki Nakagawa	71	70	75	216	1,436
*Taijiro Tanaka	70	70	76	216	
Hideto Shigenobu	72	71	74	217	1,049
Jaime Gonzalez	69	74	74	217	1,049
Toshiharu Kusaka	70	76	71	217	1,049
Hsu Sheng San	73	73	71	217	1,049
Hajime Meshiai	73	73	71	217	1,049
Hisao Inoue	69	76	72	217	1,049
Chang Ming Tsung	71	74	72	217	1,049
Mikio Ichikawa	71	69	77	217	1,049
Lim Swee Wah	71	75	72	218	860
Skip Tredway	69	72	77	218	860
Ikuo Shirahama	73	72	73	218	860
Priscillo Diniz	69	75	75	219	771
Lai Chum Hui	73	75	71	219	771
Mario Siodina	72	74	73	219	771
Kim Seung Hack	71	75	73	219	771
Alan Pate	70	75	74	219	771
Jeff Sluman	73	70	77	220	698
Pete Izumigawa	71	74	75	220	698

Thailand Rattanakosin Bicentennial Open

Royal Thai Army Golf Club, Bang Khen   March 11–14
Par 36–36—72; 7,023 yards   purse, US$100,000

	SCORES				TOTAL	MONEY
Hsu Sheng San	70	73	72	66	281	US$16,660
Shen Chung Shyan	69	74	70	68	281	11,110
(Hsu defeated Shen on first hole of sudden-death playoff.)						
Stewart Ginn	70	70	74	68	282	5,630
Sukree Onsham	70	69	74	69	282	5,630
Jerry Anderson	72	70	68	73	283	4,240
Mike Clayton	71	75	67	71	284	3,500
John McGough	69	73	71	72	285	3,000
Hsu Chi San	71	70	72	73	286	2,500
May Aye	73	73	68	73	287	1,845
Ikuo Shirahama	73	71	72	71	287	1,845
Rafael Alarcon	72	70	75	70	287	1,845
Lu Hsi Chuen	72	72	72	71	287	1,845
Kurt Cox	73	71	69	74	287	1,845
Robert Michael	71	72	70	74	287	1,845
Mario Siodina	71	70	73	74	288	1,406.67
Somsak Srisa Nga	67	73	74	74	288	1,406.67
Seng Suwannakas	71	76	73	68	288	1,406.67
Priscillo Diniz	70	71	73	75	289	1,208
Takahiro Takeyasu	74	74	69	72	289	1,208
Eleuterio Nival	73	74	71	71	289	1,208
Tsao Chien Teng	72	74	72	71	289	1,208
Chen Tze Ming	71	67	74	77	289	1,208
Ben Arda	72	72	75	71	290	1,072.50
Chen Tze Chung	75	72	72	71	290	1,072.50
Tom Anton	74	72	72	72	290	1,072.50
Marimuthu Ramayah	76	71	72	71	290	1,072.50
Hsieh Min Nan	73	72	74	72	291	955
Chris Moody	71	75	73	72	291	955
Don Klenk	74	70	72	75	291	955

	SCORES				TOTAL	MONEY
Denny Hepler	70	76	74	71	291	955
Hiroshi Yamada	72	72	71	77	292	813.33
Larry Collins	75	72	72	73	292	813.33
Tom Sieckmann	71	75	76	70	292	813.33
Ray Arinno	72	72	72	76	292	813.33
David Ogrin	75	73	72	72	292	813.33
Samreuy Krutkaew	75	73	71	73	292	813.33
*Boonchoo Ruengkit	72	71	72	77	292	
Yoshio Fumiyama	70	71	78	74	293	672.50
Liao Kuo Chih	73	75	73	72	293	672.50
Chung Chun Hsing	72	75	69	77	293	672.50
Suthep Meesawat	71	77	74	71	293	672.50
Hung Wen Neng	71	75	74	74	294	586.67
Curt Byrum	75	71	76	72	294	586.67
Choi Sang Ho	72	73	72	77	294	586.67
Norio Adachi	74	70	74	77	295	535
Rafael Mena	74	74	75	72	295	535
Ireneo Legaspi	73	73	74	75	295	535
Lee Booker	75	73	73	74	295	535
Ian Baker-Finch	74	73	72	77	296	457.14
Hisao Inoue	77	71	77	71	296	457.14
Yoshiyuki Isomura	76	71	79	70	296	457.14
Poh Eing Chong	70	71	81	74	296	457.14
John Hamarik	73	75	75	73	296	457.14
Jim Blair	74	72	75	75	296	457.14
Sanchai Senaprom	77	71	78	70	296	457.14

Indian Open

Royal Calcutta Golf Club, Tollygunge
Par 36–37—73; 7,235 yards

March 18–21
purse, US$75,000

	SCORES				TOTAL	MONEY
Hsu Sheng San	70	70	68	69	277	US$12,495
Ikuo Shirahama	69	67	73	71	280	8,332
Kyi Hla Han	69	71	74	72	286	3,562
Lu Hsi Chuen	72	68	73	73	286	3,562
Hung Wen Neng	69	73	68	76	286	3,562
Hsieh Min Nan	68	72	73	73	286	3,562
Chen Tze Chung	75	69	73	70	287	1,826
Ray Arinno	69	72	74	72	287	1,826
Robert Michael	73	70	72	72	287	1,826
Mya Aye	71	70	71	75	287	1,826
Curt Byrum	73	73	71	71	288	1,395
Brian Jones	73	73	74	70	290	1,211
Kurt Cox	71	71	76	72	290	1,211
Larry Collins	71	70	74	75	290	1,211
Wayne Grady	73	71	70	76	290	1,211
Jaime Gonzalez	75	73	69	74	291	1,023
Archin Sopon	71	72	73	75	291	1,023
Sukree Onsham	72	75	73	72	292	949
Sandy Harper	71	77	68	76	292	949
Gaylord Burrows	76	70	75	72	293	866
Liao Kuo Chih	74	70	77	72	293	866
Sasadali	74	73	73	73	293	866
Mike Cunning	73	75	71	74	293	866
Lai Chum Hui	74	72	76	72	294	806

	SCORES				TOTAL	MONEY
Jeff Short	71	76	73	74	294	806
Yasutomo Ishii	75	72	76	72	295	717
Scott Spence	75	72	76	72	295	717
John McGough	79	71	73	72	295	717
Masakatsu Sano	72	72	77	74	295	717
Deray Simon	75	75	72	73	295	717
Eugene Nava	74	72	73	76	295	717
Stewart Ginn	76	71	78	71	296	609
Rohtas	72	74	74	76	296	609
Brad Sherfy	73	77	70	76	296	609
Billy Pierot	71	75	73	77	296	609
Hiroshi Yamada	75	73	77	72	297	495
Shigeru Takeuchi	74	76	76	71	297	495
Tsao Chien Teng	74	74	76	73	297	495
Ryoichi Furugori	70	72	80	75	297	495
Peter Fowler	73	70	79	75	297	495
Jamshed	74	74	74	75	297	495
Bob Henderson	75	75	71	76	297	495
Cheng Chung Hsing	73	77	73	75	298	396
Ken Kreiger	71	73	78	76	298	396
Suthep Meesawat	74	70	77	77	298	396
Kathamuthu Selaruas	72	73	77	76	298	396
Hisao Inoue	75	73	74	76	298	396
Mike Clayton	75	73	73	77	298	396
Priscillo Diniz	69	73	75	81	298	396
*Taijiro Tanaka	72	70	76	80	298	
Hsu Chi San	75	73	78	73	299	349
Hatsuo Ito	74	72	72	81	299	349

Singapore Open

Singapore Island Country Club, Bukit Course
Par 35–36—71; 6,645 yards

March 25–28
purse, US$100,000

	SCORES				TOTAL	MONEY
Hsu Sheng San	68	67	68	71	274	US$16,660
Terry Gale	64	68	73	74	279	11,110
Chen Tze Chung	71	75	68	68	282	6,260
Ken Kreiger	71	71	69	72	283	5,000
Chen Tze Ming	73	72	69	70	284	3,870
Robert Wrenn	74	69	71	70	284	3,870
Jaime Gonzalez	70	73	72	70	285	2,750
Ben Arda	68	73	72	72	285	2,750
Jim Blair	73	72	72	69	286	1,960
Ray Arinno	70	75	70	71	286	1,960
David Ogrin	73	72	69	72	286	1,960
Lin Chia	72	72	67	75	286	1,960
Lu Ho Tsai	74	73	73	67	287	1,490
Jeff Sluman	76	69	73	69	287	1,490
Rafael Alarcon	71	74	71	71	287	1,490
Hsu Chi San	72	72	72	71	287	1,490
Brian Jones	74	71	70	72	287	1,490
Lim Leng Ann	76	71	75	66	288	1,225
Curt Byrum	70	75	75	68	288	1,225
Lim Swee Wah	72	72	74	70	288	1,225
E. Bagtas	75	71	71	71	288	1,225
Mike Harwood	70	73	70	76	289	1,071.50

	SCORES				TOTAL	MONEY
Sukree Onsham	71	70	73	75	289	1,071.50
Stewart Ginn	71	73	71	74	289	1,071.50
Tadashige Kusano	71	72	75	71	289	1,071.50
Yoshihisa Kosaka	69	72	76	72	289	1,071.50
Ikuo Shirahama	73	68	74	74	289	1,071.50
Mya Aye	77	70	67	76	290	759
Daisuke Nakajima	75	70	70	75	290	759
Hajime Meshiai	72	73	71	74	290	759
Jeff Short	73	71	73	73	290	759
Fung Hee Kwan	70	72	75	73	290	759
Larry Collins	72	75	71	72	290	759
Kathamuthu Selaruas	72	75	71	72	290	759
Eleuterio Nival	69	75	76	70	290	759
Lu Hsi Chuen	74	71	76	69	290	759
Hung Wen Neng	71	73	76	70	290	759
Lim Swee Chew	69	75	75	71	290	759
Chang Toang Liang	68	78	74	70	290	759
Lim Kian Tiong	72	74	73	71	290	759
Tom Sieckmann	72	74	72	72	290	759
Tsao Chien Teng	69	75	73	73	290	759
Denny Hepler	71	69	75	75	290	759
*Frankie Minoza	73	75	71	71	290	
Lindsay Stephen	73	73	74	71	291	521.50
Kim Suk Bong	73	74	73	71	291	521.50
Robert Michael	77	70	72	72	291	521.50
Marimuthu Ramayah	73	73	73	72	291	521.50
Chang Chung Fa	72	70	75	74	291	521.50
Hsieh Min Nan	73	71	73	74	291	521.50
Norio Adachi	73	71	75	73	292	465
Somsak Srisa Nga	73	72	76	71	292	465

Indonesia Open

Jaya Ancol Golf Course, Jakarta
Par 36–35—71; 6,731 yards

April 1–4
purse, US$60,000

	SCORES				TOTAL	MONEY
Eleuterio Nival	69	72	71	69	281	US$9,996
Rodger Davis	72	72	69	69	282	5,211
Denny Hepler	71	69	71	71	282	5,211
Brian Jones	74	70	71	69	284	2,772
Ray Arinno	69	71	71	73	284	2,772
David Ogrin	73	75	70	67	285	1,588.80
Ray Stewart	71	71	75	68	285	1,588.80
Robert Wrenn	69	75	73	68	285	1,588.80
Jaime Gonzalez	74	69	73	69	285	1,588.80
Peter Fowler	73	71	71	70	285	1,588.80
Lu Hsi Chuen	73	71	73	69	286	998.40
Chen Tze Ming	72	73	72	69	286	998.40
Hsu Chi San	72	75	69	70	286	998.40
Robert Michael	73	72	71	70	286	998.40
Mya Aye	71	73	70	72	286	998.40
Chang Chung Fa	68	77	69	73	287	840
Jeff Sluman	70	73	71	74	288	798
Sukree Onsham	75	71	70	73	289	724.80
Lindsay Stephen	72	72	74	71	289	724.80
Hisao Inoue	71	75	71	72	289	724.80

	SCORES				TOTAL	MONEY
Chen Tze Chung	72	76	68	73	289	724.80
Liao Kuo Chih	70	73	72	74	289	724.80
Toshiaki Nakagawa	71	74	77	68	290	643.50
Danny Walters	73	75	71	71	290	643.50
George Serhan	71	72	74	73	290	643.50
John Fiedler	78	70	67	75	290	643.50
Mike Malaska	73	74	75	69	291	573
Ireneo Legaspi	74	76	72	69	291	573
Shen Chung Shyan	72	73	74	72	291	573
Randy Cavanaugh	72	73	73	73	291	573
Jeff Short	76	73	74	69	292	496.80
John Benda	71	77	75	69	292	496.80
Ben Arda	73	75	74	70	292	496.80
Paterno Braza	73	73	73	73	292	496.80
John Hamarik	71	71	75	75	292	496.80
Rafael Alarcon	71	76	75	71	293	420
Gemmy	75	73	73	72	293	420
Tsao Chien Teng	75	72	73	73	293	420
Jimmy Paschal	69	73	74	77	293	420
*Frankie Minoza	73	71	73	76	293	
Eugene Nava	70	74	73	78	295	378
Hung Wen Neng	69	77	78	72	296	357
Alex Bonnington	71	76	71	78	296	357
Jeff Jones	68	81	75	73	297	317
Lim Swee Chew	72	73	77	75	297	317
Poh Eing Chong	75	75	72	75	297	317
Chang Ming Tsung	73	72	75	77	297	317
Lee Booker	75	73	72	77	297	317
Archin Spoon	73	74	72	78	297	317
Mario Siodina	76	73	67	81	297	317

Republic of China Open

Taiwan Golf and Country Club, Tamsui
Par 36–36—72; 7,152 yards

April 8–11
purse, US$100,000

	SCORES				TOTAL	MONEY
Chen Tze Ming	69	72	75	73	289	US$20,000
Kuo Chi Hsiung	73	73	73	72	291	12,500
*Chien Shun Lu	72	72	75	72	291	
*Chung Jen Lai	71	76	71	74	292	
David Ogrin	71	79	71	74	295	4,375
Chen Chien Chung	71	78	70	76	295	4,375
Hsu Sheng San	71	75	71	78	295	4,375
Lu Liang Huan	69	74	74	78	295	4,375
*Wen Sheng Lee	74	76	72	73	295	
Hsieh Yung Yo	69	77	80	70	296	2,500
Lu Hsi Chuen	73	79	72	73	297	2,000
Denny Hepler	72	77	74	74	297	2,000
Shigeru Takeuchi	74	77	73	74	298	1,685
Jeff Sluman	74	76	73	75	298	1,685
Rafael Alarcon	72	77	71	78	298	1,685
Chen Tze Chung	66	74	78	80	298	1,685
*Frankie Minoza	74	74	78	72	298	
Shen Chung Shyan	73	77	71	78	299	1,500
*Chie Hsiang Lin	71	78	74	76	299	
Tsao Chien Teng	75	75	77	73	300	1,390

	SCORES				TOTAL	MONEY
Hsieh Min Nan	72	72	79	77	300	1,390
Hsu Chi San	71	77	75	78	301	1,275
Ray Arinno	76	74	72	79	301	1,275
Don Klenk	75	77	76	74	302	1,153.33
Lu Ho Tsai	72	80	75	75	302	1,153.33
Randy Cavanaugh	77	76	71	78	302	1,153.33
Priscillo Diniz	71	76	80	76	303	1,033.33
Rodger Davis	74	79	72	78	303	1,033.33
Robert Michael	71	79	74	79	303	1,033.33
Ray Stewart	74	78	77	75	304	891.66
Chen Chien Chi	77	75	75	77	304	891.66
Brad Sherfy	72	80	75	77	304	891.66
Chang Toang Liang	74	78	75	77	304	891.66
Hung Wen Neng	76	73	77	78	304	891.66
Lindsay Stephen	73	76	75	80	304	891.66
Tom Sieckmann	77	78	78	72	305	800
K.C. Lin	72	81	74	78	305	800
John McGough	73	73	78	81	305	800
Norio Adachi	78	77	79	72	306	724
Robert Wrenn	75	80	78	73	306	724
Lin Chia	76	77	78	75	306	724
Toru Nakayama	73	79	78	76	306	724
Tom Nosewicz	73	78	76	79	306	724
Kathamuthu Selaruas	74	81	80	72	307	612
Ikuo Shirahama	73	80	78	76	307	612
Toshiaki Nakagawa	72	78	80	77	307	612
Fong Chou Chen	73	76	79	79	307	612
Toru Iuchi	79	76	72	80	307	612
*Yun Shin Chen	76	79	73	79	307	
Mike Colandro	73	78	78	79	308	550
Daisuke Nakajima	73	78	77	80	308	550

Korea Maekyung Open

Seoul Country Club, Seoul
Par 36–36—72; 6,995 yards

April 15–18
purse, US$90,000

	SCORES				TOTAL	MONEY
*Kim Joo Heun	74	69	72	70	285	
Rafael Alarcon	71	71	74	72	288	US$15,000
Lu Hsi Chuen	69	73	73	74	289	10,000
Mike Cunning	75	73	71	71	290	5,050
Ikuo Shirahama	75	72	70	73	290	5,050
Hahn Chang Sang	72	75	76	69	292	3,800
Go Shiono	78	72	71	72	293	3,200
Hsu Sheng San	75	77	73	69	294	2,192.50
Denny Hepler	73	76	72	73	294	2,192.50
Chen Tze Ming	72	79	69	74	294	2,192.50
Yoshiyuki Isomura	69	73	74	78	294	2,192.50
Chen Tze Chung	74	75	74	72	295	1,535
Brad Sherfy	71	70	82	72	295	1,535
Hiroshi Yamada	72	72	78	73	295	1,535
Park Shi Hwan	75	74	74	72	295	1,535
Ray Stewart	75	77	72	72	296	1,216
Robert Michael	76	74	73	73	296	1,216
Tsao Chien Teng	75	74	72	75	296	1,216
Lim Jin Han	74	73	75	74	296	1,216

		SCORES			TOTAL	MONEY
Tom Sieckmann	67	76	76	77	296	1,216
Ray Arinno	77	75	76	69	297	1,065
Hisao Inoue	70	75	76	76	297	1,065
Scott Spence	76	77	74	71	298	1,030
Lee Kang Sun	78	72	76	73	299	976.66
Yasushi Taki	70	80	75	74	299	976.66
Vic Tortorici	75	74	74	76	299	976.66
Sandy Harper	75	74	80	81	300	887.50
Liao Kuo Chih	72	77	79	72	300	887.50
Osamu Watanabe	74	76	78	72	300	887.50
Chen Chien Chin	78	73	76	73	300	887.50
Choi Sang Ho	75	78	75	73	301	770
Cho Am Gil	76	74	77	74	301	770
Robert Wrenn	78	73	74	77	301	770
Tom Anton	75	75	74	77	301	770
Cho Tae Woon	75	76	73	77	301	770
T. Kubota	73	74	79	76	302	690
Makoto Goto	75	77	77	74	303	618
Choi Youn Soo	76	74	75	78	303	618
Yeom Sae Woon	76	73	75	79	303	618
Priscillo Diniz	75	72	76	80	303	618
*Jang Do Heun	75	78	78	72	303	
David Ogrin	79	73	76	76	304	540
George Serhan	74	77	79	75	305	507.50
Hsu Chi San	71	76	79	79	305	507.50
Takashi Funayama	73	74	78	80	305	507.50
Mike Malaska	78	74	71	82	305	507.50
Kim Hak Seh	75	78	81	72	306	443.33
E. Yabe	76	77	78	75	306	443.33
Kim Duk Joo	73	79	79	75	306	443.33
John Hamarik	74	78	76	78	306	443.33
Toshihiro Takata	70	81	76	79	306	443.33
Seh Jung Bok	78	73	74	81	306	443.33
*Kim Seung Ho	74	75	82	75	306	

Dunlop International Open

Ibaraki Golf Club, Tokyo
Par 36–36—72; 7,006 yards

April 22–25
purse, US$150,000

		SCORES			TOTAL	MONEY
Tsuneyuki Nakajima	71	66	68	71	276	US$25,000
Saburo Fujiki	74	71	66	70	281	16,500
Isao Aoki	72	70	72	68	282	7,075
Yashikazu Tokoshima	77	70	68	67	282	7,075
Graham Marsh	72	68	73	69	282	7,075
Liao Kuo Chih	70	73	68	71	282	7,075
Katsunari Takahashi	71	73	70	69	283	3,866.66
Hsu Sheng San	71	72	71	69	283	3,966.66
Satsuki Takahashi	71	72	68	72	283	3,866.66
Yutaka Hagawa	73	70	70	71	284	2,900
Hsieh Min Nan	68	72	72	72	284	2,900
Terry Gale	73	74	69	69	285	2,200
Denny Hepler	75	70	71	69	285	2,200
Craig Stadler	73	68	72	72	285	2,200
Fujio Kobayashi	70	73	70	72	285	2,200
Haruo Yasuda	70	73	70	72	285	2,200

	SCORES				TOTAL	MONEY
Greg Norman	69	70	73	73	285	2,200
Toshiharu Kawada	68	73	71	73	285	2,200
Naomichi Ozaki	73	69	70	73	285	2,200
Namio Takasu	69	75	68	73	285	2,200
Toru Nakamura	72	71	74	69	286	1,625
Yasunori Uehara	75	69	71	71	286	1,625
Pete Izumigawa	70	71	73	72	286	1,625
Ho Ming Chung	69	75	68	74	286	1,625
Kenji Mori	72	72	74	69	287	1,425
Chen Tze Ming	74	72	71	70	287	1,425
Tom Sieckmann	71	76	68	72	287	1,425
Ray Stewart	70	71	73	72	287	1,425
Eitaro Deguchi	72	72	73	71	288	1,200
Rodger Davis	72	73	72	71	288	1,200
Norihiko Matsumoto	71	73	71	73	288	1,200
Yasuhiro Funatogawa	76	69	70	73	288	1,200
Brian Jones	69	71	72	76	288	1,200
Kikuo Arai	77	68	72	72	289	1,020
Hajime Meshiai	71	72	74	72	289	1,020
Masahiro Kuramoto	74	71	68	76	289	1,020
Alex Bonnington	72	70	74	74	290	890
Lu Liang Huan	72	71	76	71	290	890
Teruo Sugihara	73	71	72	74	290	890
Hisao Inoue	73	72	72	73	290	890
Seiichi Kanai	70	73	71	76	290	890
Chen Tze Chung	74	68	71	77	290	890
Stewart Ginn	72	73	71	75	291	800
Yoshiyuki Isomura	72	71	74	74	291	800
*Tetsuo Handa	73	74	69	75	291	
*Chukei Kaneko	73	72	76	71	292	
Yurio Akitomi	72	73	72	75	292	760
Masayuki Imai	74	73	68	77	292	760
Shinsaku Maeda	76	70	74	73	293	680
Koichi Uehara	72	71	75	75	293	680
Masaru Amano	72	74	75	72	293	680
Osamu Watanabe	72	73	74	74	293	680
Shoichi Sato	73	71	74	75	293	680
Minoru Nakamura	69	76	73	75	293	680

Shizuoka Open

Shizuoka Country Club, Hamaoka Course
Par 36-36—72; 6,859 yards

March 18–21
purse, Y30,510,000

	SCORES				TOTAL	MONEY
Eitaro Deguchi	74	69	71	68	282	Y6,000,000
Nobumitsu Yuhara	67	70	76	71	284	3,000,000
Akira Yabe	72	72	71	70	285	1,333,333
Lu Liang Huan	69	71	74	71	285	1,333,333
Koichi Inoue	72	70	73	70	285	1,333,333
Toshikazu Torisawa	74	71	69	72	286	760,000
Akio Kanamoto	75	72	65	74	286	760,000
Yasuhiro Funatogawa	69	70	72	75	286	760,000
Teruo Sugihara	71	70	78	67	286	760,000
Takaaki Kono	70	69	72	75	286	760,000
Saburo Fujiki	74	71	74	68	287	585,000
Masahiro Kuramoto	73	67	74	73	287	585,000

	SCORES				TOTAL	MONEY
Tsuneyuki Nakajima	74	72	74	68	288	470,000
Yasushi Katayama	73	72	74	69	288	470,000
Haruo Yasuda	73	72	73	70	288	470,000
Yoshikazu Yokoshima	72	72	75	69	288	470,000
George Yokoi	74	73	77	64	288	470,000
Hsieh Yung Yo	74	69	74	71	288	470,000
Masahiko Yamamoto	71	74	74	70	289	385,00
Takashi Murakami	69	71	71	78	289	385,000
Yutaka Hagawa	69	75	71	75	290	365,000
Yasuhiro Miyamoto	70	72	78	70	290	365,000
Takahiro Takeyasu	70	77	71	73	291	330,000
Minoru Nakamura	75	72	75	69	291	330,000
Norio Mikami	72	76	72	71	291	330,000
Shigeru Noguchi	72	72	77	70	291	330,000
Katsuji Hasegawa	75	71	75	70	291	330,000
Toru Nakamura	77	71	74	70	292	290,000
Hisashi Suzumura	75	73	75	69	292	290,000
Masashi Ozaki	75	73	72	72	292	290,000
Pete Izumikawa	75	73	71	74	293	270,000
Chen Chien Chung	76	68	72	77	293	270,000
Motomasa Aoki	71	72	77	73	293	270,000
Naomichi Ozaki	77	71	72	73	293	270,000
Kenji Sogame	70	73	74	77	294	254,000
Joji Furuki	76	70	73	75	294	254,000
Shoji Kikuchi	75	70	73	76	294	254,000
Kazuo Yoshikawa	73	74	73	74	294	254,000
Tomishige Ikeda	71	74	74	75	294	254,000
Takeshi Shiono	75	70	75	75	295	227,500
Masayuki Imai	71	73	78	73	295	227,500
Kazushige Kono	80	68	76	71	295	227,500
Shigeo Kanaumi	73	75	76	71	295	227,500
Norio Suzuki	72	72	77	75	296	210,000
Koichi Uehara	74	72	77	73	296	210,000
Yoshiharu Takai	74	70	79	73	296	210,000
Keiichi Kobayashi	74	71	76	75	296	210,000
Takashi Kurihara	72	72	80	73	297	200,000
Toshiharu Kawada	75	71	81	72	299	200,000
Toyotake Nakao	73	74	77	75	299	200,000
Yoshihiko Kudoh	73	75	77	74	299	200,000

Kagawa Open

Shido Country Club
Par 71; 6,445 yards

March 27–28
purse, Y10,000,000

	SCORES		TOTAL	MONEY
Shigeru Uchida	68	71	139	Y2,000,000
Kikuo Arai	71	69	140	1,000,000
Satsuki Takahashi	71	70	141	700,000
Norio Mikami	73	69	142	550,000
Pete Izumikawa	74	69	143	350,000
Toshimitsu Kai	73	70	143	350,000
Masahiro Kuramoto	72	71	143	350,000
Chen Chien Chin	72	71	143	350,000
Akio Teramoto	69	74	143	350,000
Masami Nishiyama	74	70	144	160,000
Yasuhiro Daio	73	71	144	160,000

	SCORES		TOTAL	MONEY
Suichi Sano	72	72	144	160,000
Kazuki Nagao	71	73	144	160,000
Hiroshi Ishii	70	74	144	160,000
Katsunari Takahashi	74	71	145	135,000
Futoshi Irino	74	71	145	135,000
Osami Matsuoka	75	71	146	115,000
Tatsuo Fujima	75	71	146	115,000
Yoshitaka Yamamoto	74	72	146	115,000
Shinsaku Maeda	74	72	146	115,000
Kazuo Yoshikawa	73	73	146	115,000
Toru Nakamura	73	73	146	115,000
Atsuo Suemura	73	73	146	115,000
Ichiro Teramoto	72	74	146	115,000
*Kozo Matsuura	77	70	147	
Eizo Matsuoka	75	72	147	102,500
Hiroshi Tahara	74	73	147	102,500
Tadami Ueno	73	74	147	102,500
Yukimasa Nakamura	72	75	147	102,500
Yasushi Taki	74	74	148	96,700
Minoru Kawakami	73	75	148	96,700
Katsumi Hara	72	76	148	96,700
Norio Suzuki	75	74	149	90,000
Michiyuki Kawanami	74	75	149	90,000
Kosaku Shimada	73	76	149	90,000
Shimon Takamatsu	75	75	150	83,000
*Fumio Hamanishi	73	77	150	
Shiro Matsuda	73	77	150	83,000
Takashi Miyoshi	72	78	150	83,000
*Haruyoshi Takemoto	76	75	151	
Junichi Takahashi	75	76	151	80,000
Seiji Katayama	74	77	151	80,000
*Mamoru Kusumoto	74	77	151	
*Seiichi Inoue	74	77	151	
Hideto Shigenobu	75	77	152	73,300
Hiroshi Makino	75	77	152	73,300
Yosuke Tadakuma	75	77	152	73,300
Masao Kaneya	75	78	153	67,500
Kenji Sogame	74	79	153	67,500
Tsunenori Tanaka	73	80	153	67,500
Koichi Nishimura	70	83	153	67,500

Kuzuha Kokusai

Kuzuha Public Golf Course, Osaka
Par 70; 6,238 yards

April 3–4
purse, Y15,000,000

	SCORES		TOTAL	MONEY
Namio Takasu	35	67	102	Y3,000,000
Yoshikazu Yokoshima	38	65	103	1,500,000
Yasuhiro Funatogawa	37	67	104	900,000
Minoru Nakamura	39	66	105	600,000
Toyotake Nakao	38	68	106	343,334
Koichi Inoue	38	68	106	343,334
Tsuneyuki Nakajima	36	70	106	343,333
Toru Nakamura	36	70	106	343,333
Tadami Ueno	36	70	106	343,333
Teruo Sugihara	34	72	106	343,333

	SCORES			TOTAL	MONEY
Saburo Fujiki	36	71		107	250,000
Naomichi Ozaki	36	71		107	250,000
Yoshitaka Yamamoto	35	72		107	250,000
Hideto Shigenobu	35	72		107	250,000
Toshiharu Kawada	34	73		107	250,000
Chen Chien Chung	40	68		108	201,200
Hideyo Sugimoto	38	70		108	201,200
Ichiro Teramoto	38	70		108	201,200
Akio Kanamoto	36	72		108	201,200
Nobumitsu Yuhara	35	73		108	201,200
Akira Yabe	40	69		109	165,572
Kazuo Yoshikawa	40	69		109	165,572
Kikuo Arai	39	70		109	165,572
Tadashi Kitta	37	72		109	165,571
Lu Liang Huan	36	73		109	165,571
Fujio Kobayashi	36	73		109	165,571
Kenji Mori	35	74		109	165,571
Takaaki Kono	42	68		110	142,313
Masaji Kusakabe	39	71		110	142,313
Shigeru Uchida	38	72		110	142,313
Sadao Sakashita	38	72		110	142,313
Masashi Ozaki	37	73		110	142,312
Hsieh Yung Yo	37	73		110	142,312
Yurio Akitomi	36	74		110	142,312
Norio Suzuki	36	74		110	142,312
Tsutomu Irie	42	69		111	133,000
Katsuji Hasegawa	36	75		111	133,000
Akimitsu Tokita	36	75		111	133,000
Seiichi Kanai	40	72		112	127,072
Shinsaku Maeda	40	72		112	127,072
Shozo Miyamoto	40	72		112	127,072
Takahiro Takeyasu	40	72		112	127,071
Yasuhiro Miyamoto	39	73		112	127,071
Hisashi Suzumura	37	75		112	127,071
Toshimitsu Kai	37	75		112	127,071
Hahn Chang Sang	40	73		113	123,000
Satsuki Takahashi	40	73		113	123,000
Tomishige Ikeda	39	74		113	123,000
Haruo Yasuda	38	75		113	123,000
Katsunari Takahashi	38	75		113	123,000

Hakuryuko Open

Hakuryuko Country Club　　　　　　　　　　　　　　　April 8–11
Par 72; 6,824 yards　　　　　　　　　　　　　purse, Y15,000,000

	SCORES				TOTAL	MONEY
Toshimitsu Kai	73	66	74	70	283	Y3,000,000
Tsuneyuki Nakajima	73	71	74	69	287	1,600,000
Masahiro Kuramoto	68	76	72	72	288	1,200,000
Kikuo Arai	75	72	75	68	290	800,000
Toru Nakamura	73	72	72	73	290	800,000
Saburo Fujiki	72	75	74	70	291	466,666
Naomichi Ozaki	75	72	73	71	291	466,666
Hajime Meshiai	75	71	74	71	291	466,666
Takashi Kurihara	71	79	73	69	292	264,285
Eitaro Deguchi	71	76	74	71	292	264,285

	SCORES				TOTAL	MONEY
Yoshiharu Takai	72	73	75	72	292	264,285
Yoshio Fumiyama	67	75	77	73	292	264,285
Satsuki Takahashi	72	70	76	74	292	264,285
Shinichi Hayashi	73	72	74	73	292	264,285
Shigeru Uchida	70	73	76	73	292	264,285
Motomasa Aoki	74	75	73	71	293	180,000
Masaru Amano	75	70	73	75	293	180,000
Shinsaku Maeda	73	72	73	75	293	180,000
Yasuhiro Miyamoto	74	75	75	70	294	155,000
Takumi Horiuchi	71	71	78	74	294	155,000
Kazuo Kanayama	75	74	76	70	295	140,000
Yurio Akitomi	71	75	76	73	295	140,000
Norio Mikami	70	76	76	73	295	140,000
Tadami Ueno	73	77	75	71	296	135,000
Hidenori Nakajima	72	76	76	72	296	135,000
Mitoshi Tomita	74	70	79	73	296	135,000
Suichi Sano	72	76	75	73	296	135,000
Norihiko Matsumoto	75	74	77	71	297	130,000
Keiichi Kobayashi	70	74	79	74	297	130,000
Takaaki Kono	72	76	77	73	298	122,000
Koji Nakajima	71	77	75	75	298	122,000
Yozo Okabe	68	78	81	71	298	122,000
Kenji Sogame	73	77	72	76	298	122,000
Mamoru Takahashi	77	72	73	76	298	122,000
Nobumitsu Yuhara	72	75	78	74	299	112,500
Osami Kitano	74	72	78	75	299	112,500
Michiyasu Okunobu	70	76	77	76	299	112,500
Seiichi Kanai	74	76	78	71	299	112,500
Hideto Shigenobu	72	78	78	71	299	112,500
Tomishige Ikeda	73	75	79	73	300	102,500
Yoichi Yamamoto	71	74	79	76	300	102,500
Takashi Miyoshi	72	76	76	76	300	102,500
Mahito Ito	77	70	80	73	300	102,500
George Yokoi	69	74	83	75	301	100,000
Yoshihiko Kudo	70	77	80	74	301	100,000
Toshikazu Torisawa	70	77	78	76	301	100,000
Shoji Kikuchi	71	76	80	74	301	100,000
Mitsuhiko Masuda	71	78	77	76	302	100,000
Hideo Ishii	73	76	78	75	302	100,000
Koichi Uehara	76	73	76	77	302	100,000
Yasushi Taki	75	75	79	73	302	100,000
Joji Furuki	70	76	83	73	302	100,000
Sadao Sakashita	71	77	81	73	302	100,000
Namio Takasu	73	77	78	74	302	100,000

Bridgestone Aso Open

Aso Golf Club, Kunamoto   April 15–18
Par 72; 7,020 yards   purse, Y30,000,000

	SCORES				TOTAL	MONEY
Toru Nakamura	74	72	68	69	283	Y5,000,000
Shigeru Uchida	69	72	73	72	286	2,500,000
Tsuneyuki Nakajima	72	75	71	69	287	1,800,000
Seiichi Kanai	72	72	70	74	288	1,200,000
Isamu Sugita	70	75	74	70	289	900,000
Kikuo Arai	71	71	75	74	291	785,000

	SCORES				TOTAL	MONEY
Motomasa Aoki	69	76	77	69	291	785,000
Saburo Fujiki	74	70	77	71	292	700,000
Tsutomu Irie	70	75	74	74	293	670,000
Sadao Sakashita	76	74	75	69	294	615,000
Yasuhiro Miyamoto	72	75	74	73	294	615,000
Hidenori Nakajima	75	73	77	70	295	508,000
Noboru Sugai	70	79	76	70	295	508,000
Fumio Tanaka	71	75	76	73	295	508,000
Eitaro Deguchi	73	71	78	73	295	508,000
Masahiro Kuramoto	72	75	74	74	295	508,000
Kenji Mori	72	77	71	76	296	415,000
Shozo Miyamoto	74	71	78	73	296	415,000
Takashi Murakami	70	79	73	75	297	370,000
Namio Takasu	78	70	75	74	297	370,000
Shinsaku Maeda	75	74	75	73	297	370,000
Haruo Yasuda	76	73	72	76	297	370,000
Rodger Davis	74	75	70	79	298	325,000
Toyotake Nakao	73	76	75	74	298	325,000
Kazushige Kono	70	75	79	74	298	325,000
Takaaki Kono	72	74	79	73	298	325,000
Takahiro Takeyasu	70	76	77	76	299	260,000
Satsuki Takahashi	73	75	76	75	299	260,000
Isao Isozaki	72	75	78	74	299	260,000
Masahiko Yamamoto	76	73	77	73	299	260,000
Yoshikazu Yokoshima	74	75	78	72	299	260,000
Joji Furuki	75	75	80	69	299	260,000
Teruo Suzumura	74	75	73	78	300	160,000
Reiji Bando	74	72	77	77	300	160,000
Motomasa Nishikawa	71	76	79	74	300	160,000
Takashi Kurihara	76	73	78	73	300	160,000
Fujio Kobayashi	73	77	80	70	300	160,000
Yoshio Fumiyama	71	79	74	77	301	108,570
Pete Izumikawa	76	74	80	71	301	108,570
Tadashige Kusano	75	75	76	75	301	108,570
Kuniharu Nakagawa	73	74	78	76	301	108,570
Hiroshi Ishii	75	72	83	71	301	108,570
Hiroshi Makino	75	73	78	75	301	108,570
Norifumi Mizuno	75	75	77	74	301	108,570
Minoru Nakamura	73	74	81	76	304	100,000
*Shigemi Nakazono	75	72	76	82	305	
Kenji Ueda	73	74	80	78	305	100,000
Shoji Kikuchi	73	75	81	76	305	100,000
Kazuo Yoshikawa	74	76	80	75	305	100,000
*Masaki Yamashita	77	75	79	74	305	

Chunichi Crowns

Nagoya Golf Club, Nagoya
Par 70; 6,492 yards

April 29–May 2
purse, Y70,000,000

	SCORES				TOTAL	MONEY
Gary Hallberg	69	67	66	70	272	Y14,000,000
Shigeru Uchida	70	69	68	68	275	7,500,000
Tsuneyuki Nakajima	69	72	70	65	276	4,300,000
Peter Jacobsen	72	73	67	68	280	3,000,000
Lu Hsi Chuen	74	66	72	69	281	2,233,334
Sadao Sakashita	72	70	68	71	281	2,233,334

	SCORES				TOTAL	MONEY
Saburo Fujiki	71	73	66	71	281	2,233,334
Isao Aoki	72	71	69	70	282	1,800,000
Naomichi Ozaki	70	71	72	70	283	1,566,667
Shinsaku Maeda	72	72	68	71	283	1,566,667
Johnny Miller	69	74	67	73	283	1,566,667
Yutaka Hagawa	72	68	75	69	284	1,216,667
Koichi Inoue	68	71	74	71	284	1,216,667
Tadashi Kitta	73	71	68	72	284	1,216,667
Yurio Akitomi	73	67	74	71	285	987,500
Akira Yabe	71	72	71	71	285	987,500
Eitaro Deguchi	73	69	72	71	285	987,500
Fujio Kobayashi	71	71	71	72	285	987,500
Takashi Murakami	73	70	74	69	286	800,000
Toshimitsu Kai	72	69	71	74	286	800,000
Katsuji Hasegawa	74	71	68	73	286	800,000
Hsieh Min Nan	75	70	73	69	287	680,000
Kenichi Yamada	70	74	72	71	287	680,000
Kenji Mori	71	70	74	72	287	680,000
Hideto Shigenobu	71	75	70	71	287	680,000
Nobumitsu Yuhara	75	68	72	72	287	680,000
Greg Norman	70	75	67	75	287	680,000
Craig Stadler	72	74	76	66	288	572,000
Masamitsu Oguri	75	72	72	69	288	572,000
Takeru Shibata	75	70	74	69	288	572,000
*Kazuhiko Kato	73	70	72	73	288	
Toru Nakamura	70	70	74	74	288	572,000
Satsuki Takahashi	73	74	72	70	289	505,000
Masahiko Yamamoto	74	70	73	72	289	505,000
Seiichi Kanai	76	70	71	72	289	505,000
Toshihiro Matsuda	72	74	71	72	289	505,000
Joji Furuki	70	72	73	74	289	505,000
Lu Liang Huan	72	73	70	74	289	505,000
Masami Ito	76	67	74	73	290	460,000
Denny Hepler	75	70	72	73	290	460,000
Namio Takasu	68	70	72	80	290	460,000
Kikuo Arai	76	71	73	71	291	425,000
Katsunari Takahashi	70	74	73	74	291	425,000
Terry Gale	75	69	72	75	291	425,000
Minoru Nakamura	74	69	72	76	291	425,000
Seiji Mitsuki	69	76	76	71	292	385,000
Kuo Chi Hsiung	72	75	74	71	292	385,000
Kurt Cox	76	71	72	73	292	385,000
Choi Sang Ho	74	71	73	74	292	385,000
Masaji Kusakabe	77	70	74	73	294	350,000
Graham Marsh	71	75	75	73	294	350,000
Toshiki Matsui	75	72	71	76	294	350,000

Fuji Sankei Classic

Kawana Hotel, Fuji Course, Ito
Par 71; 6,694 yards

May 6–9
purse, Y40,000,000

	SCORES				TOTAL	MONEY
Tsuneyuki Nakajima	67	73	66	71	277	Y7,000,000
Graham Marsh	70	69	69	69	277	4,000,000
(Nakajima defeated Marsh on first hole of sudden-death playoff.)						
Saburo Fujiki	68	73	68	69	278	2,500,000

	SCORES			TOTAL	MONEY
Isao Aoki	68	72	72	69	281	1,800,000
Kenji Mori	71	71	70	70	282	1,450,000
Toshiharu Kawada	69	70	70	73	282	1,450,000
Kikuo Arai	71	73	69	70	283	1,066,667
Eitaro Deguchi	72	67	71	73	283	1,066,667
Toru Nakamura	69	71	68	75	283	1,066,667
Masashi Ozaki	72	71	73	69	285	737,500
Seiichi Kanai	68	73	73	71	285	737,500
Kazushige Kono	71	72	68	74	285	737,500
Chen Tze Ming	74	69	69	73	285	737,500
Shinsaku Maeda	71	71	71	73	286	575,000
Naomichi Ozaki	71	71	71	73	286	575,000
Katsuji Kikuchi	71	73	70	73	287	500,000
Lu Hsi Chuen	67	79	68	73	287	500,000
Mark O'Meara	74	71	65	77	287	500,000
Mararu Amano	70	67	72	78	287	500,000
Teruo Sugihara	72	70	74	72	288	430,000
Hsieh Min Nan	74	69	72	73	288	430,000
Taiichi Nakagawa	70	74	71	73	288	430,000
Tadashi Kitta	71	71	71	75	288	430,000
Pete Izumikawa	70	70	72	76	288	430,000
Koichi Uehara	74	73	72	70	289	385,000
Haruo Yasuda	72	71	74	72	289	385,000
Yurio Akitomi	70	73	74	72	289	385,000
Satsuki Takahashi	75	69	70	75	289	385,000
Yoshitaka Yamamoto	75	72	72	71	290	345,000
Tsutomu Irie	73	70	73	74	290	345,000
Ikuo Shirahama	70	72	74	74	290	345,000
John Cook	73	71	71	75	290	345,000
Hiroshi Ishii	69	77	75	70	291	280,555
Chen Chien Chung	72	73	73	73	291	280,555
Mya Aye	73	74	71	73	291	280,555
Masaji Kusakabe	72	73	72	74	291	280,555
Noboru Sugai	72	74	70	75	291	280,555
Takaaki Kono	70	74	72	75	291	280,555
Yasushi Taki	70	71	74	76	291	280,555
Katsunari Takahashi	72	72	71	76	291	280,555
Namio Takasu	76	70	69	76	291	280,555
Kazuo Yoshikawa	71	75	74	72	292	232,500
Masahiko Yamamoto	74	73	72	73	292	232,500
Sadao Sakashita	74	72	72	74	292	232,500
Seiji Ebihara	70	72	73	77	292	232,500
Akio Kanamoto	73	74	73	73	293	215,000
Toshiki Matsui	69	72	78	74	293	215,000
Yoshihisa Iwashita	73	70	72	78	293	215,000
Terry Gale	69	74	78	73	294	200,000
*Minoru Azuma	72	75	75	72	294	
Akimitsu Tokita	72	74	74	74	294	200,000
Hiroshi Tahara	73	73	73	75	294	200,000

Japan Match Play Championship

Totsuka Country Club, West Course, Yokohama
Par 72; 7,046 yards

May 13–16
purse, Y32,000,000

FIRST ROUND
Isao Aoki defeated Seiichi Kanai, 2 and 1.

Saburo Fujiki defeated Yoshikazu Yokoshima, 5 and 3.
Nobumitsu Yuhara defeated Satsuki Takahashi, 1 up.
Yoshitaka Yamamoto defeated Kosaku Shimada, 1 up.
Masaji Kusakabe defeated Tsuneyuki Nakajima, 2 and 1.
Hsieh Min Nan defeated Yasuhiro Funatogawa, 1 up, 20 holes.
Norio Suzuki defeated Fujio Kobayashi, 1 up.
Yasuhiro Miyamoto defeated Katsuji Hasegawa, 4 and 3.
Masahiro Kuramoto defeated Shigeru Uchida, 3 and 2.
Koichi Uehara defeated Akira Yabe, 1 up, 19 holes.
Kikuo Arai defeated Naomichi Ozaki, 3 and 2.
Takaaki Kono defeated Toshiharu Kawada, 6 and 5.
Toru Nakamura defeated Ako Kanamoto, 3 and 2.
Namio Takasu defeated Hideto Shigenobu, 1 up, 20 holes.
Yutaka Hagawa defeated Haruo Yasuda, 1 up, 19 holes.
Teruo Sugihara defeated Masaru Amano, 2 and 1.
  (All losers in first round received Y150,000.)

SECOND ROUND
Aoki defeated Fujiki, 5 and 4.
Yuhara defeated Yamamoto, 1 up, 20 holes.
Hsieh defeated Kusakabe, 4 and 2.
Miyamoto defeated Suzuki, 5 and 4.
Uehara defeated Kuramoto, 1 up.
Kono defeated Arai, 2 and 1.
Nakamura defeated Takasu, 1 up.
Hagawa defeated Sugihara, 2 and 1.
  (All losers received Y300,000.)

QUARTER-FINALS
Aoki defeated Yuhara, 3 and 2.
Hsieh defeated Miyamoto, 1 up.
Hagawa defeated Nakamura, 3 and 2.
Kono defeated Uehara, 4 and 3.

SEMI-FINALS
Aoki defeated Hsieh, 3 and 2.
Hagawa defeated Kono, 2 and 1.

FINAL
Aoki defeated Hagawa, 4 and 2.

CONSOLATION FOR THIRD PLACE
Hsieh defeated Kono, 1 up.

CONSOLATION FOR FIFTH PLACE
Nakamura defeated Yuhara, 3 and 2.

CONSOLATION FOR SEVENTH PLACE
Miyamoto defeated Uehara, 2 and 1.

  (Aoki won Y7,000,000, Hagawa Y3,500,000, Hsieh Y2,200,000, Kono Y1,700,000, Nakamura Y1,200,000, Yuhara Y1,000,000, Miyamoto Y800,000, Uehara Y600,000.)

Pepsi Ube

Ube Country Club, Yamaguchi
Par 72; 6,849 yards

May 20–23
purse, Y30,000,000

	SCORES				TOTAL	MONEY
Kikuo Arai	67	68	70	72	277	Y6,000,000
Motomasa Aoki	75	64	68	72	279	3,000,000
Isao Aoki	69	70	70	71	280	1,333,400
Yasuhiro Funatogawa	72	70	69	69	280	1,333,400
Graham Marsh	70	69	69	72	280	1,333,400
Yutaka Hagawa	72	71	70	68	281	870,000
Saburo Fujiki	71	73	71	67	282	706,700
Fujio Kobayashi	71	69	72	70	282	706,700
Hsieh Min Nan	71	71	65	75	282	706,700
Toru Nakamura	74	68	72	69	283	580,000
Koichi Inoue	75	68	66	74	283	580,000
Chen Tze Ming	69	71	69	74	283	580,000
Yasuhiro Miyamoto	69	72	71	72	284	510,000
Shinsaku Maeda	68	70	71	75	284	510,000
Akira Yabe	68	76	70	71	285	450,000
Toshiyuki Tsuchiyama	70	73	70	72	285	450,000
Namio Takasu	72	69	72	72	285	450,000
Masahiro Kuramoto	73	68	71	73	285	450,000
Akio Kanamoto	75	69	74	68	286	381,700
Tadami Ueno	71	73	73	69	286	381,700
Kuniharu Nakagawara	75	68	72	71	286	381,700
Akio Toyoda	72	71	73	71	287	309,300
Seiichi Kanai	71	72	73	71	287	309,300
Yoshihisa Iwashita	72	72	72	71	287	309,300
Yoshiharu Takai	72	73	71	71	287	309,300
Yoshikazu Yokoshima	69	75	71	72	287	309,300
Katsuji Hasegawa	70	67	75	75	287	309,300
Hiroshi Ishii	71	68	72	76	287	309,300
Tateo Ozaki	68	76	73	71	288	255,000
Koichi Uehara	72	73	71	72	288	255,000
Kazushige Kono	70	70	73	75	288	255,000
Seiji Ebihara	72	74	73	70	289	220,000
Naomichi Ozaki	72	72	73	72	289	220,000
Hideto Shigenobu	74	72	71	72	289	220,000
Katsunari Takahashi	69	75	71	74	289	220,000
Toshimitsu Kai	72	73	71	74	290	200,000
Takashi Miyoshi	74	71	74	72	291	187,500
Norio Mikami	73	70	74	74	291	187,500
Nobumitsu Yuhara	70	73	72	76	291	187,500
Minoru Kawakami	72	68	74	77	291	187,500
Takashi Murakami	70	75	74	73	292	165,000
Kenji Ueda	76	69	73	74	292	165,000
Yozo Okabe	69	75	72	76	292	165,000
Toshiharu Kawada	69	77	70	76	292	165,000
Tsutomu Irie	70	71	73	78	292	165,000
Masashi Ozaki	70	72	81	70	293	150,000
Lu Hsi Chuen	74	72	76	71	293	150,000
Lu Liang Huan	73	70	78	72	293	150,000
Seiji Katayama	73	72	74	74	293	150,000
Tadao Nakamura	66	75	77	76	294	142,000
Chen Tze Chung	68	72	77	77	294	142,000
Shigeru Uchida	74	72	71	77	294	142,000
Kazuo Kanayama	75	70	78	71	294	142,000

Mitsubishi Galant

Kume Country Club, Okayama
Par 71; 6,679 yards

May 27–30
purse, Y40,000,000

	SCORES				TOTAL	MONEY
Graham Marsh	66	69	69	67	271	Y7,000,000
Teruo Sugihara	68	68	67	68	271	3,500,000
(Marsh defeated Sugihara on first hole of sudden-death playoff.)						
Tsuneyuki Nakajima	70	70	63	69	272	2,300,000
Saburo Fujiki	66	65	73	70	274	1,600,000
Isao Aoki	66	73	65	72	276	1,250,000
Hsieh Min Nan	66	75	67	69	277	1,050,000
Kakaaki Kono	67	71	65	74	277	1,050,000
Naomichi Ozaki	71	72	64	71	278	945,000
Toru Nakamura	69	71	68	71	279	900,000
Michiyuki Kawanami	70	70	72	69	281	825,000
Toshimitsu Kai	72	69	69	71	281	825,000
Toyotake Nakao	68	74	72	68	282	725,000
Masaji Kusakabe	67	74	70	71	282	725,000
Masahiko Yamamoto	69	70	77	67	283	602,500
Katsunari Takahashi	70	71	72	70	283	602,500
Lu Hsi Chuen	69	73	69	72	283	602,500
Fujio Kobayashi	69	68	67	79	283	602,500
Hideto Shigenobu	66	75	74	69	284	520,000
Akio Kanamoto	65	74	72	73	284	520,000
Seiichi Kanai	69	70	71	74	284	520,000
Satsuki Takahashi	71	72	74	68	285	470,000
Yoshiyuki Isomura	68	72	75	70	285	470,000
Norihiko Matsumoto	71	69	72	73	285	470,000
Hubert Green	70	72	74	70	286	430,000
Kikuo Arai	71	68	74	73	286	430,000
Hideo Ishii	70	70	74	72	286	430,000
Hiroshi Tahara	68	71	73	74	286	430,000
Toshiharu Kawada	67	68	74	77	286	430,000
Noboru Sugai	71	72	70	74	287	395,000
Chen Tze Chung	68	75	69	75	287	395,000
Tateo Ozaki	67	73	78	70	288	365,000
Koichi Uehara	73	69	74	72	288	365,000
Ben Arda	68	69	75	76	288	365,000
Ikuo Shirahama	66	75	69	78	288	365,000
Hiromi Sugitani	71	73	74	71	289	340,000
Brian Jones	69	72	76	73	290	315,000
Takashi Kubota	70	69	76	75	290	315,000
Masami Nishiyama	64	75	71	80	290	315,000
Yasuhiro Miyamoto	69	71	69	81	290	315,000
Shigeru Uchida	73	70	73	75	291	276,250
Pete Izumikawa	72	72	71	76	291	276,250
Yoshitaka Yamamoto	71	70	72	78	291	276,250
Shinsaku Maeda	65	70	77	79	291	276,250
Hajime Meshiai	74	70	76	72	292	255,000
Yoshihisa Iwashita	72	72	75	73	292	255,000
Motomasa Aoki	69	73	74	76	292	255,000
Mitsuhiko Masuda	71	73	78	71	293	230,000
Sukree Onsham	72	72	76	73	293	230,000
Tsutomu Irie	71	73	74	75	293	230,000
Koichi Inoue	70	71	76	76	293	230,000
Toru Kurihara	71	70	75	77	293	230,000
Masami Aihara	74	70	72	77	293	230,000

	SCORES			TOTAL	MONEY
Katsuji Hasegawa	73	70	73	77	293	230,000
Atsuo Suemura	70	71	72	80	293	230,000

Tohoku Classic

Nishi Sendai Country Club, Miyagi
Par 72; 6,993 yards
(First round rained out; tournament shortened to 54 holes.)

June 4–6
purse, Y30,000,000

	SCORES			TOTAL	MONEY
Shinsaku Maeda	72	70	66	208	Y6,000,000
Tsuneyuki Nakajima	72	70	70	210	1,875,000
Saburo Fujiki	69	71	70	210	1,875,000
Graham Marsh	72	67	71	210	1,875,000
Toshiyuki Tsuchiyama	70	69	71	210	1,875,000
Toru Nakamura	72	69	70	211	900,000
Hiroshi Ishii	72	74	67	213	775,000
Toyotake Nakao	70	70	73	213	775,000
Fujio Kobayashi	70	76	68	214	675,000
Pete Izumikawa	71	72	71	214	675,000
Lu Liang Huan	72	69	74	215	575,000
Akira Yabe	71	71	73	215	575,000
Katsuji Hasegawa	71	72	73	216	432,500
Chen Tze Chung	75	68	73	216	432,500
Eitaro Deguchi	72	71	73	216	432,500
Kikuo Arai	70	70	76	216	432,500
Teruo Sugihara	71	74	72	217	308,571
Teruo Suzumura	70	75	72	217	308,571
Takaaki Kono	72	73	72	217	308,571
Hsieh Yung Yo	73	72	72	217	308,571
Shigeru Uchida	72	72	73	217	308,571
Hiroshi Makino	70	72	75	217	308,571
Norio Suzuki	71	68	78	217	308,571
Masaru Amano	73	72	73	218	255,000
Yoshimi Watanabe	75	73	70	218	255,000
Masahiro Kuramoto	72	75	72	219	208,750
Takashi Murakami	69	77	73	219	208,750
Naomichi Ozaki	70	79	70	219	208,750
Tsutomu Irie	72	73	74	219	208,750
Katsunari Takahashi	73	72	74	219	208,750
Chen Tze Ming	75	73	71	219	208,750
Yurio Akitomi	74	70	75	219	208,750
Akio Kanamoto	72	68	79	219	208,750
Seiichi Kanai	73	75	72	220	190,000
Satsuki Takahashi	73	73	74	220	190,000
Isao Matsui	75	73	73	221	178,333
Akio Toyoda	73	75	73	221	178,333
Hisashi Suzumura	74	72	75	221	178,333
Mitsuo Hirukawa	73	73	75	221	178,333
Toshimitsu Kai	75	74	72	221	178,333
Taiichi Nakagawa	74	71	76	221	178,333
Hsieh Min Nan	74	73	75	222	170,000
Yasushi Taki	71	77	74	222	170,000
Yoshitaka Yamamoto	72	72	78	222	170,000
Masahiko Yamamoto	73	75	75	223	165,000
Lu Hsi Chuen	75	70	78	223	165,000
Toshiharu Kawada	72	74	78	224	160,000

	SCORES			TOTAL	MONEY
Kenji Ueda	74	75	75	224	160,000
Taisei Inagaki	75	74	75	224	160,000
Masashi Ozaki	75	73	76	224	160,000

Sapporo Tokyu Open

Sapporo International Country Club, Shimamatsu Course, Hokkaido June 10–13
Par 72; 6,949 yards   purse, Y30,000,000

	SCORES			TOTAL	MONEY
Yasuhiro Funatogawa	68	69	67	72	276	Y6,000,000
*Kazuhiko Kato	72	71	71	69	283	
Naomichi Ozaki	70	71	72	72	285	3,100,000
Hsieh Yung Yo	74	72	70	70	286	1,180,000
Isao Aoki	72	71	72	71	286	1,180,000
Koichi Uehara	73	69	72	72	286	1,180,000
Toru Nakamura	67	72	74	73	286	1,180,000
Tsuneyuki Nakajima	70	67	72	77	286	1,180,000
Terry Gale	72	68	74	73	287	700,000
Shinsaku Maeda	70	70	73	74	287	700,000
Tadami Ueno	73	69	68	77	287	700,000
Shoji Kikuchi	72	70	75	71	288	467,500
Mitsuhiro Kitta	72	72	72	72	288	467,500
Suichi Sano	76	71	72	69	288	467,500
Chen Tze Ming	71	68	73	76	288	467,500
Seiji Ebihara	69	72	76	72	289	360,000
*Tetsuo Sakata	71	71	73	74	289	
Yoshitaka Yamamoto	73	71	70	75	289	360,000
Takaaki Kono	75	70	72	72	289	360,000
Akio Toyoda	72	73	71	74	290	325,000
Seiichi Kanai	72	73	73	72	290	325,000
Mitoshi Tomita	71	74	72	73	290	325,000
Eitaro Deguchi	71	75	67	77	290	325,000
Nobumitsu Yuhara	73	72	74	72	291	276,666
Hisataka Fujii	73	72	74	72	291	276,666
Michiyuki Kawanami	73	71	75	72	291	276,666
Norio Suzuki	72	72	70	77	291	276,666
Tsutomu Irie	76	71	71	73	291	276,666
Teruo Sugihara	71	73	69	78	291	276,666
Wataru Murakami	72	70	75	75	292	242,500
Chen Tze Chung	73	73	75	71	292	242,500
Katsunari Takahashi	75	71	74	72	292	242,500
Saburo Fujiki	73	72	74	73	292	242,500
Takashi Murakami	71	76	70	76	293	210,000
Kosaku Shimada	74	71	76	72	293	210,000
Yutaka Suzuki	76	70	70	77	293	210,000
Hideto Shigenobu	71	72	73	77	293	210,000
Hsieh Min Nan	75	71	70	77	293	210,000
Masashi Ozaki	71	72	77	73	293	210,000
Satsuki Takahashi	75	66	74	78	293	210,000
Hisao Inoue	73	73	73	74	293	210,000
Katsuji Hasegawa	73	68	77	75	293	210,000
Isao Isozaki	71	71	75	77	294	184,000
Kenji Ueda	76	68	73	77	294	184,000
Yasuhiro Miyamoto	70	69	76	79	294	184,000
Akira Yabe	68	71	75	80	294	184,000
Hidenori Nakajima	72	71	75	76	294	184,000

	SCORES				TOTAL	MONEY
Chen Chien Chung	73	71	77	74	295	177,000
Takashi Kurihara	71	69	75	80	295	177,000
Kikuo Arai	74	70	78	74	296	172,000
Yasushi Katayama	72	70	74	80	296	172,000
Fujio Ishii	75	70	72	79	296	172,000

Yomiuri Open

Yomiuri Country Club, Osaka
Par 73; 7,049 yards

June 17–20
purse, Y30,000,000

	SCORES				TOTAL	MONEY
Terry Gale	70	70	68	68	276	Y6,000,000
Tsuneyuki Nakajima	70	73	64	72	279	1,800,000
Nobumitsu Yuhara	69	65	70	75	279	1,800,000
Masahiro Kuramoto	72	69	68	70	279	1,800,000
Namio Takasu	70	68	75	66	279	1,800,000
Lu Hsi Chuen	71	71	71	67	280	1,000,000
Tateo Ozaki	71	69	70	71	281	900,000
Chen Chien Chung	70	71	68	73	282	750,000
Teruo Sugihara	72	72	68	70	282	750,000
Yutaka Hagawa	70	71	69	73	283	563,333
Tsutomu Irie	73	73	70	67	283	563,333
Kenji Mori	74	73	69	67	283	563,333
Toru Nakamura	73	71	72	68	284	392,500
Seiji Ebihara	72	72	71	69	284	392,500
Koichi Inoue	75	68	71	70	284	392,500
Yoshitaka Yamamoto	70	69	71	74	284	392,500
Yutaka Suzuki	74	72	70	69	285	335,000
Saburo Fujiki	74	71	71	70	286	305,000
Akira Yabe	70	73	70	73	286	305,000
Masaji Kusakabe	69	71	71	75	286	305,000
Shinsaku Maeda	75	70	72	69	286	305,000
Hsieh Yung Yo	72	72	74	70	288	260,000
Shigeru Uchida	73	72	73	70	288	260,000
*Tetsuo Sakata	76	71	71	70	288	
Mitsuhiro Kitta	74	72	72	70	288	260,000
Teruo Suzumura	72	70	75	71	288	260,000
Shozo Miyamoto	72	75	71	70	288	260,000
Yasushi Katayama	71	71	74	72	288	260,000
Masahiko Yamamoto	76	70	70	72	288	260,000
Tadami Ueno	73	72	71	72	288	260,000
Pete Izumikawa	70	69	74	75	288	260,000
*Isamu Kanamoto	68	74	75	72	289	
Hisao Inoue	73	72	72	72	289	235,000
Katsuji Hasegawa	73	72	73	72	290	212,500
Koichi Uehara	72	73	73	72	290	212,500
Hsieh Min Nan	75	71	72	72	290	212,500
Tatsuo Fujima	73	72	73	72	290	212,500
Junichi Takahashi	72	73	72	73	290	212,500
Katsunari Takahashi	76	70	70	74	290	212,500
Tadashi Kitta	73	72	76	69	290	212,500
Motomasa Aoki	74	71	75	70	290	212,500
Kikuo Arai	71	72	75	73	291	186,600
Yoshikazu Yokoshima	72	74	72	73	291	186,600
Kenichi Yamada	71	72	75	73	291	186,600
Takashi Kurihara	75	71	71	74	291	186,600

	SCORES				TOTAL	MONEY
Masashi Ozaki	75	70	70	76	291	186,600
Eitaro Deguchi	74	70	76	72	292	179,000
Yurio Akitomi	69	70	75	78	292	179,000
Hiromi Sugitani	72	72	75	74	293	173,000
Shinichi Hayashi	75	72	76	70	293	173,000
Yasuhiro Funatogawa	76	70	75	72	293	173,000
Shuichi Sano	74	71	76	72	293	173,000

Mizuno

Tokinodai Country Club June 24–27
Bijodai Course — Par 72; 7,046 yards
Nozudai Course — Par 71; 6,868 yards purse, Y21,000,000

	SCORES				TOTAL	MONEY
Teruo Sugihara	70	68	71	73	282	4,000,000
Yutaka Hagawa	69	69	68	76	282	2,000,000
(Sugihara defeated Hagawa on second hole of sudden-death playoff.)						
Shigeru Uchida	72	70	69	72	283	1,250,000
Satsuki Takahashi	68	72	71	72	283	1,250,000
Tsuneyuki Nakajima	70	72	71	71	284	750,000
Norio Suzuki	69	70	74	71	284	750,000
Katsuji Hasegawa	71	70	71	74	286	600,000
Kikuo Arai	71	74	71	71	287	426,666
Yasuhiro Funatogawa	71	71	69	76	287	426,666
Seiichi Kanai	73	75	69	70	287	426,666
Nobumitsu Yuhara	72	74	72	70	288	330,000
Kazunori Mizuno	71	74	70	73	288	330,000
Akira Yabe	68	74	73	73	288	330,000
Hideto Shigenobu	67	74	75	72	288	330,000
Koichi Uehara	71	72	72	74	289	250,000
Namio Takasu	69	72	74	74	289	250,000
Isao Matsui	71	73	72	73	289	250,000
Yasushi Katayama	68	72	71	78	289	250,000
Akio Kanamoto	69	71	77	73	290	187,500
Tsutomu Horiuchi	69	70	74	77	290	187,500
Masaji Kusakabe	76	69	72	73	290	187,500
Takao Kage	74	74	69	73	290	187,500
Toshiyuki Tsuchiyama	69	72	73	77	291	180,000
Toyotake Nakao	69	74	73	75	291	180,000
Toru Nakamura	70	68	78	75	291	180,000
Kiyonori Tamura	71	72	79	70	292	170,000
Yoshikazu Yokoshima	71	72	75	74	292	170,000
Kazuo Yoshikawa	73	73	73	73	292	170,000
Hideo Noyama	69	72	72	79	292	170,000
Tsutomu Irie	72	75	70	75	292	170,000
Susumu Murai	76	69	74	74	293	160,000
Koichi Inoue	75	69	72	77	293	160,000
Kosaku Shimada	72	75	73	73	293	160,000
Toshimitsu Kai	71	76	76	71	294	154,000
Hisao Inoue	71	73	78	72	294	154,000
Masahiko Yamamoto	72	76	71	75	294	154,000
Naomichi Ozaki	73	70	74	77	294	154,000
Shiro Kubo	72	72	71	79	294	154,000
Shigeru Kawamata	72	74	78	71	295	150,000
Susumu Hano	71	76	75	73	295	150,000
Masami Aihara	69	76	79	72	296	137,142

	SCORES				TOTAL	MONEY
Sadao Sakashita	73	72	74	77	296	137,142
Takeshi Matsukawa	75	73	73	75	296	137,142
Akimitsu Tokita	74	72	74	76	296	137,142
Mario Siodina	68	75	74	79	296	137,142
Yoshihiro Takada	73	73	72	78	296	137,142
Minoru Kawakami	68	76	74	78	296	137,142
Shichiro Enomoto	72	72	79	74	297	130,000
Kinshiro Tsukimoto	73	75	75	74	297	130,000
Hideo Ishii	70	72	78	77	297	130,000

Nagano Open

Suwako Country Club, Nagano
Par 72; 6,642 yards

June 30–July 1
purse, Y17,900,000

	SCORES		TOTAL	MONEY
Tsuneyuki Nakajima	70	67	137	Y3,000,000
Yoshiharu Takai	68	70	138	1,600,000
Hidenori Nakajima	71	69	140	950,000
Toshimitsu Kai	69	71	140	950,000
Kikuo Arai	72	69	141	600,000
Akira Yabe	70	71	141	600,000
Saburo Fujiki	73	69	142	450,000
Norio Suzuki	71	71	142	450,000
Isao Isozaki	69	73	142	450,000
George Yokoi	74	69	143	301,430
Koichi Uehara	74	69	143	301,430
Seiichi Kanai	74	69	143	301,430
Isao Matsui	73	70	143	301,430
Ben Arda	72	71	143	301,430
Masaji Kusakabe	72	71	143	301,430
Nobumitsu Yuhara	71	72	143	301,430
Haruo Yasuda	74	70	144	212,500
Hsieh Yung Yo	73	71	144	212,500
Mitsuo Watanabe	72	72	144	212,500
Takaaki Kono	72	72	144	212,500
Tsutomu Horiuchi	75	69	144	212,500
Katsuji Hasegawa	72	72	144	212,500
Namio Takasu	71	73	144	212,500
Naomichi Ozaki	69	75	144	212,500
Fujio Kobayashi	74	71	145	183,340
Toshiyuki Tsuchiyama	74	71	145	183,340
Suichi Sano	73	72	145	183,330
Michiyuki Kawanami	72	73	145	183,330
Sichiro Enomoto	72	73	145	183,330
Masayuki Imai	71	74	145	183,330
Yutaka Suzuki	75	71	146	160,000
Masahiko Yamamoto	72	74	146	160,000
Minoru Hatsumi	71	75	146	160,000
Yoshimi Watanabe	72	75	147	154,000
Toshikazu Torisawa	72	75	147	154,000
Kazuo Kataoka	75	72	147	154,000
Mitsuo Hirukawa	75	72	147	154,000
Takeo Abe	72	75	147	154,000
Toshiharu Kawada	74	74	148	142,860
Mitoshi Tomita	73	75	148	142,860
Sadao Sakashita	73	75	148	142,860

	SCORES		TOTAL	MONEY
Takashi Miyoshi	73	75	148	142,860
Yoshio Ichikawa	73	75	148	142,860
Masami Aihara	75	73	148	142,850
Masaru Amano	74	74	148	142,850
Fumio Tanaka	74	75	149	130,000
Koichi Inoue	73	76	149	130,000
Kazunori Mizuno	73	76	149	130,000
Hideyo Sugimoto	73	77	150	126,670
Shigeru Uchida	73	77	150	126,670
Yasushi Katayama	74	76	150	126,660

Kanagawa Open

Yokohama Country Club, West Course July 3–4
Par 72; 6,925 yards purse, Y15,000,000

	SCORES		TOTAL	MONEY
Akio Toyoda	72	68	140	Y3,000,000
Isao Aoki	73	69	142	1,000,000
Teruo Sugihara	72	70	142	1,000,000
Namio Takasu	68	74	142	1,000,000
Takashi Kurihara	72	71	143	450,000
Toru Nakamura	71	72	143	450,000
Akira Yabe	74	70	144	340,000
Sadao Sakashita	73	71	144	340,000
Yoshitaka Yamamoto	72	72	144	340,000
Naomichi Ozaki	71	73	144	340,000
Kenji Mori	70	74	144	340,000
Hsieh Yung Yo	73	72	145	260,000
Keiji Yoshitake	70	75	145	260,000
Motomasa Aoki	71	74	145	260,000
Toshihiro Hitomi	71	75	146	172,500
Seiichi Kanai	71	75	146	172,500
Fujio Kobayashi	71	75	146	172,500
Kazuo Yoshikawa	74	72	146	172,500
Toyotake Nakao	74	72	146	172,500
Kikuo Arai	74	72	146	172,500
Norio Suzuki	73	73	146	172,500
Takaaki Kono	73	73	146	172,500
Shigeru Uchida	73	73	146	172,500
Haruo Yasuda	72	74	146	172,500
Masashi Ozaki	72	74	146	172,500
Tatsuo Fujima	71	75	146	172,500
Tomohiro Maruyama	74	73	147	120,000
Toshiharu Kawada	73	74	147	120,000
Shichiro Enomoto	73	74	147	120,000
Satsuki Takahashi	73	74	147	120,000
Kazuo Kanayama	72	75	147	120,000
Hisao Inoue	72	75	147	120,000
Yasuhiro Miyamoto	72	75	147	120,000
Noboru Sugai	72	75	147	120,000
Shuichi Sano	70	77	147	120,000
Fumio Tanaka	71	76	147	120,000
Keiichi Kobayashi	74	74	148	100,000
Joji Furuki	73	75	148	100,000
Hiroshi Tahara	73	75	148	100,000
Masaji Kusakabe	73	75	148	100,000

	SCORES		TOTAL	MONEY
Koichi Hirabayashi	73	75	148	100,000
Toshiyuki Tsuchiyama	73	75	148	100,000
Chen Chien Chung	71	77	148	100,000
Mitsuo Watanabe	74	75	149	100,000
Yoshiharu Takai	74	75	149	100,000
Minoru Nakamura	74	76	150	100,000
Tsukasa Hirakawa	74	76	150	100,000
Michiyuki Kawanami	74	76	150	100,000
Kazushige Kono	74	76	150	100,000
Saburo Fujiki	74	76	150	100,000
Koichi Inoue	74	76	150	100,000
Isao Matsui	74	76	150	100,000
Toru Nakayama	74	76	150	100,000

Toyama Open

Kureha Country Club
Par 72; 6,821 yards

July 9–10
purse, Y15,000,000

	SCORES		TOTAL	MONEY
Shigeru Uchida	68	67	136	Y3,000,000
Masaru Amano	68	68	136	1,300,000
(Uchida defeated Amano in sudden-death playoff.)				
Mitoshi Tomita	70	67	137	900,000
Nobumitsu Yuhara	71	67	138	600,000
Toshimitsu Kai	67	74	141	450,000
Norio Mikami	74	68	142	330,000
Kazushige Kono	73	69	142	330,000
Shigeo Kanaumi	73	69	142	330,000
Kazuhiro Tamura	72	70	142	330,000
Naomichi Ozaki	70	72	142	330,000
Ichiro Teramoto	70	72	142	330,000
Yozo Okabe	74	69	143	247,500
Teruo Suzumura	73	70	143	247,500
Akio Kanamoto	72	71	143	247,500
Toshikazu Torisawa	71	72	143	247,500
Norihiko Maei	73	71	144	205,000
Akio Toyoda	73	71	144	205,000

Wakayama Open

Kunikihara Golf Cl b, Wakayama Prefecture
Par 72; 6,649 yards

July 9–10
purse, Y8,000,000

	SCORES		TOTAL	MONEY
Hisashi Kaji	69	69	138	Y1,500,000
Shiro Kubo	72	66	138	625,000
Yuji Takagi	69	69	138	625,000
(Kaji defeated Kubo and Takagi on first hole of sudden-death playoff.)				
Yoshiyuki Isomura	72	68	140	375,000
Kozo Tamada	69	71	140	375,000
Katsumi Hara	69	72	141	300,000
Takeshi Matsukawa	72	70	142	210,000
Katsumi Yoshijima	71	71	142	210,000
Motomasa Nishikawa	71	71	142	210,000
Hiromichi Takezaki	71	71	142	210,000

	SCORES		TOTAL	MONEY
Masato Nishii	71	71	142	210,000
Nobuhiro Sakata	70	72	142	210,000
Tatsuo Nakaue	73	69	142	210,000

Niigata Open

Ooniigata Country Club, Niigata Prefecture
Par 72; 6,896 yards

July 10–11
purse, Y15,000,000

	SCORES		TOTAL	MONEY
Yoshitaka Yamamoto	69	69	138	Y3,000,000
Hsieh Min Nan	68	70	138	1,500,000
(Yamamoto defeated Hsieh on fourth hole of sudden-death playoff.)				
Kenji Mori	70	70	140	900,000
Norio Suzuki	70	71	141	650,000
Yurio Akitomi	70	72	142	450,000
Hiroshi Makino	70	72	142	450,000
Kikuo Arai	72	71	143	312,000
Hisashi Suzumura	71	72	143	312,000
Takaaki Kono	72	71	143	312,000
Yasushi Katayama	72	71	143	312,000
Seiji Ebihara	71	72	143	312,000
Katsuji Hasegawa	72	72	144	230,000
Koichi Uehara	70	74	144	230,000
Akira Yabe	70	74	144	230,000
Satsuki Takahashi	70	74	144	230,000
Shinsaku Maeda	70	74	144	230,000

Gunma Open

Ikaho International Country Club
Par 72; 7,013 yards

July 16–18
purse, Y15,000,000

	SCORES			TOTAL	MONEY
Fujio Kobayashi	68	68	75	211	Y3,000,000
Hiroshi Ishii	71	70	74	215	1,500,000
Yoshimi Niizeki	74	74	68	216	833,333
Shinobu Tonooka	72	71	73	216	833,333
Tatsuo Fujima	73	69	74	216	833,333
Takaaki Kono	75	71	71	217	450,000
Koichi Suzuki	74	70	73	217	450,000
Kikuo Arai	76	72	70	218	350,000
Toshiharu Kawada	76	74	69	219	263,333
Tateo Ozaki	74	76	69	219	263,333
Taiichi Nakagawa	74	74	71	219	263,333
Koichi Uehara	76	70	73	219	263,333
Kenji Mori	73	74	72	219	263,333
Katsuji Hasegawa	74	70	75	219	263,333
Haruo Yasuda	78	71	71	220	212,500
Akira Yabe	76	73	71	220	212,500
Shigeo Kanaumi	72	75	73	220	212,500
Toru Nakayama	77	69	74	220	212,500
Shigeru Noguchi	72	76	73	221	200,000
Yutaka Hagawa	73	72	76	221	200,000
Seiichi Kanai	75	75	72	222	150,000
Yoshihisa Iwashita	74	77	71	222	150,000

Hyogo Open

Akashi Shin Nippon Golf Club, Kobe
Par 72; 6,602 yards

July 16–17
purse, Y6,000,000

	SCORES		TOTAL	MONEY
Kazuo Kanayama	65	71	136	Y1,200,000
Hisashi Morioka	65	72	137	650,000
Hisao Inoue	68	72	140	450,000
Kosaku Shimada	73	68	141	300,000
Koichi Nishimura	71	70	141	300,000
Ikuji Kashiwagi	70	72	142	200,000
Osamu Watanabe	74	69	143	155,000
Toshitsugu Kitta	73	70	143	155,000
Shiro Matsuda	73	70	143	155,000
Ichiro Teramoto	73	70	143	155,000
Yoshio Ichikawa	74	70	144	112,500
Hisashi Terada	74	70	144	112,500
Tadashi Kitsuta	73	71	144	112,500
Minoru Kawakami	73	71	144	112,500

Descente Osaka Open

Ibaraki Kogen Country Club, Osaka
Par 72; 6,966 yards
(second round cancelled because of rain.)

July 18–19
purse, Y6,000,000

	SCORES	TOTAL	MONEY
Teruo Sugihara	68	68	Y1,200,000
Hiromichi Takezaki	70	70	350,000
Kazuo Yoshikawa	70	70	350,000
Toyotake Nakao	70	70	350,000
Minoru Kawakami	70	70	350,000
Shiro Kubo	70	70	350,000
Motomasa Nishikawa	71	71	180,000
Akio Kanamoto	71	71	180,000
Takemitsu Uranishi	71	71	180,000

Japan PGA Championship

Meishin Yokaichi Country Club, Shiga Prefecture
Par 72; 6,931 yards

July 22–25
purse, Y32,000,000

	SCORES				TOTAL	MONEY
Masahiro Kuramoto	67	69	69	69	274	Y5,600,000
Hsieh Min Nan	67	72	70	69	278	2,800,000
Fujio Kobayashi	66	72	74	69	281	1,270,000
Saburo Fujiki	68	72	71	70	281	1,270,000
Tsuneyuki Nakajima	70	70	70	71	281	1,270,000
Toru Nakamura	70	70	72	69	281	1,270,000
Isao Aoki	72	70	71	69	282	800,000
Haruo Yasuda	71	69	67	76	283	738,000
Teruo Sugihara	73	68	69	73	283	738,000
Yutaka Hagawa	68	70	71	75	284	609,600
Kikuo Arai	69	70	73	72	284	609,600
Akimitsu Tokita	69	68	73	74	284	609,600
Michiyuki Kawanami	70	73	72	69	284	609,600

	SCORES				TOTAL	MONEY
Motomasa Aoki	71	70	73	70	284	609,600
Nobumitsu Yuhara	70	72	73	71	286	512,000
Norio Mikami	70	71	70	76	287	472,000
Toyotake Nakao	75	71	66	75	287	472,000
Namio Takasu	71	68	76	73	288	448,000
Naomichi Ozaki	70	73	74	72	289	424,000
Yoshitaka Yamamoto	70	72	79	68	289	424,000
Yoshimi Niizeki	67	69	77	77	290	376,000
Koji Takahashi	71	73	72	74	290	376,000
Shigeru Kubota	71	71	74	74	290	376,000
Satsuki Takahashi	71	75	68	76	290	376,000
Toshiharu Kawada	72	73	73	72	290	376,000
Takaaki Kono	73	70	71	76	290	376,000
Shinsaku Maeda	73	72	75	70	290	376,000
Hisao Inoue	70	72	73	76	291	340,000
Yoshiyuki Isomura	73	70	72	76	291	340,000
Noriji Asai	70	75	71	76	292	316,000
Tadami Ueno	71	72	77	72	292	316,000
Yoshikazu Yokoshima	72	70	75	75	292	316,000
Takashi Kurihara	73	71	72	76	292	316,000
Tadashige Kusano	68	74	78	73	293	268,000
Suichi Sano	70	75	75	73	293	268,000
Shigeru Noguchi	72	73	71	77	293	268,000
Akira Yabe	72	72	73	76	293	268,000
Koichi Inoue	73	73	72	75	293	268,000
Kazuo Yoshikawa	73	73	73	74	293	268,000
Kenji Mori	74	72	72	75	293	268,000
Kazunori Mizuno	74	72	75	72	293	268,000
Masaru Amano	69	76	77	72	294	228,000
Shigeo Kanaumi	72	72	75	75	294	228,000
Shoji Ozaki	72	71	79	72	294	228,000
Keiichi Kobayashi	71	73	76	75	295	214,000
Akio Toyoda	72	70	79	74	295	214,000
Teruo Suzumura	73	72	74	76	295	214,000
Seiji Ebihara	74	71	76	74	295	214,000
Tsutomu Irie	70	76	71	79	296	198,000
Yoshiharu Takai	71	74	76	75	296	198,000
Yoshimi Watanabe	71	73	76	76	296	198,000
Tsukasa Watanabe	74	72	72	78	296	198,000

Kanto PGA Championship

Kanuma Koryo Country Club, Tochigi Prefecture
Par 72; 6,704 yards

July 29–August 1
purse, Y20,000,000

	SCORES				TOTAL	MONEY
Motomasa Aoki	70	65	67	72	274	Y4,000,000
Kenji Mori	69	69	69	69	276	2,000,000
Kikuo Arai	73	64	68	72	277	1,500,000
Nobumitsu Yuhara	69	70	71	69	279	1,100,000
Haruo Yasuda	70	70	67	72	279	1,100,000
Tsuneyuki Nakajima	68	68	74	72	282	800,000
Katsuji Hasegawa	69	71	70	73	283	650,000
Seiji Ebihara	69	71	69	74	283	650,000
Yoshimi Niizeki	73	72	69	71	285	500,000
Yutaka Hagawa	68	73	70	74	285	500,000
Hsieh Min Nan	69	65	73	78	285	500,000

	SCORES				TOTAL	MONEY
Kazushige Kono	71	71	73	71	286	375,000
Takashi Kubota	72	71	70	73	286	375,000
Isao Aoki	69	73	69	75	286	375,000
Norio Adachi	71	69	71	75	286	375,000
Chen Chien Chung	71	71	72	73	287	300,000
Taiichi Nakagawa	70	73	73	72	288	280,000
Toshiyuki Tsuchiyama	71	73	69	75	288	280,000
Isao Isozaki	71	71	70	76	288	280,000
Yasuhiro Yamazaki	72	73	73	71	289	235,000
Kazunori Mizuno	74	71	73	71	289	235,000
Shigeru Kubota	71	70	75	73	289	235,000
Koichi Moriguchi	69	73	74	73	289	235,000
Namio Takasu	68	71	74	76	289	235,000
Yoshikazu Yokoshima	70	70	71	78	289	235,000
Satsuki Takahashi	70	71	76	73	290	171,429
Ikuo Shirahama	72	72	73	73	290	171,429
Michiyuki Kawanami	67	71	78	74	290	171,429
Keiji Yoshitake	73	71	72	74	290	171,429
Keiichi Hoshino	72	72	75	71	290	171,428
Shigeru Noguchi	72	69	74	75	290	171,428
Toshiaki Nakamura	68	70	74	78	290	171,428
Hsieh Yung Yo	70	73	77	71	291	140,000
Shigeo Kanaumi	71	71	77	72	291	140,000
Chen Ching Po	72	72	74	74	292	128,000
Koichi Hirabayashi	71	71	75	75	292	128,000
Shotaro Watanabe	71	72	74	75	292	128,000
Eiichi Yabe	69	76	75	72	292	128,000
Hideyo Sugimoto	69	76	75	72	292	128,000
Toru Nakayama	74	69	75	75	293	120,000
Tatsuo Fujima	74	69	73	78	294	110,000
Hirosuke Sakai	69	75	74	77	295	110,000
Choji Noguchi	72	73	75	75	295	110,000
Hideo Kishiro	72	73	79	72	296	110,000
Sadao Sakashita	72	72	76	76	296	110,000
Tsutomu Horiuchi	75	69	76	76	296	110,000
Yohichi Miyashiro	72	73	75	77	297	110,000
Seiichi Sato	72	73	75	77	297	110,000
Saburo Fujiki	75	70	74	78	297	110,000
Takashi Murakami	74	71	72	81	298	101,667
Renkyoku Sugiyama	69	71	81	77	298	101,667
Akira Yabe	71	73	77	77	298	101,667
Shichiro Enomoto	69	75	77	77	298	101,667
Mitsuhiro Yamashita	72	73	75	78	298	101,666
Kazumi Terashima	72	71	76	79	298	101,666

Kansai PGA Championship

Ogori Country Club, Fukuoka Prefecture
Par 72; 6,693 yards

July 29–August 1
purse, Y13,000,000

	SCORES				TOTAL	MONEY
Hideto Shigenobu	68	70	68	71	277	Y2,625,000
Teruo Sugihara	73	72	69	67	281	1,312,500
Tadami Ueno	72	68	70	72	282	900,000
Toshiaki Nakagawa	72	72	72	70	286	464,062
Masahiro Kuramoto	80	66	70	70	286	464,062
Toshiharu Kusaka	74	71	71	70	286	464,062

	SCORES				TOTAL	MONEY
Masahiko Yamamoto	74	69	71	72	286	464,062
Tsuguhiko Bando	73	74	67	73	287	354,375
Kanehachi Yoshimura	72	72	76	68	288	310,312
Koichi Inoue	71	73	72	72	288	310,312
Eitaro Deguchi	70	71	73	74	288	310,312
Norio Mikami	73	72	69	74	288	310,312
Kenji Ueda	79	70	71	69	289	247,500
Shinsaku Maeda	71	72	75	71	289	247,500
Yoshitaka Yamamoto	70	73	74	72	289	247,500
Norio Suzuki	73	73	71	72	289	247,500
Shoji Miyamoto	70	73	77	70	290	202,500
Yoshiyuki Isomura	73	71	76	70	290	202,500
Akio Toyoda	71	74	72	73	290	202,500
Akio Kanamoto	72	71	73	74	290	202,500
Toru Hayami	74	71	70	75	290	202,500
Mitoshi Tomita	75	74	71	71	291	181,875
Tetsuhiro Ueda	72	70	73	76	291	181,875
Tsutomu Irie	76	72	72	72	292	166,875
Noboru Fujiike	74	72	73	73	292	166,875
Sadatoshi Makimura	73	73	72	74	292	166,875
Takeshi Yamamoto	72	73	72	75	292	166,875
Kunio Koike	70	74	72	76	292	166,875
Toshimitsu Kai	74	71	70	77	292	166,875
Yoshinori Ichioka	76	70	74	73	293	148,125
Yuji Takagi	74	71	74	74	293	148,125
Yoichi Yamamoto	72	75	72	74	293	148,125
Mitsuhiro Kitsuta	73	74	71	75	293	148,125
Yoshiki Yamazaki	74	75	70	75	294	133,125
Kazuo Kanayama	77	71	76	70	294	133,125
Toru Nakamura	75	69	73	77	294	133,125
Toshiki Matsui	72	74	77	71	294	133,125
Motomasa Nishikawa	72	74	75	74	295	116,250
Yutaka Suzuki	77	70	73	75	295	116,250
Hiroshi Oku	73	76	76	70	295	116,250
Shiro Matsuda	77	71	75	72	295	116,250
Hisashi Suzumura	72	76	74	73	295	116,250
Noboru Shibata	74	73	74	75	296	102,187
Shigemi Nakazono	76	73	78	69	296	102,187
Shinichi Hayashi	76	73	71	76	296	102,187
Natsuo Ito	75	73	79	69	296	102,187
Shiro Kubo	76	72	76	72	296	102,187
Rikizo Kato	75	71	78	72	296	102,187
Kazumi Nakao	77	72	77	71	297	93,750
Kenji Tokuyama	75	73	75	74	297	93,750
Yoshiharu Harato	74	70	77	76	297	93,750

Descente Cup Hokkoku Open

Katayamazu Golf Club, Ishikawa Prefecture
Par 72; 6,973 yards

August 5–8
purse, Y30,000,000

	SCORES				TOTAL	MONEY
Kikuo Arai	71	67	71	67	276	Y6,000,000
Tsuneyuki Nakajima	66	71	69	72	278	2,700,000
Yutaka Suzuki	69	71	70	71	281	2,000,000
Toru Nakamura	71	72	69	70	282	1,166,666
Saburo Fujiki	71	69	70	72	282	1,166,666

	SCORES				TOTAL	MONEY
Tateo Ozaki	70	69	69	74	282	1,166,666
Takeshi Shibata	72	75	68	68	283	800,000
Haruo Yasuda	71	68	66	79	284	750,000
Masahiko Yamamoto	72	70	73	70	285	675,000
Teruo Suzuki	71	72	70	72	285	675,000
Taiichi Nakagawa	72	73	70	71	286	520,000
Lu Liang Huan	71	70	72	73	286	520,000
Norio Suzuki	67	73	73	73	286	520,000
Nobumitsu Yuhara	72	72	68	74	286	520,000
Toyotake Nakao	72	75	71	70	288	430,000
Koichi Inoue	73	72	74	69	288	430,000
Chen Tze Ming	70	76	70	72	288	430,000
Noboru Sugai	71	73	72	72	288	430,000
Yoshitaka Yamamoto	72	71	72	73	288	430,000
Hsieh Min Nan	73	72	72	72	289	332,500
Tadao Nakamura	76	70	68	75	289	332,500
Yutaka Hagawa	74	70	69	76	289	332,500
Yoshimi Niizeki	69	70	73	77	289	332,500
Teruo Sugihara	73	72	72	73	290	303,333
Tatsuo Fujima	74	72	70	74	290	303,333
Shoji Ozaki	71	72	72	75	290	303,333
Akio Toyoda	74	71	74	72	291	270,000
Yoshikazu Yokoshima	73	70	74	74	291	270,000
Hsieh Yung Yo	69	74	78	70	291	270,000
Naomichi Ozaki	71	71	70	79	291	270,000
Hisao Inoue	74	72	71	75	292	230,000
Lu Hsi Chuen	72	72	73	75	292	230,000
Shinsaku Maeda	74	69	74	75	292	230,000
Katsuji Hasegawa	74	72	70	76	292	230,000
Isao Isozaki	71	73	75	74	293	210,000
Toru Nakayama	71	74	72	76	293	210,000
Isao Matsui	70	72	72	79	293	210,000
Toshimitsu Kai	75	72	71	76	294	185,000
Hiroshi Makino	75	70	73	76	294	185,000
Pete Izumikawa	76	71	70	77	294	185,000
Seiichi Kanai	70	71	75	78	294	185,000
Suichi Sano	74	71	76	73	294	185,000
Takaaki Kono	74	72	73	75	294	185,000
Masaji Kusakabe	74	72	75	74	295	170,000
Satsuki Takahashi	74	71	71	79	295	170,000
Kenji Ueda	71	75	74	75	295	170,000
Masaji Ebihara	73	72	77	74	296	170,000
Shigeru Uchida	73	72	76	75	296	170,000
Eitaro Deguchi	73	72	75	76	296	170,000
George Yokoi	72	74	69	81	296	170,000

Saitama Open

Kasumigaseki Country Club, Saitama Prefecture
Par 72; 6,702 yards

August 11–12
purse, Y10,000,000

	SCORES		TOTAL	MONEY
Kikuo Arai	72	67	139	Y2,000,000
Yutaka Hagawa	72	70	142	616,666
Mitsuo Watanabe	69	73	142	616,666
Takashi Kurihara	70	72	142	616,666
Hidenori Nakajima	71	72	143	300,000

	SCORES		TOTAL	MONEY
Junichi Takahashi	73	71	144	265,000
Hideo Kishiro	69	75	144	265,000
Yasuhiro Funatogawa	70	75	145	250,000
Kiyokuni Kimoto	74	72	146	226,666
Tsutomu Fukazawa	73	73	146	226,666
Masao Suzuki	73	73	146	226,666
*Sojiro Tanaka	73	74	147	
Noboru Sugai	73	74	147	200,000

East-West Match Play

Asahigaoka Country Club, Tochigi Prefecture

Par 72; 6,639 yards

August 14–15

purse, Y10,000,000 (Team)
Y8,000,000 (Individual)

FINAL RESULTS: WEST (KANSAI) 26; EAST (KANTO) 22.

FIRST ROUND
Motomasa Aoki (KT) defeated Kosaku Shimada, 72–74.
Toru Nakamura (KS) defeated Seiichi Kanai, 68–70.
Kikuo Arai (KT) defeated Tsutomu Irie, 66–77.
Shigeru Uchida (KS) defeated Yutaka Hagawa, 68–69.
Saburo Fujiki (KT) defeated Teruo Sugihara, 69–74.
Norio Suzuki (KS) defeated Nobumitsu Yuhara, 65–73.
Tsuneyuki Nakajima (KT) defeated Shinsaku Maeda, 65–69.
Koichi Inoue (KS) tied Katsuji Hasegawa, 71–71.
Akio Kanamoto (KS) defeated Namio Takasu, 70–72.
Yoshitaka Yamamoto (KS) tied Toshiharu Kawada, 68–68.
Hideto Shigenobu (KS) defeated Akira Yabe, 69–70.
Masahiro Kuramoto (KS) tied Masaji Kusakabe, 74–74.
EAST (KANSAI) leads, 13–11.

SECOND ROUND
Irie (KS) defeated Kusakabe, 70–73.
Inoue (KS) defeated Takasu, 70–72.
Kanai (KT) defeated Shimada, 69–74.
Aoki (KT) defeated Maeda, 69–72.
Hasegawa (KT) defeated Shigenobu, 67–77.
Sugihara (KS) defeated Yabe, 71–73.
Kanamoto (KS) defeated Kawada, 67–69.
Yamamoto (KS) tied Fujiki, 68–68.
Nakamura (KS) defeated Yuhara, 68–73.
Kuramoto (KS) defeated Hagawa, 69–70.
Arai (KT) defeated Uchida, 69–73.
Nakajima (KT) defeated Suzuki, 62–68.

INDIVIDUAL STANDINGS AND MONEY WINNINGS

	ROUNDS		TOTAL	INDIVIDUAL MONEY	TEAM MONEY	TOTAL MONEY
Tsuneyuki Nakajima	65	62	127	Y1,500,000	Y307,692	Y1,807,692
Norio Suzuki	65	68	133	1,000,000	461,538	1,461,538
Kikuo Arai	66	69	135	700,000	307,692	1,007,692
Toru Nakamura	68	68	136	550,000	461,538	1,011,538
Yoshitaka Yamamoto	68	68	136	550,000	461,538	1,011,538
Toshiharu Kawada	68	69	137	400,000	307,692	707,692

				SCORES	TOTAL	MONEY
Saburo Fujiki	69	68	137	400,000	307,692	707,692
Akio Kanamoto	70	67	137	400,000	461,538	861,538
Katsuji Hasegawa	71	67	138	300,000	307,692	607,692
Yutaka Hagawa	69	70	139	225,000	307,692	532,692
Seiichi Kanai	70	69	139	225,000	307,692	532,692
Shigeru Uchida	68	73	141	175,000	461,538	636,538
Shinsaku Maeda	69	72	141	175,000	461,538	636,538
Koichi Inoue	71	70	141	175,000	461,538	636,538
Motomasa Aoki	72	69	141	175,000	307,692	482,692
Akira Yabe	70	73	143	145,000	307,692	452,692
Masahiro Kuramoto	74	69	143	145,000	461,538	606,538
Namio Takasu	72	72	144	130,000	307,692	437,692
Teruo Sugihara	74	71	145	120,000	461,538	581,538
Hideto Shigenobu	69	77	146	105,000	461,538	566,538
Nobumitsu Yuhara	73	73	146	105,000	307,692	412,692
Masaji Kusakabe	74	73	147	100,000	307,692	407,692
Tsutomu Irie	77	70	147	100,000	461,538	561,538
Kosaku Shimada	74	74	148	100,000	461,538	561,538

Nihon Kokudo Keikaku Summers

Budo Country Club, Ishihara
Par 72; 7,035 yards

August 19–22
purse, Y30,000,000

		SCORES			TOTAL	MONEY
Teruo Sugihara	65	69	70	71	275	Y6,000,000
Norio Suzuki	68	66	73	73	280	2,250,000
Isao Isozaki	64	70	73	73	280	2,250,000
Norio Mikami	69	72	72	68	281	1,000,000
Chen Tze Ming	72	69	74	68	283	850,000
Shinsaku Maeda	70	69	74	71	284	685,000
Naomichi Ozaki	67	72	71	74	284	685,000
Yasuhiro Funatogawa	71	67	70	76	284	685,000
Toshimitsu Kai	74	69	67	74	284	685,000
Motomasa Nishikawa	70	71	73	72	286	575,000
Masaji Kusakabe	69	73	73	71	286	575,000
Yoshikazu Yokoshima	72	71	70	73	286	575,000
Toru Nakamura	70	73	73	71	287	467,500
Lu Hsi Chuen	70	74	70	73	287	467,500
Hsieh Min Nan	70	72	71	74	287	467,500
Kikuo Arai	71	72	70	74	287	467,500
Seiichi Kanai	73	71	72	72	288	366,916
Hiroshi Makino	70	71	74	73	288	366,916
Koichi Inoue	71	69	73	75	288	366,916
Shoji Kikuchi	73	70	70	75	288	366,916
Masahiko Yamamoto	70	71	71	77	288	366,916
Tateo Ozaki	69	73	70	76	288	366,916
Hajime Meshiai	74	72	71	72	289	322,750
Mitsuo Kaneko	71	72	73	73	289	322,750
Nobumitsu Yuhara	76	69	72	73	290	289,000
Minoru Kumabe	73	71	73	73	290	289,000
Seiji Ebihara	72	73	72	73	290	289,000
Takashi Kurihara	68	72	75	75	290	289,000
Liao Kuo Chih	73	69	73	75	290	289,000
Yoshitaka Yamamoto	72	73	74	71	290	289,000
Hiromi Sugita	72	70	71	77	290	289,000
Ben Arda	72	72	73	74	291	255,250

	SCORES			TOTAL	MONEY
Pete Izumikawa	73	70	77	71	291	255,250
Shinobu Tonooka	72	74	70	76	292	232,000
Sadatoshi Makimura	72	71	77	72	292	232,000
Motomasa Aoki	69	72	77	74	292	232,000
Hisataka Fujii	73	72	73	74	292	232,000
Yutaka Hagawa	68	73	76	75	292	232,000
Brian Jones	70	72	75	76	293	212,000
Saburo Fujiki	71	71	75	76	293	212,000
Akira Yabe	71	72	76	74	293	212,000
Toshiharu Kusaka	71	75	74	74	294	205,000
Toshiyuki Tsuchiyama	66	75	75	79	295	197,500
Yasushi Katayama	71	73	77	74	295	197,500
Yoshiharu Takai	75	69	76	75	295	197,500
Yoshimi Niizeki	73	73	74	75	295	197,500
Yoshiyuki Isomura	71	73	78	74	296	185,500
Namio Takasu	73	72	77	74	296	185,500
Hsieh Yung Yo	69	75	77	75	296	185,500
Satsuki Takahashi	72	70	73	81	296	185,500

KBC Augusta

Fukuoka Country Club, Fukuoka Prefecture   August 26–29
Par 72; 6,649 yards   purse, Y32,000,000
(Tournament shortened to 54 holes because of rain.)

	SCORES			TOTAL	MONEY
Chen Tze Ming	68	71	70	209	Y6,000,000
Hal Sutton	69	72	69	210	3,000,000
Toshiaki Sekimizu	71	74	66	211	2,000,000
Norio Suzuki	75	70	68	213	1,100,000
Shigeru Uchida	70	71	72	213	1,100,000
Minoru Kawakami	68	73	72	213	1,100,000
Kikuo Arai	73	71	70	214	700,000
Pete Izumikawa	75	69	70	214	700,000
Teruo Suzumura	72	71	71	214	700,000
Takahiro Takeyasu	71	72	71	214	700,000
Namio Takasu	70	72	72	214	700,000
Fujio Kobayashi	74	73	69	216	496,666
Hisashi Suzumura	75	71	70	216	496,666
Akira Yabe	72	73	71	216	496,666
Masaji Kusakabe	77	67	72	216	496,666
Tsutomu Irie	72	72	72	216	496,666
Kenji Mori	73	70	73	216	496,666
Masunobu Nakamura	72	74	71	217	376,750
Minoru Kumabe	75	71	71	217	376,750
Hsieh Min Nan	74	74	69	217	376,750
Toru Nakamura	72	75	70	217	376,750
Seiichi Kanai	70	74	73	217	376,750
Noboru Fujiike	73	71	73	217	376,750
Yoshinori Ichioka	70	72	75	217	376,750
Yurio Akitomi	68	73	76	217	376,750
Shigemi Nakazono	72	74	72	218	318,500
Masayuki Imai	73	75	70	218	318,500
Hiroshi Ishii	71	74	73	218	318,500
Shinsaku Maeda	75	70	73	218	318,500
Kazuo Yoshikawa	74	71	73	218	318,500
Chen Chien Chin	71	72	75	218	318,500

	SCORES			TOTAL	MONEY
Toshiharu Kawada	72	74	73	219	273,500
Shigeru Noguchi	74	72	73	219	273,500
Eitaro Deguchi	74	72	73	219	273,500
Tatsuo Fujima	74	72	73	219	273,500
Toyotake Nakao	74	71	74	219	273,500
Haruo Yasuda	69	73	77	219	273,500
Koji Takahashi	73	74	73	220	228,833
Noriji Asai	72	76	72	220	228,833
Hsieh Yung Yo	73	75	72	220	228,833
Katsuji Hasegawa	72	75	73	220	228,833
Toshimitsu Kai	72	72	76	220	228,833
Yasuhiro Miyamoto	72	70	78	220	228,833
Yasushi Katayama	75	72	74	221	195,142
Brian Jones	73	73	75	221	195,142
Akio Toyoda	74	72	75	221	195,142
Nobuhiro Sakata	72	76	73	221	195,142
Teruo Sugihara	73	75	73	221	195,142
Isao Isozaki	73	75	73	221	195,142
Misao Yamamoto	72	75	74	221	195,142

Kanto Open

Fujioyama Golf Club, Shizuoka Prefecture　　　　　　　　September 2–5
Par 72; 6,953 yards　　　　　　　　　　　　　　　purse, Y20,000,000

	SCORES				TOTAL	MONEY
Masashi Ozaki	73	72	73	72	290	Y4,000,000
Yutaka Hagawa	74	71	77	69	291	2,000,000
Isao Isozaki	74	72	73	75	294	1,350,000
Fujio Kobayashi	75	69	74	76	294	1,350,000
Shoji Kikuchi	72	70	77	76	295	775,000
Hideyo Sugimoto	72	71	77	75	295	775,000
Tsuneyuki Nakajima	75	69	76	75	295	775,000
Keiji Yoshitake	73	75	77	70	295	775,000
Akira Yabe	76	75	73	72	296	500,000
Namio Takasu	73	77	75	72	297	353,333
Katsuji Hasegawa	77	71	74	75	297	353,333
Haruo Yasuda	73	78	77	69	297	353,334
Takaaki Kono	76	73	76	73	298	330,000
Yoshikazu Yokoshima	73	76	77	72	298	330,000
Hsieh Min Nan	73	74	75	77	299	283,333
Saburo Fujiki	75	75	74	75	299	283,333
Takashi Murakami	73	78	74	74	299	283,334
Seiji Ogawa	75	72	77	76	300	236,000
Takashi Kurihara	76	75	74	75	300	236,000
Taiichi Nakagawa	73	74	75	78	300	236,000
Shigeru Noguchi	74	75	77	74	300	236,000
Kenji Mori	78	69	80	73	300	236,000
Masaji Kusakabe	79	73	74	75	301	200,000
Suichi Sano	76	74	79	72	301	200,000
*Hiroshi Tominaga	76	77	73	75	301	
Shichiro Enomoto	76	76	76	74	302	160,000
Seiji Ebihara	74	75	76	77	302	160,000
Seiichi Kanai	73	72	85	72	302	160,000
Minoru Nakamura	79	75	74	74	302	160,000
*So Minoru	79	75	73	75	302	
Tatsuo Fujima	76	72	74	80	302	160,000

	SCORES				TOTAL	MONEY
Naomichi Ozaki	76	74	79	74	303	135,000
Shigeo Kanaumi	75	72	81	75	303	135,000
Mikio Ichikawa	74	77	76	77	304	120,000
*Kazuhiko Kato	77	74	76	77	304	
Minoru Kumabe	77	73	77	77	304	120,000
Ikuo Shirahama	74	74	80	76	304	120,000
Hiromi Sugitani	79	74	76	75	304	120,000
Kikuo Arai	74	73	85	73	305	100,000
Makoto Ioka	78	74	77	76	305	100,000
Hiroshi Takenaka	77	76	75	77	305	100,000
Motomasa Aoki	73	73	80	80	306	95,000
Yasushi Katayama	80	73	77	76	306	95,000
Toshiharu Kawada	76	75	83	72	306	95,000
Shotaro Watanabe	74	73	83	76	306	95,000
Satsuki Takahashi	80	72	77	78	307	90,000
Tadao Murata	76	75	81	75	307	90,000
Nobuyuki Ikenoya	77	74	78	79	308	90,000
*Sojiro Tanaka	77	74	75	82	308	
*Yasuo Hiraga	76	77	75	80	308	

Kansai Open

Rokko International Golf Club, Kobe
Par 72; 7,065 yards

September 2–5
purse, Y15,000,000

	SCORES				TOTAL	MONEY
Teruo Sugihara	72	68	75	70	285	Y4,000,000
Toru Nakamura	75	69	73	72	289	2,000,000
Yoshinori Ichioka	74	71	75	72	292	1,000,000
Toshitaka Yamamoto	73	76	73	71	293	800,000
Shinsaku Maeda	72	76	76	70	294	616,666
Toyotake Nakao	73	74	73	74	294	616,666
Yasuhiro Miyamoto	75	74	72	73	294	616,666
Shiro Kubo	74	76	75	70	295	425,000
Yoshiyuki Isomura	74	72	77	72	295	425,000
Hiromi Watanabe	70	75	78	72	295	425,000
Keiichi Kobayashi	72	75	75	73	295	425,000
Ryoji Yokoyama	74	73	77	73	297	250,000
Ichiro Teramoto	73	76	76	72	297	250,000
*Isamu Kanamoto	73	74	75	75	297	
Kosaku Shimada	74	71	77	75	297	250,000
Toshiaki Nakagawa	72	76	76	74	298	135,000
Hideo Hashimoto	75	75	72	76	298	135,000
Katsumi Hirai	72	79	73	75	299	120,000
Toshimitsu Kai	71	79	79	71	300	112,000
Osami Kitano	73	77	77	73	300	112,000
Tadashi Kitsuta	75	75	78	72	300	112,000
Keizo Yamada	75	75	74	76	300	112,000
Hisao Inoue	72	76	74	78	300	112,000
Mahito Ito	73	74	81	73	301	100,000
Tsuneo Uchida	75	76	75	75	301	100,000
*Shinsuke Maeda	73	75	74	79	301	
Minoru Kawakami	76	72	80	74	302	86,666
Masaharu Oshima	73	77	76	76	302	86,666
Hisashi Nakase	74	76	83	69	302	86,666
Tsutai Shimojo	75	71	82	75	303	74,285
Hiroshi Oku	76	76	76	75	303	74,285

	SCORES			TOTAL	MONEY
Matsuo Kimura	76	75	77	75	303	74,285
Hisashi Terada	72	76	81	74	303	74,285
Mazumi Kanayama	76	74	78	75	303	74,285
Yasuo Tanabe	76	75	76	76	303	74,285
Takeshi Okumura	77	72	82	72	303	74,285
*Uichiro Okada	78	74	76	76	304	
Takeshi Kitadai	75	77	77	75	304	70,000
*Risaku Ikuchi	77	75	77	75	304	
Hisashi Kaji	74	75	81	75	305	60,000
Yoshiki Yamazaki	75	74	80	76	305	60,000
Tsutomu Ikeya	74	78	79	74	305	60,000
Toshimi Kimoto	72	77	80	77	306	60,000
Susumu Wakita	77	75	78	76	306	60,000
Takeshi Matsukawa	76	75	80	76	307	50,000
*Yoshiaki Kimura	77	75	81	74	307	
Yuji Takagi	73	78	78	79	308	50,000
Motomasa Nishikawa	75	75	81	77	308	50,000
Tetsuo Ishii	72	76	80	81	309	50,000
Hisashi Morioka	75	76	77	81	309	50,000
*Takahiro Nakagawa	75	77	80	79	311	
Susumu Hano	77	75	86	77	315	50,000

Chubu Open

Katayamazu Golf Club, Ishikawa Prefecture
Par 72; 6,869 yards

September 2–5
purse, ¥12,500,000

	SCORES			TOTAL	MONEY
Shigeru Uchida	69	68	75	70	282	¥3,000,000
Masahiko Yamamoto	71	73	74	70	288	1,250,000
Teruo Suzumura	72	71	74	71	288	1,250,000
Koichi Inoue	73	73	75	68	289	700,000
Lu Liang Huan	72	74	72	71	289	700,000
Kakuji Matsui	71	72	75	72	290	416,667
Kiyonori Tamura	72	71	74	73	290	416,667
Hisashi Suzumura	74	69	73	74	290	416,666
Lu Hsi Chuen	69	75	74	74	292	300,000
Hiroshi Ishii	74	70	75	74	293	250,000
Kazuhiro Tamura	73	76	74	71	294	200,000
Shunji Kanazawa	72	73	75	75	295	190,000
Hideo Ishii	74	74	74	74	296	170,000
Mitsuo Hirukawa	72	73	77	74	296	170,000
Muneyoshi Nakayama	68	79	74	75	296	170,000
Yutaka Suzuki	74	75	78	70	297	150,000
Akio Toyoda	73	74	77	74	298	135,000
Teruo Nakamura	77	71	73	77	298	135,000
Hatsutoshi Sakai	72	75	74	78	299	115,000
Kazuo Hanamura	72	72	78	77	299	115,000
Yuzo Noda	75	74	80	71	300	100,000
Norifumi Mizuno	74	78	77	72	301	100,000
Tsutomu Kakuta	74	77	76	74	301	100,000
Masamitsu Oguri	75	75	76	75	301	100,000
Norihiko Matsumoto	77	69	79	76	301	100,000
*Yoshiaki Ono	76	74	75	76	301	
Hiroaki Uenishi	74	76	77	75	302	90,000
Norihiko Maei	76	76	75	75	302	90,000
Tsuguhiko Bando	73	77	75	77	302	90,000

	SCORES				TOTAL	MONEY
*Yoki Sawada	73	73	78	78	302	
Seiji Mitsuki	75	73	78	77	303	90,000
Seiji Terashima	75	74	81	74	304	90,000
Toshihiro Matsuda	79	71	77	78	305	80,000
Kizo Ogino	73	76	78	78	305	80,000
*Hisao Takeuchi	76	76	79	75	306	
Rikizo Kato	76	75	78	77	306	80,000
Shigehisa Kano	74	77	76	79	306	80,000
*Hideo Hayama	72	76	83	76	307	
Kiyoshi Nomura	76	73	85	74	308	73,334
Yoshihiko Nagata	74	74	82	78	308	73,333
Katsuyuki Hirano	73	74	78	83	308	73,333
*Shunichiro Tsuruta	78	73	84	74	309	
Yasutoshi Terashita	73	79	81	76	309	70,000
*Mitsuo Maki	77	75	80	78	310	
Takeru Shibata	73	78	80	79	310	70,000
Yutaka Kondo	75	76	84	76	311	63,334
*Yoshihiko Nakamura	72	77	84	78	311	
Koji Tanaka	71	78	83	79	311	63,333
Koichi Okuno	76	75	80	80	311	63,333
Nobuyoshi Tajima	77	74	82	79	312	60,000

Chugoku Open

Hakuryuko Country Club, Hiroshima Prefecture
Par 72; 6,824 yards

September 2–4
purse, Y5,000,000

	SCORES				TOTAL	MONEY
Masahiro Kuramoto	67	70	73	68	278	Y1,200,000
Norio Mikami	72	72	68	70	282	700,000
Tadami Ueno	71	72	71	70	284	500,000
Katsumi Hara	74	68	73	71	286	350,000
Atsuo Suemura	68	69	73	77	287	250,000
Hideto Shigenobu	69	71	77	71	288	190,000
Yasuhiro Daio	69	72	75	72	288	190,000
Yozo Okabe	72	71	73	73	289	165,000
Kazuki Nagao	74	77	69	71	291	150,000
Takashi Watanabe	73	72	74	72	291	150,000
Takashi Nakatani	72	74	71	75	292	125,000
Mitoshi Tomita	75	74	71	73	293	110,000
Takafumi Ogawa	72	74	73	75	294	100,000
*Junji Takigawa	70	76	73	75	294	
Takashi Miyoshi	75	73	71	76	295	75,000
Mitsuji Tanaka	73	75	72	75	295	75,000
Hiroshi Taninaka	72	73	74	77	296	65,000
Mitsuhiko Masuda	71	77	75	74	297	55,000
Eizo Matsuoka	73	73	78	73	297	55,000
Yoshinori Ushijima	74	74	73	76	297	55,000
*Yoshiaki Nomura	73	74	74	76	297	
*Keisuke Miyano	70	76	75	76	297	
Nobuo Sato	67	82	76	74	299	40,000
Seiji Katayama	73	77	78	72	300	40,000
Kunio Yamashita	74	74	76	76	300	40,000
Tsunenori Tanaka	74	72	75	79	300	40,000
*Naoyasu Okunobu	72	76	75	77	300	
*Ikuo Saeki	73	77	70	80	300	
Satoshi Haga	74	74	79	74	301	30,000

	SCORES				TOTAL	MONEY
Yoshihiro Miyanaka	69	74	77	82	302	30,000
Yasushi Shiomi	72	78	74	78	302	30,000
*Kinji Ando	77	75	80	70	302	
*Kazushi Hamanou	76	79	75	72	302	

Kyushu Open

Kyushu Shima Country Club, Fukuoka Prefecture   September 2–5
Par 72; 7,129 yards   purse, Y12,000,000

	SCORES				TOTAL	MONEY
Norio Suzuki	71	72	77	71	291	Y2,500,000
Kaneya Yoshimura	70	79	74	70	293	1,250,000
*Kiyotaka Oke	73	75	77	71	296	
Shigemi Nakazono	73	76	76	72	297	700,000
Tatsuya Shiraishi	72	73	75	77	297	700,000
Kuniharu Nakagawara	74	76	78	71	299	416,666
Sadatoshi Makimura	74	74	79	72	299	416,666
Mineyuki Yoshimatsu	75	72	78	74	299	416,666
*Takehisa Shinozuka	73	77	77	73	300	
Tetsuhiro Ueda	73	77	77	73	300	235,000
Norikazu Kawakami	73	76	77	74	300	235,000
Hisataka Fujii	76	69	79	76	300	235,000
Yurio Akitomi	72	75	79	75	301	180,000
Tadayoshi Bando	75	74	79	74	302	160,000
Noboru Fujiike	74	73	79	76	302	160,000
Yoshiaki Arai	75	75	74	78	302	160,000
Masayuki Shoji	71	82	79	71	304	130,000
Kenji Ueda	73	79	78	74	304	130,000
Isamu Sugita	78	75	77	74	304	130,000
Kosei Sakai	76	76	78	75	305	110,000
Tadashige Kusano	80	77	77	72	306	100,000
Norihiko Inoue	71	82	79	74	306	100,000
Ryutaro Arima	76	78	80	73	307	96,000
Kenichi Kawano	77	77	80	73	307	96,000
Keiji Tejima	78	72	81	76	307	96,000
Yoshimasa Fujii	80	75	75	77	307	96,000
Yoshinari Shikoda	81	74	75	77	307	96,000
Nobuhiro Sakata	75	74	85	74	308	90,000
*Fumiaki Nakajima	74	75	81	78	308	
Hideyuki Tada	76	79	77	77	309	83,000
*Masanori Yamashita	78	75	79	77	309	
Reiji Bando	73	75	80	81	309	83,000
*Masanori Itoyama	74	81	79	76	310	
Yoshihito Murayama	81	75	77	81	310	80,000
Sato Tsuyoshi	78	75	77	80	310	80,000
Seiji Miyazaki	76	75	84	76	311	70,000
*Shizuo Shizuura	78	78	80	75	311	
*Keiji Takayama	79	77	78	77	311	
Masayuki Shimamura	77	81	76	77	311	70,000
*Hiromi Yokoyama	76	78	75	82	311	
Noboru Shibata	77	77	81	77	312	60,000
Makoto Nanbu	76	76	83	77	312	60,000
Yukio Makiyama	76	79	79	76	312	60,000
Hiroaki Yoshioka	78	77	80	78	313	54,000
Tatsuyuki Nishimiya	74	81	81	77	313	54,000
Atsuo Takahashi	78	80	82	78	313	54,000

	SCORES				TOTAL	MONEY
Yuji Sato	78	80	77	78	313	54,000
Misao Yamamoto	77	79	77	77	313	54,000
*Yohichi Imamura	73	75	72	83	313	
Masamitsu Urata	74	80	81	79	314	50,000
*Teruo Ikebe	75	79	83	77	314	

Hokkaido Open

Onuma International Country Club   September 3–5
Par 72; 7,122 yards   purse, Y5,000,000

	SCORES				TOTAL	MONEY
Koichi Uehara	71	72	76	70	289	Y1,500,000
Katsunari Takahashi.	72	75	75	72	294	700,000
Kesahiko Uchida	80	72	70	74	296	450,000
Ryoichi Takagi	74	73	76	73	296	450,000
Mitsuyoshi Goto	75	73	79	70	297	300,000
Soichi Sato	76	73	77	72	298	200,000
Hiroshi Yamada	75	74	78	71	298	200,000
Kanae Nobechi	71	75	78	75	299	115,000
Yutaka Ikawa	75	77	76	71	299	115,000
Toshiaki Nakamura	75	75	77	74	301	100,000
Kazumi Takai	72	77	82	71	302	70,000
Yoshiharu Takai	75	81	76	70	302	70,000
Yasuo Kuninaka	78	77	72	75	302	70,000
Harunobu Fujii	77	70	76	79	302	70,000
Shinji Kubota	78	75	76	74	303	70,000
Kenji Takeda	75	77	78	74	304	50,000
*Masanori Bimizu	77	78	79	71	305	
Masaaki Yamamoto	76	74	81	74	305	50,000
Jun Nobechi	80	75	76	75	306	50,000
Masaru Sato	79	79	76	73	307	50,000
Seiji Takahashi	75	78	76	79	308	50,000
Tetsuo Katsumata	78	74	79	78	309	50,000
Noritaka Shiraishi	83	75	75	76	309	50,000
Mamoru Takahashi	75	77	81	76	309	50,000
*Yoshinaga Sarazu	81	74	82	74	311	
*Kazuo Nishikawa	73	77	85	76	311	
*Hideo Kinoshita	83	83	72	73	311	
*Yoshimi Aisawa	79	74	78	84	315	
Shimizu Kubota	80	77	82	76	315	50,000
*Mitsuhiro Ohno	81	77	82	76	316	

Suntory Open

Narashino Country Club, Chiba Prefecture   September 9–12
Par 72; 7,138 yards   purse, Y50,000,000
(Tournament reduced to 54 holes because of rain.)

	SCORES			TOTAL	MONEY
Pete Izumikawa	67	68	72	207	Y9,000,000
Bill Rogers	66	73	70	209	5,000,000
Masahiro Kuramoto	70	70	70	210	2,667,000
Norio Suzuki	65	73	72	210	2,667,000
Tateo Ozaki	70	71	69	210	2,667,000
Minoru Kawakami	70	74	67	211	1,900,000

	SCORES			TOTAL	MONEY
Takaaki Kono	73	71	68	212	1,370,000
Seiichi Kanai	70	73	69	212	1,370,000
Isao Aoki	71	71	70	212	1,370,000
Yoshimi Niizeki	67	72	73	212	1,370,000
Tadami Ueno	69	67	76	212	1,370,000
Hiroshi Makino	71	68	74	213	1,000,000
Shinsaku Maeda	71	72	71	214	713,500
Saburo Fujiki	69	76	69	214	713,500
Nobumitsu Yuhara	72	70	72	214	713,500
Toshiharu Kawada	70	71	73	214	713,500
Masaji Kusakabe	70	69	75	214	713,500
Koichi Inoue	71	69	74	214	713,500
Toru Nakamura	72	73	70	215	472,000
Hisashi Suzumura	72	72	71	215	472,000
Hideto Shigenobu	69	74	72	215	472,000
Koichi Uehara	76	7˚	69	215	472,000
Seiji Ebihara	75	71	69	215	472,000
Tsutomu Irie	68	74	73	215	472,000
Kikuo Arai	67	77	72	216	410,000
Mitsuo Watanabe	74	72	70	216	410,000
Hideyo Sugimoto	70	72	74	216	410,000
Akira Yabe	71	73	73	217	356,500
Katsunari Takahashi	72	73	72	217	356,500
Kazuo Kanayama	73	72	72	217	356,500
Isao Isozaki	73	72	72	217	356,500
Kenji Mori	71	72	74	217	356,500
Yoshitaka Yamamoto	71	75	71	217	356,500
Tom Kite	70	72	75	217	356,500
Kosaku Shimada	71	76	70	217	356,500
Yasushi Katayama	69	75	74	218	294,000
Kuo Chi Hsiung	71	73	74	218	294,000
Toshiki Matsui	71	74	73	218	294,000
Shoji Ozaki	75	68	75	218	294,000
Akio Kanamoto	72	74	72	218	294,000
Tsuguhiko Bando	69	78	71	218	294,000
Noriji Asai	69	69	80	218	294,000
Chen Tze Ming	75	69	75	219	250,000
Yutaka Hagawa	74	72	73	219	250,000
Scott Simpson	71	75	73	219	250,000
Toyotake Nakao	70	77	72	219	250,000
Katsuji Hasegawa	72	72	76	220	222,000
Shigeru Noguchi	74	71	75	220	222,000
Hideo Ishii	72	73	75	220	222,000
Akio Toyoda	69	76	75	220	222,000
Norio Mikami	75	71	74	220	222,000
Koji Takahashi	70	77	73	220	222,000

ANA Sapporo Open

Sapporo Golf Club, Watsu Course, Hokkaido   September 16–19
Par 72; 7,098 yards   purse, Y40,000,000

	SCORES				TOTAL	MONEY
Norio Suzuki	74	63	69	72	278	Y8,000,000
Isao Aoki	71	72	67	69	279	4,000,000
Masashi Ozaki	70	71	70	69	280	1,775,000
Tsuneyuki Nakajima	72	68	70	70	280	1,775,000

		SCORES			TOTAL	MONEY
Akira Yabe	74	68	65	73	280	1,775,000
Yutaka Hagawa	72	68	67	73	280	1,775,000
Tateo Ozaki	74	74	68	66	282	1,100,000
Haruo Yasuda	70	72	70	71	283	950,000
Pete Izumikawa	70	71	71	71	283	950,000
Naomichi Ozaki	71	71	72	71	285	750,000
Chen Chien Chung	75	68	70	72	285	750,000
Kikuo Arai	69	72	72	72	285	750,000
Seiichi Kanai	72	71	71	72	286	655,000
Shinsaku Maeda	69	72	73	72	286	655,000
Takashi Kurihara	73	68	76	70	287	580,000
Hsieh Yung Yo	72	68	73	74	287	580,000
Toru Nakamura	69	73	69	76	287	580,000
Saburo Fujiki	74	72	72	70	288	490,000
Taiichi Nakagawa	74	71	72	71	288	490,000
Koichi Uehara	71	74	71	72	288	490,000
Masahiro Kuramoto	70	73	70	75	288	490,000
Hsieh Min Nan	72	76	71	70	289	423,333
David Ishii	74	73	70	72	289	423,333
Koichi Inoue	75	68	72	74	289	423,333
Toshiaki Sekimizu	69	71	75	75	290	400,000
Hidenori Nakajima	73	72	73	73	291	380,000
Yasuhiro Funatogawa	71	78	69	73	291	380,000
Kosaku Shimada	75	70	72	74	291	380,000
Namio Takasu	75	72	72	73	292	330,000
Tadao Nakamura	75	72	72	73	292	330,000
Yoshihisa Iwashita	73	73	75	71	292	330,000
Hiroshi Ishii	75	73	70	74	292	330,000
Motomasa Aoki	70	75	72	75	292	330,000
Yoshitaka Yamamoto	71	74	71	76	292	330,000
Akio Toyoda	72	75	69	76	292	330,000
Koji Nakajima	75	72	73	73	293	260,000
Hideyo Sugimoto	72	75	73	73	293	260,000
Lu Hsi Chuen	73	74	72	74	293	260,000
Mitsuhiro Kitta	73	75	71	74	293	260,000
Katsunari Takahashi	72	77	69	75	293	260,000
Hideto Shigenobu	74	73	78	68	293	260,000
Taisei Inagaki	73	72	71	77	293	260,000
Satsuki Takahashi	73	73	71	77	294	222,500
Seiji Ebihara	70	77	67	80	294	222,500
Toyotake Nakao	77	71	72	75	295	212,500
Hiroshi Makino	70	74	76	75	295	212,500
Yurio Akitomi	74	74	73	75	296	197,500
Teruo Sugihara	74	74	74	74	296	197,500
Toshiaki Nakamura	70	78	75	73	296	197,500
Fujio Kobayashi	76	73	77	70	296	197,500

Hiroshima Open

Hiroshima Country Club, Hiroshima
Par 71; 6,644 yards

September 23–26
purse, Y30,000,000

		SCORES			TOTAL	MONEY
Takashi Kurihara	69	67	70	66	272	Y6,000,000
Yutaka Hagawa	71	66	66	73	276	3,000,000
Yoshitaka Yamamoto	72	67	71	67	277	2,150,000
Tadami Ueno	70	68	69	70	277	2,150,000

	SCORES				TOTAL	MONEY
Namio Takasu	69	74	68	67	278	1,350,000
Hsieh Min Nan	68	72	68	70	278	1,350,000
Ichiro Teramoto	69	70	71	69	279	925,000
Fujio Kobayashi	69	65	72	73	279	925,000
Toru Nakamura	71	66	76	67	280	533,300
Hideo Ishii	70	70	71	69	280	533,300
Seiji Ebihara	72	66	72	70	280	533,300
Yoshiharu Takai	70	74	66	70	280	533,300
Toshiharu Kawada	67	70	72	71	280	533,300
Kenji Mori	69	70	69	72	280	533,300
Hideto Shigenobu	73	68	72	68	281	390,000
Yoshihisa Iwashita	73	67	71	70	281	390,000
Haruo Yasuda	69	72	73	68	282	340,000
Norio Suzuki	72	67	74	69	282	340,000
Kasaji Kusakabe	67	72	73	70	282	340,000
Norio Mikami	71	73	72	67	283	270,000
Kuo Chi Hsiung	70	74	70	69	283	270,000
Koichi Inoue	71	71	72	69	283	270,000
Yoshinori Ichioka	71	69	72	71	283	270,000
Norio Adachi	71	72	69	71	283	270,000
Toshimitsu Kai	71	66	73	73	283	270,000
Sadao Sakashita	68	70	70	75	283	270,000
Takao Kage	73	71	72	68	284	238,000
Akira Yabe	72	69	74	69	284	238,000
Akio Toyoda	70	73	73	68	284	238,000
Shinsaku Maeda	68	70	75	71	284	238,000
Motomasa Aoki	73	70	69	72	284	238,000
Koichi Uehara	73	69	74	69	285	230,000
Lu Liang Huan	70	73	71	71	285	230,000
Mamoru Takahashi	70	72	68	75	285	230,000
George Yokoi	74	70	74	68	286	222,000
Yurio Akitomi	69	75	73	69	286	222,000
Seiichi Kanai	72	71	74	69	286	222,000
Lu Hsi Chuen	67	74	75	70	286	222,000
Hidenori Nakajima	68	74	71	73	286	222,000
Shinichi Hayashi	71	70	75	71	287	220,000
Satsuki Takahashi	70	72	73	73	288	210,000
Hisashi Suzumura	72	71	72	73	288	210,000
Takashi Watanabe	73	71	72	73	289	206,000
Tateo Ozaki	71	69	75	74	289	206,000
Chen Chien Chung	69	72	74	74	289	206,000
Mitoshi Tomita	73	69	73	74	289	206,000
Yasuhiro Miyamoto	71	72	70	76	289	206,000
Nobumitsu Yuhara	75	68	74	73	290	200,000
Yoshikazu Yokoshima	69	72	74	75	290	200,000
Ben Arda	72	72	79	68	291	200,000

Gene Sarazen Jun Classic

Jun Classic Country Club, Tochigi Prefecture
Par 72; 6,982 yards

September 30–October 3
purse, Y50,000,000

	SCORES				TOTAL	MONEY
Teruo Sugihara	69	70	70	66	275	Y9,000,000
Norio Suzuki	69	68	67	74	278	4,500,000
Tateo Ozaki	72	69	71	67	279	3,200,000
Terry Gale	65	72	74	72	283	2,050,000

	SCORES				TOTAL	MONEY
Toru Nakamura	72	67	69	75	283	2,050,000
Tsuneyuki Nakajima	71	75	71	67	284	1,400,000
Shinsaku Maeda	70	73	69	72	284	1,400,000
Takashi Murakami	73	70	68	74	285	1,200,000
Kikuo Arai	69	72	70	75	286	1,100,000
Eitaro Deguchi	70	68	77	72	287	975,000
Graham Marsh	72	71	71	73	287	975,000
Yoshiyuki Isomura	72	74	75	67	288	850,000
Koichi Uehara	66	73	78	71	288	850,000
Seiji Ebihara	74	71	70	73	288	850,000
Naomichi Ozaki	72	76	72	69	289	725,000
Yutaka Hagawa	70	74	70	75	289	725,000
Haruo Yasuda	71	72	74	73	290	650,000
Isao Aoki	71	73	73	73	290	650,000
Masahiro Kuramoto	75	69	72	74	290	650,000
Hiroshi Ishii	76	70	70	74	290	650,000
Motomasa Aoki	70	75	75	71	291	550,000
Akira Yabe	74	74	74	69	291	550,000
Nobumitsu Yuhara	69	70	78	74	291	550,000
Pete Izumikawa	70	72	74	75	291	550,000
Hsieh Min Nan	71	75	73	72	291	550,000
Hideo Ishii	72	73	73	73	291	550,000
Ho Ming Chung	70	73	77	72	292	460,000
Saburo Fujiki	72	73	75	72	292	460,000
Satsuki Takahashi	72	72	74	74	292	460,000
Soichi Sato	75	72	73	73	293	397,500
Kuo Chi Hsiung	72	71	75	75	293	397,500
Chen Chien Chung	76	71	72	74	293	397,500
Chi Chi Rodriguez	71	74	72	76	293	397,500
Kesahiko Uchida	74	71	77	72	294	365,000
Noboru Fujiike	71	72	74	77	294	365,000
Mitsuhiro Kitsuta	72	74	75	74	295	330,000
Hidenori Nakajima	72	74	75	74	295	330,000
Kosaku Shimada	72	73	75	75	295	330,000
Taisei Inagaki	70	76	74	75	295	330,000
Isao Matsui	74	72	73	76	295	330,000
David Ishii	72	74	73	76	295	330,000
Akio Kanamoto	73	73	73	76	295	330,000
Masaru Amano	74	73	76	72	295	330,000
Tsutomu Irie	74	73	71	77	295	330,000
Katsuji Hasegawa	73	75	71	77	296	302,500
Takashi Kurihara	73	70	75	78	296	302,500
Yoshimi Niizeki	70	75	78	74	297	292,500
Yoshikazu Yokoshima	73	75	76	73	297	292,500
Mitsutaka Kohno	74	73	74	77	298	280,000
Ben Arda	73	75	75	75	298	280,000
Norio Mikami	73	74	77	74	298	280,000

Tokai Classic

Miyoshi Country Club, Nagoya
Par 72; 7,065 yards

October 7–10
purse, Y40,000,000

	SCORES				TOTAL	MONEY
Hsieh Min Nan	64	71	72	67	274	Y8,000,000
Larry Nelson	71	70	71	67	279	4,000,000
Tateo Ozaki	69	74	68	69	280	2,150,000

	SCORES				TOTAL	MONEY
Hideto Shigenobu	69	70	69	72	280	2,150,000
Yoshitaka Yamamoto	70	72	71	68	281	1,175,000
Chen Tze Ming	71	68	68	74	281	1,175,000
Toru Nakamura	67	72	71	72	282	1,000,000
Kikuo Arai	67	76	69	71	283	900,000
Fujio Kobayashi	69	73	71	70	283	900,000
Tsuneyuki Nakajima	67	71	70	75	283	900,000
Teruo Suzumura	71	72	71	70	284	780,000
Bobby Clampett	67	76	72	69	284	780,000
Toshiharu Kawada	72	69	74	70	285	700,000
Shoji Kikuchi	72	70	72	71	285	700,000
Kosaku Shimada	66	74	71	75	286	595,000
Akio Toyoda	71	73	73	69	286	595,000
Seiichi Kanai	71	74	72	69	286	595,000
Yasuhiro Miyamato	71	72	73	70	286	595,000
Masaji Kusakabe	69	69	77	72	287	510,000
Hiroshi Ishii	67	73	76	71	287	510,000
Terry Gale	70	74	69	74	287	510,000
Koichi Uehara	71	73	76	69	287	510,000
Seiji Ebihara	69	72	69	78	288	430,000
Tadashi Kitsuta	72	72	72	72	288	430,000
Ho Ming Chung	71	70	74	73	288	430,000
Teruo Sugihara	72	70	73	73	288	430,000
Akira Yabe	70	72	73	73	288	430,000
Tadami Ueno	74	69	73	72	288	430,000
Lu Hsi Chuen	74	72	70	72	288	430,000
Motomasa Aoki	70	75	74	69	288	430,000
Isao Isozaki	69	74	71	74	288	430,000
Isao Aoki	71	73	70	75	289	365,000
Namio Takasu	73	70	72	74	289	365,000
Koichi Inoue	71	71	73	74	289	365,000
Eitaro Deguchi	72	70	75	72	289	365,000
Masashi Ozaki	73	72	75	70	290	330,000
Akio Kanamoto	75	68	72	75	290	330,000
Bruch Lietzke	73	73	73	71	290	330,000
Toshihiro Matsuda	71	74	73	73	291	305,000
Taiichi Nakagawa	69	74	74	74	291	305,000
Shinsaku Maeda	70	74	76	72	292	275,000
Hidenori Nakajima	72	74	71	75	292	275,000
Isao Matsui	70	75	74	73	292	275,000
Hisashi Suzumura	69	75	74	74	292	275,000
Haruo Yasuda	70	72	75	76	293	250,000
*Minoru Azuma	74	78	67	74	293	
Masahiro Kuramoto	71	74	74	75	294	235,000
Tsutomu Irie	72	72	77	73	294	235,000
Naomichi Ozaki	70	76	73	76	295	220,000
Takeshi Shibata	69	77	74	76	296	205,000
Lu Liang Huan	70	74	74	78	296	205,000

Golf Digest

Tomei Country Club, Shizuoka Prefecture   October 14–17
Par 72; 6,857 yards   purse, Y30,000,000

	SCORES				TOTAL	MONEY
Hsieh Min Nan	64	70	65	75	274	Y6,000,000
Akira Yabe	69	70	70	66	275	3,000,000

	SCORES				TOTAL	MONEY
Bruce Lietzke	68	72	67	69	276	1,800,000
Takao Kage	70	69	70	68	277	1,150,000
Hsu Sheng San	71	66	71	69	277	1,150,000
Teruo Sugihara	66	73	69	70	278	800,000
Masashi Ozaki	72	69	71	67	279	750,000
Kikuo Arai	70	70	67	73	280	700,000
Seiichi Kanai	64	71	73	73	281	650,000
Danny Edwards	69	71	71	70	282	550,000
Hiroshi Makino	72	68	71	71	282	550,000
Yasuhiro Miyamoto	68	70	70	74	282	550,000
Shigeru Uchida	72	70	73	68	283	402,000
Yoshikazu Yokoshima	71	73	67	72	283	402,000
Chen Tze Ming	72	70	69	72	283	402,000
Yoshinori Ichioka	69	72	70	72	283	402,000
Masahiko Yamamoto	69	71	68	75	283	402,000
Tateo Ozaki	73	67	72	72	284	312,500
Tadashi Kitsuta	71	69	71	73	284	312,500
Norio Mikami	68	73	69	74	284	312,500
Tsuneyuki Nakajima	67	73	68	76	284	312,500
Katsunari Takahashi	70	74	69	72	285	280,000
Lu Liang Huan	69	70	71	75	285	280,000
Hisashi Suzumura	69	70	71	75	285	280,000
Teruo Suzumura	65	71	72	77	285	280,000
Koichi Inoue	69	75	71	71	286	260,000
Isao Isozaki	70	71	73	72	286	260,000
Satsuki Takahashi	70	71	71	74	286	260,000
Takashi Kurihara	70	71	71	74	286	260,000
Minoru Nakamura	70	74	68	75	287	240,000
Masaru Amano	69	73	70	75	287	240,000
Takashi Murakami	72	68	71	76	287	240,000
Hideto Shigenobu	68	72	71	76	287	240,000
Shigeru Noguchi	68	75	70	75	288	220,000
Junichi Takahashi	70	72	71	75	288	220,000
Namio Takasu	72	68	72	76	288	220,000
Takaaki Kono	73	70	69	76	288	220,000
Koichi Uehara	70	74	71	74	289	203,333
Chen Chien Chung	70	72	72	75	289	203,333
Go Shiono	72	71	68	78	289	203,333
Katsuji Hasegawa	71	69	77	73	290	190,000
Masaji Kusakabe	71	70	75	74	290	190,000
Sakio Ishida	76	67	76	72	291	180,000
Saburo Fujiki	73	68	76	74	291	180,000
Hiroshi Ishii	67	76	73	75	291	180,000
Fujio Kobayashi	71	71	75	75	292	170,000
David Ishii	73	70	74	75	292	170,000
Kenji Mori	69	72	71	80	292	170,000
Yasuzo Hagiwara	72	72	74	75	293	164,000
Yoshiyuki Isomura	74	70	74	75	293	164,000
Norio Adachi	72	72	74	75	293	164,000
Tsao Chien Teng	73	71	75	77	293	164,000
Naomichi Ozaki	73	71	70	79	293	164,000

Bridgestone

Sodegaura Country Club, Chiba Prefecture
Par 72; 7,151 yards

October 21–24
purse, Y50,000,000

		SCORES			TOTAL	MONEY
Hsieh Min Nan	64	70	71	74	279	Y9,000,000
Kikuo Arai	70	74	66	69	279	5,400,000
(Hsieh defeated Arai on second hole of sudden death playoff.)						
Lee Trevino	70	75	70	67	282	2,425,000
Motomasa Aoki	73	67	72	70	282	2,425,000
Tom Weiskopf	68	71	71	72	282	2,425,000
Seiichi Kanai	71	71	69	71	282	2,425,000
Teruo Suzumura	72	74	69	68	283	1,675,000
Saburo Fujiki	68	72	70	74	284	1,550,000
Bruce Lietzke	72	76	67	70	285	1,350,000
Tsuneyuki Nakajima	71	70	73	71	285	1,350,000
Tadami Ueno	69	71	70	75	285	1,350,000
Chen Chien Chung	71	73	72	70	286	950,000
Isao Isozaki	73	74	67	72	286	950,000
Yutaka Hagawa	74	71	73	68	286	950,000
Satsuki Takahashi	69	73	75	69	286	950,000
Hiroshi Makino	73	74	70	69	286	950,000
Fujio Kobayashi	69	71	76	70	286	950,000
Chen Tze Ming	70	71	77	69	287	630,000
Teruo Sugihara	75	72	71	69	287	630,000
Yoshitaka Yamamoto	72	71	73	71	287	630,000
Masashi Ozaki	78	70	68	71	287	630,000
Nobumitsu Yuhara	70	73	72	72	287	630,000
Tateo Ozaki	71	73	68	75	287	630,000
Koichi Inoue	71	72	75	70	288	415,000
Hale Irwin	69	72	77	70	288	415,000
Namio Takasu	73	73	72	70	288	415,000
Shigeru Uchida	76	72	68	72	288	415,000
Masahiro Kuramoto	71	72	73	72	288	415,000
Kosaku Shimada	74	73	70	72	289	311,071
Shigeru Noguchi	72	74	71	72	289	311,071
Yoshimi Watanabe	69	77	71	72	289	311,071
Lu Hsi Chuen	70	72	74	73	289	311,071
Koichi Uehara	70	72	73	74	289	311,071
Naomichi Ozaki	73	70	72	74	289	311,071
Yasuzo Hagiwara	72	71	70	76	289	311,071
Takao Kage	73	73	72	72	290	235,500
Katsunari Takahashi	74	74	72	70	290	235,500
Isao Aoki	72	72	76	70	290	235,500
Noboru Fujiike	76	69	72	73	290	235,500
Yasuhiro Funatogawa	76	71	68	75	290	235,500
Koji Nakajima	70	76	72	73	291	195,000
Seiji Ogawa	74	71	74	72	291	195,000
Akira Yabe	72	70	73	76	291	195,000
Liao Kuo Chih	73	72	74	73	292	155,400
Hideo Ishii	71	72	74	75	292	155,400
Eitaro Deguchi	72	74	75	71	292	155,400
Tsao Chien Teng	73	73	75	71	292	155,400
Masaji Kusakabe	73	72	69	78	292	155,400
Yasuhiro Miyamoto	75	70	74	74	293	123,400
Yoshiyuki Isomura	74	73	73	73	293	123,400
Toru Nakamura	72	75	74	72	293	123,400
Junichi Takahashi	76	71	69	77	293	123,400
Masaaki Shiraishi	74	72	78	59	293	123,400

Japan Open

Musashi Country Club, Toyooka Course, Saitama Prefecture   October 28–31
Par 71; 6,678 yards   purse, Y50,000,000

	SCORES				TOTAL	MONEY
Akira Yabe	71	70	67	69	277	Y8,000,000
Naomichi Ozaki	71	75	70	66	282	433,334
Yutaka Hagawa	70	71	71	70	282	433,333
Ikuo Shirahama	72	70	67	73	282	433,333
Tsuneyuki Nakajima	68	74	69	72	283	1,800,000
Kazunori Mizuno	74	70	69	71	284	1,400,000
Masashi Ozaki	68	73	70	73	284	1,400,000
Takashi Kurihara	71	71	73	70	285	1,100,000
Saburo Fujiki	72	69	72	72	285	1,100,000
Chen Tze Ming	70	71	69	75	285	1,100,000
Isao Isozaki	71	76	71	68	286	850,000
Teruo Suzumura	70	74	73	69	286	850,000
Isao Aoki	71	74	71	70	286	850,000
Seiji Ebihara	73	71	72	70	286	850,000
Lu Hsi Chuen	71	77	68	70	286	850,000
Katsuji Hasegawa	69	76	72	70	287	562,858
Fujio Kobayashi	73	74	70	70	287	562,857
Teruo Sugihara	74	72	70	71	287	562,857
Yoshitaka Yamamoto	70	74	71	72	287	562,857
Toyotake Nakao	68	76	71	72	287	562,857
Satsuki Takahashi	73	73	69	72	287	562,857
Kuo Chi Hisung	71	73	70	73	287	562,857
Yoshihisa Iwashita	72	72	74	70	288	440,000
Yasuhiro Miyamoto	73	73	73	70	289	401,667
Minoru Nakamura	74	72	69	74	289	401,667
Masahiro Kuramoto	70	70	74	75	289	401,666
Koichi Inoue	73	73	73	71	290	348,750
Nobumitsu Yuhara	71	72	74	73	290	348,750
Kazuo Yoshikawa	72	74	70	74	290	348,750
Hsu Sheng San	71	75	68	76	290	348,750
Hideo Kishiro	76	70	73	72	291	300,000
Ho Ming Chung	72	75	72	72	291	300,000
Tsutomu Irie	71	73	73	74	291	300,000
Shigeru Uchida	71	77	69	74	291	300,000
Hideyo Sugimoto	68	73	74	76	291	300,000
Akio Toyoda	74	74	72	72	292	257,834
Hideto Shigenobu	71	74	75	72	292	257,834
Junichi Takahashi	72	73	74	73	292	257,833
Kenji Mori	74	74	71	73	292	257,833
Hsieh Yung Yo	73	74	70	75	292	257,833
Hideo Ishii	67	75	71	79	292	257,833
Motomasa Aoki	69	75	74	75	293	242,500
Koichi Uehara	72	73	73	75	293	242,500
Namio Takasu	78	70	74	72	294	235,000
Ichiro Teramoto	76	72	73	73	294	235,000
Yoshimi Watanabe	76	72	72	74	294	235,000
*Tersuo Sakata	75	73	73	74	295	
*Ginjiro Nakabe	75	73	74	73	295	
Toshiharu Kawada	72	72	75	76	295	229,000
Yuzo Noda	76	71	75	74	296	224,500
Yoshikazu Yokoshima	72	75	74	75	296	224,500

Goldwin Cup (U.S. vs Japan)

Sobu Country Club, Tokyo
Par 71; 7,187 yards

November 4–7
purse, US$440,000

FINAL RESULT : UNITED STATES 33, JAPAN 15

THURSDAY

FOUR-BALL: Ray Floyd and Lanny Wadkins defeated Isao Aoki and
Yutaka Hagawa, 62–69.
Masahiro Kuramoto and Kikuo Arai defeated Bob Gilder
and Craig Stadler, 65–67.
Tom Kite and Calvin Peete defeated Teruo Sugihara and
Toru Nakamura, 65–68.
Jerry Pate and Tom Watson defeated Tsuneyuki Nakajima
and Norio Suzuki, 62–67.
U.S. leads, 6–2.

FRIDAY

Gilder and Wadkins defeated Suzuki and Kuramoto, 68–79.
Floyd and Pate tied Hagawa and Nakajima, 63–63.
Aoki and Arai defeated Peete and Watson, 66–67.
Sugihara and Nakamura defeated Kite and Stadler, 66–67.
U.S. leads, 9–7.

SATURDAY

SINGLES: Peete defeated Sugihara, 66–71.
Gilder defeated Arai, 65–72.
Pate tied Nakamura, 70–70.
Wadkins tied Suzuki, 71–71.
Watson defeated Kuramoto, 67–68.
Kite defeated Hagawa, 68–71.
Aoki defeated Floyd, 67–69.
Stadler defeated Nakajima, 68–73.
U.S. leads 21–11.

SUNDAY

Wadkins tied Nakajima, 70–70.
Arai defeated Pate, 70–76.
Floyd tied Hagawa, 73–73.
Stadler defeated Suzuki, 70–75.
Kite defeated Sugihara, 77–78.
Watson defeated Nakamura, 73–75.
Peete defeated Kuramoto, 68–71.
Gilder defeated Aoki, 69–73.

INDIVIDUAL STANDINGS AND MONEY WINNINGS

	SINGLES ROUNDS	TOTAL	INDIVIDUAL MONEY	TEAM MONEY	TOTAL MONEY
Bob Gilder	65 69	134	$15,000	$30,000	$45,000
Calvin Peete	66 68	134	15,000	30,000	45,000
Craig Stadler	68 70	138	5,000	30,000	35,000
Masahiro Kuramoto	68 71	139	3,000	20,000	23,000
Isao Aoki	67 73	140	1,000	20,000	21,000

	SCORES				TOTAL	MONEY
Tom Watson	67	73	140	1,000	30,000	31,000
Lanny Wadkins	71	70	141		30,000	30,000
Ray Floyd	69	73	142		30,000	30,000
Kikuo Arai	72	70	142		20,000	20,000
Tsuneyuki Nakajima	73	70	143		20,000	20,000
Yutaka Hagawa	71	73	144		20,000	20,000
Toru Nakamura	70	75	145		20,000	20,000
Tom Kite	68	77	145		30,000	30,000
Norio Suzuki	71	75	146		20,000	20,000
Jerry Pate	70	76	146		30,000	30,000
Teruo Sugihara	71	78	149		20,000	20,000

Taiheiyo Club Masters

Taiheiyo Club, Gotemba Cpirse, Shizuoka Prefecture   November 11–14
Par 72; 7,114 yards   purse, Y80,000,000

	SCORES				TOTAL	MONEY
Scott Hoch	73	70	66	69	278	Y17,397,250
Masahiro Kuramoto	68	73	69	71	281	8,698,625
Calvin Peete	73	71	68	71	283	4,683,875
Wayne Levi	72	67	69	75	283	4,683,875
Lee Elder	73	74	68	69	284	2,542,675
Naomichi Ozaki	71	70	73	70	284	2,542,675
Sam Torrance	71	71	70	73	285	1,820,020
Toshiharu Kawada	72	73	74	67	286	1,405,162
Yutaka Hagawa	71	71	70	74	286	1,405,162
Tateo Ozaki	71	73	72	70	286	1,405,162
Norio Suzuki	67	71	74	74	286	1,405,162
Tsuneyuki Nakajima	71	73	73	70	287	1,097,365
Isao Isozaki	74	71	72	70	287	1,097,365
Tom Watson	72	74	69	72	287	1,097,365
Hsieh Min Nan	72	71	71	73	287	1,097,365
Kikuo Arai	70	77	70	71	288	963,540
Takashi Kurihara	74	73	73	69	289	910,010
Satsuki Takahashi	72	72	67	79	290	789,567
Phil Hancock	75	67	82	66	290	789,567
Doug Tewell	71	74	70	75	290	789,567
Isao Aoki	73	74	69	74	290	789,567
Yoshitaka Yamamoto	74	74	71	71	290	789,567
Akio Toyoda	75	72	73	70	290	789,567
Hideto Shigenobu	75	73	73	70	291	658,419
Masashi Ozaki	74	72	74	71	291	658,419
Yasuhiro Funatogawa	75	73	71	72	291	658,419
Koichi Inoue	69	79	69	74	291	658,419
Seiichi Kanai	73	73	69	76	291	658,419
Jerry Pate	72	73	76	71	292	582,138
Minoru Nakamura	69	76	76	71	292	582,138
Seiji Ebihara	76	71	74	71	292	582,138
Namio Takasu	74	70	73	75	292	582,138
Nobumitsu Yuhara	71	71	74	76	292	582,138
Chen Tze Ming	72	68	76	76	292	582,138
Lu Hsi Chuen	74	74	72	73	293	535,300
Akio Kanamoto	70	73	76	75	294	512,917
Shoji Kikuchi	74	73	75	73	295	495,152
Koichi Uehara	74	73	71	77	295	495,152

	SCORES				TOTAL	MONEY
Howard Twitty	74	72	74	75	295	495,152
Ed Sneed	79	67	78	72	296	461,696
Barry Jaeckel	72	74	74	76	296	461,696
Kosaku Shimada	72	74	77	74	297	421,548
Masaji Kusakabe	75	73	74	75	297	421,548
Seiichi Sato	76	72	73	76	297	421,548
Bob Byman	76	72	74	75	297	421,548
Gay Brewer	76	72	75	75	298	401,475
David Edwards	73	75	75	75	298	401,475
Shigeru Uchida	75	72	70	81	298	401,475
Pete Izumikawa	70	76	77	78	301	401,475
Kenichi Yamada	70	75	77	79	301	401,475
*Kazuhiko Kato	76	76	74	75	301	

Dunlop Phoenix

Phoenix Country Club, Miyazaki Prefecture   November 18–21
Par 72; 6,989 yards   purse, Y90,000,000

	SCORES				TOTAL	MONEY
Calvin Peete	73	69	67	72	281	Y16,000,000
Severiano Ballesteros	71	76	70	67	284	7,800,000
Larry Nelson	70	70	74	70	284	7,800,000
Bobby Wadkins	73	73	68	73	287	3,900,000
Hsieh Min Nan	72	72	70	73	287	3,900,000
Bernhard Langer	72	72	73	72	289	3,200,000
Naomichi Ozaki	77	74	71	68	290	2,618,000
Shinsaku Maeda	70	74	76	70	290	2,618,000
Teruo Suzumura	72	70	77	71	290	2,618,000
Tom Watson	71	71	75	73	290	2,618,000
Wayne Levi	72	72	71	75	290	2,618,000
Sandy Lyle	74	73	72	72	291	1,764,000
Graham Marsh	73	74	72	72	291	1,764,000
Chen Tze Ming	73	72	73	73	291	1,764,000
Kikuo Arai	73	71	73	74	291	1,764,000
Fujio Kobayashi	73	71	72	75	291	1,764,000
Scott Simpson	76	73	74	69	292	1,395,000
Bob Gilder	72	73	73	74	292	1,395,000
Saburo Fujiki	73	69	76	75	293	1,215,000
D.A. Weibring	74	74	70	75	293	1,215,000
Koichi Inoue	72	74	74	74	294	1,050,000
Masashi Ozaki	73	70	76	75	294	1,050,000
Takashi Kurihara	74	71	77	73	295	795,000
Namio Takasu	72	77	71	75	295	795,000
Craig Stadler	73	73	73	76	295	795,000
Danny Edwards	69	73	75	78	295	795,000
Motomasa Aoki	73	74	69	79	295	795,000
Haruo Yasuda	71	74	70	80	295	795,000
Tom Purtzer	71	70	78	77	296	660,000
Seiji Ebihara	74	77	72	74	297	570,000
Toru Nakamura	71	73	78	75	297	570,000
Scott Hoch	72	70	78	77	297	570,000
Shoji Kikuchi	72	76	71	78	297	570,000
Tateo Ozaki	76	70	71	80	297	570,000
Lu Hsi Chuen	78	72	75	73	298	445,000
Liao Kuo Chih	74	74	75	75	298	445,000
Teruo Sugihara	72	78	74	74	298	445,000

	SCORES				TOTAL	MONEY
Yasuhiro Miyamoto	76	70	75	77	298	445,000
Hubert Green	73	75	73	77	298	445,000
Norio Suzuki	73	78	70	77	298	445,000
Yoshikazu Yokoshima	77	74	74	74	299	395,000
Akio Kanamoto	73	75	76	75	299	395,000
Ed Sneed	78	72	74	76	300	370,000
Hiroshi Makino	73	74	76	77	300	370,000
Seiichi Kanai	75	73	75	77	300	370,000
Hsieh Yung Yo	71	77	77	76	301	340,000
Lu Liang Huan	78	72	75	76	301	340,000
Gary Hallberg	78	73	72	78	301	340,000
Tsutomu Irie	74	75	76	77	302	300,000
Dan Pohl	75	72	77	78	302	300,000
Ikuo Shirahama	74	75	74	79	302	300,000

Casio World Open

Ibusuki Golf Club, Kagoshima Prefecture
Par 72; 6,966 yards

November 25–28
purse, Y65,000,000

	SCORES				TOTAL	MONEY
Scott Hoch	72	71	69	70	282	Y12,000,000
Tsuneyuki Nakajima	71	66	70	76	283	6,700,000
Severiano Ballesteros	70	69	75	70	284	3,750,000
Isao Aoki	73	70	71	70	284	3,750,000
Kikuo Arai	70	72	69	74	285	2,700,000
Chen Tze Ming	67	74	71	74	286	2,400,000
Hsieh Min Nan	76	67	73	71	287	2,000,000
Lu Hsi Chuen	69	69	76	73	287	2,000,000
Masashi Ozaki	74	70	73	71	288	1,550,000
Bobby Wadkins	71	73	72	72	288	1,550,000
Fujio Kobayashi	70	72	71	75	288	1,550,000
Masahiro Kuramoto	73	68	73	75	289	1,300,000
Nobumitsu Yuhara	72	71	77	70	290	1,120,000
Tateo Ozaki	73	70	74	73	290	1,120,000
Jim Simons	75	69	71	75	290	1,120,000
Koichi Inoue	70	76	71	74	291	821,667
Johnny Miller	74	69	73	75	291	821,667
Larry Nelson	75	71	70	75	291	821,667
Vance Heafner	73	69	73	76	291	821,667
Naomichi Ozaki	70	70	75	76	291	821,667
Yoshitaka Yamamoto	73	70	72	76	291	821,667
Akira Yabe	75	74	72	71	292	592,000
Akio Kanamoto	76	70	74	72	292	592,000
Saburo Fujiki	72	73	74	73	292	592,000
Koichi Uehara	75	68	75	74	292	592,000
Yoshikazu Yokoshima	74	71	73	74	292	592,000
Kaneya Yoshimura	73	75	72	73	293	451,667
Toshiharu Kawada	71	75	71	76	293	451,667
Katsunari Takahashi	75	71	71	76	293	451,667
Norio Adachi	73	75	69	76	293	451,667
Fred Couples	68	77	71	77	293	451,667
Scott Simpson	78	68	70	77	293	451,667
Toru Nakamura	75	73	72	74	294	400,000
Victor Regalado	72	73	74	76	295	390,000
Hsieh Yung Yo	73	75	74	74	296	360,000
Kuo Chi Hsiung	73	72	76	75	296	360,000

	SCORES				TOTAL	MONEY
Kosaku Shimada	70	74	77	75	296	360,000
Bernhard Langer	74	70	74	78	296	360,000
Hideo Ishii	72	71	72	81	296	360,000
Takaaki Kono	73	72	77	75	297	322,500
Satsuki Takahashi	77	71	74	75	297	322,500
Nirihiko Matsumoto	74	67	77	79	297	322,500
Shoji Kikuchi	71	73	74	79	297	322,500
Seiichi Kanai	77	72	73	76	298	305,000
Seiji Ebihara	73	75	73	77	298	305,000
D.A. Weibring	74	71	76	77	298	305,000
Hubert Green	71	71	78	79	299	300,000
Haruo Yasuda	74	71	72	83	300	300,000
Lee Trevino	74	73	75	79	301	300,000
Hideto Shigenobu	73	73	76	82	304	300,000

Japan Series

Yomiuri Country Club, Osaka (First 2 rounds) December 1–5
Par 73; 7,079 yards purse, Y17,000,000
Yomiuri Country Club, Tokyo (Final 2 rounds)
Par 72; 7,017 yards

	SCORES				TOTAL	MONEY
Tsuneyuki Nakajima	72	72	66	73	283	Y5,000,000
Fujio Kobayashi	69	71	71	74	285	2,600,000
Masahiro Kuramoto	70	72	72	72	286	1,300,000
Masashi Ozaki	74	71	69	72	286	1,300,000
Akira Yabe	70	71	73	73	287	1,000,000
Teruo Sugihara	71	72	71	74	288	800,000
Isao Aoki	73	75	70	72	290	700,000
Toru Nakamura	73	70	73	75	291	533,333
Saburo Fujiki	74	73	74	70	291	533,333
Hsieh Min Nan	72	70	74	75	291	533,333
Hideto Shigenobu	76	73	72	74	295	400,000
Naomichi Ozaki	73	72	74	77	296	400,000
Motomasa Aoki	67	80	74	76	297	350,000
Norio Suzuki	71	77	77	75	300	316,666
Yutaka Hagawa	77	73	78	72	300	316,666
Shinsaku Maeda	74	72	80	74	300	316,666
Kikuo Arai	82	72	73	76	303	300,000
Shigeru Uchida	77	75	73	82	307	300,000

Australasian Tour

Tooth Illawarra Open

Port Kembla Golf Club, Port Kembla,
New South Wales
Par 36–36—72; 6,594 yards

January 14–17
purse, A$25,000

	SCORES				TOTAL	MONEY
Bob Shaw	71	64	67	75	277	A$4,500
Col Bishop	72	67	69	70	278	2,700
Russell Swanson	70	69	70	73	282	1,485
Ted Ball	66	73	69	74	282	1,485
Chris Tickner	67	73	74	69	283	997.50
Peter Fowler	72	69	69	73	283	997.50
Billy Dunk	75	67	69	73	284	800
Vaughan Somers	74	74	66	70	284	800
Greg Hohnen	68	71	73	73	285	632.50
Peter Senior	70	70	72	73	285	632.50
Stewart Ginn	67	74	73	72	286	456.67
Mike Ferguson	71	68	71	76	286	456.67
Vic Bennetts	70	67	71	78	286	456.66
Ian Brander	73	74	71	70	288	360
Guy Wolstenholme	77	69	69	73	288	360
Mark Holland	72	70	76	72	290	315
Wayne Grady	70	70	76	74	290	315
Richard Lee	73	70	72	75	290	315
Rodger Davis	70	73	74	74	291	260
Ken Dukes	73	72	71	75	291	260
Bruce Hodson	72	74	71	74	291	260
Michael Mills	69	74	73	75	291	260
Wayne Riley	71	69	75	76	291	260
Steven Bann	72	72	70	77	291	260
Glen Goodwin	69	74	74	75	292	210
Frank Nobilo	75	69	72	76	292	210
Garry Overy	72	75	68	77	292	210
Richard Beer	71	72	71	78	292	210
John Clifford	74	74	72	73	293	185
Frank Conallin	72	77	72	73	294	170
Len Korn	71	76	73	74	294	170
Charles Henderson	77	71	71	75	294	170
Mike Clayton	72	78	73	72	295	152.50
Brett Wilson	70	76	74	75	295	152.50
Ray Hore	71	72	77	75	295	152.50
Chris Hearn	76	72	72	75	295	152.50
Bruce Smith	74	73	75	74	296	132.50
Michael Harwood	71	77	73	75	296	132.50
George Serhan	71	72	76	77	296	132.50
Ron Braithwaite	73	70	76	77	296	132.50
*Brad Doolan	75	70	77	74	296	
Robert Stephens	76	74	76	71	297	115
Alan Schenk	74	73	75	75	297	115
David Gannon	75	72	73	77	297	115

	SCORES				TOTAL	MONEY
Doug Maggs	74	75	76	73	298	105
*Chris Barrett	75	71	79	73	298	
David Saunders	78	72	76	73	299	97.50
*Jim Robertson	74	73	77	75	299	
John Kelly	76	73	75	75	299	97.50
*Jim Mooney	76	74	72	77	299	

Ford Dealers' South Australian Open

Kooyonga Golf Club, Adelaide, South Australia   January 21–24
Par 37–35—72; 6,740 yards   purse, A$25,000

	SCORES				TOTAL	MONEY
Graham Marsh	71	67	67	70	275	A$4,500
Billy Dunk	68	68	73	74	283	2,700
Peter Senior	73	68	73	73	287	1,725
Mike Clayton	69	74	72	73	288	1,245
Charles Henderson	73	69	72	75	289	1,040
Bob Shearer	74	72	69	75	290	955
Ian Baker-Finch	74	73	69	75	291	800
Alan Schenk	73	70	70	78	291	800
Bob Shaw	72	76	74	71	293	591.67
Guy Wolstenholme	73	72	74	74	293	591.67
Lyndsay Stephen	70	68	72	83	293	591.66
Frank Nobilo	70	77	69	78	294	450
Vaughan Somers	76	72	75	72	295	376.67
Col Bishop	72	72	74	77	295	376.67
Wayne Grady	70	72	75	78	295	376.66
Richard Lee	74	73	76	73	296	307.50
Garry Merrick	73	77	72	74	296	307.50
Stewart Ginn	76	73	72	75	296	307.50
Ray Hore	75	72	70	79	296	307.50
Robert Stephens	77	74	71	75	297	270
Michael Harwood	76	69	74	78	297	270
Walter Godfrey	76	76	74	72	298	250
Rob McNaughton	71	77	71	79	298	250
Doug Maggs	70	79	76	74	299	215
Mark Holland	80	74	72	73	299	215
John Clifford	74	75	75	75	299	215
Ron Wood	74	78	73	74	299	215
Ian Stanley	71	74	75	79	299	215
*Mark Milbank	77	78	75	70	300	
Bill Britten	75	72	80	73	300	168.34
Russell Swanson	75	76	74	75	300	168.34
Mike Ferguson	72	81	73	74	300	168.33
David Galloway	76	72	75	77	300	168.33
Glen Vines	77	73	73	77	300	168.33
Brett Wilson	77	72	73	78	300	168.33
*Graham Stevens	77	76	75	73	301	
Ted Ball	74	76	78	74	302	142.50
Terry Gilmore	80	75	72	75	302	142.50
Kel Nagle	75	77	74	76	302	142.50
Wayne Riley	74	76	73	79	302	142.50
Bob Beauchemin	75	79	77	72	303	127.50
David Gannon	74	81	75	73	303	127.50
John Kelly	77	77	79	71	304	112.50
Michael Judd	73	73	81	77	304	112.50

	SCORES				TOTAL	MONEY
Mark Griffin	75	73	79	77	304	112.50
Steve Montgomerie	75	78	72	79	304	112.50
*Kari Heikkonen	75	79	75	75	304	
Peter Headland	76	79	78	72	305	95
Michael Mills	76	75	78	76	305	95
Jeff Woodland	78	73	78	76	305	95
*Max Dale	77	78	73	77	305	
*Dean Wiles	81	74	73	77	305	

Tattersalls' Tasmanian Open

Tasmania Golf Club, Hobart, Tasmania
Par 35–37—72; 6,783 yards

February 4–7
purse, A$30,000

	SCORES				TOTAL	MONEY
Col Bishop	73	74	68	71	286	A$5,400
Mike Cahill	77	69	74	67	287	2,013
Rodger Davis	75	66	74	72	287	2,013
Stewart Ginn	73	68	71	75	287	2,013
Jack Newton	75	71	72	69	287	2,013
Rob McNaughton	72	72	74	70	288	1,146
Vaughan Somers	77	72	69	71	289	1,026
Peter Senior	74	72	69	75	290	894
Charles Henderson	75	71	74	73	293	710
Guy Wolstenholme	71	74	74	74	293	710
John Clifford	71	76	74	72	293	710
Peter Fowler	75	74	74	71	294	516
David Good	70	78	74	72	294	516
*Philip Glass	75	74	71	74	294	
Ian Baker-Finch	75	74	72	74	295	409.50
John Downs	75	75	72	73	295	409.50
Lyndsay Stephen	75	73	73	74	295	409.50
Russell Swanson	73	74	70	78	295	409.50
Peter Headland	75	73	73	75	296	351
Ian Stanley	75	74	78	69	296	351
Billy Dunk	79	74	72	72	297	318
Walter Godfrey	75	75	73	74	297	318
Roger Stephens	77	73	70	77	297	318
Jerry Anderson	74	71	78	75	298	288
Wayne Grady	74	76	72	76	298	288
Chris Tickner	78	72	71	78	299	270
*Elliott Booth	76	74	78	71	299	
*Paul Beard	77	76	74	73	300	
Brett Wilson	77	73	74	76	300	258
Alex Bonnington	75	73	77	76	301	234
John Victorsen	75	77	76	73	301	234
Glen Vines	76	76	75	74	301	234
Greg Dowling	77	76	74	75	302	207
Doug Maggs	76	77	74	75	302	207
Terry Gilmore	77	76	74	76	303	189
Mike Ferguson	73	77	73	80	303	189
Mike Clayton	76	76	75	76	303	189
Peter Croker	79	74	73	77	303	189
*Richard Boxall	79	78	74	72	303	
*Doug Thorp	77	80	72	75	304	
Greg Alexander	74	76	73	81	304	156
Mike Colandro	77	72	75	80	304	156

	SCORES				TOTAL	MONEY
Michael Harwood	73	76	76	79	304	156
Chris Hearn	76	74	80	74	304	156
Alan Schenk	77	74	74	79	304	156
Jeff Woodland	78	72	78	76	304	156
Ron Wood	73	79	76	76	304	156
Ken Dukes	77	75	76	77	305	126
Bruce Sorrenson	77	74	79	75	305	126
Gerry Taylor	77	75	77	76	305	126

Victorian Open

Metropolitan Golf Club, Melbourne, Victoria
Par 37–35—72; 7,000 yards

February 11–14
purse, A$100,000

	SCORES				TOTAL	MONEY
Mike Clayton	67	72	74	68	281	A$18,000
Bob Shearer	69	71	71	73	284	10,800
Lee Trevino	70	68	73	74	285	5,346.67
Jerry Anderson	71	70	71	73	285	5,346.67
Graham Marsh	73	71	70	71	285	5,346.66
Garry Merrick	74	74	70	68	286	3,620
Ian Stanley	69	73	71	73	286	3,620
Vaughan Somers	71	70	71	76	288	2,520
Greg Norman	73	72	68	75	288	2,520
Trevor McDonald	71	68	77	72	288	2,520
Paul Foley	73	76	72	67	288	2,520
John Victorsen	73	75	70	71	289	1,580
Alex Bonnington	69	73	74	73	289	1,580
Art Russell	70	76	72	71	289	1,580
Bob Shaw	73	68	74	75	289	1,580
Terry Gale	73	73	73	71	290	1,320
Billy Dunk	69	71	75	76	291	1,175
Peter Headland	71	74	70	76	291	1,175
Ian Baker-Finch	77	72	72	70	291	1,175
Roger Stephens	74	75	73	69	291	1,175
*Ian Hood	72	73	73	74	292	
Michael Harwood	69	76	77	70	292	1,060
Rodger Davis	74	73	73	73	293	960
Russell Swanson	78	73	69	73	293	960
Chris Tickner	69	73	76	75	293	960
Stewart Ginn	72	74	71	76	293	960
Pat Mateer	72	74	74	74	294	840
Mike Colandro	69	78	73	74	294	840
*Peter Sweeney	72	76	74	72	294	
Jack Newton	73	74	75	73	295	740
David Good	73	72	78	72	295	740
Ted Ball	73	71	76	75	295	740
Robert Stephens	74	73	71	78	296	640
Walter Godfrey	72	76	71	77	296	640
Bruce Green	72	70	78	76	296	640
Kel Nagle	74	75	74	73	296	640
Guy Wolstenholme	73	71	79	73	296	640
Mike Cahill	72	78	73	74	297	560
Peter Senior	73	75	79	70	297	560
Rob McNaughton	70	73	75	79	297	560
Alan Schenk	73	76	73	76	298	510
Ken Dukes	68	79	75	76	298	510

	SCORES				TOTAL	MONEY
*Tony Gresham	75	75	76	74	300	
Frank Nobilo	74	76	78	72	300	440
Greg Alexander	76	74	75	75	300	440
Lyndsay Stephen	75	75	73	77	300	440
Col Bishop	70	76	75	79	300	440
Noel Ratcliffe	75	76	71	78	300	440
*Stephen Hanson	77	74	75	75	301	
Mike Ferguson	75	74	72	80	301	370
David Armstrong	71	75	75	80	301	370
*Chris Tatt	72	75	73	81	301	

Australian Masters

Huntingdale Golf Club, Melbourne, Victoria
Par 37–36—73; 6,955 yards

February 18–21
purse, A$100,000

	SCORES				TOTAL	MONEY
Graham Marsh	71	72	71	75	289	A$18,000
Stewart Ginn	78	69	70	73	290	10,800
Mike Ferguson	73	70	75	74	292	6,900
Frank Nobilo	75	73	71	74	293	4,570
Akira Yabe	71	72	75	75	293	4,570
Guy Wolstenholme	73	76	74	71	294	3,620
Rob McNaughton	74	70	74	76	294	3,620
Greg Norman	73	73	78	71	295	2,142.86
Peter Senior	71	77	76	71	295	2,142.86
Yutaka Hagawa	78	70	75	72	295	2,142.86
Norio Suzuki	75	77	72	71	295	2,142.86
Jerry Anderson	75	77	72	71	295	2,142.66
Peter Fowler	74	74	74	73	295	2,142.85
Jeff Woodland	71	77	74	73	295	2,142.85
Noel Ratcliffe	75	68	78	75	296	1,264
Chris Tickner	71	78	73	74	296	1,264
Bob Shearer	70	70	80	76	296	1,264
Vaughan Somers	77	73	70	76	296	1,264
Bernhard Langer	74	73	72	77	296	1,264
*Peter Sweeney	74	74	74	74	296	
Ian Baker-Finch	81	71	73	72	297	1,080
Mike Colandro	72	71	78	76	297	1,080
Frank Conallin	75	76	73	74	298	960
Trevor McDonald	75	71	77	75	298	960
Tony Jacklin	72	75	76	75	298	960
Doug Murray	75	71	75	77	298	960
Garry Merrick	75	76	76	72	299	800
Mark Victorsen	76	74	74	75	299	800
Wayne Meikle	77	73	73	76	299	800
Mike Clayton	75	73	74	77	299	800
Arnold Palmer	76	73	74	77	300	690
Glen Vines	71	74	77	78	300	690
Charles Henderson	76	77	76	72	301	620
Art Russell	75	75	78	73	301	620
Mark Griffin	73	79	76	73	301	620
Kel Nagle	74	78	74	75	301	620
Col Bishop	75	77	73	76	301	620
Brian Jones	78	75	76	73	302	500
Ron Wood	74	70	82	76	302	500
Terry Gale	72	74	80	76	302	500

	SCORES				TOTAL	MONEY
Nobumitsu Yuhara	81	72	74	75	302	500
David Galloway	71	80	74	77	302	500
Ted Ball	75	78	72	77	302	500
Michael Harwood	73	76	74	79	302	500
*John Lindsay	76	70	82	74	302	
Bill Britten	73	73	81	76	303	410
Walter Godfrey	75	76	74	78	303	410
*Chris Tatt	72	76	77	78	303	
Saburo Fujiki	78	74	77	75	304	350
Wayne Grady	76	74	79	75	304	350
John Clifford	74	77	77	76	304	350
Terry Gilmore	73	76	78	77	304	350

Halls Head Western Open

Mandurah Country Club, Perth, Western Australia   May 13–17
Par 37–35—72; 6,699 yards   purse, A$35,000

	SCORES				TOTAL	MONEY
Mike Cahill	70	68	71	70	279	A$6,300
Wayne Grady	71	68	72	69	280	2,646
Bob Shaw	68	71	70	71	280	2,646
Terry Gale	67	67	70	76	280	2,646
Guy Wolstenholme	74	73	66	71	284	1,456
Richard Lee	71	74	70	70	285	1,267
Lyndsay Stephen	72	70	69	74	285	1,267
Stewart Ginn	70	75	72	69	286	938
Vaughan Somers	69	73	70	74	286	938
Rob McNaughton	70	68	71	77	286	938
Col Bishop	75	72	71	69	287	672
Ian Stanley	73	71	69	74	287	672
Ian Baker-Finch	71	73	72	72	288	511
Peter Senior	70	75	71	72	288	511
Simon Owen	71	73	72	72	288	511
Mike Ferguson	69	71	76	72	288	511
Frank Conallin	74	72	72	71	289	420
Wayne Riley	73	73	73	70	289	420
Billy Dunk	71	75	69	74	289	420
Walter Godfrey	71	74	76	69	290	378
John Kelly	73	71	73	73	290	378
*Andrew Mowatt	72	73	73	73	291	
Jeff Woodland	77	70	73	71	291	350
Mike Clayton	69	78	70	74	291	350
*Barry Trevenen	72	73	72	75	292	
Garry Merrick	70	76	74	72	292	315
Frank Nobilo	75	71	74	72	292	315
Roger Stephens	72	73	72	75	292	315
Peter McWhinney	71	79	72	71	293	280
Ken Dukes	74	75	72	72	293	280
Alan Schenk	73	77	75	69	294	243.25
Peter Fowler	74	74	75	71	294	243.25
John Clifford	77	71	74	72	294	243.25
Michael Judd	70	69	78	77	294	243.25
Ron Wood	73	75	75	72	295	210
Perry Somers	74	76	72	73	295	210
Len Korn	77	73	71	74	295	210
Taylor Murphy	76	74	68	77	295	210

	SCORES				TOTAL	MONEY
Paul Foley	74	69	74	78	295	210
Deray Simon	72	73	76	75	296	185.50
David Galloway	75	73	72	76	296	185.50
*Ken Bloomfield	75	74	72	76	297	
Michael Harwood	73	75	75	74	297	171.50
Glen Vines	75	77	72	73	297	171.50
Mark Griffin	74	76	70	78	298	157.50
Peter Headland	76	70	71	81	298	157.50
*Roger Mackay	76	71	74	78	299	
Steve Light	74	73	77	75	299	140
Mark Victorsen	73	76	76	74	299	140
Ross Metherell	74	73	76	76	299	140

Town and Country Channel Nine Western Australian Open

Mount Lawley Golf Club, Perth, Western Australia — May 20–23
Par 36–36—72; 6,764 yards — purse, A$25,000

	SCORES				TOTAL	MONEY
Terry Gale	71	68	65	71	275	A$4,500
Vaughan Somers	69	73	68	65	275	2,700
(Gale defeated Somers on first hole of sudden-death playoff.)						
Peter Croker	70	71	69	72	282	1,725
Chris Tickner	76	68	68	72	284	1,245
Michael Harwood	75	68	70	73	286	1,040
Peter Fowler	69	75	71	73	288	955
Walter Godfrey	70	72	74	73	289	800
Stewart Ginn	74	70	72	73	289	800
Bob Shaw	72	76	71	71	290	632.50
Simon Owen	72	70	74	74	290	632.50
Billy Dunk	69	76	72	74	291	510
Lyndsay Stephen	71	73	74	74	292	430
Steven Bann	69	72	77	74	292	430
Mike Ferguson	74	76	73	70	293	350
Ross Metherell	69	75	76	73	293	350
Peter Senior	72	77	70	74	293	350
Peter Jones	75	73	71	75	294	300
Ian Baker-Finch	74	71	72	77	294	300
Frank Nobilo	70	77	71	76	294	300
Doug Maggs	74	74	78	69	295	255
Ron Wood	75	70	76	74	295	255
Ian Stanley	70	75	74	76	295	255
Peter Headland	75	73	72	75	295	255
Wayne Grady	72	75	72	76	295	255
*Roger Mackay	71	76	72	76	295	
John Clifford	76	70	72	78	296	225
Richard Lee	77	72	80	68	297	195
James Wright	76	75	75	71	297	195
Deray Simon	76	75	74	72	297	195
John Downs	71	74	79	73	297	195
Mike Cahill	73	73	77	74	297	195
Graham Johnson	74	74	79	71	298	167.50
Frank Conallin	78	74	70	76	298	167.50
Michael Judd	75	76	74	74	299	157.50
Rob McNaughton	75	74	76	74	299	157.50
Glen Vines	75	72	78	75	300	142.50
Paul Foley	75	73	73	79	300	142.50

	SCORES				TOTAL	MONEY
Ted Ball	75	73	73	79	300	142.50
Peter Hamblett	71	80	72	77	300	142.50
Mark Griffin	74	75	77	75	301	127.50
Robert Stephens	73	78	74	76	301	127.50
Col Bishop	77	73	77	75	302	117.50
Jeff Woodland	74	75	75	78	302	117.50
Mike Clayton	74	77	75	77	303	105
Peter Randall	74	77	74	78	303	105
Charles Henderson	77	73	74	79	303	105
Roy Draddy	75	78	76	75	304	95
*Tim Elliott	70	79	81	74	304	
*Don Leary	76	74	78	77	305	
*Glen Carbon	75	76	73	81	305	
Doug Murray	77	76	75	77	305	85
John Kelly	76	77	72	80	305	85
Perry Somers	76	76	72	81	305	85

C.I.G. Channel Nine Nedlands Masters

Nedlands Golf Club, Perth, Western Australia May 27–30
Par 36–36—72; 6,352 yards purse, A$40,000

	SCORES				TOTAL	MONEY
Mike Cahill	72	71	68	68	279	A$7,200
John Clifford	68	71	70	70	279	4,320
(Cahill defeated Clifford on first hole of sudden-death playoff.)						
Wayne Grady	69	69	73	71	282	2,376
Bob Shaw	74	66	70	72	282	2,376
Terry Gale	70	71	70	72	283	1,664
*Glen Carbon	72	69	69	74	284	
Peter Jones	71	73	70	71	285	1,362.67
Col Bishop	72	68	73	72	285	1,362.67
Lyndsay Stephen	71	72	70	72	285	1,362.66
Peter Croker	75	73	67	71	286	1,012
Chris Tickner	72	68	72	74	286	1,012
Peter Fowler	72	73	71	71	287	768
Richard Lee	68	70	72	77	287	768
Michael Harwood	71	71	72	74	288	624
Frank Nobilo	69	72	72	75	288	624
Trevor Downing	70	72	74	73	289	518
Simon Owen	73	71	73	72	289	518
Charles Henderson	73	71	72	73	289	518
Graham Johnson	75	69	71	74	289	518
*Tim Elliott	76	66	73	75	290	
Ron Wood	73	74	73	70	290	448
Wayne Riley	69	75	70	76	290	448
Ian Stanley	69	75	73	74	291	408
Mike Clayton	71	70	75	75	291	408
Peter Headland	73	73	70	75	291	408
Doug Murray	72	73	75	72	292	360
Peter Senior	74	73	71	74	292	360
Garry Merrick	69	75	70	78	292	360
*Roger Mackay	71	75	73	74	293	
Deray Simon	76	69	77	71	293	286.86
Stewart Ginn	75	72	74	72	293	286.86
Vaughan Somers	73	72	74	74	293	286.86
Peter McWhinney	73	72	74	74	293	286.86

	SCORES				TOTAL	MONEY
Walter Godfrey	72	72	73	76	293	286.86
Ross Metherell	71	70	76	76	293	286.85
Billy Dunk	71	74	73	75	293	286.85
Steve Light	75	77	74	68	294	228
Robert Stephens	73	77	73	71	294	228
Paul Foley	73	77	72	72	294	228
Bruce Smith	76	73	71	74	294	228
Len Korn	72	77	70	75	294	228
Mike Ferguson	74	70	74	76	294	228
Steven Bann	73	71	77	74	295	196
Mark Griffin	73	71	77	74	295	196
Peter Hamblett	71	74	77	74	296	180
Greg Alexander	73	74	72	77	296	180
Glen Vines	78	74	76	69	297	168
*Andrew Mowatt	76	74	75	73	298	
Frank Conallin	76	74	73	75	298	144
Mark Victorsen	74	74	76	74	298	144
Roger Stephens	79	73	72	74	298	144
James Wright	75	73	74	76	298	144
Ken Dukes	73	72	75	78	298	144

Resch's Pilsener New South Wales PGA Championship

Federal Golf Club, Canberra, A.C.T. September 23–26
Par 36-37—73; 6,853 yards purse, A$25,000

	SCORES				TOTAL	MONEY
Frank Nobilo	72	74	67	66	279	A$4,500
Lyndsay Stephen	69	68	74	69	280	2,700
Gerry Taylor	71	71	71	70	283	1,485
Wayne Grady	71	66	72	74	283	1,485
Mike Clayton	73	68	72	72	285	997.50
Bob Shaw	68	73	72	72	285	997.50
Peter Fowler	71	75	71	71	288	855
Terry Perfrement	73	76	71	70	290	745
Sandy Kurceba	74	73	74	70	291	556.25
Roger Stephens	75	74	70	72	291	556.25
Robert Stephens	74	73	71	73	291	556.25
Frank Conallin	76	68	75	72	291	556.25
Alan Schenk	69	71	80	72	292	410
Col Bishop	75	70	77	71	293	311.25
Stewart Ginn	73	72	76	72	293	311.25
Ken Dukes	72	71	76	74	293	311.25
Paul Foley	72	75	71	75	293	311.25
Steve Andersen-Chapman	71	75	70	77	293	311.25
Ian Baker-Finch	69	73	74	77	293	311.25
John Clifford	71	72	74	76	293	311.25
Doug Maggs	73	72	70	78	293	311.25
George Serhan	73	75	75	73	296	240
Paul Hart	76	75	72	73	296	240
Greg Hohnen	74	71	77	74	296	240
David Galloway	72	72	75	77	296	240
Billy Dunk	75	74	76	72	297	187.15
Chris Tickner	76	71	77	73	297	187.15
Wayne Riley	77	72	74	74	297	187.14
Steven Bann	76	76	70	75	297	187.14
Jerry Stolhand	76	73	72	76	297	187.14

	SCORES				TOTAL	MONEY
Tim Ireland	75	74	72	76	297	187.14
Greg Watton	72	73	75	77	297	187.14
Mike Ferguson	76	73	79	70	298	155
Brent Murray	75	75	75	73	298	155
Peter Croker	77	73	73	75	298	155
Garry Doolan	74	76	74	75	299	142.50
Stephen Bishop	74	73	74	78	299	142.50
Peter Headland	79	73	77	71	300	130
Ted Ball	76	73	77	74	300	130
Greg Alexander	74	76	73	77	300	130
Russell Swanson	73	79	71	78	301	120
Charles Henderson	76	73	80	73	302	102.50
Ron Wood	75	76	76	75	302	102.50
David Botten	76	74	78	74	302	102.50
John Kelly	76	75	76	75	302	102.50
Neil Ulmer	72	76	77	77	302	102.50
David Gannon	78	73	73	78	302	102.50
Larry Canning	74	73	81	75	303	72.50
Mark Griffin	79	73	75	76	303	72.50
David Leary	72	72	81	78	303	72.50
Walter Godfrey	78	70	77	78	303	72.50
Bruce Sorrenson	76	70	78	79	303	72.50
Graeme Bugden	75	75	74	79	303	72.50

Kooralbyn Valley Golf Classic

Kooralbyn Valley Country Club, Kooralbyn, Queensland   October 7–9
Par 36–36—72; 7,021 yards   purse, A$30,000
(Tournament reduced to 54 holes, final round rained out.)

	SCORES			TOTAL	MONEY
Col Bishop	66	71	73	210	A$5,400
Bob Shaw	71	66	75	212	3,240
Alex Bonnington	70	70	74	214	1,782
Peter Fowler	69	72	73	214	1,782
Paul Foley	73	73	69	215	1,140
Gerry Taylor	70	74	71	215	1,140
Ian Baker-Finch	71	68	76	215	1,140
Michael Harwood	71	73	72	216	852
Stewart Ginn	72	73	71	216	852
Ossie Moore	70	75	72	217	620
Mike Cahill	70	74	73	217	620
Perry Somers	72	73	72	217	620
Art Russell	73	73	72	218	452
Jeff Senior	69	75	74	218	452
Jerry Anderson	69	74	75	218	452
Mike Clayton	75	71	73	219	361.20
Bruce Smith	71	75	73	219	361.20
Mark Victorsen	71	74	74	219	361.20
John Clifford	71	72	76	219	361.20
Wayne Riley	74	68	77	219	361.20
Frank Nobilo	70	76	74	220	306
Lyndsay Stephen	70	75	75	220	306
Richard Lee	73	70	77	220	306
Ken Dukes	73	75	73	221	270
Rob McNaughton	71	75	75	221	270
Peter Senior	71	74	76	221	270

	SCORES			TOTAL	MONEY
Garry Doolan	76	74	72	222	234
Bryan Smith	73	72	77	222	234
Walter Godfrey	70	72	80	222	234
Kevin Smallbeck	75	75	73	223	207
Mike Kelly	69	79	75	223	207
Steve Andersen-Chapman	74	76	74	224	186
Charles Henderson	71	78	75	224	186
John Victorsen	73	76	75	224	186
Robert Richardson	77	72	75	224	186
Deray Simon	74	73	77	224	186
Thad Daber	76	74	75	225	159
Glen Vines	74	75	76	225	159
Peter Headland	73	75	77	225	159
David Galloway	73	72	80	225	159
Brent Murray	74	76	76	226	129
John Downs	73	76	77	226	129
Glen Gammon	71	79	76	226	129
Roger Stephens	70	77	79	226	129
Adam Nance	74	73	79	226	129
Simon Gore	68	75	83	226	129
Larry Canning	75	75	77	227	96
Peter Croker	72	78	77	227	96
Robert Stephens	71	76	80	227	96
Don Portway	76	72	79	227	96
Len Korn	73	74	80	227	96

Dunhill Queensland Open

Royal Queensland Golf Club, Brisbane, Queensland
Par 36–36—72; 6,951 yards

October 14–17
purse, A$30,000

	SCORES				TOTAL	MONEY
Graham Marsh	73	69	70	73	285	A$5,400
Wayne Grady	70	71	70	74	285	3,240
(Marsh defeated Grady on first hole of sudden-death playoff.)						
Bob Shaw	72	71	75	73	291	1,396.80
John Downs	73	72	72	74	291	1,396.80
Paul Foley	75	69	72	75	291	1,396.80
George Serhan	74	70	71	76	291	1,396.80
Rob McNaughton	71	75	69	76	291	1,396.80
Stewart Ginn	69	72	78	73	292	804
Roger Stephens	69	73	75	75	292	804
John Victorsen	72	69	74	77	292	804
John Lister	71	72	77	73	293	612
Perry Somers	75	71	71	77	294	540
Jeff Senior	76	73	74	72	295	452
Stuart Reese	72	75	72	76	295	452
Bruce Smith	74	70	73	78	295	452
Art Russell	73	75	72	76	296	387
John Clifford	71	75	74	76	296	387
Ossie Moore	71	72	75	79	297	360
Glen Vines	71	75	78	74	298	324
Gerry Taylor	74	74	75	75	298	324
Peter Jones	74	73	72	79	298	324
Robert Stephens	72	70	73	83	298	324
Peter Fowler	76	74	74	75	299	264
Mike Ferguson	71	75	77	76	299	264

	SCORES				TOTAL	MONEY
Frank Nobilo	76	74	73	76	299	264
Mark Victorsen	72	76	73	78	299	264
Charles Henderson	74	72	74	79	299	264
Ian Baker-Finch	73	76	71	79	299	264
Ashleigh Gerhardt	73	77	75	75	300	195.75
Brian Jones	72	76	76	76	300	195.75
Garry Merrick	74	77	73	76	300	195.75
Mike Clayton	74	76	73	77	300	195.75
Col Bishop	80	69	73	78	300	195.75
Harry Berwick	70	76	75	79	300	195.75
Wayne Riley	72	78	70	80	300	195.75
Steve Montgomerie	73	71	75	81	300	195.75
*Tod Power	75	74	75	77	301	
Sandy Harper	74	74	78	75	301	156
Deray Simon	71	80	74	76	301	156
Ken Dukes	74	75	74	78	301	156
Robert Michael	72	76	73	80	301	156
Steve Andersen-Chapman	76	70	71	84	301	156
Walter Godfrey	74	77	74	77	302	123
Michael Harwood	72	74	77	79	302	123
Alan Schenk	69	75	79	79	302	123
Randall Vines	74	73	75	80	302	123
Peter Senior	69	81	71	81	302	123
Warren Young	71	73	77	81	302	123
*Mark Officer	75	76	73	79	303	
*Trevor Poetschka	76	75	75	77	303	
Ian Stanley	78	73	76	76	303	99
Terry Perfrement	74	75	77	77	303	99

National Panasonic New South Wales Open

Manly Golf Club, Sydney, New South Wales   October 21–24
Par 36-35—71; 6,433 yards   purse, A$100,000

	SCORES				TOTAL	MONEY
Bob Shearer	71	66	66	69	272	A$18,000
Graham Marsh	70	70	69	64	273	10,800
Ian Mosey	68	67	72	68	275	6,900
Chris Tickner	68	67	69	72	276	4,980
John Lister	73	68	68	68	277	3,990
Roger Stephens	65	71	71	70	277	3,990
Rodger Davis	68	74	72	64	278	3,200
Denny Hepler	68	66	72	72	278	3,200
Michael Harwood	70	67	71	71	279	2,700
Maurice Bembridge	72	67	76	65	280	2,360
Bill Rogers	66	72	73	70	281	1,920
Trevor McDonald	70	69	70	72	281	1,920
Art Russell	69	71	74	68	282	1,560
Peter Senior	70	73	68	71	282	1,560
Dennis Clark	72	69	74	68	283	1,326.67
Paul Foley	69	69	71	74	283	1,326.67
Payne Stewart	72	71	67	73	283	1,326.66
Stewart Ginn	74	71	72	68	285	1,146.67
Simon Owen	71	69	75	70	285	1,146.67
Brian Jones	70	68	74	73	285	1,146.66
Jack Newton	74	68	73	71	286	1,020
Ron Wood	71	75	68	72	286	1,020

	SCORES				TOTAL	MONEY
Vaughan Somers	70	72	72	72	286	1,020
John Kelly	71	74	73	69	287	900
Billy Dunk	67	73	75	72	287	900
Mike Colandro	72	69	69	77	287	900
*Eric Couper	72	73	74	69	288	
*Colin Hallam	74	70	75	69	288	
Robert Richardson	72	74	72	70	288	744
Doug Maggs	70	72	74	72	288	744
Mike Cahill	69	73	74	72	288	744
Kel Nagle	68	69	77	74	288	744
Stuart Reese	74	71	70	73	288	744
Wayne Grady	76	70	73	70	289	600
Gerry Taylor	74	70	73	72	289	600
Peter McWhinney	71	74	71	73	289	600
Robert Stephens	71	75	70	73	289	600
Chris Hearn	70	74	72	73	289	600
Rob McNaughton	73	73	70	73	289	600
Wayne Riley	70	73	72	74	289	600
*Tony Gresham	72	73	74	71	290	
*Colin Kaye	75	70	74	71	290	
Walter Godfrey	70	74	76	70	290	490
Richard Lee	69	77	72	72	290	490
Greg Alexander	73	73	72	72	290	490
Ian Stanley	73	69	73	75	290	490
Shizuo Mori	68	74	77	72	291	400
Randall Vines	74	71	72	74	291	400
Jeff Senior	74	71	72	74	291	400
Glen Vines	70	72	75	74	291	400
Harvey Graham	72	69	74	76	291	400

Westpac Golf Classic

Royal Adelaide Golf Club, Adelaide, South Australia
Par 37–36—73; 6,978 yards

October 28–31
purse, A$100,000

	SCORES				TOTAL	MONEY
Ian Stanley	69	67	77	72	285	A$18,000
Stewart Ginn	67	77	75	69	288	10,800
Payne Stewart	68	71	79	73	291	6,900
Graham Marsh	76	73	73	71	293	4,980
Jack Newton	74	70	72	78	294	3,990
Bob Charles	70	72	76	76	294	3,990
Bob Shearer	75	76	74	70	295	3,033.34
Ossie Moore	74	71	79	71	295	3,033.33
Wayne Grady	74	76	75	70	295	3,033.33
Ian Mosey	73	75	76	72	296	1,960
Maurice Bembridge	73	71	79	73	296	1,960
Chris Tickner	69	72	79	76	296	1,960
John Clifford	72	72	75	77	296	1,960
Art Russell	74	72	76	75	297	1,365
Terry Gale	73	72	75	77	297	1,365
Billy Dunk	75	72	74	76	297	1,365
Simon Owen	75	73	74	75	297	1,365
Vaughan Somers	72	73	78	75	298	1,146.67
Mike Clayton	76	70	76	76	298	1,146.67
Denny Hepler	72	75	73	78	298	1,146.66
Mike Ferguson	76	70	82	71	299	1,040

	SCORES				TOTAL	MONEY
Stuart Reese	76	74	76	73	299	1,040
Gerry Taylor	72	74	79	75	300	940
Peter Senior	71	76	77	76	300	940
Peter Croker	73	74	76	77	300	940
Guy Wolstenholme	75	78	76	72	301	780
Richard Coombes	74	76	76	75	301	780
Bill Longmuir	72	75	78	76	301	780
Walter Godfrey	72	75	77	77	301	780
Michael Harwood	72	73	78	78	301	780
Alan Schenk	73	78	78	73	302	630
George Serhan	77	74	78	73	302	630
Trevor McDonald	78	71	78	75	302	630
Lyndsay Stephen	71	75	78	78	302	630
Mike Moynihan	72	75	77	78	302	630
Noel Ratcliffe	76	73	75	78	302	630
Perry Somers	74	79	78	72	303	520
Jerry Anderson	73	76	77	77	303	520
Bob Shaw	74	74	78	77	303	520
Doug Maggs	75	77	74	77	303	520
Alan Cooper	71	76	76	80	303	520
Col Bishop	78	72	79	75	304	420
Mike Colandro	73	75	81	75	304	420
Rob McNaughton	76	75	76	77	304	420
John Godwin	74	73	79	78	304	420
Robert Michael	73	75	77	79	304	420
Rodger Davis	74	75	81	75	305	350
Brian Jones	74	73	78	80	305	350
Kyi Hla Han	76	77	76	77	306	320
Robert Richardson	75	77	77	78	307	280
Mike Cahill	71	79	76	81	307	280
Bruce Smith	75	75	74	83	307	280

Mayne Nickless PGA Championship

Royal Melbourne Golf Club (Composite Course), Black Rock,
 Victoria   November 4–7
Par 35–37—72; 6,979 yards   purse, A$175,000

	SCORES				TOTAL	MONEY
Graham Marsh	71	69	70	72	282	A$31,500
John Clifford	68	71	69	77	285	13,230
Bob Shearer	69	67	72	77	285	13,230
Ben Crenshaw	69	65	75	76	285	13,230
Greg Norman	68	69	73	76	286	7,280
Wayne Grady	70	71	73	73	287	6,685
Payne Stewart	70	71	78	69	288	5,985
Terry Gale	76	70	70	73	289	5,215
Art Russell	73	75	73	71	292	4,427.50
Ian Stanley	73	70	69	80	292	4,427.50
Mike Cahill	74	72	73	75	294	3,196.67
Chris Tickner	71	70	78	75	294	3,196.67
Simon Owen	70	71	74	79	294	3,196.66
Col Bishop	76	74	74	71	295	2,450
Bruce Green	73	69	74	79	295	2,450
Stuart Reese	76	67	75	77	295	2,450
Billy Dunk	72	76	75	73	296	2,056.25
Rob McNaughton	70	76	77	73	296	2,056.25

	SCORES				TOTAL	MONEY
Ian Mosey	76	72	73	75	296	2,056.25
Guy Wolstenholme	77	66	74	79	296	2,056.25
Trevor McDonald	71	72	80	74	297	1,785
John Godwin	76	70	75	76	297	1,785
Richard Lee	78	72	70	77	297	1,785
Russell Swanson	75	72	77	74	298	1,505
Denny Hepler	74	73	77	74	298	1,505
Mike Ferguson	75	75	74	74	298	1,505
Mike Clayton	74	75	73	76	298	1,505
Noel Ratcliffe	73	70	79	76	298	1,505
Frank Nobilo	78	69	79	73	299	1,160
Jack Newton	74	71	80	74	299	1,160
Rodger Davis	73	72	79	75	299	1,160
Roger Stephens	78	70	76	75	299	1,160
Ossie Moore	75	73	77	74	299	1,160
John Lister	75	74	74	76	299	1,160
Peter Fowler	78	72	71	78	299	1,160
Gerry Taylor	70	75	80	75	300	997.50
Glen Vines	74	73	77	76	300	997.50
Paul Foley	74	73	76	78	301	840
Steve Andersen-Chapman	76	73	73	79	301	840
Ian Baker-Finch	79	69	78	75	301	840
Lyndsay Stephen	73	77	77	74	301	840
David Armstrong	77	73	76	75	301	840
Vaughan Somers	74	76	76	75	301	840
Brett Wilson	75	74	75	77	301	840
Peter Croker	72	76	78	76	302	682.50
Robert Michael	72	78	76	76	302	682.50
Mike Colandro	74	74	83	72	303	612.50
Alex Bonnington	80	69	77	77	303	612.50
Bill Britten	74	75	77	78	304	525
Geoff Parslow	71	76	78	79	304	525
Mike Krantz	72	78	74	80	304	525

Resch's Pilsener Golf Classic

Coolangatta-Tweed Heads Golf Club, Coolangatta,
    Queensland
Par 36–36—72; 6,641 yards

November 11–14
purse, A$150,000

	SCORES				TOTAL	MONEY
Payne Stewart	71	65	71	72	279	A$27,000
Kyi Hla Han	66	70	72	73	281	16,200
Bob Shaw	76	70	69	68	283	8,910
Bob Charles	70	73	71	69	283	8,910
Trevor McDonald	72	73	70	69	284	6,240
Greg Norman	74	73	73	66	286	5,430
Stewart Ginn	69	74	72	71	286	5,430
Bob Shearer	74	74	73	67	288	4,260
Billy Dunk	74	70	70	74	288	4,260
Bruce Smith	72	75	73	69	289	3,100
Maurice Bembridge	77	72	68	72	289	3,100
Mike Cahill	73	70	73	73	289	3,100
Lyndsay Stephen	75	71	68	76	290	2,130
Mike Clayton	77	73	70	70	290	2,130
John Godwin	72	72	73	73	290	2,130
John Lister	74	71	71	74	290	2,130

	SCORES				TOTAL	MONEY
Noel Ratcliffe	71	71	72	76	290	2,130
Jack Newton	73	73	75	70	291	1,720
Peter McWhinney	73	73	72	73	291	1,720
Stuart Reese	77	71	74	69	291	1,720
Ian Baker-Finch	76	74	74	68	292	1,440
Terry Gale	74	73	74	71	292	1,440
Brent Murray	73	74	73	72	292	1,440
Jerry Anderson	75	73	72	72	292	1,440
Gerry Taylor	75	71	73	73	292	1,440
Mike Ferguson	73	70	72	77	292	1,440
Peter Fowler	75	72	75	71	293	1,095
Bill Longmuir	76	74	72	71	293	1,095
George Serhan	75	70	75	73	293	1,095
Wayne Grady	75	72	73	73	293	1,095
Richard Lee	72	73	74	74	293	1,095
Col Bishop	76	70	72	75	293	1,095
Graham Marsh	78	71	75	70	294	885
Mark Victorsen	76	71	77	70	294	885
Michael Harwood	77	71	74	72	294	885
Jeff Senior	76	71	71	76	294	885
Rob McNaughton	74	70	73	77	294	885
Denny Hepler	77	71	70	76	294	885
Ian Mosey	78	71	77	69	295	720
Simon Owen	74	76	74	71	295	720
Alex Bonnington	74	74	73	74	295	720
Mike Colandro	75	74	72	74	295	720
Ossie Moore	74	68	75	78	295	720
Greg Hohnen	75	74	76	71	296	615
Mike Krantz	78	72	74	72	296	615
Mark Holland	79	70	79	70	298	555
Paul Foley	74	76	74	74	298	555
Peter Beard	78	72	76	73	299	480
Kathamuthu Selaruas	76	73	75	75	299	480
Frank Nobilo	76	74	72	77	299	480

Australian Open Championship

Australian Golf Club, Kensington, New South Wales November 18–21
Par 36-36—72; 7,058 yards purse, A$225,000

	SCORES				TOTAL	MONEY
Bob Shearer	75	70	72	70	287	A$40,500
Payne Stewart	77	72	72	70	291	19,912.50
Jack Nicklaus	75	70	74	72	291	19,912.50
Wayne Grady	78	71	70	73	292	11,205
Bob Shaw	77	71	72	75	295	9,360
Terry Gale	74	75	72	75	296	8,595
Bill Rogers	72	79	73	73	297	7,695
David Good	74	74	74	77	299	6,390
Peter Senior	76	78	71	74	299	6,390
*Eric Couper	76	75	75	73	299	
Noel Ratcliffe	80	76	69	75	300	4,410
Mike Cahill	75	76	75	74	300	4,410
Peter Headland	78	75	75	72	300	4,410
Mike Krantz	75	78	74	73	300	4,410
Simon Owen	80	73	76	72	301	3,150
Rodger Davis	76	72	77	76	301	3,150

	SCORES				TOTAL	MONEY
Peter Fowler	74	77	73	77	301	3,150
Bob Stanton	75	79	75	74	303	2,592
Gerry Taylor	73	80	75	75	303	2,592
Robert Richardson	79	71	76	77	303	2,592
Art Russell	77	76	72	78	303	2,592
Roger Stephens	74	72	78	79	303	2,592
Jack Newton	79	70	72	83	304	2,295
Jerry Anderson	74	78	74	79	305	1,935
Paul Foley	76	75	79	75	305	1,935
John Lister	77	77	79	72	305	1,935
Stuart Reese	81	71	77	76	305	1,935
Ian Stanley	75	79	76	75	305	1,935
Brent Murray	75	76	76	78	305	1,935
John Godwin	78	72	76	79	305	1,935
Kyi Hla Han	78	78	79	71	306	1,530
Col Bishop	76	79	74	77	306	1,530
David Armstrong	79	76	72	79	306	1,530
Maurice Bembridge	75	80	75	77	307	1,417.50
Frank Nobilo	78	77	72	80	307	1,417.50
Chris Tickner	77	75	81	75	308	1,327.50
Vaughan Somers	78	76	75	79	308	1,327.50
Richard Lee	73	80	77	79	309	1,260
Bruce Smith	75	80	78	77	310	1,192.50
*Tony Gresham	76	80	76	78	310	
Trevor McDonald	73	78	75	84	310	1,192.50
Bobby Heins	82	75	76	78	311	1,035
Lyndsay Stephen	76	78	82	75	311	1,035
Bob Charles	73	82	79	77	311	1,035
Alex Bonnington	76	76	81	78	311	1,035
David Saunders	79	70	79	83	311	1,035
Ken Dukes	78	77	77	80	312	877.50
Ian Baker-Finch	79	76	77	80	312	877.50
Garry Merrick	79	78	78	79	314	810
Mike Clayton	82	74	83	76	315	742.50
Greg Hohnen	77	80	83	75	315	742.50

New Zealand BP Open

Christchurch Golf Club, Shirley, Christchurch
Par 36—36—72; 7,007 yards

November 25–28
purse, NZ$80,000

	SCORES				TOTAL	MONEY
Terry Gale	75	66	74	69	284	NZ$14,400
Bob Charles	70	74	69	73	286	8,640
Mike Colandro	73	71	75	71	290	5,520
Maurice Bembridge	72	71	74	75	292	3,456
Simon Owen	73	74	69	76	292	3,456
Art Russell	70	70	75	77	292	3,456
Michael Harwood	71	74	74	74	293	2,736
Mike Ferguson	77	70	77	70	294	2,272
Dennis Clark	75	70	71	78	294	2,272
Mike Clayton	76	74	74	72	296	1,568
Bob Shearer	74	72	77	73	296	1,568
Richard Coombes	75	75	73	73	296	1,568
Jack Newton	74	74	73	75	296	1,568
Noel Ratcliffe	77	70	74	76	297	1,120
Brian Jones	77	71	70	79	297	1,120

	SCORES				TOTAL	MONEY
Ian Baker-Finch	71	78	72	76	297	1,120
Robert Michael	75	68	82	73	298	960
Col Bishop	74	78	71	75	298	960
Mike Krantz	76	75	72	75	298	960
Steve Andersen-Chapman	73	74	77	75	299	848
Thad Daber	78	75	75	71	299	848
John Lister	75	74	74	76	299	848
Vaughan Somers	77	73	74	76	300	752
Peter Hamblett	71	75	76	78	300	752
Ian Stanley	76	76	71	77	300	752
Ian Mosey	74	76	79	72	301	656
*John Williamson	77	71	75	77	301	
Scott Knapp	75	72	76	78	301	656
Stuart Reese	73	72	71	85	301	656
Ken Dukes	75	76	78	73	302	556
Alex Bonnington	78	72	79	73	302	556
Geoff Clarke	77	77	75	73	302	556
Ken Tarling	73	78	73	78	302	556
Wayne Grady	74	72	79	78	303	512
Stewart Ginn	75	72	81	76	304	488
Ron Wood	76	76	75	77	304	488
John Godwin	79	73	80	73	305	416
Bob Stanton	79	74	78	74	305	416
Ed Fisher	76	77	79	73	305	416
Doug Maggs	76	70	81	78	305	416
Billy Dunk	77	76	75	77	305	416
Mark Tapper	77	72	77	79	305	416
Robert Stephens	72	76	78	79	305	416
*Grant Waite	70	74	80	81	305	
Wayne Riley	78	71	80	77	306	336
John Clifford	73	76	77	80	306	336
Ian Smalley	74	75	74	83	306	336
Frank Conallin	74	80	81	72	307	296
Kel Nagle	79	72	76	80	307	296

Air New Zealand-Shell Open

Titirangi Golf Club, Auckland
Par 35–35—70; 6,287 yards

December 2–5
purse, NZ$100,000

	SCORES				TOTAL	MONEY
Terry Gale	66	68	65	74	273	NZ$18,000
Wayne Grady	71	67	67	68	273	10,800
(Gale defeated Grady on second hole of sudden-death playoff.)						
Jack Newton	70	71	68	66	275	5,940
Sandy Lyle	65	67	73	70	275	5,940
Bob Charles	66	70	68	72	276	4,160
Art Russell	66	74	68	69	277	3,620
Bruce Devlin	70	68	70	69	277	3,620
Graham Marsh	69	73	68	68	278	2,520
Ian Mosey	68	70	72	68	278	2,520
John Godwin	72	70	67	69	278	2,520
Mike Colandro	69	70	68	71	278	2,520
Noel Ratcliffe	66	73	71	69	279	1,640
Bob Shearer	68	74	66	71	279	1,640
Bruce Lietzke	69	68	68	74	279	1,640
David Graham	71	71	70	68	280	1,360

	SCORES				TOTAL	MONEY
Ken Dukes	70	72	66	72	280	1,360
Stewart Ginn	73	72	69	67	281	1,260
Brian Jones	67	73	70	72	282	1,200
Wayne Riley	72	69	69	73	283	1,140
Simon Owen	75	71	68	70	284	1,080
Steve Stull	72	75	66	71	284	1,080
Guy Wolstenholme	65	75	71	74	285	1,000
Billy Dunk	72	70	69	74	285	1,000
Vaughan Somers	72	69	74	72	287	860
Frank Conallin	70	73	70	74	287	860
Peter Thomson	72	70	69	76	287	860
Col Bishop	70	71	70	76	287	860
Jerry Anderson	72	72	67	76	287	860
Stuart Reese	69	74	75	70	288	706.67
Brent Murray	73	73	70	72	288	706.67
Ossie Moore	67	72	76	73	288	706.66
Pat Mateer	74	71	76	68	289	620
Doug Maggs	71	71	78	69	289	620
Michael Harwood	70	77	70	72	289	620
Thad Daber	69	76	69	75	289	620
Steve Andersen-Chapman	66	73	73	77	289	620
Walter Godfrey	72	75	71	72	290	520
Scott Knapp	73	74	71	72	290	520
Lyndsay Stephen	69	74	73	74	290	520
Ian Baker-Finch	77	69	68	76	290	520
Don Klenk	73	74	65	78	290	520
Mark Tapper	75	72	74	70	291	430
John Clifford	73	73	71	74	291	430
Mike Ferguson	71	75	71	74	291	430
Ed Fisher	73	67	71	80	291	430
Kim Southerden	73	74	74	71	292	340
Dennis Clark	72	72	75	73	292	340
Robert Stephens	76	71	73	72	292	340
Kel Nagle	75	71	73	73	292	340
Terry Kendall	71	72	75	74	292	340

New Zealand PGA Championship

Mount Maunganui Golf Club, Tauranga   December 9–12
Par 36–36—72; 6,572 yards   purse, NZ$25,000

	SCORES				TOTAL	MONEY
Stuart Reese	70	63	71	73	277	NZ$4,500
Jack Newton	70	67	68	73	278	2,350
Simon Owen	68	66	70	76	280	1,475
John Lister	72	70	65	73	280	1,475
Guy Wolstenholme	71	70	66	74	281	840
Kel Nagle	73	67	69	72	281	840
Frank Conallin	75	70	69	67	281	840
Art Russell	68	70	70	74	282	682.50
Barry Vivian	71	69	69	73	282	682.50
Alex Bonnington	68	71	72	71	282	682.50
Bob Charles	69	69	72	72	282	682.50
Thad Daber	72	68	70	73	283	560
Ed Fisher	70	68	73	72	283	560
Michael Harwood	77	71	70	65	283	560
Billy Dunk	68	70	71	76	285	475

	SCORES				TOTAL	MONEY
Richard Coombes	72	71	69	73	285	475
Jerry Anderson	74	69	70	72	285	475
Dennis Clark	70	70	73	74	287	425
Kim Southerden	69	67	76	76	288	387.50
Pat Mateer	69	72	73	74	288	387.50
Simon Bittle	72	70	71	76	289	319
Vijay Singh	71	71	72	75	289	319
Mike Colandro	72	73	70	74	289	319
Walter Godfrey	68	73	76	72	289	319
Steven Bann	74	73	71	71	289	319
Ian Smalley	68	73	71	78	290	255
Frank Nobilo	70	71	72	77	290	255
Wayne Riley	67	75	72	76	290	255
Brent Murray	70	73	72	76	291	220
Steve Stull	74	70	76	71	291	220
Murray Young	70	74	74	74	292	205
Craig Owen	74	75	71	73	293	190
Robert Stephens	72	72	75	75	294	180
Brandon Perry	72	76	70	77	295	170
Mike Moynihan	74	74	70	78	296	157.50
Steve Andersen-Chapman	71	71	76	78	296	157.50
Adam Nance	77	72	73	75	297	145
Michael Dodd	78	74	72	74	298	140
Steve Bidwell	77	72	69	81	299	27.78
Ken Tarling	75	68	75	81	299	27.78
Mats Lanner	74	72	73	80	299	27.78
Mark Tapper	81	68	72	78	299	27.78
Tim Ireland	73	75	73	78	299	27.78
Alan Johnston	72	73	76	78	299	27.78
Geoff Smart	73	79	73	74	299	27.78
David Leary	74	73	79	73	299	27.77
Doug Milne	75	75	72	77	299	27.77

Miscellaneous

Canadian PGA Championship
(Labatt's International)

Cherry Hill Club, Ridgeway, Ontario
Par 35–36—71; 6,751 yards

July 8–11
purse, Can $100,000*

	SCORES				TOTAL	MONEY
Jim Thorpe	72	72	70	69	283	Can$20,000
Dave Barr	70	72	69	72	283	11,800
(Thorpe defeated Barr on third hole of sudden-death playoff.)						
Dan Halldorson	74	68	70	73	285	6,750
Ben Crenshaw	72	70	70	73	285	6,750
Bob Charles	74	72	70	72	288	4,200
Ray Floyd	71	74	73	70	288	4,200
Antonio Garrido	70	68	77	74	289	3,400
Craig DeFoy	77	71	69	73	290	2,800
Jerry Anderson	74	72	73	71	290	2,800
Norm Jarvis	68	68	76	79	291	2,400
Jim Nelford	72	73	73	73	291	2,400
Daniel Talbot	72	72	75	73	292	2,100
Bob Panasiuk	71	73	68	81	293	1,800
Juan Pinzon	74	71	71	77	293	1,800
Jim Rutledge	68	70	81	74	293	1,800
Erin Fostey	73	75	73	72	293	1,800
Ray Stewart	73	75	74	71	293	1,800
Scott Knapp	74	74	70	76	294	1,300
Graham Gunn	71	74	74	75	294	1,300
Vincente Fernandez	71	75	73	75	294	1,300
Moe Norman	77	71	71	75	294	1,300
Sandy Harper	74	72	78	70	294	1,300
Gar Hamilton	71	81	69	74	295	950
Yves Tremblay	72	75	73	75	295	950
Tom Smack	71	70	79	76	296	753.33
Tamon Munoz	77	71	73	75	296	753.33
Herb Holzscheiter	75	75	73	73	296	753.33
Liam Higgins	72	75	70	80	297	640
Bob Cox	73	71	80	73	297	640
Bernie Starchuk	74	72	76	76	298	550
Ken Fulton	76	71	75	76	298	550
Jean Louis Lamarre	74	76	73	75	298	550
Antonio Evangelista	75	74	75	74	298	550
Serge Thivierge	69	74	80	76	299	460
Don Graham	73	73	77	76	299	460
Peter Townsend	75	71	79	74	299	460
Pat O'Donnell	77	74	74	74	299	460
George Knudson	75	75	76	73	299	460
Denis Watson	75	68	74	83	300	360
Bob Breen	79	70	74	77	300	360
Kelly Kurray	76	74	76	74	300	360
Al Balding	74	76	77	73	300	360
Terry Miskoiczi	79	73	77	71	300	360

	SCORES				TOTAL	MONEY
Mark Shushack	73	79	73	76	301	300
Tim McCutcheon	76	75	74	77	302	270
Paul Kennedy	80	77	76	69	302	270
William Kozak	73	76	76	78	303	223.33
Gilles Larochelle	77	76	75	75	303	223.33
Bruce Bundy	78	77	74	75	303	223.33
Robbie Phillips	75	76	75	78	304	195
Bill Bevington	79	74	77	74	304	195

*One Canadian dollar = 80 Cents US

The LPGA Tour

Whirlpool Championship of Deer Creek

Deer Creek Country Club, Deerfield Beach, Florida January 28–31
Par 36–36—72; 6,079 yards purse, $125,000

	SCORES				TOTAL	MONEY
Hollis Stacy	67	70	72	73	282	$18,750
JoAnne Carner	73	71	67	71	282	12,250
(Stacy defeated Carner on 5th hole of sudden-death playoff.)						
Nancy Lopez	69	78	70	67	284	8,750
Lynn Adams	69	69	76	73	287	6,250
Cindy Hill	69	74	72	73	288	5,000
Betsy King	72	72	74	71	289	3,562.50
Bonnie Bryant	72	75	70	72	289	3,562.50
M.J. Smith	76	70	71	72	289	3,562.50
Beth Daniel	77	71	69	72	289	3,562.50
Judy Clark	71	74	71	73	289	3,562.50
Lynn Stroney	71	73	72	73	289	3,562.50
Dot Germain	70	74	75	71	290	2,315.50
Jane Blalock	72	73	72	73	290	2,315.50
Gail Hirata	72	73	71	74	290	2,315.50
Jerilyn Britz	69	75	70	76	290	2,315.50
Kathy Whitworth	71	71	75	74	291	1,925
Pat Bradley	72	73	72	75	292	1,572.60
Dale Eggeling	71	74	72	75	292	1,572.60
Patty Sheehan	74	71	72	75	292	1,572.60
Mary Dwyer	71	69	76	76	292	1,572.60
Sandra Spuzich	78	69	68	77	292	1,572.60
Jo Ann Washam	74	74	74	71	293	1,225
Patti Rizzo	74	74	73	72	293	1,225
Beverly Huke	74	75	69	75	293	1,225
Holly Hartley	73	68	74	78	293	1,225
Joyce Kazmierski	71	73	70	79	293	1,225
Barbara Moxness	73	73	69	79	294	952.16
Silvia Bertolaccini	71	75	71	77	294	952.16
Sandra Haynie	73	73	72	76	294	952.17
Sandra Palmer	71	76	74	73	294	952.17
Sandra Post	69	78	74	73	294	952.17
Alexandra Reinhardt	72	73	77	72	294	952.17
Sally Little	76	71	75	73	295	762.33
Shelley Hamlin	72	72	77	74	295	762.33
Vicki Fergon	76	73	71	75	295	762.33
Donna White	73	75	75	73	296	589.13
Vicki Tabor	73	73	76	74	296	589.13
Le Ann Cassaday	70	76	75	75	296	589.13
Susie McAllister	75	74	72	75	296	589.13
Pam Gietzen	73	72	75	76	296	589.12
Donna Caponi	73	72	75	76	296	589.12
Pat Meyers	73	76	71	76	296	589.12
Cathy Sherk	74	74	71	77	296	589.12
Connie Chillemi	76	72	79	70	297	432.40

	SCORES				TOTAL	MONEY
Kelly Fuiks	69	76	76	76	297	432.40
Marga Stubblefield	73	76	73	75	297	432.40
Yuko Moriguchi	73	72	74	78	297	432.40
Atsuko Hikage	74	73	72	78	297	432.40
Janet Alex	78	70	77	73	298	368.75
Beth Solomon	73	76	74	75	298	368.75
Roberta Speer	76	73	72	77	298	367.75
Muffin Spencer-Devlin	74	74	72	78	298	368.75

Elizabeth Arden Classic

Turnberry Isle Country Club, Miami, Florida   February 4–7
Par 36–36—72; 6,048 yards   purse, $125,000

	SCORES				TOTAL	MONEY
JoAnne Carner	70	70	71	72	283	$18,750
Jo Ann Washam	74	71	71	68	284	12,250
Sally Little	69	71	71	74	285	7,500
Vicki Singleton	71	66	73	75	285	7,500
Hollis Stacy	69	71	74	72	286	4,250
Jane Blalock	69	71	73	73	286	4,250
Pat Bradley	70	70	71	75	286	4,250
Brenda Goldsmith	70	70	71	75	286	4,250
Donna Caponi	69	75	71	72	287	3,125
Nancy Lopez	74	69	70	74	287	3,125
Betsy King	68	72	73	74	287	3,125
Amy Alcott	73	74	71	70	288	2,315.50
Kathy Martin	75	74	66	73	288	2,315.50
Joyce Kazmierski	71	70	73	74	288	2,315.50
Patty Sheehan	69	71	74	74	288	2,315.50
Yuko Moriguchi	71	71	77	70	289	1,680
Judy Clark	72	73	72	72	289	1,680
Patti Rizzo	76	72	69	72	289	1,680
Kathy Whitworth	75	73	69	72	289	1,680
Dale Eggeling	70	75	71	73	289	1,680
Lynn Stroney	71	75	71	73	290	1,329.34
Dot Germain	76	70	70	74	290	1,329.33
Mary Dwyer	71	73	69	77	290	1,329.33
Bonnie Lauer	77	72	73	69	291	1,225
Muffin Spencer-Devlin	73	74	75	70	292	1,025
Sue Fogleman	72	75	75	70	292	1,025
Sandra Palmer	73	73	75	71	292	1,025
Carolyn Hill	78	71	72	71	292	1,025
Carole Jo Callison	77	70	73	72	292	1,025
Gail Hirata	75	71	72	74	292	1,025
Pam Gietzen	70	74	73	75	292	1,025
Kathy Postlewait	73	73	75	72	293	762.60
Ayako Okamoto	72	76	72	73	293	762.60
Kyle O'Brien	72	72	75	74	293	762.60
Cathy Sherk	73	71	75	74	293	762.60
Joan Joyce	75	69	74	75	293	762.60
Julie Stanger Pyne	75	73	74	72	294	562.50
Beverley Davis-Cooper	71	76	74	73	294	562.50
Therese Hession	74	72	74	74	294	562.50
Lynn Adams	75	75	70	74	294	562.50
Vicki Tabor	74	72	73	75	294	562.50
Bonnie Bryant	71	75	73	75	294	562.50

	SCORES				TOTAL	MONEY
Alice Ritzman	72	73	73	76	294	562.50
Beverly Klass	70	72	75	77	294	562.50
Sandra Spuzich	73	75	75	72	295	429
Cindy Hill	70	74	75	76	295	429
Silvia Bertolaccini	72	73	73	77	295	429
Chris Johnson	73	74	77	72	296	356.25
Jan Ferraris	72	73	78	73	296	356.25
Barbara Moxness	75	74	73	74	296	356.25
Kathy Hite	77	72	73	74	296	356.25
Sandra Post	72	74	75	75	296	356.25
Becky Pearson	69	74	78	75	296	356.25
Donna H. White	71	73	76	76	296	356.25
Pat Meyers	75	69	71	81	296	356.25

S & H Golf Classic

Pasadena Golf Club, St. Petersburg, Florida
Par 36—36—72; 6,023 yards

February 12–14
purse, $125,000

	SCORES			TOTAL	MONEY
Hollis Stacy	66	71	67	204	$18,750
Patty Sheehan	67	71	67	205	12,250
JoAnne Carner	68	70	70	208	8,750
Carole Charbonnier	69	72	68	209	6,250
Amy Alcott	73	70	68	211	4,687.50
Kathy Whitworth	71	70	70	211	4,687.50
Dot Germain	71	73	68	212	3,400
Sue Fogleman	69	75	68	212	3,400
Donna Caponi	71	73	68	212	3,400
Betsy King	71	69	72	212	3,400
Debbie Austin	70	70	72	212	3,400
Alexandra Reinhardt	71	73	69	213	2,500
Bonnie Lauer	70	71	72	213	2,500
Ayako Okamoto	73	72	69	214	2,062.34
Jeannette Kerr	68	72	74	214	2,062.33
Vicki Fergon	71	68	75	214	2,062.33
Cathy Sherk	75	71	69	215	1,675
Sandra Spuzich	73	71	71	215	1,675
Myra Van Hoose	71	71	73	215	1,675
Kellii Rinker	71	74	71	216	1,332.60
Yuko Moriguchi	76	71	69	216	1,332.60
Therese Hession	71	72	73	216	1,332.60
Pat Bradley	69	73	74	216	1,332.60
Connie Chillemi	71	69	76	216	1,332.60
Bonnie Bryant	76	72	69	217	1,050
Kathy Postlewait	74	72	71	217	1,050
Sandra Haynie	68	78	71	217	1,050
Cindy Hill	70	75	72	217	1,050
Lynn Stroney	72	72	73	217	1,050
Pam Gietzen	71	71	75	217	1,050
Dale Eggeling	79	68	71	218	781.34
Kathy McMullen	72	74	72	218	781.33
Cindy Lincoln	71	74	73	218	781.33
Jane Blalock	71	74	73	218	781.33
Jo Ann Washam	76	69	73	218	781.33
Beverly Klass	68	71	79	218	781.33
Debbie Raso	72	73	74	219	637.50

	SCORES			TOTAL	MONEY
Sandra Palmer	71	72	76	219	637.50
Gail Hirata	73	76	71	220	537.50
Catherine Duggan	72	76	72	220	537.50
Penny Pulz	74	73	73	220	537.50
Janet Alex	74	73	73	220	537.50
Vicki Tabor	74	72	74	220	537.50
M.J. Smith	70	73	77	220	537.50
Jan Ferraris	73	76	72	221	382.50
Beverley Davis-Cooper	76	73	72	221	382.50
Martha Hansen	75	73	73	221	382.50
Shelley Hamlin	72	75	74	221	382.50
Beth Solomon	74	72	75	221	382.50
Barbara Barrow	72	74	75	221	382.50
Sandra Post	74	72	75	221	382.50
Robin Walton	76	70	75	221	382.50
Donna H. White	74	70	77	221	382.50
Chris Johnson	68	71	82	221	382.50

Bent Tree Ladies Classic

Bent Tree Golf and Racquet Club, Sarasota, Florida February 18–21
Par 36–36—72; 6,128 yards purse, $150,000

	SCORES				TOTAL	MONEY
Beth Daniel	71	71	66	68	276	$22,500
Amy Alcott	68	70	72	70	280	14,700
Kathy Postlewait	66	71	73	71	281	10,500
Pam Gietzen	72	69	73	68	282	7,500
Barbara Moxness	67	71	72	73	283	6,000
JoAnne Carner	69	71	72	72	284	4,800
Sally Little	72	71	70	71	284	4,800
Sue Ertl	74	66	70	74	284	4,800
Alexandra Reinhardt	73	73	69	70	285	3,600
Ayako Okamoto	73	70	72	70	285	3,600
Lori Garbacz	75	70	69	71	285	3,600
Hollis Stacy	74	72	66	73	285	3,600
Dot Germain	70	72	73	71	286	2,655
Cathy Mant	72	73	69	72	286	2,655
Beth Solomon	71	72	70	73	286	2,655
Lynn Stroney	68	71	78	70	287	2,160
Terri Moody	74	73	70	70	287	2,160
Becky Pearson	71	71	72	73	287	2,160
Vicki Tabor	71	76	73	68	288	1,677
Chris Johnson	71	74	73	70	288	1,677
Jane Blalock	72	74	71	71	288	1,677
Beverly Klass	75	68	74	71	288	1,677
Cathy Sherk	74	69	73	72	288	1,677
Patti Rizzo	77	70	72	70	289	1,410
Dianne Dailey	71	72	73	73	289	1,410
Sandra Haynie	71	70	73	75	289	1,410
Jo Ann Washam	73	71	74	72	290	1,230
Holly Hartley	72	75	70	73	290	1,230
Gail Hirata	70	74	70	76	290	1,230
Lenore Muraoka	70	73	76	72	291	985
Cindy Hill	72	71	76	72	291	985
Cathy Morse	73	73	73	72	291	985
Laura Hurlbut	72	73	73	73	291	985

	SCORES				TOTAL	MONEY
Nancy Rubin	73	73	71	74	291	985
Therese Hession	77	71	69	74	291	985
Pat Bradley	72	76	72	72	292	785
Kathy Martin	76	72	72	72	292	785
Pat Meyers	75	69	74	74	292	785
Vicki Fergon	76	73	72	72	293	660
Sandra Spuzich	73	74	74	72	293	660
Judy Clark	73	70	77	73	293	660
Martha Hansen	72	74	74	73	293	660
Marlene Hagge	72	72	72	77	293	660
M.J. Smith	72	76	73	73	294	501.43
Bonnie Bryant	70	76	74	74	294	501.43
Donna White	73	74	73	74	294	501.43
Lori Huxhold	73	74	73	74	294	501.43
Sandra Post	74	71	74	75	294	501.43
Jerilyn Britz	72	71	74	77	294	501.43
Joan Joyce	74	72	72	76	294	501.42

Arizona Copper Classic

Randolph Park North Golf Course, Tucson, Arizona   February 25–28
Par 35–37—72; 6,206 yards   purse, $125,000

	SCORES				TOTAL	MONEY
Ayako Okamoto	70	72	70	69	281	$18,750
Sally Little	73	70	72	66	281	12,250
(Okamoto defeated Little on second hole of sudden-death playoff.)						
Amy Alcott	71	70	70	73	284	8,750
Lynn Adams	72	72	70	71	285	5,625
Patti Rizzo	71	65	73	76	285	5,625
Joan Joyce	74	74	67	71	286	4,000
Becky Pearson	73	70	72	71	286	4,000
Janet Coles	70	70	73	73	286	4,000
Sydney Cunningham	74	69	71	73	287	3,250
Terri Moody	72	71	72	72	287	3,250
Myra Van Hoose	77	70	74	67	288	2,625
Kathy Whitworth	75	71	72	70	288	2,625
Chris Johnson	72	77	69	70	288	2,626
Marlene Floyd	76	73	70	70	289	1,868.67
Kathy Martin	72	73	73	71	289	1,868.67
Nancy Lopez	74	69	74	72	289	1,868.67
Pat Bradley	73	69	73	74	289	1,868.67
Yuko Moriguchi	71	71	74	73	289	1,868.66
Donna Caponi	74	75	68	72	289	1,868.66
Jan Ferraris	78	74	69	69	290	1,387.67
Karolyn Kertzman	74	72	73	71	290	1,387.67
Beth Daniel	71	73	75	71	290	1,387.66
Kathy Hite	74	68	77	72	291	1,250
Laura Hurlbut	73	70	74	74	291	1,250
Alison Sheard	73	71	78	70	292	1,025
Mary Dwyer	74	75	71	72	292	1,025
Tatsuko Ohsako	71	73	74	74	292	1,025
Carole Jo Callison	73	71	74	74	292	1,025
Barbara Moxness	71	74	73	74	292	1,025
Gail Hirata	74	71	72	75	292	1,025
Beverly Klass	73	68	73	78	292	1,025
Kathy Young	73	69	79	72	293	781.25

	SCORES				TOTAL	MONEY
Patty Hayes	72	74	74	73	293	781.25
Alice Ritzman	72	72	74	75	293	781.25
Pam Gietzen	73	72	72	76	293	781.25
*Nancy Tomich	71	72	72	78	293	
Betty Burfeindt	75	71	77	71	294	654.34
Lori Garbacz	76	73	73	72	294	654.33
Shelley Hamlin	75	68	74	77	294	654.33
Therese Hession	74	75	76	70	295	575
Penny Pulz	72	73	75	75	295	575
Marlene Hagge	74	72	74	75	295	575
Bonnie Lauer	73	77	74	72	296	500
Muffin Spencer-Devlin	76	74	73	73	296	500
Jeannette Kerr	75	74	74	73	296	500
Alexandra Reinhardt	74	75	76	72	297	415
Sharon Barrett	75	72	77	73	297	415
Jane Crafter	77	75	73	72	297	415
Rosey Bartlett	73	75	76	73	297	415
Julie Stanger Pyne	76	75	73	73	297	415
Marty Dickerson	75	72	76	75	298	356.25
Sandra Haynie	74	75	76	73	298	356.25
Atsuko Hikage	74	75	74	75	298	356.25
Carole Charbonnier	76	75	72	75	298	356.25

American Express Sun City Classic

Hillcrest Golf Course, Sun City, Arizona
Par 36–36—72; 6,232 yards

March 4–7
purse, $100,000

	SCORES				TOTAL	MONEY
Beth Daniel	70	67	71	70	278	$15,000
Carole Jo Callison	68	71	70	69	278	9,800
(Daniel defeated Callison on second hole of sudden-death playoff.)						
Dianne Dailey	70	70	70	69	279	7,000
Pat Bradley	69	71	72	69	281	4,500
Myra Van Hoose	71	71	70	69	281	4,500
Patti Rizzo	70	71	71	70	282	3,200
Ayako Okamoto	69	71	71	71	282	3,200
Tatsuko Ohsako	70	67	67	78	282	3,200
*Lauri Merten Peterson	67	77	71	68	283	
Carole Charbonnier	71	68	74	70	283	2,210
Barbara Barrow	70	70	72	71	283	2,210
Donna H. White	73	69	71	70	283	2,210
Marga Stubblefield	72	69	72	70	283	2,210
Janet Coles	69	73	70	71	283	2,210
Barbara Moxness	70	70	71	72	283	2,210
Terri Moody	69	72	73	70	284	1,543.34
M.J. Smith	73	69	70	72	284	1,543.33
Donna Caponi	70	71	69	74	284	1,543.33
Betsy King	74	71	71	69	285	1,290
Becky Pearson	71	72	73	69	285	1,290
Kathy Postlewait	74	71	70	71	286	1,100
Kyle O'Brien	71	70	73	72	286	1,100
Julie Stanger Pyne	69	71	73	73	286	1,110
Jane Blalock	73	73	71	70	287	1,000
Lori Huxhold	71	74	70	72	287	1,000
Sandra Haynie	71	73	74	71	289	820
Rosey Bartlett	70	75	73	71	289	820

	SCORES				TOTAL	MONEY
Jeannette Kerr	71	72	74	72	289	820
Martha Hansen	72	70	74	73	289	820
Bonnie Lauer	74	74	68	73	289	820
Lynn Adams	72	68	74	75	289	820
Penny Pulz	69	70	74	76	289	820
Kathy Martin	74	71	74	71	290	640
Marilynn Smith	72	70	76	72	290	640
Patty Hayes	71	74	73	72	290	640
Alice Ritzman	76	71	75	69	291	526
*Heather Farr	72	75	74	70	291	
Yuko Moriguchi	76	72	71	72	291	526
Jerilyn Britz	73	74	71	73	291	526
Kathy Young	72	73	71	75	291	526
Sally Little	71	71	72	77	291	526
Cathy Sherk	75	72	73	72	292	410
Alexandra Reinhardt	76	70	73	73	292	410
Pam Higgins	74	72	73	73	292	410
Shelley Hamlin	74	70	74	74	292	410
Atsuko Hikage	72	75	71	74	292	410
Betty Burfeindt	73	71	73	75	292	410
Cindy Lincoln	70	73	76	74	293	335
Alice Miller	73	70	76	74	293	335
Jane Crafter	73	75	75	71	294	300
Karolyn Kertzman	71	75	76	72	294	300
Roberta Speer	79	69	74	72	294	300
Kelly Fuiks	72	72	77	73	294	300
Kathy Whitworth	75	73	73	73	294	300

Olympia Gold Classic

Industry Hills Golf Course, City of Industry, California
Par 36–37—73; 6,006 yards

March 11–14
purse, $150,000

	SCORES				TOTAL	MONEY
Sally Little	75	74	69	70	288	$22,500
Donna H. White	73	68	73	76	290	14,700
Ayako Okamoto	75	72	70	74	291	9,000
Nancy Lopez	78	73	72	68	291	9,000
Vicki Tabor	75	73	72	72	292	5,625
Marlene Floyd-DeArman	71	76	74	71	292	5,625
Amy Alcott	75	70	74	74	293	4,400
Cindy Hill	76	72	74	71	293	4,400
JoAnne Carner	76	73	74	70	293	4,400
Patty Sheehan	72	75	73	76	296	3,300
Mardell Wilkins	75	72	74	75	296	3,300
Tatsuko Ohsako	75	77	71	73	296	3,300
Alexandra Reinhardt	73	73	76	74	296	3,300
Beth Daniel	77	73	71	76	297	2,557.50
Sandra Post	75	76	75	71	297	2,557.50
*Juli Inkster	72	77	75	73	297	
Janet Coles	70	74	75	79	298	1,905
Vicki Fergon	76	72	73	77	298	1,905
Cindy Lincoln	76	73	73	76	298	1,905
Kathy Whitworth	74	75	77	72	298	1,905
Chris Johnson	71	77	77	73	298	1,905
Terri Moody	76	75	74	73	298	1,905
Kathy Postlewait	76	76	72	74	298	1,905

	SCORES				TOTAL	MONEY
Julie Stanger Pyne	76	75	74	74	299	1,440
Muffin Spencer-Devlin	74	76	75	74	299	1,440
Marga Stubblefield	76	74	73	76	299	1,440
Barbara Barrow	74	74	74	77	299	1,440
Robin Walton	76	68	82	74	300	1,170
Debbie Austin	76	75	76	73	300	1,170
Rosey Bartlett	73	77	77	73	300	1,170
Janet Alex	77	73	77	73	300	1,170
Atsuko Hikage	75	75	74	76	300	1,170
Judy Clark	74	76	77	74	301	872.13
Betsy King	77	75	79	70	301	872.13
Joan Joyce	77	73	76	75	301	872.14
Mary Dwyer	78	72	75	76	301	872.14
Jeannette Kerr	74	73	77	77	301	872.14
Yuko Moriguchi	76	77	72	76	301	872.14
Pat Meyers	76	77	70	78	301	872.14
Therese Hession	79	73	77	73	302	720
Cathy Morse	79	75	73	76	303	660
Penny Pulz	77	76	75	75	303	660
Martha Hansen	71	79	74	79	303	660
Gail Hirata	75	76	77	76	304	555
Kyle O'Brien	79	72	77	76	304	555
Holly Hartley	77	73	78	76	304	555
Shelley Hamlin	78	75	73	78	304	555
Silvia Bertolaccini	81	73	73	78	305	465
Joyce Kazmierski	76	77	75	77	305	465
Jo Ann Prentice	78	74	76	77	305	465
Louise Parks	78	75	77	75	305	465
Lori Garbacz	75	74	81	75	305	465

J & B Scotch Pro-Am

Desert Inn Golf and Country Club/Las Vegas Country Club, Las Vegas, Nevada
Par 36–36—72; 6,237 yards — Desert Inn
Par 36–37—73; 6,059 yards — Las Vegas CC

March 18–21
purse, $200,000

	SCORES				TOTAL	MONEY
Nancy Lopez	70	67	69	73	279	$30,000
Sandra Haynie	71	68	72	73	284	19,600
Kathy Whitworth	72	73	71	69	285	12,000
Alice Miller	71	72	70	72	285	12,000
Patty Sheehan	72	74	68	72	286	8,000
Donna Caponi	73	69	74	72	288	7,000
Hollis Stacy	73	70	76	70	289	5,866.67
Judy Clark	69	71	74	75	289	5,866.67
Ayako Okamoto	74	70	68	77	289	5,866.66
Kathy Hite	76	68	78	68	290	5,000
Myra Van Hoose	76	73	76	68	293	4,200
Janet Coles	72	72	74	75	293	4,200
Barbara Moxness	73	75	72	73	293	4,200
Amy Alcott	75	75	73	71	294	3,300
Jane Blalock	73	72	75	74	294	3,300
Dot Germain	75	72	73	74	294	3,300
Dianne Dailey	80	72	74	69	295	2,450
Beth Daniel	73	74	77	71	295	2,450
Alice Ritzman	69	78	75	73	295	2,450

	SCORES				TOTAL	MONEY
Marlene Floyd-DeArman	71	70	73	75	295	2,450
Sally Little	71	75	74	75	295	2,450
Pat Bradley	71	75	69	80	295	2,450
Jo Ann Washam	76	76	73	71	296	2,000
Patti Rizzo	74	70	78	74	296	2,000
Barbara Barrow	82	70	72	73	297	1,840
Bonnie Lauer	72	72	79	74	297	1,840
Vicki Fergon	76	71	80	71	298	1,600
Cathy Morse	82	69	74	73	298	1,600
JoAnne Carner	80	74	71	73	298	1,600
Therese Hession	75	77	71	75	298	1,600
Barbara Mizrahie	75	76	77	71	299	1,310
Pam Higgins	76	72	77	74	299	1,310
Jerilyn Britz	77	75	73	74	299	1,310
Carole Jo Callison	81	72	71	75	299	1,310
Lori Garbacz	78	74	75	73	300	1,075
Julie Stanger Pyne	75	77	74	74	300	1,075
Shelley Hamlin	77	73	73	77	300	1,075
Gail Hirata	77	76	70	77	300	1,075
Jeannette Kerr	75	77	78	71	301	880
Dale Eggeling	80	76	74	71	301	880
Jan Stephenson	79	71	78	73	301	880
Cindy Hill	77	76	75	73	301	880
Alexandra Reinhardt	75	77	75	74	301	880
Muffin Spencer-Devlin	77	75	79	71	302	692
Vicki Singleton	82	72	75	73	302	692
Cathy Mant	77	73	75	77	302	692
Silvia Bertolaccini	80	74	71	77	302	692
Betsy King	73	73	76	80	302	692
Louise Parks	81	73	77	72	303	580
Judy Rankin	75	78	78	72	303	580
Joyce Kazmierski	78	75	75	75	303	580
Marlene Hagge	74	78	76	75	303	580
Beverly Klass	78	73	72	80	303	580

Women's Kemper Open

Royal Kaanapali (North Course), Lahaina, Hawaii
Par 35-38—73; 6,390 yards

March 25–28
purse, $175,000

	SCORES				TOTAL	MONEY
Amy Alcott	72	74	69	71	286	$26,250
JoAnne Carner	74	70	70	73	287	17,150
Nancy Lopez	70	75	69	74	288	12,250
Myra Van Hoose	72	76	71	70	289	8,750
Betsy King	76	71	77	68	292	6,562.50
Donna Caponi	76	73	70	73	292	6,562.50
Carolyn Hill	77	74	70	72	293	4,579.17
Vicki Tabor	75	73	72	73	293	4,579.17
Dale Eggeling	74	75	71	73	293	4,579.17
Pat Bradley	73	73	73	74	293	4,579.17
Jo Ann Washam	73	74	72	74	293	4,579.16
Sandra Haynie	76	74	69	74	293	4,579.16
Cindy Hill	78	71	71	74	294	3,097.67
Lori Garbacz	79	75	70	70	294	3,097.67
Donna H. White	78	71	75	70	294	3,097.66
Debbie Massey	79	74	73	69	295	2,695

	SCORES				TOTAL	MONEY
Jeannette Kerr	74	71	78	73	296	2,432.50
Holly Hartley	77	72	73	74	296	2,432.50
Judy Clark	73	80	74	70	297	1,916.17
Dianne Dailey	80	69	75	73	297	1,916.17
Yuko Moriguchi	74	76	75	72	297	1,916.17
Debbie Austin	75	77	71	74	297	1,916.17
Janet Coles	74	75	72	76	297	1,916.16
Kathy Young	70	80	70	77	297	1,916.16
Tatsuko Ohsako	78	77	72	72	299	1,610
Jenny Lee Smith	78	79	77	69	299	1,610
Jan Ferraris	77	73	77	73	300	1,273.13
Alexandra Reinhardt	78	78	72	72	300	1,273.13
Patty Sheehan	74	76	78	72	300	1,273.13
Sue Ertl	75	80	74	71	300	1,273.13
Jan Stephenson	76	79	75	70	300	1,273.12
Jerilyn Britz	77	76	78	69	300	1,273.12
Alison Sheard	76	73	77	74	300	1,273.12
Sharon Barrett	78	74	75	73	300	1,273.12
M.J. Smith	79	76	73	73	301	962.34
Kathy Martin	80	76	73	72	301	962.33
Kathy Postlewait	82	74	75	70	301	962.33
Marga Stubblefield	72	78	78	74	302	840
Mardell Wilkins	75	79	72	76	302	840
Jane Crafter	74	75	74	79	302	840
Joan Joyce	80	75	74	74	303	682.50
Atsuko Hikage	80	75	74	74	303	682.50
Mary Dwyer	79	78	72	74	303	682.50
Laura Hurlbut	75	75	79	74	303	682.50
Hollis Stacy	80	74	77	72	303	682.50
Deanie Wood	78	72	74	79	303	682.50
Becky Pearson	77	78	73	76	304	569
Janet Alex	74	79	76	75	304	569
Mary Bea Porter	74	77	79	75	305	525
Lenore Muraoka	79	74	74	78	305	525
Cathy Reynolds	76	73	77	79	305	525

Nabisco Dinah Shore Invitational

Mission Hills Country Club, Rancho Mirage, California   April 1–4
Par 36–36—72; 6,200 yards   purse, $300,000

	SCORES				TOTAL	MONEY
Sally Little	76	67	71	64	278	$45,000
Sandra Haynie	73	69	74	65	281	25,200
Hollis Stacy	73	65	71	72	281	25,200
Amy Alcott	74	74	69	67	284	13,500
Kathy Whitworth	75	72	68	69	284	13,500
Pat Bradley	72	69	74	71	286	10,500
Beth Daniel	72	71	72	72	287	8,800
Nancy Lopez	77	71	67	72	287	8,800
JoAnne Carner	73	71	69	74	287	8,800
Kathy Postlewait	78	75	68	67	288	6,900
Patty Sheehan	76	68	72	72	288	6,900
Jan Stephenson	76	69	68	75	288	6,900
Kyle O'Brien	71	76	74	68	289	5,490
Cindy Hill	75	69	70	75	289	5,490
Cathy Sherk	73	73	75	69	290	4,477

	SCORES				TOTAL	MONEY
Betsy King	79	67	73	71	290	4,477
Lori Garbacz	71	74	70	75	290	4,477
Donna Caponi	73	71	71	75	290	4,477
Cathy Morse	73	74	74	71	292	3,510
Carole Jo Callison	77	70	71	74	292	3,510
Janet Coles	76	74	70	72	292	3,510
Vicki Singleton	77	74	73	69	293	3,000
Vicki Tabor	76	73	74	70	293	3,000
Martha Hansen	75	75	73	70	293	3,000
Debbie Austin	74	75	72	72	293	3,000
Judy Clark	73	77	74	70	294	2,400
Judy Rankin	75	76	73	70	294	2,400
Dot Germain	77	74	75	68	294	2,400
Clifford Ann Creed	79	73	71	71	294	2,400
Sandra Palmer	75	76	71	72	294	2,400
Chris Johnson	75	71	75	73	294	2,400
Myra Van Hoose	78	73	73	71	295	1,785
Janet Alex	78	76	70	71	295	1,785
Joyce Kazmierski	75	75	74	71	295	1,785
Kathy Hite	80	73	77	65	295	1,785
Alice Ritzman	77	70	75	73	295	1,785
Ayako Okamoto	75	73	73	74	295	1,785
Barbara Moxness	78	74	72	72	296	1,320
Donna H. White	75	74	75	72	296	1,320
Julie Stanger Pyne	77	70	76	73	296	1,320
Dianne Dailey	75	72	74	75	296	1,320
Tatsuko Ohsako	74	74	73	75	296	1,320
Jane Blalock	73	77	70	76	296	1,320
Shelley Hamlin	74	78	65	79	296	1,320
Beth Solomon	78	72	74	73	297	1,030
Silvia Bertolaccini	78	75	72	72	297	1,030
Sandra Post	80	76	71	70	297	1,030
Penny Pulz	81	75	69	73	298	930
Bonnie Lauer	77	72	76	73	298	930
Pat Meyers	79	74	70	75	298	930

CPC International

Moss Creek Plantation, Hilton Head, South Carolina
Par 36–36—72; 6,290 yards

April 15–18
purse, $150,000

	SCORES				TOTAL	MONEY
Kathy Whitworth	73	68	73	67	281	$22,500
Patty Sheehan	75	71	72	72	290	14,700
Sally Little	71	80	73	69	293	8,000
Penny Pulz	78	70	75	70	293	8,000
Alice Ritzman	74	76	68	75	293	8,000
Nancy Lopez	75	72	75	72	294	5,025
Beth Daniel	71	71	76	76	294	5,025
JoAnne Carner	75	70	76	74	295	4,200
Julie Stanger Pyne	74	71	74	76	295	4,200
Marlene Hagge	75	74	76	71	296	3,750
Debbie Austin	72	73	75	77	297	3,450
Hollis Stacy	72	74	79	73	298	3,000
Sandra Palmer	77	75	72	74	298	3,000
Kyle O'Brien	76	74	73	76	299	2,557.50
Lynn Adams	76	72	76	75	299	2,557.50

	SCORES				TOTAL	MONEY
Jane Blalock	80	73	73	75	301	2,085
Kathy Postlewait	76	77	73	75	301	2,085
Donna H. White	72	75	77	77	301	2,085
Sandra Haynie	74	72	77	78	301	2,085
Barbara Moxness	78	76	76	72	302	1,631.25
Alice Miller	79	75	78	70	302	1,631.25
Sandra Post	70	82	77	73	302	1,631.25
Jeannette Kerr	74	73	80	75	302	1,631.25
*Juli Inkster	76	77	74	76	303	
Vicki Fergon	77	70	78	78	303	1,440
Judy Clark	75	72	73	83	303	1,440
Bonnie Lauer	76	78	76	74	304	1,320
Dianne Dailey	77	73	77	77	304	1,320
Mary Dwyer	78	79	73	75	305	1,170
Dale Eggeling	77	74	77	77	305	1,170
Cathy Morse	72	74	81	78	305	1,170
Marlene Floyd-DeArman	80	77	75	74	306	1,005
Beth Solomon	79	82	74	71	306	1,005
Betsy King	76	75	78	77	306	1,005
Chris Johnson	78	75	78	76	307	870
Lori Garbacz	77	80	73	77	307	870
Vicki Tabor	73	76	79	79	307	870
Louise Parks	74	77	79	78	308	720
Janet Coles	74	77	79	78	308	720
Myra Van Hoose	78	78	76	76	308	720
Kathy McMullen	75	81	77	75	308	720
Debbie Massey	78	76	75	79	308	720
Dot Germain	78	75	78	78	309	600
*Amy Benz	79	78	80	72	309	
Silvia Bertolaccini	85	74	79	71	309	600
Sandra Spuzich	75	77	77	80	309	600
Judy Rankin	75	78	79	78	310	515
Cathy Sherk	80	73	81	76	310	515
Kathy Hite	79	74	82	75	310	515
Susie McAllister	80	78	76	77	311	480

Orlando Classic

Rio Pinar Country Club, Orlando, Florida
Par 36–36—72; 6,214 yards

April 23–25
purse, $150,000

	SCORES			TOTAL	MONEY
Patty Sheehan	70	69	70	209	$22,500
Kathy Postlewait	66	71	72	209	14,700
(Sheehan defeated Postlewait on fourth hole of sudden-death playoff.)					
Dot Germain	70	71	69	210	10,500
Chris Johnson	73	68	70	211	7,500
Kathy Hite	77	70	65	212	5,350
Jan Stephenson	71	71	70	212	5,350
Nancy Lopez	71	71	70	212	5,350
Alice Ritzman	75	68	70	213	4,050
Janet Alex	72	69	72	213	4,050
Janet Coles	70	68	75	213	4,050
Sandra Haynie	70	73	71	214	3,300
Cathy Morse	75	68	71	214	3,300
JoAnne Carner	72	69	74	215	2,850
Silvia Bertolaccini	73	69	74	216	2,640

	SCORES			TOTAL	MONEY
Sharon Barrett	72	74	71	217	2,392.50
Betsy King	76	68	73	217	2,392.50
Dale Eggeling	72	75	71	218	1,887
Beverly Klass	74	73	71	218	1,887
Holly Hartley	78	69	71	218	1,887
Sally Little	71	74	73	218	1,887
Dianne Dailey	73	72	73	218	1,887
Lori Garbacz	74	74	71	219	1,440
Barbara Barrow	74	74	71	219	1,440
Beth Daniel	75	72	72	219	1,440
Bonnie Bryant	76	71	72	219	1,440
Cindy Hill	74	72	73	219	1,440
Amy Alcott	75	70	74	219	1,440
Penny Pulz	72	77	71	220	1,062.86
Jenny Lee Smith	77	71	72	220	1,062.86
Judy Clark	73	74	73	220	1,062.86
Carolyn Hill	73	74	73	220	1,062.86
Debbie Massey	74	73	73	220	1,062.86
Cathy Mant	74	71	75	220	1,062.85
Kelly Fuiks	71	72	77	220	1,062.85
Hollis Stacy	77	74	70	221	756.43
Sandra Post	72	77	72	221	756.43
Carole Charbonnier	76	72	73	221	756.43
Lori Huxhold	72	75	74	221	756.43
Marga Stubblefield	75	72	74	221	756.43
Carole Jo Callison	72	74	75	221	756.43
Kyle O'Brien	71	74	76	221	756.42
Vicki Tabor	77	73	72	222	536.25
Pat Bradley	76	72	74	222	536.25
Patti Rizzo	77	71	74	222	536.25
Louise Bruce Parks	73	74	75	222	536.25
Susie McAllister	73	74	75	222	536.25
Vicki Fergon	76	71	75	222	536.25
Jane Blalock	75	72	75	222	536.25
Debbie Austin	72	74	76	222	536.25
Bonnie Lauer	73	74	76	223	435
Sydney Cunningham	74	73	76	223	435
Donna H. White	70	75	78	223	435

Birmingham Classic

Green Valley Country Club, Hoover, Alabama   April 30–May 2
Par 36–36—72; 6,043 yards   purse, $100,000

	SCORES			TOTAL	MONEY
Beth Daniel	64	70	69	203	$15,000
Patty Sheehan	69	67	71	207	9,800
Sandra Haynie	71	68	70	209	6,000
Bonnie Lauer	68	69	72	209	6,000
Penny Pulz	73	67	70	210	4,000
Jeannette Kerr	72	70	69	211	3,200
Cindy Hill	73	66	72	211	3,200
Carole Jo Callison	69	70	72	211	3,200
Janet Alex	70	72	70	212	2,700
Pat Bradley	72	70	71	213	2,500
Barbara Moxness	74	71	69	214	2,200
Jan Stephenson	74	67	73	214	2,200

	SCORES			TOTAL	MONEY
Dianne Dailey	74	74	67	215	1,712.50
Janet Coles	74	70	71	215	1,712.50
Carolyn Hill	70	73	72	215	1,712.50
Debbie Austin	73	69	73	215	1,712.50
Silvia Bertolaccini	71	74	71	216	1,390
Alice Ritzman	72	73	71	216	1,390
Jan Ferraris	74	73	70	217	1,118
Jane Crafter	72	73	72	217	1,118
Barbara Mizrahie	71	74	72	217	1,118
Barbara Barrow	72	73	72	217	1,118
Vicki Tabor	74	69	74	217	1,118
Beverley Davis-Cooper	78	71	69	218	900
Holly Hartley	76	71	71	218	900
Betsy King	73	73	72	218	900
Lynn Adams	72	72	74	218	900
Patti Rizzo	74	70	74	218	900
Kathy Hite	77	72	70	219	658.75
Kathy Postlewait	70	75	74	219	658.75
Alexandra Reinhardt	74	72	73	219	658.75
Kathy Martin	72	73	74	219	658.75
Judy Rankin	71	72	76	219	658.75
Rosey Bartlett	70	73	76	219	658.75
Sally Little	71	71	77	219	658.75
Shelley Hamlin	69	71	79	219	658.75
Marga Stubblefield	72	77	71	220	450
Susie McAllister	76	73	71	220	450
Chris Johnson	73	75	72	220	450
Alison Sheard	72	75	73	220	450
Connie Chillemi	75	72	73	220	450
Terri Moody	73	73	74	220	450
Roberta Speer	73	73	74	220	450
Jo Ann Washam	74	70	76	220	450
Colleen Walker	77	72	72	221	332
Sandra Post	76	73	72	221	332
Beverly Klass	74	74	73	221	332
Lori Garbacz	74	73	74	221	332
Beth Solomon	71	75	75	221	332
Silvia Ferdon	78	72	72	222	265
Sandra Palmer	72	77	73	222	265
Karolyn Kertzman	75	74	73	222	265
Elaine Hand	72	76	74	222	265
Cindy Lincoln	72	76	74	222	265
Robin Walton	71	76	75	222	265
Alice Miller	77	70	75	222	265
Vicki Fergon	76	70	76	222	265

UVB Golf Classic

Sleepy Hole Golf Course, Portsmouth, Virginia   May 7–9
Par 36–37—73; 6,174 yards   purse, $125,000

	SCORES			TOTAL	MONEY
Sally Little	72	69	67	208	$18,750
Kathy Whitworth	68	69	71	208	12,250
(Little defeated Whitworth on first hole of sudden-death playoff.)					
Jan Stephenson	68	67	74	209	7,500
Beth Daniel	69	69	71	209	7,500

	SCORES			TOTAL	MONEY
Janet Coles	71	74	70	215	4,458.34
Lenore Kuraoka	72	73	70	215	4,458.33
Pat Bradley	71	71	73	215	4,458.33
Penny Pulz	73	69	74	216	3,625
Donna Caponi	71	75	72	218	3,375
Dianne Dailey	72	76	72	220	2,750
Lori Huxhold	71	77	72	220	2,750
Debbie Austin	74	73	73	220	2,750
Chris Johnson	71	75	74	220	2,750
Patty Sheehan	74	76	71	221	2,062.34
M.J. Smith	79	69	73	221	2,062.33
Alexandra Reinhardt	73	73	75	221	2,062.33
Dot Germain	75	76	71	222	1,737.50
Vicki Tabor	70	73	79	222	1,737.50
Janet Alex	75	75	73	223	1,500
Julie Stanger Pyne	76	71	76	223	1,500
Betsy King	79	73	72	224	1,329.34
Sharon Barrett	78	74	72	224	1,329.33
Beverly Klass	71	71	82	224	1,329.33
Lynn Adams	80	71	74	225	1,150
Carole Jo Callison	73	76	76	225	1,150
Lori Garbacz	74	75	76	225	1,150
Peggy Conley	74	73	78	225	1,150
Nancy Rubin	75	75	76	226	975
Cindy Lincoln	74	75	77	226	975
Gail Hirata	75	74	77	226	975
Jan Ferraris	82	73	72	227	745.38
Brenda Goldsmith	75	79	73	227	745.38
Sandra Haynie	72	79	76	227	745.38
Cindy Hill	77	73	77	227	745.38
Kathy Martin	76	74	77	227	745.37
Mardell Wilkins	76	73	78	227	745.37
Susie McAllister	76	73	78	227	745.37
Robin Walton	74	72	81	227	745.37
Jane Crafter	80	75	73	228	525
Jo Ann Washam	81	72	75	228	525
Beth Solomon	78	75	75	228	525
Carole Charbonnier	76	76	76	228	525
Mary Dwyer	76	76	76	228	525
Sylvia Ferdon	76	75	77	228	525
Sandra Post	76	74	78	228	525
Cathy Mant	81	75	73	229	412.34
Sue Fogleman	75	76	78	229	412.33
Kellii Doherty Rinker	76	75	78	229	412.33
Alice Ritzman	78	78	74	230	375
Shelley Hamlin	79	75	76	230	375
Laura Hurlbut	73	79	78	230	375

Lady Michelob

Brookfield West Golf and Country Club, Atlanta, Georgia   May 14–16
Par 36–36—72; 6,139 yards   purse, $150,000

	SCORES			TOTAL	MONEY
Kathy Whitworth	69	68	70	207	$22,500
Sharon Barrett	71	72	68	211	12,600
Barbara Moxness	70	70	71	211	12,600

	SCORES			TOTAL	MONEY
Amy Alcott	70	74	69	213	6,250
Sue Ertl	71	70	72	213	6,250
Julie Stanger Pyne	68	71	74	213	6,250
Janet Coles	70	72	72	214	4,800
Judy Clark	74	74	67	215	3,900
Joan Joyce	73	75	67	215	3,900
Lori Huxhold	70	75	70	215	3,900
Donna Caponi	72	73	70	215	3,900
Jeannette Kerr	72	76	68	216	2,880
Hollis Stacy	75	70	71	216	2,880
Kelly Fuiks	68	70	78	216	2,880
Silvia Bertolaccini	76	70	71	217	2,238.75
Alexandra Reinhardt	75	70	72	217	2,238.75
Dot Germain	72	72	73	217	2,238.75
Myra Van Hoose	69	73	75	217	2,238.75
Barbara Barrow	71	77	70	218	1,642.50
Lori Garbacz	72	76	70	218	1,642.50
Debbie Austin	76	71	71	218	1,642.50
Robin Walton	74	73	71	218	1,642.50
Pat Bradley	72	68	78	218	1,642.50
Beverly Klass	71	70	77	218	1,642.50
Gail Hirata	73	76	70	219	1,350
Chris Johnson	72	76	71	219	1,350
Mary Dwyer	71	75	73	219	1,350
Vicki Tabor	75	74	71	220	1,113
JoAnne Carner	73	74	73	220	1,113
Susie McAllister	77	69	74	220	1,113
Laura Hurlbut	75	70	75	220	1,113
M.J. Smith	75	70	75	220	1,113
Colleen Walker	76	72	73	221	937.50
Shelley Hamlin	71	72	78	221	937.50
Dale Eggeling	70	79	73	222	806.25
Kathy Postlewait	70	78	74	222	806.25
Kathy Martin	72	76	74	222	806.25
Jerilyn Britz	70	77	75	222	806.25
Marlene Floyd-DeArman	74	77	72	223	690
Sandra Post	69	80	74	223	690
Pat Meyers	74	75	74	223	690
Rosey Bartlett	73	78	73	224	570
Elaine Hand	73	77	74	224	570
Sandra Spuzich	76	74	74	224	570
Alice Miller	72	76	76	224	570
Beverley Davis-Cooper	76	72	76	224	570
Carole Charbonnier	73	78	74	225	450
Lenore Muraoka	71	79	75	225	450
LeAnn Cassaday	74	77	74	225	450
Louise Bruce Parks	78	72	75	225	450
Vivian Brownlee	71	78	76	225	450
Terri Moody	73	75	77	225	450
Connie Chillemi	75	73	77	225	450

Chrysler Plymouth Charity Classic

Wykagyl Country Club, New Rochelle, New York   May 21–23
Par 35–37—72; 6,084 yards   purse, $125,000

	SCORES			TOTAL	MONEY
Cathy Morse	70	72	74	216	$18,750
Sally Little	68	71	80	219	12,250
Sandra Spuzich	74	72	75	221	8,750
JoAnne Carner	72	75	75	222	5,625
Pat Bradley	76	71	75	222	5,625
Pat Meyers	75	76	72	223	3,700
Joan Joyce	74	73	76	223	3,700
Nancy Lopez	75	72	76	223	3,700
Amy Alcott	69	77	77	223	3,700
Donna Caponi	70	75	78	223	3,700
Beverly Klass	74	77	73	224	2,343.67
Sue Ertl	76	74	74	224	2,343.67
Sandra Palmer	75	73	76	224	2,343.67
Kathy Hite	71	76	77	224	2,343.67
Kathy Young	74	73	77	224	2,343.66
Vicki Tabor	71	74	79	224	2,343.66
Shelley Hamlin	75	73	77	225	1,800
Debbie Massey	73	80	73	226	1,612.50
Kathy Postlewait	77	74	75	226	1,612.50
Lori Garbacz	75	77	75	227	1,359.50
Kathy Whitworth	73	77	77	227	1,359.50
Amelia Rorer	72	76	79	227	1,359.50
Myra Van Hoose	72	73	82	227	1,359.50
Hollis Stacy	76	75	77	228	1,150
Janet Alex	75	74	79	228	1,150
Susie McAllister	74	72	82	228	1,150
Judy Rankin	73	73	82	228	1,150
Mary Dwyer	75	78	76	229	927.60
Muffin Spencer-Devlin	77	74	78	229	927.60
Jane Blalock	73	77	79	229	927.60
Patty Hayes	74	75	80	229	927.60
Dale Eggeling	73	74	82	229	927.60
Jerilyn Britz	81	72	77	230	781
Barbara Mizrahie	77	74	79	230	781
Jeannette Kerr	76	78	77	231	687.67
Vicki Singleton	78	76	77	231	687.67
Elaine Hand	78	76	77	231	687.66
Robin Walton	78	78	76	232	587.50
Mindy Moore	76	78	78	232	587.50
Jo Ann Washam	74	75	83	232	587.50
LeAnn Cassaday	74	73	85	232	587.50
Peggy Conley	73	83	77	233	500
Nancy Maunder	78	77	78	233	500
Holly Hartley	73	75	85	233	500
Vivian Brownlee	73	84	77	234	401.72
Silvia Bertolaccini	81	77	76	234	401.72
Carole Charbonnier	75	78	81	234	401.72
Laura Hurlbut	75	76	83	234	401.71
Catherine Duggan	77	74	83	234	401.71
Bonnie Lauer	77	74	83	234	401.71
Carole Jo Callison	73	77	84	234	401.71

Corning Classic

Corning Country Club, Corning, New York
Par 36–36—72; 6,286 yards

May 27–30
purse, $125,000

	SCORES				TOTAL	MONEY
Sandra Spuzich	69	72	70	69	280	$18,750
Patty Sheehan	67	75	69	69	280	12,250
(Spuzich defeated Sheehan on first hole of sudden-death playoff.)						
Sandra Haynie	70	70	70	71	281	7,500
Amy Alcott	72	70	68	71	281	7,500
Cindy Hill	72	71	72	67	282	5,000
Shelley Hamlin	71	74	69	69	283	4,000
Cathy Morse	72	70	70	71	283	4,000
Kathy Hite	70	67	71	75	283	4,000
Jo Ann Washam	74	69	69	72	284	3,375
Chris Johnson	72	72	71	70	285	2,875
Sandra Palmer	73	68	73	71	285	2,875
Jan Stephenson	71	73	69	72	285	2,875
Lynn Adams	72	72	73	69	286	2,287.50
Beth Daniel	73	72	70	71	286	2,287.50
Cathy Sherk	71	71	75	70	287	1,929
Vicki Fergon	70	76	72	69	287	1,929
Nancy Lopez	67	74	70	76	287	1,929
M.J. Smith	73	78	66	71	288	1,515.75
Kathy Whitworth	74	71	72	71	288	1,515.75
Barbara Moxness	71	73	72	72	288	1,515.75
Sally Little	74	74	67	73	288	1,515.75
Dianne Dailey	72	73	73	72	290	1,250
Gail Hirata	72	72	72	74	290	1,250
Mary Dwyer	73	73	72	72	290	1,250
Alexandra Reinhardt	74	74	68	74	290	1,250
Judy Rankin	72	71	75	73	291	1,100
Donna H. White	69	74	75	73	291	1,100
Jerilyn Britz	71	74	76	71	292	906.33
Vivian Brownlee	75	77	72	68	292	906.34
Jan Ferraris	75	71	74	72	292	906.33
Bonnie Lauer	76	69	74	73	292	906.33
Becky Pearson	75	71	74	72	292	906.33
Nancy Rubin	73	76	76	67	292	906.34
Carolyn Hill	76	73	76	68	293	762
Marty Dickerson	74	71	75	74	294	725
Lenore Muraoka	72	77	71	75	295	654.33
Pat Meyers	74	72	75	74	295	654.33
Alice Ritzman	74	68	79	74	295	654.34
Sue Fogleman	74	76	75	71	296	562.50
Kathy Martin	71	76	76	73	296	562.50
Patti Rizzo	76	76	74	70	296	562.50
Hollis Stacy	74	79	70	73	296	562.50
Sydney Cunningham	72	79	76	70	297	475
Joyce Kazmierski	73	73	75	76	297	475
Kathy McMullen	72	77	73	75	297	475
Janet Alex	72	77	73	76	298	406.25
Martha Hansen	76	76	72	74	298	406.25
Muffin Spencer-Devlin	73	76	74	75	298	406.25
Colleen Walker	75	77	72	74	298	406.25
Deanie Wood	70	77	77	75	299	350
Jane Crafter	76	75	74	74	299	350
Betsy King	76	74	76	73	299	350

	SCORES				TOTAL	MONEY
Beth Solomon	75	76	73	75	299	350
Robin Walton	74	72	77	76	299	350

McDonald's Kids Classic

White Manor Country Club, Malvern, Pennsylvania
Par 36–36—72; 6,154 yards

June 3–6
purse, $250,000

	SCORES				TOTAL	MONEY
JoAnne Carner	68	73	68	67	276	$37,500
Sandra Haynie	74	71	66	71	282	24,500
Patty Sheehan	69	71	73	70	283	17,500
Kathy Postlewait	69	68	73	74	284	12,500
Sally Little	74	73	72	69	288	9,375
Sandra Palmer	70	72	74	72	288	9,375
Barbara Moxness	76	72	71	70	289	7,062.50
Janet Alex	71	69	76	73	289	7,062.50
Gail Hirata	70	76	71	72	289	7,062.50
Pat Meyers	73	73	72	71	289	7,062.50
Chris Johnson	69	71	79	71	290	5,250
Nancy Lopez	70	73	71	76	290	5,250
Beth Daniel	74	72	69	75	290	5,250
Donna Caponi	73	77	71	70	291	4,400
Debbie Massey	72	75	73	72	292	3,731.25
Carole Jo Callison	71	71	76	74	292	3,731.25
Debbie Austin	71	76	69	76	292	3,731.25
Amy Alcott	73	71	72	76	292	3,731.25
Hollis Stacy	75	72	74	73	294	3,100
Cindy Hill	70	77	76	72	295	2,612.50
Cathy Morse	76	75	72	72	295	2,612.50
Sandra Spuzich	74	75	74	72	295	2,612.50
Martha Hansen	73	77	72	73	295	2,612.50
Dale Eggeling	74	75	72	74	295	2,612.50
Silvia Bertolaccini	73	73	73	76	295	2,612.50
Jeannette Kerr	77	75	73	71	296	2,150
Barbara Barrow	74	71	79	72	296	2,150
Patti Rizzo	73	74	75	74	296	2,150
Sydney Cunningham	72	73	80	72	297	1,646.88
Vicki Tabor	75	75	75	72	297	1,646.88
Vicki Singleton	78	75	72	72	297	1,646.88
Bonnie Lauer	75	73	76	73	297	1,646.88
Kathy Martin	74	74	76	73	297	1,646.87
M.J. Smith	77	73	74	73	297	1,646.87
Beverly Klass	77	72	74	74	297	1,646.87
Kelly Fuiks	75	72	76	74	297	1,646.87
Lynn Adams	76	76	77	69	298	1,250
Susie McAllister	77	74	76	71	298	1,250
Mary Dwyer	75	76	74	73	298	1,250
Carole Charbonnier	78	72	79	70	299	1,050
Sandra Post	75	75	79	70	299	1,050
Mindy Moore	78	75	75	71	299	1,050
Pat Bradley	75	77	73	74	299	1,050
Betsy King	73	74	75	77	299	1,050
Jo Ann Washam	76	76	76	72	300	830
Judy Clark	75	74	79	72	300	830
Dot Germain	76	73	76	75	300	830
Marga Stubblefield	78	73	73	76	300	830

	SCORES				TOTAL	MONEY
Alice Ritzman	76	72	74	78	300	830
Clifford Ann Creed	76	76	75	74	301	700
Deanie Wood	76	72	78	75	301	700
Cathy Mant	70	76	77	78	301	700
Jan Stephenson	76	76	71	78	301	700
Dianne Dailey	75	75	71	80	301	700

LPGA Championship

Jack Nicklaus Sports Center, Kings Island, Ohio June 10–13
Par 36–36—72; 6,298 yards purse, $200,000

	SCORES				TOTAL	MONEY
Jan Stephenson	69	69	70	71	279	$30,000
JoAnne Carner	71	70	71	69	281	19,600
Janet Alex	72	72	72	67	283	12,000
Pam Gietzen	72	69	71	71	283	12,000
Kathryn Young	72	74	70	68	284	7,500
Amy Alcott	74	68	72	70	284	7,500
Sandra Haynie	73	69	73	70	285	5,866.67
Hollis Stacy	73	70	69	73	285	5,866.67
Beth Daniel	69	70	71	75	285	5,866.66
Sally Little	71	73	71	71	286	4,800
Sandra Palmer	70	70	74	72	286	4,800
Donna H. White	73	76	70	68	287	3,705
Pat Bradley	71	69	76	71	287	3,705
Jeannette Kerr	72	68	76	71	287	3,705
Janet Coles	70	70	76	71	287	3,705
Judy Rankin	71	74	72	71	288	2,980
Lori Garbacz	71	71	74	72	288	2,980
Barbara Barrow	73	73	73	70	289	2,493.34
Kathy Postlewait	74	76	69	70	289	2,493.33
Therese Hession	69	73	72	75	289	2,493.33
Debbie Massey	71	75	72	72	290	2,044
Mardell Wilkins	75	71	71	73	290	2,044
Betsy King	72	70	74	74	290	2,044
Kathy Whitworth	72	69	74	75	290	2,044
Jane Blalock	71	71	73	75	290	2,044
Myra Van Hoose	72	75	76	68	291	1,760
Chris Johnson	74	74	70	73	291	1,760
Beverly Klass	73	74	74	71	292	1,417.15
Donna Caponi	73	74	74	71	292	1,417.15
Carole Charbonnier	72	74	74	72	292	1,417.14
Becky Pearson	74	75	71	72	292	1,417.14
Shelley Hamlin	76	71	72	73	292	1,417.14
Carole Jo Callison	74	73	72	73	292	1,417.14
Dianne Dailey	74	74	71	73	292	1,417.14
Cathy Morse	78	69	76	70	293	1,030
Barbara Moxness	78	70	75	70	293	1,030
Alice Miller	76	74	72	71	293	1,030
Bonnie Lauer	75	75	71	72	293	1,030
Nancy Lopez	75	75	71	72	293	1,030
Penny Pulz	72	73	70	78	293	1,030
Beth Solomon	75	74	72	73	294	780
Alexandra Reinhardt	75	74	72	73	294	780
Debbie Austin	74	74	72	74	294	780
Silvia Bertolaccini	74	71	74	75	294	780

	SCORES				TOTAL	MONEY
Muffin Spencer-Devlin	70	73	76	75	294	780
Lynn Adams	72	72	73	77	294	780
Sydney Cunningham	74	73	76	72	295	650
Connie Chillemi	76	72	74	73	295	650
Cathy Sherk	77	72	74	73	296	580
Gail Hirata	75	71	76	74	296	580
Rosey Bartlett	74	75	73	74	296	580
Dot Germain	72	73	76	75	296	580
Susie McAllister	77	74	69	76	296	580

Lady Keystone Open

Hershey Country Club, Hershey, Pennsylvania
Par 36–36—72; 6,205 yards

June 18–20
purse, $200,000

	SCORES			TOTAL	MONEY
Jan Stephenson	71	71	69	211	$30,000
Barbara Moxness	69	68	75	212	16,800
Alexandra Reinhardt	74	69	69	212	16,800
Sandra Paynie	70	70	73	213	10,000
Pat Bradley	70	73	71	214	8,000
Susie McAllister	73	74	68	215	7,000
Lynn Adams	73	72	71	216	6,400
JoAnne Carner	76	68	73	217	5,200
Dot Germain	73	72	72	217	5,200
Shelley Hamlin	73	71	73	217	5,200
Sandra Spuzich	75	71	71	217	5,200
Jane Blalock	72	72	74	218	3,463.33
Kathy McMullen	75	70	73	218	3,463.33
Nancy Rubin	73	72	73	218	3,463.34
Marilyn Smith	76	69	73	218	3,463.33
Alison Sheard	70	74	74	218	3,463.33
Jo Ann Washam	70	76	72	218	3,463.34
Janet Alex	72	72	75	219	2,078.18
Jerilyn Britz	74	67	78	219	2,078.18
Silvia Bertolaccini	72	69	78	219	2,078.18
Carole Charbonnier	74	73	72	219	2,078.19
Vicki Fergon	67	73	79	219	2,078.18
Gail Hirata	74	70	75	219	2,078.18
Beverly Klass	73	71	75	219	2,078.18
Beth Solomon	75	70	74	219	2,078.18
Myra Van Hoose	75	74	70	219	2,078.19
Mardell Wilkins	70	73	76	219	2,078.18
Donna H. White	73	73	73	219	2,078.18
Debbie Austin	75	73	72	220	1,445
Janet Coles	70	74	76	220	1,445
Cathy Reynolds	71	76	73	220	1,445
Kathy Whitworth	72	72	76	220	1,445
Beverley Davis-Cooper	72	73	76	221	1,160
Mindy Moore	75	74	72	221	1,160
Penny Pulz	74	71	76	221	1,160
Vicki Tabor	74	73	74	221	1,160
Colleen Walker	79	69	76	221	1,160
Bonnie Bryant	75	73	74	222	900
Jane Crafter	73	73	76	222	900
Elaine Hand	72	75	75	222	900
Bonnie Lauer	73	71	78	222	900
Kathy Martin	73	71	78	222	900

	SCORES	TOTAL	MONEY
Cathy Sherk	78 71 73	222	900
Barbara Barrow	76 71 76	223	680
Dianne Dailey	75 74 74	223	680
Catherine Duggan	77 74 72	223	680
Sue Ertl	77 71 75	223	680
Chris Johnson	74 74 75	223	680
Martha Hansen	75 74 74	223	680

Rochester International

Locust Hill Country Club, Pittsford, New York   June 24–27
Par 35–37—72; 6,149 yards   purse, $200,000

	SCORES	TOTAL	MONEY
Sandra Haynie	72 68 69 67	276	$30,000
Hollis Stacy	69 73 71 69	282	16,800
Nancy Lopez	70 70 70 72	282	16,800
JoAnne Carner	67 68 75 73	283	10,000
Jan Stephenson	73 72 73 66	284	8,000
Patty Sheehan	71 72 72 70	285	7,000
Pat Bradley	68 72 72 75	287	6,400
Sally Little	69 72 75 72	288	5,400
Cathy Morse	74 70 72 72	288	5,400
Patti Rizzo	72 68 75 73	288	5,400
Lynn Adams	74 72 72 71	289	4,400
Barbara Barrow	76 74 72 73	289	4,400
Sandra Palmer	70 75 75 70	290	3,540
Donna H. White	75 74 71 70	290	3,540
Shelley Hamlin	73 70 71 76	290	3,540
Janet Coles	71 74 74 72	291	2,980
Connie Chillemi	74 69 75 73	291	2,980
Donna Caponi	77 72 73 70	292	2,493.34
Penny Pulz	78 72 72 70	292	2,493.33
Sandra Spuzich	72 73 75 72	292	2,493.33
Kathy Whitworth	71 80 74 68	293	2,003.34
Jerilyn Britz	71 78 74 70	293	2,003.34
Janet Alex	75 72 75 71	293	2,003.33
Amy Alcott	75 75 72 71	293	2,003.33
Cathy Reynolds	72 71 76 74	293	2,003.33
Alice Ritzman	71 75 73 74	293	2,003.33
Beverley Davis-Cooper	68 77 75 74	294	1,600
Linda Hunt	73 72 75 74	294	1,600
Marty Dickerson	72 73 74 75	294	1,600
Carole Charbonnier	74 75 70 75	294	1,600
Pam Gietzen	70 77 76 72	295	1,340
Alexandra Reinhardt	74 75 73 73	295	1,340
Mindy Moore	73 74 73 75	295	1,340
Clifford Ann Creed	73 75 74 74	296	1,220
Lori Garbacz	75 73 76 73	297	1,130
Therese Hession	77 72 74 74	297	1,130
Jane Blalock	75 75 76 72	298	940
Amelia Rorer	75 76 74 73	298	940
Joan Noyce	74 76 74 74	298	940
Kathy McMullen	72 75 75 76	298	940
Cindy Lincoln	74 76 73 75	298	940
Robin Walton	73 72 76 77	298	940
Kathryn Young	73 74 79 73	299	760

	SCORES				TOTAL	MONEY
Sydney Cunningham	79	72	75	73	299	760
Silvia Bertolaccini	73	78	75	73	299	760
Dianne Dailey	80	69	79	72	300	640
Murle Breer	74	76	76	74	300	640
Carole Jo Callison	76	75	74	75	300	640
Dale Eggeling	73	71	80	76	300	640
Judy Clark	73	73	74	80	300	640

Peter Jackson Classic

St. George's Golf & Country Club, Islington, Ontario
Par 36–36—72; 6,071 yards

July 1–4
purse, $200,000

	SCORES				TOTAL	MONEY
Sandra Haynie	71	71	70	68	280	$30,000
Beth Daniel	67	75	70	69	281	19,600
JoAnne Carner	74	71	69	69	283	12,000
Donna Caponi	70	73	69	71	283	12,000
Sally Little	71	73	73	70	287	7,500
Beverly Klass	72	71	71	73	287	7,500
Jan Stephenson	70	73	74	71	288	6,100
Dale Eggeling	70	72	72	74	288	6,100
Sandra Palmer	74	74	77	65	290	5,200
Nancy Lopez	74	72	75	69	290	5,200
Patty Sheehan	72	74	73	72	291	4,600
Donna H. White	74	72	75	71	292	3,840
Betsy King	69	76	74	73	292	3,840
Marlene Floyd-DeArman	69	75	75	73	292	3,840
*Nancy White	75	71	73	73	292	
Lori Garbacz	72	76	76	69	293	3,086.67
Gail Hirata	71	75	74	73	293	3,086.67
Hollis Stacy	69	73	75	76	293	3,086.66
Sandra Spuzich	74	76	71	73	294	2,364
Alice Miller	72	73	77	72	294	2,364
Janet Coles	72	73	75	70	294	2,364
Beth Solomon	73	72	73	76	294	2,364
Patty Hayes	75	74	69	76	294	2,364
Catherine Duggan	78	75	69	73	295	2,040
Silvia Bertolaccini	74	76	75	71	296	1,680
Dot Germain	72	72	76	76	296	1,680
Muffin Spencer-Devlin	77	74	72	73	296	1,680
Judy Clark	75	75	72	74	296	1,680
Vicki Tabor	71	77	74	74	296	1,680
Jane Blalock	75	69	77	75	296	1,680
Mardell Wilkins	73	74	74	75	296	1,680
Robin Walton	71	75	72	78	296	1,680
Sandra Post	70	69	77	81	297	1,220
Lynn Adams	74	77	78	68	297	1,220
Susie McAllister	75	74	76	72	297	1,220
Cathy Reynolds	77	73	74	73	297	1,220
Sharon Barrett	73	74	76	74	297	1,220
Beverley Davis-Cooper	74	79	73	72	298	920
Pat Bradley	73	74	78	73	298	920
Therese Hession	71	78	75	74	298	920
Becky Pearson	75	76	73	74	298	920
Cathy Morse	77	72	74	75	298	920
Kathy Whitworth	75	74	74	75	298	920

	SCORES				TOTAL	MONEY
Judy Rankin	74	73	74	77	298	920
Marty Dickerson	74	78	73	74	299	740
Kathy Martin	71	80	73	75	299	740
Alexandra Reinhardt	77	75	75	73	300	670
Shelley Hamlin	70	78	77	75	300	670
Barbara Barrow	80	74	76	71	301	590
Cathy Sherk	78	76	73	74	301	590
Lori Huxhold	71	75	79	76	301	590
Kathy Postlewait	71	75	79	76	301	590
Vicki Fergon	75	75	73	78	301	590
Cindy Lincoln	72	76	74	79	301	590

West Virginia LPGA Classic

Speidel Golf Club, Wheeling, West Virginia   July 9–11
Par 36–36—72; 6,150 yards   purse, $125,000

	SCORES			TOTAL	MONEY
Hollis Stacy	71	66	72	209	$18,750
Kathy Postlewait	70	68	71	209	12,250
(Stacy defeated Postlewait on first hole of sudden-death playoff.)					
Alice Miller	70	69	71	210	7,500
Cathy Morse	70	68	72	210	7,500
Cathy Reynolds	75	67	69	211	5,000
Dianne Dailey	72	73	69	214	4,187.50
Silvia Bertolaccini	75	69	70	214	4,187.50
Jan Stephenson	73	72	70	215	3,125
Judy Clark	73	71	71	215	3,125
M.J. Smith	72	71	72	215	3,125
Beverly Klass	73	69	73	215	3,125
Kathryn Young	71	70	74	215	3,125
Jane Blalock	72	72	72	216	2,375
Beth Daniel	72	73	72	217	2,062.34
Bonnie Lauer	72	72	73	217	2,062.33
Alexandra Reinhardt	72	70	75	217	2,062.33
Sandra Post	74	73	71	218	1,494.72
Mary Dwyer	72	74	72	218	1,494.72
Janet Alex	74	71	73	218	1,494.72
Martha Hansen	72	73	74	218	1,494.71
Marty Dickerson	73	71	74	218	1,494.71
Vicki Tabor	73	71	74	218	1,494.71
Alison Sheard	72	71	75	218	1,494.71
Carolyn Hill	74	74	71	219	1,200
Jan Ferraris	71	70	78	219	1,200
Shelley Hamlin	74	73	73	220	1,000
Kathy Martin	73	74	73	220	1,000
Carole Charbonnier	76	71	73	220	1,000
Marlene Hagge	74	72	74	220	1,000
Lynn Adams	75	71	74	220	1,000
Janet Coles	69	74	77	220	1,000
Lori Huxhold	75	72	74	221	819
Vicki Singleton	75	71	75	221	819
Debbie Austin	76	73	73	222	690
Lori Garbacz	72	75	75	222	690
Amelia Rorer	77	71	74	222	690
Barbara Mizrahie	74	73	75	222	690
Jerilyn Britz	74	72	76	222	690

	SCORES			TOTAL	MONEY
Kathy Hite	77	73	73	223	525
Elaine Hand	78	71	74	223	525
Carole Jo Callison	72	75	76	223	525
Susie McAllister	74	72	77	223	525
Beverly Huke	75	71	77	223	525
Patty Hayes	76	70	77	223	525
Barbara Moxness	71	73	79	223	525
Millie Keeter	81	70	73	224	412.34
Dot Germain	76	71	77	224	412.33
Sylvia Ferdon	72	74	78	224	412.33
Mardell Wilkins	71	72	82	225	388
Joyce Kazmierski	75	77	74	226	356.25
Sue Ertl	74	77	75	226	356.25
Becky Pearson	73	76	77	226	356.25
Nancy Rubin	75	74	77	226	356.25

Mayflower Classic

Country Club of Indianapolis, Indianapolis, Indiana
Par 36–36—72; 6,101 yards

July 15–18
purse, $200,000

	SCORES				TOTAL	MONEY
Sally Little	71	66	70	68	275	$30,000
Beth Daniel	69	74	72	65	280	19,600
Sandra Haynie	68	71	68	75	282	14,000
Donna Caponi	71	69	72	72	284	9,000
Amy Alcott	72	71	69	72	284	9,000
Donna H. White	69	74	74	68	285	7,000
Patty Sheehan	72	72	73	69	286	6,100
Pat Bradley	73	72	70	71	286	6,100
Barbara Moxness	75	72	70	70	287	4,800
Sandra Spuzich	71	70	75	71	287	4,800
Alexandra Reinhardt	70	75	70	72	287	4,800
Bonnie Lauer	70	72	70	75	287	4,800
Nancy Rubin	70	73	73	73	289	3,660
Chris Johnson	68	73	75	73	289	3,660
Beverley Davis-Cooper	73	72	72	73	290	3,086.67
Jan Ferraris	72	74	69	75	290	3,086.67
Patti Rizzo	71	73	71	75	290	3,086.66
Silvia Bertolaccini	74	72	71	74	291	2,493.34
Debbie Austin	70	74	71	76	291	2,493.33
Jan Stephenson	71	70	73	77	291	2,493.33
Betsy King	75	73	73	71	292	2,085
Janet Alex	69	75	77	71	292	2,085
Alice Ritzman	74	71	74	73	292	2,085
Lori Huxhold	72	72	73	75	292	2,085
Kathy Postlewait	75	74	72	72	293	1,880
Myra Van Hoose	72	75	75	72	294	1,640
Kathy Martin	74	73	74	73	294	1,640
Cathy Morse	72	74	74	74	294	1,640
Dale Eggeling	74	76	68	76	294	1,640
Kathy Hite	68	74	76	76	294	1,640
Mindy Moore	73	71	80	71	295	1,340
Dianne Dailey	72	72	77	74	295	1,340
Marlene Floyd-DeArman	75	71	74	75	295	1,340
Martha Hansen	74	77	78	67	296	1,104
Vicki Tabor	75	75	75	71	296	1,104

	SCORES				TOTAL	MONEY
Becky Pearson	72	79	73	72	296	1,104
Carole Charbonnier	73	73	73	77	296	1,104
Dot Germain	75	76	69	76	296	1,104
Jerilyn Britz	75	77	73	74	299	920
Clifford Ann Creed	74	73	75	77	299	920
Beth Solomon	74	74	72	79	299	920
M.J. Smith	79	72	77	72	300	728.58
Rosey Bartlett	75	75	77	73	300	728.57
Robin Walton	75	71	80	74	300	728.57
Brenda Goldsmith	75	78	72	75	300	728.57
Beverly Klass	75	75	75	75	300	728.57
Joan Joyce	72	77	74	77	300	728.57
Lynn Stroney	77	74	71	78	300	728.57
Susie McAllister	75	75	79	72	301	600
Bonnie Bryant	74	72	80	75	301	600
Murle Breer	75	76	73	77	301	600

U.S. Women's Open

Del Paso Country Club, Sacramento, California   July 22–25
Par 37–35—72; 6,342 yards   purse, $175,400

	SCORES				TOTAL	MONEY
Janet Alex	70	73	72	68	283	$27,315
Sandra Haynie	70	74	74	71	289	10,659.25
Donna H. White	70	74	73	72	289	10,659.25
JoAnne Carner	69	70	75	75	289	10,659.25
Beth Daniel	71	71	71	76	289	10,659.25
Susie McAllister	77	70	75	71	293	5,673
Nancy Lopez	78	73	74	69	294	4,539.67
Vicki Tabor	70	76	75	73	294	4,539.67
Carole Jo Callison	76	69	72	77	294	4,539.67
Muffin Spencer-Devlin	76	71	76	72	295	3,637.33
Stephanie Farwig	75	76	72	72	295	3,637.33
Beverley Davis-Cooper	73	72	76	74	295	3,637.33
Sally Little	71	77	75	73	296	3,085.50
Dale Eggeling	72	74	76	74	296	3,085.50
Amy Alcott	75	74	71	76	296	3,085.50
Alexandra Reinhardt	73	75	71	77	296	3,085.50
*Kathy Baker	75	70	72	79	296	
Lynn Adams	71	76	77	73	297	2,744
Sandra Palmer	78	71	75	73	297	2,744
*Amy Benz	79	70	72	76	297	
Donna Caponi	73	76	78	71	298	2,474
Janet Coles	77	77	74	70	298	2,474
Pat Bradley	77	74	72	75	298	2,474
Jeannette Kerr	74	77	71	76	298	2,474
Betsy King	75	77	76	71	299	2,178.50
Jane Blalock	77	77	72	73	299	2,178.50
Yuko Moriguchi	73	74	77	75	299	2,178.50
Kathy Postlewait	76	73	75	75	299	2,178.50
*Juli Inkster	75	77	77	71	300	
Patty Sheehan	78	75	76	71	300	1,869.40
Nancy Rubin	74	78	76	72	300	1,869.40
Kathy Whitworth	74	75	75	76	300	1,869.40
Terri Moody	73	79	72	76	300	1,869.40
Bonnie Lauer	73	71	78	78	300	1,869.40

	SCORES				TOTAL	MONEY
*Carol Semple	76	72	74	78	300	
Penny Pulz	78	75	76	72	301	1,700
*Mary Zimmerman	72	74	77	78	301	
Jerilyn Britz	74	79	74	75	302	1,620
Ayako Okamoto	74	76	74	78	302	1,620
Barbara Moxness	76	78	77	72	303	1,481
Cathy Morse	76	75	78	74	303	1,481
*Anne Sander	77	76	75	75	303	
Alice Ritzman	74	77	74	78	303	1,481
Chris Johnson	74	76	79	75	304	1,364
*Dana Howe	71	77	82	75	305	
*Caroline Gowan	77	74	78	76	305	
Valerie Skinner	75	73	79	78	305	1,310
*Cindy Pleger	78	74	75	78	305	
Hollis Stacy	78	73	79	76	306	1,229.50
Myra Van Hoose	74	78	78	76	306	1,229.50

Columbia Savings Classic

Columbine Country Club, Littleton, Colorado
Par 36–36—72; 6,500 yards

July 26–August 1
purse, $200,000

	SCORES				TOTAL	MONEY
Beth Daniel	72	68	72	64	276	$30,000
Patty Sheehan	70	70	71	67	278	19,600
Sally Little	68	69	72	71	280	14,000
Sandra Haynie	72	71	68	71	282	10,000
Pat Bradley	76	68	67	72	283	8,000
JoAnne Carner	73	73	69	69	284	7,000
Chris Johnson	72	70	73	71	286	6,400
Sandra Spuzich	76	70	73	69	288	5,000
Beverley Davis-Cooper	75	73	70	70	288	5,000
Vicki Tabor	75	74	70	69	288	5,000
Cathy Reynolds	76	71	70	71	288	5,000
Beverly Klass	71	71	72	74	288	5,000
Alexandra Reinhardt	75	73	73	68	289	3,425
Sharon Barrett	77	74	70	68	289	3,425
Carole Jo Callison	75	73	71	70	289	3,425
Donna H. White	72	70	72	75	289	3,425
Mindy Moore	77	74	71	68	290	2,680
Shelley Hamlin	71	69	76	74	290	2,680
Nancy Rubin	73	72	71	74	290	2,680
Mardell Wilkins	72	75	77	67	291	2,090
Vicki Fergon	75	77	72	67	291	2,090
Sandra Palmer	74	69	77	71	291	2,090
Janet Alex	73	72	72	74	291	2,090
Jane Blalock	72	78	68	73	291	2,090
Beth Solomon	73	70	72	76	291	2,090
Amy Alcott	76	69	76	71	292	1,562.86
Kathy Hite	71	73	76	72	292	1,562.86
Jeannette Kerr	80	71	69	72	292	1,562.86
Jan Ferraris	76	69	75	72	292	1,562.86
Carole Charbonnier	74	72	72	74	292	1,562.86
Hollis Stacy	76	73	69	74	292	1,562.85
Lenore Muraoka	71	69	76	76	292	1,562.85
Jane Lock	73	77	76	67	293	1,190
Muffin Spencer-Devlin	79	72	73	69	293	1,190

		SCORES			TOTAL	MONEY
Lynn Adams	76	70	76	71	293	1,190
Sue Ertl	76	72	71	74	293	1,190
Myra Van Hoose	75	75	75	69	294	960
Bonnie Lauer	71	76	77	70	294	960
Betsy King	79	72	71	72	294	960
Kathy Whitworth	78	72	71	73	294	960
Jo Ann Washam	75	72	69	78	294	960
Pam Gietzen	74	73	79	69	295	780
Susie McAllister	76	76	74	69	295	780
Joyce Kazmierski	73	74	76	72	295	780
Nancy Lopez	75	77	71	72	295	780
Bonnie Bryant	80	69	76	71	296	660
Dale Eggeling	76	74	72	74	296	660
Debbie Austin	74	72	74	76	296	660
Janet Coles	73	76	74	74	297	620
Patty Hayes	71	73	80	74	298	600

Boston Five Classic

Radisson Ferncroft Country Club, Danvers, Colorado — August 5–8
Par 35–37—72; 6,008 yards — purse, $175,000

		SCORES			TOTAL	MONEY
Sandra Palmer	74	67	71	69	281	$26,250
Terri Moody	71	71	70	70	282	17,150
Muffin Spencer-Devlin	70	71	73	69	283	12,250
Vicki Tabor	71	74	70	69	284	7,875
Judy Clark	70	75	67	72	284	7,875
Vivian Brownlee	70	71	76	68	285	5,862.50
JoAnne Carner	74	68	74	69	285	5,862.50
Jane Lock	73	70	71	72	286	4,725
Jo Ann Washam	77	68	70	71	286	4,725
Patty Sheehan	73	70	70	73	286	4,725
Lynn Adams	72	73	70	72	287	3,850
Kathy Whitworth	74	69	74	70	287	3,850
Jeannette Kerr	73	70	72	73	288	2,997
Hollis Stacy	69	76	76	67	288	2,997
Jane Blalock	70	71	72	75	288	2,997
Jan Stephenson	72	70	72	74	288	2,997
Sandra Post	73	73	73	70	289	2,520
Donna Caponi	77	68	71	74	290	2,181.67
Beth Solomon	71	77	71	71	290	2,181.67
Patty Hayes	75	72	73	70	290	2,181.66
Kathy McMullen	78	73	72	68	291	1,752.84
Kathy Postlewait	70	76	76	69	291	1,752.84
Beverley Davis-Cooper	74	73	74	70	291	1,752.83
Sharon Barrett	74	75	72	70	291	1,752.83
Patti Rizzo	73	71	75	72	291	1,752.83
Silvia Bertolaccini	75	70	74	72	291	1,752.83
Carole Charbonnier	71	73	77	71	292	1,435
Bonnie Lauer	71	73	76	72	292	1,435
Pat Bradley	69	75	72	76	292	1,435
Mindy Moore	75	74	72	72	293	1,260
Holly Hartley	75	74	71	73	293	1,260
Cathy Sherk	72	76	74	72	294	1,041.17
Joyce Kazmierski	70	74	77	73	294	1,041.17
Janet Alex	74	73	73	74	294	1,041.17

	SCORES				TOTAL	MONEY
Dianne Dailey	74	72	73	75	294	1,041.17
Pam Gietzen	74	74	70	76	294	1,041.16
Janet Coles	71	74	71	78	294	1,041.16
Amy Alcott	75	76	74	70	295	805
Dale Eggeling	73	70	78	74	295	805
Sue Ertl	72	76	73	74	295	805
Debbie Austin	73	74	73	75	295	805
Cathy Morse	73	75	72	75	295	805
Vicki Singleton	72	74	76	74	296	665
Stephanie Farwig	75	76	71	74	296	665
Martha Hansen	76	72	70	78	296	665
Becky Pearson	72	76	77	72	297	551.34
Sydney Cunningham	71	78	76	72	297	551.34
Gail Hirata	74	77	73	73	297	551.33
Catherine Duggan	76	74	74	73	297	551.33
Marlene Floyd-DeArman	73	77	70	77	297	551.33
Joan Joyce	70	76	72	79	297	551.33

WUI Classic

Meadow Brook Club, Jericho, New York   August 9–15
Par 36–36—72; 6,305 yards   purse, $125,000

	SCORES				TOTAL	MONEY
Beth Daniel	68	68	67	73	276	$18,750
Martha Hansen	69	73	73	69	284	10,500
Ayako Okamoto	73	71	72	68	284	10,500
Lynn Adams	69	72	72	73	286	6,250
Pam Gietzen	75	71	70	71	287	4,687.50
Barbara Barrow	77	68	69	73	287	4,687.50
Carole Jo Callison	67	76	73	72	288	3,666.67
Sandra Spuzich	73	73	68	74	288	3,666.67
Silvia Bertolaccini	73	71	71	73	288	3,666.66
Judy Clark	74	74	71	70	289	2,875
Jane Blalock	74	75	69	71	289	2,875
Dot Germain	71	72	74	72	289	2,875
Dianne Dailey	69	73	68	80	290	2,375
Jerilyn Britz	76	77	72	66	291	1,665
Jo Ann Washam	75	74	72	70	291	1,665
Cathy Morse	75	73	72	71	291	1,665
Nancy Rubin	73	75	72	71	291	1,665
M.J. Smith	73	73	73	72	291	1,665
Beverley Davis-Cooper	75	69	75	72	291	1,665
Amy Alcott	72	74	72	73	291	1,665
Julie Pyne	73	72	73	73	291	1,665
Donna Caponi	78	72	68	73	291	1,665
Debbie Massey	76	72	70	73	291	1,665
Debbie Austin	72	76	73	71	292	1,150
Marty Dickerson	71	72	76	73	292	1,150
Patti Rizzo	71	75	71	75	292	1,150
Sharon Barrett	71	75	71	75	292	1,150
Janet Coles	76	73	72	72	293	1,000
Sandra Palmer	70	76	74	73	293	1,000
Jeannette Kerr	73	76	73	72	294	879.34
Patty Hayes	73	76	72	73	294	879.33
Alice Miller	75	74	72	73	294	879.33
Sandra Post	75	75	75	70	295	781

	SCORES				TOTAL	MONEY
Gail Hirata	72	75	71	77	295	781
Joyce Kazmierski	70	78	77	71	296	630.43
Elaine Hand	71	73	81	71	296	630.43
Carole Charbonnier	77	76	72	71	296	630.43
Vicki Singleton	79	70	73	74	296	630.43
Karen Permezel	78	73	69	76	296	630.43
Shelley Hamlin	73	74	72	77	296	630.43
Cathy Mant	75	72	71	78	296	630.42
Jane Lock	77	75	74	71	297	455.29
Lynn Stroney	70	79	76	72	297	455.29
Lori Huxhold	73	78	74	72	297	455.29
Penny Pulz	73	76	75	73	297	455.29
Becky Pearson	76	72	75	74	297	455.28
Chris Johnson	75	76	73	73	297	455.28
Bonnie Lauer	73	74	73	77	297	455.28
Kathy Hite	72	74	78	74	298	368.75
Myra Van Hoose	75	74	73	76	298	368.75
Robin Walton	73	74	74	77	298	368.75
Marlene Floyd-DeArman	74	74	73	77	298	368.75

Chevrolet World Championship of Women's Golf

Shaker Heights Country Club, Cleveland, Ohio — August 19–22
Par 35–37—72; 6,225 yards — purse, $150,000

	SCORES				TOTAL	MONEY
JoAnne Carner	72	70	71	71	284	$50,000
Ayako Okamoto	73	72	75	69	289	26,000
Amy Alcott	74	69	75	72	290	17,000
Jan Stephenson	76	70	73	73	292	11,500
Patty Sheehan	76	73	71	72	292	11,500
Hollis Stacy	72	74	80	68	294	6,500
Janet Alex	74	75	74	71	294	6,500
Sandra Haynie	75	71	80	71	297	4,000
Nancy Lopez	74	77	75	72	298	3,000
*Marta Figueras-Dotti	75	71	79	77	302	
Beth Daniel	76	78	75	75	304	2,000
Sally Little	78	76	77	74	305	1,500

Henredon Classic

Willow Creek Golf Club, High Point, North Carolina — August 26–29
Par 36–36—72; 6,191 yards — purse, $165,000

	SCORES				TOTAL	MONEY
JoAnne Carner	70	71	69	72	282	$24,750
Sandra Haynie	73	64	71	74	282	16,170

(Carner defeated Haynie on fifth hole of sudden-death playoff.)

Janet Coles	71	72	72	68	283	8,800
Kathy Whitworth	75	72	68	68	283	8,800
Hollis Stacy	68	71	73	71	283	8,800
Patti Rizzo	70	72	74	68	284	5,527.50
Nancy Lopez	72	72	69	71	284	5,527.50
Pat Bradley	72	70	70	73	285	4,785
Patty Sheehan	72	71	72	71	286	4,455
Sandra Spuzich	76	68	71	72	287	4,125

	SCORES				TOTAL	MONEY
Silvia Bertolaccini	72	72	74	70	288	3,465
Donna H. White	72	70	74	72	288	3,465
Dianne Dailey	71	68	75	74	288	3,465
Judy Clark	73	76	71	69	289	2,635.88
Stephanie Farwig	74	74	67	74	289	2,635.88
Cathy Sherk	69	72	72	76	289	2,635.87
Amy Alcott	69	73	69	78	289	2,635.87
Alexandra Reinhardt	70	74	74	72	290	2,128.50
Penny Pulz	73	70	73	74	290	2,128.50
Lori Huxhold	73	71	76	71	291	1,794.38
Beverley Davis-Cooper	76	72	72	71	291	1,794.38
Susie McAllister	72	72	74	73	291	1,794.37
Donna Caponi	68	73	74	76	291	1,794.37
Bonnie Lauer	76	74	70	72	292	1,551
Vicki Tabor	71	75	73	73	292	1,551
Jerilyn Britz	70	73	74	75	292	1,551
Jan Ferraris	72	71	77	73	293	1,353
Kathy Hite	69	75	76	73	293	1,353
Lynn Adams	75	72	73	73	293	1,353
Charlotte Montgomery	76	74	72	72	294	1,134.38
Beth Solomon	73	74	73	74	294	1,134.38
Sandra Palmer	77	71	72	74	294	1,134.37
Karen Permezel	76	70	69	70	294	1,134.37
Pam Gietzen	71	75	76	73	295	910.80
Sally Little	75	71	76	73	295	910.80
Jane Lock	75	74	73	73	295	910.80
Nancy Rubin	76	72	73	74	295	910.80
Cindy Lincoln	72	76	71	76	295	910.80
Beverly Klass	77	71	77	71	296	709.50
Dale Eggeling	76	74	74	72	296	709.50
Marty Dickerson	80	68	75	73	296	709.50
Kathy Postlewait	75	73	74	74	296	709.50
LeAnn Cassaday	74	74	74	74	296	709.50
Dot Germain	72	76	73	75	296	709.50
Vicki Fergon	76	75	77	69	297	539
Chris Johnson	79	70	74	74	297	539
Jane Crafter	77	73	72	75	297	539
Alice Miller	75	72	74	76	297	539
Debby Rhodes	75	70	75	77	297	539
Connie Chillemi	73	75	72	77	297	539

Rail Charity Classic

Rail Golf Club, Springfield, Illinois
Par 36–36—72; 6,281 yards

September 4–6
purse, $125,000

	SCORES			TOTAL	MONEY
JoAnne Carner	69	66	67	202	$18,750
Susie McAllister	65	74	69	208	12,250
Cathy Morse	70	71	68	209	7,500
Jo Ann Washam	64	74	71	209	7,500
Janet Coles	68	71	72	211	4,458.34
Pat Bradley	71	67	73	211	4,458.33
Janet Alex	68	70	73	211	4,458.33
Stephanie Farwig	70	72	70	212	3,375
Martha Hansen	67	73	72	212	3,375
Alice Ritzman	70	70	72	212	3,375

	SCORES			TOTAL	MONEY
Vicki Singleton	71	73	69	213	2,750
Alice Miller	71	70	72	213	2,750
Barbara Mizrahie	72	74	68	214	2,072.40
Patty Hayes	72	71	71	214	2,072.40
Silvia Bertolaccini	71	71	72	214	2,072.40
Penny Pulz	71	70	73	214	2,072.40
Jeannette Kerr	70	70	74	214	2,072.40
Jane Crafter	74	69	72	215	1,515.75
Therese Hession	74	68	73	215	1,515.75
Cathy Mant	71	70	74	215	1,515.75
Kathy Postlewait	72	69	74	215	1,515.75
Barbara Barrow	71	75	70	216	1,175
Alexandra Reinhardt	69	76	71	216	1,175
Lynn Adams	71	74	71	216	1,175
Marlene Hagge	74	71	71	216	1,175
Betsy King	73	71	72	216	1,175
Bonnie Lauer	72	69	75	216	1,175
Carole Charbonnier	67	73	76	216	1,175
Jane Blalock	74	73	70	217	862.50
Kathy Hite	68	76	73	217	862.50
Colleen Walker	72	72	73	217	862.50
Rosey Bartlett	72	71	74	217	862.50
Dianne Dailey	72	69	76	217	862.50
Rose Jones	70	69	78	217	862.50
Sue Ertl	74	73	71	218	643.84
Sandra Spuzich	75	71	72	218	643.84
Debbie Massey	74	72	72	218	643.83
Pam Gietzen	70	73	75	218	643.83
Sandra Post	74	70	74	218	643.83
Barbara Moxness	70	72	76	218	643.83
Kathy McMullen	74	73	72	219	487.50
Kathy Martin	72	74	73	219	487.50
Dale Eggeling	73	73	73	219	487.50
Vicki Tabor	73	73	73	219	487.50
Connie Chillemi	77	69	73	219	487.50
Beth Solomon	70	74	75	219	487.50
Jerilyn Britz	71	75	74	220	393.75
Mary Dwyer	70	75	75	220	393.75
Hollis Stacy	73	72	75	220	393.75
Pat Meyers	71	72	77	220	393.75

Mary Kay Classic

Bent Tree Country Club, Dallas, Texas
Par 36–36—72; 6,274 yards

September 10–12
purse, $155,000

	SCORES			TOTAL	MONEY
Sandra Spuzich	70	69	67	206	$23,250
Carole Charbonnier	67	72	68	207	15,190
Chris Johnson	66	69	74	209	10,850
Lynn Adams	69	72	69	210	7,750
Beverley Davis-Cooper	72	70	69	211	5,812.50
Patti Rizzo	73	66	72	211	5,812.50
Janet Coles	69	75	68	212	4,727.50
Pat Bradley	67	72	73	212	4,727.50
Jo Ann Washam	74	70	69	213	3,875
Shelley Hamlin	69	74	70	213	3,875

	SCORES			TOTAL	MONEY
Janet Alex	74	68	71	213	3,875
Dale Eggeling	70	75	69	214	2,597.43
Alice Miller	73	72	69	214	2,597.43
Betsy King	75	69	70	214	2,597.43
Jane Blalock	74	69	71	214	2,597.43
Barbara Barrow	69	73	72	214	2,597.43
Hollis Stacy	69	73	73	214	2,597.43
Beth Daniel	68	70	76	214	2,597.42
Sandra Haynie	69	75	71	215	1,922
Kathy Whitworth	75	73	68	216	1,619.67
Sandra Post	75	70	71	216	1,619.67
Patty Hayes	71	73	72	216	1,619.67
Barbara Moxness	69	73	74	216	1,619.67
Vivian Brownlee	68	74	74	216	1,619.66
Judy Clark	69	72	75	216	1,619.66
Cathy Morse	68	77	72	217	1,364
Mary Dwyer	71	69	77	217	1,364
Gail Hirata	76	73	69	218	1,123.67
Rose Jones	70	77	71	218	1,123.67
Judy Rankin	70	75	73	218	1,123.67
Susie McAllister	71	73	74	218	1,123.67
Jan Stephenson	76	68	74	218	1,123.66
Beth Solomon	69	74	75	218	1,123.66
Kathy Postlewait	72	77	70	219	875.75
Vicki Tabor	73	74	72	219	875.75
Jane Lock	71	74	74	219	875.75
Marlene Hagge	70	74	75	219	875.75
Jan Ferraris	76	73	71	220	744
Myra Van Hoose	76	71	73	220	744
Cathy Reynolds	74	72	74	220	744
Joyce Kazmierski	75	72	74	221	620
LeAnn Cassaday	73	73	75	221	620
Kathy Martin	71	74	76	221	620
Terri Moody	72	73	76	221	620
Marlene Floyd-DeArman	74	71	76	221	620
Marty Dickerson	71	78	73	222	465
Sharon Barrett	72	76	74	222	465
Jerilyn Britz	76	72	74	222	465
Nancy Rubin	76	71	75	222	465
Bonnie Lauer	75	72	75	222	465
Judy Ellis	71	74	77	222	465
Pat Meyers	73	72	77	222	465
Laurie Rinker	75	70	77	222	465
Amelia Rorer	74	71	77	222	465

Portland Ping Team Championship

Columbia-Edgewater Country Club, Portland, Oregon
Par 36–36—72; 6,233 yards

September 16–19
purse, $120,000

	SCORES			TOTAL	MONEY (EACH)
Sandra Haynie—Kathy McMullen	67	64	65	196	$10,800
Sharon Barrett—Nancy Rubin	66	65	67	198	5,400
Lori Garbacz—Patti Rizzo	66	64	68	198	5,400
Donna Caponi— Kathy Whitworth	67	67	66	200	2,966.67

	SCORES			TOTAL	MONEY
Chris Johnson—Robin Walton	65	67	68	200	2,966.67
Nancy Lopez—Jo Ann Washam	68	65	67	200	2,966.66
Beth Daniel—Sally Little	70	65	66	201	2,350
Myra Van Hoose— Donna H. White	66	68	68	202	2,060
Silvia Bertolaccini— Dot Germain	65	67	70	202	2,060
Mary Hafeman—Jane Lock	68	70	65	203	1,530
Rica Comstock— Stephanie Farwig	71	66	66	203	1,530
Barbara Moxness—Beth Solomon	69	67	67	203	1,530
Jerilyn Britz—Martha Hansen	66	69	68	203	1,530
Rosey Bartlett—Becky Pearson	68	66	69	203	1,530
Mindy Moore—Lenore Muraoka	69	69	66	204	1,063.34
Mary Dwyer—Sandra Post	70	67	67	204	1,063.33
Therese Hession— Vicki Singleton	68	67	69	204	1,063.33
Jan Ferraris—Beverly Huke	69	70	66	205	823.34
Janet Alex—Judy Clark	69	67	69	205	823.33
Beverley Davis-Cooper— Patty Sheehan	69	67	69	205	823.33
Joyce Kazmierski— Sandra Spuzich	73	68	65	206	663.34
Lori Huxhold—Cindy Lincoln	73	66	67	206	663.33
Carole Jo Callison— Dale Eggeling	70	67	69	206	663.33
Dianne Dailey— Alexandra Reinhardt	72	68	67	207	565
Marlene Hagge—Beverly Klass	69	68	70	207	565
Penny Pulz—Debbie Skinner	71	68	69	208	500
Connie Chillemi— Kathryn Young	68	69	71	208	500
Le Ann Cassaday—Rose Jones	65	70	73	208	500
Vicki Fergon—Joan Joyce	71	68	70	209	450
Marty Dickerson— Colleen Walker	67	69	73	209	450
Susie Berning— Vivian Brownlee	70	70	70	210	
Patty Hayes—Cathy Mant	70	69	73	212	
Shelley Hamlin— Marilynn Smith	68	70	74	212	
Lynn Stroney—Deanie Wood	72	68	73	213	
Linda Hunt— Kellii Doherty Rinker	70	71	73	214	

Safeco Classic

Meridian Valley Country Club, Seattle, Washington
Par 36–36—72, 6,084 yards

September 23–26
purse, $175,000

	SCORES				TOTAL	MONEY
Patty Sheehan	68	69	69	70	276	$26,250
JoAnne Carner	68	71	67	71	277	17,150
Dale Eggeling	71	70	69	68	278	12,250
Kathy Whitworth	69	67	73	70	279	8,750
Jo Ann Washam	71	67	74	68	280	7,000

	SCORES				TOTAL	MONEY
Donna H. White	67	70	73	71	281	6,125
Beth Solomon	73	70	68	71	282	5,337.50
Barbara Moxness	70	70	70	72	282	5,337.50
Nancy Lopez	68	72	71	72	283	4,550
Sandra Haynie	70	71	68	74	283	4,550
Cathy Morse	71	72	70	71	284	3,675
Jan Stephenson	71	69	70	74	284	3,675
Donna Caponi	73	69	66	76	284	3,675
Therese Hession	73	72	69	71	285	2,984
Barbara Barrow	68	69	70	78	285	2,984
Myra Van Hoose	70	78	72	66	286	2,520
Robin Walton	71	74	72	69	286	2,520
Sandra Post	74	71	72	69	286	2,520
Sally Little	68	73	76	70	287	2,170
Mary Dwyer	70	76	72	70	288	1,865.40
Judy Clark	73	73	70	72	288	1,865.40
Sharon Barrett	70	74	71	73	288	1,865.40
Pat Bradley	72	72	71	73	288	1,865.40
Sandra Spuzich	68	69	74	77	288	1,865.40
Beth Daniel	74	73	71	71	289	1,540
Debbie Skinner	73	72	72	72	289	1,540
Lynn Adams	73	71	73	72	289	1,540
Judy Ellis	75	69	71	74	289	1,540
Vicki Fergon	74	71	75	70	290	1,295
Vivian Brownlee	71	70	74	75	290	1,295
Susie McAllister	71	70	71	78	290	1,295
Dot Germain	73	70	78	70	291	1,041.17
Kathy McMullen	72	75	73	71	291	1,041.17
Connie Chillemi	71	75	72	73	291	1,041.17
Becky Pearson	70	71	76	74	291	1,041.17
Betsy King	73	73	71	74	291	1,041.16
Marlene Hagge	74	74	69	74	291	1,041.16
Judy Rankin	74	71	71	73	292	805
Bonnie Lauer	71	73	75	73	292	805
Jane Lock	69	72	76	75	292	805
Vicki Tabor	74	73	70	75	292	805
Sandra Palmer	74	70	72	76	292	805
Colleen Walker	72	70	77	74	293	665
Kellii Doherty Rinker	73	73	73	74	293	665
Hollis Stacy	68	76	73	76	293	665
Debbie Massey	73	72	77	72	294	577.67
Janet Coles	71	72	78	73	294	577.67
Jerilyn Britz	74	72	73	75	294	577.66
Nancy Rubin	75	71	75	74	295	490
Vicki Singleton	72	73	75	75	295	490
Debbie Austin	74	73	72	76	295	490
Shelley Hamlin	71	76	71	77	295	490
Rose Jones	72	76	70	77	295	490
Stephanie Farwig	69	73	75	78	295	490
Silvia Bertolaccini	73	73	71	78	295	490

Inamori Classic

Almaden Golf & Country Club, San Jose, California   September 30–October 3
Par 37-36—73; 6,290 yards   purse, $150,000

	SCORES				TOTAL	MONEY
Patty Sheehan	69	70	69	69	277	$22,500
Joyce Kazmierski	70	72	69	69	280	14,700
Dale Eggeling	70	74	68	70	282	10,500
Sally Little	70	72	71	71	284	6,750
Jerilyn Britz	72	69	71	72	284	6,750
Myra Van Hoose	69	74	70	72	285	5,025
Kathy Whitworth	69	69	74	73	285	5,025
Beth Daniel	68	72	76	70	286	4,200
Amy Alcott	69	74	71	72	286	4,200
Sandra Haynie	70	67	76	74	287	3,450
Vicki Fergon	69	75	69	74	287	3,450
Chris Johnson	73	72	67	75	287	3,450
Karen Permezel	75	75	70	68	288	2,568.75
Betsy King	71	72	75	70	288	2,568.75
Pat Bradley	73	75	70	70	288	2,568.75
Pam Gietzen	71	68	75	74	288	2,568.75
Lynn Adams	74	71	74	70	289	1,942.50
Sandra Palmer	73	72	74	70	289	1,942.50
Hollis Stacy	72	72	74	71	289	1,942.50
Sharon Barrett	70	76	70	73	289	1,942.50
Beverly Klass	75	66	78	71	290	1,472.15
Cathy Morse	76	71	72	71	290	1,472.15
Lori Huxhold	71	71	76	72	290	1,472.14
Patti Rizzo	73	73	72	72	290	1,472.14
Donna H. White	70	71	76	73	290	1,472.14
Julie Pyne	73	71	72	74	290	1,472.14
Barbara Barrow	72	70	74	74	290	1,472.14
Kathy McMullen	75	72	75	69	291	1,170
Donna Caponi	76	73	70	72	291	1,170
Muffin Spencer-Devlin	74	68	76	73	291	1,170
Silvia Bertolaccini	71	72	79	70	292	915
Debbie Meisterlin	73	72	77	70	292	915
Penny Pulz	74	74	72	72	292	915
Marty Dickerson	75	72	72	73	292	915
Barbara Moxness	73	71	74	74	292	915
Debbie Skinner	77	72	69	74	292	915
Judy Rankin	74	69	72	77	292	915
Janet Coles	72	75	75	71	293	705
Stephanie Farwig	75	75	72	71	293	705
Mary Dwyer	73	71	76	73	293	705
*Juli Inkster	68	82	69	74	293	
Dot Germain	73	73	72	75	293	705
Colleen Walker	74	72	73	75	294	570
Alison Sheard	74	71	74	75	294	570
Laurie Rinker	74	74	71	75	294	570
Gail Hirata	74	74	70	76	294	570
Debbie Austin	72	71	72	79	294	570
Jane Crafter	79	70	77	69	295	465
Jan Ferraris	72	75	78	70	295	465
Beverley Davis-Cooper	74	74	75	72	295	465
Beth Solomon	76	70	77	72	295	465
LeAnn Cassaday	72	74	73	76	295	465

Pioneer Cup

Genjiyama Golf Club, Ichihara City, Japan   October 29–31
Par 36–36—72; 6,312 yards   purse, $125,000

FINAL RESULTS: UNITED STATES 24, JAPAN 16

	SINGLES ROUNDS		TOTAL	INDIVIDUAL MONEY	TEAM MONEY	TOTAL MONEY
Nayoko Yoshikwa	68	73	141	$10,000	$2,500	$12,500
Yuko Moriguchi	72	72	144	6,500	2,500	9,000
Beth Daniel	73	73	146	5,000	5,000	10,000
Kathy Whitworth	74	73	147	2,666.67	5,000	7,666.67
Kathy Postlewait	73	74	147	2,666.67	5,000	7,666.67
Pat Bradley	72	75	147	2,666.66	5,000	7,666.67
Atsuko Hikage	73	75	148	1,750	2,500	4,250
Yuko Kobayashi	77	72	149	937.50	2,500	3,437.50
Sally Little	76	73	149	937.50	5,000	5,937.50
Patty Sheehan	76	73	149	937.50	5,000	5,937.50
Hollis Stacy	72	77	149	937.50	5,000	5,937.50
Chako Higuchi	78	72	150		2,500	2,500
Janet Coles	76	74	150		5,000	5,000
Ritzu Imahori	74	76	150		2,500	2,500
Shinako Yoshimochi	73	77	150		2,500	2,500
Sandra Haynie	75	76	151		5,000	5,000
Ayako Okamoto	74	77	151		2,500	2,500
Barbara Moxness	73	78	151		5,000	5,000
Jan Stephenson	78	74	152		5,000	5,000
Tatsuko Ohsako	77	75	152		2,500	2,500
Sandra Palmer	75	77	152		5,000	5,000
Setsuko Masuda	81	73	154		2,500	2,500
Keiko Matsuda	79	78	157		2,500	2,500
Reiko Kashiwado	75	85	160		2,500	2,500

Each member of winning team earned $5,000
Each member of losing team earned $2,500

Mazda Classic

Meishin Yokaichi Country Club, Yibjauchi, Japan   November 5–7
Par 36–36—72; 6,002 yards   purse, $250,000

	SCORES			TOTAL	MONEY
Nancy Lopez	66	70	71	207	$30,000
Amy Alcott	69	69	75	213	19,600
Beth Daniel	69	72	73	214	14,000
Pat Bradley	72	73	70	215	10,000
Yuko Moriguchi	75	70	71	216	6,520
Jan Stephenson	75	70	71	216	6,520
Dianne Dailey	70	71	75	216	6,520
Sandra Haynie	71	72	73	216	6,520
Alexandra Reinhardt	72	69	75	216	6,520
Sally Little	76	75	66	217	4,600
Silvia Bertolaccini	77	70	70	217	4,600
Ai-Yu Tu	75	69	73	217	4,600
Donna H. White	72	73	73	218	3,660
Nayoko Yoshikawa	72	74	72	218	3,660
Hiroko Inoue	73	75	71	219	2,790

	SCORES			TOTAL	MONEY
Alice Miller	74	74	71	219	2,790
Chako Higuchi	74	73	72	219	2,790
Tatsuko Ohsako	73	74	72	219	2,790
Angie Tsai	75	70	74	219	2,790
Mieko Suzuki	71	73	75	219	2,790
Setsuko Masuda	77	71	72	220	2,220
Janet Coles	73	77	71	221	2,000
Patty Sheehan	73	75	73	221	2,000
Ritsu Imahori	73	74	74	221	2,000
Kathy Postlewait	77	70	74	221	2,000
JoAnne Carner	77	74	71	222	1,640
Patti Rizzo	78	73	71	222	1,640
Vicki Tabor	79	72	71	222	1,640
Ayako Okamoto	76	73	73	222	1,640
Hollis Stacy	73	75	74	222	1,640
Susako Nagata	77	71	75	223	1,370
Masayo Fujimura	75	73	75	223	1,370
Atsuko Hikage	74	76	74	224	1,190
Sandra Palmer	77	74	73	224	1,190
Kathryn Young	78	76	70	224	1,190
Yoko Kobayoshi	75	70	79	224	1,190
Keiko Matsuda	73	76	76	225	900
Masumi Inaba	76	74	75	225	900
Dale Eggeling	74	77	74	225	900
Carole Jo Callison	77	75	73	225	900
Chris Johnson	78	74	73	225	900
Bonnie Lauer	77	72	76	225	900
Kathy Hite	73	75	77	225	900
Lynn Adams	72	75	78	225	900
Sachiko Takahashi	75	76	75	226	664
Barbara Moxness	75	78	73	226	664
Barbara Barrow	76	73	77	226	664
Kathy Whitworth	77	71	78	226	664
Tomiko Ikebuchi	73	73	80	226	664

J C Penney Mixed Team Classic

Bardmoor Country Club, Largo, Florida
Par 36–36—72; 7,019 yards

December 9–12
purse, $500,000

	SCORES				TOTAL	MONEY (EACH)
JoAnne Carner/John Mahaffey	68	67	63	70	268	$46,500
Hollis Stacy/Jay Haas	66	67	68	68	269	26,500
Betsy King/Ed Fiori	70	70	64	67	271	16,740
Jan Stephenson/Ferd Couples	67	66	72	67	272	12,462
Patty Sheehan/Al Geiberger	71	67	69	66	273	9,300
Barbara Moxness/Doug Tewell	71	65	70	68	274	8,370
Carole Charbonnier/ Leonard Thompson	65	68	69	73	275	7,789
Alice Ritzman/Fuzzy Zoeller	68	73	67	68	276	6,277.50
Beth Daniel/Tom Kite	68	69	70	69	276	6,277.50
Pat Bradley/Mark McCumber	69	70	66	71	276	6,277.50
Vivian Brownlee/Lou Graham	69	68	67	72	276	6,277.50
Bonnie Lauer/Gary Koch	68	69	66	73	276	6,277.50
Nancy Lopez/Curtis Strange	70	70	68	69	277	4,359.37
Patti Rizzo/Andy Bean	71	68	71	67	277	4,359.37

	SCORES				TOTAL	MONEY
Beverly Klass/						
Steve Melnyk	70	67	66	74	277	4,359.37
Jo Ann Washam/Jerry Pate	67	67	68	75	277	4,359.37
Silvia Bertolaccini/						
Jim Colbert	73	69	67	69	278	2,841.67
Chris Johnson/Brad Bryant	69	64	74	71	278	2,841.67
Myra Van Hoose/Dan Pohl	69	69	70	70	278	2,841.67
Terry Luckhurst/Scott Hoch	72	64	73	69	278	2,841.67
Donna H. White/Larry Nelson	72	69	69	68	278	2,841.67
Janet Coles/						
Peter Jacobsen	70	69	68	71	278	2,841.67
Sandra Haynie/Charles Coody	70	66	70	72	278	2,841.67
Lynn Adams/						
Chi Chi Rodriguez	65	71	70	72	278	2,841.67
Kathy Postlewait/Hal Sutton	70	67	68	73	278	2,841.66
Sandra Spuzich/						
Giddy Gilbert	71	70	68	70	279	1,825.13
Alexandra Reinhardt/						
Andy North	69	69	70	71	279	1,825.13
Janet Alex/Dennis Watson	70	70	69	71	280	1,674
Jane Blalock/Tom Purtzer	72	66	70	72	280	1,674
Cathy Morse/Vance Heafner	66	72	73	69	280	1,674
Kathy Whitworth/Calvin Peete	70	69	70	72	281	1,418.25
Sandra Post/						
Peter Oosterhuis	70	67	71	73	281	1,418.25
Vicki Tabor/Keith Fergus	71	69	70	71	281	1,418.25
Dale Eggeling/Wayne Levi	69	72	70	70	281	1,418.25
Alice Miller/						
Morris Hatalsky	72	68	71	70	281	1,418.25
Lori Garbacz/Scott Simpson	72	70	69	70	281	1,418.25
Sandra Palmer/Mark Hayes	67	70	69	75	281	1,418.25
Dianne Dailey/Bill Kratzert	72	72	70	67	281	1,418.25
Dot Germain/Joe Inman	70	70	69	74	283	1,209
Carole Jo Callison/						
Jim Simons	70	68	72	74	284	1,162.50
Judy Rankin/John Cook	69	74	70	72	285	1,116
Murle Breer/						
Dave Eichelberger	72	75	70	69	286	1,059.50
Susie McAllister/						
Tom Valentine	70	72	68	77	287	1,013.70
Marlene Hagge/Gil Morgan	70	69	72	76	287	1,013.70
Sally Little/Ed Sneed	72	71	74	73	290	985.80
Pam Gietzen/Don Pooley	74	71	76	75	296	967.20
Judy Clark/						
Gardner Dickinson	72	76	75	74	297	948.60
Cindy Hill/Mike Souchak	76	73	76	76	301	930